The Divine Charter

The Election of 1813 to the Ayuntamiento of México City.
Source: Archivo General de la Nación, México

The Divine Charter

Constitutionalism and Liberalism in Nineteenth-Century Mexico

Edited by
Jaime E. Rodríguez O.

ROWMAN & LITTLEFIELD PUBLISHERS, INC.
Lanham • Boulder • New York • Toronto • Plymouth, UK

ROWMAN & LITTLEFIELD PUBLISHERS, INC.

Published in the United States of America
by Rowman & Littlefield Publishers, Inc.
A wholly owned subsidiary of The Rowman & Littlefield Publishing Group, Inc.
4501 Forbes Boulevard, Suite 200, Lanham, MD 20706
www.rowmanlittlefield.com

Estover Road, Plymouth PL6 7PY, UK

British Library Cataloguing-in-Publication Information Available

The hardback edition of this book was previously cataloged by the Library of
Congress as follows:

The divine charter : constitutionalism and liberalism in nineteenth-century Mexico /
edited by Jaime E. Rodríguez O.
        p. cm. — (Latin American silhouettes)
    Includes bibliographical references and index.
1. Constitutional history—Mexico. 2. Mexico—Politics and government—19th
century. 3. Liberalism—Mexico—History—19th century. I. Rodríguez O., Jaime E.,
1940– II. Series.
    KGF2919.D58 2005
    342.7202'9 dc22
                                                                            2004014122

ISBN-13: 978-0-7425-3710-1 (cloth : alk. paper)
ISBN-10: 0-7425-3710-2 (cloth : alk. paper)
ISBN-13: 978-0-7425-3711-8 (pbk. : alk. paper)
ISBN-10: 0-7425-3711-0 (pbk. : alk. paper)

Printed in the United States of America

♾™ The paper used in this publication meets the minimum requirements of
American National Standard for Information Sciences—Permanence of Paper
for Printed Library Materials, ANSI/NISO Z39.48-1992.

[The Constitution of 1812] was welcomed with great joy. It received the most tender praises. No public paper nor poem was published that did not have as its object to praise it and recommend it [to the people]. They referred to the Constitution as "The Sacred Code," the "Divine Charter" . . .

—Vicente Rocafuerte

A
Linda

Mexico City at mid-century.
Source: J. Decaen, *México y sus alrededores*, 2nd ed. (Mexico, 1864)

Contents

Part II: The Church

Part III: The Military

Part IV: The Economy

Preface

For nearly three decades I have been exploring the process of nation build-ing in Spanish America. In my first book, *The Emergence of Spanish America: Vicente Rocafuerte and Spanish Americanism, 1808-1832* (Berkeley: University of California Press, 1975), I challenged the widely held view that liberalism was alien and ill-suited to the Spanish world; instead, I argued that liberalism constituted an integral part of Hispanic political culture. During the last decade, a new political history has gained prominence, particularly in Mexico. This work, which is reexamining the nature of political institu-tions and processes, complements my own studies. It advances our under-standing of liberalism and its role in the formation of the new nations that emerged from the collapse of the Spanish Monarchy.

Hispanic liberalism assumed a new and revolutionary form after Napoleon invaded the Spanish peninsula in 1808 and forced the king to abdicate in fa-vor of his brother Joseph. That event unleashed the great Hispanic Revolu-tion that culminated with the promulgation of the Constitution of 1812 in the city of Cádiz, Spain. (It was lovingly called: the *Divine Charter.*) That char-ter, which was written by both Spanish and American—as the people of the New World called themselves—deputies, created the nineteenth-century's most liberal representative government. New Spain/Mexico participated more fully in the Hispanic liberal revolution than any other part of the Span-ish Monarchy.

This volume focuses on the evolution of Mexican liberalism during the nineteenth century from the perspectives of politics, the military, the Church, and finances. The essays demonstrate that—contrary to widely held as-sumptions—liberalism was not alien ideology unsuited for Mexico's suppos-edly traditional, conservative, and multiethnic society. On the contrary, these essays, which are based on extensive archival research, demonstrate that liberalism in New Spain (colonial Mexico) arose from Hispanic culture.

The present volume synthesizes discussions about liberalism and constitutionalism among a distinguished group of historians from Mexico, the United States, Canada, Spain, and Italy engaged in the new political history. It provides the first broad examination of the evolution of Mexican liberal traditions in the nineteenth century. The essays examine the changes in liberal ideology, the nature of federalism, the efforts to create stability with a liberal monarchy in the 1860s, the manner in which the Church accommodated the new liberal order, the role of the army and of the civil militias, the liberal tax system, and the efforts to modernize the economy in the latter part of the nineteenth century. As a whole, they provide the most nuanced analysis available of the transformation of liberalism in Mexico.

A number of persons and institutions contributed to the preparation and publication of this volume. I am grateful to my colleagues in the Latin American Studies Program at the University of California, Irvine, for their support and encouragement. Karen Lawrence, Dean of the School of Humanities, Kenneth Pomeranz, Chair of the Department of History, and William Parker, Vice Chancellor for Research at the University of California, Irvine, generously contributed financial backing for the project. The UCI Latin American Studies Program and the Humanities Center of the School of Humanities provided additional financial support. I also thank Carolyn Boyd, Roderic A. Camp, David Mares, Steven Topik, and Eric Van Young for their excellent commentaries. Linda Alexander Rodríguez and Kathryn Vincent assisted in editing the papers. Their valuable suggestions were extremely helpful and contributed substantially to the volume. Carla Duke proved invaluable in assisting with the project and in preparing the papers for publication. Finally, I am grateful to Colin M. MacLachlan for his continuous support and his help during the final stages of the publication process.

Jaime E. Rodríguez O.
Los Angeles
November 24, 2003

Introduction

The Origins of Constitutionalism and Liberalism in Mexico

Jaime E. Rodríguez O.

> Was it probable, was it possible, that . . . a free government . . . should be introduced and established among such a people . . . ? It appeared to me . . . as absurd as . . . [it] would be to establish democracies among the birds, beasts, and fishes.
>
> —John Adams[1]

John Adams was not the only one to believe the Hispanic world incapable of self-government. Most scholars then and now have been convinced that constitutionalism and liberalism are alien and unsuited to the supposedly conservative society of the Hispanic world, particularly Mexico. Many believe that the Spanish Monarchy was highly centralized and confuse absolute with autocratic rule. The modern concept of colony further obscures the nature of government in Spanish America. As a result of these misconceptions many have assumed wrongly that the political structures established in the post-independence period were alien systems imported from Great Britain, the United States, and France. That is not correct. To understand the nature of constitutionalism and liberalism in Mexico during the nineteenth century, it is necessary to dispel misperceptions about the political system of the Spanish Monarchy and the nature of Hispanic political theory and practice.[2]

THE *ANTIGUO RÉGIMEN*

Throughout most of their history, particularly during the sixteenth and seventeenth centuries, the Spanish possessions in America constituted part of the worldwide Spanish Monarchy—a confederation of disparate kingdoms and lands, which extended throughout portions of Europe, Africa, Asia, and America.[3] Only very late in its history, during the reign of Carlos III (1759–1788), did the Crown attempt to centralize the monarchy and create a true empire with Spain as the metropolis. That effort, widely known as the Bourbon reforms, had not been implemented fully by 1808. Americans everywhere either objected to or opposed these innovations and modified many to suit their own interests. On the eve of independence, the leaders of the New World retained a significant degree of autonomy and control over their regions.[4]

The Spanish Monarchy was not only representative and decentralized, but also responsive to the needs of its many constituents. As John L. Phelan has indicated:

> The Spanish monarchy was absolute only in the original medieval sense. The king recognized no superior inside or outside his kingdoms. He was the ultimate source of all justice and all legislation. The late medieval phrase was, "The king is emperor in his realm." [It is worth noting here that the Castilian verb *imperar* meant "to govern."] The laws that bore the royal signature, however, were not the arbitrary expression of the king's personal wishes. Legislation, and the extent to which it was enforced, reflected the complex, and diverse aspirations of all, or at least several, groups in that corporate, multi-ethnic society. The monarchy was representative and decentralized to a degree seldom suspected. Although there were no formal representative assemblies or cortes in the Indies, each one of the major corporations, such as the [*repúblicas*—the Indian governments], the *cabildos* (city governments), the various ecclesiastical groups, the universities, and the craft guilds, all of which enjoyed a large measure of self-government, could and did speak for their respective constituents. Their views reached the king and the council of the Indies, transmitted directly by their accredited representatives or indirectly through the viceroys and the audiencias, and their aspirations profoundly shaped the character of the ultimate decisions.[5]

Hispanic political theory evolved in a fashion parallel to the development of political thought in Protestant countries and in Italy and France. As a major segment of Occidental civilization, the Hispanic world drew upon a shared Western European culture. The intellectuals of the Spanish Monarchy based their political ideas on ancient classical thought, on Catholic theories, and on the writings of a group of sixteenth- and seventeenth-century Hispanic thinkers—Francisco de Vitoria, Diego de Covarrubias, Domingo de Soto, Luis de Molina, Juan de Mariana, Francisco Suárez, and most important of all, Fernando Vázquez de Menchaca. As Quentin Skinner has observed, these Hispanic political theorists "helped to lay the foundations for the so-called 'social contract' theories of the seventeenth century. . . . [Moreover, the] Jesuit Mariana . . . [advanced] a theory of popular sovereignty which, while scholastic in origins and Calvinist in its later developments, was in essence independent of either religious creed, and was thus available to be used by both parties. . . ."[6] Some of the Hispanic theorists' ideas, particularly those of Vitoria, Covarrubias, and Vázquez de Menchaca, entered English and French political thought through the works of Johannes Althusius and Hugo Grotius.[7]

Hispanic intellectuals, like their counterparts in other regions of the Western world, believed in the ideal of a *res publicae* or mixed government. The term *republic*, however, did not mean a kingless form of government. Rather it referred to a system of government in which civic virtue ensured liberty and stability. The true republican citizen placed the common good of the res publicae, or commonwealth, above his own.[8] Based upon the political cultures of ancient Greece, Rome, and the Italian Renaissance states, mixed government was a regime in which the one (the ruler), the few (the prelates and the nobles), and the many (the people) shared sovereignty. Mixed governments were considered the best and most lasting because they established severe limitations upon arbitrary or tyrannical power—of the king, the nobles, or the people.[9] Moreover, as John Pocock has demonstrated, Niccolò Machiavelli's thought influenced significantly the concept of mixed government in England and elsewhere in the Atlantic world.[10] Educated Hispanics on both sides of the Atlantic turned to Aristotle, Polybius, and Machiavelli to understand the nature of classical republicanism.

During the late eighteenth century, nationalists on the Peninsula reinterpreted history to create a new national myth. Enlightened Spaniards argued that the early Visigoths had enjoyed a form of tribal democracy. Supposedly, these Germanic ancestors forged the first Hispanic constitution. Later, in the thirteenth century, Spain developed the first parliament in Europe, the cortes. As David Brading has observed: "it was Alfonso de Wise, the thirteenth-century king of Castile, who had created the medieval constitution, summoning to the Cortes not merely the nobility and prelates but also the representatives of the cities."[11] According to this interpretation of history, medieval Spain had enjoyed democracy only to have it destroyed by the despotic Habsburg kings. Although earlier cortes represented individual kingdoms such as Aragón and Castile and not the entire nation, eighteenth-century reformers had a unified body in mind when they spoke of reconvening a cortes. Their ideas culminated in the works of Spain's foremost legal historian, Francisco Martínez Marina, whose massive *Teoría de las cortes* implied that the restoration of a national representative body was necessary to revitalize the country.[12]

The ideas of those Hispanic theorists were reinterpreted in the universities and colleges of Spain and America and provided the basis of modern Hispanic political thought during the late eighteenth and early nineteenth centuries. Among the concepts advanced by the sixteenth- and seventeenth-century legal commentators, such as Vázquez de Menchaca and Suárez, two would become significant in the early nineteenth century—the notion of a compact (*pactum translationis*) between the people and the king and the idea of popular sovereignty.[13] Natural law theories of government also were widespread in the Hispanic world. Joaquín Marín y Mendoza, appointed by King Carlos III to the chair of law at San Isidro, for example, published *Historia del derecho natural y de gentes* in 1776. He and other professors of law introduced their students to a number of European authors who developed natural law and contract theories of government, among them Gaetano Filangieri, Christian Wolf, Emmerich de Vattel, and, most important of all, Samuel Pufendorf. These lesser-known authors, rather than the more famous Jean-Jacques Rousseau, prepared several generations of Hispanic students to reinterpret the relationship between the people and the government.[14]

In the 1780s, the University of Salamanca became a center of liberalism; its graduates would later become some of the revolutionary leaders in the Cortes of Cádiz. They were influenced by the Synod of Pistoia and two prominent theologians, Pietro Tamburini and Giuseppe Zola, who favored a less centralized Church and greater Episcopal authority. Politically, these concepts translated into representative government with a weak executive branch.[15] The ideas of Anglophone intellectuals from England, Scotland, and the United States—among them John Locke, Adam Smith, Adam Furguson, and Benjamin Franklin—were also well received. This intellectual interchange was a continuation of an ongoing dialog that began in the sixteenth century. British ideas, particularly the principle of mixed government exemplified by the unwritten English Constitution, merged well with Hispanic thought because Hispanic theorists, such as Vázquez de Menchaca, had influenced earlier British thinkers, like Thomas Hobbes.[16]

The scientific thought of the Enlightenment did not suddenly transform the Neoscholastic intellectual climate of Habsburg Spain and America. Instead, change began in the 1670s and 1680s when some Spanish scholars started questioning aspects of Scholasticism. These individuals, who are known as *eclectics*, introduced *modern philosophy*, as it came to be called, to the Hispanic world at the end of the seventeenth and early decades of the eighteenth century.[17] The new critical approach was widely disseminated through the writings of Benito Gerónimo Feijóo, who sought to introduce and popularize the scholarly and scientific achievements of the age. He insisted that the Spanish Monarchy required modern science, which did not clash with religion. Starting in 1739 with the nine-volume *Teatro crítico universal*, Feijóo discussed art, literature, philosophy, theology, mathematics, natural science, geography, economics, and history. Subsequently, he published five additional volumes of essays entitled *Cartas eruditas*. His approach was critical, exposing the fallibility of physicians, false saints, and miracles, and in all cases advancing the cause of modern analytical thought. Feijóo, as Richard Herr has observed, "never questioned the greatness of

Spain's former intellectual figures or expressed a view that he believed was the least opposed to the Catholic religion."[18] However, he upheld the experimental method of Protestant English science and rejected the highly theoretical systems and materialist philosophy of some of the French authors.[19] Although Feijóo's publications aroused great controversy, his works became extremely popular, appearing in countless editions in subsequent decades. Indeed, they were the best sellers of the age, second only to Cervantes' *Don Quijote*. Feijóo's works have been found in most colonial libraries in Spanish America, particularly those in New Spain. In 1750 King Fernando VI issued a royal decree prohibiting criticism of Feijóo because his writings merited "the royal pleasure."[20]

Spanish intellectuals were also abreast of evolving economic thought. The late seventeenth-century British proponents of free market economics[21] influenced Hispanic *tratadistas* (commentators). During the second half of the eighteenth century, societies for the promotion of useful knowledge became vehicles for disseminating economic ideas. The *Sociedad Vazcongada de Amigos del País* (Basque Society of Friends of the Country), an organization inspired by the Royal Society of London, the Society of Dublin, and the royal academies of Paris, Berlin, and St. Petersburg, was founded in the provincial city of Vergara in 1764 to support education in the region. The Sociedad Vazcongada became a major center for discussion of all sorts of useful knowledge, including science and technology. It attracted the most important men from the Basque Provinces as its members. Soon it admitted other prominent Spaniards and distinguished foreigners. As it gained influence, the Sociedad expanded its membership to include Americans. By 1773 it had admitted numerous overseas members, the vast majority in New Spain: 120 in Mexico City, 5 each in Querétero and San Luis Potosí, 4 in Oaxaca, 3 in Valladolid, 2 in Zacatecas, and 1 each in Guadalajara and Veracruz. Subsequently, other *sociedades de amigos del país* were established in Spain and in America. Inevitably, the societies turned to questions of the economy and the latest economic theories. In their discussions and publications, these bodies disseminated the works of exponents of laissez-faire economics.[22]

During the reign of Carlos III a number of distinguished reformers applied the new philosophy and economic theory to the Spanish Monarchy. Their work culminated in the activities of the great Spanish economist and statesman, Gaspar Melchor Jovellanos, who like Feijóo was an admirer of British thought. In 1774, two years before Adam Smith published the *Wealth of Nations*, Jovellanos issued a legal opinion that supported the free market: "We would like to restore liberty completely, which is the soul of commerce, the one which grants merchandize its value, based on its abundance or scarcity, and the one that establishes prices with natural justice. . . ." Both in his political actions and in his subsequent published work, Jovellanos sought to eliminate privilege and to foster commercial and political liberty.

He declared: "The first political principle is to provide men the greatest freedom possible. Protected by liberty, industry, commerce, population, and wealth will increase."[23] During his long and distinguished career, Jovellanos continued to advocate free trade and to attack all privilege. He defended property rights and self-interest and therefore opposed government interference in the economy. In his view, the role of government was to protect property and private interests with laws that ensured economic liberty and to provide education to its people and infrastructure—such as roads, canals, irrigation, ports and other facilities—to its economy. Most of all, it should impose just taxes, which everyone—without exception—should pay according to their ability.[24]

Educated groups in America were familiar with European economic, legal, and political concepts. During the late eighteenth and early nineteenth centuries, New World legal scholars—especially professors in the law faculties of the continent's universities—reinterpreted Vázquez de Menchaca's and Suárez's compact theory to further their interests.[25] Americans, like Spaniards, based their national myths on a historic constitution. According to this interpretation, Americans derived their rights from two sources: their Indian progenitors, who originally possessed the land, and their Spanish ancestors, who in conquering the New World obtained privileges from the Crown, including the right to convene their own cortes. That early compact, however, was not made between America and Spain, but between each New World kingdom and the king. The laws of the Indies affirmed the special status of the Americas within the Spanish Monarchy. Since the sixteenth century, European as well as New World legal scholars had commented on the unique nature of *derecho indiano* (the law of the Indies). The publication of the great *Recopilación de leyes de los Reynos de las Indias* in 1680 provided the impetus for extensive new interpretations of the nature of American rights. In the second half of the eighteenth century, a number of jurists published new collections of laws issued in America.[26]

Such works contributed to the notion that the New World possessed its own "unwritten constitution." As Father Servando Teresa de Mier, one of the most distinguished advocates of the thesis of American rights, declared: "Our kings, far from having considered establishing in our Americas the modern system of colonies of other nations, not only made our [kingdoms] the equals of Spain but also granted us the best [institutions] she possessed." And he maintained: "In conclusion it is evident that: under the constitution granted by the kings of Spain to the Americas, these lands are kingdoms independent of her [Spain] without any other link but the king . . . who, according to political theorists, must govern us as though he were the king of each of them [the American realms]." Moreover he noted: "When I refer to the social pact of the Americans, I do not refer to Rousseau's implicit pact. Rather, it consists of the pact between the Kingdom of New Spain and the sovereign of Castile.

The rupture or suspension of that pact . . . results, as an inevitable consequence, in the resumption of sovereignty by the Nation. . . . When that occurs, sovereignty reverts to its original owner."[27] Such notions, of course, are derived directly from Soto, Suárez, and Vázquez de Menchaca.[28]

The great-enlightened monarch Carlos III presided over a major transformation in the Hispanic world. During his reign, the Enlightenment spread throughout his realms. The Hispanic variant was neither radical nor anti-Christian, as in France. But like the Enlightenment everywhere, the Hispanic movement admired classical antiquity, preferring science and reason to authority and useful knowledge to theory. As José Miranda indicated, "The Enlightenment was neither a theory nor a doctrine, but a new way of looking at things and interpreting life. . . . The Enlightenment possessed, however, a principle common to the multitude of ideas that sprouted in its bosom: the liberty or autonomy of reason."[29] Although the Hispanic Enlightenment did not challenge the authority either of the Church or of the crown, its emphasis on science and reason created the intellectual climate that would ultimately incline some to embrace new political ideas. Although a few, particularly in the Church, opposed aspects of the new system of thought, their concerns were muted by the support that the monarch lent to the movement.[30]

Periodical publications, called *gazetas*, played a central role in disseminating "the new way of looking at things and interpreting life" in the Hispanic world. The *Gazeta de Madrid*, which appeared in 1701, and the *Gazeta de México* (1722, 1728–1730, 1784–1809) sought to record important political and cultural occurrences, other events of interest, and significant medical and scientific discoveries. The *Diario de Madrid*, founded in 1758, became the first daily newspaper in Europe. The pace of publication accelerated in the 1780s when large numbers of periodicals, which addressed a variety of issues, appeared in Spain and America. Madrid and Mexico City became the principal centers of publication. Among the important Madrid periodicals were the *Semanario erudito* (1781–1791), *El Observador* (1781–1877), *El Correo literario de Europa* (1781–1791), *El Mercurio de España* (1784–1830), *El gabinete de la lectura Española* (1787–1791), and the *Espiritu de los mejores diarios* (1787–1791), a digest of the leading European publications that circulated widely in America as well as in Spain. Influential Mexico City publications included the *Diario literario de México* (1768), the *Mercurio volante* (1772–1773), and the *Gazeta de literatura de México* (1788–1795). By the turn of the century, the press flourished both in the capital of New Spain and in important provincial cities like Veracruz.[31]

Periodicals also informed their readers about history, art, literature, philosophy, and major events. The works of the principal writers of the age, including the English and the French *philosophes*, were either translated or presented in summary form. In some cases, the periodicals reported that certain works, such as Edward Gibbon's *Decline and Fall of the Roman Empire*, had been prohibited "because . . . [they] contained false, heretical doctrines, inimical to the Catholic religion."[32] But other writers, such as Thomas Paine, were translated or paraphrased without comment. Moreover, events that might have had revolutionary implications were openly reported; for example, Madrid newspapers carried accounts of the U.S. struggle for independence and subsequently published a Spanish edition of the U.S. Constitution of 1787.[33] Similarly, periodicals such as *La Gazeta de México* discussed aspects of the French Revolution while defending the Catholic faith and the Spanish Monarchy.[34]

New ideas were widely disseminated. Periodicals and pamphlets, which became increasingly popular after the French Revolution, reached an important but limited audience in Spain and America. One should not assume, however, as many often do, that literacy rates were small relative to other nations at the time. As François-Xavier Guerra has observed, "the *Diario de México* published three editions on November 4, 1811, with a run of more than 7,000 copies. That is a huge number for a city which then had around 140,000 persons; it constitutes one newspaper for every 20 inhabitants, including children."[35]

Oral communication in the public space, a concept popularized by Jürgen Habermas,[36] played a central role in disseminating ideas to a broader public. *Tertulias*, originally informal family occasions in which men and women were joined by friends and acquaintances, expanded in the second half of the eighteenth century to become social gatherings to discuss literature, philosophy, science, and current events. In Spain and America tertulias brought elites—noble and nonnoble—merchants, government officials, clergymen, professionals, and other educated people together to discuss a variety of topics. In the 1770s it became common for some tertulias to be held in private rooms at inns. By the end of the next decade, cafes and taverns became new arenas for social discourse. At the turn of the century, distinguished noblewomen of the large capital cities, such as Madrid and Mexico, held fashionable tertulias in their homes that attracted the leading personages of the region.[37]

Cafes evolved from places where one went to *merendar* (to eat something light in the afternoon) to locations where society engaged in animated discussion. It became common for subscribers of periodicals to read them aloud in cafes and for patrons to talk for hours about important issues. As Antonio Alcalá Galiano observed "In the poor cafes [of Madrid] at that time, it was the custom to read the *Gazeta* [aloud] next to a brazier in the winter and by the window in the summer. Everyone talked with great enthusiasm. . . . Often, I played the role of reader among those in attendance."[38] Mexico City also possessed cafes that by the 1780s had become places where individuals read gazetas and discussed current events, history, art, and philosophy. As one writer commented: "The public frequents the cafes. And although science may not be cultivated there, everyone can enrich his command of our Spanish language and exercise reason while developing the ideas that occur to him." Similarly, provincial capitals became centers of an active public life.[39]

Whereas tertulias and cafes catered to the wealthier segments of society, taverns, avenues, parks, and other public places became centers of discussion for the broader public. There the popular segments of society—craftsmen, small shopkeepers, lower-level employees, muleteers, and often the unemployed—gathered to talk about events of the day. As the *Diario de México* noted in 1806, "Even though rude and coarse people do not read the dailies and other public papers, perhaps even ignoring their very existence, the useful information which they contain is transmitted imperceptibly by enlightened persons. Thus, little by little knowledge is spread."[40] With such open and widespread interest in the ideas and events of the day, it was only natural that the authorities in Spain and America became concerned that discussions might foster unrest. Taverns particularly worried government officials who perceived them as places where popular discontent might erupt. In 1791, when fear of French revolutionary ideas became paramount, the authorities briefly restricted activities in public places. Later, in 1809 in Mexico City, for example, "Nicolás Calero, a business agent, was denounced of having taken an anonymous paper to the Café Medina where he read aloud [anti-government statements]."[41]

The numerous universities and colleges of Spain and America also became centers of intellectual ferment in the latter part of the eighteenth century. Although the Jesuits and the Franciscans had been active in introducing modern philosophy, the major transformation occurred in 1771 with the reform that modernized the curriculum of the University of Salamanca, the premier institution in Spain and the model for American universities. Thereafter, despite conservative opposition, modern scientific views were taught at the institutions of higher learning in the Spanish world. The new curriculum had a profound effect. University graduates of the 1780s and 1790s, both from Spain and from America, led the great political revolution of the Spanish world after 1808.[42]

At the end of the eighteenth century, New Spain possessed one of the most extensive and diverse networks of educational and scientific institutions in the Western world. Its capital, the city of Mexico, the largest in the Western Hemisphere, was endowed with a great university (the oldest in the continent), the Royal School of Surgery, the School of Mines (the second founded in the world after the one in Paris), the Botanical Gardens, the Academy of Art of San Carlos, several important colleges, and various seminaries. According to Alexander von Humboldt, "no city in the new continent, including in the United States, possesses such great and solid scientific establishments as the capital city of Mexico."[43] Guadalajara, the capital of the kingdom's second Audiencia, also possessed a university, colleges, and seminaries. Moreover, virtually all the capitals of the other ten intendancies possessed colleges and seminaries. In addition, countless primary schools were found in all the cities of the realm, and more than a thousand schools were located in towns and villages, many of them in Indian *repúblicas*. Indeed, Guerra considered the educational establishment of New Spain "analogous to that of Spain or France [at that time]."[44]

Educated *novohispanos*, like their Spanish counterparts, were modern, enlightened individuals who were well prepared to address the many complex problems of their age. They were well versed in contemporary political thought, which emphasized liberty, equality, civil rights, the rule of law, representative constitutional government, and laissez-faire economics. Many were *liberal* before the term was coined in the Cortes of Cádiz in 1810; that is, they embraced the new ideology. They were engaged in a process of transforming the Spanish Monarchy into a modern liberal state. Such a change would neither have been easy nor rapid because important interest groups defended the status quo. The French invasion of Spain and the collapse of the Monarchy in 1808, however, provided the liberal minority with an unprecedented opportunity to implement its goals of liberty, equality, civil rights, the rule of law, representative constitutional government, and laissez-faire economics.

THE HISPANIC CONSTITUTIONAL REVOLUTION

The disintegration of the Spanish Monarchy triggered a series of events, which culminated in the establishment of representative government in the Spanish world. The initial step in that process was the formation of governing juntas in Spain and America that invoked the Hispanic legal principle that, in the absence of the king, sovereignty reverted to the people. In Spain, the provinces asserted their autonomy by insisting that sovereignty now belonged to them. While the Peninsular provinces made that transition easily, the American kingdoms faced the opposition of royal officials, resident Europeans, and their New World allies.

News of events on the Peninsula reached Mexico City in June and July 1808. Throughout the viceroyalty, people expressed their support for Fernando VII and their opposition to Napoleon. The capital and the leading provincial cities held festivities in honor of the king that, according to Hira de Gortari Rabiela, constituted "a brief collective catharsis which immediately alleviated the insecurity and concern. Thus, the festivities allowed the people temporarily to forget the uncertainty and fear provoked by the French occupation of Spain."[45]

Despite the show of unity, the new situation divided the upper classes. Most European Spaniards wanted either to temporize or to recognize an authority—any authority—in Spain. In Mexico City, many Americans, on the other hand, favored autonomy. On July 19 the American-dominated Ayuntamiento of Mexico City submitted a resolution to Viceroy José de Iturrigaray asking him to continue *provisionally* in charge of the government. The *ayuntamiento* (city council) justified its position on the basis of traditional Hispanic political theory, reminding Iturrigaray that "in the absence or during the impediment [of the king], sovereignty lies represented in all the kingdom and the classes that form it; and more particularly in those superior tribunals that govern it and administer justice and in those corporations that represent the public voice."[46] They proposed that a junta similar to those formed in Spain be convened to govern New Spain. Viceroy Iturrigaray acquiesced and, on September 1, 1808, requested that the ayuntamientos of New Spain appoint representatives to a meeting in the capital. The *peninsulares* (those born in the Spanish Peninsula), however, overthrew the viceroy on the night of September 15, 1808, to prevent the congress of cities from taking place. Many Americans were incensed by the *golpe de estado* of 1808 because the Europeans had broken the law and taken control of the kingdom. Rumors of conspiracies became common throughout New Spain.[47] The golpe was the most important cause of the insurgency that would emerge in 1810.

The creation in Spain of the Junta Suprema Central Gubernativa del Reino as a government of national defense in September 1808 appeared to provide a solution to the crisis of the Monarchy. That body not only recognized the rights of Spanish provinces but also acknowledged the Americans' claims that their lands were not colonies but kingdoms, that they constituted equal and integral parts of the Spanish monarchy, and that they possessed the right of representation in the national government, something no other European nation had granted its possessions. Each province of Spain sent two deputies to the Junta Central while nine American kingdoms were allocated one apiece. Many Americans, however, objected to the fact that they would not have equal representation.[48]

In 1809 the kingdoms of America held the first elections for representatives to a Monarchy-wide government, the Junta Central. The complicated and lengthy elections constituted a profound step forward in the formation of modern representative government for the entire Spanish Nation, as the Monarchy was now called. The electoral processes—the use of the *terna*, for example—clearly relied upon existing election procedures for corporate bodies. The major difference was that traditional electoral processes were being adapted for new political purposes. Furthermore, the process implicitly recognized the ancient putative right of the provincial capitals of America to representation in congresses of cities.[49]

New World authorities, however, implemented the election decree in various ways. In New Spain, the peninsulares *golpistas* (Europeans who overthrew the government) who controlled the kingdom interpreted the decree in its narrowest form, granting only the capitals of the twelve intendencies and two other cities, which managed to convince the authorities of their rights, the privilege of holding elections. Antequera, Arizpe, Durango, Guadalajara, Guanajuato, Mérida, México, Puebla, Querétaro, San Luis Potosí, Tlaxcala, Valladolid, Veracruz, and Zacatecas were authorized to hold elections.[50] The elections were complicated and lengthy. In New Spain, according to Virginia Guedea, "the majority [of those elected]—eight of fourteen—had been born in the Peninsula and were closely aligned with its interests . . . and had distinguished themselves, or would distinguish themselves, as ardent defenders of the . . . status quo."[51] Although family, regional, business, and professional interests influenced the elections, in many cases the conflict pitted the "European party" against the "American party." The predominance of peninsulares in the elections of New Spain undoubtedly reflected the control that Europeans had exercised over that kingdom since their golpe de estado of 1808. It would be the last election dominated by the peninsulares.

The ayuntamientos of New Spain provided their representatives to the Junta Central with very detailed instructions. All declared their loyalty to Fernando VII, and most insisted upon equality for America. Thus, the inhabitants of the New World reaffirmed their support of the Monarchy while simultaneously asserting their rights within the Spanish Nation. The City of Guanajuato declared, "This America should not be considered a colony, but a very essential part of the Spanish Monarchy. . . . Under this fundamental and invariable constitutional concept, New Spain shall be considered equal to Old Spain, without any difference whatsoever, in all provisional actions, deliberations, and even variations of the laws and the national government."[52] The City of Zacatecas voiced its desire for reform most clearly. It demanded, "that legislative power be restored to the nation represented in the Cortes, that the abuses introduced by the executive branch be reformed, and that the king's ministers be held responsible for any future wrongdoings. . . ." That was a clear reference to the administration of Minister Manuel Godoy, widely considered to have been corrupt. Zacatecas also insisted "that the most perfect, just, and inviolable equilibrium be established not only between the two powers [the executive and the legislative], but also in national representation in a future cortes by means of increased representation [for the New World] resulting from the sovereign declaration that the Americas are an integral and essential part of the Monarchy. . . ."[53]

The decisive French victories of 1809, however, destroyed the fragile balance established by the Junta Central. When the body dissolved itself in January 1810, appointing a Council of Regency in its place, some provinces of Spain and several kingdoms of America refused to recognize the legitimacy of the new government. Some Americans believed that the time had come to establish autonomous governments in their lands. The Council's decision to convene a cortes, however, addressed the concerns of the provinces of Spain and many parts of the New World. In 1810 Americans held widespread elections, not for a governing junta but for a parliament for the entire Monarchy, which possessed the authority to transform the Spanish world. The cortes provided Americans who desired autonomy with a peaceful means of obtaining home rule. Moreover, the extensive debates in that parliament, which were widely disseminated by the press during the 1810–1812 period, significantly influenced both those Spanish Americans who supported as well as the insurgents who opposed the new Spanish government.

The deputies of Spain and America, who enacted the Constitution of the Spanish Monarchy in 1812, transformed the Hispanic world. They initiated one of the greatest revolutions in modern times. The Constitution of 1812 was not a Spanish document; it was a charter for the Spanish world. The American deputies to the cortes played a central role in drafting the constitution. Their arguments and proposals convinced Spaniards to embrace substantial change in the Peninsula as well as in America. Moreover, many of the liberal reforms that characterized the Hispanic Constitution of 1812 are directly attributable to deputies from New Spain, such as Miguel Ramos Arizpe and José Miguel Guridi y Alcocer.[54] They took the lead in introducing the principal institutions of local government, the *ayuntamiento constitucional* and the *diputación provincial*.[55]

The Constitution of Cádiz, the most radical charter of the nineteenth century, abolished seigniorial institutions, the Inquisition, Indian tribute, and forced labor and asserted the state's control of the Church. It created a unitary state with equal laws for all parts of the Spanish monarchy, substantially restricted the authority of the king, and entrusted the Cortes with decisive power. When it enfranchised all men, except those of African ancestry, members of regular orders, domestic servants, convicted criminals, and public debtors, without requiring either literacy or property qualifications, the Constitution of 1812 surpassed all existing representative governments, such as Great Britain, the United States, and France, in providing political rights to the vast majority of the male population.[56] François-Xavier Guerra's analysis of the 1813 election census in Mexico City, for example, concludes that 93 percent of the adult male population of the capital possessed the right to vote.[57]

The liberal tradition that emerged in Cádiz formed the basis of later Mexican political, economic, and institutional development. The Constitution of 1812 established representative government at three levels: the cities and towns (the constitutional ayuntamiento), the provinces (the provincial deputations), and the Monarchy (the Cortes). When it allowed cities and towns with one thousand inhabitants or more to form ayuntamientos, it transferred political power from the center to the periphery and incorporated a great number of persons in the political process.[58] The Constitution of Cádiz also addressed important socio-economic questions. Although some American and Spanish deputies favored abolishing slavery, the majority was unwilling to end that odious form of property. Similarly, the deputies were divided over the question of free trade. Many American and Spanish deputies believed that free trade would greatly expand the economy and contribute to the national well being. However, the majority of American and Spanish deputies favored protection for their industries. The deputies from New Spain were divided on the question and many abstained on the final vote.[59] The vast majority supported *contribuciones directas*, direct taxes, as the best and most equitable form of financing the government. Similarly, they agreed that all men had the responsibility of defending the nation. As the *Catecismo político*, a primary school text, noted in 1813:

> Every Spaniard must love his patria, be just and kind, obey the Constitution, obey the laws, respect established authorities, contribute, without any distinction, in proportion to his wealth, to the expenses of the state, and defend the patria with arms when called upon by the law. That is, there can be no privilege whatsoever with regards either to taxation or to military service.[60]

The new liberal, representative government was introduced more fully in the Viceroyalty of New Spain than in any other region of the Spanish Monarchy, including the Spanish Peninsula. Despite confusion, conflict, and delay, the first constitutional elections in New Spain contributed to the formation of a new political culture. Citizens participated in government both at the local and provincial levels. More than a thousand constitutional ayuntamientos were established throughout the land. In some areas, such as the territories of the Diputaciones Provinciales of Yucatán and of Nueva Galicia, as many as three successive ayuntamiento elections were held during the 1812–1814 period. Five provincial deputations were established during those years; those of Yucatán and Nueva Galicia held two elections during the period, first to establish and then to renew the provincial governments.[61] The people of the former Viceroyalty of New Spain were learning the nature and importance of self-government and local autonomy through their own experience. Their appreciation of self-government would expand and mature with time.

THE INSURGENCY

The constitutional revolution, however, was not the only transformation that occurred in New Spain. The 1808 golpe had exacerbated the divisions between Europeans and Americans. The *novohispano* (people of New Spain) autonomists never accepted the Spaniard's actions. Some resorted to violence to achieve self-government. In the fall of 1809, the authorities discovered a serious conspiracy in the city of Valladolid. Iturrigaray's overthrow in September 1808 and the subsequent arrogance of the Spaniards had galvanized the Americans. The conspirators had supporters in other provincial cities, such as Guanajuato, Querétaro, San Miguel el Grande, and Guadalajara. They prepared an uprising for December 21, 1809, and expected backing from the army and the militia. They hoped to attract thousands of men from among the Indians and castas by promising to abolish tribute. The plan differed from the early autonomy movement in Mexico City only in that the conspirators had to rely on force because the Spaniards had seized the government. When the movement was exposed, the authorities chose to exercise leniency because many important persons openly declared that the conspirators were guilty only of seeking to redress rightful grievances in an inappropriate manner.[62]

The Valladolid conspiracy encouraged a similar movement in Querétaro, where militia captains Ignacio Allende and Juan Aldama and corregidor Miguel Domíguez began informal talks. By March 1810, the plotters had recruited Father Miguel Hidalgo and other disaffected criollos. They, like the Valladolid group, sought to depose the European Spaniards with the aid of the rural and urban workers of the Bajío and to establish an American junta to govern in the name of King Fernando VII. The conspirators planned the uprising for October 1810, but the authorities discovered them on September 13, and the Querétaro group was arrested.

Hidalgo, Allende, and Aldama, however, launched the revolt from the prosperous town of Dolores on the morning of September 16, 1810. According to Aldama, about eight o'clock in the morning:

> There were gathered more than six thousand men on foot and horseback for it was Sunday and they had come to mass from the nearby ranches [medium-sized farms], and the cura [Hidalgo] exhorted them to join him and help defend the Kingdom because they [the European Spaniards] wanted to turn it over to the French; that now oppression had reached an end; that there was no longer any tribute; and that those who enlisted with horses and arms would be paid a peso daily, and those on foot four reales.[63]

The Hidalgo revolt, which began as a movement for autonomy, was initially favorably received by the elite of New Spain. However, the upper classes withdrew their support when it became evident that the rebel leaders could not control their followers. The sack of Guanajuato constituted the turning point in the revolt. The looting, carnage, and destruction of the Bajian city clearly indicated that the insurrection promoted uncontrollable class conflict. The elite feared that a revolution would spark a race war. Indians and campesinos with communal lands also were afraid that the landless poor in Hidalgo's forces might dispossess them. The royal army and most of the militia, which were 95 percent American, remained loyal to the Crown. Ultimately, the royalists defeated the insurgents. Hidalgo was subsequently captured, tried, degraded from the priesthood, and executed.[64]

His death did not end the insurgency. Ignacio Rayón, a lawyer who served as the secretary of state, assumed leadership of the movement after Hidalgo's execution in 1811. Initially, Rayón attempted to effect reconciliation with the royal authorities. When they rejected his attempt to obtain autonomy, Rayón and other insurgent leaders organized the Suprema Junta Nacional Americana as an alternative government. In January 1812, royalist forces captured the town of Zitácuaro, where the Junta was based. Although Rayón escaped, he gradually lost his position as leader of the rebels. Father José María Morelos, who had been waging a guerrilla campaign in the south, emerged as the most important insurgent chieftain.[65]

In contrast to the Hidalgo revolt, the Morelos insurgency flourished because he directed an orderly movement that reduced the specter of race and class warfare. During 1811 and 1812, Morelos and his commanders concentrated on cutting the capital's lines of communication and on gaining control of the south. Morelos's greatest success came in 1812, when he captured Oaxaca. The following spring, he initiated a seven-month siege of Acapulco. Despite his military achievements, he could not claim authority merely by force of arms, particularly since the Hispanic Cortes had ratified the notion of popular sovereignty and representative government. After the promulgation of the Hispanic Constitution of 1812 and the holding of popular elections throughout New Spain, Morelos's urban supporters urged the convening of a congress.

In June 1813 Morelos convened elections in the regions controlled by the insurgents for a congress to be held at Chilpancingo, a small, easily defended, friendly town. Elections appear to have been held in the provinces of Oaxaca, Puebla, Veracruz, and Michoacán, areas held by the insurgents; in the insurgent Province of Tecpan; and secretly in Mexico City and possibly in other urban centers. Unlike elections under the Hispanic Constitution of 1812, the insurgent elections were less popular and appear to have been controlled or influenced by the insurgent leaders.[66]

Conflict ensued from the outset between the insurgent executive and the legislature. Although Congress ratified Morelos's command as generalísimo and declared the independence of *América Septentrional* (North America), the body assumed national sovereignty and attempted to exercise supreme power. On October 22, 1814, Congress issued the Constitutional Decree for the Liberty of Mexican America, known as the Constitution of Apatzingán, after the town where it was promulgated. The new charter established a republic with a plural executive and a powerful legislature. Congress rejected Morelos's pretensions to power and stripped him of supreme authority, but it retained his support by appointing him a member of the executive triumvirate. On November 1815, however, royalist forces defeated Morelos. He was captured, tried, degraded from the priesthood, and executed on December 22, 1815. Earlier that month, other insurgent leaders dissolved Congress. The Constitution of Apatzingán was never implemented and exercised no influence on subsequent constitutional development in New Spain/Mexico.[67]

THE CONSTITUTION RESTORED

The first constitutional period ended in 1814 when Fernando VII returned and abolished the Cortes and the Constitution, restoring absolutism. The Antiguo Régimen, which Fernando VII had reinstated in 1814, lasted until March 1820. In Spain, the liberals exploited the military's disenchantment with the war in America and eventually forced the king to restore the Constitution. The restored Antiguo Régimen (1814–1820) had demonstrated the value of the institutions of self-government created by the Charter of Cádiz. The inhabitants of New Spain enthusiastically reestablished the institutions that granted them political control in their territories.

News of the restoration of the Constitution of 1812 unleashed widespread political activity in New Spain. Without waiting for instructions from the viceroy, the coastal cities of Mérida and Campeche swore allegiance to the Charter at the beginning of May. Veracruz and Jalapa followed later that month. Public pressure forced the viceroy to proclaim the Constitution in the capital May 31.[68] Shortly thereafter, the authorities dispatched nearly a thousand copies of the Constitution throughout the kingdom.[69] In the following months, cities and towns established or restored more than a thousand constitutional ayuntamientos. In the Province of Puebla alone, 164 constitutional ayuntamientos, among them many in Indian towns, had been erected by January 1821. The people of the former Viceroyalty of New Spain also restored the second tier of local government, the provincial deputations. By the end of the year, six newly elected provincial deputations were functioning in the former viceroyalty.[70]

The printing press, which became the indispensable instrument of politics, fueled the explosion of political activity. Important notices, decrees, laws, circulars, minutes of special meetings, reports of elections, statements from prominent persons, and other matters of interest were published almost immediately, both in Mexico City and in the provincial capitals. Thousands of pamphlets, newspapers, and single sheets circulated. The ayuntamientos of Mexico City and other provincial capitals as well as the diputaciones provinciales informed their counterparts of their activities, often sending them printed documents. Politically active novohispanos learned of significant events within days of their occurrence; they possessed copies of important documents; and they made certain that they exercised their rights.[71] A national political culture had begun to form before the nation was formally established.

Although political debate attracted public attention, elections, perhaps more than any other activity, politicized New Spain's society. Since there were neither literacy nor property qualifications for voting, nearly all adult males had the right to participate. More than a thousand cities and towns held elections for constitutional ayuntamientos during the second half of 1820. Additional elections for the 1821 ayuntamientos were held in December 1820. Elections for deputies to the Cortes and for members of the six diputaciones provinciales occurred between August and November 1820. New elections for the 1822–1823 Cortes and to replace half of the members of the Diputationes Provinciales started in December 1820 at the parish level and concluded at the provincial capitals in March 1821. Thus, from June 1820 until March 1821, electioneering and elections preoccupied the politically active population of Nueva España—numbering more than a million.[72] These intense activities provided a practical political education that ensured that *el pueblo* remained active and engaged in the new liberal political culture.

In the second constitutional period, the provinces were not content with the small number of deputations allocated to the Viceroyalty of New Spain by the earlier Cortes, and they organized to obtain their own provincial deputation. Shortly after being reestablished, the Constitutional Ayuntamiento de Puebla, for example, sent a formal representation to the Cortes requesting that it be allocated a provincial deputation in accord with Article 325 of the Constitution, which stated: "In each province there will be a deputation called provincial to promote its prosperity, presided by the jefe superior."[73] Although each province of New Spain insisted that it be granted a provincial deputation, the Cortes authorized only one new deputation in 1820, that of Michoacán and Guanajuato, with its seat at Valladolid.

During the parliamentary recess from November 10, 1820, to March 1, 1821, the American deputies organized to mount a unified effort to expand provincial government in America. The arrival in Madrid of new proprietary deputies increased their numbers, and the American provinces themselves strengthened the hands of their representatives by submitting detailed petitions justifying the creation of new deputations. The big push occurred in the 1821 Cortes when the American deputies insisted that each former intendancy in the New World be granted a provincial deputation. After considerable debate, on May 8, 1821, the Cortes agreed.[74] The American representatives had won a significant concession in their effort to obtain home rule.

In Mexico City members of the national elite, who were concerned about the need to retain self-government, kept in close touch with like-minded individuals in the provincial capitals. Many issues worried them. The intense involvement of the people in the political process was new and unsettling.

Some members of the military and the clergy became hostile to the constitutional system because the Cortes enacted measures suppressing the Jesuits and the monastic orders and abolishing ecclesiastic and military immunity from civil prosecution.

Perhaps most distressing to the autonomists were reports about the political disintegration of the Peninsula. Was political and social revolution imminent? If so, what should be done to protect orderly representative government in New Spain? Perhaps the time had come to assume control of their political destiny. Some spoke openly of independence. One group, which included various factions, among them discontented clergymen, army officers, and government officials as well as large number of autonomists, concluded that independence might be necessary to retain home rule under the Constitution of 1812, that is, to establish a limited constitutional monarchy in New Spain.

During 1820–1821, the leaders of New Spain pursued two courses of action. New Spain's deputies to the Cortes proposed a project for New World autonomy that would create three American kingdoms governed by Spanish princes under the Constitution of 1812, and allied with the Peninsula. At the same time, New Spain's autonomists also encouraged and supported the royalist Colonel Agustín de Iturbide, who accepted *their* plan for autonomy,[75] a version of the proposal then being debated in the Cortes in Madrid. The Spanish majority in the Cortes, although initially favorable, ultimately rejected the proposal that would have granted Americans the home rule they had been seeking since 1808.

INDEPENDENCE

The leaders of New Spain declared independence when they realized that the mother country would not grant them the autonomy they desired. While New Spain's elite proposed to govern at home, they nonetheless sought to retain strong ties with Spain. Their Plan of Iguala proposed establishing a constitutional monarchy called the Mexican Empire with the Spanish king or a member of the royal family as sovereign, and acknowledged the Hispanic Constitution of 1812 and the statutes enacted by the Cortes as the law of the land. Independence was assured when Juan O'Donojú, the last jefe político superior of New Spain, ratified the Plan of Iguala by signing the Treaty of Córdoba. He reached an accord quickly with Iturbide because the Plan of Iguala was essentially the proposal for American regencies that the American deputies had presented to the Cortes, and which O'Donojú believed that parliament had approved. As Iturbide later declared, the Spaniard accepted the American's proposal "as though he had helped me write the plan [of Iguala]."[76]

The founders of the Mexican Empire considered their actions consistent with Hispanic political traditions, which they considered their legitimate patrimony. They recognized the primacy of the Hispanic Constitution of 1812 and the laws passed by the Hispanic Cortes because they were part of their recent political experience. Distinguished novohispanos had participated in its writing and for many Mexicans it was *their* Constitution as much as it was the Charter of the Spanish Monarchy. However, the extraordinary circumstances of the new nation would channel politics in directions that few might have imagined in 1821.

The autonomists considered independence the culmination of their more than a decade-long effort to achieve power. Emancipation, however, had required the aid of the military. Thus, while the autonomists believed it to be their triumph, the army, headed by Iturbide, considered independence its victory.[77] Although Mexico had achieved its emancipation, tension existed between the civilians and the military. As I have indicated: "two opposing political traditions . . . emerged between 1808 and 1821 . . . ; one forged in the crucible of war emphasized executive power and the other, based on civilian parliamentary experience, insisted upon legislative dominance."[78] It is possible that an experienced administrator and a committed liberal like O'Donojú would have succeeded in peacefully resolving those tensions. Unfortunately, he became ill immediately after entering the capital and could not attend the ceremonies of the Declaration of Independence on September 28. He died of pleurisy on October 8, 1821.

The newly independent Mexicans carefully followed the precedents of the Spanish political system. They formed a Council of Regency to govern them and a Soberana Junta Provisional Gubernativa to function as a legislature until a Mexican Cortes convened. When Spain rejected their proposal, and faced with popular and military demands, the country's political leaders reluctantly accepted a native, Agustín de Iturbide, as the nation's first emperor. Soon, however, conflict erupted between Emperor Agustín I, who believed in executive power, and the Constituent Cortes, which insisted upon legislative dominance. Although Iturbide dissolved the Cortes in October 1822, the provinces forced him to abdicate in March 1823.[79]

THE CONFEDERAL REPUBLIC

The provinces of Mexico, governed by provincial deputations established by the Constitution of 1812, insisted on electing a new constituent congress charged with ensuring their autonomy. They rejected the Constituent Cortes's claim, based on the actions of the Spanish Cortes, that it was the repository of national sovereignty. Instead, the provinces held that they possessed sovereignty and that they were relinquishing a portion of that sovereignty to create a national government. The provinces considered themselves the arbiters of the nation in mid-1823.

The Second Constituent Congress, which met on November 7, 1823, faced very different circumstances than its predecessor. Since the provinces, many already organized as states, determined that Mexico must have a federal republic, debate in Congress centered on the critical issue of who was sovereign: the nation or the states. On this question the deputies were divided into four factions: extreme defenders of states' rights; those who favored a federal system but who believed only the nation could be sovereign; those who believed in shared sovereignty between the nation and the states (confederalists); and a tiny minority of centralists who desired a highly centralized government. Neither the advocates of states' rights nor the proponents of national sovereignty triumphed. Instead a form of shared sovereignty emerged as a compromise. Nevertheless, the states gained considerable power of taxation at the expense of the national government, which lost approximately half the income formerly collected by the viceregal administration. To compensate for that loss, the states agreed to pay the national government a *contingente* assessed on each state according to its means.

The compromise to share sovereignty did not settle the question of the division of powers within the national government. Following Hispanic traditions, most congressmen believed that the legislature should be dominant. After Iturbide's abdication, the Constituent Cortes had established a triumvirate called the Supremo Poder Ejecutivo, which alternated the presidency on a monthly basis. The majority of the members of the Second Constituent Congress favored a plural executive of some kind. But a revolt on January 20, 1824, and the difficulty which the Supremo Poder Ejecutivo had in maintaining order, convinced them of the unwieldiness of the plural executive. Eventually Congress opted for a president and a vice president. That decision, however, did not mean that congress accepted a strong presidency. Most Mexicans continued to favor congressional superiority. They created a quasi-parliamentary system, making the secretaries of state responsible to Congress.

The Mexican Constitution of 1824 was modeled on the Hispanic Constitution of 1812, not, as is often asserted, on the U.S. Constitution of 1787. If the Mexican constitution possessed any similarity with a United States charter, it was with that country's first constitution, the Articles of Confederation, since Mexico's republic was *confederalist* rather than federalist. Entire sections of the Cádiz Charter were repeated verbatim in the Mexican document because the individuals who drafted the Mexican constitution were distinguished novohispanos who had served in the Cortes of Cádiz and had helped write the 1812 charter. Both the Spanish Constitution of 1812 and the Mexican Constitution of 1824 established powerful legislatures and weak executives. But it would be an error to consider the Constitution of 1824 a mere copy of the 1812 document. Events in Mexico, particularly the assertion of states' rights by the former provinces, forced Congress to frame a constitution to meet the unique circumstances of the nation.

The principal innovations—republicanism, confederalism, and a presidency—were adopted to address Mexico's new reality. The monarchy was abolished because both Fernando VII and Agustín I had failed as political leaders. Confederalism arose naturally from Mexico's earlier political experience. In most cases, the provincial deputations created by the Constitution of Cádiz simply converted themselves into states. The distinguished novohispanos, who had assumed a role of leadership in the Spanish Cortes, continued to promote their views in the new Mexican nation they were forming.[80]

The Constitution of 1824, with its weak executive, strong legislature, and mass political participation, failed to meet the challenges of the first decade of independent life. The Charter not only granted authority to the states but also empowered the *pueblos de campesinos*, the former Indian repúblicas. As a result of the extension of the franchise to large sectors of the population, the national elites found themselves in competition not only with the provincial elites but also with campesinos who challenged their power in the countryside. The vast number of ayuntamientos, originally authorized by the Hispanic Constitution of 1812, complicated the struggle at the local level and threatened regional elites. The new political structures failed to resolve conflicting demands. To end the "anarchy" that they believed dominated the region, the proponents of order often resorted to force to severely restrict the franchise, strengthen executive power, and centralize the national government. The national and the provincial elites eventually agreed on the need to limit political participation to a small group in the national and in the regional capitals.[81]

THE SEARCH FOR ORDER

After partial efforts to eliminate popular confederalism in the period 1830–1832, the proponents of order triumphed in 1835. The Constitution of 1836, known as the Siete Leyes because it contained seven sections, established a central state divided into departments. The presidential term was extended to eight years. However, the legislature remained dominant and the executive weak. A special body, known as the Supremo Poder Conservador, was established to moderate among the three branches of government. Stringent property qualifications were introduced for political participation and for office holders. The most radical change, however, consisted of the concentration of power in the hands of the few. Not only were elected state governors and legislatures eliminated in favor of departmental officials appointed by the national government—the governor and the departmental councils—but the number of ayuntamientos was drastically reduced, virtually eliminating direct political participation in the countryside. Municipal government was limited to departmental capitals, cities which had possessed such bodies before 1808, ports with populations larger than 4,000 people, and towns with more than 8,000 residents, a far cry from the 1,000 souls required by the Hispanic Constitution of 1812. Local town government and, therefore, the power of rural communities was virtually eliminated throughout the nation. The political arena was subsequently further reduced when the constituent congress, which convened in 1842, drafted the 1843 charter known as the Bases Orgánicas. The document restricted suffrage even more and attempted to strengthen the power of the president. Nevertheless, the legislature remained dominant.[82]

Provincial discontent thwarted centralist dreams of order and prosperity. Opposition, particularly in the towns and among campesinos, which took the form of federalist and rural revolts, plagued the regime. In August 1846, Mexicans terminated their experiment with centralism and returned to federalism, restoring the Constitution of 1824. The country, however, remained divided and political upheavals continued even as the United States invaded Mexico.

A new generation of political leaders, who came of age after Independence, began to reach positions of power and influence by mid-century. Unlike their predecessors, they had not experienced Spanish rule. Since the mother country, like Mexico, had experienced economic decline and political disruption in the post-independence period, the group turned to more advanced nations, particularly France and Great Britain, for examples of stable, prosperous, and modern societies. While Britain provided an important model of economic development, French socio-political structures gained prominence among Mexican leaders. The European Revolutions of 1848, in particular, inspired many who wished to bring their countries into the modern age.

THE NEW LIBERAL ORDER

A new form of liberalism, which stressed political stability and economic modernization, began to gain adherents. The pace of social, political, and economic reform quickened. The new liberals severely restricted the power of the Catholic Church by separating church and state. They eliminated military and ecclesiastical fueros, making all citizens equal under the law. Moreover, they ended the right of traditional corporations—primarily the Church and the native communities—to own land by decreeing individual ownership of property. Most of all, they sought to form a stronger and more effective national state. This meant abandoning confederalism for a much more powerful national government. Still, most liberals continued to prefer a strong legislature and a slightly stronger executive branch.[83]

A new generation of Mexican conservatives allied themselves with the strongman Antonio López de Santa Anna to thwart the liberal project. In 1852, they succeeded in imposing a stronger centralism. The conservative project favored individual property rights and a market economy, but it restored Church influence and even proposed establishing a monarchy. Most important, the conservatives again restricted local government and widespread political participation.

Opposition emerged from two sources: the new liberals who wished to establish a modern federal republic and the leaders of rural communities who insisted on retaining a popular confederalism. The latter initiated the Revolution of Ayutla, which ousted Santa Anna and the conservatives. The rural leaders favored a political system that distributed power widely and guaranteed state and local autonomy. They also demanded universal male suffrage and low taxes.[84] The new liberals, while agreeing with parts of the rural project, favored a stronger state, which they hoped would foster national economic growth and modernization.

The new liberals ultimately prevailed. Their project became enshrined in the Constitution of 1857. The new charter created a federal republic with a somewhat stronger president and a unicameral legislature. It granted the national government greater power, particularly in the area of taxation, while reserving considerable authority for the states. It established equality under the law; that is, it eliminated clerical and military fueros. It also separated church and state, eventually providing for religious toleration. Further, it abolished corporate and communal property in favor of individual property rights. The document also enumerated individual rights and guarantees such as freedom of religion, press, speech, and assembly, and introduced free and compulsory education.

The Constitution of 1857, designed to further the liberal project of capitalist modernization, could not be fully implemented for a decade. First, conservatives rebelled, unleashing a civil war known as the War of the Reform; then, conservatives with the aid of France imposed a foreign monarch, Maximilian of Austria,[85] thereby initiating another conflict, the War of the French intervention. The liberals' triumph of 1867 finally enabled them to initiate the transformation of Mexico.

As a result of the great political revolution of the Hispanic world, Mexico developed a new legitimacy that lasted for a century. Despite numerous political upheavals, most Mexicans believed in the principles of popular sovereignty, local rights, and civilian, representative, constitutional government. They disagreed about the degree of popular participation and local government, but they did not question the validity either of representative government or of legislative supremacy. Although Mexicans established a central republic in 1836, they did not succeed in imposing either a highly centralized government or a powerful presidency. Instead, they reduced the political role of the towns, concentrating power in the principal cities. Under the centralist constitutions the legislature remained dominant. Even those who sought to restore the monarchy favored a constitutional monarchy. The Constitution of 1857, promulgated to resolve the perceived flaws of the earlier federal charter, neither concentrated power in the national government nor established a strong presidency. No president, including Benito Juárez and Porfirio Díaz, dominated Mexico during the nineteenth century. Although the Mexican Revolution of 1910 and the subsequent post-revolutionary governments transformed the country's political system, concentrating power in the capital and in the president, the ideals of popular sovereignty, local rights, and representative government remained the goals of the Mexican people.

NOTES

1. John Adams, *The Works of John Adams* (Boston: Little, Brown, and Company, 1850), 10: 145.

2. See, for example, Claudio Véliz, *The Centralist Tradition in Latin America* (Princeton: Princeton University Press, 1980); and Frank Safford, "Politics, ideology, and society in post-Independence Spanish America" in Leslie Bethell, ed., *The Cambridge History of Latin America* (Cambridge: Cambridge University Press, 1984–1992), 3: 347–421.

3. Older historians, such as Roger B. Merriman, thought in terms of the Spanish Empire in the Old World and the New, as the title of his great work indicates: *The Rise of the Spanish Empire in the Old World and the New* (New York: The Macmillan Co., 1918–1934). Recently, Henry Kamen has reasserted this view in a "modern" fashion; see: *Empire: How Spain Became a World Power, 1492–1763* (New York: Harper Collins Publishers, 2003).

4. On this point consult Jaime E. Rodríguez O., *The Independence of Spanish America* (Cambridge: Cambridge University Press, 1998), 19–35.

5. John L. Phelan, *The People and the King: The Comunero Revolution in Colombia, 1781* (Madison: University of Wisconsin Press, 1978), 82.

6. Quentin Skinner, *The Foundations of Modern Political Thought* (Cambridge: Cambridge University Press, 1978), 2: 159, 347.

7. In Anthony Pagden's view: "Despite its absence from most contemporary scholarship the Controversiarum illustrium [of Fernando Vázquez de Menchaca] was to have a massive and sustained influence on Grotius—whose own attack on universalism is little more than a summary of Vázquez's conclusions—and through Grotius on much later discussions of the juridical basis of the relationship between states." *Lords of all the Word: Ideologies of Empire in Spain, Britain, and France c. 1500–c.1800* (New Haven: Yale University Press, 1995), 56. Vázquez de Menchaca's thought is examined by Annabel S. Brett in *Nature, Right, and Liberty: Individual*

Rights in Later Scholastic Thought (Cambridge: Cambridge University Press, 1997), 165–204. She concludes: "Vázquez's political construction, founded on the legal notion of an original absolute natural liberty . . . stands behind a tradition of radical juristic political thought which is generally recognized as beginning with Grotius, for whom Vázquez was a major source" (p. 204).

8. John Adams, for example, advanced a threefold classification of *republics*—democratic, aristocratic, and monarchical in his "A Defense of the Constitution of the Government of the United States," in Adams, *The Works of John Adams*, 4: 271–588, 5: 3–490.

9. José Antonio Maravall, *La philosophie politique espagnole au XVIIe siècle dans ses rapports avec l'esprit de la contre-réforme* (Paris: J. Vrin, 1955), 137–141.

10. John G. A. Pocock, *The Machiavellian Moment: Florentine Political Thought and the Atlantic Republican Tradition* (Princeton: Princeton University Press, 1975), 628–631. On this see also: Maurizio Viroli, *For Love of Country: An Essay on Patriotism and Nationalism* (New York: Oxford University Press, 1995), 18–94.

11. David A. Brading, *The First America: The Spanish Monarchy, Creole Patriots, and the Liberal State, 1492–1867* (Cambridge: Cambridge University Press, 1991), 541. On the cortes see: Joseph F. O'Callaghan, *The Cortes of Castile-León, 1188–1350* (Philadelphia: University of Pennsylvania Press, 1989). It is interesting to note that John Adams, who believed Castilian culture to be backward, authoritarian, and dominated by obscurantist Catholic clergy, nevertheless considered the ancient constitution of the mythical Basque Republic—which he called "Biscay" and classified as one of the "Modern Democratic Republics"— important in his defense of the United States Constitution of 1787. See his "A Defense of the Constitution of the Government of the United States," in Adams, *The Works of John Adams*, 4: 310–314.

12. Richard Herr, *The Eighteenth-Century Revolution in Spain* (Princeton: Princeton University Press, 1958), 337–347. Francisco Martínez Marina, *Teoría de las Cortes*, Biblioteca de Autores Españoles (Madrid: Ediciones Atlas, 1968–1969). His critical introduction to the *Siete Partidas* has been reissued together with an excellent study of his thought as vol. 194 of Biblioteca de Autores Españoles (Madrid: Ediciones Atlas, 1966).

13. Francisco Suárez, *Tratado de las leyes y de Dios legislador*, trans. Jaime Torrubiano Ripoll (Madrid: Reus, 1918). See also O. Carlos Stoetzer, *The Scholastic Roots of the Spanish American Revolution* (New York: Fordham University Press, 1979).

14. Herr, *The Eighteenth Century Revolution in Spain*, 172–183; José Carlos Chiaramonte, "Fundamentos iusnaturalistas de los movimientos de independencia," in Marta Terán and José Antonio Serrano Ortega, eds., *Las guerras de independencia en la América española* (Zamora: El Colegio de Michoacán, 2002), 99–122.

15. Juan Marichal, "From Pistoia to Cádiz: A Generation's Itinerary, 1786–1812," in A. Owen Aldridge, ed., *The Ibero-American Enlightenment* (Urbana: University of Illinois Press, 1971), 97–110.

16. John H. R. Polt, *Jovellanos and His English Sources, Economic, Philosophical, and Political Writings* (Philadelphia: Transactions of the American Philosophical Society, 1964); Manuel Moreno Alonso, *La forja del liberalismo en España. Los amigos españoles de Lord Holland, 1793–1840* (Madrid: Publicaciones del Congreso de Diputados, 1997). On Vázquez de Menchaca's influence on Hobbes, see Brett in *Nature, Right, and Liberty*, chapters 5 and 6.

17. Olga Victoria Quiroz-Martínez, *La introducción de la filosofía moderna en España* (Mexico: El Colegio de México, 1949). See also, Bernabé Navarro, *La introducción de la filosofía moderna en México* (Mexico: El Colegio de México, 1948).

18. Ibid.

19. José Antonio Pérez-Rioja, *Proyección y actualidad de Feijoo (ensayo de interpretación)* (Madrid: Instituto de Estudios Políticos, 1965), 40–41, 163.

20. Herr, *The Eighteenth-Century Revolution*, 39.

21. On the seventeenth-century British commentators, see Joyce Appleby, *Economic Thought and Ideology in 17th Century England* (Princeton: Princeton University Press, 1978). On Spain, see Herr, *The Eighteenth-Century Revolution*, 52; and Marcelo Bitar Letayf, *Los economistas españoles del siglo XVII y sus ideas sobre el comercio con las Indias* (Mexico: Instituto Mexicano de Comercio Exterior, 1975).

22. Robert J. Shafer, *The Economic Societies in the Spanish World, 1763–1821* (Syracuse: Syracuse University Press, 1958); Robert Sidney Smith, "The *Wealth of Nations* in Spain and Hispanic America, 1780–1830," *The Journal of Political Economy* 65: 2 (April 1957): 104–125.

23. Quoted in Polt, *Jovellanos and His English Sources*, 25.

24. Ibid., 15–43.

25. Virginia Guedea, "Criollos y peninsulares en 1808: Dos puntos de vista sobre lo español" (Licenciatura Thesis: Universidad Iberoamericana, 1964); and José Castán, *La influencia de la literatura jurídica española en las codificaciones americanas* (Madrid: Instituto de Estudios Jurídicos, 1984).

26. Collections of laws, such as Eusebio Ventura Beleño's *Recopilación sumaria de los autos acordados de la Real Audiencia y Sala del Crimen de esta Nueva España*, ed. María del Refugio González (Mexico: Universidad Nacional Autónoma de México, 1981), provided Americans with a sense of their own unique identity.

27. Servando Teresa de Mier, "Idea de la Constitución dada a las Américas por los reyes de España antes de la invasión del antiguo despotismo," in Jaime E. Rodríguez O., ed., *Obras completas de Servando Teresa de Mier: La formación de un republicano*, (México: Universidad Nacional Autónoma de México, 1988), 4: 57, 31–91.

28. These questions are treated in a different way, but at greater length, in Stoetzer, *The Scholastic Roots of the Spanish American Revolution*.

29. José Miranda, *Humboldt y México* (Mexico: Universidad Nacional Autónoma de México, 1962), 11.

30. Various aspects of the Enlightenment are discussed in: Jorge Cañizares-Esguerra, *How to Write the History of the New World: Historiographies, Epistomologies, and Identities in the Eighteenth-Century Atlantic World* (Stanford: Stanford University Press, 2001).

31. Herr, *The Eighteenth-Century Revolution*, 183–200; Virginia Guedea, *Las gacetas de México y la medicina: Un índice* (Mexico: Universidad Nacional Autónoma de México, 1991); Ruth Wold, *Diario de México: Primer cotidiano de Nueva España* (Madrid: Editorial Gredos, 1970); Ignacio Bartolache, *Mercurio volante,* ed. Roberto Moreno (Mexico: Universidad Nacional Autónoma de México, 1979); José Antonio Alzate, *Obras,* vol 1. *Periódicos,* ed. Roberto Moreno (Mexico: Universidad Nacional Autónoma de México, 1980).

32. Wold, *Diario de México,* 2: 1454 (September 24, 1809).

33. The *Gazeta de Madrid* (May 7, 1776) and the *Mercurio histórico y político* (July 1776), for example, note the appearance of Thomas Paine's *Common Sense*. With regard to the independence of the United States, see José de Covarruvias, *Memorias históricas de la última guerra con la Gran Bretaña, desde el año de 1774: Estados Unidos de América* (Madrid: Imprenta de Antonio Ramírez, 1783). See also Luis Angel García Melero, *La independencia de los Estados Unidos de Norteamérica a través de la prensa española* (Madrid: Ministerio de Asuntos Exteriores, 1977); and Mario Rodríguez, *La revolución Americana de 1776 y el mundo hispánico: ensayos y documentos* (Madrid: Editorial Tecnos, 1976).

34. Carlos Herrejón Peredo, "México: Luces de Hidalgo y de Abad y Queipo," *CARAVELLE: Cahiers du Monde Hispanique el Luso-Brasilien* 54 (1990), 107–135.

35. François-Xavier Guerra, *Modernidad e independencias. Ensayos sobre la revoluciones hispánicas* (Madrid: Editorial MAPFRE, 1992), 281.

36. Jürgen Habermas, *The Structural Transformation of the Public Sphere: An Inquiry into a Bourgeois Category* (Cambridge: MIT Press, 1989).

37. On the role of women, see Alfonso E. Pérez Sánchez and Eleanor A. Sayre, *Goya and the Spirit of the Enlightenment* (Boston: Little, Brown, 1989). In Mexico City, for example, María Ignacia Rodríguez de Velasco, popularly known as *la Güera Rodríguez,* hosted one of the most prominent tertulias during the independence period. Jaime E. Rodríguez O., "The Transition from Colony to Nation: New Spain, 1820–1821," in Jaime E. Rodríguez O., ed., *Mexico in the Age of Democratic Revolutions, 1750–1850* (Boulder: Lynne Rienner, 1994), 116. On popular tertulias and gatherings, see Virginia Guedea, *En busca de un gobierno alterno: Los Guadalupes de México* (Mexico: Universidad Nacional Autónoma de México, 1992).

38. Cited in Guerra, *Modernidad en independencias,* 292.

39. Wold, *Diario de México,* 12: 1616 (March 5, 1810); Isabel Olmos Sánchez, *La sociedad mexicana en vísperas de la independencia (1787–1821)* (Murcia: Universidad de Murcia, 1989), 277–278.

40. Wold, *Diario de México,* 2: 105 (January 13, 1806). A decade and a half later, Joel R. Poinsett remarked that in Mexico "Most of the people in the cities can read and write. I would not be understood as including the *leperos;* but I have frequently remarked men, clothed in the garb of extreme poverty, reading Gazettes in the streets." *Notes on Mexico made in the Autumn of 1822* (Philadelphia: H. C. Carey and Lea, 1824), 277–278.

41. Cited in Guerra, *Modernidad en independencias,* 292. On taverns, see Virginia Guedea, "México en 1812: Control político y bebidas prohibidas," *Estudios de Historia Moderna y Contemporánea de México,* 8 (1980): 23–65.

42. George M. Addy, *The Enlightenment in the University of Salamanca* (Durham: Duke University Press, 1966). See also Batia B. Siebzehner, *La universidad Americana y la ilustración: Autoridad y conocimiento en Nueva España y el Río de la Plata* (Madrid: Editorial MAPFRE, 1992).

43. Quoted in Guerra, *Modernidad e independencias,* 277.

44. Ibid. On primary education, see Dorothy Tanck de Estrada, *La educación ilustrada (1786–1836)* (Mexico: El Colegio de México, 1977); and *Pueblos de indios y educación en el México colonial, 1750–1821* (Mexico: El Colegio de México, 1999). On Guadalajara, see Carmen Castañeda, *La educación en Guadalajara durante la colonia, 1552–1821* (Mexico: El Colegio de México, 1984).

45. Hira de Gortari Rabiela, "Julio-agosto de 1808: 'La lealtad mexicana,'" *Historia Mexicana* 39: 1 (July–September 1989), 201.

46. "Testimonio de la session celebrada por el Ayuntamiento de México, el 19 de julio de 1808," in *Documentos históricos mexicanos*, ed. Genaro García (Mexico: Museo Nacional de Arqueología Historia y Etnología, 1910), 1: 27.

47. Guedea, "Criollos y peninsulares en 1808"; Jaime E. Rodríguez O., "From Royal Subject to Republican Citizen: The Role of the Autonomists in the Independence of Mexico," in Jaime E. Rodríguez O., ed., *The Independence of Mexico and the Creation of the New Nation* (Los Angeles: UCLA Latin American Center, 1989), 19–43. The Audiencia de Guadalajara opposed the convening of any congress of cities. Later, the Ayuntamiento de Guadalajara supported the overthrow of Iturrigaray. Lucas Alamán, *Historia de Méjico* (Mexico: Fondo de Cultura Económica, 1985), 1: 212, 258.

48. Rodríguez O., *The Independence of Spanish America*, chapter 2.

49. Ibid.; Julio V. González, *Filiación histórica del gobierno representativo argentino* (Buenos Aires: Editorial "La Vanguardia," 1937–1938), 1.

50. See, for example, "Sobre derecho de las Provincias Internas para elegir en cada una Diputado que sea comprendido entre los demas del Reyno donde se ha de sortear el que baya a la Suprema Junta," Archivo General de la Nación, México (hereafter AGN), Historia, vol. 416.

51. Virginia Guedea, "The First Popular Elections in Mexico City, 1812–1813," in Jaime E. Rodríguez O., ed., *The Evolution of the Mexican Political System* (Wilmington: SR Books, 1993), 46–47. See also Nettie Lee Benson, "The Elections of 1809: Transforming Political Culture in New Spain," *Mexican Studies/Estudios Mexicanos*, 20: 1 (winter 2004), 1–20.

52. Quoted in José Miranda, *Las ideas y las instituciones políticas mexicanas, primera parte, 1521–1820*, 2d ed. (Mexico: Universidad Nacional Autónoma de México, 1978), 227–228.

53. Quoted in Guerra, *Modernidad e independencias*, 212–213.

54. Rodríguez O., *The Independence of Spanish America*, chapter 3; see also Manuel Chust, "De esclavos, encomenderos y mitayos. El anticolonialismo en las Cortes de Cádiz," *Mexican Studies/Estudios Mexicanos*, 11: 2 (summer 1995), 179–202.

55. Nettie Lee Benson, *La Diputación Provincial y el federalismo mexicano* (Mexico: El Colegio de México, 1955), 13–21; Manuel Chust, "Legislar y revolucionar. La trascendencia de los diptados novohispanos en las Cortes hispanas, 1810–1814," in Virginia Guedea, coord., *La independencia de México y el proceso autonomista novohispano, 1808–1824* (Mexico: Universidad Nacional Autónoma de México and Instituto Mora, 2001), 23–82.

56. Rodríguez O., *The Independence of Spanish America*, 49–92; Manuel Chust, *La cuestión nacional americana en las Cortes de Cádiz* (Valencia: Fundación Instituto Historia Social, 1999).

57. François-Xavier Guerra, "El soberano y su reino: Reflexiones sobre la génesis del ciudadano en América Latina," in Hilda Sabato, coord., *Ciudadanía política y formación de la naciones: Perspectivas históricas de América Latina* (Mexico: Fondo de Cultura Económica, 1999), 45.

58. Later, a decree from the Cortes reduced to two hundred the number of inhabitants necessary to form an ayuntamiento constitucional. Studies of the popular elections in

Spanish America demonstrate that, while the elites controlled politics, hundreds of thousands of middle- and lower-class men, including Indians, mestizos, and castas, participated in those processes. See: Nettie Lee Benson, "The Contested Mexican Election of 1812," *Hispanic American Historical Review*, 26 (August 1946), 336–350; Virginia Guedea, "Las primeras elecciones populares en la ciudad de México, 1812–1813", *Mexican Studies/Estudios Mexicanos* 7: 1 (winter 1991), 1–28; Virginia Guedea, *En busca de un gobierno alterno: Los Guadalupes de México* (Mexico: Universidad Nacional Autónoma de México, 1992), 233–315; and Virginia Guedea, "El pueblo de México y la política capitalina, 1808–1812," *Mexican Studies/Estudios Mexicanos*, 10: 1 (winter 1994), 27–61; Jaime E. Rodríguez O., "La revolución hispánica en el Reino de Quito: las elecciones de 1809–1814 y 1821–1822," in Marta Terán and José Antonio Serrano Ortega, eds., *Las guerras de Independencia en la América española* (Zamora, Mexico and Morelia: El Colegio de Michoacán, INAH y Universidad Michoacana de San Nicolás de Hidalgo, 2002), 485–508; and Peter Guardino, "'Toda libertad para emitir sus votos': Plebeyos, campesinos y elecciones en Oaxaca, 1808–1850," *Cuadernos del Sur* 6: 15 (June 2000), 87–114. Studies of elections in Mexico City, Veracruz, Guadalajara, Guatemala, and Guayaquil demonstrate that people of African ancestry were allowed to vote; see: Guedea, "Las primeras elecciones populares"; Patrick J. Carroll, *Blacks in Colonial Veracruz* (Austin: University of Texas Press, 1991), 134–141; Jordana Dym, "A Sovereign State in Every Village: City, State and Nation in Independence-era Central America, ca. 1760–1850" (Ph.D. Diss.: New York University, 2000); Jaime E. Rodríguez O., *"Rey, religion, yndependencia, y Unión": el proceso político de la Independencia de Guadalajara* (Mexico: Instituto de Investigaciones José Luis Mora, 2003); and Jaime E. Rodríguez O., "La independencia de Guayaquil," in Jaime E. Rodríguez O., ed., *Revolución, Independencia y la nuevas naciones de América* (Mexico: Fondo de Cultura Económica, in press).

59. Two deputies from New Spain voted against the free trade proposal, eight abstained, and nine voted in favor; see: John H. Hann, "The Role of the Mexican Deputies in the Proposal and Enactment of Measures of Economic Reform Applicable to Mexico," in Nettie Lee Benson, ed., *Mexico and the Spanish Cortes, 1810–1822* (Austin: University of Texas Press, 1966), 167–168.

60. D. J. C., *Catecismo político arreglado a la Constitución de la Monarquía Española; para la ilustración del Pueblo, instrucción de la juventud, y uso de las escuelas de primeras letras*, 2d ed. (Puebla: Imprenta San Felipe Neri, 1820).

61. Jaime E. Rodríguez O., "Las elecciones a las Cortes Constituyentes Mexicanas," in Louis Cardaillac and Angélica Peregrina, coords., *Ensayos en homenaje a José María Muriá* (Zapopan: El Colegio de Jalisco, 2002), 80–85; Rodríguez O., *"Rey, religion, yndependencia, y Unión,"* 28–37.

62. Rodríguez O., *The Independence of Spanish America*, 72–73.

63. Juan Aldama, "Declaración rendida por … en la causa que se le instruyó por haber sido caudillo insurgente," in García, ed., *Documentos*, 6: 529.

64. The best study of the Hidalgo Revolt remains Hugh M. Hamill, *The Hidalgo Revolt: Prelude to Mexican Independence* (Gainesville: University of Florida Press, 1966). Lucas Alamán, *Historia de Méjico desde los primeros movimientos que prepararon su independencia en el año de 1808 hasta la época presente* (Mexico: Fondo de Cultura Económica, 1985), although originally published in 1849, is still the best, most detailed, and most subtle account of those events.

65. Alamán, *Historia de Méjico*, 3: 443–580; Virginia Guedea, *En busca de un gobierno alterno: Los Guadalupes de México* (Mexico: Universidad Nacional Autónoma de México, 1992), 48–125.

66. Virginia Guedea, "Los procesos electorales insurgentes," *Estudios de Historia Novohispana* 11 (1991): 222–248.

67. Ibid., 203–249; Ana Macías, *Génesis del gobierno constitucional en México, 1808–1820* (Mexico: Secretaría de Educación Pública, 1973); and Alamán, *Historia de Méjico*, 3: 545–584.

68. Rodríguez O., *"Rey, religion, yndependencia, y Unión"*; Rodríguez O., "The Transition from Colony to Nation," 101–102.

69. "Número de ejemplares de la Constitución repartidos en el circular de 19 de junio de 1820," AGN, Historia, vol. 404, f. 329.

70. "Bando de la Junta Preparatoria de Nueva España," *Gazeta del Gobierno de México*, 40: 91 (July 13, 1820), 683–688; Rodríguez O., *"Rey, religion, yndependencia, y Unión"*; Rodríguez O., "The Transition from Colony to Nation," 101–102; Benson, *La Diputación Provincial*, 47; Herrejón Peredo, Carlos, ed., *Actas de la Diputación Provincial*," 26; "Actas de la Diputación Provincia de Yucatán, 1820," Centro de Apoyo a la Investigacón Histórica de Yucatán; "Actas de la Diputación Provincial de Nueva Galicia, 1820–1821," Nettie Lee Benson Papers, Benson Latin American Collection, University of Texas, Austin.

71. Rodríguez O., "The Transition from Colony to Nation," 102–103.

72. The actas of the elections to the Cortes and the Provincial Deputations for 1820 and 1821 are located in the Archivo del Congreso de Diputados de las Cortes en Madrid and the Archivo General de Indias en Sevilla. See also: "Diputados a Cortes para los años de 1822 y 1823," AGN, Gobernación: Sin Sección, Caja 16, exp. 2, ff. 1–86.

73. Articulo 325, "Constitución Política de la Monarquía Española," in Felipe Tena Ramírez, *Leyes fundamentales de México, 1808–1991*. 16th ed. (Mexico: Editorial Porrúa, 1991), 97; Ayuntamiento de Puebla, *Representación que hace a S. M. Las Cortes el . . . , para que en esta ciudad, cabeza de provincia, se establezca Diputación provincial, como dispone la Constitución* (Puebla: Imprenta del Gobierno, 1820); Junta Electoral, *Representación, que hace al soberano congreso de Cortes la . . . de la provincia de Puebla conforme al artículo 325 de la Constitución* (Puebla: Imprenta de Pedro de la Rosa, 1820).

74. Rodríguez O., "The Transition from Colony to Nation," 108–110; Benson, *La Diputación Provincial*, 49–55.

75. I maintain that the autonomists were the intellectual authors of the Plan of Iguala, not Agustín de Iturbide. See: Rodríguez O., "The Transition from Colony to Nation," 113–124; and Jaime E. Rodríguez O., "Los caudillos y los historiadores: Riego, Iturbide y Santa Anna," in Manuel Chust and Víctor Mínguez, coords, *La construcción del héroe en España y México, 1789–1847* (Valencia: Universitat de Valencia, 2003). For a different interpretation of these events see: Manuel Ferrer Muñoz, *La formación de un estado nacional en México. El Imperio y la República Federal, 1821–1835* (Mexico: Universidad Nacional Autónoma de México, 1995). I do not cite Timothy E. Anna's apologia of Iturbide, *The Mexican Empire of Iturbide* (Lincoln: University of Nebraska Press, 1990), because it suffers from serious flaws and because my research of the period is broader and more complete.

76. Quoted in Nettie Lee Benson, "Iturbide y los planes de Independencia," *Historia Mexicana* 2: 3 (Jan.-March 1953), 442.

77. Agustín de Iturbide expresses that opinion in his *Memorias escritas desde Liorna* (Mexico: Editorial Jus, 1973), 27: "Cuando entré en México mi voluntad era ley, yo mandaba la fuerza pública, los tribunals no tenían más facultades que las que emanaban de mi autoridad. ?Pude ser más absoluto?"

78. Quote in Jaime E. Rodríguez O., "The Struggle for Dominance: The Legislature versus the Executive in Early Mexico," in Christon I. Archer, ed., *The Birth of Modern Mexico* (Wilmington: SR Books, 2003), 205; Rodríguez O., "The Transition from Colony to Nation," 97–132.

79. Ibid.

80. See my essays: "The Transition from Colony to Nation" and "The Constitution of 1824 and the Formation of the Mexican State," in Jaime E. Rodríguez O., ed., *The Evolution of the Mexican Political System* (Wilmington: SR Books, 1993), 71–90; "The Struggle for Dominance" and "Las Cortes Mexicanas y el Congreso Constituyente," in Virginia Guedea, coord., *La independencia de México y el proceso autonomista novohispano, 1808–1824* (Mexico: Universidad Nacional Autónoma de México and Instituto Mora, 2001), 285–320; and "The Struggle for the Nation: The First Centralist-Federalist Conflict in Mexico," *The Americas* 49: 1 (July 1992), 1–22. See also Benson, *La Diputación Provincial* and José Barragán Barragán, *Introdución al federalismo (la formación de los poderes 1824)* (Mexico: Universidad Nacional Autónoma de México, 1978).

81. José Antonio Serrano provides an excellent account of these conflicts in *Jerarquía territorial y transición política: Guanajuato, 1790–1836* (Zamora and Mexico: El Colegio de Michoacán and Instituto Mora, 2001).

82. Reynaldo Sordo Cedeño, *El congreso en la primera República Centralista* (Mexico: El Colegio de México and Instituto Tecnológico Autónomo de México, 1993); Cecilia Noriega Elío, *El Constituyente de 1842* (Mexico: Universidad Nacional Autónoma de México, 1986); and Michael P. Costeloe, *The Central Republic in Mexico, 1835–1846: Hombres de bien in the Age of Santa Anna* (New York: Cambridge University Press, 1993).

83. Alicia Hernández Chávez, *La tradición republicana del buen gobierno* (Mexico: Fondo de Cultura Económica, 1993), 46–117; Charles Hale, *The Transformation of Liberalism in Late Nineteenth-Century Mexico* (Princeton: Princeton University Press, 1989).

84. Peter F. Guardino, *Peasants, Politics, and the Formation of Mexico's National State: Guerrero, 1800–1857* (Stanford: Stanford University Press, 1996), 178–210.

85. Maximilian, however, disappointed the conservatives who supported him because he attempted to rule as a liberal monarch. See: Robert H. Duncan, "For the Good of the Country: State and Nation Building during Maximilian's Mexican Empire, 1864–67" (Ph.D. Dissertation: University of California, Irvine, 2001); and Erika Pani, *Para mexicanizar el Segundo Imperio: el imaginario político de los imperialistas* (Mexico: El Colegio de México and Instituto José María Luis Mora, 2001).

I

POLITICS

1

From *res publicae* to Republic: The Evolution of Republicanism in Early Mexico

Alicia Hernández Chávez

This chapter analyzes the evolution of Mexican government during the first half of the nineteenth century based on the political catechisms (manuals for teaching in the form of questions and answers) of the time.[1] During this period, a proliferation of civics readers, catechisms, and leaflets served as vehicles for transmitting the new constitutionalism and creating public opinion. Political catechisms are a valuable source for understanding the transformation of law and how basic constitutional precepts were propagated among the general public. Most importantly, they express the nuances and interests of the divergent factions within society, as each political group responded with modified interpretations of basic issues such as the role and balance among the branches of government; the institutions representing the people; what was to be understood as the people; and the definition of citizens' rights.

THE QUEST FOR EQUAL REPRESENTATION WITHIN THE SPANISH MONARCHY

The political processes that led to the adoption of the republican form of government in Mexico were not the direct result of U.S. independence in 1776, of the French Revolution of 1789, or an immediate product of New Spain's independence in 1821. The concept of a republic and of republicanism arose from the ideas, principles, historical concepts, and idiosyncrasies of the people of the land that was to become Mexico. Internal and external historical processes, in existence for half a century before, contributed to the establishment of the Mexican republic.

At the time of the American and French revolutions, the people of New Spain did not favor a republican form of government. Politically active *novohispanos* (the people of New Spain) continued to favor monarchy during the first two decades of the nineteenth century, a period that encompassed the first movements for autonomy and subsequent independence from Spain. When the Spanish monarchy collapsed in 1808, rather than forming an independent nation, novohispanos instead chose to remain part of a constitutional Hispanic Monarchy until 1821.

With the phrase "Death to bad government, long live the king!" as their battle cry, these Americans (as they called themselves) established a distinction between tyrannical and inept governments and their loyalty to the monarch. The king offered justice and mercy to his vassals, who were organized socially and culturally into corporate bodies and estates. Novohispanos expressed their religious unity by emphasizing the monarch's role as the representative of Catholicism, the one and exclusive true religion of the realm.

The Enlightenment, a movement that emphasized the primacy of reason and that revolutionized the world through scientific discoveries, stimulated reforms in New Spain. The notion of progress provided fertile ground for achieving material gain and economic growth. These ideological transformations led to the reevaluation of the individual, his history, and his ability to transform his surroundings. Although the independence of the British American colonies in 1776 was the object of heated discussion in New Spain, as were the French Revolution ten years later and the black rebellion in Antilles, domestic issues shaped the novohispano reformist agenda, which emphasized equality rather than independence.[2]

Champions of reform, within the Church and secular society, faced government repression and resistance from proponents of the status quo in the two decades before 1808. For example, prominent American clergymen, including Fray Servando Teresa de Mier and Miguel Hidalgo, and his followers in the San Nicolás seminary of Valladolid, were prosecuted because they rekindled the conflict over the relationship between the Church and crown. The struggle was reflected in the ever-present tensions over the preeminence of the regular and secular clergy, over the Spanish Crown's role vis à vis the Pope in Rome, and over the royalist effort to restrict the disruptive ideas advanced by such French philosophers as Descartes and Rousseau.[3] Manuel Godoy, the king's prime minister in the period 1793–1808, curtailed reform, allied the Spanish Monarchy with the European powers that opposed the French Revolution, and ensured that every royal official sent to New Spain would resist change. The political and social cost of these policies was exacerbated by the Crown's demands for painful economic sacrifices from its American possessions to finance European wars. The two social sectors hardest hit by the new taxes were the Indians and the Church. In 1804, the

Crown confiscated the Indians' *Cajas de Comunidad*, their communal treasuries, and the Church's *Cajas de la Iglesia*. The Indian communities were angered, but so were landowners, merchants, and mine operators who were accustomed to financing their operations with Church loans. At the end of the eighteenth and the beginning of the nineteenth century, these factors fueled the discontent of broad segments of the society including wealthy *criollos* (as the Americans were also called), Indian communities, and *castas* (people of mixed ancestry).

Simultaneously, a non-religious movement led by enlightened novohispanos challenged European claims of superiority, thus raising the question of the equality of all men, including the Indians and the blacks. Of course, the institution of slavery was also questioned. The ideas of this group were circulated in periodicals such as *La Gaceta de Literatura*, edited in Mexico City by José Antonio Alzate. Educated residents of New Spain also participated in scientific expeditions and discussion circles and organized and promoted archeological research in order to revive the land's ancient past. These and other activities exemplified the optimism of Americans at the end of the eighteenth century and the exaltation of the country's richness, the land's historical roots, its scientific advances, and the individual potential of its inhabitants.

Although such ideological movements did not lead to a struggle for independence from Spain, they demonstrated a desire to curb the excesses of the crown and to establish a new relationship within the Spanish Monarchy that would allow Americans to strengthen local governments and liberate themselves from economic, political, and social constraints. Throughout the vast Spanish Monarchy there emerged a widespread demand for representation and autonomy.

THE CLAIM OF SOVEREIGNTY

Jaime E. Rodríguez's studies of the processes that led to independence serve as a foundation for the interpretation of the ideas found in constitutional catechisms.[4] In 1808, Napoleon's invasion of Spain and the king's abdication forced both Spaniards and Americans to take measures to preserve the integrity of the Monarchy as a whole and the Kingdom of New Spain in particular. Some political factions argued that—as a result of the crisis of the Monarchy—sovereignty reverted to the people of New Spain, while others challenged the people's authority to deprive the king of his sovereignty.

The criollo argument may be summarized as follows: "In the absence of the king, where does the sovereignty of the Spanish Nation [as the Spanish world came to be called] reside?" If "the king is separated from his crown and the Prince of Asturias [the heir to the crown] from his rights and the Crown of Spain and the Indies renounced by royal decree on May 8, 1808: what happens when this [news] reaches New Spain?" The most prominent citizens of New Spain, as they themselves acknowledged, being "criollos, were heirs to the rights that from the conquest of this empire were handed down to our elders by the conquistadores."[5] Therefore, they convened a special session of the Ayuntamiento (municipal council) of Mexico City and declared that the Kingdom of New Spain could not be transferred to any other sovereign or nation. As a Noble City, Head of the Kingdom in the New World in "use and representation of its rights and in the name of the People," the City of Mexico declared that the "laws, royal orders and decrees that have, until now, governed the empire will remain [in force], with full vigor and strength."

HISTORICAL CONSTITUTIONALISM VERSUS ROYAL SOVEREIGNTY

The leaders of New Spain claimed the heritage of historical constitutionalism; they did not intend to establish a modern constitution. Historical constitutionalists justified the rule of customary law and were fearful of negotiating new rights and obligations, which could endanger their traditional privileges. Thus, when the Americans convened a meeting on July 19, 1808, the capital's ayuntamiento declared that the sitting viceroy should retain his position for the time being. The other ayuntamientos in the viceroyalty ratified that action and resolved to convene a congress with representation from all the major cities of New Spain. The congress would function as a provisional body until the restoration of Fernando VII, the legitimate monarch.

Viceroy José de Iturrigaray accepted these decisions, but they met with immediate disapproval at the highest levels of the bureaucracy from the *gachupines*, conservative Spaniards, who held positions in the *Real Audiencia* (high court), the Royal Treasury, and the *Real Acuerdo*, another judicial body. To counteract these forces, the viceroy convened a general junta with representatives from all the corporations in the capital, including the merchant, mining, and military guilds, the Church, the Indian cabildos, the titled nobility, and the university. The advocates of autonomy proposed that a local junta and the viceroy's council govern until the restoration of the legitimate king. This is what the provinces in Spain had done, where local committees governed in the name of Fernando VII. But in New Spain, the royalist gachupines opposed the proposal as subversive. They organized a coup d'etat on September 16, 1808, arrested the viceroy and the autonomist leadership, and took control of the government.

The coup exacerbated the divisions between those who demanded self-government and those who opposed it. The absolutists held power until

1810, while autonomist groups, who favored equal representation for Peninsulars and those born in New Spain, seethed. The persecution of autonomists by the gachupín government united criollos, Indians, and castas in their desire for home rule. A small group planned an armed uprising to seize power in the name of the legitimate government approved by the ayuntamientos in 1808. They proposed to establish a provisional government in New Spain, representing all political groups in a council of cities, which would assume sovereignty in the name of King Fernando VII.

Although the absolutist defenders of the old order had gained control of important government positions in September 1808, they gradually lost political strength. In 1809, the acting government in Spain, the Central Governing Junta, instructed the New World to elect representatives to that body. The absolutists who controlled the higher administration of New Spain were unable to ensure that gachupines won the elections. Although the absolutist minority monopolized the principal political positions, it was outnumbered by Americans occupying posts in ayuntamientos and in intermediate positions of the bureaucracy. Americans won the elections, first to the Junta Central, and subsequently to the extraordinary *Cortes* (parliament) convened to govern the Spanish world as it struggled against Napoleon's forces.

A NATIONAL AWAKENING: THE HIDALGO-MORELOS REVOLT AND THE CORTES OF CÁDIZ

Between July 1808 and September 1810, developments in Old and New Spain strengthened the autonomists' position and even advanced the idea of complete independence. The interests of different actors converged in a process that incorporated criollos, mestizos, castas, and Indians forming an inclusive, cross-class, and multi-ethnic national awakening. This fostered a rapid spread of a variety of political movements in New Spain—the formation of an insurgent force by the priest Miguel Hidalgo, the proliferation of secret societies and armed groups in various cities and areas of the kingdom, and the formation of the revolutionary army by the priest José María Morelos.

Simultaneously, a constitutional reorganization of the Spanish world was taking place in Spain at the port of Cádiz. Novohispano deputies participated prominently at the Cortes of Cádiz, the first joint Spanish and American parliament. They contributed significantly to political and cultural change in both Europe and America. Understandably, the American deputies, particularly those from New Spain, insisted on equal rights for all the people of the New World. Moreover, they insisted on the right of equal representations of the American kingdoms based on their population. There emerged a debate about who possessed full citizenship rights. The Peninsular majority in the

Cortes agreed that criollos, Indians, and mestizos had full rights as citizens of the Spanish Nation. However, people of African ancestry, blacks and the colored castas, were defined as Spaniards but not full citizens. In New Spain, the criollos, Indians, mestizos, blacks, and other castes continued to insist on full political rights for all people.

While the Spanish and American deputies to the Special and General Cortes in Cádiz grappled with the problem of political representation and political rights in the Spanish Nation, profound political changes were occurring in New Spain. What had begun as a movement to establish provisional structures to govern in the name of the king became a drive to govern at home. On September 15, 1810, Father Miguel Hidalgo pronounced the *Grito de Dolores*. He exhorted those gathered in his parish to defend the country from the Spanish, who, he said, wanted to deliver the kingdom to the French. Moreover, he called upon his parishioners to establish a new government. Hidalgo's movement gained immediate popularity because Indians, castas, criollos, and even some Spaniards, in the words of a bitter opponent of the rebels, "were convinced of the benefits that would result from an independent government."

Hidalgo soon lost the support of the criollos. They were frightened by the anarchy, violence, and destruction of their properties that accompanied the insurrection. By mid-1811, after Hidalgo was defeated and executed, the uprising subsided. The revolt did not cause the criollos to abandon their search for autonomy and surrender to the absolutists. Rather, they preferred a reformist movement to an armed insurrection. Between 1810 and 1812, members of the American elite participated in diverse conspiratorial activities to establish home rule.

The effort to restore an absolutist government encountered two major obstacles. The first, essentially a problem in New Spain, was the southern insurgency headed by the priest José María Morelos and Vicente Guerrero, son of a prominent landowner. The other, larger, obstacle was the 1812 Constitution promulgated by the Cortes of Cádiz. Its application in New Spain seriously undercut the foundation of existing political arrangements. In fact, the insurgents at home and the delegates from New Spain to the Cortes of Cádiz complemented rather than hindered each other. They agreed on a number of essential points. Constitutional government based on a written constitution was absolutely necessary. The constitution should be framed by a congress composed of elected deputies. It should establish the form of government, the division of power among the branches of government, the rights and obligations of citizens, and a manner of electing representatives. In Cádiz, the deputies proposed radical reforms to transform an absolute monarchy into a constitutional one that consisted of a community of independent kingdoms organized federally under a single crown and parties to a written constitution.

The new revolutionary ideas were founded on ancient Hispanic precedents. The Spanish legal scholar Francisco Martínez Marina published his massive *Teoría de las Cortes* (Theory of the Cortes), which maintained that before absolutism had been imposed in Spain three centuries earlier, the cortes shared legislative power with the king. In this fashion, he and others spread the myth that the medieval cortes had represented the various social orders.[6] For some, it was a way to stop the "seditious republican" ideas "usurpers of thrones and enemies of the altar"[7]—imported from France—from corrupting Hispanic society. Instead, traditional institutions and concepts, such as the *nation represented in the cortes,* would unite the people of the Spanish Monarchy.

In New Spain, Americans found the approach appealing. It enabled them to advance their own hypothetical traditions founded on historic constitutionalism. They maintained that as the descendants of the land's "original" inhabitants—the discoverers, conquistadores, and the Indians—they were the heirs to the rights, exemptions, and privileges their ancestors had obtained through a compact with the monarchy. They possessed rights and privileges from "ancient times." An 1821 catechism, for example, declared: "after the conquest of Mexico, Carlos V himself had wanted to grant them independence."[8] Moreover, "the Cortes—which is the nation because it consists of the representatives of the people—and the people, who constitute political society, had only to revive the rules previously in use but now broken and forgotten" to restore constitutional government.[9] The members of the *repúblicas de Indios* (the governments of those legally considered Indians) formulated their own myths based on the historical rights of the indigenous populations. They asserted that the Spanish Crown had recognized not only their titles of nobility as Indians, but also rights to their lands as the original inhabitants of the country. Therefore, they demanded rights similar to those of the criollo descendants of the conquistadores.[10] Authorities of the Indian pueblos advanced this argument to demand the "restitution" of ancient rights, a movement that continued throughout the nineteenth century and much of the twentieth.

THE CONSTITUTION OF CÁDIZ

The Constitution of Cádiz, which was applied in America from 1812 to 1814, stimulated the political reorganization in New Spain. The kingdom was divided into provinces administered by provincial deputations elected locally. Local political elites took charge of regional governments. The provincial deputations, precursors to the Mexican states, oversaw the establishment of constitutional ayuntamientos that would be transformed some decades later into municipalities. The provincial deputations and the municipalities were the basic institutions of the federalist structure and the political arena for democratic change.

Constitutional ayuntamientos were organized in urban centers with at least one thousand inhabitants, providing they had sufficient resources to afford self-government. In the midst of a large-scale insurrection, most town folk willingly accepted the ayuntamiento as an orderly option much more attractive than war. Thus, calls for rebellion were subordinated to a profound political and social restructuring process. The establishment of ayuntamientos in villages and towns diverted the people's attention to local matters and contained the insurgency. The right to form an ayuntamiento not only meant electing local officials, but it also granted the community jurisdiction over its territory and control of its resources. Moreover, the new municipalities could determine who could exercise the rights of citizenship. Individuals, who previously had possessed only transient residential rights, were granted an opportunity to acquire full *vecino* status; that is, the right to full citizenship, to elect and to be elected, and to exploit the towns' agricultural resources, such as land, water, and forests. In return, they were obligated to contribute certain dues, taxes, and community services.

In New Spain, the insurgent leaders also proposed creating a government. Ignacio Rayón assumed the leadership of the movement after Hidalgo's execution. He and other insurgent leaders formed a national junta, the Suprema Junta Nacional Americana, to govern in the king's name. The royal authorities, however, rejected with force the efforts to establish an autonomous government. As a result, a great war of insurgency erupted in many regions of the kingdom. José María Morelos, who had been waging a guerrilla campaign in the south, emerged as the most important insurgent leader. In June 1813, he convened elections in the regions controlled by insurgents for a congress to form a national government. Moreover, he rejected the earlier assertion that they were acting to preserve the throne for King Fernando VII. In essence, he declared the independence of New Spain, called Anáhuac by the insurgents, from the Spanish Crown. Morelos assumed the title of Servant of the Nation and Generalísimo of its forces.

THE ARMY: PROTECTOR OF THE NATION

The congress, which met in the town of Chilpancingo, ratified his actions and declared the independence of América Septentrional (North America) from all kingdoms or nations. On October 22, 1814, Congress issued the Constitutional Decree for the Liberty of Mexican America, popularly known as the Constitution of Apatzingan, after the town where it was promulgated. The new charter established a republic with a plural executive and a powerful legislature. All those born or residing in American territory, regardless of race or social status, were recognized as citizens.[11] The project had a short life and was barely enforced, but it did play an important role by Americanizing constitutionalism. In that respect, Morelos and the representatives of the Congress of Chilpancingo established an American legal tradition that was not easily ignored by their successors and from which Mexico's legal tradition is drawn.

Between 1808 and 1821, other changes occurred that not only transferred government decision making to Americans, but also reinforced the power of different factions. As a result of widespread warfare, the army and its leaders became the representatives of the people and the nation, guaranteeing their safety, security, unity, and territorial integrity. The armed forces soon became an essential component in the construction of a modern state. The concept of the army as the protector of the nation, an inheritance of the French Revolution, became prominent. Similarly, the military *caudillo* (political leader), in the manner of Napoleon Bonaparte, emerged as a key figure in constructing the new nation.[12] The new political and cultural environment glorified the energy and creativity of the individual and elevated the soldier to the status of hero; as one catechism noted: the soldier was "a citizen armed to defend his *patria*, the constitution, and his king . . . and any man armed at the whim of a tyrant is a mercenary. . . ."[13] In addition to the regular army, the Constitution of Cádiz and later the new Mexican government established the civic militia to protect the territory of the ayuntamientos, as Manuel Chust demonstrates in this volume.[14] Through service under arms, the soldier obtained full citizenship rights as well as land or other resources to pay his taxes. The political actor was no longer the family, but the independent male who did not have to be pater familia to exercise political rights.

POLITICAL CATECHISMS

The catechisms issued from 1813 to 1821, which transmitted political concepts to wide sectors of society, represent the political discourse of the time, particularly regarding the nature of the new rights of citizens. The most popular political views held by the people of New Spain were based on Christian doctrine—the myth that the king governed with the advice of the medieval cortes, and on the belief that political representation was the responsibility of the fittest and most virtuous. A catechism, for example, asserted that "the people do not create laws for themselves; that would not be possible among such distant regions were it not through subjects carefully chosen, named by the people and designated as their deputies or representatives."[15] Electors had be virtuous, noble, talented, and love their equals as required by the Catholic religion; they also had to know how to read and write. Another publication noted that: "Christianity with its divine morality necessarily produces all the civic virtues needed by a republic."[16]

The predominant view as expressed by the catechisms was that the constitution—by limiting the king's authority—transferred the vast majority of power to the Cortes. Initially, most believed that the nation, that is to say the Cortes, was constituted by the estates as the representatives of political society, a conception of the *antiguo régimen* that prevailed until the concept of the people as a subject of sovereignty was fully understood. Representatives to the Cortes were elected in a similar manner as in the classic aristocratic states, such as the Dutch, Venetian, Genoese, or Hanseatic republics. Nonetheless, the elective character of the Cortes was a great innovation that generated significant divisions among the elite. Moreover, at intermediate levels the electoral bodies became powerful political mechanisms for social change.

The first to condemn the authority of the Cortes was the Church. In an 1817 ruling, the Tribunal of the Inquisition ruled that the acts of the Cortes restricting the legislative authority of the king were heretical because in 1615 Pope Alexander VII had declared, under threat of excommunication, that the legislative powers of the king could not be limited. Starting with that first challenge, the Church continued to oppose the Cortes.

The Church was particularly distressed that catechisms, texts used to teach its doctrine, were being used to "transmit subversive ideas." They not only "contained concepts that threatened public and social order, [but also] the Crown." The Church maintained "[t]hat a good citizen has as his only aim to serve his patria and to enjoy, for the services he offers to it, the honors, rewards, and privileges his patria bestows upon him." The Church also asserted that representative government was "a secular idea that does not direct individuals to serve, love, and know God over all things and, in this way, be granted eternal life."[17] Moreover, defining the nature of the 1812 Constitution as good, wise, just, and equitable constituted a usurpation of attributes that belonged only to God. The heart of the problem resided in the fact that the catechisms, by spreading new secular and anti-religious beliefs, could lead public opinion toward a profound revolution that established the basis of a secular political culture.

On the other hand, the new constitutionalism was eagerly accepted by most social sectors because it responded to their demands for self-government. The Constitution of 1812 created two institutions of local government: the provincial deputations and the constitutional ayuntamientos. The two new institutions brought about significant changes at the provincial and municipal level. These new bodies, which held periodic elections and forbade reelection, provided Americans the opportunity to assume control of local government. As a result, local entrepreneurs and prominent men quickly gained importance in their provinces. In the words of the above mentioned catechism: "in a vast nation, divided into provinces and composed of different populations, auxiliary authorities are needed to administer local government and to foster order and general prosperity."[18]

The catechism, thus, indicated that home rule was best exercised through the constitutional ayuntamientos and the provincial deputations. These were much more than new versions of the old ayuntamientos, the twelve intendancies, two provinces, and the government of Tlaxcala that comprised New Spain at the end of the eighteenth century. The 1812 Constitution of Cádiz and Mexico's independence in 1821 transformed military and administrative divisions into political entities with their own jurisdiction, where every individual was included in the census to ensure proper representation. Consequently, geographic issues and territorial limits assumed an important role in defining sovereignty.[19]

CONSTITUTIONALISM AT WORK

The Constitution of 1812 reduced the viceroy of New Spain to the status of *jefe político superior* (superior political chief) with authority over only six of the provinces. The intendants or the governors assigned to the other 10 provinces were no longer under his direct jurisdiction. Instead, they reported to the government of the Spanish Nation in the Peninsula. According to the Constitution, the citizens elected deputies to the Cortes through indirect elections, and then they elected seven individuals to the provincial deputation.[20] In this way, the vast Spanish Nation was divided into provinces administered by provincial deputations, jefes políticos, and intendants.[21] Those elected to the Cortes represented their provinces in the legislature of the Spanish Nation, and the provincial deputies were responsible for the correct application of the Constitution of 1812 in their jurisdictions.

The new political system favored the election of prominent local citizens, firmly rooted and well known in their own territories. As a result, Americans gained access to public posts, weakening the power of *peninsulares* (Spanish-born citizens). In addition, between 1812 and 1823 the new institutions set the firm foundations for provincial autonomy. Although King Fernando VII suspended the Constitution in 1814, the changes that had taken place between 1808 and 1814 in New Spain fractured the viceroyal government and created a power vacuum. In the absence of authority, the provincial deputations, the ayuntamientos, and their territorial elite were able to maintain order in their provinces. In this way, the provincial deputations and the constitutional ayuntamientos reinforced each other as territorial governments that weakened—through the electoral process and the prohibition on reelection—the hierarchy of both the Indian and American estates, which had controlled local government. Thus, inter-ethnic ayuntamientos emerged.

A catechism's question identified the transformation: "Is it true that there are no longer either *regidores* [councilmen] or *oficios perpetuos* [permanent officials] in the ayuntamientos? Answer: there are none; these permanent offices have been justly abolished. . . ."[22] Moreover, the ethnic and estate-centered order was gradually dissolved by the new requirements for being elected and for who had the right to vote: only "citizens twenty-five years of age or older, with five years of residency and in full exercise of their rights."[23]

The elective nature of political office introduced by the Constitution of Cádiz undermined the authority of the traditional repúblicas de indios. In the antiguo régimen, these polities—divided into *cabeceras* (head towns) and *pueblos sujetos*—were governed by *caciques* (Indian political bosses) who possessed hereditary office. The constitutional system with its emphasis on the individual and equality under the law privileged the mestizo-criollo culture. The cabildos of the repúblicas de indios and the *cacicazgos* (hereditary political offices) disappeared with the law. To survive, they mutated and transformed into constitutional ayuntamientos. The change was necessary because of a new definition of citizenship. The roles of cities and towns changed; many lost status as seats of government with their own territorial jurisdictions. The Constitution established ayuntamientos on the basis of population and not ethnicity. The *civitas* or citizenship—located in the cities and capitals of provincial deputations with their resident citizens—encouraged individuals to exercise their rights.[24]

A NATIONALIZED VERSION OF A
CONSTITUTIONAL MONARCHY

It is helpful to examine the historical development of this process. In 1821, New Spain declared its independence and established a constitutional monarchy. Deputies were elected to a cortes that served as a constituent congress. They were to draft a charter for a constitutional monarchy in accordance with the Plan de Iguala and the Treaty of Córdoba, which recognized the rights of all the people of Mexico as well as the Cádiz Constitution of 1812. During the sessions, the justice commission of the Mexican Cortes insisted on the need to control abuses, already emerging, that were attacking the bases of the union by proposing ideas of republicanism. In reality, only a few deputies favored a republican form of government. Nevertheless, some legislators proposed tempering the naturally democratic impulses of popular groups. Finally, a moderate faction refuted the aristocratic pretensions of those who wanted to restrict voting rights to property owners and convert the legislative body into an assembly of notables.

In those early years, the difference between the monarchical and the republican form of government was, according to an 1820 catechism, "the position and distinction of the three branches." It defined republican government as one in which "all the people, under certain fundamental rules and conditions, exercise legislative power and bestow executive and judiciary authority for a limited time on those whom they have elected."[25] The monarch—according to the catechism—holds executive power perpetually and exclusively and possesses final review of the judiciary. The first two estates—the clergy and the nobility—enjoyed hereditary representation in the Cortes while the third estate obtained representation through elections. The monarchy avoided despotic power through a constitution that defined the institutions that protected and implemented it.

An 1821 catechism indicates that the potentates and notables of the time were in favor of an aristocratic form of government that "is a gradation of the republic or democratic government, which in its true sense is government by the best. However, the difficulty of establishing a government composed only of the best men of the nation has resulted in defining aristocratic government as one in which only the nobility has power, unlike the republican or the democratic government where power is held by all people indiscriminately."[26] In reply to the question of which is the best, the catechism answered, "All are good if power is balanced, no branch of government is superior to the others, and the rights of citizens are protected from arbitrary acts." The text specified that "for smaller states a republican government may be preferable; for a larger state a constitutional monarchy is preferable because the executive branch must extend its field of action and, if it is not adequately concentrated, many causes may contribute to its weakening."[27]

The persistence of the concept of the ancient republic, where public issues were debated among the potentates in the public square, is evident in the catechisms. In contrast, in the imaginary of the time, they conceived a constitutional monarchy as a confederation of kingdoms united under one crown. Few supported a moderate republican form of government in Mexico while the monarchy still had many adherents, according to deputy José María Luis Mora, because of an "esprit de corps widespread among all the social classes, [the product of] a marked tendency to establish corporations even if they did not enjoy equal privileges." Therefore, Mora concluded that "the republican voice was not adequate for representing a society that was really nothing more than the viceroyalty of New Spain with a few [individuals] who wanted it to be something else."[28] In his view, if independence had not occurred, the interests developed by the monarchy were such that "had a congress met, there is no doubt that the deputies would have been named by the different corporations and not by the electoral juntas. Each deputy would have considered himself a representative of the corporations and not of the nation."[29]

Mora portrays an early republicanism—cautious of democracy and its potential for anarchy—a defender of the republic "of notables" that excluded from citizenship rights "those who were not trustworthy—that is to say, all those without property."[30] Citizens with voice and vote should possess, according to Mora, the qualities that economic security provided. Such security would foster true civic virtues, such as charity, personal decorum, good manners, and love of the public well-being; all, he declared, are virtues exclusive to property owners.[31]

Although the Constitution of Cádiz was in effect for only a brief period between 1812 and 1814, the concepts and institutions it introduced endured. When it was reestablished in 1820, the same town councils, deputies, and local politicians re-emerged. The catechisms of the time highlighted the historic continuity: "Q: Who drafted this Constitution? A: The General and Special Cortes set up on the Island of León on September 14, 1810. Q: Is the Constitution a novelty among us? A: No; its principal rules have been in use earlier; but since they neither constituted a single body of law nor was their application guaranteed, those interested in violating the Constitution had caused it to fall into disuse. The Cortes have made the Constitution live again."[32] The Catholic religion was another element of continuity. It was defined as the religion of the nation because it "is convenient for the well being and harmony of the state; the unity of religious sentiments is as convenient as the unity of political sentiments."[33]

Most political factions agreed on one issue: the need for continuity. They first proposed a constitutional monarchy—an empire—that avoided a civil war in 1821 and facilitated Mexico's recognition as a sovereign nation by the European powers. The empire was described as "the walls of a building that once erected and finished cannot be modified without destroying the building itself." Its constitution had to be flexible and capable of change in order to avoid chaos as the government evolved from a national constitutional monarchy toward a republic. A catechism on the empire identified the classic forms of government: the monarchy and the aristocratic republic, which entrusts government to the hands of the wisest or the eldest; an oligarchy—it asserted—is more stable and limited than other forms of government; and popular democracy, in which people congregated to exercise authority by themselves. The catechism concluded that monarchy was the most appropriate form of government for Mexico and the one that also enjoyed the greatest recognition among nations.[34]

The specific form of monarchical republicanism recommended by the catechism derived from the classic doctrines of theorists who refer to the Venetian, Genoese, Hanseatic, and Helvetian republics. They considered the republic in its three forms: the monarchic, the aristocratic, and the so-called popular or democratic. The 1820 catechism rejected the latter form of republic because people who frequently deliberate are often angered and "since they lack either firm judgment or solid virtue, they would be easily manipulated by speakers or led into civil war because republican virtues are not very common among them."[35] The catechism did not reject the democratic republic, but it did not endorse it for Mexico because "the people lack the universal nature of disinterest and the wisdom needed to govern a republic."[36]

The regency of the Mexican Empire, presided by Agustín de Iturbide, fundamentally consisted of a government of Spaniards and criollos whose numbers had "increased considerably [in relation to the castas] and possessed enlightenment and knowledge to overcome their [the castas] advantage in number."[37] According to the catechism: liberty is a gift from God, and electors had to be men of Christian virtue, as well as possessing noble and elevated principles. Although the castes were granted active citizenship, they should remain passive citizens until they acquired the necessary education; in short, careers were open to them according to merit. Consequently, the first concept of a republic was rooted in the ancient tradition in which republican virtues are those of the Christian prince; it was a government called aristocratic in the hands of a select few who dominated national representation in the Cortes or parliament.[38]

The opposite republican model, the one established in the United States, was unique in the Western world and held great interest for the new American nations, which did not possess a nobility. The Spanish-speaking countries of South America that had gained independence opted for republics with aristocratic features. Thus, when Spain refused to send a member of the Bourbon house to reign in Mexico, most agreed that the *people* could not choose a king from among themselves. However, with military and popular support, Agustín de Iturbide forced Congress to appoint him emperor. Nevertheless, following ancient tradition, Congress remained identified with the nation and served as a source of unity.[39] Tadeo Ortiz has correctly described this first independent government as a "nationalized constitutional monarchy." He contends that it could have lasted longer had it not been for Iturbide's arbitrary dissolution of Congress under the excuse that he understood "the customs of the Mexican people and the inspiration behind the country's legislation."[40] According to Ortiz, there were individuals in congress who believed that "the republican system could have been perfected and have flourished with the experience and protection of liberty;"[41] that is, the deputies could have gained experience as legislators and formed a more perfect government. In some ways they did mature. Servando Teresa de Mier asserts that the deputies delayed their work in the constituent congress to avoid ratification of an imperial constitution that would have confirmed Agustín de Iturbide's stay in power.[42]

The first empire collapsed, according to Iturbide himself, when three provincial deputations and a section of the army disagreed with the path taken by the emperor.[43] A crisis erupted on August 30, 1821, when Iturbide dissolved the congress and arrested a number of its members, violating article 172 of the Constitution of 1812.[44] As a result, some ayuntamientos, electors, members of the provincial deputations, militia and army officers, and many citizens at Soto de la Marina pronounced themselves in opposition to the emperor's actions because of "the imprisonment of the deputies that has reduced national representation to zero."[45]

CONSTITUTIONAL CRISIS AND REPUBLICANISM

The political and constitutional crisis allowed factions in favor of a republican government to flourish. They demanded new elections, free from all constraints, to select a congress that could establish the form of government best suited to the nation. They denounced the first constituent congress because it had not been elected in accordance with the Constitution of 1812 and because it had been convened to form a constitutional monarchy. Moreover, some maintained that it was necessary to establish a form of government that would secure the support of the United States as well as of Great Britain because Mexico was making a definitive break with Spain.[46]

Agreement proved difficult to obtain because the provinces opposed the authority and power of Mexico City. Some insisted on establishing a confederation, which they called a federation. The inability to obtain a European monarch and the failure of the native ruler, Agustín I, ended the possibility of restoring the constitutional monarchy. Only a republic was now feasible. However, some traditionalists identified a republic with the old repúblicas de indios founded by the Spanish Monarchy in the sixteenth century. This explains a request to the constituent congress from the citizens of Matehuala, a town in San Luis Potosí, who asked for "the reestablishment of the government of the repúblicas." When a deputy asked the commission on the constitution to rule "over a possible reestablishment of the ancient system of repúblicas," the committee replied in the negative because such an act "was not in agreement with the Empire's Constitution."[47]

The concerns of popular groups, particularly those of the members of the Indian communities, were eased by the expansion of constitutional ayuntamientos. These local governments could be established in areas with a population of a thousand persons and the means to support the town government. The Constitution eliminated traditional rights and permitted new groups to participate in local administration without regard to ethnicity. Moreover, the elimination of traditional hereditary office opened new opportunities to individuals hitherto excluded from government. Elections to municipal office and appointment to the local militia strengthened identification with republicanism. Popular political participation, however, was restricted by the three-tiered indirect elections and by property requirements for office. Nevertheless, social and political mobility flourished at the level of the municipalities, thereby strengthening the local character of government as the deliberative seat of the collective interest.

REPUBLICANISM AND THE RIGHT TO RESIST TYRANNY

Mexico's first republicanism included different imaginaries that had to be transformed to produce a modern republic founded on universal citizen rights. Republicanism, as an integrative phenomenon, had to include different ethnic and social groups, ideas, and cultures. Therefore, its evolution was not the work of a group of enlightened individuals or even a single generation. The formation of a genuine republican system of government required several generations in which elites and common citizens, recognizing that constitutional authority was paramount, interacted with the national government through ayuntamientos and militias. The transition from a nationalized monarchy in 1821 to the confederated republic in 1824 probably resulted from Spain's refusal to allow a member of the ruling house—as occurred in the case of Brazil—to assume the throne of the Mexican Empire. In the resulting power vacuum, it was inevitable that Colonel Agustín de Iturbide, as *primus inter-pares*, would become emperor. However, when he sought to centralize authority, members of Congress opposed him. When Iturbide responded by arresting some deputies and ultimately dismissing Congress, the provinces of Mexico rose in revolt against him. The empire collapsed in the midst of a constitutional crisis.

Political commentators argued that, historically, insurrection was an extraordinary measure to enforce the public will against tyrants. Therefore, it should only be employed in rare cases. As a catechism asserted: the Mexican people, being morally and materially mature, "made use of its right to insurrection."[48] The concept of the right to insurrection blended well with a new political practice that emerged at independence. A nascent caudillo and his followers advanced a political plan to implement certain reforms and appealed to the provinces for support. In the language of the time, it became known as a *pronunciamiento*. As the catechism noted: "The plan and the pronunciamiento of Iguala [issued at independence in September 1821 to form a constitutional empire] resulted in the creation of a new nation, known today as the United States of Mexico, which adopted a representative, republican, and federal government." It is representative because the legislative branch is entrusted by the people to persons elected by it for fixed periods of time; it is republican because the legislature in its totality is named by the people and no one in that body holds permanent office; it is federal because it unites a number of independent regional governments in the exercise of certain aspects of sovereignty and is superior to them in the exercise of other aspects of sovereignty.[49] As a new nation, it established its limits, territories, districts, and states, an essential aspect of a modern state because "the entities that constitute the [national] territory have legal personalities with sovereign rights over their own territories."[50]

POLITICAL REPRESENTATION

The role of the people was fundamental in the catechism's view. It recognized that the country's population was mixed: "Mexicans are the result of the intermingling of the ancient inhabitants, the dominant groups, and, in some places, the black slaves transported from Africa." Mexico had obtained its independence because of "the general will, in other words, the formation of a public opinion strong enough to be recognized. The general will is expressed through the votes of the representatives of the 'people.' However, since the people do not possess and cannot possess the information required [to express that will] . . . , a system of proxies has been invented to represent them [the people] who may be removed if they [the people] believe they [the proxies] are not acting according to their [the people's] will."[51]

The congress of the new republic consisted of two chambers of representatives elected under conditions defined locally because each state was sovereign.[52] Initially, Congress was the dominant branch of the national government, a situation mirrored in the state legislatures. The confederate form of government and the imbalance of power among its branches protected local freedoms. The deputies and senators elected by each state were expected to defend, above all, local interests, that of their patrias. Hence, they arrived in Congress with either wide or limited authority, depending on their state's mandate. In theory, a large body of representatives, whose mandates could be revoked or renewed by elections, prevented the emergence of a tyrannical executive branch. In fact, the first republic was a confederation of parliamentarians with different levels of authority, a mechanism designed to ensure that local interests were not subverted. Far from being deputies of the nation, they were the defenders of the *res publicae* of each territory.

CONGRESSIONAL POWER

The sovereign states of the Union exercised considerable power. Their legislatures established the criteria for citizenship within their own territories. The national congress introduced its own requirements for federal elections. Each state legislature regulated internal trade while the national congress regulated commerce at the interstate level. A similar division of responsibilities applied to management of roads and waterways. Local authorities regulated local economies through their right to impose *alcabalas* (sales taxes) and other internal tariffs on consumption and land use.

Congress, not the executive branch, controlled the fiscal sector. It established the annual budget and approved the taxes needed to fund it; Congress also determined expenditures and audited the executive branch. The executive was in charge of foreign relations, including the task of negotiating agreements or treaties with the Holy See and with the governments of Roman Catholic nations regarding ecclesiastical issues. The executive branch was also charged with administering the *patronato*, understood as the nominating of those who were to govern the Church and supervise the conduct of its civil and ecclesiastic obligations, the bishops.

Congress also controlled the nation's armed forces. It determined the size of the permanent army and navy and regulated the armed forces. Local militias were under the jurisdiction of the states, unless needed by the national government in case of emergency. The relationship between the legislature and the armed forces reflected the political mobility present between the two bodies during the first half of the century. A regional and national political class formed through the intertwining of these two organs, the legislature and the armed forces. The close relationship between the two sectors and the resolution of common concerns gradually allowed them to counterbalance parochial interests.

THE CITIZEN MILITIA

The linking mechanisms for citizens became the military and the three levels of government: municipal, state, and national. The electoral processes, political practices derived from voting procedures, organized public opinion, and the factions within the three levels of government provided ample opportunity for all groups. At the top of the pyramid, the national congress and the state legislatures, which assumed the task of representing the nation, established their power with a nexus between parliament and army. The armed forces—the keepers of the peace, unity, and religion, in other words, the protectors of the nation's sovereignty—became the superior among equals. As the armed sector of Congress, the nation's new heroes were armed citizens who protected the national territory and the national well-being.

Initially, the executive branch was reduced to carrying out legislative policies. After overthrowing Iturbide, Congress entered an anti-centralist stage, the result of factions that successfully resisted the emperor's demands for greater government authority. Federal, confederal, and openly separatist interests flourished. The new constitution granted the executive branch limited authority: appointing public officials, conducting diplomatic negotiations, controlling the armed forces, investing public funds, and limited control over the federation's economic and internal issues. The executive was elected for a four-year term, without the possibility of immediate reelection. State legislatures were the first to vote for a president; then the chamber of deputies selected the winner from among those who had obtained the greatest number of votes. In 1824, the country was governed by a weak federal administration; most authority remained in the hands of the state legislatures. Within each state, the ayuntamientos exercised strong control over their jurisdictions. The precarious state of most government administrative institutions, at both the state and federal level, also contributed to local municipal dominance.

MUNICIPAL AUTHORITY

The municipality became the basic institution of the federal structure. By the late 1820s it had become a territorial jurisdiction with its own main town council (ayuntamiento) and auxiliary town councils (*alcaldías* and *ayudantías municipales*). The municipality became the foundation of the political system because it was a source of unity and identity for most residents. In this period of transition, local governments had been capable of protecting their resources because only local folk were familiar with the area's wealth. As a result, municipalities were not only able to collect but also to retain taxes; rarely were local funds sent to the state government. The municipality also gained strength because of the tiered nature of elections. Since the first-level vote included most male residents, local authorities obtained a large base of support. A similar situation occurred with the local electors picked by the municipality to represent it at the district-level. Since the district electors were not eligible for high-ranking posts, their primary interest lay in retaining the support of local municipal citizens. Their intermediary position also allowed the district electors to establish inter-regional networks linking other districts within a growing electoral body.

At the other extreme of the government, federal and state authorities were elected from among the potentates. Their selection was intended to separate parochial interests—those of the municipality—from those of the states and the nation. In this way, a political class that would represent the interests of the nation prospered at the higher levels of government. In addition, elite dominance avoided the anarchy that democracy might bring if people who lacked civility participated fully. Thus, the broad-based municipal-level voters were contained at the first stage since stricter property requirements blocked their upward mobility.

CONFEDERATE RULE

The confederacy resulted in great instability because the national government could not be consolidated. During these years, Mexico experienced repeated changes in the national executive. However, local and state officials, members of the military and of the national congress enjoyed a longer tenure. Liberal and republican political elites, who realized that the power of the states undermined the efforts of the executive to govern, gradually shifted their support toward a central republic. The debate over centralism and federalism divided all social sectors and affected the precarious balance among the federal entities. The situation, moreover, led to the eruption of disputes over boundaries and jurisdictions between states and municipalities.

The debate over the nature of government required a clear definition of the term republic. The liberal centralists were the first to define the concept. As a result, the traditional notion of good government or res publicae faded away. The 1833 *Cartilla Social*, and its 1836 edition, defined a modern republic as liberal, central, and endowed with the classical division of powers, executive, legislative, and judicial. It categorically established representation, and for the first time included the rights of man: liberty, property, and the free circulation of ideas and goods, and social rights, such as the right to education and employment. Republican values to liberal centralists were secular and placed particular emphasis on tolerance and respect for the individual.

LIBERALISM AND THE RIGHTS OF MAN

The catechisms of the 1830s start with individual rights and progress to social rights. In that respect, the two editions of the *Cartilla Social* (1833 and 1836), which were substantially different from the concepts of 1824, reflect an important evolution in the debate. The first chapter of the 1833 edition considers civil society, while the 1836 Cartilla addresses from the very beginning men's individual rights and obligations. Both editions advocate a liberal and secular view of society. Virtues, conceived as individual, social, and moral, are useful to the individual and to society. Individual virtue refers to the science that fosters prudence and judgment, moderation and temperance, and gives strength and courage to the body and the soul as well as emphasizing purity of body, or neatness, and attractiveness in dress and in one's dwelling. Social virtue consists of justice, which encompasses all socially useful actions, such as love and patriotism. Civil society is the union of many people with tacit or explicit agreements to ensure common security, tranquility, and a comfortable life without fear of danger or of disturbance.[53]

The two editions of the *Cartilla Social* enunciate an important transformation in political concepts. Both abandon tradition and historic constitutionalism in favor of a new perception of republicanism. They conceive the republic as a polity formed by the social contract, or new compact, that citizens establish to create a civil society. The compact establishes order in society and imposes rights and obligations on all citizens to promote the well-being of the republic.[54] All citizens are obliged "to always prefer the common over the individual good." In that respect, civil government imposes rights that are linked to obligations based on the social contract formed by civil society. For example, taxes and their payment are an obligation with a corresponding right: the right to vote and to be elected to office. A citizen's liberties are limited by the common well-being of the republic. However, civil society can also impose restrictions on its representatives by limiting their authority. No representative may perform a sovereign act without it first being approved by the people.

A REPUBLICAN POLITICAL COMMUNITY

The new republic was based on a revolutionary and modern principle: the sense of belonging to a political community with common secular values and principles, such as liberty, equality, representation, and citizenship based on merit rather than inheritance or privilege. The notion of a single political community that did not acknowledge the various cultural and ethnic groups within it remained controversial. Because of the multi-ethnic composition of Mexican society, legislative factions arose in response to the pressures of armed ethnic groups and their leaders. In some instances, indigenous groups demanded the restitution of their lands and resources on the grounds of traditional rights. Such demands ran counter to the policies of establishing constitutional municipal governments, which introduced a modern administrative and political organization. In the latter instance, the political unit was based on population size, while in the former, members of corporate estates or of ethnic groups considered the republic as a synonym for local autonomy.

The two editions of the *Cartilla Social* perceive the republic as a system of government in a profoundly different way than those of the first republicanism in 1824. The earlier view was founded on the classical conception of the nature of republics: monarchical, aristocratic, and democratic. Initially, Mexico privileged the aristocratic republic of "notable citizens" in which the common good or general interest is synonymous with res publicae that is characterized by a form of government opposed to despotic rule.

The cartillas sociales of 1833 and 1836, in contrast, maintain that men enjoy greater liberty in a democracy than in other forms of government. "That is to say, they are freer than in a monarchic or aristocratic government because in a democracy each individual exercises, alternatively, a function of government. Every citizen has access to public jobs and has an active and passive vote in all councils and public deliberations. That is why, everyone is considered an equal. Moreover, the government is obliged to treat the people with respect and does not dare commit excesses. If excesses are committed, those who later assume office will correct and change them. For all these valid reasons, in a popular government there is greater freedom and equality than in other governments."[55]

The way in which the 1836 *Cartilla Social* conceived the relationship between the people and the governing elites is significant. It recognized that "in a popular government, the people have their juntas (meetings), which must be held with the consent of all citizens, or, if the importance of the issue required, the consent of the majority of the inhabitants of the district or locality. . . . They must follow a preordained order to be established by each society according to its fundamental laws. If order is lacking in such events, they will not be popular juntas, but preparations for popular mutinies." The catechism then poses a series of questions and answers: "Do all citizens have the right to vote during the junta? All those who are capable of explaining their will should have part in the government and, therefore, vote in the juntas. If the community is very large can all individuals gather? Yes, divided by states, cantons, districts or departments, they will establish a special junta to elect their deputies who will form the provincial junta that will later name deputies who, informed of the needs of the inhabitants of each town, will constitute a congress or general junta in which authority resides, inasmuch as it represents the whole nation, and which possesses of the powers necessary to govern it."[56] The *Cartilla Social*'s dialogue is fundamental for understanding all the linking mechanisms of the representative system and the connections established among the different levels of government.

What are the continuities and differences with the recent past? The *Cartilla Social* reiterates the right to resistance, or what had been previously called pronunciamiento or insurrection. The catechism states: "the nature of authority consists precisely of leading the actions and forces of the members of society towards the common good, in other words, to achieve the ends of society. Later, if the authorities clearly depart from that goal and use those forces to ruin the state, all the people and all the individuals that constitute [the political entity] have the right, based on the primitive social compacts, to resist; not to do so would constitute a violation of their basic obligations."[57]

According to the *Cartilla Social* the wealth of a nation, or republic—terms that are now synonymous—resides in agriculture, trade, and industry as well as on an educated and moral society where justice is imparted with rectitude and poverty and laziness are abolished. It rejected the latter vices because they formed beings useless to society and because "this class of people are purely consumers and are in no way productive; society must destroy them if they cannot become useful." With relation to political tolerance, it affirmed that "it consists of respecting the individual opinions of each citizen as long as he has fulfilled his obligations and has not broken any laws of behavior."[58]

CITIZEN RIGHTS AND REPUBLICAN VALUES

The catechism defined equality as that which everyone possesses simply for being a member of society. All possessed equal rights to protection, security, and tranquility. All citizens also had the obligation to contribute to the maintenance of social order through equal sacrifice. The catechism taught that equality "could be called legal equality, which is the only equality possible, since nature itself has established certain inequalities among men, such as talent, instruction, virtue, valor, wealth, and education."[59] Through these five variables, men can improve their qualities and obtain full citizen rights with active and passive votes. "It is the law that balances these inequalities, always protecting the weakest from the strongest." In other words, a man of virtue and courage has primacy over a talented and educated individual with little sense of patriotism. Also, citizenship may be lost, since it is a right as well as an obligation, if citizens do not fulfill their obligations to the republic. These include "those of any member of a society to which he belongs since the republic is nothing more than a political society. As a result of the primordial compact, members of the society are obligated to employ their goods, strengths and, even, their lives to preserve society and ensure that it fulfills its goals—security, tranquility and public happiness—because society's survival depends on each individual."[60] At the same time, the citizen is free to leave civil society if it suffers from disorder and lacks the strength or the means to ensure the citizen's access to security and tranquility. The catechism insists on the citizen's right to insurrection, to the pronunciamieto—under specific circumstances—considering it an extraordinary right of the citizen. In such circumstances, it constitutes a political measure and not a rebellion. Not until the Constitution of 1917 were political factions legally denied the use of insurrection to obtain power.

The *Cartilla Social* does not take a stand for or against centralism or federalism. It mentions only indirectly that the national guards and the citizen militias were abolished while the regular army was strengthened. Nevertheless, during the 1830s there was evidence of a more open, more secular society that favored social and political mobility. Religious tolerance emerged as a new issue when only twenty years before the only acceptable religion was Catholicism. Clearly, fundamental change had occurred.

LINKAGES WITHIN SOCIETY AND LEVELS OF GOVERNMENT

The path that society took during the years 1808 to 1836, the span of a full generation, may be perceived in the following example, which initiates the popular foundation of republican federalism, which is fundamental to understanding of the republican triumph. The southern leader Juan Álvarez wrote in 1842 to the great legislator of central Mexico, Mariano Riva Palacio: "Our elections in this area have been conducted to our full satisfaction. Secondary electors upon arriving in that city (Mexico) will seek you to reach an understanding. They are carrying a list of candidates that I am also sending to General Bravo so that he may have it adopted by the electors of Chilapa. The electors of Taxco will also accept that list and united those districts will cooperate with their votes in the elections of other districts, thereby establishing a mutual correspondence."[61] The quote is important for the purposes of this essay because it demonstrates that the electoral process organized the popular will around a political faction, that of the caudillo or regional leader, through the military organization and the national guard, that, together with the legislative branch, connects the various municipal, district, and state interests with the national congress.

The civic militias, under the control of the regional caudillos, had been able to establish vertical links, reaching upward to the national congress and to the elites. Simultaneously, they also created other links that interacted with the different government levels. Education, or patriotic values, became a powerful mechanism for advancement that resulted in mobility among the different levels of representation. Mobility became the trait of the new era. As the 1836 *Cartilla Social* observed: the ability to obtain a certain office with neither "riches, nor the merits of forefathers, nor ancient family splendor, nor any other considerations of that nature, as the basis for the election [constituted the essence of the new republicanism]."[62] Access to full citizenship, granted because of a patriotic act in defense of the nation, facilitated the correlation among the different levels of representation.

This essay has sought to portray the socio-political transformations of the time through an analysis of the political catechisms of the years 1810 to 1836. It demonstrates how the changing concept of sovereignty and representation, founded on the criteria of population, replaced the earlier system of representation by corporate estates. The new electoral processes transformed the old corporate society and led to the formation of new institutions. Indeed, elections became a powerful mechanism for molding public opinion and public life. As the national congress, the state legislatures, and the municipal governments consolidated their roles, Mexico embraced the new republican order. In that respect, the liberal and federal Constitution of 1857 not only defined the nature of government, but also represented the country's definitive rejection of monarchy and the acceptance of a modern republic.

NOTES

1. On catechisms as an educational source see Javier Ocampo López, *Los Catecismos Políticos de la Independencia de Hispanoamérica. De la Monarquía a la República* (Tunja: Publicación del Magister en Historia, UPTC, 1988).

2. Silvio Zavala, "Tres acercamientos de la Ilustración Francesa a Nuestra Historia," in Solange Alberro, Alicia Hernández Chávez, and Elías Trabulse, coords., *La Revolución Francesa en México* (Mexico: El Colegio de México, CIESAS, 1991), 9–46.

3. Germán Cardozo Galue, *Michoacán en El Siglo de las Luces* (Mexico: El Colegio de México, 1973).

4. Jaime E. Rodríguez O., "From Royal Subject to Republican Citizen: The role of the Autonomists in the Independence of Mexico," in Jaime E. Rodríguez O., ed., *The Independence of Mexico and the Creation of the New Nation* (Los Angeles: UCLA Latin American Center Publications, 1989), 1–43. The following are the essential sources for this period: Jaime E. Rodríguez O., *La independencia de la América Española* (Mexico: Fideicomiso Historia de las Américas/El Colegio de México/Fondo de Cultura Económica, 1996), published in English by Cambridge University Press, 1998; Virginia Guedea, *En busca de un gobierno alterno: Los Guadalupes de México* (Mexico: Universidad Nacional Autónoma de México, 1992); Charles A. Hale, *El liberalismo mexicano en la época de Mora, 1821–1853* (Mexico: Siglo XXI, 1968). This period is also studied in some of my own work: Alicia Hernández Chávez, *Anenecuilco. Memoria y vida de un pueblo* (Mexico: Fideicomiso Historia de las Américas/El Colegio de México/Fondo de Cultura Económica, 1993); *La tradición republicana de un buen gobierno* (Mexico: Fideicomiso Historia de las Américas/El Colegio de México/Fondo de Cultura Económica, 1993); *México. Breve historia contemporánea*, Colección Popular (Mexico: Fondo de Cultura Económica, 2000) (forthcoming in English: University of California Press). Regarding the first problems faced by federalism see Marcello Carmagnani, "Del territorio a la region" in Alicia Hernández Chávez/Manuel Miño Grijalva, coords., *Cincuenta años de historia en México en el cincuentenario del Centro de Estudios Históricos*, 2 vols. (Mexico: El Colegio de México, 1991), 2: 221–241; Michael P. Costeloe, *La Primera república federal de México, 1824–1835* (Mexico: Fondo de Cultura Económica, 1975); Michael P. Costeloe, *La república central en México, 1835–1846. "Hombres de bien" en la época de Santa Anna* (Mexico: Fondo de Cultura Económica, 2000).

5. Acta del Ayuntamiento de México, 1809, in Felipe Tena Ramírez, *Leyes Fundamentales de México, 1808–1983* (Mexico: Porrúa, 1983), 4–20. The document indicates that the abdication of Carlos IV and Fernando VII is declared void; any official named in Spain will not be recognized; the only authority recognized is the viceroy who will govern through a mandate of the Ayuntamiento in representation of the whole territory.

6. Wladimiro Piskorski, *Las Cortes de castilla en el periodo de tránsito de la Edad Media a la Moderna 1188–1520* (Barcelona: Ediciones El Albir, S. A., 1977).

7. Edicto del 16 de febrero de 1816 dado en la Inquisición de México. Here are listed all the leaflets, political catechisms, pamphlets, reflections, sermons, and theater scripts forbidden in Mexico City, the states and provinces of New Spain, Guatemala, Nicaragua, the Philippines, its districts and jurisdictions.

8. *Catecismo de la Independencia en Siete Declaraciones, por Ludovico LatoMonte, quien lo dedica al Excmo. Señor don Agustín de Iturbide y Aramburu, Generalísimo de las armas de mar y tierra y Presidente de la Regencia Gobernadora del Imperio Mexicano* (Mexico: Imprenta de Mariano Ontiveros, 1821). Hereafter, I will cite the catechism, followed by the date printed and, when so needed, the title of the chapter.

9. *Catecismo político arreglado a la Constitución de la Monarquía Española para Ilustración del Pueblo, Instrucción de la Juventud y Uso de las Escuelas de Primeras Letras. Por D. J. C.* (Puebla: Imprenta de San Felipe Neri, 1820), 4.

10. The claims of restitution were based on those rights and are found in litigation initiated by the ancient towns that demanded the restitution of property during the nineteenth century and for a good part of the twentieth. These republics were conceived as autonomous governments with corporate and individual properties and wealth. They were the foundation of the society of New Spain; their existence was threatened in the eighteenth century, and this created the first autonomy movements and the refounding of towns that would have room for new social actors. Hernández Chávez, *La tradición republicana*; and ibid., *Anenecuilco*.

11. Juan A. Mateos, *Historia Parlamentaria* (Mexico: Congress of the Union. Instituto de Estudios Parlamentarios, 1997), 1: 194.

12. Carl von Clausewitz, in his theory on war, systemizes the function of the army in the creation of new states in the eighteenth and nineteenth centuries. See Peter Paret, *Clausewitz and the State. The Man, His Theories and His Times* (Princeton: Princeton University Press, 1985).

13. *O se descoyota a la nación o cesa su libertad* (Puebla: Imprenta Liberal de Moreno Hermanos, 1824). It tells of cavalry regiment No. 11 as it headed to a sovereign Congress in 1824 with a proposal of stripping all Spanish of their jobs.

14. Manuel Chust, "Armed Citizens: The Civic Militia in the Origins of the Mexican National State, 1812–1827," in this volume.

15. *Catecismo 1821*, "Declaración Quinta de la forma de gobierno," 38–39.

16. *Catecismo 1820*, "Lección XI," 47.

17. Archivo General de la Nación, México (hereafter, AGN), Ramo Inquisición, Legajo 4489, No. 11. *Sentencia del 1 de Agosto de 1815 al Catecismo Político o Doctrina del Buen Ciudadano, amante de su religión, de su patria y de su rey* (Zaragoza: printed in Madrid, reprinted in Zaragoza, Spain, 1814).

18. Ibid., chapter 15. "Del gobierno interior de las provincias y de los pueblos," 63.

19. With regard to this, Edmundo O'Gorman says in *Historia de las Divisiones Territoriales de México* (Mexico: Editorial Porrúa, 1985): "[I]n a system of government as ours, fixing precise limits is indispensable because the entities that conform our territory enjoy legal personality with sovereignty over their territory. During the colonial era, this was not so; it was enough to list the seats, along with the towns, boroughs, and ranches that were under their authority." Note 1 of the "Introducción histórica."

20. Nettie Lee Benson, *La diputación provincial y el federalismo mexicano* (Mexico: El Colegio de México *primera parte, 1521–1820* 1994), 35; and ss. José Miranda, *Las ideas y las instituciones políticas mexicanas, primera parte, 1521–1820* (Mexico: Universidad Nacional Autónoma de México, 1978).

21. *Catecismo 1820*, "Lección XVI. De las diputaciones provinciales," 67; and Benson, *La diputación provincial*.

22. *Catecismo 1820*, 64.

23. *Catecismo 1820*, "Lección XVI. Del Gobierno Interior."

24. *Civitas*, as a political organization of citizens when a state or nation is in the making, is best analyzed in Pietro Costa, *Civitas. Storia della Cittadinanza in Europa I Dalla. Civilita Communale al Settecento* (Bari: Editorial Laterza, 1999).

25. *Catecismo 1820*, "Lección 4. Del Gobierno," 23.

26. Ibid., 24.

27. Ibid., 26.

28. "Programa de los Principios Políticos que en México ha profesado el partido del progreso, y de la manera en que una sección de este partido pretendió hacerlos valer en la administración de 1833 a 1834," in José María Luis Mora, *Obras Completas. Política*, 3 vols. (Mexico: Instituto Mora-SEP, 1986), 2: 370–376.

29. Ibid., 371.

30. "Discurso sobre la necesidad de fijar el derecho de ciudadanía en la república y hacerlo afecto esencialmente a la propiedad 14 abril 1830," in Mora, *Obras Completas*, 1: 370.

31. Ibid., 374–375.

32. *Catecismo 1820*, "Lección Primera De la Constitución," 3–4.

33. Ibid., 8.

34. *Catecismo 1821*, "Declaración quinta. De la forma de gobierno." It states "[Monarchy] is the only one that can bestow felicity upon us, given the character and circumstances of the Mexican people [...] Because it is the one that receives the greatest recognition from other peoples and can avoid the evils of the others," 34.

35. Ibid., 35.

36. Ibid., 37.

37. *Catecismo 1821*, "Declaración segunda. De la Independencia mexicana," 14–15.

38. *Catecismo 1821*, "Declaración primera. De la Independencia en común," 10, 11.

39. *Catecismo 1820*, "Lección XI. De los secretarios de despacho," 47.

40. Tadeo Ortiz, *México considerado como Nación Independiente y Libre según algunas indicaciones sobre los Deberes más Esenciales de los Mexicanos* (Mexico: Cien de México, 1996), 38.

41. Ibid., 19.

42. Servando Teresa de Mier, *La formación de un republicano*, compilation and introduction by Jaime E. Rodríguez O. (Mexico: Universidad Nacional Autónoma de México, 1988).

43. AGN, Col. Folletería, Vol. 2, f. 45. *Catástrofe de D. Agustín de Iturbide aclamado emperador el 18 de mayo de 1822 o relación exacta de las circunstancias que han acompañado el desembarco y la muerte de este hombre célebre* (Paris: 1825).

44. Manuel Calvillo, *La consumación de la Independencia y la Instauración de la República Federal Mexicana Gestación y Nacimiento* I. (Mexico: Distrito Federal, 1974).

45. *Planes de la Nación*, 138.

46. Mier, *La formación de un republicano*.

47. Mateos, *Historia Parlamentaria*, vol. 1, December 5, 1821, session, and January 5, 1822, session.

48. "Catecismo Político de la Federación Mexicana," in José María Luis Mora, *Obras Completas. Política* (Mexico: Instituto Mora-SEP, 1987), 3: 31. The year is not

mentioned, but the contents can be dated to after the Federal Republic's Constitution of 1824. It will be cited hereafter as: Mora, "Catecismo Político."

49. Mora, "Catecismo Político": Chapter 2. "De la Nación Mexicana, sus partes constituyentes, su forma de gobierno y religión, " *Obras Completas*, 3: 432–433.

50. O'Gorman, *Historia de las Divisiones Territoriales*, 3.

51. Mora, "Catecismo Político," *Obras Completas*, 1: 8.

52. Ibid., 438.

53. José Gómez de la Cortina, *Cartilla Social o Breve Instrucción sobre los Derechos y Obligaciones del Hombre en la Sociedad Civil*, 2nd ed. (Mexico: Ignacio Cumplido, 1836). The first edition, from 1833, was published in Mexico by Imprenta Galván. I will make reference to both editions, distinguishing them by the year of publication.

54. *Cartilla Social 1833*, capítulo I. "De la sociedad Civil y del Imperio que resulta de ella"; ibid., *Cartilla Social 1836*, capítulo II. "De la sociedad Civil y del Imperio que resulta de ella."

55. *Cartilla Social 1836*, capítulo III. "De las diferentes especies de repúblicas."

56. *Cartilla Social 1836*, capítulo IV. "De las Juntas populares."

57. *Cartilla Social 1836*, capítulo VI. "Sobre la seguridad y la tranquilidad de la república."

58. *Cartilla Social 1836*, capítulo III. "De las diferentes especies de repúblicas".

59. *Cartilla Social 1836*, capítulo VIII. "De la igualdad."

60. *Cartilla Social 1836*, capítulo X. "Obligaciones de los ciudadanos."

61. Quoted in Cecilia Noriega Elío, *El Constituyente de 1842* (Mexico: Universidad Nacional Autónoma de México, 1986), 68.

62. *Cartilla Social 1836*, Capítulo V. "Naturaleza de la majestad, sus obligaciones y derechos," 21, 32.

2

"Ningún pueblo es superior a otro": Oaxaca and Mexican Federalism

Jaime E. Rodríguez O.

Oaxaca sola e independiente de Méjico eres feliz. . . . Separate de Méjico, y esta acción misma, la veras identificada con tu felicidad: establece un nuevo orden de cosas: muda el sistema que has observado hasta aqui, y dentro de pocos años, seras la embidia de las Naciones. . . . Considera el estado actual de Méjico, y . . . veras . . . que ocupado el Soberano Congreso en las vastas atenciones que demanda el Septentrión entero; no puede dedicarse a este punto solo, con aquel empeño, que seguramente tendran sus propios indigenas.

—Antequera de Oaxaca, May 25, 1823

El pueblo de Oaxaca en asonada y tumulto riguroso proclamó la Independencia de México, que apoyó el Diputado D. Antonio León, Jefe militar interino, pero de una manera tan grosera que no pudo disimular su intervención en este hecho, más ridículo que inocuo. . . . No fueron cien personas las que convocaron y causaron el motín, siendo el alma de él el subdiácono D. Ignacio Ordoño, hombre de una inmoralidad escandalosa. . . . León el Comandante militar, ha sido manejado por este hombre atolondrado, y los que han intervenido en la farsa son no menos criminales que estúpidos. Han expedido su Convocatoria para instalar un Congreso provincial el 1 de julio, congregación que semejará en mucho a la reunión que hizo Júpiter de todos los animales.

—Carlos María de Bustamante, Mexico, June 1823

Los principios que dirigen las operaciones de México, son la infracción del último pacto, y la violación de los sagrados derechos que tienen los pueblos para promover por todos los medios la felicidad. ¡Vicios inherentes a la capital del despotismo, que hace muchos siglos alimenta y sostiene su

65

pompa y grandeza con el sudor, y sangre de la victima! Allí reconcentraron los antiguos visires todo el poder, y toda la grandeza: allí pusieron el despacho universal de los negocios, y los que participan aun de tales usurpaciones, no conocen otros derechos que su interés particular. Se olvidan de que cuando las provincias convinieron despues del plan de Casa Mata en que reuniese el Congreso, fue solamente, para que espidiese la convocatoria para otro nuevo: que . . . los pueblos se manifestaron de un modo inequívoco por el sistema de república federal. . . . A México lo han reconocido los Estados por centro de unión: no tiene duda; pero esto ha sido por política, por conveniencia, y por el bien general de la nación, y de ninguna manera por estar persuadidos de que allí existe la representación nacional. . . . Todo lo contrario. El corto número de individuos que quedan [en el Congreso] no es otra cosa, sino una juntilla de facciosos que apoyados del gobierno, bien hallado con ostentar un poder absoluto, estan sofocando, y reprimiendo por medio de fuerza armada la libre voz del resto de las provincias. . . . ¡O Iturbide! Acuerdales a esos hombres descarriados, que tales medidas no te valieron en tus agonias: que con ellas te hiciste mas odioso, y te precipaste a tu ruina.

—Ignacio Ordoño, Antequera de Oaxaca, September 12, 1823

On the morning of Sunday, June 1, 1823, large numbers of people congregated in the plaza mayor of the city of Antequera de Oaxaca demanding the establishment of a "Republican Federal Government, Independent of that Capital [México City]."[1] As a result, the Province of Oaxaca became the first to establish an interim government and the first to convert itself into an independent and sovereign state within the larger Mexican nation.

The triumph of federalism in Oaxaca was the culmination of several decades of institutional, economic, political, and ideological change. This essay analyzes Oaxacan events, placing them within the broader context of the extraordinary transformations within the Hispanic world during the previous years.

During the latter part of the eighteenth century, the region prospered as the result of the production of *grana de cochinilla* (scarlet cochineal dye) and textiles. By the end of the century, the capital city of Antequera had a population of about 19,000 people. It was the principal non-Indian city in an area of large native population. The *alcaldes mayores* (magistrates), most of them European Spaniards, administered the region and served as middlemen between producers and merchants, primarily in Mexico City, through the system of *repartimiento de comercio*. Power relationships changed in 1786 when Oaxaca became an intendancy; *subdelegados* replaced the alcaldes mayores and the repartimiento de comercio was abolished. Since the repartimiento functioned as an important system of credit and the alcaldes mayores facilitated the marketing and export of local products, the modifications occasioned considerable discontent. The establishment of the Consulado (merchants' guild) of Veracruz also undermined long-established credit and trade connections with the large merchants of the Consulado of Mexico. The European wars unleashed by the French Revolution of 1789 curtailed and further transformed commerce. The Intendancy of Oaxaca was in the process of accommodating these far-reaching changes when the region was engulfed in the upheavals of 1808.[2]

THE HISPANIC REVOLUTION

The collapse of the Spanish Monarchy in 1808, as a result of the French invasion of the Peninsula and the abdication of its rulers, triggered a series of events that initiated the great political revolution of the Hispanic world. The first step in that process was the formation of local governing juntas in Spain, which invoked the Hispanic legal principle that, in the absence of the king, sovereignty reverted to the people.

News of events in Spain, as well as in other parts of the monarchy, was rapidly and widely disseminated. In the *Antiguo Régimen*, news and information was spread in a variety of ways. Printed laws, decrees, and official notices were distributed to the relevant authorities who, in turn, informed the people by posting them in public places and by employing town criers to read them to the public. Public officials and private individuals often wrote letters that contained information or comment about the events of the day to friends and colleagues. The recipients of this mail in turn informed their friends, colleagues, and neighbors. Much information was transmitted orally. *Curas* often discussed important questions both formally, during mass, and informally outside the church. Public scribes informed the illiterate public of the latest events. Muleteers, merchants, and travelers kept the inhabitants of towns and villages abreast of events occurring in the viceregal capital or in Europe. People talked about the events of the day in social gatherings, such as those at *tertulias*, cafés, taverns, and *paseos*. Thus, even the vast illiterate population was much better informed than is generally believed. Of course, rumor and misinformation were also widespread.[3] Frequently, the rapidly changing circumstances confused and disturbed the people of New Spain.

Public discourse intensified after 1808. The printing press, which became the indispensable instrument of politics, fueled an explosion of political activity in the entire Hispanic world. In the months and years that followed, important notices (particularly about the struggle against the French), decrees, laws, minutes of special meetings, reports of elections, statements from prominent persons, and other matters of interest were published rapidly. News from Europe and America circulated widely in Mexico City and in the provincial capitals. Politically active *novohispanos* (people of New Spain) learned of significant events shortly after their occurrence; they quickly received copies of important documents; and they learned to exercise their rights.[4]

Although political ideas, structures, and practices changed with vertiginous rapidity after 1808, much remained from the Old Regime. The nature of social, economic, and institutional relations changed slowly; the new liberal processes and institutions required time to take hold. As this essay will show, the Province of Oaxaca experienced drastic political change during the first decades of the nineteenth century. Yet, the new liberal institutions and processes were often intermingled with traditional patterns and practices. Concepts such as authority, sovereignty, legitimacy, the people, representation, and independence changed but also remained unclear. There were no sharp breaks with the past; the Antiguo Régimen and the new liberalism blended throughout the process.[5]

News of the collapse of the Spanish Monarchy mystified both the authorities and the people. Who ruled in Spain? Who, if anyone, should be obeyed? What should be done? Suddenly, the nature of authority, legitimacy, and sovereignty was called into question, dividing the ruling groups in Antequera. Most European Spaniards believed that anyone in authority in Spain should be obeyed, while many Americans favored some form of local government in New Spain. For some, the crisis provided an opportunity to undermine and possibly reverse the changes introduced with the intendancy in 1786. The merchants, particularly the *peninsulares* (people from the Spanish peninsula), also complained about *mal gobierno* (bad government). They accused the intendant of corruption, identifying him with the ministerial despotism of the discredited Manuel Godoy in Madrid.

In the Antiguo Régimen, *ayuntamientos* (city governments) functioned as provincial capitals. By tradition, ayuntamientos possessed the voice and representation of the region. In the sixteenth century King Carlos I had recognized the right of New Spain's ayuntamientos to participate in a regional *cortes* (parliament). Indeed, he had granted the city of Mexico, as the viceregal capital, a prominent position in any future assembly of cities. In June 1808, invoking the principle that in the absence of the king sovereignty reverted to the people, the Ayuntamiento of Mexico proposed that a junta similar to those being formed in Spain be convened to govern New Spain. Viceroy José Iturrigaray appeared to accept the corporation's arguments when, on September 1, 1808, he requested that the ayuntamientos of New Spain send representatives to a meeting in the capital. To prevent the congress of cities from taking place the peninsulares overthrew Viceroy Iturrigaray on the night of September 15, 1808. The event had significant repercussions in Oaxaca, where the European Spaniards took control of the city and ousted several criollos from important positions. In Antequera, as in the rest of New Spain, peninsulares governed disgruntled Americans.[6]

The following year, the Junta Central Gubernativa del Reino, which had been formed in the Peninsula to oppose the French, invited the kingdoms of America to elect delegates to that body. As Virginia Guedea indicates, "as a consequence of these elections, the ayuntamientos of New Spain began to regain the role, which . . . the Ayuntamiento of Mexico sought in 1808, that those corporations obtain the right to represent the provinces of the kingdom [of New Spain]."[7] The Ayuntamiento of Antequera de Oaxaca, like those of other intendancies in New Spain, was instructed to elect three individuals of well-known probity, talent, and learning and select one by lot. Then the Real Acuerdo in Mexico City would elect three from among the provincial representatives and would choose the delegate of New Spain by lot. In addition, the ayuntamientos of provincial capitals were to provide their delegates with credentials and instructions. The electoral process—the use of the *terna* (selection from among three candidates), for example—clearly relied upon existing election procedures to corporate bodies. The major difference was that traditional electoral processes were being adapted for new political purposes.[8]

The Ayuntamiento of Antequera, dominated by Europeans, elected as its representative Fr. Ramón Casar, auxiliary bishop of Jaca, Aragón. More significant, however, the ayuntamiento submitted a very somber *Instrucción*, which argued that the reforms of King Carlos III had severely damaged the region's economy. The ayuntamiento attributed the fall in the production of grana de cochinilla to the abolition of the alcaldías mayores and the elimination of the repartimiento de comercio. Since then, the ayuntamiento argued, Indians worked less, resulting in a corresponding decline in the collection of *alcabalas* (sales taxes), tribute, and *obvenciones parroquiales* (parish fees). To reinvigorate the economy, the ayuntamiento requested the abolition of the intendancy system and many taxes, the establishment of a *consulado de comercio* (merchants' guild) in Antequera, and free trade with ports in Guatemala and Peru. In addition, it asked for local improvements, including a university.[9]

The elites of the area had a second opportunity to express their views about their needs and about the nature of government when on May 22, 1809, the Junta Central requested that Spain and America respond to a *Consulta a la Nación* (Consultation to the Nation). The Consulta asked provincial juntas, ayuntamientos, tribunals, bishops, universities, and erudite individuals to recommend the best method of organizing the government.[10] The action of the Junta Central significantly changed traditional political practices. In ways that we have yet to understand, that request initiated the process of devolution of political power to the localities and engendered new sociopolitical relations.

On January 1, 1810, the Junta Central decreed that elections be held for a national Cortes. This time, each province in the New World was allocated a deputy to be elected by the ayuntamiento of the provincial capital. In addition to providing America greater representation, the decree stated that the deputies had to be natives of the provinces they represented. That requirement strengthened the political rights of Americans. The action not only substantially weakened the political power of European Spaniards, it also legitimized the concept of local rights.[11] The Ayuntamiento of Antequera elected Manuel María Mexía, cura of Tamasulapa, as its deputy to the Cortes. When the clergyman resigned, the ayuntamiento named *regidor honorario* Juan María Ibáñez Corbera to replace him.[12] Although its delegate was unable to travel to Spain, Antequera, like the rest of America, received detailed accounts of the activities of the Cortes. Newspapers and pamphlets also reported and analyzed the debates and decisions of that congress.

The deputies of Spain and America, who enacted the Constitution of the Spanish Monarchy, in March 1812, transformed the Hispanic world. The Charter of Cádiz created a unitary state with equal laws for all parts of the Spanish Monarchy, now called the Spanish Nation. When it enfranchised all men, except those of African ancestry, without requiring either literacy or property qualifications, the Constitution of 1812 expanded the electorate and dramatically increased the scope of political activity. The new charter established representative government at three levels: the municipality (the constitutional ayuntamiento), the province (the provincial deputation), and the monarchy (the Cortes). By authorizing cities and towns with one thousand or more inhabitants to form ayuntamientos, the Constitution transferred political power from the center to the localities and incorporated vast numbers of people into the political process.[13]

THE INSURGENT REGIME IN OAXACA

Although the Constitution of the Spanish Monarchy was published in New Spain during the months of September, October, and November 1812, it did not end the insurgency that emerged in the wake of the 1808 coup in Mexico City. The constitutional system had little impact on the Province of Oaxaca because on November 25, 1812, José María Morelos—an insurgent leader who rejected the constitutional process as a means of achieving home rule—occupied the city of Antequera and governed the region until March 1814.[14]

The insurgent victory in Oaxaca profoundly influenced the province's politics. Leading royalists, such as Bishop Agustín Bergoza y Jordán, fled as the insurgents captured, tried, and executed high-ranking royalist army officers. Morelos then expropriated the property of European Spaniards, particularly the merchants.[15] Although the Hispanic Constitution had replaced the hereditary elites, who had hitherto controlled the ayuntamientos, with popularly elected officials, the insurgent occupation of Oaxaca prevented the holding of popular elections in the province. Instead, after receiving oaths of allegiance from the established institutions, such as the *cabildo eclesiástico* (cathedral chapter), the ayuntamiento, and the guilds, Morelos retained the old corporate structures, but named criollos to government posts. He appointed the prominent hacendado José María Murgía y Galardi intendant and named a new ayuntamiento for Antequera consisting entirely of criollos. He also named Americans to replace peninsulares in all government offices, including that of subdelegado.[16] Although the changes eliminated European Spaniards from office, they did not constitute a social revolution. The American appointees, like their predecessors, were members of the province's social and economic elite.[17]

The extraordinary circumstances of the time influenced and complicated politics. Numerous individuals and groups in Oaxaca and other parts of New Spain had opposed the insurgents, particularly at the beginning, because they considered them violent, disorderly, and destructive. Even those who were disaffected with the existing royal authorities were distrustful of the insurgents. To allay those fears, in 1811 the insurgent leaders decided to institutionalize the movement. After extensive consultation, they established the Suprema Junta Nacional Americana as "a center of authority over all the [insurgent] leaders, which would uniformly and effectively direct all [insurgent] movements."[18] The Suprema Junta consisted of four members, Ignacio Rayón, José María Liceaga, José Sixto Verduzco, and José María Morelos; others would be elected as more provinces of New Spain came under insurgent control. Early in 1812, groups in Mexico City and other locations began secretly to support the insurgents, particularly Morelos who had emerged as the most important leader. Even as they won the Hispanic constitutional elections of 1812–1813, discontented groups in Mexico City, who sought to obtain autonomy by any means, also considered the possibility of joining the insurgent government. For example, Carlos María de Bustamante, a *oaxaqueño* lawyer and journalist who had been living in the viceregal capital for nearly a decade and who was selected parish elector in November 1812, fled Mexico City in December and joined the insurgents because his incendiary articles had aroused the ire of the authorities.[19]

The occupation of Oaxaca provided the opportunity to elect a fifth member to the Suprema Junta Nacional Americana. On April 30, 1813, Morelos sent to the ayuntamiento and the cabildo eclesiástico of Antequera de Oaxaca the *convocatoria* to elect the new member. The electoral process was a strange mixture of traditional corporate practices and the new procedures introduced by the Cortes of Cádiz. As Virginia Guedea indicates: "The principal subjects, both secular and ecclesiastic, with the exception of the regulars, 'all the criollos and those who supported the cause' together with the higher ranking officers were to meet in a 'Junta General Provincial' to elect the fifth member through a terna."[20]

The election of the fifth member provided the elites of Oaxaca an opportunity to play a significant role in restructuring the insurgent government. Upon receiving the convocatoria, the governor of the diocese, doctor Antonio José Ibáñez y Corbera, and the intendant, José María Murgía y Galardi, convened a meeting of the cabildo eclesiástico and the ayuntamiento on May 22, 1813. The sixteen members of the two corporations who met that day agreed to hold the election. Subsequently, Carlos María de Bustamante, who had arrived in his hometown of Antequera as Inspector General of the American Cavalry, proposed to the military governor of the city, Benito Rocha, that Oaxaca request the convening of an insurgent congress. Rocha agreed and convened "a solemn and general junta to be attended by the secular and ecclesiastic cabildos, the prelates of the religious orders, field grade military officers, other functionaries and the leading and distinguished persons [of the region]."[21]

On May 31, sixty-nine individuals met at the cathedral. Carlos María de Bustamante urged those present to sign a representation to Morelos, as individuals and as representatives of their corporations as well as *vecinos* (citizens) of the city, requesting the convening of a congress. He argued that "an August Body, the repository of Sovereignty" should be formed to exercise authority in America. Such a body required "a significant number of individuals who, although substitutes, represent the rights of their provinces."[22] (The election of substitutes to represent their provinces was clearly based on the election of substitutes to the Cortes of Cádiz in 1810.) In addition, he proposed Antequera as the seat of the new insurgent congress.

Bustamante, who had participated in the constitutional elections in Mexico City and who assumed the title Elector del Pueblo de México (Elector of the people of Mexico [City]), enunciated two important principles established by the Hispanic revolution: the notions that sovereignty resided in a congress of deputies of the nation and that those individuals represented "the rights of their provinces." Those principles embodied conflicting views of the nature of sovereignty. The first held that the people were sovereign. Congress, as the representative of the people, embodied national sovereignty. Therefore, it alone possessed the right to organize and administer the nation. That had been the position taken by the Cortes of Cádiz. The second principle held that sovereignty resided in the provinces, a portion of which they collectively ceded in order to form a national government. The provinces, however, as the original possessors of sovereignty, could reclaim what they had relinquished. The latter principle contained the germs of the subsequent confederalism that erupted in Mexico after independence.

The debate in the cathedral about Bustamante's proposal revealed divisions about the insurgency among Oaxaca's elites. The clergy, which included European Spaniards, opposed the insurgents and did not want the corporation to contribute to the legitimation of that movement. However, they felt compelled to favor holding elections for the fifth member to the Suprema Junta because Morelos had warned them not to criticize the insurgent government.[23] The ayuntamiento, although composed entirely of Americans, also had reservations about the insurgent movement. The representatives of the insurgent military, however, naturally desired to strengthen their government. After some discussion, the cabildo eclesiástico, with the exception of Canon Dr. José de San Martín, voted to hold the election for the fifth member and to treat Bustamante's proposal separately. "This way, [the chastened corporation argued,] the Cabildo will neither directly nor indirectly influence matters of the government, which is uniquely charged with making political arrangements and this Ecclesiastic Corporation with obeying with all deference."[24] The ayuntamiento, with the exception of two of its members, concurred. The military favored both the election of the fifth member and "that a National Congress composed of the representatives of the Provinces of the Kingdom of New Spain be established."[25] Those favoring only the election of the fifth member prevailed.

After extensive consultations about procedures, the final election was held in the cathedral on August 3, 1813. The eighty-five participants represented the cabildo eclesiástico, the ayuntamiento, commerce, functionaries, religious orders, field grade officers, the principal vecinos, and the electors of the eight quarters of Antequera and the five *partidos* (districts), three *doctrinas*, and seventeen *subdelegaciones* of the province. The procedure authorized by Morelos mixed traditional and new liberal practices; it began as a traditional terna, the electors placed their votes in "three crystal glasses with the signs 1, 2 y 3," but it ended in the new style when it awarded the position to José María Murgía y Galardi, the individual who obtained the majority of the votes.[26]

Morelos, who already had decided to hold elections for a Soberano Congreso Nacional (Sovereign National Congress), determined that Murgía y Galardi should be considered Oaxaca's representative to that body. The other regions controlled by the insurgents—Puebla, Veracruz, Michoacán, and the insurgent Province of Tecpan—held elections for the Soberano Congreso. Secret elections were also held in Mexico City and, possibly, in other urban areas. Unlike elections under the Hispanic Constitution, the insurgent elections were less inclusive and appear to have been controlled. Although the Soberano Congreso issued the Decreto Constitucional para la Libertad de la América Mexicana, better known as the Constitución de Apatzingán, in October 1814, that charter was never applied and had little influence in the later constitutional development of Mexico.[27]

HISPANIC CONSTITUTIONALISM

As a result of royalist victories, the insurgents abandoned Oaxaca in March 1814. Intendant Murgía y Galardi surrendered the city of Antequera to royalist commander Melchor Alvarez at the end of the month. Alvarez published the Hispanic Constitution on April 12, and held elections for the *ayuntamiento constitucional* of Antequera on the 16th. The electoral procedures were indirect, lengthy, and complex. There were two stages for elections to the constitutional ayuntamientos: the selection of parish electors and the designation by these electors of the new *alcaldes, regidores,* and *síndicos.* For electoral purposes, the city was divided into four *cuarteles mayores.* The vecinos of the four cuarteles selected the thirty-two parish electors allocated to the city. Those parish electors subsequently elected the sixteen members of Antequera's constitutional ayuntamiento. The first popular election in the capital of Oaxaca yielded interesting results; half of those selected were European Spaniards and half Americans, including an Indian and a mestizo.[28] Unlike the elections under the insurgents that were dominated by elite groups, the new constitutional elections appeared to reflect changing power relationships in the city. [29]

The constitutional system lasted only a few months, however; it was abolished at the end of August 1814, and the Antiguo Régimen was reestablished. But, as Silke Hensel observes, many of the members of the former ayuntamiento were no longer around; some had died and others had fled. Moreover, many Europeans had abandoned the province because of the dangers of the insurgency.[30] Thus, the changing political conditions prevented the old order from being fully restored and strengthened the role of Americans who replaced European Spaniards in a number of government posts.

The restored Antiguo Régimen survived until 1820. In Spain the liberals exploited the army's disenchantment with the war in America, eventually forcing the king to restore the Constitution in March 1820. The return of the constitutional order transformed the Hispanic political system for the third time in a decade. In the case of Oaxaca, which had been occupied by the insurgents, it constituted the fourth political change in a dozen years. The restoration of the Constitution unleashed widespread political activity in New Spain. In early May, without waiting for instructions from the viceroy, the coastal cities of Mérida and Campeche took oaths of allegiance to the charter of Cádiz. Veracruz and Jalapa followed later that same month. Although he would have preferred to await formal instructions, public pressure forced Viceroy Juan Ruiz de Apodaca to proclaim the Constitution in the capital on May 31. The Ayuntamiento of Antequera swore obedience to the Constitution on June 7, 1820, and restored to office the individuals elected to the constitutional ayuntamiento in April 1814. The Constitution was formally published and public swearing ceremonies were held in the plaza mayor on June 12.[31]

The political transformation also stimulated widespread public discussion about the importance of the recently restored constitutional order. As Vicente Rocafuerte later recalled, "The rebirth of . . . [the Constitution's] second epoch was welcomed with great joy. It received the most tender praises. No public paper nor poem was published that did not have as its object to praise it and recommend it [to the people]."[32] The voluminous political literature that appeared is indicative not only of the public's enthusiasm for the constitutional system, but also of the intense debate generated about the kind of government novohispanos favored. Politically active groups in Oaxaca participated in the discussion. On June 16, a broadside appeared in Antequera titled *Oaxaqueños,* which praised the Constitution, "whose object is to make us happy," and declared that the charter contained the fundamental bases for good government: "They are: protect Religion, defend and respect the Monarch, and conserve and save the outraged rights of man."[33]

Although political debate attracted public attention, elections, perhaps more than any other activity, politicized New Spain's society. From June 1820 until March 1821, electioneering and elections occupied the politically active population. Elections were held for the constitutional ayuntamientos of 1820 and later for those of 1821. Two separate elections were held for the Cortes: one rapidly in the autumn of 1820 for the Cortes of 1820–1821, and a second for the 1822–1823 session of parliament. Elections also were held for the six diputaciones provinciales of the viceroyalty.[34]

During the period, Oaxaca was inundated with documents from the authorities in Mexico City: copies of the constitution, instructions for holding elections, decrees of the Cortes, and even an exhortation from the king in support of the constitution. In addition, the constitutional Ayuntamiento of Mexico City distributed printed reports on its organization and activities.[35] Armed with that information, the authorities in Antequera rapidly proceeded to reintroduce the constitutional system. Elections were held for the Ayuntamiento of Antequera on Sunday, July 2, 1820. As in the earlier 1814 elections, the city was divided into four cuarteles for electoral purposes. This time, however, the authorities authorized only twenty-five electors as opposed to the thirty-two in 1814. Although the election followed the new liberal procedures, the authorities resorted to traditional practices to resolve a three-way tie for the twenty-fourth and twenty-fifth electors. Three individuals received fifty-six votes each. Since only twenty-five electors could be chosen, one had to be eliminated; the loser was selected by lot. The following Sunday, July 9, the electors chose the city's two alcaldes, twelve regidores, and two síndicos. As in 1814, the voters elected both European Spaniards and Americans, and as in 1814, some represented non-elite groups. This time, "four regidores of humble social status were elected."[36]

The details of the elections in the rural ayuntamientos remain unclear. A recent study indicates that in 1810 there were 928 pueblos in the Province of

Oaxaca. Since the size of the population of the pueblos is not given, it is impossible to determine how many would have qualified to be ayuntamientos constitucionales under the Constitution of 1812. Sources for the period provide numbers ranging from 128 to 413 ayuntamientos constitucionales. The elections in rural areas are little studied, but Peter Guardino's examination of the political practices of the campesinos of at least one area, Villa Alta, indicates that the new popular elections had a profound impact at the pueblo level where local residents were elected. At the partido level, however, villagers tended to select curas and functionaries as their representatives because they trusted them and because they believed that these individuals possessed the education and the experience necessary to defend local interests.[37]

The curas in rural partidos exercised great influence because of the complex nature of the elections for deputies to the Cortes and the diputaciones provinciales. "Elections to these two bodies occurred at three levels: parish, partido, and province. Because of their complexity, preparatory juntas were necessary to organize and conduct them."[38] The Intendancy of Oaxaca was included in the region of New Spain for the purpose of elections to the Cortes and the diputación provincial. As a result, the Junta Preparatoria de México issued the instructions for those elections. It determined that according to the last census, Oaxaca had a population of 411,336 inhabitants of whom 16,767 were not eligible to be active citizens. This reduced the population with the right of representation to 394,569; therefore, Oaxaca was entitled to six deputies and two *suplentes* (substitutes) to the Cortes. The province was divided into twenty partidos, each subdivided into one or more parishes. The Junta's instruction allocated much authority to the curas. They were to establish the number of citizens in their parish, to determine who was eligible to vote, and to "explain to their faithful the object of these electoral processes, the dignity to which the vecinos of each town are elevated in the process as well as the fact that the high character of the representatives of the Sovereign Nation had its origins in their vote and will."[39]

The elections for deputies to the Cortes of 1820–1821, held in August and September, highlight the vast differences between rural and urban voting practices. The parish elections were held on Sunday, August 13, 1820, and the partido elections on the following Sunday, August 20. The partido electors subsequently met in Antequera on September 17, 1820, to select the province's six deputies and two suplentes. The parish, partido, and provincial elections for the nineteen rural partidos occurred in different and, often, distant pueblos and in Antequera. In contrast, in the capital, the parish, partido, and provincial elections were held within the city. Rural voters tended to elect curas or functionaries who understood and would represent their interests in the higher levels of government. In Antequera, where the economic and political elite dominated the elections, the winners included prominent merchants. The capital's elite, however, failed to dominate the province-wide elections despite efforts to challenge the selection of several electors from rural partidos. They argued that some partido electors were not eligible to hold that office either because they had been associated with the insurgency or because they were military men on active duty. After an extensive debate, however, the Junta Electoral de Provincia concluded that, under the Constitution of 1812, citizens could not be excluded from office because of their political opinions and that officers on active duty could be chosen provincial electors. Consequently, unlike the elections to the Ayuntamiento of Antequera, no merchants were elected to the Cortes. Nonetheless, prominent oaxaqueños, who were ecclesiastics, military men, and functionaries, were selected: Francisco María Ramírez, Luis Castellanos, Mariano Castillejos, Tomás Bustamante, Patricio López, and José María Murgía y Galardi as well as the suplentes, Mariano Calvo and Ramón María Castellanos. Only Murgía y Galardi, López, and Ramírez attended the Cortes in Madrid.[40]

Elections for deputies to the 1822–1823 Cortes, held in March 1821, exhibited the same pattern. Once again the electors of the nineteen rural partidos dominated the provincial election held on March 12. They again selected ecclesiastics, military men, and functionaries: José Miguel Valentín, Antonio Mantecón, Gregorio Miguel Vasconcelos, Domingo Garfías, Francisco Estevez, and José Ortiz de la Torre deputies, and Domingo Rocoy and Nicolás Fenández del Campo suplentes.[41]

The Intendancy of Oaxaca, which earlier had constituted part of the Diputación Provincial of New Spain, did not obtain its own provincial deputation until 1822. Because the region had been then under insurgent control, the people of Oaxaca had not elected a provincial deputy during the first constitutional period, 1812–1814. At that time, suplentes were chosen in Mexico City to represent the province: José María Fagoaga in 1812 and Juan Bautista Lobo in 1813.[42] Oaxaqueños had the first opportunity to elect their own provincial deputy in 1820. As was customary, the same partido electors who chose the deputies to the Cortes also selected the members of the Diputación Provincial the following day, September 18, 1820. The Penitenciario Lic. Francisco Ignacio Mimiaga was chosen proprietary deputy and Dr. José Mariano Amable, suplente. The records of the *Actas de la Diputación Provincial de Nueva España* indicate that Lic. Mimiaga joined the Diputación Provincial of New Spain in Mexico City on October 7, 1820, as the deputy from Oaxaca.[43] The following year, on March 13, the Oaxaqueños elected Lic. José Mariano Fernández Arteaga, their representative to the Diputación Provincial de México.[44]

Oaxaca, like the other provinces of New Spain, was not content with the small number of deputations allocated to the viceroyalty by the Cortes of Cádiz. Each immediately organized to obtain approval for its own provincial deputation from that parliament. Shortly after being reestablished, the Constitutional Ayuntamiento of Puebla, for example, sent a formal representación to the Cortes requesting that it be allocated a provincial deputation in accord with article 325 of the Constitution, which stated: "In each province there shall be a deputation called provincial, to promote its prosperity, presided by a political chief."[45] The big push for local provincial government occurred in the 1821 Cortes when the American deputies, among them Oaxaca's Murgía y Galardi, insisted that the Cortes grant each former intendancy in the New World a provincial deputation. After considerable debate, on May 8, 1821, the parliament agreed.

THE MEXICAN EMPIRE

Before those changes could be introduced, New Spain separated from the Península. Concerned that Spain would not grant them the full autonomy that they sought, the elites of the kingdom pursued alternative means of achieving home rule. They convinced an efficient and ruthless officer, Colonel Agustín de Iturbide, to assume the leadership of an autonomy movement. With their help, he formulated a program for autonomy that he issued at the village of Iguala on February 24, 1821. A carefully crafted compromise document, the Plan of Iguala provided a way of retaining representative constitutional government that did not preclude reconciliation with the Spanish Monarchy. The Plan provided protection for the clergy, the army, and Europeans. It established the Roman Catholic faith as the official religion "without tolerance for any other," declared "the absolute independence of this kingdom," instituted a constitutional monarchy, and invited Fernando VII, a member of his family, or someone from another ruling dynasty to govern.[46] As Iturbide noted, the desire for autonomy was widespread in New Spain. Provincial elites, among them some from Oaxaca, supported the movement.[47]

Although many of Oaxaca's elites favored autonomy, most were ambivalent about the Plan of Iguala. The restored Constitution of 1812 ended their obligation to finance the war effort.[48] And the Hispanic Cortes appeared willing to grant them greater autonomy by approving diputaciones provinciales for each intendancy. The constitutional ayuntamiento of Antequera, which opposed the Plan of Iguala on March 13, 1821, believed that the prudent course of action was to support the restored constitutional order. Those elites, who feared that Iturbide's movement appealed to the popular classes, favored the ayuntamiento's decision. Other elites, particularly the clergy, were concerned about the radical nature of the Cortes, which had passed laws restricting the *fueros* (privileges) of the clergy and the military. They favored the Plan of Iguala because it protected the rights of the Church and the armed forces. The issue was settled on June 19 when Antonio de León, a former royalist officer who had earlier accepted the Plan of Iguala, declared the independence of the Province of Oaxaca from his hometown of Huajuapan. Royalist forces capitulated at the end of July, and León and his troops occupied the city of Antequera. Iturbide promoted León to the rank of lieutenant colonel, appointing him military commander of Oaxaca.[49]

The independence of New Spain was assured in September when Juan O'Donojú, the last jefe político superior of the realm, ratified the Plan of Iguala by signing the Treaty of Córdoba. The newly independent Mexicans carefully followed the precedents of the Hispanic political system. They formed a Council of Regency to serve as the executive and a Soberana Junta Provisional Gubernativa (Sovereign Provisional Governing Junta) to function as the legislative branch until a Mexican Cortes convened. At its first session in Mexico City, the Soberana Junta reviewed and approved the appointments of the thirty-two members present. Then it selected the five individuals who would compose the Council of Regency, naming Iturbide its president. Disagreement ensued immediately over the nature of the convocatoria to elect the Constituent Cortes. The Soberana Junta proposed to follow the procedures established by the Hispanic Cortes, that is, indirect elections based on proportional representation. However, the Regency and Iturbide recommended changes, which included electing representatives of the estates and corporations. As a result, the convocatoria provided for a congress elected on the basis of a complex mixture of corporate interests and partidos. Since there was no relationship between the number of partidos in a province and its population, the measure resulted in regional imbalance that favored the less-populated peripheral provinces.[50]

The Soberana Junta issued a convocatoria on November 17, 1821, which intermingled liberal processes with traditional practices. First, there would be elections in two stages for ayuntamientos constitucionales. Electors would be chosen on December 21 and they, in turn, would select the alcaldes, regidores, and síndicos on December 24. The new ayuntamientos, elected under liberal rules, would then choose partido electors on the 27th much as those bodies had elected other kinds of representatives during the Antiguo Régimen. The partido electors would then select the provincial electors on January 14, 1822, who subsequently would elect the deputies to the Cortes on the 28th and, later, deputies to the Diputación Provincial. The large provinces, including Oaxaca, "will name the [number of] deputies to which they are entitled . . . , and from among them, there will be precisely and indispensably three: an ecclesiastic of the secular clergy, a military man, native or foreign, and a magistrate, *juez de letras* or lawyer."[51]

Under the new electoral formula, the Province of Oaxaca elected fourteen deputies to the Cortes constituyentes mexicanas (Mexican Constituent Cortes), among them Dr. José San Martín as the ecclesiastic, Lic. Carlos María de Bustamante as the lawyer, and Lieutenant Colonel Antonio de León as the military man. Oaxaca also elected its first diputación provincial in January 1822. As had occurred in the earlier province-wide elections, those chosen were lawyers, military men, and clergymen.[52]

The introduction of a new institution, the diputación provincial, with authority over the ayuntamientos resulted in confusion and conflict in the province. The new system divided executive authority in the province between a new official, the jefe político, who assumed responsibilities in the areas of *policía* (or public tranquility, public works, provisions, etc.), *justicia* and, in unusual cases, *guerra*, and the older official, the intendent, who became responsible for the financial administration of the area. The situation was further complicated by the fact that the jefe político—who was to reside in the capital of the intendancy and preside over that city's ayuntamiento— also presided over the diputación provincial.[53]

As a result of conflicts with the Ayuntamiento of Antequera, the diputación provincial failed to establish a strong presence in Oaxaca. In the Antiguo Régimen, ayuntamientos had often functioned as provincial capitals. That had been the case for Antequera. Under the Constitution of 1812, the Ayuntamiento of Antequera, however, became one of many ayuntamientos in the intendancy. Initially, the economic elite of the province assumed that they would control the provincial deputation as they had the ayuntamiento. But the 1820 and 1821 elections for deputies to the Cortes demonstrated that in such province-wide elections the nineteen rural partidos prevailed and elected curas and functionaries who did not necessarily support the interests of the province's economic elite. The commercial elite who dominated the Ayuntamiento of Antequera, therefore, resisted such a diminished role for their institution.[54]

The provincial elite quickly sought to emasculate the new body. Neither the jefe político nor the intendant was in the city when the diputación provincial began to meet. Since the decree of the Hispanic Cortes on provincial government did not provide for such an eventuality, the leaders of the ayuntamiento imposed a solution that enhanced that corporation's status. Article XIX of the decree on *gobierno de las provincias* stated that "the alcalde of the first vote named by the ayuntamientos of the *cabezas de partido* where there is no subaltern jefe político" should assume that official's role in the interim. Therefore, Antequera's *alcalde primero*, Juan José Estrella, assumed the role of jefe político and insisted on presiding over the provincial deputation. Furthermore, José de Micheltorena, an official of the provincial finance office, insisted that, as the substitute for the intendant, he had the right to participate in the sessions of the diputación provincial. The Ayuntamiento of Antequera also refused to cooperate with the diputación on a variety of matters. The new institution appealed to the government in Mexico City for relief, but the national government, which faced numerous problems, failed to provide a remedy. In July, it appointed "the member of the Diputación Provincial with the greatest seniority" interim jefe político.[55] Oaxaca's deputy Pedro Labayru also raised the issue in the Cortes, noting that several provincial deputations lacked jefes políticos. He urged the government to resolve the question as soon as possible.[56] Subsequently, the administration appointed José María Murgía y Galardi jefe político of Oaxaca. The appointment did not establish the primacy of the diputación provincial because the new official first took the oath of office before the ayuntamiento and, subsequently, before the provincial body, actions that appeared to recognize the preeminence of the city's government.[57]

The national government failed to resolve the conflicts in Oaxaca, in part, because it too was divided internally. Almost from the outset, conflict erupted between the president of the Regency and the legislature, first under the Soberana Junta and later the Cortes. The struggle centered on different conceptions of sovereignty and national power. Following the precedent established by the Cortes of Cádiz, Mexican legislators believed that the Cortes mexicanas, as the representative of the nation, possessed sovereignty. Conversely, Iturbide was convinced that he embodied the national will because he had directed the movement that achieved independence. Unwilling to compromise, Iturbide crowned himself emperor on May 19, 1822, with the backing of the army and with strong popular support. Like Fernando VII before him, the emperor of Mexico subsequently jailed dissenting legislators and ultimately dissolved the Cortes on October 31, 1822. He appointed a Junta Nacional Instituyente, a substitute congress that he hoped would follow his dictates.[58]

It would be difficult to impose order by force, however, because the level of political participation had increased vastly between 1820 and early 1823. To ensure rapid communications, the independent government issued a decree in 1822 dismissing any official who did not disseminate information within three days of its receipt.[59] Requests from all parts of the country for clarification of articles x, y, and z of specific decrees and with inquiries as to their relationship to earlier laws fill the Archivo General de la Nación. The voluminous documentation indicates that the ayuntamientos had become the focus of Mexican political life. The major provincial cities, for example, took the lead in expanding the number of diputaciones provinciales in the country. There had been six in 1814. When the Hispanic Constitution was restored in 1820, novohispanos insisted on increasing the number. The number of provincial deputations grew to thirteen in 1821, eighteen in 1822, and twenty-three in 1823.[60]

Iturbide's new political system proved unworkable. As had occurred earlier in Spain, discontent led to rebellion in the provinces. Although civilians orchestrated several revolts throughout the country, the opposition to the emperor coalesced around senior army officers. During the struggle for independence many commanders had become accustomed to governing their regions, often overruling civilian authorities. The restoration of the Hispanic Constitution in 1820 reduced the power of the military. After independence, however, Iturbide created new commands, giving those men who had supported the Plan of Iguala important posts.[61]

Instead of restoring order, the new military leaders contributed to the unrest that would culminate in the ouster of the emperor. Although provincial discontent had erupted first in the north, it was Brigadier Antonio López de Santa Anna who, with his Plan of Veracruz of December 2, 1822, initiated the successful insurrection against the emperor. Other generals, including Spaniards who had chosen to serve the new nation, issued the Plan of Casa Mata on February 1, 1823, and carried the revolt to its conclusion. While the Plan of Casa Mata won the support of the provinces because it included a provision granting local authority to the provincial deputations, it did not contemplate a fundamental change in the national government. It neither rejected constitutional monarchy nor proposed a republic, much less a federal republic. The election of a new congress constituted the Plan's principal demand.[62] Following the precedent of the Hispanic Cortes, Mexican political leaders considered the executive subservient to the legislature. Thus a new congress, which did not possess the liabilities of the old, could restore confidence even if the executive remained in place. Mexican politicians, of course, expected the new body to keep the emperor in check. Although regional leaders sought more local control, few genuinely opposed the monarchy, and even fewer called for federalism. Neither republicanism nor federalism was yet inevitable. Most provincials desired a strong national government that guaranteed a measure of home rule, on the order of the system created by the Hispanic Constitution of 1812. Initially, they were satisfied with the slightly increased autonomy that the Plan of Casa Mata provided.[63]

The residents of Antequera, like those of other provincial capitals, were concerned about and affected by national events. At the end of 1822, they were also preoccupied by internal social and political conflict. During the earlier elections of December 1821, the "*nobleza*" (nobility) of Antequera challenged four regidores, presumably because they did not represent the elite. At that time, the authorities in Mexico City refused to overturn the elections. A year later, in 1822, the political situation in Antequera remained tense. When the ayuntamiento inquired if all members of the body should be replaced or only half as the decrees of the Hispanic Cortes indicated, the authorities in the national capital replied that the Constitution of 1812 remained in effect, and that only half the ayuntamiento should be replaced.

The ayuntamiento elections of December 1822 provoked much dissension. The electoral campaign was heated, and the losers were quick to challenge the outcome. According to the Hispanic Constitution, "bribery or collusion in order for the election to fall on a specific person" constituted grounds for its annulment. Because some questioned the loyalty of two European Spaniards, claiming that they did not favor independence, groups for and against those individuals organized. Some electors had met to agree on a list of candidates who subsequently triumphed in the elections of December 22, 1822. Those who had not participated in that agreement filed protests, demanding that the election be annulled. According to Jefe Político Murgía y Galardi, the nobleza opposed popular groups whom it called "*vinagrilla*" (vinegary). The popular group, who named the others "*aceites*" (oils), countered with a petition bearing 367 signatures, among them many from military men, that asserted that their opponents, by violating the law, had undermined the new regime. The jefe político, who acknowledged that ethnic as well as social divisions contributed to the conflict, referred the issue to the national authorities.[64]

The struggle marked the beginning of partisan tensions, which would divide Antequera for a decade. The bishop as well as the jefe político indicated that disaffected individuals, particularly three military men, had manipulated the popular groups. They accused Lieutenant Colonel Diego González, Captain Manuel María Fagoaga, and Sub Lieutenant Angel Alvarez of organizing "*la plebe*" against persons of good standing. The bishop described them as fearful revolutionaries who would destroy society to achieve their ends. Murgía y Galardi also expressed concern about all of them, but particularly about Alvarez, who seemed to exercise a great deal of influence on the lower classes. The jefe político ordered all three to Mexico City for investigation. They left under protest and ably defended themselves in the capital, claiming that they had only exercised their rights as citizens. After several months, the national authorities in the capital acquitted them and allowed them to return to Antequera.[65]

SOVEREIGNTY AND INDEPENDENCE

The conflict in Antequera coincided with an anti-Iturbide *pronunciamiento* that would draw the province into the larger struggle. In December 1822, former insurgent generals Vicente Guerrero and Nicolás Bravo pronounced against Iturbide, demanding that Congress be restored. Imperial troops defeated the two rebels at Almolonga on January 25, 1823. While Guerrero was severely wounded and believed dead, Bravo escaped to form another antigovernment force. Shortly thereafter, on February 1, other imperial troops declared the Plan of Casa Mata. Unaware of the event, Bravo moved with his forces toward Oaxaca. Lieutenant Colonel Antonio de León, who had declared independence in Oaxaca in 1821, was ordered by the imperial government to intercept Bravo. However, once again, León changed sides, joining the opposition. The combined rebel forces occupied Antequera on February 9. Two days earlier, some groups in the city had declared their support for the Plan of Casa Mata. Oaxaca became the third province, after Veracruz (February 2) and Puebla (February 6), to favor the Plan.

Unlike Veracruz and Puebla, where the provincial deputations assumed authority, in Oaxaca there was widespread support for establishing a new institution to serve as a provincial government until a new national congress was elected. Therefore, Bravo agreed to convene a joint meeting of the provincial deputation and the Ayuntamiento of Antequera to select members for the new body. Although some oaxaqueños believed that the provincial deputation should administer the province, most favored the creation of a Junta Provisional Gubernativa (Provisional Governing Junta), which was formed on February 24. It consisted of nineteen members and included the Diputación Provincial, representatives from the ayuntamiento, and representatives from the clergy and the military. Manuel Nicolás de Bustamante, Carlos María's brother who subsequently became a strong federalist, was chosen president of the Junta. An anonymous *Manifiesto*, issued on March 22, justified these actions on the grounds that a transitional government was necessary because Iturbide had been a tyrant who had made himself emperor with the support of the masses of Mexico City and the military. The document stated that Oaxaca had acted appropriately in creating the Junta Provisional Gubernativa to exercise authority in the province. It also noted that the diputación provincial had been ineffective and that the Junta, which included members from the provincial deputation, was a stronger body that could defend Oaxaca's interests.[66]

The national political situation began to change in late February 1823 when Iturbide refused to acquiesce to the demand for a new congress. The emperor's intransigence prompted the provinces to adopt more radical positions. As opposition mounted, the provincial deputations and the ayuntamientos of the provincial capitals began to discuss restructuring the national government. On March 10, 1823, Puebla invited each province to send two delegates, empowered to form a provisional government, to a convention in that city. The Junta Provisional Gubernativa of Oaxaca elected its deputies to the meeting at Puebla on March 17. But before the provincial delegates met in that city, Iturbide reconvened the Constituent Cortes and abdicated on March 19. The provincial delegates to the Puebla convention recognized the reconvened legislature, but only for the purpose of convoking a new constituent congress.[67]

The reconstituted Constituent Cortes included many deputies who favored a strong national government. Some, like Carlos María de Bustamante, were convinced that "a faction of demagogues" had misled the provinces. They believed that the provinces could decide the nature of the country's government through debate in the congress, despite the provinces' adherence to the Plan of Casa Mata. (Ironically, Carlos María de Bustamante led the opposition to the continued existence of bodies, such as the Junta Provisional Gubernativa of Oaxaca, over which his brother Manuel presided.) With 103 legislators present, the Cortes declared itself in session on March 29 and set about governing the nation. It abrogated the Plan of Iguala and the Treaty of Córdoba, thus opening the way for a full discussion of the future organization of the nation. Like the earlier Hispanic Cortes, which distrusted the executive branch, the Cortes mexicanas held that only the legislature truly represented the nation. Therefore, it established a weak executive, a triumvirate called the Supremo Poder Ejecutivo (Supreme Executive Power) that would alternate the presidency on a monthly basis. On March 31, the Cortes selected Generals Nicolás Bravo, Guadalupe Victoria, and Pedro Celestino Negrete to serve as the Supremo Poder Ejecutivo.[68]

A struggle over the nature of Mexico's government erupted between the newly reconstituted Cortes and the provinces. Oaxaca's creation of the Junta Provisional Gubernativa established a precedent in favor of local control. Fearing that the nation lacked a true representative government, the Diputación Provincial of Yucatán and the Ayuntamiento of Mérida met on April 9 to consider how to respond to the new circumstances. The Yucatecan leaders formed a Junta Provisional Administrativa (Provisional Administrative Junta), similar to the one in Oaxaca, to maintain order and tranquility in the province. The Junta de Yucatán voted on April 25 to recognize the authority of the reconvened Cortes and the Supremo Poder Ejecutivo on two conditions: that the legislature hold elections for a new congress and that the national government agree not to interfere in the province's internal affairs.[69]

Provincial leaders generally believed that sovereignty had reverted to the provinces when the Iturbide regime ceased to exist. Under these circumstances, the sole function of the reconstituted Cortes was to prepare the convocatoria for a new congress that would write the nation's constitution. The majority in the reconvened legislature, however, rejected the pretentions of the provinces. In keeping with the Hispanic constitutional tradition, they considered the Mexican Constituent Cortes the repository of national sovereignty. Like the Cortes of Cádiz, the Cortes mexicanas believed that it alone possessed the power to choose the government best suited to the nation. On April 2, the Cortes appointed a committee to determine how to proceed. The representatives of Oaxaca, Zacatecas, San Luis Potosí, Guanajuato, Michoacán, Guadalajara, and Querétaro, who had been elected to the convention of Puebla and who were in the capital to pressure the Cortes into acceding to provincial desires, met with the legislative committee of the Cortes on April 4 to demand that it recommend issuing a convocatoria, based on the Constitution of 1812, to elect a new congress. Despite their efforts, the committee of the Cortes rejected the demands of the provinces. Instead, on April 12, the committee recommended that the existing Cortes continue its functions, organize the government, and write a constitution.[70] The national legislature accepted the recommendation.

The provincial commissioners responded immediately and forcefully. On April 18, they informed the Cortes that the provinces of Mexico lacked confidence in the present legislature and demanded the election of a new constituent congress. The people, they declared, did not support the actions of "a Congress whose members were elected without appropriate liberty and named from a limited number of classes. A Congress in which national representation is monstrously established upon the number of partidos rather than on population. . . . A Congress of deputies chosen for the specific purpose of creating a monarchy, rather than the form of government most convenient to the nation. . . . A Congress in which many of its members had lost the confidence of the public and were unworthy of the high post they held." Although the commissioners had referred to "*the vote of our provinces*," they declared that in fact they reflected the will "of the entire Nation."[71]

The Cortes's decision not to hold new elections prompted some regions to withdraw their support from the national government. The Provincial Deputation of Jalisco, meeting in special session on Friday, May 9, voted to rescind its recognition of the Cortes, declaring that the Province of Jalisco had only recognized that body for the purpose of convening a new legislature. Three days later, the provincial deputation and the Constitutional Ayuntamiento of Guadalajara, meeting in extraordinary session, agreed to support the creation of a federal republic. They also resolved that they would no longer obey decrees and orders from the Cortes and the Supremo Poder Ejecutivo; that the diputación provincial together with three members of the ayuntamiento constituted the highest authority in the province; and that they would communicate in writing these dispositions to all other provincial deputations in the nation, urging them to establish a general federation. Thus, Jalisco not only followed Oaxaca's lead by forming a new provincial government, but also became the first province to reject the authority of the existing national government and to propose the creation of a federal republic.[72]

News that some regions had revolted unnerved the national government. Nearly every day *El Aguila mexicana*, the organ of the federalists, published news of provinces opposing Mexico City. The Cortes met in special sessions on Saturday, May 17, and Sunday, May 18, to discuss the national crisis. Minister of Interior Relations Lucas Alamán expressed the fear that the nation would collapse unless the government took prompt action. Many deputies, however, believed that only the convocation of a new congress would calm the provinces. At the request of the Supremo Poder Ejecutivo, the Cortes met in a special night session on Tuesday, May 20. José Mariano Michelena, then president of the Supremo Poder Ejecutivo, and minister Alamán urged conciliation. The following day, after extensive debate, the majority proposed the convening of a new legislature. Partisans of the existing body, such as Carlos María de Bustamante, sought valiantly but unsuccessfully to block the measure. The vote in favor of convening a new congress was seventy-one for and thirty-three against. Despite their loss, the proponents of a strong national government remained unwilling to capitulate. They delayed issuing the *convocatoria* and convinced the Supremo Poder Ejecutivo to dispatch armies to restore order in the recalcitrant provinces.[73] Even though his province had been the first to establish an autonomous local government, Carlos María de Bustamante wrote the authorities in Antequera declaring: "I have the honor of belonging to that small group [of deputies who opposed the measure], and not to have given my unfortunate Nation this last impulse to consummate its ruin."[74]

The unwillingness of an influential faction in the restored Cortes to accept the will of the provinces and convene a new congress disturbed many in Antequera. Rumors of *infidencia* (conspiracy) in the city became widespread. Anonymous reports reached the authorities in Mexico City that Masons were agitating in favor of independence in Oaxaca. In late May, before news of the Cortes's decision to convene a new congress was known, an imprint appeared in Antequera titled *Invitación que hace un oaxaqueño a su suelo Patrio*. The author argued that Oaxaca possessed sovereignty and should assume the responsibility to guide its own destiny. The government in Mexico City had been despotic and only as a result of "great risks and imponderable efforts" had it been overthrown. But there was no guarantee that the current regime would be any less repressive. Mexico City was too far away, and it had to address the many problems of América Septentrional (North America). Instead, he urged: "Elect leaders in whom you have confidence, from within your own bosom, leaders to whom you may appeal when necessary, and don't remain subject to seeking justice elsewhere." The government in Mexico City, he noted, was naturally corrupt; "the agents of that Court do not take a step without first receiving their expenses." The national government was irresponsible; "although all the Provinces favor a federal republic, nothing has been accomplished because the Court opposes it." El oaxaqueño concluded that it was necessary for the educated classes and for the landowners to act. If they did, the clergy and the military would support the movement for autonomy.[75]

El oaxaqueño's views were popular. The new Jefe Político Antonio de León reported that the city and region were preoccupied with the question of autonomy. When the mail arrived from Mexico City, the news spread rapidly that on May 21 the Cortes had agreed to convene a new congress. First small groups, and then larger ones, gathered to comment and to insist that Oaxaca should form its own government. Mid-level army officers, curas, and popular groups appeared to be among the most determined supporters of autonomy and the formation of a federal republic. The bishop feared that the same individuals who had manipulated the plebe during the earlier city elections were at work again. In Mexico City, Carlos María de Bustamante received similar information from Antequera.[76]

On the morning of June 1, 1823, large crowds gathered in the plaza mayor demanding separation from Mexico City and the establishment of a federal republic. Fearful of public disorders, interim Jefe Político and Commanding General Antonio de León restricted the troops to quarters, and, at 11:45 AM, hastily convened the members of the constitutional ayuntamiento of the city of Oaxaca to an extraordinary session "because public tranquility required it," warning "no one will miss the meeting without incurring the most grave responsibility . . . , and therefore all other activities must be abandoned immediately." In an effort to control the large crowds, the senior alcalde, who presided over the ayuntamiento, agreed that a delegation of citizens could meet with the body. When admitted into the chamber of the ayuntamiento, their spokesman declared: "The people has decided to constitute itself into a Free Province, independent from all others in the Mexican state, in the form of a Federal Republic." The people "requested and expected" that the constitutional ayuntamiento acquiesce.[77]

Uncertain about the appropriate course of action, the members of the ayuntamiento decided to inform Jefe Político León "about the wishes of the People," asking him to declare "if, in his opinion, the present [crowds constituted] a popular tumult or if their request [was a serious proposal], which the authorities should consider."[78] They sent a delegation to the jefe político's house to request his presence at the ayuntamiento to discuss the question. Upon learning the ayuntamiento's concerns, Jefe Político León declared: "that [the request of the People] was not, in his view, a popular tumult, but the pronouncement of a free People, whose rights he had always respected."[79] Before acting, the ayuntamiento asked the jefe político and commanding general to consult the troops.

Jefe Político Antonio de León convened a meeting at his house of sixty-three "field grade and lower ranking officers of the regular army, civic corps, and unattached and retired officers" at one that afternoon. After explaining the earlier events, Commanding General León requested "that each one express his opinion and vote, both individually for themselves and for the units, companies, and pickets under their command, regarding the free, natural, and enthusiastic proclamation of a Federal Republic, which the People of this city has made."[80] After extensive discussion, they agreed unanimously "by voice and in writing" that they endorsed "the patriotic sentiments of the . . . Constitutional Ayuntamiento and heroic people who, aware of their rights, have this memorable day known how to make noble use of their natural and indisputable Sovereignty. Therefore, they offered and committed themselves to support and carry out such a philanthropic resolution." They requested that the commanding general publish the minutes of their meeting and "circulate them to the generals of the other Provinces, inviting them to unite fraternally with the sentiments of the resolution as the only one that can bring happiness to the great Nation that we have the honor and glory to constitute." To demonstrate that their only goal was "the love for the well-being of the Patria and its greatness and felicity. . . ," they also insisted that for supporting "such separation no promotions, appointment, prizes or any distinction be granted."[81]

Upon learning the results of the Junta de Guerra (junta of military men), the ayuntamiento dispatched a commission to inform "the Citizen, his Excellency the Diocesan Prelate, of the occurrences until that moment, [requesting] that he explore the will of his secular and regular subjects, and communicate the results as soon as possible." In addition, the ayuntamiento requested that the alcaldes of the guilds, the Diputación del Comercio (merchants' deputation), and government functionaries convene their members "in order to learn their will regarding the form of government that the People desires." Although the ayuntamiento sought "to explore in so far as possible the general opinion," the people in the plaza mayor began to lose their patience and demanded an immediate decision. Jefe Político León, however, indicated that he would maintain order with military force if necessary and that the ayuntamiento "was in the most complete liberty" to act as it considered best.[82]

The ayuntamiento received reports that the guilds, the Diputación del Comercio, and the employees of Hacienda (office of finances) unanimously supported the people's desires. The bishop informed the body that he had convened the cabildo eclesiástico, which after a lengthy discussion had determined that it lacked sufficient information to judge the issues and that given "the transcendental importance" of the questions, the body would meet the following day to discuss the proposals.[83]

In view of the delicate circumstances, the ayuntamiento requested the convening of the Junta Provisional Gubernativa—formed in February and which included members of the diputación provincial and the ayuntamiento—to discuss the people's proposals. Acordingly, León formally convened that body indicating that extraordinary circumstances had arisen that required a meeting of the Junta.

The Junta Provisional Gubernativa met late in the afternoon in special session to consider the situation. After receiving reports, Junta member Ramón Ramírez opined that it was necessary to learn the views of "all the classes of the State," either individually or from representatives of their corporations. Although many members of the Junta agreed on the need for consultation, Regidor Vicente Manero Embides indicated that the ayuntamiento had already obtained those opinions, except those of the clergy who would meet the following day. Some proposed that the Junta delay its decision and remain in permanent session until it learned the opinion of the clergy. Others insisted that a decision be taken immediately. Regidor Juan Ignacio Aguirreurreta proposed "that a Provisional Government independent of Mexico [City] be declared, reserving the definition of its structure for the representation, which all the Partidos of the Province shall name." Regidor Manero Embides, however, insisted "that, in fact, a Federal Republic be declared." When the Junta opted for further consultation, Manero Embides proposed that the ayuntamiento decide the question in a secret session. At its meeting, the ayuntamiento unanimously declared "that Oajaca was Independent and absolutely Free, constituting itself into a Federal Republic with all the other Provinces of the Empire under the auspices of the one and only Roman, Catholic, Apostolic Religion." When it learned of that body's decision, the Junta voted to support the ayuntamiento, and formed a commission to establish the structure of the new government. The new body included three members from the Junta, three from the ayuntamiento, and three from the military.[84]

On June 2, 1823, a troubled cabildo eclesiástico met in the cathedral to discuss the events of the previous day. They agreed that it was important to address the question "with all the maturity, circumspection and good judgment that the gravity of such a delicate matter required." First, the members of the cabildo concluded that because the new government was proposed "in such general and imprecise terms," it was impossible to judge the proposal. They also did not know of any "new motives that had arisen [which justified] the rupture with the capital city of México," particularly since the national Cortes had agreed to hold elections for a new congress. The clergy were concerned because the opinion of the armed forces carried such weight. If it had been wrong for the garrison of Mexico to elect Iturbide emperor, as many writers proclaimed, surely it was not appropriate for the garrison of Oaxaca to transform the political system. The clergy maintained "that in all liberal systems the armed forces have neither the right to petition nor the prerogative to name or to request the form of Government that should be constituted. That is the exclusive attribution of the Sovereign People, acting in a state of complete and absolute liberty to execute it and to fulfill it." The elected representatives of the people in a congress should carry out such fundamental changes. Equally disturbing was the fact that only the people of the city of Antequera were acting. For a change of such magnitude "the general will, not only of the People of the Capital, but also of the entire Province was necessary." Indeed, the population of the rest of the province constituted the majority, "whose will had neither been expressed in any way nor had been explored, as it was certainly an absolute necessity to do." Therefore, the cabildo eclesiástico, "for the reasons expressed, did not consider convenient in the present circumstances the pronunciamiento of emancipation from the Central Government of Mexico [City], nor the installation of a new Supreme and independent Government in this Province."[85]

The delayed negative response from the cabildo eclesiástico had no impact on the political transformation. The same day, the commission composed of members from the Junta Gubernativa, the military, and the ayuntamiento issued the *Bases Provisionales con que se Emancipó la Provincia de Oajaca*. The document established the Catholic religion as the only one for Oaxaca; determined that the province exercised exclusive sovereignty, but "federally"; created a provincial congress, constituted on the basis "Equality, Liberty, Property and Security," to "be named by the electores de Partido"; and indicated that existing laws that did not contravene independence or the federal republic remained in effect, but that new laws emanating from México City would not be valid. Moreover, it instructed Oaxacan deputies to resign from the national congress and return home. Finally, it established a junta de guerra to oversee the military, but without authority either to promote individuals or, without permission from the provincial government, to wage war.[86]

On June 3, the commission issued the convocatoria for elections to the congress of the Estado de Oajaca. Modeled on the tripartite elections established by the Hispanic Constitution of 1812, parish elections were to be held on June 15, 1823, partido elections on June 22, and provincial elections on the first of July. "Election of Deputies to the General [State] Cortes will be held the following day." As in the Constitution of 1812, there were neither property nor literacy qualifications for the voters. Although it did not distinguish between men and women, one may assume that women did not obtain the franchise. Since a deputy represented "thirty thousand souls," according to the latest census the congress of Oaxaca would have fourteen deputies and four suplentes. To be a deputy one had to "be a Citizen in the exercise of his rights, older than twenty-five years, have five years of residency in the Province, [and] be well known to be committed to the system of a Federal Republic." Deputies in the national Cortes who did not resign immediately or who opposed the federal system were excluded.[87] The latter restriction was clearly intended to prevent the election of Carlos María de Bustamante, who was not only a deputy to the national Cortes from Oaxaca, but also an opponent of federalism.

As in the case of the collapse of the Spanish Monarchy in 1808, with the rejection of Iturbide's government in 1823, sovereignty returned to el pueblo de Oaxaca. In 1808, the term *el pueblo* (the people) had referred to the representatives of the corporations. On the morning of June 1, 1823, the nameless groups of persons who gathered in the plaza mayor constituted the abstraction of el pueblo. Everyone, the ayuntamiento, Jefe Político León, the military, and clergy, agreed that el pueblo possessed sovereignty and that it had the right to decide the political future of Oaxaca in an open and free forum. Reality was at odds with those assertions; on June 1, 1823, el pueblo did not act on its own. Rather it appealed to the old pueblo, the constituted authorities and corporations. Under the Constitution of 1812, which was in effect in Mexico at that time, the diputación provincial and the jefe político constituted the highest-ranking authorities in the Province of Oaxaca. The Junta Provisional Gubernativa, which included members from the diputación provincial and the Ayuntamiento of Antequera de Oaxaca, had, in theory, become the highest authority in the province. Yet, Jefe Político León did not contact either the provincial deputation or the Junta Provisional when he learned of the crowds in the plaza mayor. Instead, he convened an emergency meeting of the Ayuntamiento of Antequera, as would have been appropriate under the Antiguo Régimen. Under the Hispanic Constitution, however, that body possessed no more authority than any other ayuntamiento in the province. In the Antiguo Régimen, the Ayuntamiento of Antequera had functioned as the capital of the province. It played that role once again in June 1823. Although it did not convene a junta of notables, as had occurred in Mexico City in 1808 during the crisis of the monarchy, the Ayuntamiento of Antequera, following traditional practices, consulted the principal corporations in the capital of the province: the armed forces, the clergy, the guilds, the Diputación del Comercio, and government officials. Only after receiving replies from those groups did the ayuntamiento consult the Junta Provisional Gubernativa. When that body failed to act, the ayuntamiento declared independence and federalism.[88]

The roles of the armed forces and the clergy—the only corporations that retained fueros under the Constitution of 1812—are significant.[89] The political influence of the armed forces increased when Agustín de Iturbide and his army appeared to achieve independence in 1821. The following year, the armed forces raised him to the status of emperor. Subsequently, military men took the lead in opposing Iturbide. As a result, generals and their armies became important political actors throughout the nation. Indeed, political gatherings throughout the country always included the senior commanders of the area. This did not mean that the armed forces as an institution determined the nature of politics. Rather, it meant that army commanders made good politicians. Military men were charismatic figures who captured the popular imagination. Moreover, politically active officers attracted people from the entire political spectrum because there was a military man who held every possible political view.[90] The junta of military men, which met to approve Oaxaca's independence and federalism, was not limited to professional officers of the regular army; it included members of the civic militia, retired officers, and military men in transit. Since many of those present were really civilians, who were part-time army officers, the junta did not represent the corporate interests of the military institution.[91] Individual military men, moreover, had collaborated with popular groups in their demands to establish an independent and sovereign state in Oaxaca. They practiced the new liberal politics, but did not abandon traditional structures.

The Church, in contrast, had lost influence during the period. Bourbon reformers had eliminated some of its privileges, and the struggle for independence divided its members. The restored Hispanic Cortes of 1820–1821 introduced measures that limited clerical privilege and influence. As a result, some among the higher clergy supported the Plan of Iguala and the independence of Mexico. But the Church was not a monolithic corporation; the interests of the higher and lower clergy often were not the same. Since 1808, many individual curas had become politicians, espousing a variety of views. Some became insurgent leaders while others gained political influence and power as a result of the new constitutional order. Because many liberal politicians, among them some curas, appeared to be anticlerical, the hierarchy of the Church viewed change with alarm. Early in 1823, for example, the bishop and members of the cabildo eclesiástico expressed the fear that the Plan of Veracruz threatened the Church.[92] Thus, despite the participation of some curas in the movement, in June 1823 the higher clergy of Oaxaca questioned the proposed transformations. They inquired about the reasons for the change, asked why the army had taken such a prominent role, and argued that the capital of Oaxaca could not act without the consent of the rest of the province. Ironically, the cabildo eclesiástico used modern liberal concepts to question actions based partially on Antiguo Régimen practices.[93]

The authorities in Mexico City were not pleased with events in Oaxaca. In his report to the Cortes, Minister of Interior Relations Alamán ridiculed Oaxaca's proclamation of "Independence from Mexico." Although many deputies who heard his account laughed at acts that Carlos María de Bustamante described as stupid, they were also concerned because other provinces might follow Oaxaca's lead. Yucatán, Jalisco, and Zacatecas also had formed new governments and refused to accept instructions from the national government that conflicted with federalism. Diputaciones provinciales assumed control of the government in Veracruz, Puebla, Michoacán, Guanajuato, Querétaro, and San Luis Potosí. Those provinces accepted the authority of the national government, but declared that they expected the election of a new congress. During May and June 1823, the provinces of Mexico communicated extensively with one another, sending copies of all important decisions to the other provincial deputations.

As they had done in March, during their opposition to Iturbide, the provinces discussed convening an assembly to address matters of common interest. Indeed, the diputaciones provinciales of Michoacán, Querétaro, Guanajuato, and San Luis Potosí began to prepare for such a meeting. In response, the Supremo Poder Ejecutivo and the government ministers acted to regain control of the nation. The minister of interior relations instructed the provinces not to introduce any changes in government because the new congress would write a constitution that would organize the nation. The Cortes issued a convocatoria on June 17, 1823, which not only called for new congressional elections, following the model of Cádiz as the provinces had demanded, but also required new elections for all diputaciones provinciales. In this way, the national authorities hoped to eliminate the newly independent regimes that had formed in several provinces. But to ensure that no province separated completely, they dispatched several armies to maintain order.[94]

Initially, the national government responded moderately to Oaxaca. Minister Alamán dispatched a highly critical letter accusing the province of completely separating from the nation and calling this action unconstitutional. He urged the province to follow the orderly process that the Cortes recently had approved to elect a new congress, which would establish the future government of the nation. Carlos María de Bustamante publicly criticized his province in a pamphlet entitled *Examen crítico sobre la federación de las provincias del territorio mexicano.* He argued: "the Mexican people . . . has decided to form *only one family.* That has been accomplished by gathering together in one center of felicity, which is Congress. And as Deputy from Oaxaca, I am concerned with the felicity of Sonora, which I only know by its geographic location, with the same interest and ardor with which the Deputy from Sonora looks after my well beloved Oaxaca. There has never existed there [in congress], the odious spirit of provincialism, to which we have sworn eternal abhorrence." The nation needed unity, not division, he insisted. One had but to consider the disasters that occurred in Caracas, Santa Fe de Bogotá, and Cartagena de Indias to understand the dangers of "the diabolical genie of unlimited federalism." There was no reason to form an independent provincial government. The Cortes had already agreed to convene a new congress. That body would form a strong federation that suited the country's reality.[95]

In Antequera, the new political leaders perceived their actions differently. The president of the Junta Provisional Gubernativa, Victorés Manero, informed the Supremo Poder Ejecutivo that Oaxaca had never contemplated "the total separation from the other" provinces of México. "The Province of Oaxaca, united in its interests with those of its sister [provinces], all of whom comprise this América Septentrional," wished only to form a more effective union, one that would recognize the interests of all provinces while strengthening the nation to which they all belonged.[96]

Elections were held and the State Congress of Oaxaca convened on July 6 in Antequera amidst extensive ceremonies. In its first decree, Congress instructed the Junta Provisional Gubernativa to cease its functions, authorized all civil and military officials to continue to exercise their authority, and recognized the jefe político as the chief executive, who served at the pleasure of Congress. Until the national and provincial constitutions were promulgated, all laws were to remain in effect so long as they did not challenge either independence or the federal system of government.[97]

Not everyone in the Province of Oaxaca agreed. Teotitlán del Valle and Tehuantepec denounced the actions in the Oaxacan capital and prepared to defend themselves against those "rebels." Some frontier partidos in bordering provinces, such as Tixtla, refused to collaborate with Oaxaca and forwarded the documents sent them by Antequera to the national authorities in Mexico City.[98] Others, such as the author of an anonymous letter to the national authorities, reported that Ometepec had declared itself in favor of Mexico and was raising troops to defend itself against the federalists. Indeed, several areas of the province requested military aid from the national government in order to restore order to Oaxaca.[99]

In an attempt to reduce tensions with Mexico City, the president of the Congress of the State of Oaxaca, Florencio Castillo, notified the national government of that body's action on July 8, 1823. Concerned that Oaxaca's declaration of sovereignty and independence not be misunderstood, he indicated:

> From the moment of its installation, [the State Congress of Oaxaca] considered as one of its first and most important obligations the resolution of all differences with the Supreme Government, to maintain with it the greatest harmony and good relations, and, moreover, to recognize it as a center of unity among the various states that make up the Mexican nation.
>
> This [State] Congress is intimately convinced that a central Government should not cease to exist a single day so that unity and order exist among the provinces, which seek the general good of the Nation, as well as to avoid the anarchy and dissolution of the associated states. . . .
>
> Because the sentiments of Oaxaca are entirely consistent with those of the Sovereign General Congress and the Supreme Executive Power, which have opted for a popular, federal system of government, this [State] Congress is pleased that there being no substantive differences about the form of government [to be established], any other that may occur will be easily resolved through reason, justice, and [concern for] the public well-being.[100]

The State Congress of Oaxaca formally established its relations with the nation in its decree of July 28. Article 4 of that document defined its relations with the other provinces as follows: "This State is free, and will only recognize, with the other [states] of the Mexican nation, the relations of fraternity, friendship and confederation that the General Constitution [of the country] establishes." Article 5 indicated that "For the present, and until the General Congress of the federated states of Mexico is formed, it recognizes as the center of union of all of them the Capital [City] of Mexico." Moreover, article 6 declared: "It recognizes as well the present Congress and Supreme Executive Power with the understanding that the Congress has no other role than that of convening [a new congress]."[101]

Nevertheless, the Supremo Poder Ejecutivo decided to restore Oaxaca to the previous system. It had received information that Jefe Político León was the chief architect of that province's political transformation. Reports from the bishop and anonymous letters suggested that there were tensions in the city of Antequera. Apparently, troops in various towns had declared themselves in favor of the national government. Moreover, the new state government's moderate tone indicated that some accommodation might be possible. Therefore the Supremo Poder Ejecutivo ordered Jefe Político León to resign and General Manuel Rincón to advance to Antequera.[102]

The civil authorities in Antequera disagreed with Jefe Político León about the best course of action. In their view, the Province of Oaxaca had achieved its goals when it established its own government. The convocatoria to elect a new national congress guaranteed that it would recognize the desires of the provinces. Therefore, they favored reaching an accommodation with the national government. León, on the other hand, insisted on defending the province from the advancing national forces. To accomplish this goal, he conscripted men and released criminals from jail, provided that they join his force. Many local observers discounted the martial abilities of such troops. Indeed, they not only proved ineffective in skirmishes with recalcitrant partidos, but many deserted. In these circumstances, the bishop and the clergy argued that it was necessary to retract "the violence committed against Mexico City."[103]

Unable to force the jefe político to change his policies, many civil authorities resigned from office. The Congreso del Estado de Oaxaca, which followed the regulations of the Hispanic Cortes, consisted of fourteen deputies, most of them curas and functionaries. Two, José Esperón and Nicolás Fernández del Campo, however, had not arrived to assume their seats, possibly because they lacked confidence in the state legislature. Canon Castillo, president of the body, resigned late in July when he realized that the province was on a collision course with the national government. Five members resigned at the end of the month when orders from Mexico City arrived instructing the provinces to elect new provincial deputations. Thus, only six congressmen remained in early August, and it was reputed that they too wished to quit their office.[104] On August 4, 1823, at 4 PM, the Ayuntamiento of Antequera resigned en masse to protest the "despotism" of Comandante General León. He had disregarded the authority of the ayuntamiento when he ordered the release of a prisoner whom an alcalde was prosecuting. When questioned, he declared that he acted on his authority as military commander.[105] His primary concern was defending the province from the advancing national army under the command of General Rincón.

In early August it appeared that civil war might erupt in Mexico. National armies were poised on the borders of Jalisco, San Luis Potosí, Querétaro, and Oaxaca. The national government insisted that the provinces fully implement the electoral law, while Jalisco, Zacatecas, Yucatán, and Oaxaca declared they would obey only those parts pertaining to national elections. At issue was the nature of sovereignty. The provinces maintained that the national government held final authority only on questions affecting the entire country. Otherwise they had the right to govern themselves. By mid-August, it became obvious that only war or compromise on the part of the national government could end the conflict. On Friday, August 15, the Cortes met in a special evening session to hear a report about the state of talks on the Jalisco border.[106] After explaining the situation, Minister of Interior Relations Alamán indicated that the administration requested instructions from the legislature as to how to proceed. The following day, the Cortes voted to authorize the executive to negotiate a settlement, which included amnesty for the provinces.[107]

The Supremo Poder Ejecutivo instructed its commanders to negotiate with the recalcitrant provinces. General Rincón reached an accord with Oaxaca on September 22, 1823. Under the settlement, the Congreso del Estado de Oaxaca continued to govern, the province agreed to hold elections for the national constituent congress as well as elections for a new provincial legislature, and both sides agreed to provide amnesty. The settlement specified that the partidos of Tehuantepec and Teotitlán del Valle, which had opposed Oaxacan independence, would not suffer recriminations from the provincial government. General Rincón withdrew his troops, but transferred Lieutenant Colonel León to Veracuz. He was replaced by Murgía y Galardi, who subsequently became governor of the Estado de Oaxaca.

Elections were held throughout the nation during the next months. The new congress, which the provinces had insisted upon since March, finally met on November 7, 1823. While the executive branch remained unchanged, the second constituent congress was quite different from the first. It not only represented the provinces more equitably, but some of its members possessed instructions to form *only* a federal republic. Carlos María de Bustamante was once again elected, but from Mexico, not Oaxaca. The deputies from Oaxaca were federalists. Oaxaca, Yucatán, Jalisco, and Zacatecas, which had become states, elected state congresses rather than provincial deputations as the convocatoria required. The new constitutional congress, acknowledging the new reality, established a federal republic.[108]

THE NEW POLITICAL LEGITIMACY

The State of Oaxaca, like the Republic of México, achieved self-government after a decade and a half of vertiginous and almost constant political change. Although the insurgency affected large areas of New Spain, other than symbolically, it did not significantly affect the political institutions or ideas of the new Mexican nation. Instead, the liberal tradition that emerged in Cádiz became the basis of Mexican political and institutional development. That tradition was founded on two notions of the concept *el pueblo*. One, in the sense of *la gente* (the populace), was identified with the citizen and with popular politics; the other, in the sense of *la región*, was identified with local rights and interests. Both were often used interchangeably and in confusing and contradictory ways. The concept of the citizen, who possessed rights, rapidly became associated with representation based on the population of the regions. The citizen with individual rights, collectively, became the region, which also possessed rights and sovereignty. In 1809, the Americans protested their inequitable representation to the Junta Central, which was not based on population. Similarly, the provinces of Mexico bitterly protested the convocatoria of 1822, which also was not based on population. The protests expressed differing conceptions of the nature of representation between the center and the regions.

The transformations in political thought occurred as mass political participation emerged. The appearance of an active pueblo in 1808, the elections of 1809 and 1810 and, after 1812, the popular constitutional elections rapidly engaged the citizens, who were el pueblo, in the affairs of the day. With the rise of popular politics, there also emerged popular politicians, primarily curas, mid-level military men, lawyers, and functionaries. These politicians represented many interests, often not those of their corporations. Although, on occasion, they might support the interests of the higher clergy and the armed forces, the political activities of curas and military men should not be confused with clerical and military influence or domination.

At independence, regional and popular politics were transforming the institutions and nature of government in Mexico. Change was gradual, however, and old traditions and practices mingled with the new. Neither independence nor a republic, much less a federal republic, was inevitable. The experience of Oaxaca clearly indicates the dramatic, but, nonetheless, evolutionary transformation. It would have been impossible in 1808 to predict that the province would take the lead in establishing federalism in independent Mexico. The disenchantment of the merchant elite, particularly the European Spaniards, was evident in 1809 when they insisted in the "Instrucción" of the Ayuntamiento of Antequera that the intendancy system be abolished. They wished to control the province, but they did not consider that possible without the support of groups in Mexico City and, more important, in Madrid. Ironically, the insurgent occupation of Oaxaca (1812–1814) did not shift the relations of power in the province. The only change was to replace peninsulares with Americans, but the elite remained in control.

The popular constitutional elections transformed the nature of politics in Oaxaca, particularly after 1820 when they were fully implemented. New institutions and actors appeared. The Ayuntamiento of Antequera struggled to maintain its dominance over the province. When it realized that the rural partidos, represented by curas, military men, and functionaries, would dominate province-wide elections, it attempted to undermine the provincial deputation. But it could not control the new popular politics. New actors, some of them representing the humble classes, began to challenge the ayuntamiento itself.

The Province of Oaxaca did not exist in isolation. National events affected Oaxaca as well as other provinces. After 1820, change accelerated and the leaders of the province were constantly forced to respond to shifting conditions. Mexican independence was assured when the provinces accepted the Plan of Iguala. Similarly, Iturbide's rule ended when the provinces accepted the Plan of Casa Mata. Subsequently, the reconstituted Cortes tried unsuccessfully to oppose the will of the provinces. In those changing circumstances, the people, both as the citizen and the region, acted decisively. In Antequera, curas, military men, and functionaries led the people in demanding sovereignty and independence. Most institutions were swept along. Although the higher clergy advanced strong arguments against the June 1, 1823, movement, its voice counted little. Ultimately, the governing elites of Oaxaca, like those of Mexico City, had to accept the demands of el pueblo. That did not mean, however, that they accepted the change meekly. While they did not try to return to the Antiguo Régimen, they sought to transform the new system in ways that would be more beneficial to them.[109]

NOTES

An earlier Spanish language version of this work appeared in Brian F. Connaughton, ed., *Poder y legitimidad en México, siglo xix: Instituciones y cultura política* (Mexico: Miguel Angel Porrúa, 2003), 249–309. It is published here with permission of the editor. Research for this essay was made possible by grants from the University of California, Irvine's Academic Senate Committee on Research, and the University of California's Institute for Mexico and the United States. I am grateful to Linda Alexander Rodríguez, Peter Guardino, José Antonio Serrano, and Aldo Flores Quiroga for suggestions for improving this essay.

1. Antonio de León al Supremo Poder Ejecutivo, Oaxaca, 4 de junio de 1823, Archivo General de la Nación (hereafter cited as AGN), Gobernación, Sin Sección (hereafter cited as G: SS), Caja (hereafter cited as C) 48, ff. 18–20.

2. John K. Chance, *Race and Class in Colonial Oaxaca* (Stanford: Stanford University Press, 1978), 144–185; Marcello Carmagnani, *El regreso de los dioses. El proceso de reconstitución de la entidad étnica en Oaxaca. Siglos XVII y XVIII* (México: Fondo de Cultura Económica, 1988), 109–230; Carlos Sánchez Silva, "Indians, Merchants, and Bureaucracy in Oaxaca, Mexico, 1786–1880" (Ph.D. diss: University of California, San Diego, 1998); Brian R. Hamnett, *Politics and Trade in Southern Mexico, 1750–1821* (Cambridge: Cambridge University Press, 1971); Jeremy Baskes,

"Coerced or Voluntary? The *Repartimiento* and Market Participation of Peasants in Late Colonial Oaxaca," *Journal of Latin American Studies* 28: 1 (February 1996), 1–28. See also his *Indians, Merchants, and Markets: A reinterpretation of the Repartimiento and Spanish-Indian Economic Relations in Colonial Oaxaca, 1750–1821* (Stanford: Stanford University Press, 2000).

3. The national and ayuntamiento archives of Spanish America are replete with reports and imprints of a wide variety of events. It is common to find letters and reports discussing not only events in Spain but also throughout the American continent. An official, for example, wrote in January 1810: "y como son tan interesantes las noticias" he was sending them immediately to his colleague. AGN, Historia, vol. 326, exp. 7, f. 1. Official documents often included the following instruction: "y para que llegue la noticia a todos los habitantes, mando que se publique y se fije en los parajes acostumbrados." In addition, *pasquines* and *hojas volantes* conveyed public reaction, often in opposition to official actions. See also Eric Van Young, *The Other Rebellion: Popular Violence, Ideology, and the Mexican Struggle for Independence, 1810–1821* (Stanford: Stanford University Press, 2001), 311–349.

4. The massive growth of publications is made evident in *Impresos novohispanos, 1808–1821.* 2 vols. Amaya Garritz, Virginia Guedea, and Teresa Lozano, eds. (México: UNAM, 1990); and in Rocío Meza Olivier and Luis Olivera López, eds., *Catálogo de la colección LaFragua de la Biblioteca Nacional de México, 1800–1810* (México: Universidad Nacional Autónoma de México, 1993); and ibid, *Catálogo de la colección LaFragua de la Biblioteca Nacional de México, 1811–1821* (México: Universidad Nacional Autónoma de México, 1996). Ayuntamiento archives throughout Mexico are filled with copies of a wide variety of imprints. Although the Archivo del Ayuntamiento de Oaxaca no longer contains many of the *libros de actas del ayuntamiento* for this period, the volumes that exist include many imprints of the time.

5. For distinctions between the corporate concepts of the Antiguo Régimen and those of liberalism see Annick Lempériere, "Reflexiones sobre la terminología política del liberalismo," in Brian Connaughton, Carlos Illades, and Sonia Pérez Toledo, eds., *Construcción de la legitimidad política en México* (Zamora and México: El Colegio de Michoacán, Universidad Autónoma Metropolitana, Universidad Nacional Autónoma de México, and El Colegio de México, 1999), 35–56; and Peter Guardino, "Bourbon Judges, Spanish Liberals, and Republican Reformers: Changes in Oaxaca's Political Culture, 1750–1850," Paper presented at the annual meeting of the Conference on Latin American History, Seattle, January 9, 1998.

6. Virginia Guedea, "Criollos y peninsulares en 1808. Dos puntos de vista sobre lo española" (Licenciature thesis: Universidad Iberoamericana, 1964); Jaime E. Rodríguez O., "From Royal Subject to Republican Citizen: The Role of the Autonomists in the Independence of Mexico," in Jaime E. Rodríguez O., ed., *The Independence of Mexico and the Creation of the New Nation* (Los Angeles: UCLA Latin American Center, 1989), 19–43.

7. Virginia Guedea, "The First Popular Elections in Mexico City, 1812–1823," in Jaime E. Rodríguez O., ed, *The Evolution of the Mexican Political System* (Wilmington: SR Books, 1993), 46–47.

8. Jaime E. Rodríguez O., *The Independence of Spanish America* (Cambridge: Cambridge University Press, 1998), 59–64.

9. "Poder e Instrucciones de Antequera de Oaxaca," 18 de agosto de 1809, AGN, Historia, Vol. 417, ff. 302–316.

10. Although the replies to the Consulta have not been located in Mexico, I have found the request in the AGN, Historia, Vol. 416 and in the Archivo del Ayuntamiento de Jalapa, which indicates that it must have been sent to other ayuntamientos, such as Antequera de Oaxaca. "Consulta a la Nación," Archivo del Ayuntamiento de Jalapa, Actas del Cabildo, 1809.

11. Guedea, "The First Popular Elections," 45–48.

12. "Sobre haber sido electo diputado en Cortes por la Provincia de Oaxaca Dn. Juan María Ybáñez Corbera, Regidor honorario del Ayuntamiento de aquella Ciudad," Archivo del Congreso de Diputados de las Cortes (hereafter ACDC), Documentación Electoral (hereafter DE), No. 31, Leg 3.

13. Studies of the popular elections in Spanish America demonstrate that despite the fact that elites dominated politics, hundreds of thousands of middle and lower class men, including Indians, mestizos, and castas, participated in politics. See Guedea, "The First Popular Elections," 45–69; Virginia Guedea, *En busca de un gobierno alterno: Los Guadalupes de México* (México: Universidad Nacional Autónoma de México, 1992), 233–315; and Virginia Guedea "El pueblo de México y la política capitalina, 1808–1812," *Mexican Studies/Estudies Mexicanos* 10: 1 (winter 1994), 27–61; Jaime F. Rodríguez O., "La revolución hispánica en el Reino de Quito: Las elecciones de 1809–1814 y 1821–1822," in Marta Terán and José Antonio Serrano, eds., *Las Guerras de Independencia en la América Española* (Zamora and Morelia, Mexico: El Colegio de Michoacán, INAH and Universidad Michoacana de San Nicolás de Hidalgo, 2002), 485–508; and Jaime E. Rodríguez O., *"Rey, religión, yndependencia, y Unión": el proceso político de la Independencia de Guadalajara* (México: Instituto de Investigaciones José María Luis Mora, 2003).

14. Virginia Guedea, *José María Morelos y Pavón* (México: Universidad Nacional Autónoma de México, 1981), 107–170.

15. Lucas Alamán, *Historia de Méjico desde los primeros movimientos que prepararon su Independencia en el año de 1808 hasta la época presente.* 5 vols. (México: Fondo de Cultura Económica, 1985), 3: 318–327.

16. Ibid., 3: 327–330.

17. As Lucas Alamán observed, "todos estos nombramientos recayeron en sugetos de gran mérito." Ibid., 3: 329–330. See also Silke Hensel who indicates that Morelos did not appoint anyone of middle or lower rank to office. *Die Entstenhung des Foderalismus in Mexiko. Die politische Elite Oaxacas zwischen Stadt, Region un Staat, 1786–1835* (Stuttgart: Franz Steiner Verlag, 1997), 124–127.

18. Alamán, *Historia de Méjico*, 2: 378–379.

19. Guedea, *En busca de un gobierno*, 67–151.

20. Virginia Guedea, "Los procesos electorales insurgentes," *Estudios de Historia Novohispana* 11 (1991): 214.

21. Ibid., 215.

22. Quoted in ibid., 216.

23. Morelos complained that the clergy "son unos declamadores perpetuos del gobierno americano," and he warned that he would take action to stop it. He warned the cabildo eclesiástico that "es necesario que entienda que los derechos de la patria . . . son mas sagrados que los de qualquiera individo o corporación . . . ," "Orden del

Sr. Morelos, fecha 5 de Julio de 1813, previniendo al Cabildo Eclesiástico que se abstenga de hablar en contra del gobierno independiente," in J. E. Hernández y Dávalos, *Colección de documentos para la historia de la guerra de independencia de México de 1808–1821*, 6 vols. (México: José María Sandoval, 1882), 6: 480.

24. "Votos sobre la proposición de Bustamante," in Hernández y Dávalos, *Colección*, 6: 470.

25. Ibid.

26. Guedea, "Los procesos electorales insurgentes," 220–221.

27. Ibid., 222–249.

28. "Convocatoria," in Rosalba Montiel, ed., *Documentos de la guerra de independencia en Oaxaca* (Oaxaca: Archivo General del Estado de Oaxaca, 1986), 195–197; Hensel, *Die Entstenhung des Foderalismus*, 134–137; Peter Guardino, "'Toda libertad para emitir sus votos': Plebeyos, campesinos, y elecciones en Oaxaca, 1808–1850," *Cuadernos del Sur* 6: 15 (June 2000), 95.

29. According to Hensel, elections were also held for deputies to the Cortes and to the Diputación Provincial in August 1814. That seems unlikely, however. Elections to those bodies required establishing an electoral census that divided the province into partidos. Indirect elections would then have to be held at the parroquia, partido, and province level. That was a complex process that took much time. In the case of the Reino de Quito, which I have studied, that process took several months. Moreover, Guardino indicates: "No he encontrado evidencia de que hubiera elecciones constitucionales en ningún pueblo del distrito [de Villa Alta]." If that is so, then there could not have been elections for deputies to the Cortes and the diputación provincial either. Hensel, *Die Entstenhung des Foderalismus*, 137–138; Guardino, "'Toda libertad para emitir sus votos,'" 93; Rodríguez O., "La revolución hispánica en el Reino de Quito," 494–503.

30. Hensel, *Die Entstenhung des Foderalismus*, 256–258.

31. Jaime E. Rodríguez O., "The Transition from Colony to Nation: New Spain, 1820–1821," in Jaime E. Rodríguez O., ed., *Mexico in the Age of Democratic Revolutions, 1750–1850* (Boulder: Lynne Reinner, 1994), 101–102; Libro de Acuerdos, 1820, Archivo Histórico del Ayuntamiento de la ciudad de Oaxaca (hereafter AHAO), ff. 220–226v.

32. [Vicente Rocafuerte,] *Bosquejo ligerísimo de la Revolución de Mégico [sic] desde el grito de Iguala hasta la proclamación imperial de Iturbide* (Philadelphia: Imprenta de Teracruef y Naroajeb, 1822), 4.

33. *Oaxaqueños* (Oaxaca: Impreso en la Oficina del R. P. Preposito D. José María Idiaquez, 1820).

34. Rodríguez O., "The Transition from Colony to Nation," 104–106.

35. The documents are found in the Archivo del Estado de Oaxaca, in the Biblioteca del Estado de Oaxaca, Colección de Mariano Martínez Grácida, and in the AHAO. The bound volume, "Acuerdos, 1820," which is really the *libro de actas* for 1820, includes many of those documents. The dates of the actas indicate, more or less, when the document arrived.

36. Quote from Guardino, "'Toda libertad para emitir sus votos,'" 95; Acuerdos, 1820, ff. 37–38, 256; Hensel, *Die Entstenhung des Foderalismus*, 142–144. According to Helsel (p. 143), eleven of the sixteen individuals elected to the ayuntamiento were merchants.

37. Sánchez Silva, "Indians, Merchants, and Bureaucracy," 56. Dorothy Tanck de Estrada, however, provides the lower figure of 873 in her *Pueblos de indios y educación en el México colonial, 1750–1821* (México: El Colegio de México, 1999), 274, 579; "Lista de los Ayuntamientos Constitucionales establecidos en este Reyno como consta en las actas de su instalación recibidas hasta el del 31 de enero de 1821," AGN, Ayuntamientos, vol. 120. The same list, but with the actas, is located in Archivo General de Indias, México, 1680. Antonio Annino, "Cádiz y la revolución territorial de los pueblos mexicanos, 1812–1821," in Antonio Annino, ed., *Historia de las elecciones en Iberoamérica, siglo XIX* (Buenos Aires: Fondo de Cultura Económica, 1995), 209; Guardino, "'Toda libertad para emitir sus votos,'" 105.

38. Guedea, "The First Popular Elections," 48–49.

39. "Instrucción, que para facilitar las elecciones Parroquiales y de Partido . . . ha formado la Junta preparatoria de Méjico y remite a los pueblos para su comprehension," AHAO, Acuerdos, 1820, ff. 104 r–v. See also *Gazeta del Gobierno de México* (July 13, 1820), XI, núm. 22, pp. 684–685.

40. After the election, the president of the Junta Electoral de Provincia ordered a manuscript copy of the acta affixed in each portal of the Casas Consistoriales and appointed four members of the Junta to inform all corporations and the public of the results. "Oaxaca. Acta de elección de Diputados a Cortes para la Legislatura de los años 1820 y 1821," ACDC, DE, No. 21, leg 7.

41. "Oaxaca. Acta de elección de Diputados por esta provincia a Cortes de 1822 y 1823," ACDC, DE, No. 20, leg 9.

42. Guedea, "The First Popular Elections," 66–68; "Certificación de haberse instalado la Diputación Provincial de México," in Rafael Alba, ed., *La Constitución de 1812 en la Nueva España*, 2 vols. (México: Archivo General de la Nación, 1912), 1: 220–221.

43. "Oaxaca. Acta de elección de Diputados a Cortes para la Legislatura de los años 1820 y 1821," ACDC, DE, No. 21, leg 7. Carlos Herrejón Peredo, ed., *Actas de la Diputación Provincial de Nueva España, 1820–1821* (México: Camara de Diputados, 1985), 86.

44. "Diputados a Cortes para los años 1822–1823: Oaxaca," AGN, Gobernación, Sin Sección, Caja 16, exp. 2. f. 52.

45. Rodríguez O., "The Transition from Colony to Nation," 108–109.

46. Ibid., 109–123.

47. Carlos María de Bustamante, *Cuadro histórico de la revolución mexicana*, 4 vols. (México: Cámara de Diputados, 1961), 3: 130.

48. Christon I. Archer, "Where Did All the Royalists Go? New Light on the Military Collapse of New Spain, 1810–1821," in Jaime E. Rodríguez O., ed., *The Mexican and Mexican American Experience in the 19th Century* (Tempe: Bilingual Press, 1989), 37.

49. Guillermo Rangel Rojas, *General Antonio de León. Consumador de la Independencia de Oaxaca y Benemérito del Estado de Oaxaca* (Oaxaca: Ayuntamiento de Oaxaca de Juárez, 1997), 21–29.

50. Jaime E. Rodríguez O., "Las Cortes Mexicanas y el Congreso Constituyente," in Virginia Guedea, coord., *La independencia de México y el proceso autonomista novohispano, 1808–1824* (México: UNAM and Instituto Mora, 2001), 285–320; and Jaime E. Rodríguez O., "Las elecciones a las Cortes Constituyentes Mexicanas," in

Louis Cardaillac and Angélica Peregrina coords., *Ensayos en homenaje a José María Muriá* (Zapopan: El Colegio de Jalisco, 2002), 79–110.

51. "Decreto de 17 de noviembre de 1821, sobre convocatoria a Cortes," in Manuel Dublan and José María Lozano, *Legislación mexicana o colección de las disposiciones legislativas expedidas desde la independencia de la República,* 34 vols. (México: Imprenta Dublan y Lozano, 1876–1904), 1: 550–563. Rodríguez O., "Las elecciones a las Cortes Constituyentes Mexicanas," 90–105.

52. Ayuntamiento de Antequera al ministro de relaciones, Oaxaca, 12 de octubre de 1821, AGN, G, leg 1576, exp. 1; *Gaceta Imperial de México,* I, núm. 62 (5 de febrero de 1822), pp. 487–488. Those elected were: Lic. Luis Castellanos, cura Manuel Domínguez, Br. Lucal Almogavar, Lic. Manuel Nicolás de Bustamante (Carlos María de Bustamante's brother), Mariano Flores, colonel Manuel del Solar Campero, administrador Nicolás Fernández del Campo, and as suplentes, Lieutenant Colonel José López Ortigoza, Br. Lucas Morales Ibañez, and prepósito José María Idiáquez.

53. Manuel Chust examines the intentions of both the Americans and peninsulares in creating the diputaciones provinciales. *La cuestión nacional americana en las Cortes de Cádiz* (Valencia and México: UNED-Fundación Instituto de Historia Social and Universidad Nacional Autónoma de México, 1999), 218–238; "Del Gobierno interior de las provincias y de los pueblos," "*Constitución política de la Monarquía Española,*" in Felipe Tena Ramírez, ed., *Leyes fundamentales de México. 1808–1991,* 16th ed. (México: Editorial Porrúa, 1991), 95–99. The regulations were further explained in "Instrucciones para el gobierno económico-político de las provincias," in *Colección de decretos y órdenes de las Cortes de Cádiz,* 2 vols. (Madrid: Publicaciones de las Cortes Generales, 1987), 907–928.

54. The Ayuntamiento of Antequera de Oaxaca was not the only ayuntamiento of a provincial capital that clashed with the new provincial government because it feared losing its preeminent position in the province. A similar conflict took place between the Ayuntamiento of Guanajuato and the state constituent congress. See José Antonio Serrano, *Jerarquía territorial y transición política: Guanajuato, 1790–1836* (Zamora and Mexico: El Colegio de Michoacán and Instituto Mora, 2001), 137–202.

55. "El Soberano Congreso Constituyente para dar a la Administración pública un curso pronto y expedito cual se requiere en las presentes circunstancias, sin que se embarace por las dudas que puedan ocurrir a cerca de quien deba substituir en la muerte, ausencia, o falla del Gefe Político de la Provincias …[decretó que] 1. A falta del Gefe Político, e Intendente propietarios, sea Gefe Político y presida la Diputación Provincial el vocal mas antiguo de ella, como no sea Eclesiástico, en cuyo caso lo sera el Secular mas antiguo. 2. Que el Empleado que por Ordenanza substituya al Intendente ocupe en la Diputación el asiento inmediato despues del que preside." AGN, G, leg. 17, exp 11.

56. The extensive discussions on the matter are found in a legajo in AGN, G, SS, C. 13, exp. 7.

57. Hensel, *Die Entstenhung des Foderalismus,* 212–215. The membership of the diputación provincial changed during 1822. One member died, another failed to assume office, and a third departed for Spain. The three suplentes took their places. As the Constitution mandated, the following year three members of the body were replaced with newly elected deputies: José Javier Bustamante, Ramón Ramirez de Aguilar, and Joaquín Miura y Bustamante. Thus, in 1823, the Diputación Provincial of Oaxaca was composed of military men, functionaries, and clergy. Ibid.

58. Rodríguez O., "Las Cortes Mexicanas," 287–293.

59. "El Soberano Congreso Constituyente con el fin de asegurar la mas punctual y exacta observancia de todas sus determinaciones, ha tenido a bien resolver con esta fecha: que todo funcionario público, que recibiendo algun Decreto o orden dentro de tercero dia no cumpla en la parte que le toca, quede por solo este hecho, privado del destino que tenía." AGN, G, leg 17, exp 6.

60. Jaime E. Rodríguez O., "La Constitución de 1824 y la formación del Estado mexicano," *Historia Mexicana*, 40: 3 (January–March 1991), 514–517; Benson, *La Diputación Provincial*, 66–198.

61. Christon I. Archer, "The Royalist Army of New Spain, 1810–1821: Militarism, Praetorianism, or Protection of Interests?" *Armed Forces & Society*, 17: 1 (fall 1990), 99–116; and ibid., "The Militarization of Mexican Politics: The Role of the Army, 1815–1821," in Virginia Guedea and Jaime E. Rodríguez O., eds., *Five Centuries of Mexican History/Cinco siglos de historia mexicana*, 2 vols. (México: Instituto Mora, 1992), 1: 285–302.

62. Nettie Lee Benson, "The Plan of Casa Mata," *Hispanic American Historical Review* 25 (February 1945), 45–56.

63. On the political opinion in the provinces, see: "Informes pedidos por Don Agustín de Yturbide a los Jefes de las Provincias, con respecto a la opinion de las poblaciones, en sistema de gobierno, administración pública, etcetera, en 1822," in Benson Latin American Collection, University of Texas, Austin, García Collection.

64. The jefe político indicated that "En la representación . . . firmada por 367 individuos incluidos los Oficiales de aquella guarnición, esponen; que hallandose con derecho para representar con arreglo a la Constitución, sobre los defectos de dichas elecciones, lo verifican, sin que les mueva espiritu de partido...: que los electores abusaron de su confianza; pues nombraron los sujetos de menos concepto de luces, y amor a la Patria, y fue hecha la elección en complot por 14 o 15 que repartieron listas . . . [del] partido de la nobleza. . . ." See the expediente titled: "Sobre las desagradables ocurrencias que se originaron en Oajaca con motivo de la renovación del Ayuntamiento," AGN, G, SS, C. 58, exp. 1; Hensel, *Die Entstenhung des Foderalismus*, 32–237; Guardino, "'Toda libertad para emitir sus votos,'" 95–96.

65. "Oaxaca. Teniente Coronel González, Capitán Fagoaga y Subteniente Alvarez, revolucionarios," AGN, G: SS, C. 58, exp. 16.

66. Nettie Lee Benson, *La Diputación Provincial y el federalismo mexicano* (México: El Colegio de México, 1955), 151–151; *Manifiesto que sobre la instalación de la Junta provisional gubernativa de Oajaca, se hace a los habitantes de la provincia* (Puebla: Pedro de la Rosa, 1823); Carlos María de Bustamante, *Diario histórico de México*, 3 vols. (México: Instituto Nacional de Antropología e Historia, 1980) (26 de febrero de 1823), tomo 1, vol. 1, pp. 186, 189. Carlos María de Bustamante believed that, even if only provisional, the creation of such a body was a step toward federalism, a form of government he opposed. As a result of such criticisms, in mid-April the body "acordó no volver a reunirse, sino en caso extraordinario que exigiera sus servicios." Apparently, thereafter, the Diputación Provincial of Oaxaca functioned as the provincial government. According to Bustamante, "La Junta Gubernativa de Oaxaca se ha disuelto y merecido la aprobación y gracias del Gobierno, pero habiéndose reorganizado la antigua Provincia [diputación provincial?], resulta que ésta en la mayor

parte está plagada de serviles; esto ha provocado una providencia del Poder Ejecutivo," ibid., tomo 1, vol. 1, 224.

67. José Morán al Secretario de Relaciones Interiores, México, 23 de abril de 1823, AGN, G, leg. 25, exp. 12 (62); *Acta de la Junta de Puebla sobre la reinstalación del Congreso Mexicano* (Puebla: Pedro de la Rosa, 1823).

68. Bustamante, *Diario histórico de México*, 26 de febrero de 1823, tomo 1, vol. 1, p. 216.

69. Jaime E. Rodríguez O., "The Formation of the Federal Republic," in Guedea and Rodríguez O., eds., *Five Centuries of Mexican History*, 1: 316–319.

70. Ibid., 320–321.

71. *Representación de los comisionados de las provincias al Soberano Congreso* (México: Imprenta del Ciudadano Alejandro Valdés, 1823). The signatories were: Martín García of Michoacán, Tomás Vargas and Rafael Márquez of San Luis Potosí, Anastasio Ochoa of Querétro, Prisciliano Sánchez and Juan Cayetano Portugal of Guadalajara, Francisco de Arriera and Santos Vélez of Zacatecas, Juan Ignacio Godoy of Guanajuato and Vicente Manero Embides of Oaxaca.

72. Rodríguez O., "The Formation of the Federal Republic," 322.

73. Ibid., 324–328; Bustamante, *Diario histórico de México*, tomo 1, vol. 1, pp. 258–261. The lengthy convocatoria was published June 17, 1823: *Decreto del Soberano Congreso Mexicano para las elecciones que deberán hacer las Provincias, de los Diputados que han de componer el que constituya la Nación* (Mexico: Imprenta del Supremo Gobierno en Palacio, 1823).

74. Bustamante, *Diario histórico de México*, 21 de mayo de 1823, tomo 1, vol. 1, p. 258.

75. Y. M. O., *Invitación que hace un oaxaqueño a su suelo Patrio* (Oaxaca: n. p., 1823).

76. Antonio de León al Supremo Poder Ejecutivo, Oaxaca, 4 de junio de 1824, AGN, G, SS, C. 48, f. 20; Bustamante, *Diario histórico de México*, tomo 1, vol. 1, p. 271.

77. "Sesión extraordinaria," 1 de junio de 1823, AGN, G: SS, C 48, exp. 12, ff. 7r–v.

78. Ibid., f. 7v.

79. Ibid., f. 8r.

80. "Acta de la Junta de Guerra," ibid., ff. 15–17.

81. Ibid., 15–17. All sixty-three officers signed the acta.

82. "Sesión extraordinaria," f. 8r–v.

83. "Acta del Cabildo Eclesiástico," 1 de junio de 1823, AGN, G, SS, C 48, exp. 12, ff. 34–38.

84. "Acta de la Junta Provisional Gubernativa," 1 de junio de 1823, AGN, G, SS., C 48, exp. 12, ff. 1–3v, 7–15v. See also "Manifiesto de la Junta Provisional Gubernativa de Oajaca a los habitantes de toda la provincia," *Aguila Mexicana*, 86 (July 9, 1823), 318–319.

85. "Acta del Cabildo Eclesiástico," 2 de junio de 1823, AGN, G, SS, C. 48, exp. 12, ff. 40–43

86. *Bases Provisionales con que se Emancipó la Provincia de Oajaca* (Oaxaca, n.p., 1823).

87. "Convocatoria," AGN, G, SS, C 48, ff. 27–28v. See also "Oaxaca: Ocurrencias del Día," AGN, G, SS, C. 47, exp. 29.

88. Silke Hensel has offered a different explanation for the ayuntamiento's prominent role. She argues that the corporation was dominated by merchants who objected to the forced loans, taxes, and paper money introduced by the imperial government. As a result of these measures and the province's deteriorating economic conditions, the elites of Oaxaca, who controlled the ayuntamiento, concluded that the national government was an obstacle to their economic well-being and opted for federalism in order to control their own destiny. *Die Entstenhung des Foderalismus*, 162–163.

89. Both groups were aware of the significance of their actions and maintained a formal record of their deliberations. The large legajo titled "Oaxaca. Sobre el pronunciamiento en dicha Ciudad, de la República federada e independiente de los Supremos Poderes de la Nación" does not include the deliberations of the other corporations. There is a printed as well as a manuscript version of the deliberations of the armed forces in the legajo. There are only manuscript versions of the two meeting of the clergy, but both have written at the top "para imprimir." AGN, G, SS, C. 48, exp. 12.

90. Rodríguez O., "The Formation of the Federal Republic," 317–318.

91. According to Hensel nineteen military men were members of the elite or were related to them. Moreover, the group also included current and former regidores of the Ayuntamiento of Antequera. *Die Entstenhung des Foderalismus*, 160–162.

92. Bustamante, *Diario histórico de México*, 26 de febrero de 1823, tomo 1, vol. 1, pp. 164–165.

93. For more information on the political activities of the clergy, consult: Brian Connaughton, *Ideología y sociedad en Guadalajara (1788–1853)* (Mexico: Consejo Nacional para la Cultura y las Artes, 1992); ibid., "Troublemakers, Priests and Public Opinion in Mexico, 1821–1860," *Mexican Studies/Estudios Mexicanos*, 17: 1 (winter 2001), 41–69; and ibid., *Dimensiones de la identidad patriótica: religion, política y regions en México. Siglo xix* (Mexico: Universidad Autónoma Metropolitana and Miguel Angel Porrúa, 2001).

94. Rodríguez O., "The Formation of the Federal Republic," 324–328.

95. Carlos María de Bustamante, *Examen crítico sobre la federación de las provincias del territorio mexicano. Carta primera a un oaxaqueño* (México: Imprenta del Ciudadano Alejandro Valdés, 1823).

96. Victorés Manero al Supremo Poder Ejecutivo, Oaxaca, 24 de junio de 1824, AGN, G, SS, C. 42, exp. 12, ff. 47–48r.

97. "Ceremonial que aprobó la Junta Gubernativa" & "Congreso Provincial, Decreto núm. 1," AGN, G, SS, C. 48, exp. 12, 54–56.

98. The documents from Tixtla are found in AGN, G, SS, C. 48, exp. 12, ff. 51–52v–r; "Sobre que el Pueblo de Tehuantepec no se adherido al pronunciamiento de Oaxaca," ibid.

99. "Noticias ocurridas en esta Provincia de Oaxaca hasta hoy, 5 de agosto de 1823," ibid, f. 63r–v.

100. Florencio Castillo al Supremo Poder Ejecutivo, Oaxaca, 8 de julio de 1823, AGN, G, SS, C. 48, exp. 12, ff. 60r–v. Not all members of the Congreso Provincial de Oaxaca were so conciliatory, however: see, *Voto particular del Señor Ordoño, Diputado del Congreso Provincial de Oajaca sobre el pase a Convocatoria de México. Con notas de un Ciudadano del Estado libre de Xalisco* (Guadalajara: Imprenta del Ciudadano Urbano Sanroman, 1823). It appears that the pamphlet was circulated

throughout the country. See: "El Gefe Político de Tabasco remitiendo un impreso que se le remitió desde Jalisco, y participando haber impedido su publicación en aquella Provincia, por subversivo," AGN, G, Leg. 20(1), exp 8.

101. *Bases para el Gobierno Provincial de este Estado interin se da la Constitución General de la Nación* (Oaxaca: n.p., 1823).

102. "Resoluciones del Supremo Poder Ejecutivo," AGN, Colección José López Portillo, ff. 27v, 34v, 32r–v. Carlos María de Bustamante believed that León was the driving force behind the political changes in Oaxaca, but he was also convinced that the Subdeacon Ignacio Ordoño manipulated León. See *Diario histórico de México,* tomo 1, vol. 1, pp. 270, 279.

103. "Noticias ocurridas en esta Provincia de Oaxaca hasta hoy, 5 de Agosto de 1823," AGN, G, SS, C. 48, exp. 12, f. 63r–v

104. "Anónimo al Señor Capitán General del Sur," AGN, G, SS, C. 48, exp. 12, ff. 64–65v.

105. "Noticias occurridas en esta Provincia de Oaxaca."

106. Many provinces were opposed to the government's use of force. See, for example, "La Diputación Provincial de Puebla sobre no poder dar los tres mil pesos que pide el Sr. Rincón y ruega se evite romper las hostilidades en Oaxaca," AGN, G, SS, C. 48, exp. 12.

107. Bustamante, *Diario histórico de México,* tomo 1, vol. 2, pp. 39–40.

108. *Aguila Mexicana* 188 (October 30, 1823), 2; Rodríguez O., "The Formation of the Federal Republic," 324–328.

109. Two other explanations have been advanced for these events. Writing in 1955, Nettie Lee Benson believed that the national government, first under Iturbide and then the reconstituted first Cortes, so alienated the province that it finally separated. In her view, it was the Provincial Deputation of Oaxaca that "decidió declarar su completa independencia del gobierno central de México." Benson, *La Diputación Provincial,* 152. Recently, Silke Hensel has argued that the Ayuntamiento of Oaxaca was in the hands of the merchant elite and it was they who were most important in seeking federalism. In her view, "Fue precisamente el grupo al que tradicionalmente se ha atribuido una orientación conservadora y centralista el que se unió al ejército en su apoyo al orden federal. Pero el proyecto que los comerciantes perseguían con la 'declaración de independencia' de Oaxaca no se caracterizaba precisamente por su tenor liberal. Se trataba más bien de conseguir aquello por lo que venían luchando desde la introducción de las intendencias en 1786: el retorno a su posición poderosa antes de que los intendentes como altos funcionarios de la Corona controlasen la provincia." Silke Hensel, "Los orígenes del federalismo en México. Una perspectiva desde la provincia de Oaxaca de finales del siglo XVIII a la Primera República," *Ibero-Amerikanisches Archiv* (1999): 235.

3

Masonic Connections, Pecuniary Interests, and Institutional Development Along Mexico's Far North

Andrés Reséndez

Long regarded as hopelessly chaotic and inhabited by sycophantic *caudillos*, the history of Mexico's early nineteenth century has come of age in recent years. Scholars working in different regions have shed some light on the difficult transition from Spanish colony into independent nationhood, have examined the articulations of local, regional, and national agents, and have recast liberalism and conservatism as credible, vibrant, and changing political movements, not as timeless ideologies.[1] This scholarship is especially interested in exploring how the Mexican national project *actually* unfolded on the ground in an immense territory from Alta California to Guatemala.[2] In this process of bringing local communities into "the national grasp" two parallel developments stand out. On the one hand, there is an institutional dimension: a national *state* gradually emerges out of congeries of alternative institutions (church, corporate bodies, indigenous polities) and is able to exercise authority, however contested. On the other hand, individuals initially committed to ethnic, local, or regional identities gradually come to see themselves as members of a national community. Thus the perilous road to nationhood was dual: the Nation-State had to win out over lesser political organization and potential challengers, *and* people had to subsume or somehow rework their previous ethnic, corporate, or other subnational loyalties into a national identity.

Both of these processes should be at the heart of the story of how Mexico's Far North became the American Southwest. After all, colonial institutions and mores that had long anchored peoples' lives in far-flung places like Texas and New Mexico were the only structures that kept the Far North attached to the rest of the nation in the aftermath of Mexico's independence. Moreover, there is clear evidence that such venerable colonial institutions (i.e., patronage, royal rituals, municipal governments, the secular church, the military, etc.) were deliberately deployed, contested, and adapted in the Far North (as elsewhere in Mexico) to serve national purposes in the critical period leading up to the Mexican-American War. I do not claim that such nationalizing blitzkrieg resulted in successful dominance or that it occurred peacefully. But incomplete and fractious as this process of hegemonic incorporation was, it nonetheless proceeded in earnest at this time. A generation of frontier Hispanics, Anglo-American colonists, sedentary Indians, and nomads in the 1820s and '30s found themselves carving out spaces for themselves out of the Spanish imperial machinery and in the process chiseling out a new Mexican order.

Unfortunately, the unfolding of Mexican institutions and mores in places like Texas, New Mexico, and Alta California have traditionally received short shrift in the historiography.[3] One reason for such neglect of things Mexican in this region may have to do with the enormous influence of the "Boltonian school" and its relentless focus on missions and presidios, institutions that although vital and expanding in the Spanish era entered a period of stagnation and obvious decline after Mexico's independence. Such a perspective tends to reinforce the enduring, if inaccurate, interpretation of the Mexican period in the Far North as declension from the heights of Spanish imperialism.[4] But perhaps the most important reason for this tendency to rinse Mexico out of what became the American Southwest is that this region's history has been written primarily from the perspective of the United States' expansion across the continent. This historiography customarily downplays the Mexican context in two crucial respects: first, by depicting Mexico's Far North as largely disconnected from the politics and discussions of central Mexico; and second, by rendering this region's story as a mere prelude to annexation to the United States.[5] Teleology creates the impression that the inhabitants of Mexico's Far North were simply waiting for the inevitable to occur: revolution and war to break out and the United States to take over.

What follows is an attempt to bring some of the insights of the recent Mexican historiography of the early nineteenth century to bear on the history of the Far North, and to recast the Mexican period in Texas not as declension for old colonial glories but as an era of institutional creativity and successful expansion of peculiarly Mexican institutions to the very edge of the national territory and over a very heterogeneous frontier society.

THE ALLURE OF *BALDÍOS*

In the 1810s Texas was still a backwater province with enormous *baldíos* (vacant lands) occasionally visited by peripatetic Indians, explorers, trappers, and Spanish officials. Within two decades this corner of Mexico would emerge as the most important colonization experiment in the nation, meant to show how the forces of enlightenment and progress could work their magic on a vast and untamed wilderness. To tell this story of intrigue, high hopes, and political partisanship it is first necessary to say something about an idiosyncratic institution that would play the leading role both in early Mexican politics and in facilitating the colonization of Texas: Freemasonry. Putting aside the reputedly dark underside of these "secret societies"—their conspicuous rituals and secrecy often exaggerated by their Catholic opponents—Masonic lodges were quite simply social venues where political opinion was shaped in the absence of formal political parties.[6] Masons (invariably men, no women were allowed) would gather to discuss politics, to exchange information, and—as their political and economic influence increased—to jockey for positions in government and curry economic favors. In the immediate aftermath of Independence, Freemasonry of the Scottish Rite became particularly active in many parts of Mexico. The *escoceses* multiplied largely through the proselytizing efforts of former Mexican deputies to the Spanish Cortes who, after extensive involvement with lodges in Europe, returned to Mexico eager to promote them at home.[7] Initially, the aim of Scottish Rite Masons was to establish a republic and institute some of the reforms advocated by the Spanish Cortes.[8] Early in 1823, after a rapid and highly organized movement, Scottish Rite Masons succeeded in toppling the Mexican Empire headed by Iturbide and lived a brief but crucial heyday in 1823–1824. The escoceses dominated the Constituent Congress that yielded Mexico's first political constitution in 1824. But Scottish Rite Masons soon found themselves outflanked by a second Masonic group founded in Mexico City in the summer of 1825. Joel R. Poinsett, the first United States ambassador to Mexico, was asked to incorporate the newly formed society into the Rite of York by obtaining the regulating patents from the Grand Lodge of New York.[9] Ideologically, the York Rite Masons were more radical than their escocés counterparts, favoring popular participation through direct elections and being committed to federalist (understood as home rule) tenets.[10] Generally, their boldness earned them the names of radicals, federalists, or simply *yorkinos*. Moreover, a noticeable pro–United States stance stood in stark contrast to the distrustful attitude toward Mexico's northern neighbor evinced by the escoceses. Especially along Mexico's Far North, yorkinos had interaction with lodges in the United States and drew support from influential foreign-born residents.[11]

Both brands of Masonry had a tremendous influence on Texas, especially because the province started out its Mexican existence under the aegis of neighboring Coahuila.[12] During the early 1820s the Coahuilan Clergyman Ramos Arizpe—arguably the main leader and ideologue of the escoceses at that time—pushed for the union of Coahuila and Texas, pointing out that the latter would be better off as a "free and sovereign state" (even though it was only in partnership with Coahuila and with a minority stake at that) rather than "degrade itself" by becoming a territory under the iron grip of the national government.[13] The escocés ideals were also decisive in shaping the early political institutions of Texas. In 1824 the citizens of Coahuila and Texas elected an escocés-dominated provincial constituent assembly charged with organizing the state government, drafting a colonization law, and enacting a series of economic reforms.[14] And just as the escoceses had finished crafting a functioning government, the pendulum swung toward the radical camp. In the elections of 1827 and 1829 York Rite Masons won solid majorities in the twelve-member legislature. More important perhaps was the rise to power of the Viesca brothers. José María Viesca was elected to the governorship of Coahuila and Texas in 1827. A few months later his brother, Agustín Viesca, would be appointed to the Ministry of Foreign Relations during the radical administration of President Vicente Guerrero. Agustín Viesca had been among the founding members of the York Rite Masonry in Mexico City and together with his brother assembled an informal political group with connections stretching from Texas administrators all the way to the highest echelons of the national government. An American witness described the Viesca family as "rich, large, respectable, learned, sensible, and honorable, they believe not in this d___d foolish religion and possess two very fine libraries of miscellaneous and scientific books."[15]

From the start the baldíos of Texas had been considered the very cornerstone of the state's development strategy. State and local officials in Texas had come to the remarkable conclusion that the prosperity of the state depended on its ability to attract foreign colonists and turn them into law-abiding citizens of Mexico. The road to this decision had not been easy. For nearly a century tejanos had struggled to populate and pacify a backwater Spanish province of the size of continental Spain, France, and Holland put together. Properly monitored, Anglo Americans could speed up this process. The *jefe político* of Texas, Antonio Martínez, put it quite clearly: "the [Mexican] population in this province is too small, and yet it is absolutely essential to settle Texas so the easiest and least costly way to accomplish this is by admitting *extranjeros* (foreigners), especially those who are known to us, or have means and properties, or at least can produce certificates of orderly conduct."[16] The clearest articulation of this vision appears in the 1825 Coahuila and Texas Colonization Law. In this notable document, state legislators dreamed of sprawling new communities dotting the entire Texas territory. Any foreigner willing to embrace Catholicism and Mexican rule was free to project a new settlement on unclaimed lands. These new settlements would be located in "the most appropriate places" following the recommendations of state officials and would be free to pursue all kinds of industrial and mining enterprises. As far as possible, the new settlements would be composed of both Mexicans and foreigners living in stone or wooden houses arranged along straight streets in the Spanish grid fashion. Lot owners would pay annually one peso that would be applied to the construction of a Church. The Coahuila and Texas Colonization Law also reached out to nomadic Indians who were prepared to accept a Christian and sedentary way of life. Indians could establish themselves in any of the new and predominantly Anglo-American or Hispanic settlements, although the colonization law did not set up any explicit mechanism to provide land to entire tribes wishing to establish themselves *on their own*. In this fashion tejano leaders—at least on paper—hoped to bring peace to Texas by building a remarkable community composed of different races but united in a common quest for prosperity.[17]

These lofty ideals would be vigorously promoted from the state government by a small elite that kept a tight control of the land-granting process. Essentially, the state governor and a colonization committee in the state legislature would review all colonization projects and land petitions submitted by national and foreign *empresarios*, Indians, and individuals at large. Those projects deemed "worthy," "sound," and "beneficial to the state" would then be "elevated" to federal authorities for scrutiny. While approval at the federal level was not a foregone conclusion—disagreements sometimes occurred and indeed became a major source of friction in the 1830s—nonetheless the federal government generally went along with the state authorities' recommendations in the early years.[18] In truth, the governor and two or three state legislators, after secretive deliberations, were able to confer princely land grants, colonization enterprises, and exclusive rights to navigate Texas rivers, and made profitable appointments for Texas customs and land officials.[19] Saltillo may have been a dusty small town lost in the Coahuila plains, but after 1825 it attracted a lively cast of land speculators, settlers, empresarios, merchants, and politicians of all hues and levels bent on securing Texas land. And in this world prone to the wholesale trafficking of political influence and economic favors, Masonic lodges provided a ready-made network of personal contacts and tacit alliances.

As state legislators discussed the final draft of the state colonization law early in 1825, numerous land developers swarmed into Saltillo. The most successful turned out to be Masons. One of them was Robert Leftwich. Since 1822 Leftwich, representing a group of Tennessee investors, had spent his time dealing with bureaucracies and colonization committees in Mexico City trying to obtain a land grant in Texas. In February of 1825 he moved to Saltillo, where he finally clinched the sought-after contract from the state government.[20] Another fellow Mason, Frost H. Thorn, had also followed closely the development of Mexico's land policy both in Mexico City and then in Saltillo where he too obtained an empresario contract to introduce 400 families.[21] In addition to Leftwich and Thorn, the list of Anglo-American Freemason empresarios included David G. Burnet, John Cameron, Benjamin

R. Milam, Haden Edwards, and James Power.[22] No empresario was more successful than Stephen F. Austin of the Louisiana No. 109 Lodge. By early 1825,
Austin was already a well-established empresario and seasoned operator of
the intricate Mexican national and state bureaucracies. Austin had spent all
of 1822 and part of 1823 in Mexico City validating a Texas land grant that the
Spanish colonial government had conferred to his father. In the course of his
lobbying activities he came in contact with some of the most prominent Mexican politicians, as well as other Anglo-American would-be empresarios.[23] In
June of 1825 Austin obtained a second grant from the Coahuila and Texas
government to introduce 500 families. It was the beginning of a close relationship, as Austin was awarded three more colonization contracts: in 1827
to introduce 100 families, in 1828 to bring 300 families, and one more in
1831, in partnership with Samuel M. Williams, to introduce 800 families of
European and Mexican settlers.[24]

In addition to Anglo-American Masons, prominent Mexican Masons managed to secure empresario contracts or 11-league grants.[25] The list was
topped by none other than Ramos Arizpe himself. On November 12, 1828,
he obtained an enormous colonization contract running along the northern
margin of the Rio Grande in an irregular quadrangle comprising—by Ramos
Arizpe's own reckoning—between 800 and 1,000 square leagues of land or
over 4 million acres.[26] Interestingly, Ramos Arizpe objected to the open-door
policies introduced by several yorkino administrations that in his view had
resulted in the rapid Americanization of Texas.[27] Indeed, Ramos Arizpe justified his own enormous colonization contract as a last-ditch effort to secure
a Mexican stronghold north of the Rio Grande:

> In November of 1828 I visited the capital of the state of Coahuila and Texas and
> was dismayed to learn that due to the inconceivable stupidity of three successive
> yorkino legislatures, the exclusive rights to navigate the Rio Grande on steam boat
> were given to a company promoted by Anglo Americans and supported by capi-
> talists of their republic. This privilege extends from the mouth of the Rio Grande
> or Bravo del Norte, through the states of Tamaulipas, Coahuila and Texas, and
> Chihuahua, all the way to New Mexico. This disastrous policy in effect puts the
> line that North Americans have long coveted as the limit of their own territory in
> the hands of individuals and wealthy capitalists from the United States.[28]

Clearly, the predominance of Anglo-American empresarios in Texas constituted one of the main rifts between escoceses and yorkinos. But the state's
yorkinos, led by the Viesca brothers, remained very much in control of the
land-granting process and continued to favor both Anglo-American entrepreneurs and Mexican leaders who supported an open border with the
United States. Indeed, many of the highest-ranking yorkinos not only in
Coahuila and Texas but throughout Mexico acquired land in Texas in those
years. Texas became something of a heaven where liberal politicians pinned

their hopes and invested their personal fortunes. In case of a downturn in their political careers they could always flee to Texas, as many of them did in the mid-1830s. Such prominent York Rite Masons included the Grand Secretary of the Grand Lodge of Mexico, Colonel José Antonio Mexía. He did not secure a colonization contract but, with the blessing of Governor Viesca, Colonel Mexía bought a "princely domain" amounting to some 55 square leagues or 243,540 acres, far in excess of the 11-square-league maximum permitted by the law.[29] Another notorious case was that of Lorenzo de Zavala, one of the founders of the early yorkino lodges who went on to become governor of the state of Mexico and finance minister. The circumstances in which Lorenzo de Zavala obtained his empresario contract are indicative of the ruthless dealing-and-wheeling prevalent in Saltillo in those heady years. The colonization contract in question had originally been granted to Colonel Peter Ellis Bean, a naturalized Mexican (possibly escocés) whose services had been most valuable in putting down the Fredonia Rebellion of 1826–1827. As a reward he was offered an empresario contract to settle Indians. But after the rise to power of yorkinos in Saltillo, Colonel Bean was accused of bigamy. Colonel Bean stated in his land request that he was married to a Mexican woman, doña Magdalena Farfán de los Godos, to bolster his claim to citizenship. But Governor José María Viesca soon found out that the prospective grantee was in fact living with an American woman called Candes Marquif. Judicial proceedings were initiated against him, and even before the verdict had been reached Colonel Bean was stripped of his grant, which was quickly awarded to Governor Zavala.[30] Zavala's grant remained the most controversial decision made by the state government. Many other liberal leaders, especially yorkinos, acquired land interests in Texas, including Valentín Gómez Farías, the Vice-President of Mexico; and Father José María Alpuche, an eccentric clergyman from Tabasco who had also been among the founders of the yorkino lodges together with Lorenzo de Zavala and Agustín Viesca.[31] Well-connected Masons seemed ubiquitous. Even the Cherokee grant had been arranged through Masonic contacts. When Chief Richard Fields went to Mexico City to negotiate land for his people, he decided to join a lodge.[32] All told, more than half of all land grants in Mexican-Texas were awarded to Anglo-American, Mexican, and Indian Masons while the proportion of Masons within the population of Texas at large was less than 10 percent.[33]

Land and Masonic connections were also vital to the political and economic fortunes of Mexican-Texans. While the paucity of records makes it exceedingly difficult to locate individual tejanos as escoceses or yorkinos, it is possible to identify tejano elite members who favored Anglo-American colonization projects and were ideologically close to the positions adopted by the yorkino faction in Coahuila led by the Viesca brothers. The Seguín family is a good example. Erasmo Seguín, the patriarch, had been a consistent

supporter of Anglo-American immigration into Texas at least since 1821. He
was the first tejano to welcome Stephen F. Austin into Texas, and since that
early encounter the two men struck up a close friendship, economic partnership, and crucial political alliance.[34] Don Erasmo also blazed the way for
cooperation with Coahuila politicians, although he may have had mixed
feelings later on. In his quest to advance the interests of Texas, including
those of Austin and his Anglo-American colonists, the elder Seguín, as the
Texas representative in the Constituent Congress, accepted Ramos Arizpe's
offer to form a joint state. This arrangement at least kept land decisions
within the state. As Ramos Arizpe explained: "The Texas representative and
I have agreed to unite our provinces and are of one mind about parceling
out our baldíos in such a way that this policy will become a powerful lever
working in favor of our two provinces."[35] Juan Nepomuceno Seguín continued in his father's footsteps, cultivating close ties with the increasingly influential Anglo-American empresarios (especially Austin) and generally keeping good relations with the yorkino leadership in Coahuila. This alliance
acquired concrete form during the Texas Revolution when the Seguíns initially sided with the Viescas and sought to enlist the help of Anglo-American
settlers to their cause, as we shall see.

The early life of José María de Jesús Carvajal—one of the most colorful figures of the border, who would go on to play key roles in the Texas Revolution, the Republic of the Sierra Madre secessionist attempt, and the filibus-
tering activities in the Texas-Tamaulipas border in the 1850s, and would cap
his career attempting to raise a large mercenary force in the United States to
fight the French Intervention in Mexico in the 1860s—best illustrates the
powerful triangular alliance between tejanos, Anglo-American entrepreneurs, and Coahuila politicians. A native of San Antonio, the first turning
point in Carvajal's life occurred in 1821, when he was sponsored by a newly
arrived Austin to spend some years in Kentucky and Virginia learning the
tanning and saddle trades. This experience changed his life forever. Fluent
in English and possessing a demeanor that hinted at something foreign—to
the point where fellow tejanos called him "el norteamericano"—when he returned to Texas Carvajal naturally gravitated toward the camp of his Anglo-
American sponsors.[36] Indeed, Austin's intervention continued to be decisive
in helping him secure employment as a land surveyor and coming in contact
with well-known yorkinos in Texas (Francisco Madero and Martín de León)
and also with the Viesca faction in Coahuila. In 1835 Carvajal was elected as
one of the Texas representatives to the state legislature, turning into a fierce
supporter of Governor Agustín Viesca.[37]

The early life of Carvajal shows how prominent tejanos more generally remained involved in colonization ventures in Texas as land administrators.
With the union of Coahuila and Texas in 1824 the tejano elite in fact lost control of land decisions outside the San Antonio–Goliad region. But some of

them made up for this loss by receiving lucrative administrative appointments. Each colonization project required a land commissioner charged with hiring one or more surveyors, collecting the appropriate fees from the colonists, and issuing land titles.[38] Hence the state legislature regularly appointed "well informed, reliable persons" many of whom turned out to be influential tejanos.[39] These were extremely lucrative jobs. At first, a commissioner negotiated his pay with each colonist. This led to widespread abuse since colonists, eager to obtain land titles, were cajoled into paying large sums of money. A federally appointed official lashed out against them: "bearing the title of commissioners, the state government has sent a bunch of ignorant and destitute men who, under the pretext of giving possession to the colonists, in addition to a stipend of 50 pesos that they receive for each act of possession, conduct a shameful traffic of influence which has resulted in the wholesale transfer of baldíos that many foreigners now illegally own."[40] New regulations were introduced in 1827 whereby commissioners' fees were fixed, but even then a commissioner working on an average-size colony was able to collect what amounted to a small fortune.[41] Not only were commissioners handsomely paid but they also became key intermediaries between the state government and the empresarios who depended on their services. Carvajal's trajectory is quite illuminating in this regard and he was hardly alone. The roster of land commissioners and surveyors with close ties to Anglo-American empresarios and Coahuila politicians includes José Miguel Aldrete and Juan Nepomuceno Seguín.[42]

In the absence of a constituted nation, this vast network of landed interests running from Mexico City, through Saltillo and San Antonio, and to the various colonization projects and land grants throughout Texas is what kept an array of diverse human beings together. Land provided a stake in the nation to a very heterogeneous frontier society that otherwise had little else in common. Land grants enticed settlers, created new communities, restricted the mobility of Indians, and extended the reach of the Mexican government as it brought scattered populations into the orbit of local, state, and national bureaucracies— for instance, empresarios initially acted as civil and judicial authorities in their own communities and were required to act as intermediaries between the colonists and the state government. As we think about this impressive proto-national administrative network, it is worth keeping three points in mind. First, this nexus of interests not only involved high-ranking Mexican politicians, wealthy Anglo-American developers, and Indian leaders, but directly affected the common folk. Although the historical record focuses on the actions of prominent speculators and politicians, ordinary foreign-born settlers, Indian families living on land grants, and non-elite tejanos were the most dependent on Texas land and the machinery that validated its distribution and administration. Speculators may have seen their fortunes rise and tumble in spectacular transactions, but ordinary individuals literally lived off the land.

Second, this administrative system favored some individuals and restricted access to others, thus generating considerable conflict. Texas was literally parceled out among a few fortunate empresarios while aspiring Anglo-American colonists, Indians, and even Mexican-Texans could not gain access or at least obtain proper titles to their lands. Anglo-American colonists who had settled beyond colonization grants were perennially at risk of being evicted from their fields and improvements. Regarded as squatters, these colonists often clashed with land commissioners and other Mexican authorities as they confronted Mexico's land bureaucracy. Similarly, a few Indian groups like the Cherokee were able to secure grants after considerable efforts. But most natives had no success as it was unclear whether to negotiate with state or federal authorities, and there was no established mechanism comparable to the empresario system to give land to Indians wishing to settle on their own. Even Mexican-Texans complained about lack of access. Since 1826 the *ayuntamiento* of Goliad had vigorously protested the decision of the state government to give Irish empresarios James Power and William Wilson lands in the extinguished mission of Refugio. Ayuntamiento members objected to a land policy that so blatantly favored Anglo-American developers impinging on the rights of Mexican-Texans who had owned these lands "from time immemorial."[43] Understandably, a free-wheeling land administration making controversial decisions ended up with supporters and antagonists among all ethnic groups. But even as the system was frequently challenged, it still came to underpin the political and economic life of Texas.

The third and final point to bear in mind is that Texas land was rather more than land; it came intertwined with ideology and politics. The entire colonization experiment in Texas was guided by a conspicuous cosmopolitanism quite evident in the State Colonization Law of 1825 and the preference for Mason empresarios and Anglo-American settlers. These ideas were deeply rooted in the international liberal movement. In the early decades of the nineteenth century, liberalism was on the rise worldwide. Religious and institutional strictures of the past were being cast aside in favor of a new system of freedoms aimed at unleashing the full potential of human spirit, particularly in the pursuit of economic endeavors.[44] The colonization commissioner for Texas and former Mexican consul in Bordeaux, Tadeo Ortíz, wrote to the president in 1833 explaining that since the French Revolution Europe had been working relentlessly to abolish all obstacles to the expansion of industry, accumulation of wealth, and commerce. Above all, the commissioner pointed out, the United States furnished indisputable evidence of the validity of these new political doctrines. By bringing hard-working settlers, allowing trade to flourish, and promoting industry, the young republic to the north had become a sprawling and prosperous entity, a *Wunderkind* nation. It was now Mexico's turn to follow suit, and Texas, with her convenient ports, her proximity to the American market, and her enormous baldíos was well poised for just that feat.[45] Note that this liberal policy is far from laissez-faire but rather consisted of government intervention meant to lower barriers to trade, industry, and immigration. In this sense, the colonization experiment launched by the authorities of Coahuila and Texas became a crucial test, an ideological battleground of the virtues of liberalism, and the hopes of liberals throughout Mexico rode on its success.

Texas land and liberal politics were also inextricably intertwined with ideas of state autonomy and home rule. The one issue that dominated politics in Mexico throughout the nineteenth century was the spatial distribution of power, with centralists/conservatives generally advocating political centralization in Mexico City while federalists/liberals championed political autonomy for states and municipalities. Coahuila and Texas was a principal backer of the latter camp. Indeed, the Texas baldíos constituted the most effective way to propagate home rule ideals. After all, by parceling out land and deciding on its own natural resources, the state government of Coahuila and Texas exercised the ultimate attribute of state sovereignty.

LIBERAL PARADISE UNDER CENTRALIST PRESSURE

The rise of centralism in Mexico had profound repercussions for the liberal experiment unfolding in Texas. National leaders who took control of government, fleetingly in 1830–1832 and more permanently after 1834, pointed toward the "Texas question" as a blatant example of the pernicious effects of liberalism, lambasting the absurdly generous state colonization laws and liberal trade policies and pointedly remarking that Anglo Americans had, quite literally, taken possession of Texas.[46] Minister of Interior Affairs Lucas Alamán expressed these concerns in unmistakable terms: "instead of sending conquering armies, they [North Americans] have recourse to other means . . . they begin by introducing themselves in a territory that they desire and establish colonies and trading routes. Then they demand rights that would be impossible to sustain in any serious discussion and base their claims on historical facts that nobody admits . . . little by little these extravagant ideas, out of repetition, become sound proofs of ownership."[47] Texas may have been far away from Mexico's heartland, but in the symbolic geography of centralist politicians it was at the core. Just as federalists had used Texas as a showcase for a modern nation, the conservative rendition of the nation, built on the threat of impending territorial loss, began with the defense of Texas.

One of the most interesting features of the origins of the Texas Revolution is that Spanish-speaking politicians in Coahuila and Texas were the ones to first seriously entertain the possibility of breaking free from the rest of Mexico. Older scholarship of the Texas Revolution tends to present it as an ethnic struggle between Hispanics and Anglos. But a growing interest in

Mexican-Texans has shown that the revolution was not carried out exclusively by dissatisfied Anglo colonists, but that Hispanics were actively involved too. Indeed, the initial momentum to resist Mexico City's authority, even if that entailed using force, originated among Hispanics in Coahuila and Texas, not among Anglo-American colonists who only belatedly were invited to join the revolt.[48] As early as June of 1834, a year and a half before Anglo-American colonists themselves began considering independence in a series of conventions, a staunchly federalist governor and state legislature broke spears with the federal government, refusing to recognize any decrees from President Santa Anna. In the following months the struggle between Santa Anna's increasingly centralist government and the embattled coahuiltejano authorities would only deepen, a political crisis that would lead to the withdrawal of the state's allegiance from the Mexican federation. Such a stance was far from unprecedented. As recent Mexicanist scholarship has underscored, states were quite independent in this period and prone to defying national authorities. Zacatecas, Jalisco, and Guerrero among other states were waging similar battles against the powers of the federation.[49] But what made the case of Coahuila and Texas particularly crucial was its large pool of Anglo-American colonists, whose help could be enlisted to uphold the federalist cause.

Standing at the epicenter of this secessionist movement in Coahuila and Texas was the state legislature and, above all, Agustín Viesca, who would become governor during the most critical circumstances. The dramatic floor debates, poignant letters, and legislative work during 1834–1835 have left us a paper trail of how this group of determined state politicians came to the startling conclusion that temporary independence from Mexico was the most sensible course of action. Their debates and actions also speak eloquently about how they used the formidable machinery around land in Coahuila and Texas to advance their political goals. At first these coahuiltejano federalists were merely reacting against Mexico City's centralizing offensive.[50] In the early months of 1834 state authorities learned with dismay of President Santa Anna's dissolution of the national congress. Closer to home, the governor and state legislators came under the scrutiny of two federal envoys, Colonels José María Noriega and Juan Nepomuceno Almonte, who arrived in Coahuila and Texas as Directors of Colonization in April of 1834.[51] Colonel Noriega's orders were to go to Monclova—which had been functioning as the state capital since 1833—to review the labyrinthine maze of land grants and contracts in Texas, and to investigate the fate of the abandoned customshouses and see to it that they were reopened. Colonel Noriega also bore secret instructions that included, among other things, to spy on the American Consul in Matamoros and find out whether he was encouraging the separatist movement in Texas, and to remove rebellious Anglo colonists by buying them out of the state. Simultaneously, Colonel Almonte would travel through Texas to gather geographic, demographic, and military information, and to "ascertain the opinions of Anglo colonists concerning separation from Mexico and exploit any differences among them." With regard to Indian tribes, Colonel Almonte was to inform them that the Supreme Government was willing to give them full possession of the lands that they occupied provided that they unambiguously declared themselves to be citizens of Mexico.[52]

It is clear that the vast network of landed interests running between the state capital and Texas emerged as the main bone of contention between federalists and centralists and roughly defined the ideological and political battle lines. In the San Antonio area the largest landowners generally supported the federalist faction of Monclova. Sitting in the municipal governments of Goliad and San Antonio, the tejano elite had carried out considerable land transactions, most of which had been validated by the state government. This group included José Casiano, José Antonio Navarro, Ramón Músquiz, and the Seguíns, all generally sympathetic to the federalist camp.[53] Some went even further. Deputy of San Antonio José María Carvajal traveled through Texas in early 1835 offering land to the dispersed Anglo-American and Indian families in exchange for military support on behalf of the Monclova state government.[54] He took refuge in Austin's colony in June of 1835 and became a key link between tejano federalists and Anglo-American colonists.[55] Carvajal was elected to the convention of 1836 at Washington-on-the-Brazos that declared Texas independence but did not attend.[56] To be sure, the same patronage system could work in the opposite direction as well. Some Goliad ranchers were far more receptive to the centralist harangues that emphasized patriotism precisely because of a long-standing dispute with empresario Green DeWitt, who had close ties to the Monclova clique. Carlos de la Garza, a Goliad resident, became the most conspicuous centralist tejano leader.[57] The point to bear in mind, however, is that such centralist leanings could also be traced to the nexus of interests revolving around Texas land.

Beyond the San Antonio–Goliad region, other Mexican empresarios cast their lot with the state federalists as well. Martín de León and his family were "decidedly opposed to Santa Anna, and all exerted themselves in favor of the constitution of 1824."[58] Initially, the Mexican empresario provided cattle, horses, and money for the revolution. His son, Fernando de León, together with José María Carvajal purchased arms and ammunition in New Orleans for the Texas Army.[59] Another Mexican land owner in Texas, Colonel José Antonio Mexía, was so strenuously opposed to centralism that in November of 1835 he fitted out an expedition in New Orleans and made a disastrous attempt to occupy the port of Tampico and wrest Mexico's second most important customshouse from the hands of the centralists.[60] Lorenzo de Zavala, the most controversial Mexican empresario, upon learning of Santa Anna's abolition of the 1824 constitution, resigned his post as Mexican ambassador in France in March of 1835, and went to New York and from there to New Orleans and Texas to carry out a liberal revolution. In Lynchburg, where he established his home, Zavala delivered a speech in August of 1835 using land as an inducement:

> It is said that the inhabitants of Texas are indebted to the Supreme Government of Mexico and to state governments for the laws that gave them the land they cultivate now. This is true: but it must be remembered that those governments were formed by the same men who are now persecuted—among whom I have the honor to count myself one. A party composed of the military, ecclesiastics, and Spaniards, would never have thrown open their country to foreigners.[61]

Coahuiltejano federalists openly used the state's patronage system revolving around land to obtain arms and enlist the help of Anglo-Americans for their cause. Some Anglo-American empresarios such as John Cameron and Benjamin Milam were already part of the inner circle of Monclova's political clique and were quite sympathetic to the idea of upholding the state's rights. Clearly these empresarios, Masonic connections and all, shared with coahuiltejano federalists similar political ideas and pecuniary interests. Yet, others understandably attempted to remain neutral or refrained from taking sides in Mexico's fractious politics. But coahuiltejano authorities had few qualms about pressuring such undecided Anglo-American colonists to the federalist side. For instance, on March 30, 1835, the federation mandated drastic reductions in the size of state militias, the very bulwark of state autonomy. That decree was a watershed because it transformed what had been mere political bickering into a military showdown between state militias that refused to comply and the national army charged with enforcing the law. But far from reducing the state militia, Governor Agustín Viesca sought to expand it with the help of tejanos and Anglo-Texans.[62] He played with the fears of Anglo colonists: "the party now in power, the same that prohibited the emigration of North American colonists in 1830, has openly declared against all foreigners and secretly favors Spanish policy and Spanish despotism. The law of April 6 is about to be renewed under a still more drastic form."[63] Another way in which Monclova federalists used the land patronage system to advance their political aims was by selling land to raise cash, men, and arms. Resorting to the April 19, 1834, decree that empowered the state to sell large quantities of land to protect citizens against Indian depredations, the state legislature in Monclova sold 300 leagues of Texas land to John T. Mason, a representative of the Galveston Bay and Texas Land Company.[64] On May 13, 1835, the state legislature alienated another 1200 leagues—5 million acres— to Samuel M. Williams, Francis W. Johnson, and Robert R. Peebles in lots of 400 leagues each. In exchange, the three contractors were to raise a militia in the number of 1000 men, provide them with arms and ammunition, and keep them in the field for one year.[65]

By the spring of 1835 Mexican federalists were clearly contemplating a full-scale military engagement with the Federation and began to toy with the idea of separation from Mexico altogether. In May the state legislature issued a decree that moved the seat of government from Monclova to a more defensible place in Texas, an initiative that in effect extended the war from Coahuila to Texas. On May 21 Governor Viesca and his six–person council that included James Grant, a Texas representative to the legislature, and John Cameron and Benjamin Milam, two Anglo-Texan empresarios, rode out of Monclova in the middle of the night and headed north toward the San Juan road. The roving state government was nonetheless captured before it could reach its destination.[66] Simultaneously, prominent Mexican federalists were already thinking about secessionist schemes. In September Zavala volunteered to draft a proposal for the *temporary* separation of Texas from Mexico. Texas would secede in order to defend her rights under the social contract of 1824, and would rejoin the Mexican confederation *only as a free and independent state.* Zavala's proposal allowed for Texas to take independent action but only if "after the passage of a certain period (say two years) the Mexican states do not recover their freedom."[67]

The decision of Anglo-Texan leaders and colonists at large to pursue all-out separation from Mexico early in 1836 gave the revolutionary movement a far more definitive and ominous character and produced a grave split among Mexican federalists. As late as November of 1835, Vice President Gómez Farías—who had sought refuge in Texas and was living in New Orleans—still defended the national character of the Texas movement: "the reports are false, entirely false, that the Texans want to dismember the Mexican territory."[68] Even in December, Mexican federalists clung to the idea that Anglo-Texans genuinely fought for federalism. Addressing the citizens of San Antonio, General Mexía exclaimed: "Companions! They deceive you who inform you that the Texians wish a separation from the Mexican Federation, therefore do not believe it, what they desire is what I and all Federalists desire, that is the Constitution of 1824 and that we should not be governed neither by friars nor by aristocrats."[69] When the final break occurred in early March of 1836, many Mexican federalists felt betrayed. One high-ranking activist from New Orleans broke the news to his lover: "I cannot describe to you my anger upon learning that the Texan colonists who had pronounced themselves for the federal constitution now only aspire to become independent." The writer observed that General Mexía became furious and together with General Peraza left the place saying that "he was Mexican by birth, and would never consent to his country's dismemberment."[70]

But notwithstanding such disappointments, it is remarkable that other Mexican federalists supported the Texas Revolution to its ultimate denouement. Lorenzo de Zavala continued in Texas, became a delegate at the convention of 1836 that declared independence from Mexico, and was then elected vice-president of the Republic of Texas. Similarly many tejanos remained loyal to Texas even as secession from Mexico became permanent. The Seguíns emerged as the most conspicuous tejano leaders. Erasmo Seguín had supplied large numbers of cattle to feed the insurgents. Juan Nepomuceno Seguín raised a tejano volunteer army to fight the national troops.[71] José Casiano turned over his house and store to the Anglo troops that took possession of San Antonio in the winter of 1835. Casiano's house was used as a hospital, and the wounded were supplied from his store. Posing as a merchant, he went to Matamoros in March of 1836 to spy on the movements of Santa Anna's troops.[72] José Antonio Navarro and Francisco Ruiz, more than anyone else, symbolized the alliance between tejanos and Anglo-Texans. They were chosen to represent the Béxar district in the convention in Washington-on-the-Brazos and signed the Texas declaration of independence. It is said that Navarro "hesitated in the course which he was about to take, he had an ardent desire to establish a free government for Texas, and yet he trembled at the thought of having to sanction with his signature the eternal separation of Texas from the mother country."[73] In December of 1836, Francisco Ruiz wrote to his son-in-law: "do not oppose the Texans under any circumstance and advise your friends to do the same, only the power of God will return the territory of Texas to the Mexican government, Texas has arms and money for her defense and will be free forever."[74]

CONCLUSION

Prior to the Texas Revolution and the Mexican-American War, Mexico did not possess a full-fledged state. But it did have bureaucracies and systems of patronage that proceeded in earnest with the arduous task of nationalizing authority and weaving together disparate frontier social groups. It is time to revise the prevailing narrative of early Mexico as declension from Spanish monarchical institutions, loss of control, and chaos. Since the late eighteenth century, local and regional communities throughout Mexico had been experimenting with new ideas and institutions as they coped with the Bourbon Reforms.[75] Recent Mexicanist scholarship has emphasized the country's impressive institutional development immediately before and after independence, which introduced novel institutions like elected municipal and provincial governments, attempted to define the proper spheres of the Federation and the states, and transformed the relationship between church and state. This process, difficult as it was in some regions, slowly yielded functioning state and local governments that were more or less successfully integrated into the national domain.

This same institutional transition began to take place along Mexico's northern frontier with developments like the emergence of a land administrative system in Texas in the 1820s. Although this process of institutional development was never completed before this region ceased to be a part of Mexico, it nonetheless set the terms of the identity struggles that would rock this region in the years leading up to the Texas Revolution and the Mexican-American War. The story of how Mexico's Far North became the American Southwest begins with these institutions and the ways in which they impinged on the livelihood of frontier society. Indeed, the Texas Revolution of 1835–1836 and other revolutionary upheavals that broke out in other peripheral regions of Mexico would be incomprehensible without regard to these determined efforts at institutional consolidation and centralization—premature perhaps—and the reactions of frontier inhabitants. I have also tried to underscore that this institutional development entailed not only systems of control, coercion, and self-interest, but also various political and ideological meanings. Land in Texas was associated to ideals of liberalism and home rule; and these very notions kept the door open to Anglo Americans desirous to settle in Mexico. In the absence of other common elements, these entrenched institutions that supported a nexus of pecuniary interests, ideological beliefs, and emotional attachments constituted the very foundation of citizenship for coahuiltejanos. If, as Benedict Anderson would have it, the nation is an imagined community, Texas shows us that this imagining had concrete, institutional underpinnings.

NOTES

1. A note about terminology. It has been the curse of Mexicanists (and more generally Latin Americanists) working on the nineteenth century to be forced to grapple with notions so malleable and changing and yet so crucial to the entire historical experience as liberalism and conservatism and their forerunners, federalism, centralism, *yorkismo*, etc. As some scholars have observed, there is no point in treating these notions as fixed political ideas but rather as broad and changing political movements. Still, it is possible to get closer to the meaning and membership of these political labels at the regional level and for short periods of time. In this sense, when I write about liberalism in this paper I really mean *coahuiltejano* liberalism in the 1820s and '30s except when otherwise noted.

2. Peter F. Guardino, *Peasants, Politics, and the Formation of Mexico's National State: Guerrero, 1800–1857* (Stanford: Stanford University Press, 1996); Richard A. Warren, *Vagrants and Citizens: Politics and the Masses in Mexico City from Colony to Republic* (Wilmington: SR Books, 2001); Cynthia Radding, *Wandering Peoples: Colonialism, Ethnic Spaces, and Ecological Frontiers in Northwestern Mexico, 1700–1850* (Durham: Duke University Press, 1997); Michael T. Ducey, "Village, Nation, and Constitution: Insurgent Politics in Papantla, Veracruz, 1810–1821," *Hispanic American Historical Review* 79: 3 (Aug. 1999): 463–93; and Guy Thomson, "Bulwarks of Patriotic Liberalism: The National Guard, Philharmonic Corps and Patriotic Juntas in Mexico, 1847–88," *Journal of Latin American Studies* 22: 1 (Feb. 1990): 31–68,

among others. Jaime E. Rodríguez O. has reinterpreted the process of emancipation, emphasizing the continuity of political processes and institutions in *The Independence of Spanish America* (Cambridge: Cambridge University Press, 1998). He has also edited a number of volumes dealing with this period. See also the pioneering work of Nettie Lee Benson on the origins of federalism, which has appeared in an updated version as: *The Provincial Deputation in Mexico: Harbinger of Provincial Autonomy, Independence, and Federalism* (Austin: University of Texas Press, 1992). Among scholars working in Mexico, see Virginia Guedea, *En busca de un gobierno alterno: Los Guadalupes de México* (Mexico: Universidad Nacional Autónoma de México, 1992); and her edited volume *La independencia de México y el proceso autonomista novohispano* (Mexico: Universidad Nacional Autónoma de México, 2001); Brian Connaughton, *Dimensiones de la identidad patriótica* (Mexico: Miguel Angel Porrúa, 2001); and his edited volumes *Construcción de la legitimidad política en México* (Mexico: Universidad Autónoma Metropolitana, 1999); and *Poder y legitimidad en México, siglo xix: Instituciones y cultura política* (Mexico: Miguel Angel Porrúa, 2003); and José Antonio Serrano, *Jerarquía territorial y transición política: Guanajuato, 1790–1836* (Zamora: El Colegio de Michoacán, 2001).

3. For a discussion of such historiographical imbalances see David J. Weber, "Mexico's Far Northern Frontier, 1821–1854: Historiography Askew," in *Myth and the History of the Hispanic Southwest* (Albuquerque: University of New Mexico Press, 1988), 89–104. All along there have been exceptions to this trend. Most notably see Nettie Lee Benson, *La Diputación Provincial y el Federalismo Mexicano*, 2d ed. (Mexico City: El Colegio de México, 1994); Gerald E. Poyo, ed., *Tejano Journey, 1770–1850* (Austin: University of Texas Press, 1996); Andrés Tijerina, *Tejanos & Texas under the Mexican Flag, 1821–1836* (College Station: Texas A & M University Press, 1994). Recent work has highlighted the importance of colonial institutions in the daily lives of frontier residents. See Gerald E. Poyo and Gilberto M. Hinojosa, eds., *Tejano Origins in Eighteenth-Century San Antonio* (Austin: University of Texas Press, 1991); and Jesús F. de la Teja, *San Antonio de Bexar: A Community on New Spain's Northern Frontier* (Albuquerque: University of New Mexico Press, 1996).

4. For a thoughtful consideration of the work of Eugene Bolton and his followers see David J. Weber, "Turner, the Boltonians, and the Borderlands," and "John Francis Bannon and the Historiography of the Spanish Borderlands, Retrospect and Prospect," both in *Myth and the History of the Hispanic Southwest*, 33–54 and 55–88 respectively.

5. For an insightful discussion of scholarly trends with respect to Texas see Gerald E. Poyo and Gilberto M. Hinojosa, "Spanish Texas and Borderlands Historiography in Transition: Implications for United States History," *Journal of American History*, 75: 2 (September 1988): 395–416.

6. The role of secret societies in early Mexican politics is a crucial but still dimly understood subject. For a brief historiographical assessment see Jean-Pierre Bastian, "Una ausencia notoria: la francmasonería en la historiografía mexicana," *Historia Mexicana* 175 (Jan.–Mar., 1995): 439–460. François-Xavier Guerra contends that Masonic lodges constitute the first modern vehicle of political association. François-Xavier Guerra, *México: Del Antiguo Régimen a la Revolución*, 2 vols. (Fondo de Cultura Económica, 1988), 1: 157–170. My own work shows that Masonry's role extended far beyond the purely political and encompassed the economic realm as well. Contemporary authors, politicians (and Masons) such as Lucas Alamán and Lorenzo de Zavala provide some evidence of

the far-reaching influence of Masonic networks. See specific citations below. For a short and balanced introductions to the history of Freemasonry in Mexico see: Lillian Estelle Fisher, "Early Masonry in Mexico (1806–1828)," *Southwestern Historical Quarterly* 40: 3 (Jan. 1939): 198–214; and Virginia Guedea, "Las sociedades secretas durante el movimiento de independencia," in Rodríguez O., ed., *The Independence of Mexico and the Creation of the New Nation* (Los Angeles: UCLA Latin American Center, 1989), 45–62. The most comprehensive study of Masonry in Texas is James David Carter, *Masonry in Texas: Background, History, and Influence to 1846* (Waco: Committee on Masonic Education and Service for the Grand Lodge of Texas, 1955).

7. The life stories of Miguel Ramos Arizpe and Lorenzo de Zavala illustrate this pattern very well.

8. On the federalist movement and Ramos Arizpe see Nettie Lee Benson, *La diputación Provincial y el federalismo mexicano* (El Colegio de México, 1955); and Lucas Alamán, *Historia de México*, 5 vols. (Mexico: Fondo de Cultura Económica, 1985), 5: 357–58. For a description of the character and influence of Ramos Arizpe see Lorenzo de Zavala, *Ensayo crítico de las revoluciones de México desde 1808 hasta 1830* (Mexico City: Editorial Porrúa, 1969, c1831), 114.

9. Zavala, *Ensayo crítico de las revoluciones de México*, 252; and Alamán, *Historia de México*, 5: 411.

10. One must bear in mind that these ideologies changed according to place and time. For instance, David Brading has noted the inconsistencies between classic liberal doctrines and the *yorkino* movement. Contrary to liberal doctrines, *yorkinos* in south central Mexico advocated protectionism. David Brading, *The Origins of Mexican Nationalism* (Cambridge, U.K.: Centre of Latin American Studies, 1985), 71, 92. See also Guardino, *Peasants, Politics, and the Formation of Mexico's National State*, 122; and Timothy E. Anna, *Forging Mexico, 1821–1835* (Lincoln: University of Nebraska Press, 1998), 176–177. In the case of *yorkinos* of Coahuila and Texas, the *yorkino* movement staunchly supported free trade so there were no such inconsistencies. This underscores the fact that, far from a unified political ideology, the *yorkino* movement was very much shaped by regional concerns.

11. Zavala, *Ensayo crítico de las revoluciones de México*, 197–198, 252–253, 257; and Alamán, *Historia de México*, 5: 308, 405, 411–412, and 417–418.

12. Regino F. Ramón, *Historia general del estado de Coahuila*, 2 vols. (Saltillo: Universidad Autónoma de Coahuila, 1990, c1917), 2: 456. On the federalist movement and Ramos Arizpe see: Benson, *La diputación Provincial y el federalismo mexicano*; and Lucas Alamán, *Historia de México*, 5: 357–58.

13. See Charles A. Bacarisse, "The Union of Coahuila and Texas," *Southwestern Historical Quarterly* 51:3 (Jan. 1958), 340–349; and Ricki S. Janicek, "The Development of Early Mexican Land Policy: Coahuila and Texas, 1810–1825," Ph.D. diss. Tulane University, 1985, 180–199.

14. Some of these reforms had already been introduced by the short-lived Provincial Deputation of Texas. See Janicek, "The Development of Early Mexican Land Policy," 136–137. See also Vito Alessio Robles, *Coahuila y Texas*, 1: 155–210, 245–269. For a brief but ambitious consideration of Mexico's overall land policies along the Far North during the early decades, see Nettie Lee Benson, "Territorial Integrity in Mexican Politics, 1821–1833," in Rodriguez O., ed., *The Independence of Mexico and the Creation of the New Nation*, 275–307.

15. Robert Andrews to Stephen Austin, Parras, Sep. 5, 1823, quoted in Janicek, "The Development of Early Mexican Land Policy," 195.

16. Jefe político Antonio Martínez, "estado actual de la provincia de Texas," San Antonio, Feb. 6, 1822, Béxar Archives (hereafter BA), 70, 581–582.

17. Colonization law of the state of Coahuila and Texas, Saltillo, Mar 24, 1825, Translation in Malcolm D. McLean, *Papers Concerning Robertson's Colony in Texas*, 16 vols. (Fort Worth and Arlington: University of Texas at Arlington Press, 1974–1990), 2: 276.

18. Janicek, "The Development of Early Mexican Land Policy," 180–216; Janicek, "The Politics of Land: Mexico and Texas, 1823–1836," unpublished paper presented at the Texas State Historical Association meeting of 1996; and the report of José María Díaz de Noriega, federal commissioner of colonization, Monclova, June 23, 1834, Bolton Papers (hereafter BP), Bancroft Library, University of California, Berkeley, P 40: 673, 7.

19. On the influence of the state legislature see: Vito Alessio Robles, *Coahuila y Texas desde la consumación de la independencia hasta el tratado de paz de Guadalupe Hidalgo*, 2 vols. (Mexico City: Jus, 1945), 1: 177–269.

20. See Leftwich's diary in McLean, *Papers Concerning Robertson's Colony in Texas*, introductory volume.

21. Mary Virginia Henderson, "Minor Empresario Contracts for the Colonization of Texas, 1825–1834," *Southwestern Historical Quarterly* 31: 4 (1928): 298–299.

22. List of Texas Masons in James D. Carter, *Masonry in Texas*, 425–465.

23. José María Tornel describes Austin as that person "with whom we all became acquainted in Mexico [City]." José María Tornel, *Tejas y los Estados Unidos de América, Mexico City, 1837*, in *The Mexican Side of the Texan Revolution*, translated by Carlos E. Castañeda (Dallas: P. L. Turner Co., 1928), 309.

24. Eugene C. Barker, *The Life of Stephen F. Austin, Founder of Texas, 1793–1836* (New York: Da Capo Press, 1968), 89–134 and 141–144; Andreas V. Reichstein, *Rise of the Lone Star*, Jeane R. Wilson, trans. (College Station: Texas A&M University Press, 1989), 32–36; and Gregg Cantrell, *Stephen F. Austin: Empresario of Texas* (New Haven: Yale University Press, 1999), 132–170.

25. Nettie Lee Benson makes the point that more attention has been given to foreign *empresarios* than to Mexican *empresarios*. See "Texas as Viewed from Mexico, 1820–1834," *Southwestern Historical Quarterly* (Jan. 1987): 244–245.

26. This grant was not included in professor McLean's list. See report of José María Díaz de Noriega, federal commissioner of colonization, Monclova, Jun. 23, 1834, BP, 40:673, 7, pp. 637–638; land petition of Miguel Ramos Arizpe to the state government of Coahuila and Texas, Saltillo, Nov. 12, 1828; and clarification of Ramos Arizpe's *empresario* contract, n.p., Apr. 11, 1830, in BP 40:673, 4.

27. In 1825 Ramos Arizpe himself became a yorkino. But yorkinos were split between *moderados* and *exaltados*, and the Coahuilan politician clearly belonged to the moderate wing.

28. Miguel Ramos Arizpe to the state government of Coahuila and Texas, Saltillo, Nov. 12, 1828; and clarification of Ramos Arizpe's *empresario* contract, n.p., Apr. 11, 1830, in BP 40:673, 4.

29. C. Alan Hutchinson, "General José Antonio Mexía and His Texas Interests," *Southwestern Historical Quarterly* 85 (Oct. 1978): 125; and James D. Carter, *Masonry in Texas*, 237. See article 24 of the state colonization law on the limitations of private land ownership. The General Land Office of Texas has defined the *sitio* or square league as 4,428.4 acres.

30. Peter Ellis Bean's land petition, n.p. May 6, 1826; and Commander of the Eastern Interior Provinces to Ministry of Foreign Affairs, Mexico City, Nov. 22, 1828, BP 40:673, 4. See also Governor José María Viesca to Minister of Foreign Affairs, Leona Vicario, May 5, 1828, BP 40:673, 3.

31. On speculation on 11–league grants carried out by Masons see Janicek, "The Politics of Land: Mexico and Texas, 1823–1836," 9–10. See also C. Alan Hutchinson, "Mexican Federalists in New Orleans and the Texas Revolution," *Louisiana Historical Quarterly* 30 (Jan. 1956), 1–47; and Hutchinson, "General José Antonio Mexía and His Texas Interests," 117–142.

32. James D. Carter, *Masonry in Texas,* 231.

33. This figure was determined by comparing Professor McLean's list of Texas land grants with the list of known Masons in Texas provided by James D. Carter, *Masonry in Texas,* 425–465.

34. For sketches of the lives of Erasmo and Juan Nepomuceno Seguín see Jesús de la Teja, *A Revolution Remembered,* 3–56.

35. Miguel Ramos Arizpe to *ayuntamiento* of Saltillo, Mexico City, Mar. 8, 1824, quoted in Ramón, *Historia general del estado de Coahuila,* 2: 487. See expanded discussion in Andrés Tijerina, *Tejanos & Texas under the Mexican Flag, 1821–1836* (College Station: Texas A & M University Press, 1994), 97–99.

36. Stephen F. Austin to Mary Holley Austin, quoted in Harbert Davenport, "General José María Jesús Caravajal," *Southwestern Historical Quarterly* 40 (April 1952), 476–477. In a telling letter Carvajal wrote to his mother explaining that after two years in the United States he had become "verry wicked" and that he had found consolation in reading the Bible and thus decided to "renounce the doctrines of the Church of Rome" and become a Baptist. Carvajal also asked his mother to send him books in Spanish, "I have nearly lost my language in my own tounge. . ." Carvajal to his mother, Lexington, Jul. 2, 1826, in *The Austin Papers,* edited by Eugene C. Barker (Washington: Government Printing Office, 1924), 2: 1366–1367.

37. Frederick C. Chabot, *With The Makers of San Antonio* (San Antonio: Artes Gráficas, 1937), 33–34. Shortly after the Atascosito incident Carvajal was released and went on to serve as surveyor in the Béxar district until 1834. Carvajal's appointment in records of the General Land Office of Texas [hereafter GLO] 123: 8, 98–99; and José Antonio Padilla to jefe politico of Texas, Monclova, Jun. 13, 1834, GLO 125: 22, 265. See also Ana Carolina Castillo Crimm, "Success in Adversity: The Mexican Americans of Victoria County, Texas 1800–1880," (Ph.D. diss.: University of Texas, Austin, 1994), 142–144. On the federalist leanings of the de León family see Ana Carolina Castillo Crimm, "Finding Their Ways," in *Tejano Journey, 1770–1860,* Gerald E. Poyo, ed., (Austin: University of Texas Press, 1996), 115–118.

38. Articles 38 and 39 of the state colonization law.

39. See José Miguel Aldrete to Ramón Músquiz, Goliad, May 6, 1830, GLO 123: 7, 83; Ramón Músquiz to governor, Béxar, May 24, 1830, GLO 123: 7, 87; appointment of José María Salinas, Béxar, Oct 1, 1831, GLO 123: 8, 98–99.

40. Report of Tadeo Ortiz to the President, Matamoros, Feb. 2, 1833, BP 40:673, 4.

41. See instructions for land commissioners in GLO 123: 9, 108–109. A commissioner was allowed to collect 15 pesos for each league of *agostadero,* two pesos for each *labor* of *temporal,* and 20 reales for each *labor* of *regadío.* See also GLO 123: 7, 77.

42. For a list of land commissioners and surveyors see GLO 123, passim.

43. Members of the ayuntamiento of Goliad to Commander of Goliad Juan Manuel Sabariego, Goliad, Jul. 25, 1834. Henry Raup Wagner Collection of Texas Manuscripts, WA MSS S-339, box 3, folder 107, Beinecke Library, Yale University.

44. Brading, *The Origins of Mexican Nationalism*, 70. Brading probes the multi-layered relationship between liberalism and nationalism. For the articulation and origins of the liberal ideology in Mexico see Charles A. Hale, *Mexican Liberalism in the Age of Mora, 1821–1853* (New Haven: Yale University Press, 1968), passim.

45. Tadeo Ortiz to President of Mexico, Matamoros, Feb. 2, 1833, BP 40:673, 4. It is important to note that even Mexican politicians who later denounced the expansionism of the United States were initially quite impressed by her success as a nation and ready to follow her footsteps. See Reynaldo Sordo Cedeño, "El General Tornel y la Guerra de Texas" in *Historia Mexicana* 42:4, 934–935. See also Josefina Zoraida Vázquez, "The Colonization and Loss of Texas: A Mexican Perspective" and Jesús F. de la Teja, "The Colonization and Independence of Texas: A Tejano Perspective," both in Jaime E. Rodriguez O. and Kathryn Vincent, eds., *Myths, Misdeeds, and Misunderstandings: The Roots of Conflict in U.S.-Mexican Relations* (Wilmington: SR Books, 1997), 47–77 and 79–95 respectively.

46. For a very illuminating discussion of the politics around colonization in early Mexico see Dieter George Berninger, *La inmigración en México, 1821–1857* (Mexico City: SepSetentas, 1974).

47. Lucas Alamán, *iniciativa de ley . . .*, Mexico City, Feb. 8, 1830, in Vicente Filisola, *Memorias para la historia de la Guerra de Tejas*, 2 vols. (Mexico: Imprenta de I. Cumplido, 1849). 2: 591–593.

48. See Paul Lack, *The Texas Revolutionary Experience, A Political and Social History, 1835–1836* (College Station: Texas A&M University Press, 1992), 156–207; *A Revolution Remembered: The Memoirs and Selected Correspondence of Juan N. Seguín*, edited by Jesús F. de la Teja (Austin: State House Press, 1991), passim; and Andrés Tijerina, *Tejanos & Texas under the Mexican Flag, 1821–1836* (College Station: Texas A&M University Press, 1994), 137–144.

49. Especially Anna, *Forging Mexico*; and Guardino, *Peasants, Politics, and the Formation of Mexico's National State*.

50. The traditional liberal interpretation is that Santa Anna himself was at the head of the centralist revolution. See Michael P. Costeloe, *The Central Republic in Mexico, 1835–1846* (Cambridge: Cambridge University Press, 1993). Reynaldo Sordo Cedeño has challenged this idea, arguing that Santa Anna remained in favor of the federation until early 1835, at which time he yielded to the growing influence of the centralist movement in various parts of the country. Reynaldo Sordo Cedeño, *El congreso en la primera república centralista* (Mexico City: El Colegio de México-ITAM, 1993), 19–59, 173, and 418. For a detailed account of this reformist period and the legislation introduced see also Enrique Olavarría y Ferrari, *Episodios históricos mexicanos*, 4 vols. (Mexico City: ICH-FCE, 1987) 4: 1185–1279.

51. Reports of Almonte and Noriega, Monclova Sep. 23, 1834, BP 40:673, 5.

52. Report of Almonte to governor of Coahuila and Texas, Monclova, Sep. 23, 1834, BP 40:673, 5.

53. This was determined by comparing the list of the largest tejano land owners in the 1840 census to the list of tejano political activists in various gatherings in October 1834 through May 1835. See Gifford White, ed., *The 1840 Census of the Republic of*

Texas (Austin: Pemberton Press, 1966), 35–37 and compare that list to the list of signers of the San Antonio declaration, San Antonio, Oct. 7, 1834, BP 40:673, 5.

54. Antonio Tenorio to Ugartechea, San Felipe, Aug 24, 1835, BA, 166, 347–49. Músquiz to Dimmitt, Monclova, Mar 5, 1839, Dimmitt Papers, Eugene C. Barker Texas History Center, University of Texas, Austin.

55. Ayuntamiento of San Felipe to inhabitants, San Felipe, Jun. 25, 1835, Nacogdoches Archives (hereafter NA), 2q309, 247, 169–171.

56. American consulate in Matamoros to Colonel José Mariano Guerra, commander of Matamoros, Matamoros, Dic 12, 1835. Archivo de la Secretaría de Defensa Nacional, Mexico (hereafter ADN), 48:1657; and deposition of James W. Robinson, Victoria, Oct. 7, 1849, Unpaid Claims Collection at the Texas State Archives.

57. See Castillo Crimm, "Finding Their Ways," 119–120; Tijerina, *Tejanos & Texas under the Mexican Flag*, 123–124; Lack, *The Texas Revolutionary Experience*, 163; and Tijerina, "Under the Mexican Flag," 44–46.

58. Deposition of James W. Robinson, Victoria, Oct. 20, 1849, Unpaid Claims Collection at the Texas State Archives.

59. American consulate in Matamoros to Colonel José Mariano Guerra, Matamoros, Dec. 7, 1835, ADN 48:1657.

60. José Antonio Mexía to Agustín Viesca, Brazos Bar, Dec. 3, 1835, in John H. Jenkins, ed., *Papers of the Texas Revolution, 1835–1836*, 10 vols. (Austin: Presidial Press, 1973) (hereafter PTR), 3: 89–90; and Mexía to Henry Smith, governor of Texas, Quintana Mouth of the Brazos river, Dec. 7, 1835, PTR 3: 106–110.

61. Zavala to colonists, Lynchburg, Aug. 7, 1835, PTR 1: 313–314.

62. Vicente Arriola, military commander of Monclova, to Martín Perfecto de Cos, Monclova, Apr. 8, 1835, ADN 23:1095.

63. Address to Coahuiltexanus, Monclova, May 4, 1835, NA, 2q309, 246, 167–172.

64. See McLean's list of empresarios in his *Papers Concerning Robertson's Colony in Texas*, 2: 219–222.

65. Judge Daniel J. Toler to M. B. Lamar, n.p., 1844, in Charles A. Gulick, ed., *Papers of Mirabeau Buonaparte Lamar*, 6 vols. (Austin: A. C. Balwin Printers, [1921]) (hereafter LP 4) 3: 96–98.

66. Secret session of the state legislature in Monclova. Copy made in Leona Vicario, May 11, 1835; Vicente Arriola to Cos, Monclova, Jun. 1, 1835, ADN 23: 1095; Cos to *jefe político* of Béxar, Matamoros, Jun. 12, 1835, BA 2q309, 247, 114–115; and Judge Daniel J. Toler to M. B. Lamar, n.p., 1844, LP 4: 96–98.

67. Zavala to Austin, Lynchburg, Sep. 17, 1835, PTR 1: 453–454.

68. Gómez Farías to Estevan Moctezuma, n.p., Nov. 7, 1835, PTR 2: 346.

69. Mexía to the besieged forces in San Antonio, n.p, Dec. 1835, PTR 3: 205.

70. "El desterrado" to his lover, New Orleans, Feb. 26, 1836, NA 2q311, 253, 126–129.

71. Lack, *The Texas Revolutionary Experience*, chapter 10; and de la Teja, *A Revolution Remembered*, biographical introduction. For a brief account of the military participation of tejanos see Stephen L. Hardin, "Efficient in the Cause," in Gerald E. Poyo, ed., *Tejano Journey, 1770–1860* (Austin: University of Texas Press, 1996), 49–71.

72. José Casiano to Tribunal for the Adjudication and Settlement of Claims, San Antonio, Feb. 26, 1839, Comptroller of Public Accounts Collection, Audited Civil Claims, box 2, folder 72, Texas State Archives; and *acta levantada por Don José Casiano. . .*, Apr. 16, 1836, Casiano-Pérez Collections, Daughters of the Republic of Texas at the Alamo, box 2, file 71.

73. Taken from H. S. Thrall, *A History of Texas from the Earliest Settlements to the Year 1885* (New York: University Publishing Company, 1887), 636. Naomi Fritz disputes this idea: "José Antonio Navarro" (MA thesis: Saint Mary's University of Sant Antonio, 1941), 33–34.

74. Francisco Ruiz to Blas Herrera, Columbia, Dec. 27, 1836, Texas State Archives, box 2–22/711.

75. Among others see Ross Frank, *From Settler to Citizen: New Mexican Economic Development and the Creation of Vecino Society, 1750–1820* (Berkeley: University of California Press, 2000); De la Teja, *San Antonio de Béxar*, passim. Weber provides an overview of these new institutions and ideas in *The Mexican Frontier*, 15–42.

4

Maximilian and the Construction of the Liberal State, 1863–1866

Robert H. Duncan

Padre Francisco Javier Miranda, auxiliary to the Bishop of Puebla and the man who took part in rescinding the liberals' reform laws, eagerly anticipated the arrival of Mexico's new emperor. In April 1864, he had traveled to Miramar castle in Trieste to attend the ceremony that officially offered the throne to Austrian Archduke Ferdinand Maximilian. Like his clerical-conservative cohorts in the delegation, Miranda had high hopes for the empire.[1] His enthusiasm, however, was short-lived. After returning from Miramar, Miranda felt that he had erred in his judgment. Not only did Maximilian later declare religious toleration but also reaffirmed the hated desamortization law passed by the *Reforma* liberals a few years earlier. Miranda ultimately would describe the new emperor as a "foolish" dreamer who mistakenly believed in a liberal and democratic monarchy for Mexico. Maximilian lacked the necessary character and decisiveness for the task at hand; "he was a poet, that is, a dreamer"—an image repeated down through the years.[2]

Seen as a by-product of foreign aggression, the Second Empire's standing in Mexican history has been that of the "poor cousin." Neatly bracketed by the standard periodization, the French Intervention casts a long shadow over the empire, making the two virtually inseparable in the historiography. As a result, the Second Empire is often denied an independent place in Mexican history. Maximilian's execution on the *Cerro de las Campañas*, a hill on the outskirts of Querétaro, only furthers this perception. The fall of the empire has given the period the semblance of an interlude, a detour on the liberal republican path of state and nationbuilding. And, by extension, it has seemingly confirmed the political soundness of *juarismo* and the liberal cause. Indeed, Juárez's victory has given republicanism and radical liberalism a sort of political cachet and inevitability greater than it may have deserved at the time. Knowing the outcome of the story, however, will always be the advantage and hindrance of historical study. Dealing with a lost cause makes the task evermore difficult. The tendency to dismiss the empire and emperor as irrelevant to the course of Mexican history has been hard to resist. Only recently has the empire received more serious study.[3]

Liberal state-building in nineteenth-century Mexico, however, did not disappear during the Second Empire. The project begun in the 1850s continued, developed, and even prospered. As historian Patricia Galeana de Valadés observes, the Second Empire constituted an important stage in Mexican liberalism and "to ignore it equals denying an important part of our past."[4] Much like Juárez, Maximilian envisioned a strong constitutional state, the supremacy of civil authority, and the secular rule of law.[5] In many ways, the empire consolidated the liberal reforms that had preceded it and, at the same time, often expanded their scope by adding a measure of social justice.[6] Viewed closely, Maximilian's liberalism and the state that he contemplated reflected not only his times but also foreshadowed progressive trends of the early twentieth century. In short, the empire afforded an alternative in constructing a liberal Mexican state.

The diplomatic maneuvers that brought Maximilian to Mexico as well as the military aspects of the empire have been covered in detail elsewhere.[7] This essay instead will examine the components of Maximilian's liberalism, his concepts of state-building and their eventual realization, and where some key imperial policies—most notably on land, labor, and the Church— revealed the tensions inherent in enacting the liberal project. Maximilian, of course, did not operate in a vacuum. In Europe, he received advice and counsel from Napoleon III, King Leopold of Belgium, and even Pope Pius IX. Once in Mexico, moderate liberals such as José Fernando Ramírez, Manuel Orozco y Berra, and Manuel Siliceo, to name a few, headed the imperial ministries, councils, and administrative committees (with the exception of war and finance). Nevertheless, as archduke, then emperor, Maximilian had a direct hand in planning and constructing this new liberal state, and therefore, his ideas warrant some attention. The resultant imperial regime, with its strong executive and pursuit of liberal ideals, became the precursor to the later state that Juárez would attempt to erect.[8]

THE EARLY MEXICAN STATE

Setting up a monarchy in republican Mexico, as is often said, was doomed from the start. The obstacles that had forestalled the consolidation of earlier regimes are often ignored in favor of a simpler explanation: the impossibility of any American republic being successfully converted into an empire. Notwithstanding nations like France that had bounced between monarchy and republicanism throughout most of the nineteenth century, this belief in the sanctity of New World republicanism has been hard to dislodge. From this viewpoint, the empire failed not due to incessant political warfare, financial difficulties, or sundry other circumstances, but from the mere fact that it was a monarchy. The empire's collapse, it is argued, proved its nonviability as a political alternative. But upon closer inspection, the establishment of an empire in Mexico in itself was not nearly as inconceivable as many believe.

From 1810 onwards, Mexico would enjoy a representative, constitutional government. Deriving from the Spanish Cortes of Cádiz, the Constitution of 1812 became the centerpiece of a new political structure. While limiting the king's authority, the Cortes expanded its own power and radically altered perceptions of the state. By placing population ahead of privilege as the determinant for sovereignty, the constitution started the political transition from subject to citizen. Two new administrative institutions, the regional "provincial deputation" and the local "constitutional *ayuntamiento*" for towns exceeding one thousand residents, offered home rule to the New World for the first time. Their creation radically increased popular participation and representation in the political arena.[9] By the early 1820s, newly independent Mexico possessed a functioning electoral system and congresses at both the national and state levels. True, debate periodically arose over the extent of the franchise or the degree of local autonomy, but most of the political elite had no intention of returning to the form of Spanish absolutism existing before independence. While far from tranquil, constitutional processes and institutions did work in the early Republic and had support from the majority.

Accordingly, by the time of the liberal refashioning of government in the 1850s, the Republic "was a school with thirty years of experience."[10] This experience, however, must take into consideration the broad range of thought attached to the concepts of monarchy and republicanism. Unlike the obvious intellectual chasm existing between absolutism and democracy, the distinction between a constitutional monarchy and a republic could have far less practical significance. Ever since the Constitution of 1824, advocates of both liberal and conservative principles agreed on the need for legislative dominance and the restriction of executive power. The substantive difference between constitutional monarchism and republicanism, therefore, pretty much came down to the political mechanism used to choose the executive. So while no one wished a return to colonial absolutism, the door was left open for a limited constitutional monarch. Undoubtedly, this option made the idea of monarchy palatable for many. Constitutional monarchy, therefore, was not a theory of state thrust upon Mexico from outside but an evolutionary process in keeping with Mexico's political culture.[11]

At the same time, the wide array of opinion within the liberal and conservative camps must be kept in mind. All political affiliations and groupings in early republican Mexico, in one way or another, derived from the Cortes of Cádiz (the term *liberal* originated there to designate those who supported a constitutional system). While distinct coalitions did emerge, liberals as well as the conservatives organized themselves not as formal parties but more as factions of like-minded individuals sharing ideas and pursuing similar policy goals. The shifting nature of these affiliations, in fact, allowed flexibility on issues to arise as circumstances warranted. Yet, the literature often portrays these liberals as a single-minded, progressive force championing secular and popular values in nineteenth-century Mexico. Conservatives, on the contrary, are the reactionaries, elitist and clerical monarchists who desired nothing other than to return to colonial absolutism. In point of fact, the political elite in Mexico pretty much agreed on the need for a strong national state to protect Mexican territorial integrity and, above all, provide order against the seemingly constant state of pronouncements, bankruptcy, and political strife.[12]

Unfortunately, in the same way that conservatism has become popularly linked to monarchism, there exists an all-too-common tendency to conflate liberalism with republicanism (and even nationalism). But whereas republicans by definition perceived all monarchies as arbitrary, liberals objected only to arbitrary government.[13] The latter, therefore, might oppose an imperious dictatorship on ideological grounds but not necessarily monarchy as long as it was constitutional and followed the rule of law. Great Britain stood out as the preeminent example of a liberal parliamentary monarchy that safeguarded individual rights from tyranny. In theory, then, a limited monarchy might attract support from across a broad political spectrum.

The search for answers to Mexico's problems explains why calls for a foreign prince could be heard on both sides of the Atlantic. Prior to the Second Empire, talk of monarchy erupted periodically and in varied disguises. Some were pro-Spanish in nature like Padre Joaquín Arenas's abortive revolt in 1827, or Bermúdez de Castro's efforts to palm off one of Spain's second sons two decades later.[14] Others were French inspired with plans coming from minister plenipotentiaries Allege de Cyrez and Juan Alexis Viscount de Gabriac in the 1840s and 1850s.[15] Within Mexico itself, José María Gutiérrez de Estrada, a career diplomat and onetime Minister of Foreign Affairs, became a prominent spokesman for monarchy. Known for his clerical views and later promotion of the Second Empire, Gutiérrez de Estrada wrote an open letter to President Anastasio Bustamante advocating the adoption of a "true" monarchy—constitutional in form and headed by a foreign prince. Written in 1840, his epistle praised Britain and France, pointing out how the latter had only recently chosen Louis Philippe to head a constitutional monarchy of order and liberty.[16] Other Mexicans like Francisco de Paula de Arrangoiz, conservative author and later imperial diplomat, explained how "the disorder, the continuous unrest, [and] the loss of

Texas, daily increased the number of partisans for monarchy; there were few men of good faith that were not convinced that the republican form of government would lead the country to be seized by the United States."[17] Even Santa Anna during his last stand as president instructed that appeals for a prince be sent to the French and British courts as protection against the United States.[18] But security and order were only part of the picture. José Manuel Hidalgo y Esnaurrízar, the Secretary of Legation during the presidency of Zuloaga, believed that setting up a monarchy would no less save the Latin race and Catholicism in the New World.[19] Saving religion, as will become evident, became a recurrent theme.

The desire for a stable, economically viable, and efficient government, free from upheaval, strengthened after the territorial loss during the Mexican-American war. In fact, both liberals and conservatives began to clamor for an executive armed with broad powers—possibly a dictator—as the only solution for Mexico's problems.[20] For many, the attachment to a particular theory of state took a backseat to solving more pressing problems. Conservative spokesman Lucas Alamán advocated a strong hand, as did Mexican émigrés like Gutiérrez de Estrada, who championed the idea of a dictatorship "on the pattern of that established in France and everywhere else." As for liberty, Gutiérrez de Estrada felt, "we have had only too much of that, unfortunately without finding a dictator of the desired ability."[21] To the other extreme, radical liberals like Melchor Ocampo and even Juárez had come to feel that only a president freed from legislative and judicial control could implement the liberal program. As fellow liberal Manuel Siliceo explained, many in the *Reforma* government did not truly support the Constitution of 1857 but rather preferred a liberal dictatorship where their reforms could be imposed by presidential decree.[22]

From many quarters, then, the yearning to see an effective state, even under authoritarian control, had appeared well before French troops arrived. These ideas would lay the early groundwork for the Second Empire. As Francisco J. Bermúdez predicted in early 1864,

> If, then, our Sovereign [Maximilian] comes soon, you can be certain that he will be received by a general, unanimous, and enthusiastic acclamation of Mexican people that visibly do not want, nor still can, prolong a senseless fight. Many of the very liberals, of the very constitutionalists, of the very supporters of the Reform, see in the empire of Maximilian the only means of salvation that we have left. These are not words without feeling or significance: it is the truth, it is that for which, I see and hear, clear, distinct and perceptibly.[23]

Keep in mind, however, this longing for a savior took for granted that the chosen leader would enact the proper agendas. In other words, Gutiérrez de Estrada would have objected as vociferously to a liberal dictator as would Juárez to a conservative one.

MAXIMILIAN AS A LIBERAL

"I am liberal," declared Maximilian, "but this is nothing next to the empress, who is red."[24] That Maximilian considered himself a liberal comes as little surprise to historians and observers who have long noted this tendency. Historians, however, have grappled with the extent to which this liberalism was genuine. Some have seen his progressive liberal policies as simply a product of his royal upbringing and "the old paternal spirit of his royal ancestors."[25] For others, it was mere mimicry of pre-existing laws, political expediency, or just an ironic twist to the French Intervention—a sort of poetic justice for the conservatives who brought the archduke to Mexico. Arrangoiz, for instance, accused Maximilian of only wanting to impress German ultraliberals with his democratic ideals, "as if monarchy and democracy could exist together." In fact, he contended that the only acceptable policies undertaken by the emperor had merely imitated those of the viceroyalty.[26] While it was true that Maximilian wished to attract liberals to his cause, his belief in liberal principles was sincere and not for the sake of convenience or opportunism. If it were, abandoning conservative support made little sense.

Nephew of Austrian Emperor Ferdinand, Maximilian was two years younger than his brother Franz Josef who acceded to the Austrian throne in 1848.[27] As children, both brothers followed an identical course of study under their tutor, Count Charles de Bombelles, who instilled a practical curriculum, especially when it came to the Catholic religion.[28] Apart from Bombelles, little evidence exists as to specific intellectual influences on the archduke. But, considering his position as second in line to the throne, Maximilian most likely had at least passing familiarity with the current thinkers of the age. One suggested possibility has been the German thinker, Lorenz von Stein, whose *Der Sozialismus und Kommunismus des heutigen Frankreich* (1842) introduced French utopian socialism to Germany. Stein's contention that the state should not represent a single class interest but instead act as a peacemaker between opposing interests closely paralleled the archduke's thinking.[29] On more than one occasion, Maximilian declared his intention to rise above party factionalism in order to balance political interests. Only in this way could a monarch hope to construct a strong and efficient government.

Unlike standard portrayals of the archduke as indecisive and ill-informed, Maximilian had confidence in matching his abilities against the other crowned heads of Europe. A case in point, when visiting Belgium in 1856, he wrote to his brother Franz Josef concerning King Leopold, uncle to Britain's Queen Victoria as well as Maximilian's future father-in-law. The king had cultivated a reputation in Europe as a "political pope, before whose pronouncements all the rulers of Europe must bow." Maximilian would wryly observed how Leopold "repeated several times the hackneyed phrase that he was the Nestor among monarchs and that all of them might learn from him." However, when Leopold promised to give the archduke "a lecture upon political science and the balance of Europe," Maximilian—though just twenty-four years old—received the offer "yawning in spirit."[30] At the same time, however, he understood the importance of statecraft and a wise executive in the fate of a country. As he traveled through Belgium, Maximilian described it as

> the most lovely, blooming land that I have yet seen; a country possessing all the elements of prosperity and plenty; a fertile soil, rich cities crowded closely together, harbours, the sea, a well-laid-out network of railways, commerce and factories. . . . the whole country is well cultivated; forests of factory chimneys, industrial establishments, on a scale which I had never seen before, cover whole stretches of the landscape. Belgium fully deserves the self-chosen name of a model country; this it undoubtedly owes in the first place to the prudent procedure of the King, and it is very much to be wondered whether the peace of the kingdom and the dynasty will survive Leopold I.[31]

When the offer of a Mexican crown presented itself, Maximilian must have seen it as an opportunity to accomplish similar things in Mexico.

Maximilian saw himself as a product of his times, a "modern" individual of the nineteenth century. His progressive ideas soon attracted attention outside of Austrian circles. Government officials in Great Britain, for instance, floated the idea that the archduke should head an independent Hungarian government owing to his liberal spirit and enlightened thinking.[32] It was in Italy, however, that Maximilian got his first chance to place his liberalism into practice after being appointed governor-general of the Austrian provinces of Lombardy and Venetia. Entering Milan in April 1857, he resolved to set the provinces on a solid and equitable base and, by all accounts, undertook the mission with considerable passion. Although the symbol of colonial domination, Maximilian felt that material progress coupled with compassionate liberal rule would mitigate and even legitimate Austrian authority over Venetia and Lombardy.[33] Once there, he launched a progressive slate of public works, urban renewal, and social services to reconcile the rebellious Italian provinces to Austrian rule. Gutiérrez de Estrada, the longtime monarchist, recounted how the Italian people could not deny "the benefits lavished by the generous hand of the archduke." Each day, he recounted, witnessed some useful enterprise, a healthful reform, suppression of some abuse, or the abolition of some privilege.[34]

Maximilian, nonetheless, became depressed that he had to act "as the representative of an inactive Government with no ideas" that trifled with the goodwill of the masses. He even questioned whether he could still follow instructions from Vienna in good conscience.[35] Sentiment in the area unfortunately had passed the point where liberal reforms would have had an impact.[36] Being summarily dismissed after less than two years, the arch-duke realized the extent to which Italian nationalism and Austrian bungling had frustrated his efforts. Count Camillo di Cavour, the Foreign Minister of Piedmont-Sardinia and sworn enemy of Austrian rule, still and all, recognized the value in the archduke's approach:

> The man who was our worst enemy in Lombardy, whom we feared the most, and of whom every day we watched the progress, has been dismissed. Already his perseverance, his fair and liberal spirit, had won him many of our supporters. Lombardy had never been so prosperous, so well administered. Then, thank God, the dear Viennese government intervenes, and in its usual way manages to make a mess of everything, and to ruin its chances by recalling the Emperor's brother, because his wise reforms had displeased the old die-hards in Vienna.[37]

Despite his short tenure, the archduke's Italian experience laid the groundwork for his thinking in Mexico. Mexico offered a clean slate, so he thought, where his liberal ideas could be implemented without interference. This time, Maximilian would enter as an emperor, not as someone else's governor.

CONCEPTS OF STATE

Critical to the whole issue of the imperial state is the nature of the government that Maximilian contemplated. No doubt Maximilian intended to rule as a constitutional monarch. Less well known, however, is the form that this liberal empire in Mexico would take. Although he never introduced a formal constitution, Maximilian did promulgate an *Estatuto Provisional del Imperio Mexicano* in 1865 to serve as an interim measure until times permitted a more formal political document. These documents provide insight into what the empire might have been.

As a Habsburg, Maximilian expressed a measure of ambivalence toward constitutional regimes. This was not surprising inasmuch as Franz Josef ruled Austria in a neo-absolutist manner. After taking the throne in 1848, Franz Josef had scuttled plans for a representative diet as well as permanently "suspending" a tentative constitution in 1851. Maximilian's cynical feelings about constitutions, however, seemed prompted as much or more by notions of protocol and decorum than from any deep-seated antipathy toward representative government itself. On a visit to King Leopold in 1857, for instance, he attended a New Year's ceremony where for nearly five hours he "had to swallow all the hackneyed phrases ground out to each other by the constitutional ruler and the various authorities and corporate bodies." In fact, he felt that, the whole affair was calculated to inspire the unprejudiced observer with a profound disgust for constitutional shams. On Twelfth-night I was offered another spectacle: that of a constitutional court ball. Since the Belgian regime has not consented to establish a hard and fast rule for presentation at court, so that it is not easy to reject any application, it may be imagined how mixed the company at such a ball must be. The higher nobility of the land rubs shoulders with its own tailors and cobblers; all the English shopkeepers who have retired to Brussels on grounds of economy have access to the ball with their respective families.[38]

But when it came to himself, such as during a visit to Brazil in 1860, he "felt anxious to escape all the ceremony and etiquette appropriate to my rank, and to be left to myself to enjoy my first visit to the tropics in freedom, with impressions undisturbed by the presence of a gold stick in waiting, acting as guide."[39] Maximilian sometimes found reconciling his liberalism with his royal position troublesome.

Juárez and his followers had a powerful political symbol in the Constitution of 1857. It served not only as a banner of legitimacy but also as the proposed panacea to regenerate the country. Liberals hoped it would create a modern society based on the sovereignty of the people, legal equality, protection of private property, and individual rights. With the memory of Santa Anna's conservative dictatorship (1853–1855) still lingering in their minds, the moderate and radical liberals who drafted the constitution reasoned that centralism and executive power had been at the root of Mexico's problems. Though this was not the case, as Brian Hamnett correctly points out, the constitution constructed a federal system with a strong legislature and a weakened executive who held consultative but not veto power over legislation.[40] In fact, since true power was vested in Congress, there seemed little need for the constitution to limit presidential re-election. But faced with rising opposition from the Church, conservatives, and a disruptive legislature, the Constitution of 1857 gradually lost support from even some liberals.

Given Mexico's political past, a new empire could not realistically return to colonial absolutism but would have to have some kind of representative government. In late 1863, Maximilian met with Mexican émigrés like Gutiérrez de Estrada at Miramar castle, where the outlines of a new political system emerged. By September, Carlota took a draft of the proposed constitution to Brussels for her father's comment. Leopold responded favorably to "Max's proclaiming himself a constitutional emperor." While he endorsed the idea of a constitution, Leopold advised that it should be "very elastic," avoiding the "great mistake" made in Belgium of putting in too many points that were "capable of change or emendation." After evaluating two sample articles on press freedom, for instance, Leopold suggested adopting the simpler version. Although equality before the law went "without saying" for Leopold, he advised against the right of assembly since granting it to people of the Latin race was "impossible." He also agreed with a provision for a state religion as in Brazil but only if something could be "done" for toleration.[41] The later *Estatuto Provisional* would follow Leopold's advice by including only broad concepts and leaving the details to individual decrees.

The draft constitution then made its way to Napoleon III, who studied it with Empress Eugénie for more than two hours. The French emperor was quick to point out the paradox between the exigencies of state-building and political freedom. In summing up his views, Napoleon wrote to Maximilian:

> But allow me to call your attention emphatically to one point: a state which is sunk in anarchy is not to be regenerated by parliamentary liberty. What is wanted in Mexico is a liberal dictatorship. I mean a strong power, which shall proclaim the great basic principles of modern civilization, such as equality before the law, civil and religious liberty, an honest administration, and an equitable system of justice. As regards the constitution, that must be the work of time, and I believe that even if it has been promised and elaborated, it should not be really applied until several years have passed, the country is pacified and the Government in good working order.[42]

For the French emperor, enlightened despotism seemed a safer course of action. Just as Juárez would govern with emergency powers in times of crisis, Maximilian was counseled to do the same.

Although the proposed constitution for Mexico had been developed without Maximilian ever having visited the country that he would rule, it embodied many of the basic tenets found in the Constitution of 1857. In more than forty articles set down in Carlota's handwriting, the "Constitution for the Empire of Mexico" outlined the fundamental structures and features for the future empire.[43] The draft, however, did not just replicate other European constitutions but contained many provisions that went beyond most contemporary models. It started with a bold declaration: "Mexico is free, sovereign, and independent." At first glance, the words might seem ironic for a foreign-born emperor-designate to declare about a country currently occupied by foreign troops. But Maximilian's motives for going to Mexico contrasted with those of the French. He planned to rule as a nationalist, not as the puppet of another country. Whereas Napoleon III had imperial spoils in mind for France, Maximilian represented only himself.[44] Prior to leaving for Mexico, he had agreed to a family compact—though under protest—renouncing all future dynastic claims in Austria for himself as well as any heirs. Once signed, he had little incentive to return home.

The proposal then proceeded to define the basic principle of citizenship in Mexico. The inclusion of this article, elaborated later in the *Estatuto Provisional*, illustrated Maximilian's intention to govern "citizens" rather than imperial "subjects." These citizens would enjoy equality without regard to rank. As a liberal, Maximilian placed great stock in promoting the principle of equality before the law. Few liberal doctrines had more significance for Mexico than legal equality, which was the weapon used by *Reforma* liberals to fight corporatism. For many (including the archduke), juridical equality and the rule of law evinced modernity. *Equidad en justicia*, in fact, became the motto of the Second Empire.

As a guard against arbitrary or despotic rule, the constitution also included a slate of individual protections for its citizens that equaled or surpassed the Constitution of 1857. Naturally, the new empire would have a free press, a mainstay of liberal thought, along with the guaranteed inviolability of private property except for the public good. Individuals, moreover, could not be deprived of their liberty except by duly authorized judges or tribunals. In this way, individual liberty took precedence. Even though the draft constitution declared Roman Catholicism as the religion of state, it did not exclude the practice of other faiths. On this point, the archduke had already committed to a position that would create a major rupture with his clerical-conservative supporters.

The new empire would have a ministerial form of government consisting of a Council of Ministers, an advisory Council of State, and a unicameral senate. As emperor, Maximilian retained a full range of powers such as the right to name ministers, initiate laws, commute sentences, and make decisions on war and peace. The proposed senate chamber, however, consisted of an interesting mix of imperial control, independent authority, and popular representation. When Carlota first presented her father with the idea of a senate, King Leopold had opposed it, especially for one that held real power. Leopold believed "that a senate on the American plan would meet the case better, for that is really conservative."[45] Likewise, Napoleon III saw danger in having a one-chamber assembly as well as the provision for the franchise, as will be seen.[46] The archduke chose not to heed this advice.

This planned senate reveals much about the nature of the state that was envisioned. It would contain three sections, each with one hundred imperial senators holding legislative immunity and serving out six-year terms. The first section displayed an autocratic quality with the senators appointed personally by the emperor. The second section, far more eclectic, would reflect a broader cross-section of society. It would contain the imperial princes at their majority; the religious hierarchy of bishops, archbishops, and any future cardinals; departmental governors and the *alcaldes* of large cities; rectors of the University as well as heads of the *academias;* and, finally, the Supreme Court along with a to-be-established Court of Commerce. Forty of the section's members would derive from among the large landowners of the nation. At a later date, the senate would add ten members representing industry—a likely reflection of the archduke's optimism in reviving Mexico's economy. In this second section, it is interesting to note, the imperial government lacked direct control over selecting members except for the governors. Finally, the chamber's third section, by far the most democratic and progressive, would consist of two senators from each of the fifty departments, elected by the "vote of the citizens of the departments." This proposed enfranchisement, in fact, was an idea not yet practiced in Maximilian's own central Europe. Showing Maximilian's awareness of the sensitive nature of these provisions, he reportedly left unresolved the details of the selection process "not to provoke the conservatives."[47]

As a general rule, the Council of State would have the responsibility to initiate and prepare legislation for the emperor's approval. The senate's power, however, was far from symbolic. It also possessed legislative power to suggest or draft laws on issues of great national importance. The senate, moreover, possessed the authority to change the constitution by a two-thirds majority vote, not a small matter given its representative makeup. Of its powers, the most interesting concerned the responsibility for determining the line of succession if there existed no heir to the throne—a crucial issue for Maximilian since the royal couple had gone six years without children. Though limited, the proposed senate did have a true legislative role and a fair measure of popular representation, especially in comparison with Austria's own government. Bear in mind, its republican counterpart, the Constitution of 1857, had granted only indirect elections for president and congressional deputies.

In September 1863, José Manuel Hidalgo sent a copy of the proposed constitution to Juan Nepomuceno Almonte, the head of the Regency in Mexico.[48] A letter accompanied the draft and, in all likelihood, represented Maximilian's own views on the subject. It explained to Almonte how the "times" compelled European monarchs to reign according to liberal principles (including individual guarantees) if they did not want to be "swept away." Accordingly, the new Mexican empire needed to follow the pattern set by the British or French rather than reinstall a new absolutism in Mexico. Hidalgo made clear how, although the proposed constitution borrowed elements from its French and Belgian counterparts, many provisions came directly from the archduke's "inspiration." At this point, the letter turned conspiratorial, informing Almonte that he would be the only one of the three Regency members to know that Maximilian had written the constitution himself. The Regency, Hidalgo's letter instructed Almonte, should proceed in setting up a *cámara* according to Mexico's 1845 electoral law. This *cámara* would then vote on the constitution with minimal discussion. Then, when Maximilian arrived, he would approve the constitution and swear an oath to support it, requiring all public employees and soldiers to do the same.[49] Clearly, Maximilian wanted the constitution to seem an outgrowth of democratic processes within Mexico. In this way, the constitution would gain a degree of legitimacy that it would otherwise lack if it were imposed from outside. To all appearances, Leopold knew of this plan since he favored the idea of the constitution being approved by a national assembly rather than Maximilian promulgating it himself. "It is quite a good thing," noted Leopold, for Maximilian "to adapt himself a little to the wishes of the Mexicans, and very natural that they should demand it."[50] Due to his conservative views, however, Almonte simply dropped the whole matter.[51]

LEGITIMACY AND THE STATE

As French troops entered Mexico City in June 1863, a caretaker government chose a collection of thirty-five distinguished—and predominately conservative—residents of the city to "decide" the form of state. This junta appointed three individuals (General Mariano Salas, a former republican president; Antonio Pelagio Labastida, the exiled bishop of Puebla; and Juan N. Almonte) as an executive triumvirate. It then chose an additional 215 eminent landowners, lawyers, priests, and businessmen to round out an "Assembly of Notables." The assembly passed four resolutions accordant with French wishes: henceforth, Mexico would have a limited hereditary monarchy under a Catholic prince; the monarch would hold the title of emperor; the offer would go first to Maximilian; and if he refused, the assembly would ask Napoleon III to recommend another Catholic prince. On July 11, 1863, the executive triumvirate became the Regency.[52]

A ten-member Mexican delegation soon arrived in Trieste to present the "crown of the Mexican Empire" to Maximilian. The president of the delegation, Gutiérrez de Estrada, gave a recitation "of our tribulations and misfortunes" that had made "the name of Mexico synonymous with desolation and ruin." Gutiérrez blamed republican institutions, "so contrary to our natural constitution, to our customs and traditions," that had been unable to preserve Mexico's splendid heritage. While republicanism might be the pride of Mexico's neighbor, it had brought nothing to the country but "an incessant source of the cruelest misfortunes."[53] Maximilian then responded. He thanked the delegation (in Spanish) but informed them that his acceptance would be conditional:

> Assuring the independence and prosperity of Mexico under the aegis of stable and free institutions is a noble enterprise. I must nevertheless acknowledge, in complete agreement with His Majesty, the Emperor of the French, whose glorious initiative has made possible the regeneration of your beautiful homeland, that monarchy could not be reestablished on a solid and legitimate base unless the whole nation, expressing its will freely, desired to ratify the vote of the capital. Thus, I should first make the acceptance of the throne offered to me dependent upon the outcome of the votes from the majority of the country. On the other hand, appreciating the sacred duties of a sovereign, it is essential that I ask for indispensable guarantees for the Empire about to be reconstituted, to secure

it from the dangers that would threaten its integrity and independence. If these pledges for a secure future would be obtained and the universal selection of the noble Mexican people fell to me, with the secure consent of the august head of my family and confident in the support of the Almighty, I will be willing to accept the crown. In the event that Providence calls me to the high civilizing mission that goes together with this crown, I declare to you, gentlemen, from now on, my firm resolution of following the salutary example of my brother the emperor [Napoleon III], opening up to the country, by means of a constitutional regime, the broad avenue of progress based on order and morality and of sealing with my oath that as soon as that vast territory is pacified, the fundamental covenant with the nation. Only this way, will a new and truly national politics be inaugurated, in which the various parties, forgetting their old discord, would work in common to give Mexico the prominent position that it seems to be destined for among the pueblos under a government that has in principle, making prevail equity in justice.[54]

Thus, once a plebiscite was held, Maximilian would bring order, justice, and a constitutional government to Mexico as soon as conditions permitted.

Since these delegates hardly represented public opinion, their offer of the crown provided little reassurance. No longer could divine law alone sustain a monarch's mandate to rule. Napoleon III, in fact, prided himself that his political authority rested on universal suffrage. Maximilian as well understood that a new Mexican empire had little hope of survival without a national consensus. Prideful that he could not ascend the throne as a usurper or adventurer, Maximilian wanted a sense of legality to dispel the impression that French arms offered the throne, so he insisted on a plebiscite as "one of the essential conditions" for his acceptance.[55] Although French forces reported in late 1863 that sixty-six localities including the capital, Puebla, Veracruz, and scattered villages along the Veracruz road endorsed the empire, the future emperor made clear that the "great majority" must freely elect the political system under which they would live. Only then would he be "ready to abandon Europe to accept the vote of the Mexican people."[56]

Though confident in the ultimate outcome, Maximilian awaited confirmation until he could "know the votes of the rest of the country."[57] Known as "*actas de adhesión*," these documents, drafted by villages and cities alike, recited their community's acceptance of the intervention and then attached the signatures of local notables. Since the extent to which these *actas* reflected the true views of all the residents was doubtful, most historians have chosen to overlook them.[58] Contained within these *actas*, however, are insights into the political and social agendas held by these individuals, many of whom represented the original supporters of the empire.

Most revealing are the extent to which the ideas expressed as to the Church and monarchy differed from Maximilian's own. Documents from Puebla provide a useful illustration. In a special council meeting on June 13,

1863, the prefecto político of Puebla, Fernando Pardo, and nineteen other officials including local *alcaldes, regidores,* and the members of the *ayuntamiento* met to discuss and then grant their "solemn" adherence to the French Intervention. Not only did they accept the French intervention on behalf of the state but also dedicated "votes of eternal gratitude" to the worthy French Emperor for undertaking "the grand work of Mexico's political regeneration." The *acta* praised Napoleon III and the expeditionary army for reassuring the public that the independence of Mexico was "far from being in danger." The sole intention of the intervention, claimed the authorities, was to promote the reconstruction of the social fabric and provide happiness, and glory to the nation. Republicanism unfortunately had placed Mexico on the "edge of an abyss" and had to be replaced by a system of "order and morality." Puebla's acceptance would serve as an example to other parts of the republic.[59] In this way, the public officials in Puebla made clear their desire to see a government in Mexico that would restore order and protect religion.

The following day, Puebla's supreme tribunal added its own declaration that provides further indication of their motivation. The tribunal's *acta* related how the two political parties in Mexico had constantly disputed power. One party—the conservatives—carried as its banner the flag of the "immortal Iturbide" while the other—the liberals—proclaimed its program in two words, "freedom and progress . . . magical words in their literal sense, but ominous for men of integrity." In this struggle, explained the document, conservatives had repeatedly endured defeat that destroyed the freedoms, honor, and best interests of the nation. The liberals, in contrast, had banned public worship, attacked religious beliefs, suppressed public and private guarantees, and subverted all the principles on which the social order rested. As a result, both parties as well as the general public had come to realize that the republican system had not promoted the country's welfare. The tribunal members even questioned Mexico's future under this "disastrous" democratic principle. For them, monarchy was "consistent with the spirit of the century, with national traditions, old customs, and the hopes of men devoted to the honor and happiness of their homeland." As the depository of the grand elements of glory and greatness, it was the only system that could "preside over the noble aspirations" of the Mexican people. Monarchy had been adopted by "the most enlightened nations of the globe" and epitomized "the perfection of governments, the crown of the noble efforts of honesty and virtue, the shield of true liberty, and the most glorious triumph of social science."[60] Beneath these grandiloquent words, however, can be seen a rejection of democratic principles and a desire to return to autocratic rule for the sake of the faith.

Elsewhere in Puebla, the local *cura* of San Andrés Cholula repeated how the people coveted a government of "order and morality" that would respect "the Catholic beliefs of all Mexicans" and would grant "true guarantees to all the residents of Mexico, respect for property, [and] individual liberty."[61] These guarantees of property and liberty, of course, were not the same individual rights advocated by liberals. Instead, they were calls for protecting Church holdings and upholding privilege. Over and again, the themes of order and religion reemerged. In another pueblo, Santa Clara Ocoyucan explained how the liberal party promised freedom, enlightenment, and progress but only created divisions. Ever since the "wicked influence" of the United States Minister to Mexico, Joel R. Poinsett, who some forty years earlier had introduced "the horrible denomination of the *Yorquinos,*" Mexico had experienced continuous "pronouncements, fratricidal struggles, sieges, looting, robberies and all sorts of violations." At their core, republican theories were "pure illusions" unlike the monarchy that had governed from before the conquest and for three centuries afterwards, "in whose time was enjoyed peace, abundance, and public happiness."[62] Outside of Puebla, the Villa de Santiago del Rio in San Luis Potosí proclaimed that the "only means" to save the religion and independence of Mexico was support for foreign intervention. Experience had shown that monarchy was the form of state "that more suits Mexico," and only it could assure the "happiness of our very beloved homeland."[63] Clearly, all the signatories to these various documents favored at least some restoration of Church power and a monarchy more in keeping with colonial times than with modern constitutionalism. The political lines, in short, had been drawn with these supporters well before Maximilian arrived.

In the end, the regents claimed that all important Mexican cities and towns accepted the empire, encompassing three-quarters of the territory and four-fifths of the population. In reality, the French forces that "collected" these votes occupied only a fraction of the countryside and controlled even less.[64] Even Maximilian's cousin, Emperor Dom Pedro II of Brazil, questioned, "how do you appreciate such liberty at a distance, and across foreign bayonets?"[65] Nevertheless, Maximilian's repeated insistence on the vote and his monitoring of the tallies indicated the importance of the mandate in his thinking.

THE LIBERAL EMPEROR

"Only by means of truly free institutions, strict justice, [and] protection to people and property," Maximilian told local authorities in Puebla, "will the ruler and his representatives be able to take the country along the path of progress that leads to prosperity and true greatness."[66] Ten months later, on April 10, 1865—the anniversary of Maximilian's acceptance of the throne— the *Estatuto Provisional del Imperio Mexicano* appeared, which provided a working outline for all branches of public administration until the establishment of order permitted a permanent constitution to be enacted.[67] The *Estatuto*, as will be seen, lacked the provision for the imperial senate contained in the earlier draft constitution, but still offered many of the liberal protections and guarantees found in the Constitution of 1857. With eighty-one articles, the *Estatuto* officially established a moderate and hereditary monarchy headed by a Catholic prince. The emperor would swear an oath before the grand bodies of state "to secure by all means within my reach, the well-being and prosperity of the Nation, to defend its independence and preserve the integrity of its territory." Under the *Estatuto*, national sovereignty did not rest in the people, as it did in the Constitution of 1857, but in the emperor's representation of them. Maximilian would exercise this sovereignty through advisory bodies such as the Council of Ministers.[68]

The statute created a strong centralized government along with a strict rationalization of authority. Article 52 divided the empire into eight grand divisions, the divisions into fifty departments, the departments into districts, and the districts into municipalities. The emperor would appoint a *comisario imperial* to head each division, entrusted with encouraging development and ensuring good administration in the departments under his care. Special inspectors (*visitadores*) would be used when and where needed. *Prefectos políticos*, also named by Maximilian, would reside in each departmental capital and serve as an administrative "delegate" of the emperor. Assisting them would be *subprefectos* (appointed by the *prefecto*) and a special council comprising a "most distinguished" member of the judiciary, a fiscal administrator, a landowner, merchant, and a miner or industrialist depending on the department. Thus, imperial administrators at the intermediate and upper levels would receive their appointments directly from the emperor or through other appointed officials.

At the local level, however, the *Estatuto* granted direct representation. Each "population" would have its own municipal administration (*alcaldes, ayuntamientos,* and *comisarios municipales*) allocated proportionately. Each *ayuntamiento* would "be popularly chosen by direct election and be renewed by half each year." The subsequent *ley electoral* of November 1, 1865, detailed the naming of the *ayuntamiento* through the direct popular vote of citizens twenty-one years old and over. However, there were restrictions. Voters had to be literate and residents of their community for more than a year. Candidates for office, additionally, had to be over twenty-five years old and pay a direct annual tax of at least twenty pesos. While the Constitution of 1857 did not contain a literacy or tax requirement, those obligations in the *Estatuto* applied only to municipalities numbering more than five thousand residents. This reflected the recognition that residents of smaller communities might lack the educational facilities or the financial means to take part in the electoral system otherwise.[69] In this respect, the actual limitations on popular participation were modest. As for *alcaldes*, Maximilian would name the *alcalde* in Mexico City while elsewhere the *prefecto* would have the authority (subject to approval). A governmental re-organization in June 1866, however, expanded representation by allowing the direct election of *alcaldes*. Thus, while the empire did not yet have an elected senate, it did offer a range of local representation.

As the draft constitution had done, the *Estatuto* specified who qualified as "Mexican" and the political basis for citizenship. It defined Mexicans as fathers of legitimate children or mothers of illegitimate children living in or outside of Mexico.[70] In addition, other categories included naturalized foreigners, children born in Mexico of foreign parents who chose Mexican citizenship, and, most controversially, foreigners who acquired territory in Mexico.[71] In contrast, the statute designated citizens (race not being a factor) as those individuals over twenty-one years old and living an honest way of life. As citizens, the individuals had to register in their municipalities and discharge the duty of voting in popular elections where no legal impediment existed. In this way, the statute combined the notions of citizenship and democracy at the local level.

Included in the *Estatuto* was a laundry list of liberal protections described for the first time as "individual guarantees."[72] Granted to all citizens subject to appropriate restrictions, these guarantees ensured equality before the law, personal security as well as that of property, the free exercise of religion, and the right to publish opinions. The concept of legal equality must have seemed unambiguous since the statute contained no elaboration on the concept. As for personal rights, however, it went into greater detail. Only the competent authority, for instance, could issue a warrant to search a home or detain a suspect of a crime. By the third day after arrest, a judge would decide if enough evidence existed to hold the detainee over for trial. Only in cases of crimes against the state or disturbing the public order could individuals be detained for longer. The accused would also be entitled to know the accuser and the charges against them to prepare a defense. With all trials public, except in cases of danger to order or morals, the magistrates and judges would enjoy absolute independence and immunity in exercising their judicial functions. In short, these legal protections mirrored those granted by the *Reforma* a few years earlier.

Other liberties followed. Much the same as the Constitution of 1857, the statute prohibited slavery and specified that any slaves entering Mexico would become free—an issue of concern for the empire considering the imminent fall of the Confederacy. And like its republican predecessor, no individual could demand free or forced service of another nor contract their own service except on a temporary basis. This protection, as will be seen, would be later extended into a direct challenge to peonage. In true liberal fashion, the statute prohibited the confiscation of goods and proclaimed property to be "inviolable" except in instances of proven public utility and prompt indemnity. Finally, the empire upheld the freedom of the press, stating that no individual could be molested for their opinions or impeded in publishing them. A later press law gave all individuals the right to express their opinions freely and voice any objections to official acts as long as done with due respect. Morally offensive comments, spreading discord or political unrest, as well as libelous attacks, however, would be subject to censure.[73] In regards to all these individual rights, only the emperor or *comisarios imperiales* could temporarily suspend them for the conservation of peace and public order.

Though not quite what a liberal republican would have had in mind, the *Estatuto* did go far in granting a level of representation and protection to its citizens. Recognizing the liberal merits contained in these articles, opponents of the regime complained less about the ideas contained in the *Estatuto* itself and more about the consistency of their execution. One anonymous author charged that Maximilian had served as both legislator and executive, sometimes repealing powers and encroaching on the functions of the judiciary. The emperor "published a Statute, it is true; but he himself, or his agents, trampled it. He created a council; but not popular election, and not even followed their decisions when he consulted it." The author believed it a "crime" to have offered a system of government that set down individual guarantees along with the means to make them effective and then to "trample" and "violate" those sacred principles at each step.[74] Obviously, liberal elements contained in the imperial state had appeal.

IMPERIAL POLICIES

Maximilian felt that his "energetic and liberal" policies would win over the hearts and minds of the people, hoping some day even to shake hands with Juárez.[75] Even among imperial enemies, Maximilian's policies did have resonance at times. In Puebla's western sierra, for example, liberal commander Rafael Cravioto fought the Intervention until his capitulation in early 1865. Since the majority of the nation had accepted monarchy "tacitly or expressly," Cravioto noted how

> the acts of His Majesty the Emperor prove in an unequivocal way [his] good intention to preserve and develop the progressive liberal ideas prevailing in the country and after having accepted the throne of Mexico and giving up his future rights in Austria, he has become Mexican, and, as such, offers the glorification of the empire, the integrity of its territory, [and] the development and protection of the sciences and arts that are the source where all public wealth and the welfare of all social classes emanates.[76]

Few rulers have received such praise from their opponents. Not surprising, however, tensions soon erupted between these liberal ideas and the conservatives who first supported the empire. The emperor naturally preferred the political company of moderate liberals and his entourage brought from Europe. In turn, conservatives objected to being shut out from positions of power within the emperor's inner circle and the government in general. When Maximilian arrived, he staffed the imperial ministries with moderate liberals such as Juan de Dios Peza (War), Luis Robles Pezuela (Development), Pedro Escudero Echánove (Justice), and José Fernando Ramírez (Foreign Affairs). Conservative ministers serving the Regency such as José María González de la Vega (Government) were replaced by the more liberal ones like José María Cortes y Esparza. In fact, only the conservative Joaquín Velázquez de León had been retained from the Regency as Minister of State. The empire even packed the *prefecturas* with liberals and instructed all public officials not to molest former *juaristas*.[77]

Equally irksome to conservatives, Maximilian brought a coterie from Europe with him comprising his private cabinet. It included his former secretary at Miramar, Baron De Pont, a career diplomat from Austria's Foreign Affairs Ministry; Sebastian Scherzenlechner, a Hungarian valet at Schönbrunn who later became his personal secretary; Stefan Herzfeld, a naval officer and his aide-de-camp; and Félix Eloin, a Belgian mining engineer recommended by Leopold. The latter caused particular irritation since Eloin, as head of the private cabinet, was not only an anti-clerical Protestant but also anti-French.[78] Arrangoiz derisively described this inner circle as "a tower of Babel," filled with those who did not speak Spanish, had no knowledge of Mexico, and had little loyalty to the emperor.[79]

For staunch conservatives who had originally anticipated a restoration, Maximilian became a traitor for his failure to underwrite their agenda. Even before settling in, Maximilian had outraged many of them by lifting the Regency ban on the anti-Conservative song *Los Cangrejos* (The Crabs).[80] The most disturbing aspect of this imperial betrayal, however, involved the strengthening of the state's secular domination over the Church. Like other Catholic rulers in the nineteenth century, both Carlota and Maximilian considered themselves true believers but imbued with a healthy dose of anti-clericalism. While individual parish priests often received praise, Maximilian routinely castigated the Church hierarchy for interfering in state affairs rather than confining itself to its spiritual and educational duties. A "pure" Christianity, as many felt, would uplift and buttress the cause of civilization.[81] Through a series of decrees spanning several months, Maximilian reissued virtually all of the anti-clerical legislation passed during the *Reforma*.

Of them all, the *Ley Lerdo*, the liberal law that had eliminated corporate land ownership, had particular importance. In July 1862, even before the French forces had taken Mexico City, Napoleon III had instructed the head of the expeditionary force, General Élie Frédéric Forey, to support religion but to keep in place all transfers of Church property.[82] At this time, Maximilian admitted being "still very little acquainted with all the factors related to the so complex matter of the church property to allow me to emit a judgment, mainly since Monsignor Labastida [the bishop of Puebla] abstained to touch on the point during the talks that I had with him before his exit for Mexico."[83] Once in Mexico, however, Maximilian made up his mind. Despite negotiations with Monsignor Meglia, a special papal nuncio sent to resolve the issue, Maximilian reaffirmed the *Ley Lerdo* on December 27, 1864. The decree not only confirmed the ownership for those who had purchased the *bienes nacionales* but also renewed government sale of the property. For clerical-conservatives, this action gave unequivocal evidence of the emperor's hostility toward the Church. Two months later, an equally disturbing decree followed: religious toleration. Although the Second Empire recognized Catholicism as the religion of state, individuals were allowed to practice other religions as long as they did not violate public morals. This decision coincided with the liberal view that religious liberty would bring Mexico in line with other nations; as French General Forey noted, it was a "grand principle of modern society."[84]

The empire announced a further series of measures that continued the secularization of the state such as a civil registry, secular cemeteries, and government control over publishing papal bulls.[85] Clerical-conservative backers of the empire, of course, had expected compensation for their backing of the archduke and Napoleon III. Once these reform laws were upheld, little reason for support remained. For example, Bishop Pelagio Antonio de Labastida had resigned his seat on the Regency over the failure to return Church property even before Maximilian arrived. Other conservatives tried working with the empire but soon became disillusioned. A prime example was Francisco Arrangoiz, who resigned his imperial diplomatic posts in protest. Feeling an acute sense of betrayal, he felt that Maximilian did not appreciate how conservatives desired only "peace and union" for Mexico and not vengeance. By filling the imperial administration almost exclusively with republicans, the emperor had pushed aside those who had brought him to the throne. In the end, Arrangoiz, attributed the collapse of the empire to Maximilian's anti-clerical decrees. Granting freedom of religion, failing to return Church property, and even allowing government offices to stay open on Sunday had all openly opposed the precepts of the Catholic Church.[86]

Indeed, Maximilian did not live up to conservative expectations, but the emperor even faced opposition from some of his moderate liberal supporters when imperial policies became too socially progressive. Decrees concerning land and labor, particularly regarding indigenous communities, came under special scrutiny from all sides. By and large, liberals agreed that freeing land held in mortmain would make it available for economic development. This meant not only corporate land held by the Church but also indigenous village landholding that many saw as the cause for the "backwardness" of Mexican peasant agriculture. Breaking up communal landholding would have the added benefit of making indigenous peoples socially productive through integration. Although a steadfast believer in private property and supporter of nationalized property, Maximilian tempered his liberalism with a measure of social justice when it came to indigenous holdings. Liberal theory and practice, at times, conflicted.

Though the empire did not return the land taken under the liberals' desamortization law, it did take steps to help Indian communities deal with the disruptions.[87] In this way, historian Jean Meyer argues that Maximilian followed a version of social liberalism in Mexico "when he attempted to make less painful and unjust for '*las clases menesterosas*' the transition from the old to the new social and economic order."[88] Three decrees containing a "high spirit of social justice" had particular importance for the villages.[89] The first, the "*Ley para dirimir las diferencias sobre tierras y aguas entre los pueblos*," promulgated on November 1, 1865, detailed how pueblos could pursue claims for property or water rights against either individuals or other villages. Pueblos could present their claim to the local *prefecto superior* while the defendant, either a pueblo or individual, would do the same within one month or forfeit the claim.[90] This extra level of legal protection for land and water rights went beyond what prior governments had offered indigenous villages.

On June 26, 1866, the imperial government passed a second decree designed to help villages deal with the breakup of communal lands. While corporate bodies still could not own land outright in accordance with the *Ley Lerdo*, the empire finessed the issue by allowing full ownership of communal and *repartimiento* lands (those held in usufruct) to pueblo residents as individuals. The land would be awarded preferring poor to rich, married to single, families to those without. In a calculated move to avoid future land concentration and in line with the emperor's belief in the value of smallholdings, the law allowed the individual owners to sell or rent their land but only to landless buyers.[91] The law, however, met with systematic obstruction, taking ten months to promulgate. Resistance came from many quarters involving some inside the government itself. Opponents included moderate liberals like Manuel Siliceo (the ex-Imperial Minister of Public Instruction), Francisco Pimentel (political economist, author on indigenous cultures, and imperial advisor), and Tomás Morán y Crivelli (honorary imperial councilor) as well as conservatives like Teodosio Lares (the soon-to-be Minister of Justice) who called the law both "inconvenient and impractical."[92]

The final law, the "*Ley agraria del imperio*" of September 16, 1866, provides a good illustration of the breach between the emperor on the one side and both liberal and conservative critics on the other—a confrontation that Jean Meyer describes as "most decisive."[93] In July 1866, a proposal made its way to the imperial government for legislation granting a *fundo legal*—a town site extending 550 meters in each direction from a central plaza—as well as *ejidos* for pueblos lacking them. While under consideration, opponents drafted a response ostensibly to inform the emperor of the risks involved in such an "imprudent" act. The anonymous authors, above all, denounced the basic premise of expropriation since the "public good" applied only to such matters as road construction, canals, and railroads, but not to a *fundo legal* or a private *ejido*. These features of village life, they maintained, had always been constituted from vacant land or royal grants but never from private holdings. The government, in short, had no right to "plunder" land from private sources to distribute to Indian villages. Any move to create the fundo legal had to harmonize with the principles of justice and respect possession for "security and public tranquility."[94] In other words, private property should remain inviolable.

Three weeks after registering their complaint, the empire issued the decree. In it, the law granted pueblos containing over 400 residents a *fundo legal* and productive land for an *ejido* if the population exceeded 2,000. The *ejidos* would come from public holdings or purchases of private land and be used to support public schools for the villages. The decree, in fact, encouraged smaller pueblos to unite so they could take advantage of the new law.[95] The conservative periodical, *La Sociedad*, was quick to attack the law creating the *fundo legal* as contrary to the principles of political economy that recognized the sanctity of private property. A *fundo legal* would never bring with it the benefits found in private property.[96] But for Jean Meyer, the law qualified as a true agrarian reform since it contained two modern features: restitution and endowment.[97]

Unfortunately, when village residents often tried to use these laws, they faced local officials whom more often than not supported landowners. Florencia Mallon concludes that, "without exception, the populism of the imperial government quickly melted before the glare of local political authorities."[98] The government, in short, had to rely on the departmental prefects, subprefects, and judges who undoubtedly felt little motivation in helping Indian villages recover lost land; few, if any, liberals or conservatives wanted to restructure rural relations. In reality, a majority of those holding important government posts whether under the republic or empire were landowners determined to protect their interests. These actions to alleviate pressures on pueblos, unfortunately, only alienated the hacendados and forfeited valuable political support. In the end, the attempt to enact social justice for the villages by decree failed.

Despite Maximilian's avid interest in modern technology, his concerns for labor were just as passionate. As a twenty-year-old, he had written:

> I can never accommodate myself, or at least I cannot at present, to see the rich possessor of a factory producing in quantities articles which satisfy the extravagant luxury of the rich, whilst his workmen are serfs by the mere power of his money; pale shadows of men, who in a state of stupor and for the needs of their stomach, sacrifice their body to his money-bag. I cannot forget my fellow-men, even for the most beautiful new machines; my valuation of the so-called genius of the century does not reach to that height. . . . we live in the century of haste, and with this the factories seem to harmonise.[99]

Once in Mexico, he got the opportunity to enact protective measures for labor. The imperial decree of November 1, 1865, took an impressive step toward addressing the plight of workers by involving the state actively in correcting inequities in the countryside.[100] Maximilian would note with pride how Mexico became the first country in the world that had a law to protect work and workers. The law not only abolished debt peonage but also regulated child labor, eliminated corporal punishment, and even regulated lunch breaks. For its time, the controversial *ley de trabajo* became one of the most—if not the most—progressive laws to regulate labor and protect workers in the world. Even when compared to the progressive labor measures in the Mexican Constitution of 1917, the imperial decree holds it own.[101]

Although article 5 of the Constitution of 1857 had prohibited service for debt, no provisions specifically dealt with peonage. The *ley de trabajo*, however, was a frontal assault.[102] It granted rural workers the right to leave their employers as long as they did not have any outstanding debts. Above all, it capped worker debt by prohibiting employers from demanding repayment in excess of ten pesos. Combined with the elimination of inheritable debts, the end of forced purchases, and the abolition of corporal punishment, the law addressed the most glaring rural abuses. Moreover, the new law limited the workday from dawn to sunset, requiring two hours of rest time for meals, and gave each Sunday off as well as any state-recognized holidays. As for children under the age of twelve, the workday would be halved and proportional to their strength. While not radical by modern standards, these safeguards protected Mexican workers and greatly exceeded the European laws at the time. Although the first limit on work hours appeared in parts of Switzerland in 1848, not until 1877 did a national law restrict the workday to eleven hours. Maximilian's fellow Austrian liberals of the 1860s felt labor legislation only interfered with individual freedom. In fact, neighboring Germany had no laws regarding work hours for adult males until after World War I. As for child labor, Austria had placed some mild restrictions in their "Trade Code" of 1859 but did not pass more extensive laws until 1885.[103] Of course, had the empire survived, the ability to enforce such regulations, especially in rural areas, would have been difficult at best.

The labor legislation also promoted social justice by requiring employers to give rural workers access to water, shelter, and tools. In an early version of worker insurance, the employer had to lend assistance to ill workers and advance funds for needed medicine. All estates with more than twenty families, moreover, had to provide a free school for teaching the basic elements of reading and writing. The government placed the same obligation to factories as well as workshops that employed more than one hundred workers. Although modest, these articles expressed real concern for worker welfare and, more important, indicated a willingness to place the government between the masses and hacendados.[104]

Not surprisingly, this legislation, once again, alienated many regardless of their political philosophy. Conservatives felt the law ill-informed and feared the social consequences. *La Sociedad* editorialized that "almost always these attacks on the good name of Mexico and theories more or less unattainable and dangerous that are proposed as a remedy for our ills, come accompanied by an absolute lack of knowledge of our history, of our legislation, and even of our present social state."[105] For Arrangoiz, the blame lay with Maximilian's advisors for persuading the emperor that the law would gain him "great fame in liberal Europe" and make him appear as a great administrator and "creative genius"—that before his arrival, there "existed nothing that constituted a civilized country." The emperor needed only to look toward colonial legislation to realize a more prudent course.[106]

The move gained few admirers from among imperial liberals as well who objected to state involvement in affairs deemed outside its purview. Some like Tomás Morán y Crivelli, an honorary imperial councilor and a landowner in Tlaxcala, attacked many sections of the labor code that he felt impinged on the freedom to contract unhindered in the marketplace.[107] Likewise, Francisco Pimentel, who served on Mexico City's *ayuntamiento* and worked in the empire's colonization office, became a major critic of the *ley de trabajo*.[108] For economic liberals like himself, the government's role was to safeguard freedom and liberty—not to intervene in private affairs. The right to have Sundays and holidays off, for instance, violated individual rights since Jews did not work on Saturdays, Christians on Sundays, and others did not think they should work on *"San Lunes."* The obligation to supply tools and employer-funded schooling seemed outrageous since the law gave the owners all the responsibilities but none of the rights. Even restricting child labor would only foment laziness.[109] As evident to some, imperial liberalism had overstepped its bounds in the attempt to provide protection for labor.

By using the state to intervene in issues of social welfare and justice, Maximilian's *ley de trabajo* made an important stride toward a modern labor policy. Although written in conjunction with his imperial advisors and French expeditionary commander, François Achille Bazaine, the real impetus for the legislation undoubtedly came from the emperor. Little evidence exists, however, that officials ever tried to require compliance. Republican critic Justo

Sierra agreed that it was "a law inspired by a splendid sense of justice, but unfortunately impossible to enforce."[110] Restructuring rural relations, in fact, would take a revolution. Still, despite being short-lived, these policies on land and labor, in particular, reveal the early development of an activist state that exceeded conventional liberal limits and foreshadowed transitions half a century later.

As conditions worsened through 1866, any possibility of introducing a formal constitution disappeared. Though Maximilian continued his efforts to create a "homogeneous administration . . . [and] give political and religious peace to the Nation," circumstances forced a reversal in policy.[111] By October 1866, the evacuation of French troops left no other alternative than to "leave a great part of the country's reorganization with the elements of wealthy landowners." Thus, Maximilian re-staffed his ministries with conservatives like Teodosio Lares and prepared for a last stand to save his empire. A liberal by conviction to the very end, the emperor promised that this conservative shift would be done "without sacrificing political and religious liberty for any reason."[112] Despite his attempt, the Second Empire would fall a few months later.

CONCLUSIONS

Historians often advise against speculating on "what might have happened" even though the evaluation of historical events is frequently based, explicitly or not, on alternative choices and outcomes. Had the empire survived, Mexico would still have had the nationalization of Church property, equality under the law, a host of civil guarantees, as well as progressive legislation protecting labor and indigenous communities. The movement toward more representative government and a constitution, moreover, seemed a matter of time. The liberal project in Mexico, in other words, would have most likely survived regardless of the victor. The very fact that Maximilian did not reign as a neo-absolutist over an anti-liberal state, as Padre Miranda would have wished, actually assisted the republican cause upon its return. Church land had not reverted. *Reforma*-era laws regarding the secularization of society and individual rights had been upheld. In many ways, the *juaristas* returned to power without the added hindrance of having to re-fight old ideological battles.

As Patricia Galeana notes, "despite the good intentions of Maximilian, the Empire succumbed and his reformist laws will remain as a testament to the force of an idealist spirit that wished to contribute to the modernization of the country and the triumph of liberalism in Mexico."[113] Without doubt, Maximilian played an active part in furthering the liberal project in Mexico and stood at the forefront of a liberal constitutional movement that swept

Europe in the mid-nineteenth century. The true political legacy of Maximilian, however, might well be his status as the first strong executive in post-independent Mexico, having imposed much of his liberal agenda by decree. For the rest of the century, both Juárez and Díaz would struggle to extend their presidential power much in the same way. Despite his critics, Maximilian never intended to rule as a despot—something that would have been difficult in any event given Mexico's political culture. Maximilian envisioned himself as a constitutional monarch in true nineteenth-century style.

With the restoration of the republic, it became easy to dismiss the empire as a "romantic dream" (used in a pejorative sense) somehow detached from Mexican reality.[114] This refrain, heard ever since disenchanted conservatives unleashed their attack on the emperor, provides little in the way of understanding. If the structures of state or the policies pursued were truly out of touch, so had been those proposed by the radical liberals who planned to regenerate Mexico in no less a dramatic way. The emperor trusted that liberal laws and policies would gain acceptance and legitimacy for the empire. Unfortunately for the empire, time ran out.

NOTES

1. The term "clerical-conservatives" refers to those defenders of the Church who often were the most vocal early proponents of establishing a monarchy in Mexico.

2. Exiled from 1855 to 1856 for his conservative views, Miranda returned to become Minister of Justice for President Félix María Zuloaga in 1859. Patricia Galeana de Valadés, *Las relaciones iglesia-estado durante el segundo imperio* (Mexico: Universidad Nacional Autónoma de México, 1991), 48–49; Francisco de Paula de Arrangoiz y Berzábel, *Apuntes para la historia del segundo imperio mexicano* (Madrid: Imprenta de M. Rivadeneyra, 1869), 193.

3. See, for example, Patricia Galeana de Valadés, ed., *La definición del estado mexicano 1857–1867* (Mexico: Archivo General de la Nación, 1999).

4. Galeana, *Las relaciones iglesia-estado*, 185.

5. Brian R. Hamnett, *Juárez* (New York: Longman, 1994), 10.

6. Jean Meyer has recognized the socially progressive features of the Junta protectora de las clases menesterosas established to give voice to rural complaints; see "La Junta Protectora de las Clases Menesterosas. Indigenismo y agrarismo en el segundo imperio," in Antonio Escobar, coord., *Indio, nación y comunidad en el México del siglo XIX* (Mexico: Centro de Estudios Mexicanos y Centroamericanos, 1993), 329–375.

7. See Daniel Dawson, *The Mexican Adventure* (London: G. Bell and Sons, Ltd. 1935); Arnold Blumberg, "The Diplomacy of the Mexican Empire, 1863–1867," *Transactions of the American Philosophical Society*, New Series, 61: 8, (Philadelphia: The American Philosophical Society, 1971); Nancy Nichols Barker, "Monarchy in Mexico: Harebrained Scheme or Well-considered Prospect," *Journal of Modern History* 48 (March 1976): 51–68.

8. For an examination of the issue of presidential control, see Laurens Ballard Perry, *Juárez and Díaz: Machine Politics in Mexico* (DeKalb: Northern Illinois University Press, 1978).

9. See Nettie Lee Benson, *The Provincial Deputation in Mexico: Harbinger of Provincial Autonomy, Independence, and Federalism* (Austin: University of Texas Press, 1992); Jaime E. Rodríguez O., *The Independence of Spanish America* (Cambridge: Cambridge University Press, 1998), 87–92, and "The Constitution of 1824 and the Formation of the Mexican State," in Jaime E. Rodríguez O., ed., *The Evolution of the Mexican Political System* (Wilmington, Delaware: SR Books, 1993), 74.

10. José C. Valadés, *Maximiliano y Carlota en México: Historia del Segundo Imperio* (México: Editorial Diana, 1976), 12.

11. Jaime E. Rodríguez O., "The Struggle for Dominance: The Legislature versus the Executive in Early Mexico," in Christon I. Archer, ed., *The Birth of Modern Mexico, 1780–1824* (Wilmington: SR Books, 2003), 205–228.

12. Even an area like economic development, long deemed the bailiwick of the liberals, has been shown to have been a conservative issue as well; see Barbara Tenenbaum, "Development and Sovereignty: Intellectuals and the Second Empire," in Roderic A. Camp, et al., eds., *Intellectuals and Power in Mexico* (Los Angeles: UCLA Latin American Center Publications, 1981), 77–88.

13. Donald Fithian Stevens, "Autonomists, Nativists, Republicans, and Monarchists: Conspiracy and Political History in Nineteenth-Century Mexico," *Mexican Studies/Estudios Mexicanos* 10 (winter 1994): 251.

14. Stanley C. Green, *The Mexican Republic: The First Decade 1823–1832* (Pittsburgh: University of Pittsburgh Press, 1987), 142–144; Miguel Soto, *La conspiración monárquica* (Mexico: EOSA, 1988).

15. Barker, "Monarchy in Mexico," 55.

16. José María Gutiérrez de Estrada, *Carta dirigida al excelentísimo señor presidente de la República sobre la necesidad de buscar en una convención el posible remedio de los males que aquejan a la República, México* (Mexico: Ignacio Cumplido, 1840). Seen as a potential threat to both political groupings, Gutiérrez de Estrada fled to Europe but continued to float plans in England, Spain, and Austria that became more autocratic as time went by.

17. Arrangoiz, *Apuntes*, 9.

18. Barker, "Monarchy in Mexico," 58–59; Arrangoiz, *Apuntes*, 12.

19. Egon Caesar Count Corti, *Maximilian and Charlotte of Mexico*, trans. by Catherine Alison Phillips (New York: Archon Books, 1968), 74–75.

20. See Érika Pani, "La tentación de la dictadura 1857–1861," in Galeana, ed., *La definción del estado mexicano*.

21. Corti, *Maximilian and Charlotte*, 278.

22. Siliceo served as Minister of Fomento for President Ignacio Comonfort and later as Minister of Public Instruction for Maximilian; see Hamnett, *Juárez*, 61, 80.

23. Francisco J. Bermúdez to Ignacio Aguilar y Marocho, Mexico, March 9, 1864, in Archivo Histórico del Centro de Estudios de Historia de México [hereafter Condumex], fondo IX-I, carpeta 1, doc. 29.

24. Galeana, *Las relaciones iglesia-estado*, 50.

25. Enrique Krause, *Mexico: Biography of Power: A History of Modern Mexico, 1810–1996*, trans. by Hank Heifetz (New York: Harper Collins, 1997), 183.

26. Arrangoiz, *Apuntes*, 193–194.

27. Maximilian's uncle, Emperor Ferdinand I, abdicated in 1848 to his brother, Franz Karl, who then immediately turned over the throne to his son, Franz Josef.

28. Bombelles warned against fanatical religion including the use of rosaries, Corti, *Maximilian and Charlotte*, 41.

29. Galeana, *Las relaciones iglesia-estado*, 46.

30. Maximilian to Franz Josef, draft report, June 1856, in Corti, *Maximilian and Charlotte*, 60, 62–63.

31. Maximilian to Franz Josef, Amsterdam, June 1856, in Corti, *Maximilian and Charlotte*, 64.

32. Maximilian was also suggested for the Greek throne; see, Corti, *Maximilian and Charlotte*, 73, 389.

33. *Advenimiento de SS.MM.II Maximiliano y Carlota al trono de México*. Edición de "La Sociedad" (México: Andrade y Escalante, 1864), 15.

34. Ibid., 13–15.

35. Maximilian to Archduchess Sophia, n.p., [autumn] 1858, in Corti, *Maximilian and Charlotte*, 83–84.

36. As Egon Corti observed, "It is true that neither the most sympathetic government nor the extremest severity or mildness would have essentially altered the situation in Italy," *Maximilian and Charlotte*, 70–71, 82–83.

37. Joan Haslip, *The Crown of Mexico* (New York: Holt, Rinehart, and Winston, 1971), 117–118.

38. Maximilian to Franz Josef, draft, January 14, 1857, in Corti, *Maximilian and Charlotte*, 68–69.

39. Maximilian, *Recollections of My Life by Maximilian I. Emperor of Mexico*, vol. 3 (London: Richard Bentley, 1868), 105.

40. Hamnett, *Juárez*, 71.

41. Corti, *Maximilian and Charlotte*, 246–248.

42. Napoleon III to Maximilian, n.p., October 2, 1863, in Corti, *Maximilian and Charlotte*, 254, 260.

43. "Draft of a Constitution for the Empire of Mexico" (1863), Maximilian decree, Bancroft Library, University of California, Berkeley, BANC MSS M-M 1806, vol.2.

44. Recently, Shirley Black has examined the French desires to gain access to Mexican silver to prop up a monetary crisis; see *Napoleon III and Mexican Silver* (Silverton, Colorado: Ferrell Publications, 2000).

45. Corti, *Maximilian and Charlotte*, 246–247.

46. Corti, *Maximilian and Charlotte*, 254.

47. Johann Lubienski, "Una monarquía liberal en 1863," in Galeana, ed., *La definición del estado mexicano*, 62.

48. Illegitimate son of independence hero José María Morelos, Almonte had served as minister of war (1839–1841, 1846), variously as minister to the United States, Great Britain, and France, and presidential candidate in 1856. After 1850, he had become conservative and fled to France in 1861, returning the following year. He was chosen by Maximilian to serve as the head of the Regency from 1863–1864.

49. Lubienski, "Una monarquía liberal," in Galeana, ed., *La definición del estado mexicano*, 58–60, 65.

50. Corti, *Maximilian and Charlotte*, 246–248.

51. Lubienski, "Una monarquía liberal," in Galeana, ed., *La definición del estado mexicano*, 65. This may explain why during the empire Almonte was reduced to serving in secondary positions.

52. Valadés, *Maximiliano y Carlota*, 104, 119. The Assembly called republicanism the result of "youthful inexperience" after independence; see Rafael Tafolla Pérez, *La Junta de Notables de 1863* (México: Editorial Jus, 1977), 32–34, 67–91, 109–147.

53. José María Gutiérrez de Estrada, *Discurso pronunciado por D. J. M. Gutiérrez de Estrada presidente de la diputación, el 3 de octobre de 1863, al ofrecer en el palacio de Miramar, a nombre de la asamblea de los Notables de Mexico, la corona imperial AS.A.I. Y R. el archiduque Fernando Maximiliano* (Querétaro: Imprenta del Gobierno, 1863), 1–6.

54. Gutiérrez de Estrada, *Discurso*, 7–8.

55. Maximilian to Juan N. Almonte, Miramar, November 4, 1863, Condumex, fondo XXIII, no. 19. There had been a recent precedent for royal "elections" when the French Senate ratified a popular referendum that crowned Louis Napoleon as emperor.

56. Maximilian to Almonte, Miramar, November 4, 1863, and December 8, 1863, Condumex, fondo XXIII, no. 19 and 21; Corti, *Maximilian and Charlotte*, 263.

57. Maximilian to Almonte, Miramar, December 26, 1863, and January 10, 1864, Condumex, fondo XXIII, no. 22, 23.

58. Patricia Galeana has been a notable exception. She has pointed out that crosses next to some signatures might have even indicated that the signatory was deceased, "El concepto de soberanía en la definición del Estado mexicano," in Galeana, ed., *La definición del estado mexicano*, 19–20.

59. *Prefecto Político* Fernando Pardo, Puebla, June 13, 1863 [copy, Secretario del gabinete civil, Mexico, January 26, 1866], no. 93, in Archivo General de la Nación, Mexico (hereafter AGN), Gobernación, legajo 1332, expediente 1.

60. Manuel Fernandez Leal, Tribunal Supremo de Justicia de Puebla [copy, Secretario del gabinete civil, Mexico, January 27, 1866], AGN, Gobernación, legajo 1332, expediente 1.

61. Galeana, "El concepto de soberanía," in Galeana, ed., *La definición del estado mexicano*, 20–21.

62. Alcalde Matias Sebastian Coyott, Santa Clara Ocuyucan, June 21, 1863, [copy, Secretario del gabinete civil, Mexico, January 28, 1866], no. 99, AGN, Gobernación, legajo 1332, expediente 1.

63. Acta de adhesión al Imperio, Villa de Santiago del Río, San Luis Potosí, January 9, 1864 [copy, Secretario del gabinete civil, Mexico, December 16, 1865], AGN, Gobernación, legajo 1332, expediente 1.

64. Jasper Ridley, *Maximilian and Juárez* (New York: Ticknor and Fields, 1992), 140–148, 156–157; Corti, *Maximilian and Charlotte*, 307; Manuel Santibañez in *Reseña histórica del cuerpo de ejercito de oriente*, tomo II (México: Oficina impresora del timbre, 1893), 24–36, opines that these *actas* came not from conviction but through violence and the force of arms.

65. Harry Bernstein, *Dom Pedro II* (New York: Twayne Publishers, Inc., 1973), 89.

66. *Breve Noticia del recibimiento y permanencia de SS. MM. II. en la ciudad de Puebla* (Puebla: T. F. Neve, 1864).

67. Eugenio Maillefert, *Directorio del Comercio del Imperio Mexicano para el año de 1867* (Mexico: Instituto de Investigaciones Dr. José María Luis Mora, 1992), 21–28.

68. A minister, for instance, would introduce a draft piece of legislation to the other ministers for debate. If approved, the proposal would circulate as law under the name of the ministry that proposed it. "Instrucción para la formación de las leyes," Mexico, July 18, 1865, AGN, Gobernación, legajo 1428, expediente 1.

69. Eduardo Castellanos Hernández, "Formas de gobierno y sistemas electorales durante el periodo 1857–1867," in Galeana, ed., *La definición del estado mexicano*, 55.

70. Article 51, for the first time, also delineated the physical boundaries of Mexico.

71. This last provision, also contained in the Constitution of 1857, was intended to make foreigners who owned land in Mexico subject to Mexican laws. In response to protest from ex-Confederate immigrants, however, the provision was later changed.

72. Ángel Barroso Díaz, "Maximiliano: Legislador Liberal," in José Luis Soberanes Fernández, ed., *Memoria del II Congreso de historia del derecho Mexicano (1980)* (Mexico: Universidad Nacional Autónoma de Mexico, 1981), 554.

73. Maximilian to Velásquez de León, Mexico, August 6, 1864, in AGN, Gobernación, legajo 1515 expediente 3; Juárez's 1861 press law had similarly included an exception for disturbing public order.

74. *Examen crítico de la administración del Príncipe Maximiliano de Austria en México* (Mexico: Vicente G. Torres, 1867), 19–20.

75. Valadés, *Maximiliano y Carlota*, 163. Maximilian even contemplated offering Juárez a position as prime minister in a liberal constitutional government; see Hamnett, *Juárez*, 177.

76. Rafael Cravioto, Huachinango, January 15, 1865 [copy, Secretario del gabinete civil, Mexico, March 2, 1866], no. 295, AGN, Gobernación, legajo 1332, expediente 3. Rafael and his father Simón were placed under house arrest in Puebla city; see Florencia Mallon, *Peasant and Nation: The Making of Postcolonial Mexico and Peru* (Berkeley: University of California Press, 1995), 23.

77. Galeana, *Las relaciones iglesia-estado*, 96.

78. Joan Haslip theorizes that Eloin had been recommended by King Leopold to scout mining opportunities in Mexico; see Haslip, *The Crown of Mexico*, 238.

79. Arrangoiz, *Apuntes*, 195.

80. Arrangoiz, *Apuntes*, 200.

81. E. Bradford Burns and Thomas E. Skidmore, *Elites, Masses, and Modernization in Latin America, 1850–1930* (Austin: University of Texas Press, 1979), 23.

82. Corti, *Maximilian and Charlotte*, 181.

83. Maximilian to Juan N. Almonte, Miramar, December 8, 1863, Condumex, fondo XXIII, no. 21.

84. Galeana, *Las relaciones iglesia-estado*, 58.

85. Prefecto político José María Esteva noted that the imperial decree secularizing cemeteries actually conflicted with a Regency's law on the same subject passed before Maximilian's arrival, Esteva to Ministerio de Gobernación, Puebla, March 18, 1865, AGN, Gobernación, legajo 1716, expediente, 3.

86. Niceto de Zamacois, *Historia de Méjico desde sus tiempos mas remotos hasta nuestros días*, vol. 17 (Mexico: J. F. Parras y Compañía, 1881), 1022–1031. In fact, the conservative editor of *La Cronista*, Niceto de Zamacois, felt that these moves were all

a conspiracy by the republicans to convince Maximilian to make laws against the Church and thereby alienate his original base of support.

87. Liberals considered Indian communal landholding as an obstacle to a prosperous nation. In classic liberal terms, land needed to circulate on the open market. The Constitution of 1857 added *ejidos* to the list of property to be privatized.

88. Meyer, "La Junta Protectora," 330.

89. Valadés, *Maximiliano y Carlota*, 269.

90. Maximilian, *Decretos*. Benson Latin American Collection, University of Texas, Austin (hereafter BLAC).

91. Maximilian, *Decretos*. BLAC.

92. Meyer, "La Junta Protectora," 374.

93. Ibid., 348.

94. "Observaciones generales que se hacen por acuerdo de S.M. sobre el Proyecto de Ley concerniente a fundo Legal y Egido para los pueblos indígenas," draft reproduced in Meyer, "La Junta Protectora," 348–350.

95. Rosa Isabel Estrada Martínez, "Legislación y política agraria de la Reforma y del Segundo Imperio," in *Memoria del II Congreso del Historia del Derecho Mexicano* (Mexico: UNAM, 1981), 612.

96. *La Sociedad*, September 20, 1866.

97. Meyer, "La Junta Protectora," 351, 353.

98. Mallon, *Peasant and Nation*, 172.

99. Maximilian, *Recollections*, 2: 74.

100. Many sources have attributed the labor policy to Carlota who, in her capacity as regent during the emperor's absence, supposedly pushed forward the legislation; see Haslip, *The Crown of Mexico*, 324, and Ridley, *Maximilian and Juárez*, 216. Since Maximilian kept in regular contact with Carlota during his trips outside the capital, formulating such important legislation without his knowledge and approval would have been unlikely.

101. Valadés, *Maximiliano y Carlota*, 269. In fact, the imperial decree and Constitution of 1917 both regulated working hours, child labor, and days of rest. The imperial decree mandated cash payments, housing, schools, healthcare, worker debts, and equal pay for equal work (in the draft version) that the Constitution of 1917 also included. Only with the issues of minimum wage, leave for childbirth, and the right to strike did the 1917 Constitution go further than its predecessor. It is important to remember that the progressive article 123 was enacted only *after* the Revolution had broken vested interests. Without it, the Revolutionary legislation would have also faced entrenched opposition attempt.

102. Decree, November 1, 1865, in *Colección de leyes, decretos y reglamentos que interinamente forman el sistema político, administrativo y judicial del Imperio*, vol. 6 (Mexico: A Boix, 1865), 185–187.

103. Margarete Grandner, "Conservative Social Politics in Austria, 1880–1890," *Austrian History Yearbook* 27 (1996): 77–107.

104. One proposed measure (undoubtedly the most unusual article in the draft) never passed the discussion phase: it proposed paying female workers as much as males. Some predicted that, if instituted, the article would price women out of the workforce.

105. Quoted in Francisco de Paula de Arrangoiz, *Méjico desde 1808 hasta 1867*, vol. 3 (Madrid: Imprenta de Estrada, 1872), 339. The emperor's own minister of government, José María Esteva, felt the decree might cause riots and possibly ignite a race war; see Zamacois, *Historia de Méjico*, 84.

106. Arrangoiz, *Méjico desde 1808 hasta 1867*, 3: 339–341.

107. Tomás Morán y Crivelli, *Observaciones al proyecto de reglamento presentado por la Junta protectora de las clases menesterosas sobre el trabajo de los peones y sirvientes de fincas rústicas* (Mexico: Imprenta Literaria, 1865), 13, 21, 23.

108. Francisco Pimentel took special aim on the labor code in his book, *La economía política aplicada a la propiedad territorial en México* (Mexico: Andrade y Escalante, 1866).

109. Pimentel, *La economía política*, 153–162.

110. Justo Sierra, *The Political Evolution of the Mexican People*, trans. by Charles Ramsdell (Austin: University of Texas Press, 1969), 330.

111. Maximilian to Juan N. Almonte, Chapultepec, August 3, 1866, Condumex, fondo XXIII, no. 60.

112. Maximilian to Juan N. Almonte, Chapultepec, September 20, 1866, Condumex, fondo XXIII no. 65.

113. Galeana, *Las relaciones iglesia-estado*, 158.

114. Krause, *Mexico: Biography of Power*, 176.

5

Kaleidoscopic Views of Liberalism Triumphant, 1862–1895

William H. Beezley

"Cinco de Mayo," the date of the Mexican Liberal Army victory over invading veteran French troops at the battle of Puebla in 1862, in many ways established the frame of reference for the Liberal political currents that came to dominate Mexico until the middle of the 1890s. This battle had consequences beyond the immediate military victory for Mexican Liberals: it resulted in the first defeat for Napoleon III in his plans for a Latin world under his direction; it permanently discredited Mexican conservatives with their ties to the Papacy; and, it provided a rallying triumph for Mexican Liberals that endured into the 1890s. As new Porfirian leaders abandoned broad Liberal patterns in the 1890s, they initiated practices that helped provoke the Mexican Revolution in 1910. The Cinco de Mayo victory inspired habits of patriotic Liberalism and reinforced fundamentals of folk or popular Liberalism. Together they shaped patterns of behavior and politics that joined with those of scientific Liberalism to hold sway until the 1890s during the regime of Porfirio Díaz (1876–1911).

In the last decade of the nineteenth century, the veteran officers of the War against the French, who were the leaders of the Patriotic Liberals, died away. At the same time, the spokesmen for popular Liberals were increasingly ignored. One current of the Scientific Liberals established what today we would call a technocratic administration. These Porfirian technocrats, many of them followers of Auguste Comte, dominated the national administration until the fall of the regime in 1911. In the years of scientific Liberals, the Catholic Church reemerged in public life, especially in the guise of modern Catholicism that recognized vernacular practices and the need for social reform (in other words, these clerics were harbingers of Catholic Social Action). These churchmen represented a kind of Catholic Liberalism that resulted from the

Papal encyclical *Rerum Novarum*. The Pope issued the decree as the Roman Catholic Church's accommodation to Western Liberalism.[1] This essay concludes with some discussion of the Porfirian dismissal of popular Liberalism and the connection of this action with the outbreak and the character of the Mexican Revolution and the formation of Mexican identity.

MEXICO'S SECOND LIBERALISM

Return now to Puebla, May 5, 1862, when some 6,000 French troops, most of them veterans of the Crimean War, advanced on some 4,000 ill-equipped Mexican soldiers. On that cold, rainy day, the French commander ordered his men forward in unnecessarily desperate and careless frontal attacks that repeatedly failed, until the French line broke in disorderly retreat. Cinco de Mayo marks the day of Mexico's greatest military victory, although the French returned and placed Maximilian on a throne as emperor. Finally, in 1867, these Liberal officers succeeded in defeating the European invaders and reestablishing the republic with Benito Juárez as president.

Mexican commanding officers, because of the Cinco de Mayo victory, for the rest of their lives were bound together as brothers of the sword.[2] Despite periodic defections followed by political forgiveness, they shared a patriotic Liberalism that rested on the expulsion of the French puppet Maximilian in 1867. They came to dominate the republic from 1876 into the 1890s. Once these men had expelled the French and their emperor, they faced the same problem earlier Mexican officers had confronted with victory in the wars of independence. They needed to create a workable national government with broad-based support that required a general sense of national identity. The Independence generation ultimately failed, and the Cinco de Mayo generation ultimately succeeded.

These Liberal officers had as their beloved martyr General Ignacio Zaragoza, the commander at Puebla, who died unexpectedly shortly after the battle. Zaragoza's staff at Puebla, Generals Felipe Berriozábal, Mariano Escobedo, Miguel Negrete, Gerónimo Treviño, and, above all, Porfirio Díaz, all became national heroes and leaders among this group of Liberals. For the rest of their careers, including political and economic activities, they espoused Liberal doctrines, stiffened with military discipline. In addition, the war against the French occupation, 1862–1867, gave other officers who had opposed Benito Juárez and the Liberals in the Wars of the Reform (1858–1861) a chance for redemption. Miguel Negrete, Manuel González, and Sóstenes Rocha were three who grabbed the opportunity to fight for Mexico and in the process to fuse their patriotic views with the Liberal campaign. All these generals developed a set of shared expectations, despite some personal rivalry, that included a common suspicion of Juárez's romantic Cincinnatus ideals for them.

Juárez defined Liberalism, above all, in civilian terms. After the victory over Maximilian in 1867, he expected soldiers to return home and become independent agrarians. He angered and divided the generals and their men as he slashed the victorious national army of 60,000 by two thirds, and created five new divisions, each with 4,000 men, commanded by one of the generals who had fought against the French. Porfirio Díaz received command of one of the divisions, but it was hardly the reward he expected for his wartime service. Almost immediately, he began scheming to seize power and successfully did so in 1876.

When Porfirio Díaz took the presidential chair, he determined to redeem his fellow officers, whom he recognized as tested patriots.[3] Among the most prominent officers at the time, two were in exile, Sóstenes Rocha in Paris and Mariano Escobedo in New York City, and two others, Miguel Negrete and Felipe Berriozábal, were in political isolation. Porfirio brought them and other veterans of the officer corps into his political administration and directed economic opportunities toward them.

Díaz's treatment of the army, especially its general officers, recognized their contributions to the nation and emphasized tenets of Liberalism that reached back to the 1812 Constitution of Cádiz. Following his victory in 1876, Díaz converted short-term volunteers and militiamen into state, and then through the state, into community militia and national guard units. Díaz also ordered the transfer of many promising soldiers to the newly expanded rural constabulary, the Rurales, under the auspices of the Secretary of Gobernación. In this process, officers left without a command went into a pool from which future vacancies were filled. Of course, Díaz made these appointments in part to placate his brothers of the sword and to preempt military insurrection against his government.

Yet these steps also confirm a kind of military or patriotic Liberalism that survived into the 1890s and, in some ways, until 1903. The return of troops to community control as local militias validated the decentralized Liberal goal of the 1812 Constitution and reasserted the authority of the municipios clearly established in the same document. Both these tenets formed foundational features of the Liberal ideology that shaped much of the Constitution of 1857. The support for a strong army and the expansion of the Rurales confirmed a commitment by these patriotic Liberals to social and political stability, essential for the Liberal goal of providing security of person and property to all individuals as Mexican citizens.

Díaz skillfully worked with the heroes of Cinco de Mayo, even those who opposed him. General Mariano Escobedo and General Miguel Negrete, because of their Liberal commitment to federalism, revolted against Diaz's centralized regime in 1878. Once he suppressed the insurgents, Díaz had Escobedo brought to Mexico City and pardoned this hero of Puebla and one of the victors of the Battle of Querétaro that led to the capture of

Maximilian. He pardoned Negrete in 1878 and again in 1880. These generals and others who remained loyal benefited with political and economic preferment. General Manuel González was named Minister of War and later was tapped to serve as President from 1880 to 1884. General Gerónimo Treviño received a fiefdom in the North of some 880,000 acres in Coahuila. He soon emerged as a powerful caudillo. Another of the heroes of Cinco de Mayo, General Gaspar Sánchez Ochoa, who had received a concession from Juárez to mine sulphur from Popocatepetl and became popularly known as the man who owned a volcano, was appointed chief of engineers in the Department of War and later a member of the Supreme Court.[4]

Generals Berriózabal, Rocha, and Escobedo all served the Porfirian regime and Liberalism. Berriózabal received an appointment as minister of war (1896–1900); Rocha as director of the restored Colegio Militar (1880–1886 when Felipe Angeles, Felix Díaz, and Victoriano Huerta were cadets), as a national deputy, and as editor of the anticlerical, strongly liberal newspaper, *El Combate*; Escobedo was trotted out for ceremonial purposes until the 1890s, when he began serving eight terms in the Chamber of Deputies, interrupted from 1892 to 1894, when he presided over the military Supreme Court. All of these heroes served the Liberal cause and Porfirio in death as in life. Only Treviño survived the Porfirian regime to 1914. Each of the others received a major state funeral, providing the occasion to declaim to the public their contributions to the nation and their commitment to this military-styled Liberalism.[5] During the Díaz regime that endured from 1876 to 1911, 78 percent of Porfirio's political appointments were veterans of the war against the French, a war that he regarded as a struggle against foreign invaders, domestic conservatives, and the Roman Catholic clerics. They thus held the banner of patriotic Liberalism.

The rank and file of troops who fought at Puebla on Cinco de Mayo and afterward against the French to restore Juárez returned home with weapons and membership, for the most part, in local militias or in the national reserve. They returned with rather clear views of both their rights and responsibilities as Mexicans. Both categories of rights and responsibilities were defined in community terms, represented by the municipality that had been given corporate endorsement in the Constitution of 1812 and carried forward into the Constitution of 1857. Many of these men fought in irregular forces with their own line officers and were supported by their communities. For example women of the community often sent men off to battle with a supply of hard cooked tortillas (called *tlayudas*) as provisions and sometimes traveled with them to forage for foodstuffs during the campaign. These veterans built up what one could call a moral economy of community rights, learned through the struggle against the French, that formed a kind of particularistic folk liberalism.[6] Although this liberalism was distinct to each community, nearly every community stressed local control of taxes, lands, and the militia that along with selection of town officials formed the basis of what became the hallowed folk or popular liberal institution, the *municipio libre*. Often at this time, the community's unique personality received lyrical expression with the creation of municipal bands.[7]

The problem from the perspective of Mexico City was how to join these local communities, especially as they had developed unique senses of Mexican-ness, into a cohesive nationality. From an administrative point of view, this was the crisis of nineteenth-century liberalism that led to the strong, central government in the Constitution of 1857 and increasingly authoritarian rule first by President Juárez, and second by President Díaz, who perfected it with the use of the appointed district administrator, the *jefe político*. Certainly, Díaz and his close circle of officers, even though Liberals, had a firm belief in and experience with the habit of command.

On the level of sentiment, there was the question of uniting these particularistic communities into a shared national identity. This will be considered below, after looking at the third group, the Scientific Liberals of the Porfirian years. This term avoids confusion with the Científicos and the Positivists, although, of course, there was a great deal of overlap among the three groups. The identification of this group of Liberals draws on the innovative research of Leticia Mayer Celis, anthropologist and historian of science in the department of applied mathematics at the Universidad Autónoma Nacional de México. She has evaluated elites who had either a professional or avocational interest in science, particularly the collection of statistical information about the nation's population and the physical characteristics. She builds on the work of Ian Hacking[8] and makes a powerful case for the shift from generalizations about human nature to national identity. Mayer Celis has investigated most extensively the individuals who formed the Instituto Nacional de Geografía y Estadística, founded in 1833, and who became so disappointed by the U.S.-Mexican War that they abandoned politics and their scientific activities.[9] A new group of Mexicans interested in science, especially based on quantitative materials, appeared after 1867, that is, in the post–French Intervention years.[10]

These scientific Liberals developed their approach to social programs on the collection of numbers from the civil and criminal registers created by the Constitution of 1857. The inspiration of this program of analysis was the French astronomer, Alfonse Quetelet, who in 1835 developed the idea of the "average man" as an analytical figure that quickly became the basis for a mathematical description of national types. Moreover, this information provided a snapshot of social attributes that needed to be improved, or eliminated, or regulated by the utilitarian Liberal state. Of these Scientific Liberals, three men made signal contributions during the Juárez years. Miguel Lerdo de Tejada, in 1856, directed a demographic survey as part of the disamortization of both church and village lands. Manuel Orozco y Berra, working for the Ministry of Development, wrote the *Diccionario Universal de Historia y Geografía*, and Antonio García Cubas, also working for the Ministry of Fomento (Development), attempted to graph the changing distribution of the population in response to the sale of church and Indian municipal properties in 1861, 1869, 1871, and 1872 in *Cuadro geográfico, estadístico, descriptivo, y histórico de México* (1885). These three men laid the groundwork for the Scientific Liberals who joined the Díaz government and came to dominate in the 1890s.[11] Of this group during the Porfirian years, the best known was Antonio Peñafiel, who was the founder of the Dirección General de Estadística in 1882 as part of the Ministry of Development. For these Liberals there existed an unbreakable connection joining public health (hygiene), morality, and progress, and they believed the starting point for an analysis of the nation's people was a national census. As result they founded the Dirección General de Estadística with the primary obligation of conducting a general census. The agency first completed a census of the Federal District in 1892 and then of the nation in 1895. In their efforts, these scientific liberals strived to describe the Porfirian nation with exactness, accuracy, and elegance.[12] Their statistical findings would become a key to Porfirian policies, such as public hygiene campaigns, especially those shaped by the emerging professional organizations such as the national association of engineers in the last two decades of the regime.[13]

THE NATURE OF THE NEW LIBERALISM

The kaleidoscopic patterns of Liberalism during the Porfirian era reveal: (1) the crucial role of the Cinco de Mayo victory for defining leadership opportunities for Liberal military officers and redeeming Conservative soldiers not allied with the French; (2) a glance at national concerns reveals the military issue of Liberalism—that can be defined as municipal control of the militia and paramilitary, the Rurales, and the military enforcement of social order to ensure secure circumstances for citizens; (3) the rank and file who served against the French and in the Liberal internecine wars from 1867 to 1876 developed a moral economy with grace notes as military service confirmed municipal values and practices that can be traced back to the Constitution of 1812. Another way of saying this is that fighting for *la patria* invigorated *la patria chica*; contrary to Eugene Weber's interpretation for France, military service need not create a sense of nationalism. Rather in Mexico, it inspired a sense of *fulano*'s rights in Cuautitlán.

As a result, the general campaign to promote modernization, defined as the creation of a viable nation-state, a self-disciplined citizenry, and a secure society limped ahead until the 1890s, when Scientific Liberals came to the fore. Their zeal and their success also carried the seeds of the regime's demise in the Mexican Revolution. As these technocrats took control of the Porfirian regime, they squeezed out governors as the representatives of provincial elites and replaced the traditional families with claims for political preferment who also came from the countryside. When the revolutionaries in 1910 attacked the "full car" of the Díaz administration, they referred to the national government bureaucracy dominated by *licenciados* and *ingenieros* from Mexico City. Confirmation of the opposition to this group appeared in the revolution led by Francisco Madero, son of the powerful, but ignored, provincial family from Coahuila.[14] None of the revolutionary chiefs were from the federal district, nor could any of them be described as technocrats, although many provincial school teachers played an active role in the struggle.

The three types of Liberals, the patriotic, the folk, and the Scientific Liberals, who emerged after 1867, of course built on the earlier Liberalism of Benito Juárez and those who wrote the Constitution of 1857. What had changed most dramatically was anticlericalism. In public discussions, the anticlerical character of the Porfirians remained just as important as during the Juárez years, but as a practical policy it did not. The nature of the Porfirian Liberals might stand in greater relief if they were compared to Liberals elsewhere in Latin America. The most likely place for such a comparison would be Brazil, where veteran officers from the Paraguayan War, Comtean-influenced intellectuals, and Abolitionists overthrew the Empire of Pedro II and established the republic. No such comparative study exists.[15]

Despite the kaleidoscope of Liberalism during the nineteenth century and the persistence of local community particularism, a strong sense of national identity emerged and appeared without regard either to the repeated failures of national projects to produce citizens or to some broad-based local set of attitudes about entitlements based on military service. The appearance of individual identification as Mexicans seems to have developed in response to curiosity about the country and its people that was answered by members of the petit bourgeoisie, working people trying to make a living in any way they could. National identity was the unintended and unexpected consequence of individuals who produced and sold almanacs, provided the holiday ephemera to celebrate independence and other national days, made and marketed the games played at local fairs or in cheaper versions at home, and the entertainers who developed programs for the itinerant puppet theaters that crisscrossed the nation.[16] These individuals, in many cases nameless working-class people, merit some further discussion.

DISCOVERING NATIONAL IDENTITY

Mexicans learned about their country from a host of official, institutional, informal, and familial forms for teaching values and fashioning identity during the nineteenth century. Nevertheless, the informal sources proved especially pervasive and persuasive. They included: (1) civic and religious fiestas, including the floats and other ephemeral paraphernalia; (2) almanacs, known in the nineteenth century as *calendarios*; (3) folk art, especially the children's game *loteria de figuras*; and, (4) popular public performances, in particular itinerant puppet theater. These sources focused on the images on display in fiestas and that include statues and monuments, buildings and neighborhoods that formed the destinations and the backdrops of the fiestas; the explanations, from almanacs, of what it meant to be Mexican; the stereotypes of society displayed by loteria de figuras; and the portrayal of everyday life and its problems such as family, politics, and caciques, and the diversity of Mexican landscapes and cultures represented in puppet theater.

Consider a brief example of puppet theater. The puppet company was not simply a commercial enterprise; it was much more—it was a family's livelihood. To say its goal was to make a profit does not capture the urgency of the endeavor—puppeteers were not trying to make a profit, but to make a living, an entirely different proposition. Puppeteers had to be completely sensitive to how their shows played with audiences. If puppeteers did not gauge their audiences correctly, the people would not return for the second night of performances. The audience's judgment was immediate and final. Consequently, much more than the novelty of stringed actors drew spectators to the theater; the nature of the performance mattered.

Puppets had a prominent role during the Spanish colonial era with both entertainment and religious features. The puppet theater reflected the peninsular pattern, probably of Italian origin, brought from France to Spain by *juglares*, according to one source in 1116, who performed puppet-jousts. Puppet theater was later popularized by Alberto Naceri de Ganassa, the author of *Commedia dell'Arte* in the late sixteenth century. Soon, puppet performances dealt with the Life of Christ, the Virgin, and the Saints.[17] Puppets, perhaps because of the shortage of missionaries, were widely used in the evangelization campaign in New Spain. Performances of the Christmas story and the Holy Week passion of Christ had large followings, but the most popular sketch showed the arrival of the three kings (*El Auto de los Reyes Magos*). Satirical and burlesque marionette performances of dances, cock fights, and bull fights, accompanied by guitar music, occurred in the homes of the colonial elites.[18]

After independence, puppets became clearly related to popular culture and the people in general. The first well-known puppet ensemble featured don Folías, his wife, la Mariquita, and his nemesis, El Negrito, with his woman, Procopia, who made up the regular cast. Often the narrator, Juan el panadero, also appeared outside the stage to provide the moral of the story. These characters appeared in numerous sketches about the struggles between men and women, and of course the devil's temptations. Don Folías had a great following because whenever he got angry, which happened in every performance when El Negrito told him that his wife had cuckolded him, his neck stretched out and his nose extended, and El Negrito danced an elaborate dance of joy.

In 1835, the most important puppet company in Mexican history was born in Huamantla, Tlaxcala: this was the Rosete Aranda Company. Today the National Puppetry Museum is located in Huamantla, Tlaxcala, as a tribute to the founders of these representatives of popular art and entertainment. The Rosete Aranda Company initiated formal programs in 1850, and the troupe continued until 1943. During this era, they offered performances to persons as notable as Presidents Antonio Lopez de Santa Anna and Benito Juarez. In the years from 1835 and 1913, the Rosete Aranda Company established two famous marionettes. Vale Coyote, who represented a campesino that acted as the spokesperson for the desires and sentiments of the people, and Doña Pascarroncita Mastuerzo de Verdegay Panza de Rez y Gay Verde, the snooty woman who sang the famous "Coplas de Don Simón."[19] Other puppets included the prominent political figures, such as Padre Miguel Hidalgo, Benito Juarez, and Porfirio Díaz. They also included well-known entertainers, such as the famous clown, Ricardo Bell.[20]

In cities up and down and across the republic, all the puppets had the ability to synthesize in form and language the social inequities and complaints and the ability to create universal metaphors and popular symbols with a spirit of criticism and a sense of humor.[21] The family established an annual circuit from Mexico City, through the Bajío, north to Chihuahua or northeast to Monterrey, with occasional visits to El Paso or San Antonio, Texas. The return trip down the west side of the Sierra Madre eventually reached Oaxaca, then on to Tehuacán, Puebla, and back to Huamantla. During the winter months, the company traveled to Pachuca, El Real del Monte, Xalapa, and Veracruz. These trips enabled the company to meet the curiosity of their audiences about Mexico and Mexicans, and even to offer the examples of music from across the nation.[22] The repertory of each performance included the discourse of Vale Coyote, the "Coplas de Don Simón" by Doña Pascarroncita, traditional stories, religious scenes of Holy Week, Christmas, and other feast days, and typical scenes of Mexico—the promenade on la viga and Bucareli streets, bull fights, cock fights, independence day celebration, historical dramas, and popular folkloric figures, such as Chucho El Roto.[23]

The Rosete Aranda puppets brought together local knowledge and linked it together into a national memory. The puppets offered stereotypes of each region, the major events—both civic and clerical—in the calendar, and the heroic moments of the past. Moreover, as the puppets went about this formation of popular memory they incited, if not demanded, audience participation. This was especially the case with the *cócoros*, or hecklers, who formed a vital part of the performances and challenged the puppets to more artful performances.

The popular memory of Mexican history in the nineteenth century revolved around great men and women. To say that Hidalgo, Juárez, La Corregidora, and the Virgin of Guadalupe personified the heroic moments and tragic realities of the nation's history does not in the slightest discount the rest of the Mexican people, the *pueblo*. Only if one ignores the obvious or resorts to some theory of politics or the theater of life can one insist that this emphasis on great men and women fails as a national history. Hidalgo, for example, in his role as the father of independence is not a solitary actor, nor is he a metaphor for either a social class or a narrow elite. Rather Hidalgo is a metonym for one large segment of the Mexican people; he did form part of the same group with them—and his experience, his life's drama, was to a large extent theirs.

The national identity that emerged from these popular sources, especially the itinerant puppet theater, included these attitudes. First was a strong sense of place. That is to say, a strong sense of the physical geography and the size of Mexico. Of course this began with recognition of images of the volcanoes Popo y Itza, the peak of Orizaba, and the cataract of Tula. The size of the country came from the distances between cities and the maps of the states and cities such as México, Guadalajara, and Veracruz. Second was the knowledge that México was a land of impressive architecture from the pre-Columbian, colonial, and independent eras. The almanacs, the puppet theater backdrops, the lottery cards, and the fiestas offered examples of the fortress of San Juan de Úlua, the National Cathedral, colonial churches, and *el caballito*. Third was the knowledge of patriotic symbols, especially the eagle on the nopal with a snake in its mouth and lady liberty. Other symbols included the national flag[24] and the national seal.[25]

Fourth, the almanacs offered a civic education. One example was the "calendario de la democracia dedicado al pueblo Mexicano," for the year 1852, published by Leandro J. Valdés. This almanac (and others) featured a civic catechism. This consisted of questions and answers for the public to memorize. For example:

> What is political liberty?
> The common independence; power exercised with violence not only is an injustice, it is a sacrilege.
> What is authority and what is domination?
> The first commands for the good of all; the second is the absolutism; the first keeps us from danger; the second degrades us.[26]

The publishers of the almanacs also judged politicians. For example, the almanac editor Abraham López said that Mexico's problems came from the self-importance that each governor adopted. He said that each state governor thought of himself as more important than a king; he concluded "*Cada gobernador se cree igual a un bajá de tres colas. No obedece leyes ni las or-*

denes que dimanen del centro."[27] Finally, in various almanacs there were explications of the difference between the rights of human beings and the rights of citizens. According to one, human beings had the right to live free, with security and with protection of life and home; citizens had rights of property, to elect government officials, and to carry arms.

Here as these descriptions show there was a broad-based sense of national identity and liberal attitudes that coincided with national programs and the values of the three types of Liberals in the 1890s. The technocrats, with their scientific liberal values, unfortunately dismissed much of the rural, indigenous, and poor population as unworthy of attention. As a result, these groups became the revolutionaries who seized control of the nation after 1910.

NOTES

1. For the impact of the Papal encyclical in Mexico, the starting point is the study of Catholic Social Action by Randall S. Hanson, "The Day of Ideals: Catholic Social Action in the Age of the Mexican Revolution, 1867–1929" (Ph.D. diss., Indiana University, 1994).

2. The following discussion draws heavily on the seminar paper by David Coffey, "Brothers of the Sword: The Bond of Nationalist Struggle in Porfirian Mexico" (Unpublished seminar paper, Texas Christian University, 1996).

3. Almost no scholarly work exists on the military officers as a social group. Christon Archer has provide some discussions incidental to his other work on the independence period. Some information on the generation of military officers who ruled Mexico after independence can be found in Salvador Rueda Smithers, *El diablo de Semana Santa: El discurso político y el orden social en la ciudad de México en 1950* (México: Instituto Nacional de Antropología e Historia). Nothing exists on the officer class for the Porfiriato, but see the suggestive work of Stephan Neufeld, "The Preformative Porfirian Army" (M.A. thesis, University of British Columbia, 2003).

4. William H. Beezley, *Judas at the Jockey Club and Other Episodes of Porfirian Mexico* (Lincoln: University of Nebraska Press, 1987), pp. 36–37.

5. Matthew D. Esposito, "Memorializing Modern Mexico: The State Funerals of the Porfirian Era, 1876–1911" (Ph.D. dissertation, Texas Christian University, 1997).

6. This particularistic community outlook, formed in a more or less closed corporate community, represents the basic argument of Eric Van Young's explanation of the wars of independence in *The Other Rebellion: Popular Violence, Ideology, and the Mexican Struggle for Independence, 1810–1821* (Stanford: Stanford University Press, 2001).

7. For discussion of popular Liberalism, a starting place is Guy P. C. Thomson's recent work: "Popular Aspects of Liberalism in Mexico, 1848–1888," *Bulletin of Latin American Research* 10, 3 (1991): 265–292; "Bulwarks of Patriotic Liberalism: The National Guard, Philharmonic Corps and Patriotic Juntas in Mexico, 1847–88," *Journal of Latin American Studies* (1990): 51–61; "The Ceremonial and Political Roles of Village Bands, 1846–1974," in William H. Beezley, Cheryl English Martin, and William E.

French, eds., *Rituals of Rule, Rituals of Resistance: Public Celebrations and Popular Culture in Mexico* (Wilmington, DE: SR Books, 1994): 307–342.

8. Ian Hacking in *The Taming of Chance* (Cambridge: Cambridge University Press, 1990) and other volumes examines what he identifies as the Second Scientific Revolution with the development and use of statistics.

9. Leticia Mayer Celis, *Entre el infierno de una realidad y el cielo de un imaginario: Estadística y comunidad científica en el México de la primera mitad del siglo xix* (México: El Colegio de México, 1999).

10. Leticia Mayer Celis, "La *Ley de los Grandes Números* y La Cultura Liberal en México, 1856–1885," in François-Xavier Guerra and Mónica Quijada, eds., *Imaginar la nación* (Münster,Germany: Cuadernos de historia latinoamericana, 1994), 51–82.

11. Carlos Alberto Contreras and Peter L. Reich, "Numbers and the State: An overview of Government Statistical Compilation in Mexico Since the Colonial Period," in James W. Wilkie, Carlos Alberto Contreras, and Catherine Komisaruk, eds., *Statistical Abstract of Latin America* 31, part 2 (Los Angeles: UCLA Latin American Center Publications, 1995), 1254.

12. These terms come from Michael A. Bernstein, "Numerable Knowledge and its Discontents," *Reviews in American History* 18 (1990): 151.

13. The emergence of these Scientific Liberals who represented the first technocracy in Mexico (the beginnings of the second group appeared under Miguel Alemán in the 1950s) is discussed in François-Xavier Guerra, *Le Mexique de l'ancien regime a la revolution* (Paris: Editions L'Harmattan, 1985), tome 1. See also Claudia Agostoni, *Monuments of Progress: Modernization and Public Health, 1876–1910* (Calgary: University of Calgary Press, 2003).

14. The standard account of the Madero revolution remains Charles C. Cumberland, *The Mexican Revolution: Genesis under Madero* (Austin: University of Texas Press, 1952).

15. The important volume on this topic, Vicent C. Peloso and Barbara A. Tenenbaum, eds., *Liberals, Politics, and Power: State Formation in Nineteenth-Century Latin America* (Athens: University of Georgia Press, 1999) does not attempt such comparisons.

16. This argument is more fully developed in the forthcoming book, William H. Beezley, "Amending Memories: The Formation of National Identity in Nineteenth-century Mexico."

17. J. E. Varey, *Historia de los títeres en España (desde sus origines hasta mediados del siglo XVIII)* (Madrid: Revista de Occidente, 1957), 8–9, 99, 107, 131, 155, 239.

18. Paul McPharlin, *The Puppet Theatre in America: A History* (New York: Harper & Brothers, 1949), 6, 7, 70, 71, 73, 77, and 78. For discussion of the European origins of marionettes, pre-Columbian examples of puppets, and colonial New Spanish puppet theater, see Sonia Iglesias Cabrera and Guillermo Murray Prisant, *Piel de Papel, Manos de Palo; Historia de los Títeres en México* (México: Espase-Calpe Mexicana, 1995), 53–59.

19. *Primera Parte de las Coplas de Don Simón* (Puebla: Imprenta de Jesús Franco é hijo, 1907), 3.

20. Francisco Rosete Aranda, *La compañía de títeres de los Rosete Aranda* (Tlaxcala: Instituto Tlaxcalteca de la Cultura, 1983), 75–77.

21. For England, see Scott Cutler Shershow, *Puppets and "Popular" Culture* (Ithaca: Cornell University Press, 1995).

22. The information on the tours is contained in the Rosete Aranda family account books. See El Archivo de la familia Rosete Aranda, Libros del Cuentos, Museo Nacional de Títeres, Humantla, Tlaxcala.

23. *Catálogo del Museo Nacional de Títeres* (Huamantla, Tlaxcala: n.p., n.d.).

24. Enrique Florescano, "La creación de la bandera nacional: un encuentro de tres tradiciones," unpublished essay presented at the coloquio "México en Francia: tradición. modernidad: Actualidad de la investigación mexicana en ciencias sociales (Paris, May 1995); "La construcción de identidades colectivas en México: Etnia, estado y nación," unpublished essay, presented at the coloquio "México en Francia: Tradición, Modernidad, Actualidad de la Investigación Mexicana en Ciencias Sociales" (Paris, May 1995); *Memoria Mexicana* (México: Fondo de Cultura Económica, 1994).

25. Isabel Fernández y Carmen Nava Nava, "He de comer de esa tuna: Ensayo histórico iconográfico sobre el escudo nacional," unpublished presentation at the American Historical Association (1996). In 1996, there was a documentary exposition called "La consumación de independencia 175 años" in the Archivo General de la Nación.

26. Isabel Quiñónez, *Mexicanos en su tinta: Calendarios* (Mexico: Instituto Nacional de Antropología e Historia, 1994), 68–69.

27. Ibid., 77.

II

THE CHURCH

6

The Enemy Within: Catholics and Liberalism in Independent Mexico, 1821–1860

Brian Connaughton

As Mexico reached the mid-nineteenth century, churchmen, as other citizens, were increasingly concerned by the inability of the country to organize and overcome the devastating legacy of unruly politics since independence. A frontal assault was needed on whatever was spoiling the cultural wellsprings of Mexico's strength and dignity in the midst of the numerous challenges it was facing. Liberal spokesmen defended Mexico's democratic heritage and identified a buoyant future with continued reform in a progressive direction.[1] But the Church hierarchy and those who identified with it had settled on another view. It had become increasingly clear to them that ideological and ethical forces they had long tolerated or even promoted were indeed undermining the country in such a way that it would never recover if left unchecked. Prominent bishops discovered the origins of this problem in the regalism and Jansenism of the late eighteenth century, and in liberal republicanism which had made undue advances against Church authority and attacked dogma while pretending to reform abuses.[2] Not all Catholic thinkers agreed on when the problem began or who was to blame, but they shared a new sense of urgency and peril. An anonymous pamphlet of 1858 saw the Constitution of 1824 as the opening shot fired against the Church and the long-standing interests of the Mexican people. In fact, it stated, "after the independence of Mexico, liberalism has been the first cause of its misfortunes."[3]

Mexican liberalism, it continued, favored social reforms and was not simply a political movement. The many political and social freedoms divorced it from the Church, that "eternal pillar on which all political systems should obviously rest." Furthermore, the liberal doctrines of "freedom of conscience," "popular sovereignty," "human freedom," "human perfectibility," "general will," and "national representation" seemed at odds with the

Church's beneficial and hierarchical presence in society, giving undue pre-eminence to popular opinion, representative institutions, and individualist outbursts against authority and social hierarchy.[4] Liberalism now seemed identified with "a certain hatred, a certain vehement desire to destroy religion and the Church."[5] To this pamphleteer, such a lamentable bias, with roots deep in the eighteenth century, threatened to cripple "the elements of all our national greatness."[6]

But even at mid-century, not all defenders of Mexican Catholicism were so convinced that liberalism was the dire and unrelenting foe of Mexico's good fortune and the Church. One writer blamed the problems on "ultraliberalism" more than liberalism itself and attacked the idea that "the clergy . . . is the enemy of liberal institutions . . . the clergy neither creates disturbances, nor incites to sedition, nor is the enemy of democracy."[7] Different clerics favored different political solutions, and there were proponents of democracy, aristocracy, monarchy, and even autocracy among the clergy. But the clergy as a corporation had no political affiliation *per se.*[8] This writer was content to point out that, under the sway of ultraliberalism, the Constitution of 1857 was at odds with the "general will," that due process was not being followed, that freedom of the press was being violated, that state legislatures were guilty of arbitrariness and exceeding the limits of the law, and that the rights of persons and property were not being respected.[9]

Even at the crisis point when the Reforma got under way in 1854, there was a certain reticence on the part of defenders of the Church to condemn liberalism outright. Censure was combined with the long-standing argument that the Church was compatible with a great variety of political solutions, one of which was liberal republicanism itself. This is no great surprise. Church authorities, in their dealings with the state, had in fact supported the federal experiment in 1824, whatever the preferences of certain individuals. Bishop Antonio Joaquín Pérez Martínez in Puebla removed the ecclesiastical governor of his diocese in 1824 because of a purported lack of support for the federal constitution. Canon Toribio González in Guadalajara published an edict explicitly supporting the federal republic, notwithstanding his open opposition to article 7 of the Constitution of Jalisco, which would have put the clergy there on salary. In both dioceses, there were important conflicts between Church authorities and parish priests as the Church put into practice its new alliance with the republic.[10] Local conflicts in the states cast an occasional shadow over the national alliance, but when in the late 1820s there were repeated confrontations between dissident friars unhappy with the anticlerical tone of the times, Church authorities came out strongly once again in favor of the liberal federal State and its authority.[11]

During the 1820s, churchmen customarily used the language of liberal republicanism to defend what they considered the Church's rights, combined with a frequent resort to more traditional arguments. In 1826, Miguel Gordoa, the ecclesiastical governor of the Diocese of Guadalajara, condemned the State of Jalisco's desire to exclude certain clerics from Church appointments on the basis of suspicions of their loyalty and patriotism. To Gordoa, this violated the rights of the citizen and due process, which was entirely incompatible with the "the just and liberal system which governs us." The following year another diocesan spokesman decried the suppression of the Church's tithe offices by means of a secret session in the local legislature, drastic action taken before publication of the new law, and an obvious attempt to circumvent the Church's legal right to protest. This seemed strangely at odds with "our liberal system."[12]

Quite noticeably, from the twenties onwards, Mexican clerics had to defend the Church's presence in a more mobile society where many people demanded "progress." Here also, it was necessary to show that Catholicism and progress were entirely compatible. That meant muffling the conflict between modern and Catholic values, and showing that there was nothing of value present in modern and liberal thinking that Catholicism did not accept or, indeed, had not, itself, anticipated.[13] Science was always a contentious point in this regard. Accordingly, the Metropolitan ecclesiastical government in Mexico City in 1833 declared that "there are no connections between science and impiety: there are no affinities between enlightenment and irreligiosity." It added that "the desire to accummulate knowledge, the effort to scrutinize even the most recondite objects, the truly philosophical liberty to reason about all the beings of nature, is not at odds with, rather, it establishes liaisons with just submission, with a healthy and proper subjection to revelation."[14]

Down to 1834, Church spokesmen openly supported the republic and progressive demands while simultaneously denouncing extreme positions or dangerous radicalisms. There was no frontal assault on liberalism. They fought against "yorkinismo," the "sansculottes," and tendencies to "de-catholicize" Mexico, not against liberals or liberalism in general. In fact, the standard language of the Church in the twenties and thirties, especially when under attack, was to claim for itself the liberal benefits of independence and to specifically point out the freedoms it should have under the new regime, in contrast to the tyranny of the old colonial regime. In such arguments, the line between the secular and clerical beneficiaries of independence and liberalism was carefully obscured.

As Mexican liberalism moved from its constitutionalist to its anticorporativist phase after 1830, certainly it was more and more difficult for the Church to make the adjustments it had so adroitly made during the twenties.[15] But the change did not impede a certain continuity in Church thought and its political positioning. In a well-known pamphlet of 1833 regarding the unilateral assumption by the State of ecclesiastical patronage, Pedro Espinosa, a canon of the Guadalajara cathedral, compared the situation in Mexico with revolutionary France and blasted the "detestable [Masonic] lodges" and "[i]nfamous reformers," but at the same time he underscored the participation of clerics in Mexican independence, gave ultramontanism a wide berth, and criticized the government in power for its contradiction because while it "presumes to be liberal" it was in fact "as absolute as" the colonial Spanish government.[16]

When the ecclesiastical governor of the diocese and other clerics were accused of seditious activities, another pamphlet declared that "Ecclesiastics by belonging to the clergy do not have fewer rights than other citizens, and in their court processes the legal procedures must be followed."[17] Another pamphlet followed the same line of reasoning, defending Article 3 of the Federal Constitution and adding for good measure that if clerics in their pulpits were called seditious, "it will not be only they who deserve this praise, it will be the constituent congress which provided this immutable article, it will be the entire nation that has wanted always and wants [now] to be" Catholic. This pamphleteer declared that no other class of citizens was under such constant attack as the clergy.[18]

Still another pamphlet called out for Mexico to prove Montesquieu wrong by "presenting the new phenomenon of a civilized, Catholic republic." The author emphasized that Mexicans were not subject to the pope in temporal affairs, that they could become moral and prosperous citizens without accepting religious toleration, that the tithe system could be reformed in an agreement between Church and State, and that Article 3 of the Federal Constitution was the bedrock of the republic. Attacking it could awaken opposition to republicanism, perhaps to "any liberal government," and even associate religion with the "cloak of despotism" and an absolute monarch.[19]

Something of this kind was in the cards. The following year, 1834, Canon Pedro Espinosa of the Guadalajara Diocese would declare that "the rights of the Church . . . are indisputably more to be respected than those of private individuals: and that is why if taking property from an individual is theft, taking it from the Church is a sacrilege."[20] The Church was then in the process of disengaging from the federal republic, if not entirely from moderate liberalism.[21] There was a growing sense among Church leaders that behind anticlericalism was the growing influence of utilitarianism among liberals, associated with a secular view of human nature and life in society, which was entirely antithetical to Article 3 of the Constitution of 1824 and its protection of a privileged role for the clergy in a Catholic Mexico.[22]

The disenchantment of the Church with the federal republic would not solve the dilemmas it was facing. Liberal anticorporativism would carry over into the following decade where, according to Josefina Vázquez, what prevailed was centralist liberalism more than conservatism.[23] During this period the Church was hounded for ever more loan monies. In 1838 the government tried to convince Church authorities to fund a bank whose major purpose was lending money to the administration. The sale of Church properties, especially those belonging to religious orders, was carefully controlled and significantly impeded by the central government. Orders were given to avoid the entry into Mexico of secularized friars who had belonged to Spain's regular orders, because their conduct and antecedents were suspect to the administration.[24]

Anticlerical tendencies deepened with the indisputably liberal-leaning revolution of 1841. Late that year, Sabás Sánchez Hidalgo sent to the Council of Government a plan to take over ecclesiastical wealth and attend to the problem of the national debt, a project he stated had now been delayed since it was last attempted in 1834, in a clear reference to the liberal regime of Valentín Gómez Farías. Sánchez Hidalgo wanted territorial wealth to circulate in benefit of a larger number of citizens, and he argued that clerics could be simply salaried by the central administration. He saw no reason why the Mexican constitutional tradition should have exempted the clergy from the ban on entailed estates. He argued for the dissolution of the "baneful alliance" that united the military and the Church and demanded that the armed forces ally with "the people." With ideas such as these freely circulating, it is not surprising that the early forties were characterized by growing friction and mistrust between the central government and the Church. As tension grew, it was rumored that a priest in Puebla had declared that "The government has now taken off its mask: it directly attacks the Church; and good Christians must be ready to defend it by fire and sword until death."[25] Significantly, the government commissioned the elaboration of two judicial opinions that were strongly regalist in 1843. One of these, by José María Jáuregui, essentially argued that Church wealth belonged to the nation while, in the other, Manuel de la Peña y Peña insisted that clerics were citizens who had the same obligation as all others to obey the law under all circumstances.[26]

Church authorities and their allies reacted. Deputy Juan Rodríguez de San Miguel demanded a review of the projected 1842 constitution because it permitted unlimited freedom of expression, excepting only direct attacks against Christian dogma or public morals. He also objected that only the public exercise of other religions was prohibited while unlimited freedom was given to private education. Likewise, although there was a provision for regulatory powers to control the excesses of the executive and the judiciary, no such power was contemplated for the much-feared legislature.[27]

The ecclesiastical chapter of Guadalajara found Rodríguez's thoughts regarding freedom of expression and private teaching quite pertinent. But it also worried that the jury system in the proposed constitution would give little protection to the Church in matters of attacks on religion since uninformed laymen might eventually make key decisions. Protection of Church property was not adequately established either, it argued. The Guadalajara chapter perceived that the wording of this project suggested that the exercise of Church patronage was inherent to Mexican sovereignty and that the national government could obstruct the distribution of papal communications among the population. Neither possibility was acceptable, and the latter affected the free flow of knowledge in society. Additionally, the authority assigned to the central government for legislating on Church affairs was unlimited and could not be accepted.[28]

A translated pro-Catholic treatise published the next year by a local friar in Guadalajara made it clear that alarm was spreading in some sectors of the Church that a moral and philosophical revolution was under way in the nation and had to be stopped. Freedom of conscience, religious tolerance, the excesses of interpretation of popular sovereignty, and the attack on clerical immunities had all become worries for dedicated Catholics.[29] There was even a suggestion that the Catholic clergy and democracy might be incompatible.[30] Perhaps the propagators of change were not sure "if in [their] liberty they do not recognize a God."[31] The thirst for progress and the advance of secularization were promoting a change of custom and a more relaxed attitude even during the traditional Lenten period leading up to the great event of Christian culture. The town council of Guadalajara had to step in and prohibit a new opera program during Lent in 1844, even while quickly admitting that "man lives in continual change, that is his irresistible propensity." But following the path set out by Mexican Catholics since the twenties, the town council associated Catholic practice with constitutionality and stability in a nation that had become all too prone to political fractiousness. Secularization had crept into even the defense of the nation's Catholic tradition.[32]

The pressure by the government of Valentín Gómez Farías for 15,000,000 pesos from the Church in early 1847, while still forbidding the Church to sell its possessions, only accentuated the Church's assurance that an important change was afoot in the nation. Federalism and a modified Constitution of 1824 were restored in May 1847. A pamphlet that year reminded readers that the program to disenfranchise the Church went back to José María Luis Mora in Mexico and encompassed a whole program in these times when "*impiety can count on a great number of followers.*" On the other hand, the pamphleteer seemed quite convinced that the current government was still basing its action on the legal opinion given by Manuel de la Peña y Peña in 1843. He held that Peña's arguments had undermined Church property and immunities and put it on the defensive. While accepting Peña's demand for clerical obedience to civil laws, this writer declared that "What the Mexican Church desires, what it requests, what its Prelates demand, *are not privileges and exemptions, but, rather, since those that it possesses are not respected, the same equality and justice be granted it that are not denied to anyone.*"[33]

Church arguments were tightening and reflecting the pressure of a concerted effort by the government, now avowedly liberal. Once again it seemed to be seeking the protection of the Constitution of 1824. The basic problem was a value change in the nation which was undermining the role the Church had played in Mexico and making the population susceptible to regalist liberal persuasion:

> The young person in the midst of our society, unfortunately suckled at the breasts of the ghost of liberty and wisdom, is like the coastal inhabitant, because wherever he sets his eyes, he sees under lovely golden glows prejudicial maxims; and even if not reading, he listens to the doctrines in family conversations, in common gatherings he hears them applauded, and he finds himself impelled to attend them even inside the venerable area of the temples themselves.

The situation was serious because

> the discord of novelty has become general . . . the frenzy of modern opinions is judged an all-powerful necessity . . . the false philosophy, spread profusely in the books of the day, is the whispering bird which trills in the woods. . . . It may be said that impiety is the blood which circulates in the veins of the century; that it is the air that society breathes; that it is like the sunlight that illuminates the nation.[34]

Under these circumstances reaction was making itself felt in some sectors of the Catholic Church. But one prominent cleric still argued forcefully that the only remedy was for "Christian teaching to accommodate to the state of society, follow its movements and variations and take on forms adequate to insinuate itself to the masses, attending to the intellectual change of mankind."[35]

It is tempting to think of some or much of the Church's ideological effort to adjust to the times as a Thomistic project of pretended synthesis between religious and secular traditions. That is, not so much an abandonment of long-standing intellectual traditions as a willingness to dialogue and interact with liberal thinking as it spread its influence in Mexican society and politics. But there was a personal twist to much of this discourse, for a number of prominent clergymen had significant experience with the Spanish liberal Cortes and new liberal institutions between 1810 and 1822, and with Mexico's constituent assembly in 1823–1824. Canon Miguel Gordoa, destined to be named bishop of the Guadalajara diocese in 1832, was such a man. He in fact signed the Constitution of 1824.[36] Through such experience, which seems to have implied earlier thinking that synchronized the political culture of these churchmen with changes taking place throughout the Spanish Empire, many enlightened clerics came to at least partially identify with many of the values which would ultimately question the Church's role in society.[37] Additionally, clerics tended to have a strong identification with Mexico as a new nation, and Mexico's early nationalism was closely associated with liberal republicanism in the 1820s and early 1830s, and clearly once again in the mid-forties and early fifties. A marked alternative was slow to take shape and, as we have seen, at least one author considers the period of 1835 to 1846 as a period of centralist liberalism rather than clearly one of conservatism. And regalist tendencies during this period did not make it an easy moment for the Church. So, due to past experiences, the association between liberalism and nationalism, and the lack of clear alternatives, Mexican Church authorities did not customarily attack liberalism in the period down to the mid-fifties.

At the same time, it is clear that individual clergymen were not always capable of navigating the political waters of this period with the Olympian equanimity of Church authorities. A percentage of clerics were tempted by the desire for political participation, by the lure of liberalism and reform, and by the suasive language of republicanism to recast their own view of things and to engage in new activities and manifest their thought in ways that showed the clear influence of liberalism. In this way, the struggle over ideology and values that was straining civil society would make its way into the fabric of the Church itself. For example, Francisco Delgadillo, parish priest of Colima who had been removed from his post by the bishop for his political activities, demanded of the government in February of 1830 a law that would set out the responsibilities of Church authorities in the Republic. Until this was done, Delgadillo considered that the people and the clergy would be "under the yoke of a colossal power, which recognizes no superior on earth." Delgadillo did not tire of using liberal arguments and epithets against the Church authorities in his battle to regain his parish.[38]

In a similar fashion, José de Jesús Huerta, the parish priest of Atotonilco el Alto, Jalisco, defied Church authorities in Guadalajara during the 1820s and early 1830s, supporting the radical liberal view that patronage was inherent in the sovereignty of the nation and lambasting clerical authorities as tied to a fanatical tradition of Inquisition and tyranny. Huerta spoke out for a creative and gentle gospel of Christianity against such tendencies.[39] In like fashion, the Canon José Manuel Covarrubias carried on a protracted conflict with Church authorities in Guadalajara from the late thirties into the mid-forties over a chaplaincy. Covarrubias's favorite weapon was the pamphlet, where he hammered the Curia over its internal disorders and scoffed at its resistance to the legal order, which to his understanding, defended his individual rights to free expression and defense of his interests over whatever the Church authorities might consider appropriate.[40]

By the mid-forties, parish priests in Colima and Guadalajara were supporting liberal causes in patriotic speeches. In September of 1846 the population of Colima was told by its priest that freedom of thought was the most sacred of properties and that Church abuses must be remedied by a return to early Christian virtues, which might be achieved by adopting American institutions, which should be considered a model for Mexico. He also demanded a reform and modernization of Mexican education, the creation of civil and penal codes that could be understood by ordinary people and used by them, and an overhaul of the legal system to make it quicker and less expensive.[41] In October, the pastor of the cathedral parish in Guadalajara extolled the virtues of the "popular party" and called for spreading the "divine fire of liberty." He decried monarchy, arguing that popular sovereignty was inalienable, and demanded that "truth, justice and reason" be discovered in the "majority" of the population. He spoke out simultaneously for religion, the "republican system," and "democracy."[42]

The liberal regime of Valentín Gómez Farias would appoint the parish priest of Colotlán, Jalisco, Andrés López Nava, as Minister of Justice and Ecclesiastical Affairs in 1847. López Nava promptly found himself in a head-on collision with several Mexican bishops, defending the Mexican nation and government attempts to alienate Church wealth in a regalist manner, which liberals of all persuasions were then using. In an imperious tone, which might seem more befitting a monarchy than a republic, López Nava nonetheless supported the liberal regime against the bishops, accusing them of unholy conduct and inciting Catholics to violence against the government.[43]

Church-State conflict grew worse in the fifties. An open debate took place in Jalisco between churchmen over the Constitution of 1857 and the conduct that clerics should adopt toward it and toward the liberal government. A number of priests took their oath of allegiance to the liberal constitution and served in the constitutionalist armies. One priest defended the sacramentality of civil marriages and others defended their right to give absolution to constitutionalists on their deathbeds. As late as 1860, Canon Juan José Caserta of the cathedral defended his right to participate in politics and identify with "Christian liberty" against "false devotion." He protested the bishop's punishing him for his liberal commitment, considering the censure "unnecessary, despotic, calumnious and insidious." Still another priest in 1860 defended his right to his private opinion in questions where absolute truth had not been clearly established. Trying to find common ground with Bishop Pedro Espinosa, he proclaimed that "however much I am inclined to liberalism as a man, I am more inclined to Catholicism as a Christian." It is not surprising that under these circumstances Bishop Espinosa attempted to persuade wayward priests to rejoin the fold, and to one of them he confided his own preference for a constitutional oath that would allow convinced Catholics to swear to the constitution while adhering to the dictates of their conscience in matters of religion.[44]

If such turmoil was true of the clergy, it was also true of the Catholic laity. José María Luis Mora and a few others may have been judged to have gone beyond the pale of Catholic orthodoxy, but the borderline between what was acceptable Catholic thinking and what was not was forever escaping easy definition, especially since what appeared to be at the bottom of this unseemliness was a tidal wave of value change more than "ideas" as such.

Topics such as religious tolerance within a Catholic state began appearing as legitimate items for debate right after independence.[45] The viability of the Mexican nation-state had become a major concern of many prominent thinkers and Church wealth, Church authority, and Catholic loyalties came under serious scrutiny.[46] Long-standing friends of the Church such as Manuel de la Peña y Peña, Antonio Haro y Tamariz, and Juan Bautista Morales betrayed the Church at key moments by siding with the State or adopting avowedly liberal positions regarding government sovereignty, ecclesiastical wealth, and the moral and structural reform of the Church.[47]

The bishops' pastoral letters and other Church-oriented documents are full of references to value changes and concern with fashionable ideas in the midst of a proliferating free press and imported printed materials.[48] One author finds that beginning in the late twenties the elite and people of Mexico City celebrated Independence Day events which were "almost entirely non-religious and the role and intervention of the clergy always kept to a minimum." He finds that the attitude of the elite in this regard was fully conscious and purposeful.[49] Such resolute secularization of civic events speaks of changes in the minds and hearts of many people who seldom had direct confrontation with the Church and infrequently were disposed in any way to give up their religious beliefs.

In a similar vein, another historian finds that religious practices of the faithful in Puebla were reflecting new and more secular values before independence and that this continued more markedly thereafter.[50] Vocations for religious life were slipping significantly in the decades after independence, throughout the whole national territory, a process which merits further study.[51] There was also a growing preference for religious orders that would directly serve society by means of their educational and hospital activities.[52] Although numerous agreements were made that virtually reestablished aspects of the patronage system, formal Church-State relations were a source of constant concern for Mexican Catholics. Ecclesiastical authorities in Mexico spoke out against Leo XII's condemnation of Mexican independence in 1824, and the Church granted the State rights over ecclesiastical appointments and monies, but there was never a definitive solution, not even during the Second Empire. In this ill-defined context, Carlos María de Bustamante, a convinced Catholic and defender of the Church, could assert the anticlerical view that patronage rights were inherent to Mexican sovereignty.[53] From its initial decade of support of the Constitution of 1824, its partial loss of control over the body faithful, and an embarrassing problem with dissident priests, the Church hierarchy had to confront this disheartening prospect of internal dissention. The liberal challenge had to be domesticated by constant debate and assiduous clarifications, and liberalism itself shorn of its exaggerations and extremisms. But this challenge could not be easily or relentlessly attacked by name because it had come in through the door of the Cortes, consolidated under the federal republic, and had not lost all of its mystique and popular appeal even under the centralist experiment of 1836–1846. On the contrary, the vibrancy of liberalism in the late forties, and following upon the dictatorship of Antonio López de Santa Anna in 1853–1854, was such that it is not an exaggeration to suggest that Mexican Catholics down to 1860 were not able to fully combat this political orientation because the ranks of the laity and the clergy themselves suffered noticeably divided loyalties.

It would seem fair to say that before 1860 the relations between liberalism and Mexican Catholics was neither one of "[c]onsistent harmony" nor constant confrontation.[54] Certainly by mid-century friction was growing and common ground in political ideas between reformers and proclaimed Catholics was shrinking. Yet still in 1849 Canon Clemente de Jesús Munguía, of the Diocese of Michoacán, could find the supremacy of Catholic principles compatible with reason, science, educational reform, liberty, and the general improvement of society. At that time, Munguía seemed bent on winning over public opinion instead of suppressing it, and he even sanctioned the Church's "prudent reserve . . . towards new theories."[55]

Popular sovereignty, individual freedoms, political representation, and constitutionalism had firmly rooted in Mexico's political culture, and the Church as such did little to attack them. Thornier issues were freedoms of press and religion, the idea of a "social pact" that seemed to suggest to some that the rules of society might be arbitrarily construed, certain aspects of individualism and utilitarianism that seemed to conflict with charity, a holistic sense of society and spirituality, and, of course, anticlericalism. Property itself was frequently an issue, since Church spokesmen demanded that no distinction be made between individual and corporate holdings. But Hale found that there was no "constant ideological conflict" between 1834 and 1846.[56] And, as we have seen, before and after that period there was a rather fluid debate more than constant confrontation.

In the midst of a significant value change in the population, favoring secularization, liberalism, and a less clergy-mediated Catholicism, Church authorities tended to defend moderate reformism against radical change.[57] They had many liberal allies. Even José María Luis Mora had to confess that the great reforms of 1833–1834 divided liberals themselves into "fervent" liberals and moderates.[58] It would be hard to argue that "fervent" or later pure liberals had won a majority of political support prior to 1854.[59] So in fact the supporters of the Church had some room to operate. The political environment was becoming more complex, tense, and polemical, as ideology and values became a subject of growing debate. Yet, just as there was no concerted Catholic drive against many important aspects of liberalism, nor even against increasing secularization in education that accompanied liberal ascendancy, it would seem—on the other hand—that only a minority of clearly liberal thinkers shared the politics of Valentín Gómez Farías and José María

Luis Mora as they turned against the Constitution of 1824 and promoted liberal reforms that had a broad social and political content.[60] It would seem important to underline the point that, down to 1856–1857, mainstream liberalism in Mexico was tied to the Constitution of 1824 or to the centralist liberal constitutions in the period 1834–1846. The currents of opinion that would come to prevail in Mexican liberalism after 1857 could be combated until then as undesirable and unnecessary accretions to a body of thought that could found a republic while not necessarily imperiling the long-standing and paramount interests of the Catholic Church. Only the late fifties and early sixties would see the consolidation of a Catholic school of thought openly hostile to liberalism.[61]

True, before that time it is possible to detect some cognitive dissonance between Church spokesmen and liberal advocates. The easiest way to summarize this is to point out Church concern with assuring Mexico's present and future as a Catholic nation with transcendental Christian goals to accomplish. There was a long-standing fear that foreign, especially French, influence might derail this national project, and such an idea fueled attempts to censor public opinion, prevent religious tolerance, and even diminish direct contact with foreigners.[62] Churchmen and other Catholic thinkers tended to emphasize holistic social values in this regard and to limit their commitment to the professed liberal goals of individual liberty and freedom of thought and press. The implications of the popular vote and popular sovereignty could be questioned, while not necessarily discarding either. As evidenced in the civic discourse of Puebla State, such Catholic positions could exercise strong local influence and condition the way liberalism itself and the national identity were managed by political thinkers.[63]

The powerful thrust of Church discourse oriented to national transcendence was present in other areas besides Puebla. This was a constant in the Guadalajara diocese as well.[64] However, in formal Church discourse and in the action of individual clergymen, the Guadalajara diocese seems more fully involved in a reconciliation of the differences between Catholic preferences and liberal doctrine. Church discourse tended to be more equally divided between a commitment to the liberal order and insistence on particular Catholic social and economic premises. It is in Guadalajara that the liberating aspects of Christian dogma were more customarily underlined, and by the mid-forties there seemed to prevail the idea of a liberal-Catholic alliance.[65]

While civic discourse in Puebla showed signs of a liberalism clearly moderated by the holistic concerns of Catholic thought, churchmen in Puebla cautiously sought civic reconciliation in the thirties and forties based on a certain dose of liberal pluralism. But it did so in the midst of a remarkably strong reaction against secularization, extreme liberalism, and signs of growing religious indifference. In Puebla the promises of individualistic liberalism were denounced as chimerical in 1834. In 1838 the liberal-federal Constitution of 1824 was referred to as the "tragic system of 1824" because it was reputed to have opened the door to partisan conflict, which promised the people more equality than they wanted and tore apart society under the inspiration of the Masonic lodges. Bishop Francisco Pablo Vázquez evinced deep concern for the direction of society and the State and in one excess of emotion in 1834 struck out against "Republican despotism" in matters concerning the Church. A Church-inspired pamphlet called in 1839 for the rights and obligations of citizens to be reviewed and sanctioned by bishops. And the identification of the Mexican nation with the Virgin of Guadalupe and divine providence was simultaneously underscored by others.[66]

Social tensions seem to have run high in Puebla in these years, higher than in the Diocese of Guadalajara.[67] This might indeed account for and partially justify a marked wariness about the effects of an individualistic liberalism on the body politic. Materialism, also identified with incoming liberalism, was generally combated with a pronounced emphasis on the sacred basis of social intercourse.[68] All of this was not exclusive to Puebla, but it was very marked there and thinkers gave eloquent expression to their concerns. But their views were not necessarily at odds with moderate liberalism, despite expressions of anger and angst. Bishop Vázquez demanded in 1834 that the rights of citizens be extended to the Church and due protection be awarded it. Partisan politics were denounced by Church-oriented pamphlets in the following years of centralist liberal governments. A sermon of 1839 by a well-known local parish priest decried the false notion that there was any opposition between the Church and republican government. The true Church and true liberty were said to be above such insane ideas. Also in 1839 a re-edition of a 1822 sermon by former Bishop Antonio Joaquín Pérez Martínez underwrote a close association between the Church, the State, the nation and progress. The governor himself was moved in 1841 to suggest that partisan politics had been laid to rest in Puebla. While a sermon in 1843 demanded all sights be focused on "the progress of civilization," another in 1845 celebrated the fall of yet another dictatorship of General Antonio López de Santa Anna. It proclaimed that absolutism had been defeated by religious piety under the aegis of the Virgin of Guadalupe. The Constitution and the law had been defended against an absolutist government by the combination of civic and ecclesiastical authorities. Another sermon that same year claimed to support religion, freedom, the fatherland, and fraternal unity. The preacher expressed his hope that a just freedom would bring happiness and abundance. Still in 1851 a civic speaker could see a Christian education as the wellspring from which morality, civilization, and true democracy would develop.[69]

Crisis would come to Mexico in the form of polarizing public opinion and growing confrontation in the fifties. Clearly more studies of regional processes are needed, but throughout the country the Church and ordinary Catholics would face hard decisions.[70] As seen above, in the Diocese of Guadalajara the fifties witnessed important conflict between the bishop and priests who sided with the liberal constitutionalists. It is interesting to note that Guy Thompson found indications of a similar process in the Diocese of Puebla and an air of uncertainty as to the authority the Church might exercise there over liberal parishioners.[71]

Mexico moved quickly from the heavy-handed moderate liberal government of General Mariano Arista, to the conservative dictatorship of General Antonio López of Santa Anna, to the governments of the Reforma and civil war.[72] The properties of the clergy and the role of the Church in Mexican society were definitely at the heart of the crisis after the disastrous defeat in the war with the United States.[73] It was now that Republican liberalism and Catholicism had their hardest moments to face. Yet even with outspoken Catholics veering to the right and confrontation with the daily diet, Catholic thought still has to be carefully analyzed for the ensuing period. Even monarchical tendencies are no sure sign that Catholic thinkers had all broken with liberalism. The Second Empire itself, the most protracted experiment with monarchy ever in independent Mexico, would turn out to be an utter fiasco from the standpoint of the Church itself.[74] When the cycle of civil war ended, we still need to know how individual preference among Catholics and enduring regional variation affected political responses among the clergy and the laity.[75]

It is known that nationally Mexican Catholics split between hard-core traditionalists and Catholic Liberals. We know mostly about the traditionalists.[76] Intransigence became associated with the papal Syllabus of 1864, which blasted the "errors" of liberalism.[77] But the Roman ultramontane magazine *Cività Cattolica*, read by Mexican Catholics during the sixties, has been seen as no less pragmatical than doctrinaire.[78] Eulogio G. Gillow of Puebla, ordained in 1865 and appointed Bishop of Oaxaca in 1887, has been described as a Catholic liberal by a modern Mexican historian, and there is no doubt he collaborated intimately with the government of General Porfirio Díaz while traditionalist Catholics demanded a hostile or nonpolitical stance. The new Archbishop of Mexico in 1892, Próspero María Alarcón, had not sided with the Second Empire and was known to have Republican convictions, while more and more Catholics were warming to the regime.[79] The Church was engaged in important new educational and social programs, as well as internal reform, and was increasingly inspired by the social message of Pope Leo XIII.[80]

It is imperative that we soon have a fresh evaluation of the gamut of Catholic thought and values in Mexico during this time. Was the relationship with the Catholic liberal past lost during this period? Was popular Catholicism as closed to the liberal regime as some traditionalist Catholic thinking and values would make us believe? Was all traditionalist Catholic thinking a simple rehash of old values and ideas, or did it also more freely interact with ongoing social and ideological trends? Were the new interests among Catholics a way to fudge the implications of social change and to finally make their peace with it, or were they truly and fully the search for a totally Catholic alternative?[81] And finally, we should make less use of "Catholic" as an all-encompassing adjective and start speaking more of "Catholics" as a plural historical phenomenon quite clearly marked by time, space, and social condition in a regional and not just national dimension. Better yet, we should aim to consider the conduct, ideas, and values not only of the Church hierarchy and vociferous and self-proclaimed Catholic thinkers, but also of a larger number of more ordinary, quotidian actors in a regionally differentiated Mexican society in transition.

NOTES

I would like to thank William B. Taylor and Eric Van Young for their careful reading of an earlier version of this essay and for their very helpful suggestions.

1. Brian Connaughton, "Entre la palabra hablada y la palabra escrita: la política nacional en el foro de La Alameda," in *Cultura Impresa en México, Siglos XVI–XIX* (Guadalajara: CIESAS-Occidente) (forthcoming).

2. "Protesta del Y.S. Obispo de Puebla contra la Constitucion espedida en el presente año," Archivo General de la Nación (hereafter AGN), Justicia Eclesiástica, vol. 183, fs. 340–354; "Representaciones y protestas de varios Diocesanos contra la ley de obvenciones parroquiales," AGN, Justicia Eclesiástica, vol. 183, fs. 458, 468–484.

3. J. H., *El liberalismo y sus efectos en la República Mexicana* (Mexico: Imprenta de A. Boix, 1858), 5.

4. Ibid., 4–7. The pamphlet only details its understanding of three terms: "freedom of conscience," "popular sovereignty," and "human freedom."

5. Ibid., 7.

6. Ibid., 8–9.

7. Un jalisciense, *Tendencias de la demagogia mexicana, manifestadas por sus propios hechos* (Guadalajara: Tipografía de Rodríguez, 1857), 5, 10.

8. Ibid., 13–14.

9. Ibid., 26–27.

10. Brian Connaughton, "La Secretaría de Justicia y Negocios Eclesiásticos y la evolución de las sensibilidades nacionales: una óptica a partir de los papeles ministeriales, 1821–1854," in Manuel Ramos Medina, comp., *Memoria del I Coloquio Historia de la Iglesia en el Siglo XIX* (Mexico: Condumex, 1998), 127–147, especially pp. 132–134; *[Edicto del] . . . Dr. D. Toribio González, prebendado de la santa iglesia catedral y vicario capitular del obispado de Guadalajara, en sedevacante* (Guadalajara: Imprenta de la viuda de Romero (12 de diciembre de 1824).

11. For the case of conflict between the Church and liberals in Jalisco, see Brian F. Connaughton, "El federalismo: las élites secular y clerical en los 1820," *Estudios*

Jaliscienses 22 (1995), 23–38. Regarding dissident friars and the Church, see Connaughton, "La Secretaría de Justicia," 134–137.

12. Brian Connaughton, *Ideología y sociedad en Guadalajara, 1788–1853* (Mexico: Consejo Nacional para la Cutura y las Artes and Universidad Nacional Autónoma de México, 1992), 300–303 and 332.

13. Connaughton, "El federalismo"; James H. Lee, "Church and State in Mexican Higher Education, 1821–1861," *Journal of Church and State* 20: 1, (winter 1978), 57–72.

14. *Carta pastoral del . . . Deán y Cabildo Gobernador de la Santa Iglesia Metropolitana de México* (Mexico: Imprenta de Galván a cargo de Mariano Arévalo, 1833 [14 de mayo de 1833].

15. Charles A. Hale, *El liberalismo mexicano en la época de Mora, 1821–1853* (Mexico: Siglo XXI, 1972), 106–107, 110, 150–151.

16. Pedro Espinosa. *Patronato en la nación. Núm. 2°, Contestación al dictamen de la comisión eclesiástica del Senado sobre que el patronato de la Iglesia mexicana reside radicalmente en la nación* (Guadalajara: Imprenta de Dionisio Rodríguez, 1833).

17. A.T., *Hablen los predicadores y confundan la impiedad* (Guadalajara: Imprenta de Dionisio Rodríguez, 1833). No page numbers.

18. Un quidam, *Contestación a los enemigos de los predicadores* (Guadalajara: Imprenta de Dionisio Rodríguez a cargo de Trinidad Buitrón, 1833).

19. T.B.M., *Disertación contra la tolerancia religiosa* (Mexico: Imprenta de Galván a cargo de Mariano Arévalo, 1833), especially pp. 12–13, 31–33, 43, 46–59.

20. Pedro Espinosa, *Rentas eclesiásticas o sea impugnación de la disertación que sobre la materia se ha publicado de orden del Honorable Congreso de Zacatecas* (Guadalajara: Imprenta a cargo de Teodosio Cruz-Aedo, 1834), 11.

21. Connaughton, *Ideología y sociedad*, 355–386.

22. Hale, *El liberalismo mexicano*, 152–192, discusses the role of utilitarianism in liberal thought.

23. Josefina Zoraida Vázquez, "Centralistas, conservadores y monarquistas 1830–1853," in Humberto Morales and William Fowler, coords., *El conservadurismo mexicano en el siglo XIX (1810–1910)* (Puebla, Mexico: Benemérita Universidad Autónoma de Puebla, Saint-Andrews University, Secretaría de Cultura del Gobierno del Estado de Puebla, 1999), 115–133, especially p. 117.

24. Brian F. Connaughton, "¿Ruptura o continuidad? Federalismo, centralismo y cultura político-religiosa, 1821–1854," in *Eslabones*, 13 (January–June 1997): 6–19, especially pp. 12–13; and "Agio, clero y bancarrota fiscal, 1846–1847," *Mexican Studies/Estudios Mexicanos* 14: 2, (summer 1998) 263–285; Michael P. Costeloe, *The Central Republic in Mexico, 1835–1846* (Cambridge: Cambridge University Press, 1993), 127–131, 192–193, 223–224 and 290.

25. Connaughton, "¿Ruptura o continuidad?," 13–17.

26. Brian Connaughton, "El ocaso del proyecto de 'Nación Católica.' Patronato virtual, préstamos, y presiones regionales, 1821–1856," in Brian Connaughton, Carlos Illades, and Sonia Pérez Toledo, eds., *Construcción de la legitimidad política en México en el siglo XIX* (Mexico: El Colegio de Michoacán, Universidad Autónoma Metropolitana, UNAM/Instituto de Investigaciones Históricas, El Colegio de México, 1999), 227–262, especially pp. 230–231.

27. Juan Rodríguez de San Miguel, *Discurso pronunciado en [sic] 14 de noviembre de 1842 por el Sr. Diputado . . . contra el proyecto de Constitución en su discusión general. Tomado del Siglo Diez y Nueve Num. 410* (Guadalajara: Imprenta del Gobierno, 1842).

28. *Observaciones que hace el Venerable Cabildo de Guadalajara al Soberano Congreso Constituyente, sobre el proyecto de Constitución* (Guadalajara: Imprenta del Gobierno, 1842).

29. Conde Muzzarelli, *Cartas del Conde Muzzarelli, sobre el juramento de la Constitución Cispadana,* trans. Fr. José María Guzmán (Guadalajara: Imprenta del Gobiero, 1843).

30. Ibid., 56.

31. Ibid., 71.

32. *Exposición hecha por el M. I. Ayuntameinto de esta ciudad al Señor Prefecto del Primer Distrito, de los motivos que determinaron al primero á no contratar funciones de opera en cuaresma* (Guadalajara: Imprenta de Dionisio Rodríguez, 1844). The quote is from p. 5.

33. *Observaciones sobre el dictamen del Señor Licenciado don Manuel de la Peña y Peña relativo al decreto de 31 de agosto de 1843* (Guadalajara: Imprenta del Gobierno, 1847), especially pp. 5, 17, and 34 (emphasis in the original).

34. J. M. Cayetano Orozco, *Discurso sobre la necesidad que hay en el día, de dedicar a la juventud al estudio de las humanidades. Y principalmente sobre la elocuencia sagrada: escrito por Dr. D. . . . Catedrático de Elocuencia y de Historia en el Seminario de esta ciudad* (Guadalajara: Imprenta de Manuel Brambila, 1848), especially pp. 21, 23.

35. Ibid., 29.

36. Juan B. Iguíniz, *Catálogo Biobibliográfico de los Doctores, Licenciados y Maestros de la Antigua Universidad de Guadalajara* (Mexico: Universidad Nacional Autónoma de México, 1963), 168–171; Manuel Chust, *La cuestión nacional americana en las Cortes de Cádiz* (Valencia: Fundación Instituto Historia social and IIH/Universidad Nacional Autónoma de México, 1999), 43–44. I would also like to thank Jaime E. Rodríguez O. for documents he has shown me and comments made in this regard.

37. Jaime E. Rodríguez O., *The Independence of Spanish America* (Cambridge: Cambridge University Press, 1998); François-Xavier Guerra, *Modernidad e independencias. Ensayos sobre las revoluciones hispánicas* (Mexico: Editorial MAPFRE and Fondo de Cultura Económica, 1993).

38. Brian F. Connaughton, "Hegemonía desafiada: libertad, nación e impugnación clerical de la jerarquía eclesiástica. Guadalajara 1821–1860," in Nelly Sigaut, ed., *La Iglesia Católica en México* (Mexico: El Colegio de Michoacán and Secretaría de Gobernación, 1997), 145–169, especially pp. 145–149.

39. Sigaut, ed., *La Iglesia Católica en México,* 149–150.

40. Ibid., 151–154.

41. Ibid., 154.

42. Ibid., 155–157.

43. Ibid., 157–159.

44. Ibid., 159–168.

45. Gustavo Santillán, "La tolerancia religiosa y el Congreso Constituyente, 1823–1824," *Religiones y Sociedad* 6 (May–August, 1999): 67–80.

46. Brian Connaughton, "La Iglesia y el Estado en México, 1821–1856," in *Gran Historia de México Ilustrada* 36 (Mexico: Editorial Planeta, 2001).

47. *Observaciones sobre el dictamen*, especially p. 33; Connaughton, "El ocaso del proyecto," 231, 239, 262; Jan Bazant, *Antonio Haro y Tamariz y sus aventuras políticas, 1811–1869* (Mexico: El Colegio de México, 1985), especially pp. 47–52.

48. Sometimes controversy over new ideas grew into a storm, as it did in Guadalajara in 1850–1851. See *Censura y prohibición del libro titulado "Educación de las madres de familia, o de la civilización del género humano por medio de las mujeres", su autor L. Aymé Martin* (Guadalajara: Tipografía de Dionisio Rodríguez, 1850); *Prohibición del libro titulado: "El retrato de la Virgen María en los cielos"* (Guadalajara: Tipografía de Rodríguez, 1850); *Observaciones contra la impugnación del libro titulado El retrato de la Virgen, y su contestación por el Dr. D. Pedro Espinosa, Canónigo de Guadalajara* (Mexico: Tipografía de R. Rafael, Calle de la Cadena número 13, 1850); *Defensa de algunos puntos de la Doctrina Católica, o sea contestación a las "Nuevas observaciones sobre el opúsculo 'Lo del Señor Espinosa contra el Retrato a la Virgen'"* (Guadalajara: Tipografía de Dionisio Rodríguez, 1851).

49. Michael P. Costeloe, "The Junta Patriótica and the Celebration of Independence Day in Mexico City, 1825–1855," *Mexican Studies/Estudios Mexicanos* 13: 1 (winter 1997), 21–53, especially p. 51.

50. Francisco J. Cervantes Bello, "De la impiedad a la usura. Los capitales eclesiásticos y el crédito en Puebla (1825–1863)," (Ph.D. diss.: El Colegio de México, 1993); Francisco J. Cervantes Bello, "La piedad en la catedral angelopolitana: capellanías, aniversarios y misas, 1830–1840," in Ramos Medina, comp., *Memoria del I Coloquio*, 217–228.

51. Jan Bazant, *Los bienes de la Iglesia en México (1856–1875), Aspectos económicos y sociales de la Revolución liberal* (Mexico: El Colegio de México, 1971), 42; Anne Staples, *La Iglesia en la primera república federal mexicana (1824–1835)* (México: Secretaría de Educación Pública, Colección SepSetentas, 1976), 23.

52. Elisa Speckman, "Congregaciones femeninas en la segunda mitad del siglo XIX" (M.A. thesis: Universidad Nancional Autónoma de México, 1996); Anne Staples, "Un balance histórico: el papel de los conventos mexicanos de monjas, siglo XIX," Ramos Medina, comp., *Memoria del I Coloquio*, 199–216, especially p. 201.

53. Rodolfo Casillas R., "Del Patronato al nombramiento de obispos: El inicio de un nuevo entendimiento," *Religiones y Sociedad* 6 (May–August 1999): 83–110, especially p. 89; Michael P. Costeloe, *Church and State in Independent Mexico. A Study of the Patronage Debate, 1821–1857*, (London: Royal Historical Society, 1978); Josefina Zoraida Vázquez, "Federalismo, reconocimiento e Iglesia," in Ramos Medina, comp., *Memoria del I Coloquio*, 93–112; Connaughton, "El ocaso del proyecto"; Connaughton, "La Secretaría de Justicia"; Brian F. Connaughton, "Cultura, política y discurso religioso en Puebla: los caminos entrecruzados de la primera ciudadanía, 1821–1854," *Iztapalapa*, 39: 69–92, especially p. 74; Luis Ramos Gómez-Pérez O.P., "El Emperador, el Nuncio y el Vaticano," in Álvaro Matute, Evelia Trejo, and Brian Connaughton, coords., *Estado, Iglesia y Sociedad en México, Siglo XIX* (Mexico: Universidad Nacional Autónoma de México & Miguel Ángel Porrúa, 1995), 251–265; William Fowler, "Carlos María Bustamante: un tradicionalista liberal," in Morales and Fowler, coords., *El conservadurismo mexicano*, 59–85, especially pp. 63, 68.

54. Lee, "Church and State," 71.

55. Clemente Munguía, *Los principios de la Iglesia Católica comparados con los de las escuelas racionalistas, en sus aplicaciones a la enseñanza y educacion pública, y en sus relaciones con los progresos de las ciencias, de las letras y de las artes, la mejora de las costumbres y la perfeccion de la sociedad. Por el Lic. . . . , Rector del Seminario, Canónigo de esta Santa Iglesia Catedral, Provisor y Vicario general de este Obispado* (Morelia: Imprenta de Y. Arango, 1849), 6.

56. Hale, *El liberalismo mexicano*, 150. Hale also summarizes some of the outstanding features of Mexican liberalism on p. 42. For a broad discussion of liberalism in general, see Norberto Bobbio, Nicola Matteucci, and Gianfranco Pasquino, eds., *Diccionario de Política* (Mexico: Siglo XXI, 1995), 2: 875–901.

57. B. F. Connaughton, "Soberanía y religiosidad: la disputa por la grey en el movimiento de la Reforma," in Alicia Tecuanhuey, coord., *De clérigos y políticos durante la desacralización del poder político. Puebla siglos xix–xx* (forthcoming); Connaughton, *Ideología y sociedad*.

58. José María Luis Mora, *Obras sueltas de . . . , Ciudadano mejicano,* 2 vols. (París: Librería de Rosa, 1837), 1: lxxxvii.

59. Hale, *El liberalismo mexicano*, 18–19, 35–41.

60. Hale, *El liberalismo mexicano*, 115–117, 125; Mora, *Obras*, 1: cxi–cclxii propounds the bases of the program he and Gómez Farías fostered in 1833–1834.

61. Gastón García Cantú, *El pensamiento de la reacción mexicana*, 3 vols. (Mexico: Universidad Nacional Autónoma de México, 1994–1997), especially volumes 1 and 2.

62. William Taylor brought to my attention an interesting pre-independence pamphlet which expresses this fear for Mexico. See *Las chinches de la Europa, ó comparación de los franceses con este odioso animal. Por el autor del juego de las provincias* (Mexico: Imprenta de la calle del Espíritu Santo, c. 1809). This idea resurfaced with great force in the thirties and forties. See Connaughton, *Ideología y sociedad*, 309–418.

63. Brian F. Connaughton, "La sacralización de lo cívico: la imagen religiosa en el discurso cívico-patriótico del México independiente. Puebla (1827–1853)," in Matute, Trejo, and Connaughton. coords., *Estado, Iglesia y Sociedad en México*, 223–250.

64. Connaughton, *Ideología y sociedad*.

65. Brian F. Connaughton, "Ágape en disputa: fiesta cívica, cultura política y la frágil urdimbre nacional antes del Plan de Ayutla," *Historia Mexicana*, 45: 2, (Oct.–Dec. 1995) 281–316; Brian F. Connaughton, "Providencia y progreso, Cultura política en Guadalajara, 1821–1853," in Brian F. Connaughton, *Dimensiones de la identidad patriótica. Religión política y regiones en México, Siglo XIX* (Mexico: UAM-I and Miguel Ángel Porrúa, 2001), 123–135.

66. Connaughton, "Cultura, política y discurso," especially pp. 77–83; Connaughton, "La sacralización de lo cívico."

67. Guy P. C. Thomson, *Puebla de los Ángeles, Industry and Society in a Mexican City, 1700–1850* (Boulder: Westview Press, Dellplain Latin American Studies, 25, 1989).

68. Brian F. Connaughton, "Conjuring the body politic from the 'corpus mysticum': the post-independent pursuit of public opinion in Mexico, 1821–1854," *The Americas*, 55: 3 (1998): 459–479.

69. Connaughton, "Cultura, política y discurso," 79–86.

70. Robert J. Knowlton, *Los bienes del clero y la Reforma mexicana, 1856–1910* (Mexico: Fondo de Cultura Económica, 1985), 38–78.

71. Guy P. C. Thomson, "La contrarreforma en Puebla, 1854–1886," in Morales and Fowler, coords., *El conservadurismo mexicano*, 239–263, especially 241–242.

72. Michael P. Costeloe, "Mariano Arista y la élite de la Ciudad de México, 1851–1852," in Morales and Fowler, coords., *El conservadurismo mexicano*, 187–212; Carmen Vázquez Mantecón, *Santa Anna y la encrucijada del Estado. La dictadura (1853–1854)* (Mexico: Fondo de Cultura Económica, 1986); Knowlton, *Los bienes del clero*, 79–113.

73. Nicole Giron, "El proyecto de Folletería Mexicana del Siglo XIX: alcances y límites" *Secuencia* 39, nueva época, (Sept.-Dec. 1997): 7–24, especially p. 20. Giron argues that there was a boom in the discussion of Church-State issues after 1837, which peaked in 1851 and in fact descended significantly thereafter, as reflected in the publication of related pamphlets.

74. Ramos Gómez-Pérez O.P., "El Emperador, el Nuncio y el Vaticano."

75. Connaughton, *Dimensiones de la identidad patriótica*, explores important regional variations of the Mexican Church from the late colonial period down to the 1850s, with special attention to the Dioceses of Puebla and Guadalajara.

76. Jorge Adame Goddard, *El pensamiento político y social de los católicos mexicanos 1867–1914* (Mexico: Universidad Nacional Autónoma de México, 1981), especially pp. 27–29, 106–114.

77. A Church-inspired document of this sort appeared in Guadalajara in 1875 as a re-edition of a French text. See Monseñor Segur, *Ofrenda a los jovenes católicos liberales por . . . Vertida al castellano de la cuarta edición francesa por el C. De A.* (Guadalajara: Tipografía de Rodríguez, 1875).

78. Manuel Olimón Nolasco, "Una revista católica europea y la Reforma mexicana," in Brian F. Connaughton and Andrés Lira González, coords., *Las fuentes eclesiásticas para la historia social de México* (Mexico: Universidad Autónoma Metropolitana-Iztapalapa & Instituto Mora, 1996), 371–379, especially p. 375.

79. Manuel Esparza, "Arzobispo Eulogio G. Gillow, ¿un liberal?," in Carlos Martínez Assad, *A Dios lo que es de Dios* (Mexico: Aguilar, 1994), 217–228; Adame Goddard, *El pensamiento político*, 106–114, 161.

80. Luis Ramos Gómez-Pérez, "Escuela católica y sociedad a principios del Siglo XX," in Sigaut, ed., *La Iglesia Católica en México*, 293–306; Adame Goddard, *El pensamiento político*, 183–246; Manuel Ceballos Ramírez, *El catolicismo social: Un tercero en discordia. Rerum Novarum, la 'cuestión social' y la movilización de los católicos mexicanos (1891–1911)* (Mexico: El Colegio de México, 1991); Laura O'-Dogherty, "El ascenso de una jerarquía eclesial intransigente, 1890–1914," in Ramos Medina, comp., *Memoria del I Coloquio*, 179–198.

81. Manuel Ceballos Ramírez, "Las fuentes del catolicismo social," in Manuel Ceballos Ramírez and Alejandro Garza Rangel, coords., *Catolicismo social en México, Teoría, Fuentes e Historiografía* (Monterrey: Academia de Investigación Humanística, A.C., 2000), 75–91, especially p. 85.

III

THE MILITARY

7

The Militarization of Politics or the Politicization of the Military? The *Novohispano* and Mexican Officer Corps, 1810–1830

Christon I. Archer

> Soldados ¿Qué furor os agita? ¿qué negro velo se extiende delante vuestros ojos? ¿no ves ya en la continuación de vuestro delerio los campos de Anáhuac empapados en vuestra sangre, y nuestros cadáveres nadando en las lágrimas de nuestras desconsoladas mujeres, de nuestros hijos miserables? ¡Ea, soldados! Un instante solo de cordura, una mirada de compasión hacia vosotros mismos; vuestras familias y vuestros amigos os harán abandonar esa bandera oscura, que no es otra cosa que la nube próxima á expedir el rayo de la desolación y el extermino: corred á mis brazos, formemos una misma familia, dad á la patria un día de gloria, y borre el arrepentimiento los de duelo que le ocasionará vuestro extravío. Agustín I es nuestro padre, nuestro libertador: su devisa es amor, humanidad, filantropía. . . .
>
> —General José Antonio Echáverri, Jalapa, 6 de diciembre de 1822[1]

What hyperbole! What passion! Field Marshall José Antonio Echáverri reached out to the soldiers of his army at Veracruz with powerful words aimed to turn them against his erstwhile former royalist army comrade, Brigadier General Antonio López de Santa Anna. Having papered over what must have been the accumulated resentments between the hunter and the hunted, Santa Anna appeared to have formed an alliance with his old wartime adversary and republican, General Guadalupe Victoria. Others reported that Santa Anna had been in communication with some of the *cabecillas* (chiefs) of the insurgent bands that for years had infested the territory inland from Veracruz to Puebla.[2]

A major problem at Veracruz following independence in 1821 was the fact that a Spanish garrison continued to occupy the castle of San Juan de Ulúa that in theory protected the maritime approaches to the port city. From this stronghold, they threatened an invasion to restore King Fernando VII, occasionally raided or shelled the city, and engaged in many intrigues. On the Mexican side, frustration reigned because there were no heavy guns available to bombard the fortress into submission. Santa Anna, the commander of the Mexican forces in the region, had proposed many solutions, from assaults to quite bizarre schemes, to trick the Spanish defenders, but nothing worked. With the port blockaded and commerce stifled, merchants and civilian leaders urged the army to get on with its work. In Mexico City, Emperor Agustín de Iturbide lost confidence in Santa Anna and decided to dispatch Echáverri and an army from the interior to do the job.

On 10 November 1822, the emperor traveled to Jalapa where he met Santa Anna and tried to convince him to go to Mexico City to take up a new position and then dismissed him from command at Veracruz. Unwilling to be drawn out of his power base, Santa Anna returned to the port in a very foul mood.[3] He called out the troops of his Eighth Infantry regiment, harangued his men, and particularly denounced Emperor Iturbide for having dissolved Congress and thus delivering a severe blow to the Mexican nation. With Guadalupe Victoria and other republicans at his side, he talked about the growth of support in many provinces for a change to a republican form of government.[4] Given the highly charged emotions and strong partisan atmosphere, it is very difficult to establish when or if the major players at Veracruz supported constitutional monarchy with clear dominance of the Congress based on the well-known Constitution of Cádiz of 1812 or republicanism that few understood. As Miguel Lerdo de Tejada pointed out, Santa Anna probably knew very little about republicanism.[5] On 6 December, Santa Anna proclaimed the Plan de Veracruz, a program that lambasted Iturbide for his actions and demanded that he recall Congress as a first step and then allow the membership to debate the exact form of government. Nettie L. Benson described the plan that contained seventeen articles and twenty-two explanatory clauses as a "poorly organized verbose document" containing portions of the Plan de Iguala and other proclamations.[6] There was no reference to the establishment of a republic, but the presence of republicans and the general tone of Santa Anna's recent actions provided some hints about possible future directions.[7] Miguel de Santa María, the Colombian minister to Mexico and a native of Veracruz, drafted the document with the input of other civilians. They knew that Santa Anna opposed the emperor and convinced him to proclaim the plan.[8]

Although the Plan de Veracruz did not openly demand the overthrow of the Mexican Empire and Agustín de Iturbide, Santa Anna's activities convinced his opponents that he had such projects in mind. Field Marshall Echáverri fulminated:

This Santa Anna who now preaches republic, never had the virtues of a republican; vain, conceited, arrogant, deprecator of the rights of man, ungovernable, enemy of society, groveller in his pretensions, low in his procedures, he has no other system, nor is he animated by other desires than that of dominating the wretched.[9]

Santa Anna roared back: "Long live the nation; long live the free sovereign congress, and long live the true liberty of the motherland, without ever admitting or recognizing the orders of Don Agustín de Iturbide!"[10] Echávarri besieged the forces of Santa Anna and Guadalupe Victoria. Santa Anna defended the port city effectively and even managed to obtain some supplies from the Spanish at San Juan de Ulúa. The light mountain guns available to Echávarri's besieging force of only about 3,000 troops failed to demolish even the weak city walls of Veracruz. In the mortifying tropical heat, the unacclimatized soldiers from the highlands suffered from a lack of provisions and even adequate tents.[11] The old curse of *vomito negro* (yellow fever) eroded the numbers of the besiegers and cast fear into the hearts of their comrades who soon contemplated desertion to save their lives.

Although the forces loyal to Iturbide managed to crush the scattered revolts inspired by the Plan de Veracruz elsewhere in Mexico, the port city proved to be a most difficult objective. The emperor, who failed to understand why Echávarri could not complete his mission, pressured his commander for immediate results. However, Echávarri, who so recently had condemned Santa Anna as a traitor, now appeared to take matters into his own hands. In what was to occur, Lucas Alamán perceived the hand of the Masonic lodges that only recently had recruited Echávarri and many of his officers. Oppressed by fears of failure and loss of military honor, Alamán described a process in which these army officers—novice masons—fell under the control of "hidden superiors."[12] On 1 February 1823, Echávarri and his officers signed the Plan de Casa Mata that called for new elections to restore the congress dissolved by the emperor and recognized the political power of the provinces. This Plan pointed directly to the formation of a federal system. Although the army officer signers insisted that the plan was not aimed to discredit the emperor, Alamán argued that its concepts granted Iturbide's enemies, including the masons, some of the returned deputies of the Spanish Cortes, jailed members of the former congress, and many others the ammunition they needed to act.[13] Santa Anna and his officers joined the plan, and other garrisons and army units quickly followed suit. Under the terms of the Plan, the besieging army of Echávarri pulled back to the highland towns of Jalapa, Córdoba, and Orizaba.

The fact that the Plan de Casa Mata circulated almost immediately to nearby Veracruz and to all of the Provincial Deputations in the country illustrated Alamán's point that powerful political forces and organizers well beyond the army gave it their blessing and full backing. This time, the Masonic lodges and political leaders such as Miguel Ramos Arizpe, José Mariano Michelena, and other influential civilian politicians appear to have made the army commanders little more than couriers and not the intellectual originators of the program.[14] The experiment with monarchy and Emperor Iturbide had almost run its course. As Jaime E. Rodríguez has argued, the Plan de Casa Mata drew widespread popular support because it conceded local authority to the provincial deputations.[15] Whether antimonarchical or prorepublican, however, the politics of postcolonial shock now devoured one *libertador* first to exile in Italy and shortly thereafter to face a military firing squad at Padilla, Tamaulipas.[16]

The decade of the Independence War (1810–1821), a civil war, and a cataclysmic guerrilla-insurgent versus counterinsurgent conflict, was a refined destroyer of people, property, and of systems. For Mexico, it was a form of political and social autocannibalism that consumed human talent, wealth, and civility. The new nation of Mexico suffered a hard birth scarred by complex and multifaceted conflicts—social, economic, political, and racial—that could not be settled simply by proclamations, plans, military power, or political independence from Spain.[17] And because of the unique conclusion to the war in 1821 under the Plan de Iguala, political leaders including army commanders who fought on both sides faced the prospect of setting aside their entrenched enmities and contemplating the enormous complexities of building rather than destroying. In some respects, the compromise peace of 1821 represented the exhaustion of the belligerents—particularly the fading royalist counterinsurgency machine—rather than a definitive victory or defeat.[18]

The new nation of Mexico came into existence with two somewhat vague heterogeneous political groupings each claiming victory—a transformed but still more or less intact royalist side that tended toward centralism, and a more amorphous potentially powerful yet disunited provincial side that included former insurgents and many people who wished to protect local and provincial rights and privileges.[19] Former royalist army personnel, bureaucrats, clergy, merchants, miners, and other *criollos* of the urban centers retained deep suspicions about the revolutionary insurgent intellectuals and their followers in different plebeian sectors. With the impact of social and economic reorientation of the country through the decade of brutal warfare, the struggle to establish a victorious faction with the powers to enforce one approach to nation building would take decades to settle. Spain was the obvious loser in all of this as were those *gachupines* (European Spaniards) who failed to evade the vengeance of expulsion laws directed against them.[20] However, the mother country left behind its political infrastructure, much of the royalist army, and a large population of politically active people of the former royalist persuasion who opposed radical changes. Until the withdrawal of the Spanish garrison from San Juan de Ulúa in 1825 and the crushing defeat of the quixotic reconquest expedition of 1829 commanded by Brigadier Isidro Barradas, King Fernando VII maintained the notion that Spain could reconquer his most valuable American possession.

The hypotheses of the present essay propose a two-part approach to army politics concerning the political thinking of the officer participants and the meanings of militarization and militarism in the Mexican context. First, the wartime decade from 1810 to 1821 produced some remarkable army commander-administrator-politicians and a system of militarized regional and district governance. Under powerful commanders, some military-political jurisdictions became almost semiautonomous regional satrapies. Second, in the 1821 to 1830 decade, former army commanders who had dominated regions and districts during the war years—mostly royalists—now engaged in politics on the national scene. The conversion of these men from martial careers to politics was quite remarkable—including Iturbide, Santa Anna, Pedro Celestino Negrete, Anastasio Bustamante, and many others. From the insurgent side, notwithstanding their protracted efforts to create governments and to write constitutions through the war years, except for a relatively small number of supporters from the major cities and towns, the former insurgents lacked experience within a broad military or political jurisdiction. The rebels had operated most effectively out of isolated and rugged mountainous regions, forests, and lake or marsh environments that posed logistical and health concerns for their royalist adversaries. They evolved classic guerrilla hit and run tactics, and functioned most effectively at the level of regional districts, towns, villages, and rural communities. With some exceptions, Vicente Guerrero and Guadalupe Victoria being the most outstanding, following the attainment of national independence most former insurgent commanders did not perform as well on the broader stage of the national scene as the former royalists. It took some time for the doctrines and ideas focused upon concepts of local autonomy to erode more centralized approaches.[21]

Through the different stages of the multifaceted conflict, the royalists undertook central military and strategic planning from a high command based in Mexico City. Viceroys Francisco Javier Venegas, Félix Calleja, and Juan Ruíz de Apodaca directed the full panoply of military, political-administrative, economic, and legal structures, and notwithstanding wartime interruptions they maintained the framework of the Bourbon centralized system of governance. Throughout the period, the viceroys and their war planners viewed the conflict in its entirety as well as in its complex and confused parts. The royalist military structure controlled communications, transportation, and attempted with often limited success to keep abreast of day to day operations. Nevertheless, owing to the fragmented and regionalized nature of the conflict, both the insurgency and the counterinsurgency advanced and entrenched powerful decentralizing elements. Even if armed convoys permitted the shipment of silver bullion, livestock, some commerce, and the maintenance of essential communications, entire regions were cut off for months or even years by endemic insurgent-guerrilla activities.[22]

For all of its vaunted strength as a conventional fighting force, in some years the royalist army failed to keep open the most strategic arteries connecting Mexico City by way of Jalapa, Orizaba, and Córdoba to the port of Veracruz. Multiple demands and missions for royalist troops fragmented regiments and battalions assigned to garrison duties, patrols, and convoy duties, leaving few companies available to form operational field forces and *destacamentos volantes* (flying mobile divisions or detachments).[23] The inefficient system of transport by heavily armed military escorted convoys empowered army commanders to requisition mules and *arrieros* (muleteers) and to engage in a variety of corrupt practices. Some district commanders monopolized commerce and communications, levied illegal taxes, extorted funds from merchants and traffickers, and opened their own businesses to sell off goods confiscated from insurgents or unclaimed by former owners. Provincial or regional *gobernadores militares y políticos* held offices that combined the political and military jurisdictions. In some regions, these military bosses exerted near dictatorial control over the political, economic, and social lives of their people.

At Jalapa, Brigadier Joaquín del Castillo y Bustamante, Gobernador Político y Militar, a powerful landowner and merchant as well as an experienced army commander, dominated every aspect of life in his jurisdiction. In 1820, the administrator of the mail service at Jalapa, Faustino de Capetillo, complained that during his six-year governorship, Castillo y Bustamante afflicted the people who "saw civil liberty destroyed and discord fomented." He awarded *varas de justicia* to his followers who were "vindictive, harsh, and vicious" in their efforts to destroy the most honored residents and abandoned unfortunate prisoners in the jails.[24] With the restoration of the Spanish Constitution in 1820, apparently almost everyone at Jalapa earnestly desired the transfer of Castillo y Bustamante, but this did not occur. With scandalous disregard for the law that he had sworn to uphold, even after the local elections he attempted to dominate the *alcaldes constitucionales*. In a bid to get rid of Castillo y Bustamante, the *ayuntamiento* of Jalapa circulated a petition that charged him with opposing the Constitution.[25] Perhaps influenced by the changed political environment in New Spain and cognizant of the fact that all good things eventually come to an end, Castillo y Bustamante requested the renewal of an earlier license to return to Spain![26]

Other commanders openly disregarded the law and the jurisdiction of the provincial intendants, subdelegates, and other bureaucrats—often in their efforts to gain positions and wealth from the war. Even the viceroys acting as captains general discovered that their direct orders were sometimes difficult or impossible to enforce in a country fragmented by the conflict. Regional commanders were able to follow their own policies and if necessary to blame interdicted roads and captured dispatches for delays in enforcing specific regulations and policies.[27] Although it is difficult to trace the illegal activities of royalist army officers, there were some notable scandals involving Colonel Agustín de Iturbide, Comandante of Guanajuato and Commander of the Ejército del Norte; Brigadier Melchor Alvarez, Comandante General of Oaxaca; and Captain Antonio López de Santa Anna that compelled the senior military authorities to investigate and the viceroys to take action.[28] It is interesting that all three of these officers overcame their critics and their own dubious records to play leading roles in later events. Iturbide and Santa Anna achieved recognition and at least temporary successes that transcended almost all other officer-politicians in the post-independence epoch.

One area of chronic trouble concerned the manipulation of escorted commercial convoys by comandantes militares who siphoned off funds in special taxes and in the process created an avalanche of complaints from the consulados, ayuntamientos, mining deputations, and anyone concerned with transport by the mule trains. From the beginning of the war, the insurgents obstructed roads, in some cases collected their own transit taxes, and sought to prevent the passage of silver shipments, mail, dispatches, provisions, and any other valuable items of commerce. In 1811, a junta of senior merchant and mining bureaucrats proposed that the Consulados of México, Guadalajara, and Veracruz, and the Tribunal de Minería establish new taxes to raise 150,000 pesos annually to pay for military escorts for commercial convoys.[29] Viceroy Venegas contributed his views, arguing that another tax should be set up to establish a *camino militar* (military road) with 1,200 to 1,500 cavalry troops assigned to keep the roads open between Mexico City and Veracruz.[30]

Both the merchants and miners of New Spain were apoplectic in their responses that the viceregal regime and the army wished to prey upon their limited resources to finance royalist defenses against the insurrection. The Veracruz merchants particularly opposed a 2 percent increase in the convoy tax to pay for the *camino militar.* They argued that if the regime levied this new tax, the annual import and export traffic at Veracruz valued at about 21 million pesos would produce an income of 420,000 pesos. Since the defended road was to cost around 500,000 pesos, the consulado argued that the maritime traffic of the port should not bear the burden of paying for terrestrial defenses.[31] Given this background and the tradition of regional and district resistance to the central government, it is not surprising that civilian elements within and outside the ayuntamientos worked to oppose tax programs that originated with the central regime and military command.

When the army competed directly with the civil sector over mule transport, the struggle between the regime and the powerful regional merchants and miners over defense taxation became even more embittered. All over the country, district army commanders requisitioned mules and horses either for military use or for more dubious purposes to extort funds by claiming that the defensive effort against insurrection demanded the primacy of military need. By 1813, the arrival of European expeditionary battalions in New Spain placed even greater pressures upon available transport. In the same year, Brigadier José Olazabal, commander of the Ejército del Sur, expressed frustration that there were insufficient mules available to carry the baggage, artillery, munitions, and supplies that belonged to the recently arrived battalions of the Expeditionary Infantry Regiments of Zamora and Castilla.[32] The destructive assaults of vomito negro (yellow fever) on the unacclimatized peninsular troops required good organization and speed to move the troops inland.

Unfortunately, the arrogant demeanor of European Spanish officers exacerbated old rivalries in New Spain and especially at Veracruz. This emphasized the acute dislike of the criollos toward the haughty *gachupín* army officers long resident in New Spain who provoked strained relations by threatening to requisition mules or to use local tax funds to pay their soldiers. In 1815 for example, the arrival of the Expeditionary Infantry Regiment of Ordenes Militares and the Batallion of Volunteers of Navarra—1,718 soldiers commanded by Brigadier Fernando Miyares y Mancebo—produced heated disputes and resentment among the Veracruzano population. Pulling rank to mask their fears of contracting vomito negro, the Spaniards requisitioned all of the horses of the local militia lancer companies, took over the wagons belonging to the police authorities, and marched immediately for the highlands.[33]

In its reaction to such heavy-handed military actions, the Consulado of Veracruz resisted the army and policies that the merchants described as the negative militarization of the port and provincial economy. Beginning in 1813 and continuing up to the attainment of independence under the Plan de Iguala, the Veracruz merchants like many others in New Spain developed increasing antimilitary attitudes that resulted directly from the insatiable demands by the royalist army for additional funds and manpower. The port merchants pointed out that since the war began they had made immense sacrifices to provide financial support for the Veracruz garrison and provincial defenses. On many occasions, they offered emergency funds to incoming Spanish expeditionary battalions that arrived in New Spain sometimes destitute without a real for subsistence. During many lengthy rebel blockades of the roads to the interior—some that lasted for months or even over a year—they paid the wages of naval and merchant crews delayed at the port. Like other merchants and business people, they lamented the reductions in their income and the dangerous shortages of specie available within the economy. With commerce paralyzed and both private and public spending directed to the war effort, the Veracruz consulado informed Viceroy Félix

Calleja that the merchants could not pay more. Already, their city had raised a 300,000 peso war loan, accepted a 10 percent increase on rural and urban property taxes, and a rise of 2 percent on convoy taxes to raise funds for the construction of the costly *camino militar* to Jalapa.[34]

Despite these defensive initiatives of the royalists, by 1815 the insurgent bands in Veracruz province successfully interdicted commerce, raided district army posts, and made a complete mockery of royalist military efforts to defend the camino real. Their intimate knowledge of the rugged mountains, forests, and barrancas and an inborn ability to function effectively in the mortifying climate made Veracruz prime territory for the small guerrilla bands that fought alone or coalesced with other rebel forces to assault hard-pressed royalist towns, haciendas, garrisons, and convoys. In part, the insurgent bands supported their activities by levying transit taxes on travelers and commercial shipments between Jalapa and Córdoba to Veracruz. The response of the royalist military commanders was to place ever-tighter restrictions over travel and prohibitions against the dispatch of any commercial shipments without official army armed escorts. Unemployment produced by the conflict and the general economic dislocation of the province compelled many village and rural people to join the rebellion.[35]

Although the insurgent blockades in Veracruz Province could be viewed as a major irritant rather than a watershed crisis in the war, the reality of the situation was that the insurgents managed to stymie the royalist army and to sever communications with Spain for periods of many months. This crisis produced a corresponding negative economic impact throughout the country upon merchants, miners, and travelers. Over time, the blockades and economic disasters compelled people to reevaluate their commitment to military solutions and to consider other means to achieve peace. For example, insurgent activities in Veracruz province at the end of October 1814 forced a heavily escorted convoy that departed Mexico City with almost 2.7 million pesos belonging to private merchants and the Crown to halt for over five and a half months at Jalapa. Passengers with the convoy who traveled by coach, litter, horseback, or on foot had to seek housing at Jalapa. Many experienced severe hardships and had to sell off their possessions to pay for subsistence. Some merchants sold their goods at ridiculously low prices that ruined the local economy and most of the *mayordomos* (managers) who owned mules and employed *arrieros* (muleteers) eventually suffered financial ruin. Some of the larger wartime convoys employed as many as 400–500 arrieros who looked after 2,000 to 3,000 mules, including spare and replacement animals needed to carry the heavy cargo.[36]

During 146 days of inactive waiting, the commander of the stalled Jalapa convoy, Colonel Luis del Aguilar, ran up personal expenses of 1,425 pesos, and he took the almost unprecedented step of breaking into the sealed shipment of silver coin to requisition 139,382 pesos and four and a half reales to pay the troops of the convoy escort.[37] In the future, underpaid army garrison and division commanders along the routes to the coast came to view the convoys from the interior carrying shipments of minted pesos as something of a godsend. In the meantime, the Royal Navy warship *Prueba,* which had been lying at anchor at Veracruz since August 1814, and several other merchant ships waited for the arrival of the convoy. Without access to provisions from inland producers and because of a British wartime naval blockade of American ports during the War of 1812, the city of Veracruz was unable to purchase sufficient provisions to feed the population. As a direct result, in 1815 an epidemic of scurvy and dysentery ravaged the otherwise disease-resistant population. The consulado complained to Viceroy Calleja that the reduction of the port city to "total indigence" was not at all positive for "a felicitous outcome for the royalist cause."[38] Once again, civilian leaders had good reason to seek ways to end the war and to curb the activities of the military.

Fully aware of the failures and abuses of the military, the Veracruz merchants sought the direct intervention of the imperial government. Writing to the Secretario de Estado y del Despacho Universal de Indias, they lambasted the royalist army and the viceroy for outlawing unescorted commerce and for failing to provide adequate service. The result was the "mortal paralysis" of internal and external trade and the reduction of many merchants to destitution. With the countryside ravaged and business losses that the consulado now estimated at seventy million pesos since the beginning of the war, merchants who were still able to afford to do so had begun to flee to Spain. The consulado particularly resisted the prohibition of unescorted commerce, pointing out that the resulting economic damage was far worse than if the arrieros simply paid the insurgent tariffs. Many of the rebel bands near the port city operated close to the roads so that they could waylay the muleteers and petty traffickers in fresh provisions who entered and departed.[39]

The Veracruz consulado blamed some of the comandantes militares for exaggerating the actual situation to their superiors in Mexico City. The result had produced the total prohibition of unescorted commerce that halted the flow of trade with the interior of the country. The outcome of total economic stagnation was one that even the most intensive efforts of the enemy had failed to accomplish. The merchants complained bitterly that they lived as downtrodden subjects of "the empire of the bayonets." In 1815, the army attempted five operations—requisitioning almost all transport mules available—to crush the insurgent fort at Zopilote and to destroy the parapets and ditches that interdicted the major arterial road inland at Antigua. Instead of attacking these positions directly, however, the royalist commanders sought out minor roads, paths, and even cut new routes through the rugged terrain. All the while the officers complained bitterly about the oppressive heat and noxious climate of the country. Contrary to army officers who claimed the presence of significant enemy numbers, the consulado estimated from its own local intelligence sources that there were only about six hundred insurgents active in the Antigua district. Resentments increased when the Veracruz merchants observed that when military-escorted convoys did get through to the coast, the regime shipped silver and other precious goods, but seldom managed to include food products and other desperately needed items of ordinary consumption at the port city.[40] The consulado pointed out that even during the occupation of Spain, Cádiz had been permitted to trade with countries occupied by "el tirano de Europa." In the case of the strategic port of Veracruz, the overly restrictive military system of New Spain reduced trade to its immediate lateral coasts.

The acrimonious dispute over trade simmered through the remaining years of the war. However, in 1817 when the royalist armies achieved success in temporarily pushing back the Veracruz insurgents, Viceroy Apodaca lifted the restrictions demanding military escorts for all commercial convoys. With the return of relative tranquility and security, the port city experienced a immediate revival of trade that attracted traffickers with mules and burros and Indians on foot, some of whom traveled great distances from the Mixteca and Guadalajara to proffer their merchandise. Once again, the Veracruz economy prospered and the markets were full of good quality and inexpensively priced products. In 1819, however, renewed insurgent assaults on the roads inland from Veracruz caused the viceroy to reinstate the restrictive convoy system. The Veracruz merchants were furious—insisting that open commerce was absolutely essential and warning that a combination of unemployment and scarcity of food would drive many otherwise loyal shopkeepers to join the rebel side. They warned that the reintroduction of convoys would produce a monopoly of three or four large proprietors and mayordomos who controlled the largest herds of draft animals. These individuals would raise freight charges and negotiate monopolistic contracts with the wealthiest shippers—leaving little or nothing in the way of business opportunities for the smaller merchants and arrieros. These muleteers who owned only a few animals and the small traffickers who supplied the port city's provisions were certain to be driven out of business.[41] Frustrations with the war and with highly centralized military decision-making centered in Mexico City aggravated resentments felt in Veracruz and later increased support from the civilian sector for regional autonomy. In the near post-independence future, the Veracruzanos sought the support and protection of General Antonio López de Santa Anna, who as a politician watched over the affairs of his home province.

In a conflict involving insurgency and counterinsurgency warfare, army officers confronted military and political challenges that were quite outside of their previous military experience. Well aware that one bad decision or battlefield disaster could produce an outcome that would permanently ruin their careers, from the beginning of the war some older and more senior army commanders sought refuge outside the war zones. Since an unsullied trajectory of career promotions was the foremost element of building an officer's *hoja de servicio* (service record), sedentary garrison duty punctuated by occasional chases of guerrilla-insurgents was quite unappealing and also held many potential pitfalls. A skirmish lost or connection of an officer to abuses involving civilians could damage or even terminate the most promising of military careers. Some officers longed for safe postings to weather a messy war that was mostly devoid of glorious conventional battles and the rules that governed civilized warfare.

Brigadier José de la Cruz, Comandante General de Nueva Galicia, a tough Spanish army commander who never shirked his duty or difficult decisions, informed Félix Calleja in 1811, "I am finding out at close range that there is a certain class of men in this New World who are entirely different from those whom we know." He arrived in New Spain in 1810 and went to work immediately as a counterinsurgency commander dedicated to extirpating the rebel bands that emerged in the wake of Cura Miguel Hidalgo. For Cruz, the lack of total commitment and dedication by brother officers—especially high-ranking commanders—came as a real shock. In words dripping with irony, in April 1811 he commented to Calleja, "What different fortunes we have had in the present insurgency than those of our illustrious comrades at arms Brigadiers Nemesio Salcedo, Bernardo Bonavía, and Alejo García Conde!" Salcedo had made certain to remain in the Provincias Internas far from the insurgency, Bonavía hunkered down in his "rabbit warren of Durango," and when the revolt broke out, García Conde fled "like a bolt of lightning to Arizpe to look after his governorship and intendancy."[42] Speaking with contempt, Cruz concluded: "They will have much greater luck than us in that their reputations will be without stain or fear of loss. Here, we are exposed to the vagaries of accidents that even without eating or drinking might choke us and even may send us to the other world!"[43]

What Cruz failed to mention was that these officers were of a different generation—older, accustomed to sedentary peacetime service, and like many of their contemporaries quite incapable of making the difficult transition to wartime duty and combat in a bloody and complex war.[44] Though he remained loyal to Spain, Cruz, like many of the younger officers who survived the conflict to make their careers in independent Mexico, proposed harsh methods to suppress rebellion. He informed Calleja, "Let's spread terror and death everywhere and especially to these wicked men who have scorned to receive the pardon that we have offered them. In the end we will get to the point that not one of these depraved persons will remain on this earth."[45] As might be anticipated, this sort of gung-ho enthusiasm or commitment by royalist commanders produced a general disregard for any obstacle or jurisdiction that stood in the way of their absolute annihilation of the insurgency. Legal or constitutional niceties held little appeal for officers who dedicated their undivided attention solely to the objective of total victory. To instill the full impact of counterinsurgency terror, commanders such as Cruz wanted to allow the military untrammeled access to power. Since the royalists represented "la causa buena" against "la causa mala," his system was to "execute hundreds, to decimate towns, and to make the name of soldier as frightening as death itself."[46] Cruz often referred to the healthful example of hanging up the cadavers of dead rebels at the gates of towns and insisted that he would "completely terrorize" the population. He insisted that in New Spain, "the germ of insurrection is too deeply implanted to make it disappear without many exemplary punishments."[47]

On the one hand, the royalist response to rebellion was to militarize the governance of cities, towns, and rural districts. Félix Calleja's Plan Político-Militar of 8 June 1811,[48] proposed a detailed counterinsurgency system that would require local town, village, and rural officials to raise militia units paid for by their communities through specially levied local taxes. The concept was to compel towns and districts to create self-defense forces thus freeing the army for specific operations against larger coalesced rebel forces. For years, the royalists compelled local men to serve in garrison duty paid for through the application of taxes euphemistically called *contribuciones militares*. In some districts, property owners paid annual taxes based upon their lands and income. Although this program of militarization was unpopular and produced significant hardships for artisans, laborers, and agricultural workers, in some parts of the country the insurrection was either brought under control for some time or for the duration of the entire decade of war. Over time, however, the Plan Político Militar exhausted militiamen and their families. The removal of many community wage earners, sometimes for long periods of duty, created economic hardships, labor shortages, and the desertions of men who fled from their home regions. Their goal was to escape demanding militia service and arbitrary treatment by local *comandantes de patriotas* who held viceregal militia commissions as captains. Regular army officers tended to disparage these men, and often they refused to recognize their rank or authority.

In the district and *cabecera* (the seat of district government) town of Pachuca for example, with eight towns and villages and five mining communities, Viceroy Venegas commissioned Francisco de Paula Villaldea, a wealthy merchant mine owner and hacendado, to raise, maintain, and command the local self-defense forces. Villaldea received orders to enlist three mounted *carabinero* squadrons stationed in Pachuca, Actopan, and Zempoala and a larger number of defensive infantry companies to patrol and to guard their town gates, parapets, and guard towers. Armed with lances and machetes, or carbines and pistols if available, the carabineros also formed squadrons assigned to rural patrols, the protection of roads, and the guarding of livestock and agriculture.[49] The key element in these defense forces was the selection of a *junta de arbitrios* (committee on taxation) consisting of the *subdelegado* of the district, the local *cura*, two well-respected individuals from Pachuca as the *cabecera* (leading administrative town), and one delegate from each dependent town or village of the jurisdiction. Supported by the expertise of the local treasury official and the mining *diputado*, the first duty of the junta was to establish *contribuciones de milicias* that in this district were taxes levied on refined silver produced in mining districts, shops, market stalls, grain production, and agricultural crops.[50]

Of even greater concern to the populace, the comandante militar and junta de arbitrios gathered census data on the population required to establish *contribuciones obligatorias* (sometimes called *contribuciones patrióticas*) levied as property or income taxes upon all district residents according to their total estimated wealth. No one was exempt, and even the poorest inhabitants had to make at least a minimum payment.[51] Hacendados and rancheros paid taxes according to their overall worth—a factor that produced angry resistance from those who claimed that insurgent bands had occupied their estates for years and that they earned no income from other lands abandoned by farmers or stock raisers. The *contribuciones obligatorias* were a particularly heavy burden for village people who often lacked access to specie and suffered from unemployment, crop failures, epidemics, and insurgent activities. In 1814, the Indian Governor of Tezontepec subject to Pachuca lamented that his community was in arrears fifty pesos in its collection of militia taxes. Some women who could not pay a single real had been reduced to selling garments off their backs, and most of the men in the community had left to seek work elsewhere.[52] While this might sound like an extreme or bogus case, many other small communities made repeated complaints concerning similar abuses by the local militia authorities.

The outpouring of enthusiasm for the restored Spanish Constitution in 1820 and the election of *ayuntamientos constitucionales* and *diputaciones provinciales* in almost every region and district of New Spain related directly to war exhaustion and opposition to abusive militia taxation. Moreover, it was quite obvious that while the royalist army of New Spain had achieved a standoff, there was no legitimate hope for a total victory.[53] The strength of the backlash against the militarization of the society and spontaneous enthusiasm for a countrywide process of demobilization was quite remarkable. Moreover, the Constitution outlawed arbitrary levies of so-called vagabonds that had been used to round up young men for the regular army regiments.[54]

In 1820 and thereafter, people began to address each other as *ciudadano* or *ciudadana* and sometimes refused to recognize the constituted legal authorities. In the cities, clubs and juntas of lawyers, merchants, bureaucrats, and army officers convened to discuss the concepts of liberty and independence. There was a definite antigachupín tone to many conversations and demands for the destruction and expulsion of all abusive gachupines (European Spaniards). In Guadalajara, José de la Cruz proposed an immediate end to the destructive subdivisions that were common in army units and a halt to the transfer of regiments and battalions away from the provinces where they had served for many years. On 4 October 1820, Cruz became more concerned about disrespectful behavior, surreptitious gatherings, anonymous broadsides, and other signs of unrest. He wrote to Viceroy Venadito, ". . . everything one perceives gives indications that we are sitting on a volcano."[55] Other letters referred to suggestions that were similar in some respects to what would soon appear as proposals in the Plan de Iguala. Many recommended the immediate removal of military regulations restricting travel and the requirement that all travelers had to carry official passports. Flexibility of movement permitted a much greater exchange of ideas, and soldiers deserted and returned to their homes. Ordinary people mocked the military patrols, police authorities, and officials who had held them in check for a decade. On the roads, officials complained that since almost everyone carried arms, it was difficult to identify the thieves and bandits from the legitimate subjects.[56]

In a world lacking anything like mass communications, the massive rejection of military taxes that swept over New Spain in some respects commenced the beginning of the end for the royalist regime. This reaction in 1820 launched a falling domino process that led to the destruction or better the implosion of the royalist army and to the spectacular flight of army officers and soldiers to support Iturbide's Plan de Iguala. They joined the glorious and almost bloodless victory march of the Army of Three Guarantees. Notwithstanding the fact that all of this was all much too easy and did not solve real economic and political problems, for a short while at least enthusiasm for Iturbide's cause disguised the deep fractures and divisions within Mexican society. Once the oppression of the royalist regime ended, the rush to freedom as it was perceived produced hundreds of constitutional ayuntamientos that no longer accepted their old subservience to the *cabecera* towns, to the provincial deputations, or to a central government in Mexico City.

The reports written in 1820 by many of the newly constitutional ayuntamientos offer a poignant reminder about the horrors of war and oppression that had intruded upon the lives of ordinary Mexicans during the decade of revolutionary warfare. From Miacatlán, the municipal government informed the *Diputación Provincial de México* that the system of *contribuciones militares* had been extremely damaging and stressful for their populace. They lamented their downtrodden condition and concluded: "It is not possible to describe the supreme rigor and violence that the military taxes have exacted in these regions. It will be enough to say that there is not an unfortunate Indian who, without a real to make the required payment, has been despoiled of his miserable rags and left exposed to the most indecent and shameful nudity." Some men who suffered the constant threats and cruel treatment by the tax collectors finally reached "such heights of desperation that they took up a weapon and committed the horrible act of suicide."[57] The writers of Miacatlán supposed that those in the superior levels of government probably did not know about such cruelties.

At a meeting of rancheros in the Montes de Altamajaque in the district of Chignahuapa, two hundred rancheros gathered like so many others elsewhere during July and August 1820 to discuss the Constitution and the new system of government. They voted on the spot to terminate the *contribuciones militares* that they deemed no longer necessary. Unable to grasp the significance of the change in attitudes and behavior by these men, Colonel Manuel de la Concha dispatched a *partido volante* of twenty-five dragoons commanded by Captain José Ignacio Zuñiga of the Regiment of San Luis to warn the ranchers about the evils of clandestine meetings. Concha insisted that discussions of political subjects such as militia taxation had to take place in the context of their ayuntamiento. He misinterpreted their political activity completely as a sign of a renewed rebellion and noted that these same people had supported the rebel chief José Francisco Osorno at the beginning of the war.[58]

At Puebla, Brigadier Llano corroborated these same reactions from the ayuntamientos constitucionales of his provincial jurisdiction. Small towns of just over a thousand residents elected municipal governments and sent delegations to Llano that clamored for an immediate end to the militia taxes. Each community blamed the royalist military system for its unhappy and miserable state.[59] Viceroy Venadito did not help matters with his unhelpful response to Llano that the question of how to fund local militias was up to him as the Comandante General and Intendant of Puebla province. Llano went back to the ayuntamientos to propose more modest taxes, but received a response that neither the rich nor poor would pay. What was worse, the ayuntamientos warned Llano that it would be dangerous for his government to press the militia tax issue any further. Some towns did not bother even to complain and simply stacked their weapons at the town hall and dismissed their militiamen. Since Llano recognized that the ayuntamientos were responsible for appointing officers, recruitment, and paying all of the costs, there was nothing further that could be done.[60]

Neither the royalist comandantes nor the civil bureaucrats recognized at first that the introduction of the Spanish Constitution launched what was a peaceful and quite democratic revolution. If the military commanders who militarized New Spain to resist revolution now wished to maintain networks of local and district militias, they would have to deal with local politics and politicians rather than to impose arbitrary solutions. The Constitution turned over significant powers to people who were anxious to exercise their rights in defense of their interests. Within the ayuntamientos constitucionales and in the communities at large, local leaders discussed the meaning of articles of the Constitution while those who were illiterate listened carefully as others read the articles aloud. At Tlaxco for example, the members of the ayuntamiento debated the meanings of Article 172 and Article 338. They concluded that exorbitant taxation to support urban realista militias was now completely illegal. Moreover, if the king himself could not levy contribuciones militares, the constitutionalists at Tlaxco concluded that subordinate authorities in New Spain most certainly could not impose such taxes.[61]

Other administrators, such as Subdelegado Francisco de Ortiz at Huejutla, argued that while the Indian towns of Taltocan and Yxcatlan had populations in excess of the 1,000 inhabitants required to elect a constitutional ayuntamiento, he did not think that they could function in a truly constitutional manner. In his view, they were incapable of understanding even the most basic principles of the Constitution since they were "*mazorrales* (uncouth), without knowledge of the Castillian language, lacking in any culture, and by their habit of dependency since time immemorial upon their old superiors."[62] Since the declaration of the Constitution most of these people refused to recognize any authority, some left their communities, many drank to excess daily, and everyone refused to pay legitimate taxes, to send their children to school, or to do any work. As the subdelegado of Santa Anna near Mexico City, José María Torres, concluded about the people of his subject towns: "They believe that the Spanish Constitution is a printed license that authorizes them to violate the laws with impunity and to avoid recognizing any authority whatsoever."[63]

The debates over militia taxation also foreshadowed a general mood in some provinces that the decade of revolution was over and that it was time to restore commerce, industry, and agriculture. At San Juan del Río, members of the ayuntamiento lauded the return of peace in the country and insisted that superfluous urban infantry and cavalry companies be disbanded. They composed a legal argument against the militia taxation based upon their interpretation of Article 321 of the Constitution. An even more pressing issue was that the existing militia support fund used to pay these militiamen was over 8,000 pesos in debt. The lenders clamored for their money, and the ayuntamiento had no idea where such a large sum was to be found.[64] While the debt at San Juan del Río remained, questions about the meaning of the Constitution regarding the local militias concluded with the publication of a Royal Order issued in Madrid dated 11 February 1820. The king prohibited army generals, division commanders, and other officers from imposing and collecting their own taxes from towns to pay for the subsistence of the army.[65]

In their enthusiasm for the Constitution, elections, and for ridding themselves of oppressive military taxation, in 1820 many Mexicans conveniently forgot that in some regions the insurgency was by no means concluded.

Clearly, the regime of Viceroy Venadito and the senior army chiefs needed to rethink their approaches to the war. Some of the best commanders and certainly those with greatest longevity in the harsh climate of regional warfare were those who developed extensive networks of *amistad* and roots within the military, civilian, and religious sectors. Failure to practice effective politics set back or even terminated military careers and damaged some comandantes who failed to play an effective political game. Good professional soldiers, strategists, tacticians, and logisticians in a strictly military sense were not always the best regional or district commanders. During the war years, a new generation of young officers emerged and gained experience that kept in mind the political side of military career advancement and routes to rise in prominence. Field commanders learned how to accentuate their battlefield victories and to vie in the *Gazeta de México* for publication of their bombastic reports of charges and stalwart defenses against hordes of insurgent fighters. Officers worked to build networks based upon collegial relationships and alliances that connected them with different social, economic, and religious leaders as well as with popular sectors. Indeed, some detractors of the comandantes militares and of Agustín Iturbide in particular, complained that such men kept the war going for their own selfish career interests and to keep their commands.[66]

The war years provided a kind of apprenticeship for royalist officers—both criollos and peninsulares—who rose later to become Mexican Generals including Agustín de Iturbide, Antonio López de Santa Anna, Manuel Gómez Pedraza, Pedro Celestino Negrete, Anastasio Bustamante, Melchor Alvarez, José Joaquín de Herrera, Vicente Filisola, and others. Although the present study focuses upon the first decade of independence, even as late as the 1840s a count of the most senior Mexican army *generales de división* and *generales de brigada* reveals that the great majority were of royalist origins who commenced their military careers during the Independence epoch. Of course, prominent former insurgents also rose to the rank of army general such as Guadalupe Victoria, Nicolás Bravo, Vicente Guerrero, José María Tornel y Mendivel, Juan Alvarez, and Melchor Muzquiz.[67] Almost all of these military politicians formed linkages with civilian groups and the most successful of them dedicated their careers to politics alone.

Perhaps of all the young royalist commanders to rise to prominence before 1821, Agustín de Iturbide was the most notable and in some respects one of the least as well as one of the most effective of the officer politicians. Santa Anna had more spectacular turns in his career, but he lived a great deal longer and managed to evade the firing squads that various of his enemies hoped would shorten his earthly tenure. Iturbide was born on 27 September 1783, and grew up in Valladolid (Morelia) the pampered son of a wealthy peninsular family. He was twenty-seven when the Hidalgo Revolt commenced and in his late thirties when he became emperor of the Mexican Empire. Despite his youth, from the beginning of his army career Iturbide stood out as a force to be reckoned with in the royalist army. His remarkable ambition, loyalty to his friends and soldiers, willingness to press hard for his causes with senior officers and viceroys, his ability to create networks of friends and supporters, his high energy and persistence, and his absolute dedication to the king brought him special recognition and attention. Nevertheless, Iturbide's self-promotion was shameless, and he turned a string of royalist battlefield victories into his own personal engagements.

In 1812, still early in his career, Iturbide boasted that he had been in nine major actions—all of them more glorious than what the Reales Ordenanzas Militares identified as "distinguidos."[68] He ingratiated himself with senior well-placed military patrons who watched over his career development for years and who were willing to overlook his tendency to be arbitrary and extremely cruel. Iturbide became a scourge of the insurgents in the Bajío provinces, Valladolid, and in bordering districts of Nueva Galicia. He was a man committed absolutely to his religion, to the certainty of the absolute justice of his cause and the evils of the revolution. In a word, Iturbide emerged as a man with a mission driven by a special vision and by almost limitless ambition. The war established his career, provided him with a platform to rise to prominence, and carried him to the pinnacle of success and power as Emperor of Mexico. At the same time, however, Iturbide made powerful enemies on the road to success. He developed arbitrary behaviors and corrupt practices as military commander and ruler of Guanajuato province that would have ended the career of a lesser individual. In some respects, Iturbide failed to move beyond his training as a counterinsurgency commander. Indeed, if he was a man of destiny, there was always a dark side that marred his diplomacy and made him a bloody-minded and intolerant bludgeon of his enemies and opponents. He could be charismatic and charming to his friends and followers while at the same time acting as a self-righteous moron, fanatic, and fool.[69]

Quite unusual for army commanders in the Independence War of New Spain, Iturbide left a detailed "Diario Militar" that covered the period from January 1812 to July 1813. This quite remarkable document casts light upon his thoughts, his travels, and his ideas. Placed alongside the rough draft letterbooks in which he recorded his correspondence with friends, other officials, and sometimes with his mortal enemies, historians can gain insights into his thinking processes that is not possible for most army officers of the period. Iturbide recorded a daily tally of the number of leagues he traveled—in fact one wonders if he dragged an odometer behind his horse. In his own reckoning, he clocked a total of 3,794 leagues in a year and a half! This works out roughly to 21,000 kilometers of frenetic pursuits of rebel forces, siege preparations, convoy escort duties, and multiple visits to any and all surrounding military jurisdictions to meet regional commanders for consultations and conferences. There were also regular trips from distant towns for visits and planning sessions at Celaya and elsewhere with his immediate commander, Brigadier Diego García Conde.

At the beginning of 1812, Iturbide left Valladolid to join General Félix Calleja's Ejército del Centro at Izucar where there was a powerful insurgent gathering led by José María Morelos and other insurgent chiefs. Iturbide was fortunate to accompany Calleja's wife, Doña María Francesca de la Gándara de Calleja, who introduced him later to the general. At Maravatío, Iturbide found the Batallón Mixto, a cavalry and infantry unit that included a detachment from Tula that he was to command. He greeted his friends and "compañeros de armas" and became acquainted personally with General Calleja. He visited with his old friend, Francisco Rendón, who had been Intendant of Zacatecas until captured by the insurgents. Accompanying Rendón was his wife, Margarita, whom Iturbide knew well, and he visited with their small children. He sought out many friends in different units whom he had not encountered since the war began including Bernardo Villamil, whose wife Iturbide described as being in a delicate condition due to pregnancy. It was at Maravatío that Iturbide received his new assignment to serve in García Conde's command. Although he respected "este benemérito jefe," he expressed some sorrow that he would not be able to serve with the main body of the royalist Army of the Center.[70]

It is interesting that even at this early stage as a young officer, Iturbide knew so many of the powerful commanders of the royalist army, and he used his connections to expand his growing circle of political contacts, friends, and new acquaintances. Beginning in early February, Iturbide began to command operational elements of García Conde's division that was a mixed force including a regular army battalion of the Regimiento de Infantería de la Corona, two squadrons of the provincial Dragones de Puebla, the Batallón Mixto, and the cavalry Cuerpo de la Frontera de Nuevo Santander. On February 12, Iturbide led a mixed infantry and cavalry force on a seventeen and a half hour march, during which they rested only an hour and a half, to surprise the insurgent Albino García who was reported to be at the pueblo of Amole with 4,000 men. Attacking at 2:30 AM, the royalist forces managed to kill some insurgents, and the cavalry chased the enemy for over a league and a half. Considering their exhaustion following such a long march, Iturbide expressed admiration at the courage and determination of his soldiers. In the action, the achievement of surprise was complete, and only one royalist sergeant received a wound.[71]

During the 1812–1813 period, Iturbide operated throughout the Bajío, usually against small insurgent bands that were seldom able to stand up to the better armed and disciplined royalist troops. Employing speed and marching great distances, the royalists were able to surprise insurgent forces at night and to assault them with combinations of cavalry, dragoons, and mounted infantrymen. Sometimes the rebels possessed a few old firearms, and they attempted without much success to manufacture swords, wooden cannons, and muskets—sometimes gilding the wood with silver to make these weapons appear at a distance to be made of burnished metal.[72] The difficulty for the royalists was that they could not occupy every town and village and also have operational units available to run down the small insurgent bands. Iturbide ordered rebel prisoners captured following skirmishes to be executed by firing squads following very cursory interrogations. His forces attacked the insurgents effectively by moving rapidly, setting up ambushes in villages, dividing and subdividing their forces, and coalescing on a target village or district to overwhelm the insurgent defenders through the use of disciplined attacks and superior firepower.

In many of the towns and villages of the Bajío, the *curas, presbíteros*, doctors, and some landowners exerted political leadership over their communities and sided openly or secretly with the insurgency. Their leadership appeared to focus on regional and district questions, and in the 1812–1815 period there were few references in their correspondence to questions relating to the great issues of the revolution concerning independence or autonomy for New Spain. Royalist forces commanded by Iturbide and other royalist commanders raced from place to place, destroyed property, confiscated anything of value, and executed almost anyone who appeared capable of exerting intellectual and political leadership.

On both sides, propaganda and threats replaced any possibility for meaningful dialogue. Iturbide corresponded with suspect curas beyond his control demanding that they support the legitimate government. He pointed out that insurgent chiefs attracted new adherents through lies, calumnies, and promises designed to attract the very gullible. They concocted grand lies that Morelos had entered Mexico City or would do so in a short time, that the Rayón brothers were in Querétaro, José María Liceaga and Dr. José María Cos had occupied Guanajuato and Irapuato, and Verduzco was in Valladolid. The insurgents falsely debunked royalist amnesty programs by spreading rumors that secret executions followed pardons. Iturbide insisted that the insurgent threat was in reality quite limited. While in the absence of royalist forces they were able to influence and to control the populace, the number of rebels available for armed service in most districts of the Bajío provinces seldom exceeded 300 to 700 poorly trained and equipped fighters. They lacked access to muskets and their locally founded primitive cannon were small enough to be carried two to a mule. These guns were much too light and inaccurate to incur major damage. Iturbide argued that in his opinion, ". . . one-hundred soldiers who deserve the name could pass through districts such as Yurira, Salvatierra, and Salamanca without any danger of receiving damage."[73]

There was also the major problem of poor cooperation between the royalist military jurisdictions. To escape hot pursuit, the insurgent bands simply crossed the boundaries of provincial military jurisdictions.[74] By working out of frontier zones between Guanajuato, Valladolid, and Nueva Galicia, the insurgents compensated for their chronic weaknesses of poor military discipline and inferior weaponry. Iturbide and other field commanders recognized the essential need for military cooperation between royalist divisions based in the different provinces. He visited Valladolid where Colonel Torquato de Truxillo was uncooperative, but assisted Captains Antonio Linares and Pedro Celestino Negrete who commanded forces near the borders of Nueva Galicia under the command of Brigadier Cruz. During these years, Iturbide became a major advocate promoting cooperative military assistance, and he was more active than any other royalist commander in visiting surrounding jurisdictions on a regular basis and in getting to know his associates.

High energy and harsh persecution of insurgent forces brought Iturbide successes that impressed senior officers and the viceroys. His troops captured the insurgent chief Albino García, who was executed at Celaya, and the assault on the rebel fortress at Isla de Liceaga in Lake Cuisio overcame what other royalists considered to be an unassailable stronghold. Guarded by a well-built stone wall and a palisade woven of thorny branches, and surrounded by deep ditches, the garrison of 200 defenders at first appeared to have high morale. While his troops built rafts and assembled canoes, Iturbide employed psychological warfare to inculcate a spirit of "terror pánico" among the rebel troops. Approaching the island from different sides at 2:00 AM on September 9, the royalist soldiers yelled out, "Let's go, our comrades are already inside; Let's go, Let's go we want to get inside; Long live Fernando VII; Long live Spain; Death to all who do not surrender, Death at this moment!" The invaders carried large stones that were to be thrown when the rebels fired their cannons so as to create a diversionary splash that would confuse their aim.[75] The rebel defenses collapsed, and all of the defenders were captured or killed except those who managed to swim to shore. Iturbide paraded his captives, including the insurgent commander Juan José Ramírez, and his officers, including Pablo Nelson, known by the rebels as El Angloamericano.

With battlefield exploits such as these and with his well-developed patronage connections, Iturbide bypassed other more senior officers to become Colonel of the Provincial Infantry Regiment of Celaya, and in May 1813, Viceroy Venegas appointed him Colonel and Comandante General of Guanajuato and the Bajío. He claimed that he was not particularly pleased to have to alter his thinking from purely military matters to meet the political demands of an important administrative office that required tact and other skills to deal with the elite of Guanajuato. Responsible for provisioning and transport, he complained to Cruz that he now saw himself as transformed from the leader of an army division to commander general of mules. From the outset, Iturbide knew that he made enemies—particularly among gachupín officers who wanted him out of office. He felt that there were those who would celebrate if he lost an entire silver convoy, and bragged that in seven major shipments the rebels had not managed to steal a single mule.[76]

Notwithstanding Iturbide's successful efforts to gain the respect and friendship of army officers, he lacked appeal among some other sectors of the population. His thug-like behavior in counterinsurgency in the rural districts of Guanajuato province and on the margins of neighboring jurisdictions produced negative repercussions from powerful religious leaders, hacendados, merchants, and shippers. Hacendados such as Lieutenant Colonel Pedro Otero complained that soldiers and muleteers from Iturbide's command had invaded his lands, cut down fruit trees and vines, and totally destroyed his crops. They broke into his house, smashed his furniture, stole his doors and windows, and even ravaged his gardens and fruit trees. When Otero went to file a claim for damages, Iturbide treated him as if he were a traitor or an insurgent. He told Otero to his face: "El Rey no pagaba nada (The King did not pay for anything)." Having served under Calleja at the Battle of Calderón, and at the siege of Cuautla Amilpas, and having granted large donations to assist Spain's war effort, Otero expressed outrage and appealed directly to Viceroy Calleja for restitution of his losses. He said that others warned him against making a complaint because of the "vengeful anger" of Iturbide.[77] The viceroy censured Iturbide and ordered him to control his personal resentments.[78]

From this point forward, Iturbide came under a growing assault of complaints from Guanajuato—until Calleja had no alternative other than to order him to Mexico City where he remained in legal limbo until December 1820, when he was resurrected to fight against the tenacious guerrillas of the Dirección del Sur. At first, the complaints were that Iturbide had taken monopolistic control over the commerce of Guanajuato.[79] In early 1816, however, Dr. Antonio Labarrieta, Cura y Juez Eclesiástico of Guanajuato, submitted a detailed report to the viceroy condemning Iturbide for a variety of crimes that he also circulated widely. The charges included the unjust imprisonment of military and religious personnel and the abuse of 180 women of Pénjamo who had been locked up without any formal charges. Other complaints related to Iturbide's sacking and burning of haciendas that belonged to the Conde de Pérez Gálvez, and retired Lieutenants Colonel Pedro Otero and Francisco Crespo Gil. If these crimes were not sufficient, Labarrieta claimed that Iturbide, like so many other army commanders, monopolized commerce, bought silver at artificially low prices, and detained convoys so that he could raise the prices that the merchants paid for shipping. Within his command, Iturbide removed senior officers for not assisting his projects and outraged a number of ayuntamientos by refusing to accept their nominations of officer candidates. He was arbitrary in his political conduct and mishandled or rejected orders from the superior government. Civilian officials claimed that despite the large amounts of money spent on them, Iturbide's troops lacked discipline and sub-ordination. Finally, Labarrieta declared that Iturbide misled the viceroy about the outcome of several failed military operations.[80]

As might be expected, Iturbide responded to Labarrieta's charges with characteristic anger and by taking the offensive against his clerical tormen-tor. He wrote at great length criticizing the priest for his well-known talents for troublemaking, for corrupt customs, and for aberrations in his political opinions. Iturbide countered each charge, and a number of his supporters from the military and ecclesiastical communities submitted lengthy memori-als defending his character and his activities as Comandante General of Gua-najuato. As for the charge of imprisoning and placing women under house arrest, Iturbide responded that this was Calleja's policy in the cases of women suspected of insurgent sympathies. He noted as an aside that Hi-dalgo had not been so gentle when he executed prisoners in Valladolid and Guanajuato. However, he stressed that he had not charged the women with crimes, but simply detained them with the object of attracting them to the royalist side. Most of the women had been released under the caution that they must reside in communities protected by royalist forces. Finally, having refuted all of the charges to the best of his ability, Iturbide lamented that his enemies had transformed him from a man of educated and distinguished ori-gins to "un monstruo de maldad (a monster of wickedness)."[81]

Although some of the charges against Iturbide were quite minor and similar to complaints directed against the oppression of many royalist army com-manders in a wartime situation, there had been too many specific instances of abuses in the past. Viceroy Calleja took Labarrieta's complaint seriously and or-dered Iturbide to Mexico City.[82] He remained in the capital for four years, transformed as he put it through "a degrading metamorphosis from warrior to litigant."[83] He was convinced more than ever that his accusers represented the machinations of the rebels, "to tear from my hands command of the army that persecuted them and frustrated their plans." [84] Through his days of exile in Mexico City, Iturbide retained command of the Provincial Regiment of Celaya, and he continued to petition the viceroy and the Sub-Inspector General, Brigadier Pascual de Liñan, for a full investigation that would proclaim his in-nocence. His appointment in November 1820 as Comandante General al Rumbo de Acapulco may have represented a form of absolution, but it was a most difficult and dangerous assignment. The large insurgent bands of Gor-diano Guzmán and Isidro Montes de Oca ruled the region around Apatzingan, and the forces of Vicente Guerrero and Pedro Asencio were well known for their tenacious fighting abilities. The Captain General of Valladolid, Brigadier Luis Quintanar, expected that he might have to lead his forces on an expedi-tion to assist Iturbide.[85] For his part, however, Iturbide most certainly had other plans about how he would handle his new command.

With this background, the transformation of Iturbide from dedicated roy-alist to the political leader of independence and promoter of the Plan de

Iguala is not so difficult to comprehend. He recognized that his professional military career had received mortal blows from the Guanajuato affair. With the context of widespread political effervescence present in New Spain during 1820 and the near spontaneous collapse of the militia system that had underpinned the royalist military, Iturbide's acceptance of a most difficult assignment came after he had already made up his mind to take action. As Jaime Rodríguez pointed out, Iturbide had used his time in the capital to develop close connections with important people.[86] The existence of premeditation was obvious well before the declaration of the Plan de Iguala from the movement of army officers who migrated without army orders toward the position of Iturbide's new command. With the royalist military already under pressure, Iturbide offered an escape to all those who feared more radical solutions if they failed to act. On 19 March 1821, Brigadier José Antonio Echávarri, who is quoted in the epigraph of the present essay, wrote from Teloloapan stating that he had sworn allegiance to the Plan de Iguala that he described as "nuestra gran obra (our great project)." He was present with troops from the Infantry Regiments of the Crown, Murcia, Santo Domingo, Tres Villas, and Celaya, the Escuadrón del la Reina, and pickets of other royalist battalions. They swore to guarantee religion, wanted the king or one of his brothers to come to Mexico, and proclaimed the union of all who now came together in liberty within the new Empire. Echávarri's reasoning for all of this was "because we found ourselves in danger of becoming the prisoners of another nation, and of continuing the destructive war of eleven years that we have carried on and perhaps would find it very hard to conclude unless we adopted these means."[87]

The rapid collapse of the royalist army followed. From Mexico City, Viceroy Venadito looked on in horror as "the perfidious and ungrateful" Iturbide raised the banner of a new rebellion. The rise of Iturbide to emperor marked what was a remarkable rehabilitation of a man condemned and almost forgotten. However, in a very short time enthusiasm for new solutions once again would pass Iturbide and cast him aside. During the 1820s, Mexico's direction was unclear as competing factions and ideas struggled for supremacy. For army officers—especially the former royalists—politics and political activities often became much more important than professional military activity. There would be no militarization of society or of politics following the experience of eleven years of brutal warfare. If military men entered politics, they would have to act more as politicians than as representatives of the armed forces.

NOTES

1. Proclama del Capitán General de Veracruz, José Antonio de Echáverri, Jalapa, 6 December 1822, in José María Bocanegra, *Memorias para la historia de México*

independiente, 1822–1846, 3 vols. (Mexico: Fondo de Cultura Económica, 1987), 1: 167–168.

2. Lucas Alamán, *Historia de México desde los primeros movimientos que prepararon su independencia en el año de 1808 hasta la época presente* (Mexico: J. Mario Lara, 1852), 5: 686. This was the opening for Alamán's famous statement, "La Historia de Méjico desde el periodo en que ahora entramos, pudiera llamarse con propiedad la Historia de las revoluciones de Santa Anna." Today, many historians seek to revise this view and to place Santa Anna into the context of a much more complex and textured epoch. See Will Fowler, *Tornel and Santa Anna: The Writer and the Caudillo, Mexico 1795–1853* (Westport, Connecticut: Greenwood Press, 2000), 26–28.

3. Alamán, *Historia de México*, 5: 678; and Alfredo Avila Rueda, "Para la libertad. Los republicanos en tiempos del imperio, 1821–23," (Ph.D. diss.: Universidad Nacional Autónoma de México, 2001), 240–243.

4. Nettie Lee Benson, *The Provincial Deputation in Mexico: Harbinger of Provincial Autonomy, Independence, and Federalism* (Austin: University of Texas Press, 1992), 64.

5. Miguel Lerdo de Tejada, *Apuntes históricos de la heróica ciudad de Veracruz* (Mexico: Secretaría de Educación Pública, 1940), 2: 237–238. Other historians picked up the same theme and stressed the role of Miguel de Santa María in the preparation of the Plan de Veracruz. See for example, Felipe Victoria Gómez, *Guadalupe Victoria: Primer Presidente de México* (Mexico: Ediciones Botas, 1962), 104–105.

6. Benson, *The Provincial Deputation*, 64. For the test of the Plan de Veracruz, see Miguel Lerdo de Tejada, *Apuntes históricos*, 2: 238–245.

7. Avila Rueda, "Para la libertad," 244–245.

8. Benson, *The Provincial Deputation*, 64.

9. Proclama del Capitán General de Veracruz, José Antonio de Echávarri, 6 December 1822, in Bocanegra, *Memorias*, 1: 169.

10. Proclamación de D. Antonio López de Santa Anna y D. Guadalupe Victoria, Cuartel General en Casa Mata, Veracruz, 1 February 1823, in Bocanegra, *Memorias*, 1: 191.

11. Alamán, *Historia de México*, 5: 707–708.

12. Ibid., 709.

13. Ibid., 711–713.

14. Benson, *The Provincial Deputation*, 65.

15. Jaime E. Rodríguez O., "'Ningun pueblo es superior a otro': Oaxaca y el federalismo mexicano," in Brian Connaughton, coord., *Poder y legitimidad en México, siglo xix. Instituciones y cultura política* (Mexico: Universidad Autónoma Metropolitana, Iztapalapa & Miguel Angel Porrúa, 2003), 249–309.

16. See Alamán, *Historia de México*, 5: 797–802; William Spence Robertson, *Iturbide of Mexico* (Durham: Duke University Press, 1952), 294–297; and Timothy E. Anna, *The Mexican Empire of Iturbide* (Lincoln: University of Nebraska Press, 1990), 233–235.

17. Jaime E. Rodríguez O., "Down from Colonialism: Mexico's Nineteenth-Century Crisis," in Jaime E. Rodríguez O., ed., *The Mexican and Mexican American Experience in the 19th Century* (Tempe: Bilingual Press, 1989), 7–23, 103–106.

18. Christon I. Archer, "Where Did All the Royalists Go? New Light on the Military Collapse of New Spain, 1810–1822," in Jaime E. Rodríguez O., ed., *The Mexican and*

Mexican American Experience, 24–43, 106–110; and Archer, "Fighting for Small Worlds: Wars of the People during the Independence Era in New Spain, 1810–1821," *Cuadernos de Historia de América* 6 (1998): 87–92.

19. See for example Peter F. Guardino, *Peasants, Politics, and the Formation of Mexico's National State: Guerrero, 1800–1857* (Stanford: Stanford University Press, 1996), 211–220. Guardino noted, "Elite and popular politics were intertwined. It is impossible to write one without the other."

20. Manuel Ferrer Muñoz, *La formación de un estado nacional en México (El Imperio y la República Federal: 1821–1835)* (Mexico: Universidad Nacional Autónoma de México, 1995), 169–173; and Harold Dana Simms, *The Expulsion of Mexico's Spaniards, 1821–1836* (Pittsburgh: University of Pittsburgh Press, 1990).

21. See Guardino, *Peasants, Politics, and the Formation of Mexico's National State*, 81–98.

22. Christon I. Archer, "'La Causa Buena': The Counterinsurgency Army of New Spain and the Ten Years' War," in Jaime E. Rodríguez O., ed., *The Independence of Mexico and the Creation of the New Nation* (Los Angeles: UCLA Latin American Center Publications, 1989), 85–108.

23. Ibid.

24. Faustino de Capetillo, Administrador de Correos de Jalapa to Governor José Dávila, 6 July 1820, Archivo General de la Nación, Mexico, Sección de Operaciones de Guerra (Cited hereinafter as AGN:OG), vol. 266.

25. Petition of the Ayuntamiento of Jalapa, 10 July 1820, AGN:OG, vol. 216.

26. Viceroy Conde de Venadito (Juan Ruíz de Apodaca) to the Ministro de Hacienda, no. 1101, 31 July 1820, Archivo General de Indias, Sevilla, Sección de Méjico (cited hereinafter as AGI, Mexico), legajo 2420.

27. See Christon I. Archer, "Politicization of the Army of New Spain during the War of Independence, 1810–1821," in Jaime E. Rodríguez O., ed., *The Evolution of the Mexican Political System* (Wilmington, Delaware, Scholarly Resources Inc., 1993), 17–43; and Archer, "The Militarization of Mexican Politics: The Role of the Army, 1815–1821," in Virginia Guedea and Jaime E. Rodríguez O., eds., *Five Centuries of Mexican History/ Cinco siglos de historia de México* (Mexico: Instituto Mora, 1992), 1: 285–302.

28. Archer, "Politicization of the Army of New Spain," in Jaime E. Rodríguez O., ed., *The Evolution of the Mexican Political System*, 34–39.

29. Juan Bautista Lobo to the Prior y Consules del Real Tribunal del Consulado de Veracruz, 30 June 1811, AGN:OG, vol. 215.

30. Viceroy Miguel Xavier de Venegas to the Consulado of Mexico, 4 July 1811, AGN:OG, vol. 215.

31. Consulado of Veracruz to Venegas, 7 December 1811, AGN:OG, vol. 215.

32. Gobernador y Intendente de Veracruz José de Quevedo to the Prior of the Consulado of Veracruz, 10 February 1813, AGN:OG, vol. 215.

33. Interim Governor Pedro Quevedo to Viceroy Félix Calleja, 18 June 1815, AGN:OG, vol. 698.

34. Consulado of Veracruz to the Conde de Castro Terreño, Comandante General of the Ejército del Sur, 17 May 1813; and Consulado of Veracruz to Calleja, 12 June 1813, AGN:OG, vol. 215.

35. Royal Order of Viceroy Calleja, 4 April 1814, AGN:OG, vol. 216. By this order, Calleja halted all commerce without official military convoy escorts.

36. See for example Estado que manifiesta los arrieros, mulas, cargas del comercio, de Hacienda Pública, salidas de Veracruz en el presente convoy del mando de Teniente Coronel Saturnino Samaniego, Puebla, 3 December 1813, AGN:OG, vol. 215.

37. Juan Montoto y Garza, Diputado del Comercio en el presente convoy to the Prior and Consules of the Consulado of Veracruz, 18 April 1815, AGN:OG, vol. 216. Once funds had been withdrawn from one convoy, army commanders along the route from Mexico City through Jalapa preyed upon the shipments of minted silver. In the convoy of October 1815, from Mexico City, Colonel José Joaquín Marqués at Jalapa withdrew 15,168 pesos to meet the expenses of his division; Colonel Francisco Hevia requisitioned 66,725 pesos 4 reales under a commission to do so issued by the commander of the Ejército del Sur; Brigadier Fernando Mijares y Mancebo took 175,000 for his activities in Jalapa; and the commander at Veracruz took 150,000 pesos to pay for defensive requirements. See Consulado of Veracruz to Calleja, 8 January 1816, AGN:OG, vol. 217.

38. Consulado of Veracruz to Viceroy Calleja, 13 April 1815, AGN:OG, vol. 216.

39. Ibid.

40. Consulado of Veracruz to the Secretario de Estado y del Despacho Universal de Indias, 23 June 1815, AGN:OG, vol 216.

41. Consulado of Veracruz to Viceroy Conde de Venadito (Apodaca), 9 June 1819, AGN:OG, vol. 217.

42. José de la Cruz to Félix Calleja, Guadalajara, 8 April 1811, AGN:OG, vol. 145.

43. Ibid.

44. See Senior Officers of the Army of New Spain, 1811, in AGI, Mexico, Sección 5 legajo 1321. Brigadier Bonavía died in 1816, and his widow, Doña Clara de Torre, requested and received permission to return to Spain. See Viceroy Juan Ruíz de Apodaca to the Ministro de Hacienda, no. 190, 7 August 1817, AGI, Mexico, legajo 2420.

45. Cruz to Calleja, Guadalajara, 8 April 1811, AGN:OG, vol. 145.

46. Cruz to Calleja, 15 July 1811, AGN:OG, vol. 145.

47. Cruz to Calleja, 2 January 1811, AGN:OG, vol. 143; and Cruz to Calleja, Huichapan, 2 December 1810, AGN:OG, vol. 140.

48. Reglamento político militar que deberán observar bajo las penas que señala los pueblos, haciendas, y ranchos a quienes se comunique por las autoridades legítimas y respectivas . . . , Aguascalientes, 13 June 1811, AGN:OG, vol. 278. Also see Archer, "The Counterinsurgency Army and the Ten Years' War," 96–97.

49. Viceroy Venegas to Francisco de Paula Villaldea, 2 August 1812; and Villaldea to Venegas, Pachuca, 24 August 1814, AGN:OG, vol. 894.

50. Ibid.

51. Report of Villaldea, 23 March 1812, AGN:OG, vol. 894.

52. Br. Francisco Javier Viera, Cura of Tezontepec to Viceroy Venegas, August 1814; and Report of George Alejandro, Gobernador de Tezontepec to Venegas, August 1814, AGN:OG, vol. 894. For an interesting comparison, see Lista de la Contribución Patriótica Militar del Partido de Tlayacapa para el mes de agosto de 1820, AGN:OG, vol. 377.

53. See for example Brigadier Domingo Luaces to Viceroy Venadito, no. 119, Querétaro, 17 July 1820. Without pay, discipline in the garrison of Querétaro declined, and soldiers who lacked provisions had begun to beat and to rob civilians.

54. Viceroy Venadito to Luaces, 16 December 1820, AGN:OG, vol. 512. Although the viceroy stated that he could not allow a levy of vagabonds, he proposed that Luaces meet with the *alcaldes constitucionales* and the *jueces de letras* of Querétaro to see if means could be found under the Constitution to round up these elements.

55. Cruz to Venadito, 4 October 1820; and José María Alfaro to Manuel Pesquera, Valladolid, 12 September 1820, AGN:OG, vol. 157.

56. Brigadier Ciriaco de Llano, Capitán General and Intendant of Puebla to Venadito, Reservado, 12 October 1820, AGN:OG, vol. 461.

57. Ayuntamiento of Miacatlán to the Presidente y Vocales del la Exma. Diputación de México, 4 November 1820, AGN:OG, vol. 455.

58. Manuel de la Concha to Venadito, Tulancingo, 25 August 1820, AGN:OG, vol. 118.

59. Llano to Venadito, Puebla, no. 566, 28 July 1820, AGN:OG, vol. 325.

60. Llano to Venadito, Puebla, no. 1050, 11 September 1820, AGN:OG, vol. 461.

61. Ayuntamiento of Tlaxco to Concha, 12 August 1820, AGN:OG, vol. 118.

62. Francisco de Ortiz to the Intendant of Mexico Ramon Gutiérrez del Mazo, Huejutla, 22 January 1821, AGN:OG, vol. 455.

63. José María Torres to Venadito, Santa Ana de México, 23 November 1820 AGN:OG, vol. 457.

64. Ayuntamiento of San Juan del Río to Venadito, 24 July 1820, AGN:OG, vol. 512.

65. José Dávila to Venadito, 7 November 1820, AGN:OG, vol. 266.

66. Anonymous Representation signed by Pedro Somoza to the Consejo de las Indias, 26 February 1817, AGI, Mexico, legajo 1147.

67. Alberto M. Carreño, *Jefes del Ejército Mexicano en 1847: Biografías de Generales de División y de Brigada y de Coroneles del Ejército Mexicano por fines del año de 1847* (Mexico: Imprenta y Fototipia de la Secretaría de Fomento, 1914). Of eighteen Generales de División, six were of insurgent origin and twelve were former royalists. Of twenty Generales de Brigada, four were of insurgent origin and sixteen were former royalists.

68. Relación de los Méritos de Iturbide, 31 de agosto de 1812, AGN:OG, vol. 426. These included his role at Las Cruces on 30 October 1812; at Iguala on the 3rd and 4th of July; at Acuichio and Sipimeo on the 7th and 14th of September 1811; at Valle de Santiago on 25 May 1812; in the capture of Cabecilla Albino García, June 1812; at Calpulalpam against the Cabecillas Chito Villagran and Padre José María Correa, in June 1812; in the action of 24 July 1812, in the Valle de Santiago; at Salamanca on 7 August 1812, in defense of the convoy. Iturbide noted that he had been in many lesser engagements, paid for spies and couriers in his employ, and rewarded his valiant soldiers often from his own purse.

69. The controversy over Iturbide shifts back and forth over time. See for example Robertson, *Iturbide of Mexico*. In chapter 2, "Struggles for Mexican Independence," Robertson devotes sufficient space to Iturbide's early career to develop a clear view of his potential weaknesses. Also see Anna, *The Mexican Empire of Iturbide*. Anna, who did not devote much attention to Iturbide's service as a royalist wartime commander,

declared, "To paint Iturbide as a unilateral force of evil, a usurper, a tyrant, ignores the context of his life, the challenges that he faced in creating a nation and founding a government, and the multitude of failings of his opponents and enemies (p. 237). As Anna points out in his revisionist study, almost all Mexican historians have accepted the blackest of interpretations of Iturbide's career.

70. Diario Militar, entries for January 21–23, 1812, Iturbide Papers, Library of Congress (hereafter LC), Ms. 15338, roll 1.

71. Ibid., entry for February 12, 1812.

72. Iturbide to García Conde, Hacienda de San Nicolas, 27 July 1812, LC, Ms. 15338, roll 1.

73. Ibid.

74. Brian R. Hamnett, "Royalist Counterinsurgency and the Continuity of Rebellion: Guanajuato and Michoacán, 1813–20," *Hispanic American Historical Review* 62: 1 (February 1982), 19–48.

75. Instrucción de lo que los comandantes de balsas y canoas deben executar para el asalto de la Isla Liceaga la noche del 31 de octubre de 1812, LC, Ms. 15338, roll 1.

76. Iturbide to Cruz, 4 October 1813, LC, Ms. 15338, roll 2.

77. Pedro Otero to Viceroy Calleja, Guanajuato, 12 August 1813, AGN:OG, vol. 426.

78. Calleja to Iturbide, 1 September 1813, LC, Ms. 15338, roll 4.

79. Anonymous letter of Un Fiel Servidor de VE to Félix María de Cayeta, n.d., LC, Ms. 15338, roll 4.

80. Testimony of Dr. Antonio Labarrieta, 8 July 1816, LC, Ms. 15338, roll 4. For a detailed summary, see Robertson, *Iturbide of Mexico*, 42–47.

81. Iturbide to Calleja, 14 August 1816; Iturbide to Apodaca, n.d., 1817; Report of Teniente Coronel Manuel de Yruela, Comandante del Batallón Rural de Salamanca, 21 September 1816, LC, Ms. 15338, roll 4.

82. Calleja to Iturbide, 4 April 1816, AGN:OG, vol. 434.

83. Instancia de Agustín Iturbide, July 1817, AGN:OG, vol. 502.

84. Ibid.

85. Luis Quintanar to Venadito, Valladolid, no. 5, 5 December 1820, AGN:OG, vol. 702.

86. Jaime E. Rodríguez O, "The Transition from Colony to Nation: New Spain, 1820–1821," in Jaime E. Rodríguez O., ed., *Mexico in the Age of Democratic Revolutions, 1750–1850* (Boulder: Lynne Reinner, 1994), 118–119.

87. José Antonio de Echávarri to Teniente Coronel Isidro Marron, Teloloapan, 16 March 1821, AGN:OG, vol 702.

8

Armed Citizens: The Civic Militia in the Origins of the Mexican National State, 1812–1827

Manuel Chust

After the leaders of New Spain proclaimed independence and established the Mexican Empire in September of 1821, the new nation faced several challenges. Perhaps the first was to maintain the very independence—both political and economic—they had just declared. Obviously, it was impossible for the new country to conserve both components of independence without defending itself militarily. Consequently, the new nation state was born, like all before it, with an organizational problem regarding the military. The legislature rejected the clear-cut solution of entrusting national defense entirely to the regular armed forces. Congress clashed over the matter, using both economic and political arguments, and finally determined to support a regular army and to establish an armed force comprising citizens guided by civil authority—the ayuntamiento or municipal council—a type of organization familiar in Mexico. Thus the civic militia was born in 1823.

The civic militia had a clear precedent in the national militia, which originated in the Spanish Constitution of 1812 as a defense against the absolutist whims of the monarchist army, especially the noble officers who intended to support Fernando VII in the return to absolutism. The national state forged in the Cortes of Cádiz, including its constitutional aspect, emerged with Hispanic parameters that incorporated the territories of "both hemispheres" with equal political rights and equal representation in only one Constitution.[1] Five American delegates served in the commission to draft the charter, which was adopted and proclaimed in the majority of the American territories. The Constitution of Cádiz was proclaimed in Mexico City on September 30, 1812.[2] Its transcendence is fundamental in explaining the origins of the Mexican national state in a plurality of aspects: economic, administrative, judicial, educational, social, and military.

The absolutist reaction in May 1814 prevented the Hispanic state of 1812 from triumphing. The return to absolutism also paralyzed the development of a *reglamento* (regulation) for the national militia, whose guidelines were reflected only in scarce constitutional articles and in some orders and decrees. Moreover, the few battalions of militiamen organized since 1812 were demobilized and disarmed. Following the triumph of the liberal revolution of 1820, the national militia was reorganized. The restored Cortes in Madrid swiftly drew up a reglamento, passed in April 1820, to initiate the militia units. The regulation was approved in New Spain in September of the same year and served as a precedent for post-independence developments.

MILITIA AND ARMY: CITIZENS VERSUS SOLDIERS

Following independence, Mexico's Congress took up the militia debate. The arguments on the matter were telling. Manuel Tejada first posed the question in the sessions from March 1 through 9, 1822. He requested that "the national local militia" be established in "the entire [Mexican] empire, as one of the columns upon which are supported liberty, independence, and the observance of its [the empire's] constitution, and as one of the economic means of maintaining a respectable armed force for the prosperity of the empire."[3] Two initial considerations motivated this debate: the poor state of the army and the lack of funds to reform it.[4] On April 18, 1822, the arguments made by the deputy were detailed by Florencio Castellano, who discussed the organization of armed forces in the Mexican State. This was one of the greatest concerns of the majority of the liberal Mexican deputies; one of the essential necessities of every country that was reaching national statehood; as well as one of the fundamental questions for the preservation of independence. It was not, however, a singularly Mexican concern. Similar discussions were happening in Spain, and at their origins, most European and American states experienced this dilemma. Florencio Castellano stated:

> There are two purposes that free governments have proposed in the establishment of civic militias: one, to resist, along with the military [the army], exterior enemies, and the other, to sustain liberty in the face of the despot who, making use of the veteran troops, intends to attack it: I agree that there will not be in the empire a serviceman who is not a lover of liberty; but Sir, it is the system and not the man who should inspire trust . . .[5]

His intervention was not wasted; it focused the subject. The problematic was diverse. The scarce, if not inexistent, treasury determined exceedingly the organization and maintenance of an army capable of defending its national borders (read 'national independence') at a time that it maintained the political principles for which the new nation had been planned—in this sense, the administrative structure, federal or not, of the country and the attainment of liberal rights. Liberal politics and ideology were in continual tension with the democratic demands of popular groups and the pressure from factions of the conservative bourgeoisie to control the régime. It was a true problematic in a time of revolution, as much national (read 'independence') as social: in other words, the transformation of a new state different from a metropolitan monarchy. To deal with the issue, Congress decided to create a commission; its composition does not elude interpretations. It was formed with a deputy from each province. Of course former doceañistas (participants in the drafting of the Spanish Constitution of 1812) were included: José Miguel Guridi y Alcocer from Tlaxcala and Miguel Ramos de Arizpe from Coahuila. The latter, especially, had the experience of having participated in the elaboration of a first national militia regulation in the Cortes of Cádiz as well as later in the Cortes of Madrid.

Scarcely three days later, the Mexican Congress began to debate the reglamento of the national militia on the basis of the Spanish regulation. Nevertheless, an action was undertaken by a faction of deputies who intended to change the regulation to achieve a civic militia. On the same day, April 18th, José María Cobarrubias, supported by Rafael del Castillo, presented "a civic militia plan" that was approved and sent to the congressional commissions of Guerra and Hacienda (War and Finance). The plan became the source of the subsequent regulation establishing the civic militia.

The discussion of the reglamento ended May 3, 1822, although the approval of the decree was delayed until August. Another discussion, of greater magnitude, if possible, emerged in Congress once debate on the regulation was finalized for all practical purposes. Starting from the Guerra commission reports, Congress began to discuss the necessity of augmenting the permanent army to 35,900, calculated by the president of the Regency and generalísimo of the army, Agustín de Iturbide, as the number necessary to defend the borders against a possible outside attack. During the days of the debate, Pedro José Lanuza, José María Bocanegra, José Domingo Martínez Zurita, Santiago Alcocer, and Antonio José Valdés, among others, argued for the increase on the basis of fear of an external invasion from Spain, France, the United States, and even Russia. The problem of the "barbarous" tribes of the North, the resistance of the Spaniards in San Juan de Ulúa, the distrust in the reliability of a national militia in case of war, and the prestige of the new Mexican nation's military power depended on a large army as an element of stability of the new state: "without an army there is not, nor can there be, liberty, existence, or property; everything is at risk, and sooner or later, everything is lost."[6]

But not all arguments were based on the need to defend against a foreign enemy. Lanuza insisted:

> Let us search the annals of the ages; be the form of government adopted by the people what it will; be the state of their politics and enlightenment what they may, liberal and despotic, even theocratic governments . . . recognized in principle, that

to conserve public order soldiers were necessary to consolidate the government, to make the public respect the authorities and observe the law.[7]

The deputy did not hide pretensions of doing away with interior political and social problems: "On the other hand, let us not lose sight of the fact that the authorities are not respected when they do not have a force that sustains them: let us not govern by force; but we need it to enforce [the law]."[8]

Other deputies stepped up to the podium with another proposal. Starting from analogous premises regarding the danger of invasion, they advanced economic reasons for deploying a civic militia force, since public funds were nonexistent and a larger army would require new taxes or loans.

Carlos María Bustamante and, above all, Hipólito Odoardo proposed another totally different formula for the "defense of the Patria": an army of 20,000 soldiers as well as the organization of the national militia throughout the country with sufficient arms to guarantee its success. Bustamante could not escape a romantic and almost bucolic image of the militiaman, but he combined it with empirical data from 1806 when the people of Buenos Aires had confronted the occupation by English troops:

> The militia soldier is a man bound with powerful ties; he is a citizen, a father of a family; he is a man who recognizes all the dignity of his being, and recognizes it most when he is in sight of the enemy, because then he calculates what he is going to lose and gain: he sees everything vividly in his imagination, and, full of passion, he defies danger, advances over the mouths of canons, and penetrates over the spines of bayonets. Let us spread our gaze over what happened in Buenos Aires.[9]

Nevertheless, the debate became more heated. The more liberal deputies demonstrated their distrust of a large army controlled by the executive branch. Economic justifications (scarce funds) were no longer the only ones wielded by these deputies. There was an evident lack of trust in the army that affected even Iturbide himself. What happened next was one of the most influential debates ever in Congress. The phantasm of imminent invasion pervaded the chamber. The partisans of a large army controlled by the executive branch gave alarmist speeches. Odoardo requested calm, diffused the alarm, and counterattacked:

> If the permanent military [the army] is united with the nation for the moment, if it has promoted independence and regulated the [insurgent] movement avoiding the ill-fated convulsions of peoples in similar crises, Congress should not, for that reason, forget that in time it [the army] could lose its patriotic and laudable sentiments and become an instrument in the hands of the government to destroy the liberties of the people; and among us this suspicion should endure as long as the organization of the army is not changed to conform to the political Constitution [of the nation], making it [the army] less dependent on the ex-

ecutive power, as has just been done in Spain, and is the practice among free peoples and nations with representative governments.[10]

This crucial discussion came to a close May 17th after three days of intense debate. Congress voted to approve an army of 20,000 men. Bustamante and Odoardo's plan was implemented. Thirty deputies, however, expressed the desire that the record show their dissenting vote. Not content with that, the next day José María Cobarrubias, José María Bocanegra, Valentín Gómez Farías, and Juan Miguel Riesgo challenged the previous day's vote and demanded a recount. That same day, events accelerated. The army proclaimed Iturbide to be emperor. The action was intended to reinforce executive power in Mexico.

As Jaime E. Rodríguez has demonstrated, there was a clear connection between these congressional discussions on the size and nature of the army and the elevation of Iturbide to emperor by the capital's garrison, at the front of which was General Anastasio Bustamante.[11] The struggle between the executive and legislative branches shifted to the terrain of the armed forces. It became a crucial factor in the structure of the Mexican national government. With the establishment of the federal republic, the civic militia would be configured as an armed civil bastion of the states against the centralist and conservative tendencies of the executive branch and some of its officers. In this sense the tensions would be constant. Nevertheless, the legislative battle had already been won.

ORGANIZATION OF THE CIVIC MILITIA

The Mexican Congress approved the regulation establishing the civic militia on August 3, 1822, and the earlier national militia established in 1820 was reorganized. Its name was changed from "national" to "civic" in order to differentiate it from the designation reminiscent of the former Spanish administration. Still, the "national" designation had permeated deeply into Mexican institutions and political leaders. During the initial years of the Mexican nation the nomenclature was confused in decrees, orders, and proclamations. Magistrates, *jefes políticos* (political chiefs—governors of provinces under the constitution), military commanders, and aldermen employed the terms national and civic interchangeably. Thus, the terms national militia and civic militia came to represent the same thing: the armed revolution of the citizens.[12]

Generally, the transposition of the militia from national to civic did not cause problems. The jefes políticos instructed the ayuntamientos not to dissolve their national militias and at the same time ordered them to establish the civic militia. In several instances, the requests of local authorities were met so that the battalions already constituted would not be disbanded, especially because they were a necessary force for the security of cities. This was the case, for example, made to Domingo Velásquez, jefe político of the province of Zacatecas, who on May 3, 1823, received the following observation from the ayuntamiento:

> The corporation believes that the . . . [section] of said Reglamento listing the qualities necessary for the citizens to enlist, does not require the dissolution of the Militia that still survives with the name national. Instead, its spirit appears to be that those who enlisted in the first [militia] remain in place and conform to the reforms and the rules prescribed [by the Reglamento].[13]

CIVILIAN CITIZENS, ARMED CITIZENS

The establishment of the civic militia required all "citizens" between the ages of eighteen and fifty to enlist. It is important to point out that the requirement of citizens to enlist in the militia excluded those *vecinos* (residents) who did not have the necessary income or property to hold citizenship. The theoretical and ideological difference of the most typical liberalism, among others that of L'Abbé Sièyes, between "active classes" (political and civil rights) and "passive classes" (civil rights), was used to exclude the popular strata from the organized militia. This politico-economic requirement caused various problems for the ayuntamientos—which had the responsibility of effecting enlistment and organizing and constituting the companies and battalions—not only because of the vecinos' resistance to enlisting, but also because the number of citizens in many areas was not very high.

In Mexico City enlistment was open in the town hall from nine to one o'clock and from four to six o'clock, Monday through Friday. By April 1823 the first company was formed, comprising 107 militiamen, seventeen having their own firearms; in the cavalry squadron only one man enlisted with the requisite horse. By the end of June of the same year five companies with a total of 524 militiamen had been formed. In addition, the capital's ayuntamiento reported that it had more than one hundred men enlisted and ready for organizing a second battalion, which was formed in September. In the cavalry squadron, 191 militiamen comprised three companies. Despite these successes, the ayuntamiento started a community campaign to increase the militia, a program common to most ayuntamientos throughout the 1820s and 1830s. The *alcalde* (magistrate) Melchor Muzquiz, speaking somewhere between ordering and counseling, encouraged the residents of Mexico City to enlist:

> Having painfully realized that the inhabitants of this capital are deaf to the imperious voice of the law, and that—postponing their [civic] interests and the conservation of their public liberties to the leisure and malice to which they thoughtlessly abandoned themselves—they have not complied with the com-

mand in the sovereign Decree of April 9th of the previous year, published by edict the 23rd of the same month, he has resolved that … the general enlistment for the national militia proceed [immediately].[14]

The sparse enlistment and its discontinuity represented a trend in the majority of cities, a problem experienced by nearly all the ayuntamientos, as demonstrated by my studies of Puebla, Veracruz, Zacatecas, and México.[15]

Still, this first enlistment shows the conservative nature of the regulation in requiring only those who possessed a certain level of income or property to take up arms, an aspect of moderate liberalism that was superceded in the Reglamento of 1827, which called "all Mexicans" to enlist in the civic militia. As a result, the number of militiamen not only increased, overcoming the problem of the scarcity of troops, but the sociological and professional composition of the militia also changed, the burden falling on artisans, clerical workers, and laborers.

This military organization reflects the change of the revolutionary moment, from Iturbidist moderatism to federal republicanism. Enlisted, organized, trained, and armed civilians would become one of the armed social foundations of the democratic movement started by Vicente Guerrero in 1828.

It should be emphasized that in this first moment of independence a single national identity—that is, Mexican—was not yet consolidated. The Regulation of 1822 required the condition of being "American" in order to be a cívico, a general condition sufficient for "the defense of the Patria." This definition of civic responsibility was also a strategy for the comprehensive defense of the American continent as a result of the pan-Hispanic American tendency that emerged from the experience of the Cortes of Cádiz and continued for more than two decades thereafter in a movement that Jaime E. Rodríguez has called Spanish Americanism.[16]

The "American" standard changed in Mexico with the Reglamento of 1827, when Mexican nationality became a civil and political requirement for service in the civic militia. With this change, the civic militia integrated all vecinos into its ranks, thus incorporating a fundamental principle of the national army established, among others, by Napoleon: the *leva en masa* (mass recruitment). An important difference is that the authorities favored obligatory conscription rather than voluntary enlistment. However, the indifference, aloofness, and even antagonism of the population with respect to joining the militia caused some officials to take more coercive measures to enlist the vecinos. Such methods provoked community protests and contradicted the voluntary and "patriotic" spirit of the civic militia. The amalgamative force of an incipient Mexican nationalism had not yet spread sufficiently among the popular classes to reach the level of patriotism.

The civic militia's enlistment efforts increased the number of its companies, diversified the socio-professional composition and officers, and prolif-
erated the social problem at the heart of the militia organization and beyond.
In time, militia enlistment coincided with the recruitment of the army, or active military, by means of the levy. Thus, some individuals employed the
stratagem of enlisting in the civic militia in order to be excluded from conscription in the levies of the national army and from the provincial militia's
drafts. This caused numerous conflicts between the civil and the military authorities. The local officials demanded the release of civic militiamen conscripted by force into the army, while the military authorities protested the
legal obstacles placed by civil authorities to impede the inclusion of civic
militiamen into the ranks of the army. The levy generated many conflicts and
protests in the population.[17] Faced with this manifest confusion, the captain
general of central Mexico explained to the ayuntamiento who was susceptible to be recruited by the levy:

> In our liberal system, vagrants are conscripted; those who frequent, at improper
> times, wine shops, cafés, taverns, and prohibited games; those who gamble il-
> legally and after the ringing of curfew bells wander aimlessly through the
> streets; just as all those who violate the edicts of order and good government
> should be conscripted.[18]

The recruitment squads exceeded their responsibilities and forced their
way into the houses of artisans and businessmen, pressing them into service,
a recruitment practice common during the absolutist monarchy. Many artisans who were also cívicos were affected, and this fed the conflict between
the militia and the army, between civil and military authority. In addition,
faced with legislation that did not specify exceptions, many individuals enlisted in the civic militia in order to evade recruitment into the national army
or the provincial militia, immediately asking for a certificate of membership
in the civic militia. The problem was resolved with the decree of October 16,
1824, that included cívicos in the provincial draft lotteries. This measure increased the protests by militiamen who saw in it a decline of civil rights in
deference to military power. Furthermore, the cívicos demanded a *fuero* (a
set of legal privileges), just as the members of the army possessed, which
would grant an exemption that excluded them from serving in the army.
There was the case, for example, of the "citizens" of Guadalupe in Zacatecas, who sent a manifesto to the jefe político protesting that:

> Moreover, if from this number (the quota of recruits assigned to the town) the
> majority belongs to the body of cívicos because only commanders and officers
> [of the civic militia] are excepted from conscription by Article 29 of the Decree
> of the 16th of October, 1824, will it not enervate the civic militia, created with
> the laudable purpose of protecting the internal security of the places in which it

has been established? As a result, the peaceful, unarmed, and defenseless people of the town will be deprived of this small force to protect them from the invasions and hostilities of the perverse men who are still abundant in this region. This state of affairs is all too frequent and notorious in the State to which we belong.[19]

Not all citizens had to enlist. The civic militia made exceptions for ordained clergy, sailors (clearly showing the deficiencies and needs of the virtually nonexistent Mexican Navy), those physically impaired and unable to operate firearms, civil and military public officials, and, it should be noted, *jornaleros* (ordinary day laborers). This last restriction showed the civic militia to be an armed body dictated by class and directed, controlled, and armed by landowners, provincial authorities, and the local bourgeoisie. Excluded from militia service, it must be emphasized, were the popular classes who had constituted the social foundation of the insurgency of Miguel Hidalgo and José María Morelos, who constantly threatened agrarian revolts and urban riots, and who ultimately led the assault on the Parián market in Mexico City in 1828. The bourgeoisie, what some call an oligarchy, the elite, or notables, would not permit an institution that existed for national defense to accept the popular classes, which were identified more and more with laborers, with or without work, who might question the liberal order, private property, the expropriation of land from indigenous communities, or the elimination of universal adult male suffrage as a result of the Federal Constitution of 1824.

However, Mexico did not invent anything new in its militia regulations. Rather, the exclusion of jornaleros from militia organizations was a common practice. It was a restrictive clause of the national militia in Spain.[20] The same thing happened with France's Garde Nationale and in Italy with Garibaldi's Red Shirts. The militia became an essential armed body in all the liberal revolutionary processes. The civil authorities needed faithful, devoted, controllable, "civilian," armed forces to defend the liberal principles of the nation state against the whims of absolutist kings, such as Fernando VII in the Peninsula, as well as in other territories that the monarchy had lost but still coveted, New Spain in particular. This revolutionary process brought with it the long and difficult struggle for the formation of the national state, in which the civic militia played a principal role.

Nevertheless, the word jornalero continued to cause confusion between civil and military authorities. The concept of jornalero referred to *campesinos* (peasants) without land. Proletarianized campesinos, or those who had failed to acquire land, were excluded from the militia. Still, if the liberals intended to exclude workers with this measure, they failed because artisans, who were included in the militia, were also in danger of losing their work. What were artisans if not workers?

The same discussion arose in Congress when the regulation was debated. José María Bustamante asked the commission to clarify the term jornalero or substitute it with *operario* (worker). The commission replied that "the word jornalero explains enough. . . in terms of not earning a wage on a day they do not work."[21]

All the same, the uncertainties multiplied. Many ayuntamientos raised the matter of jornaleros with the enlistment commissions of the diputaciones provinciales and, later during the federal republic, with the governor. Thus, for example, the ayuntamiento of San Alto asked the Zacatecas Congress if "the corporals, cattlemen, shepherds and other persons in continuous service in the haciendas" were included in the category of jornaleros. Of all the questions, one had priority: if the "so-called Indians of the town who have temporary work" were included in this category. If "they are excluded, we deprive ourselves of the most reliably strong and useful men and the number of cívicos then diminishes excessively" because they constituted the majority of population in many areas, while the artisans "are very few."[22]

The civic militia in Mexico had a double role, as a national force against potential invaders, especially Spaniards, and, within its boundaries, as an armed political force capable of defending liberal principles against the conservative efforts of the Iturbistas, or against popular democratic revolts such as Vicente Guerrero's, for example, that threatened the social and political stability of the new liberal state. In this sense, Article 23 of the reglamento established that the civic militia was not to provide an honor guard to anyone, "no matter how important they may be." Paradoxically, it displayed the remnants of an absolutist tendency when it refused to render honors while under arms to anyone except to the "Divine Majesty." What was to be understood by this? Could it have been a tribute to Iturbide himself?

A second relevant particularity of the civic militia was the procedure for appointing the non-commissioned, regular, and commanding officers. The officers and non-commissioned officers were elected by the rank and file "by a majority of votes." The civic militia was a military organization composed of citizens who democratically elected their superiors and whose officers maintained liberal principles proclaiming that "they will conduct themselves as citizens who command citizens."[23] This democratic practice of the militia generated a social and civil problematic between the officers and troops that reflected the contradictions of an armed organization comprising civilians whose commanding officers were elected democratically by them. The mental confusion of the militiamen was evident since the liberal representative methods of the civil institutions also applied to a military organization in which the officers received their posts by popular vote and not by privilege (a characteristic of the army officers of the ancien régime), their preparation in military academies, or their skill and/or heroism in battle (a characteristic of regular army officers). The civic or national militia would shift toward democratic positions, as much because of the socio-professional characteristics of its troops as the political inclination of its officers, who often were elected to posts of command by troops with a tendency toward radicalism. When that occurred, the political institutions, provincial or national, tried to moderate, disarm, or simply dissolve the militias.

To be an officer it was necessary to have been born in America[24] or to have a minimum of seven years' residency and to be "a well-known supporter of independence." This democratic practice transferred to the military the concept of popular representation that doceañista liberalism had inaugurated in the ayuntamientos, the diputaciones provinciales, and the Cortes. As a consequence, many of the most popular political leaders also placed themselves in command positions of militia companies and battalions, thus obtaining not only political backing but also military command. As a result, the militia companies sometimes held strong political views. Nevertheless, unlike the national militia in Spain, individuals could not choose which company to join, making it more difficult for companies to concentrate militiamen from one or another political orientation.

In this way, the civic militia constituted a peculiar organization, composed of civilians and directed by political and even popular leaders. But the characteristic that made the militia significant in a time of political upheaval was that it was armed. The militia had popular representation and an electoral legitimacy, but lacked the sovereignty that the diputaciones provinciales, and later the states, would possess.

The commanding officers of each battalion were elected by the officers of each company, developing in this way a chain of democratic representation that characterized the entire command structure. These commanding officers were faced with a particular problem because they were elected by officers who later did not always obey them. As the colonel of the Zacatecas militia complained to the ayuntamiento: "These subjects are absolutely inept or disorderly: with the result that when dealing with officers of the same quality in the militia, educated and well-behaved citizens refused to enlist and serve in such units."[25]

Another important aspect of the civic militia was that it was under the jurisdiction of the "local superior political authority," that is, of the magistrate, who in serious matters "will work with the ayuntamiento." Thus, to complete the trilogy: vecinos were led by vecinos democratically elected from among them and under the command of an authority elected by the same vecinos. Nevertheless, all of them and their institution were armed. They functioned under military regulations at a time of upheaval when independence, revolution, and war followed one another. These were sufficient reasons for the national state to maintain the civic militia.

Furthermore, the reglamento sought to resolve the potential conflict between commanders of the civic militia and of the army, or "active or permanent militia." During active duty, when both armed forces met, command corresponded to the highest-ranking officer; when of equal rank, command went to the army officer. This represented a novelty in relation to the Spanish national militia, since the members of the militia were always subordinate to the army officers. In contrast, Mexico granted equal recognition to the civilian hierarchy of officers vis-à-vis the army's, which conferred military authority to the civilian command in acts of service as well as war. Nevertheless, and in spite of the reglamento's provisions for avoiding conflict, tensions and constant confrontations between the civic militia and the army command and soldiers persisted.

MILITIAMEN AND CIVILIANS

In order to reach a real, and not de facto, equality, the militiamen had to receive instruction and preparation. Militia officers attended classes in theory taught by retired army commanding officers; if there were not enough retired officers for that task, army officers on active duty were responsible for that instruction. Once this first stage was completed, the militia officers were obligated to instruct the troops. Since militia troops consisted of vecinos who dedicated their workday to their professions and occupations, training took place on holidays and Sundays. This caused the training of militiamen and officers to be delayed, sometimes excessively, and promoted absenteeism since the militiamen had to dedicate their day of rest (sometimes a day they would have preferred to work) to an activity that they considered unproductive, dangerous, and bothersomely obligatory.

There are numerous examples of non-participation in training, and it was one of the greatest problems of the organization. Take the case, for example, of the civilian colonels of Zacatecas and Aguascalientes who complained repeatedly to the governor that the owners of haciendas, mines, and commercial and other "profitable" businesses constantly urged their employees not to attend guard duty, doctrinal exercises, and other militia activities. Likewise, the employees excused themselves from guard duty and instruction under the threat of being dismissed by their bosses. It was a socio-civilmilitary constant not easily resolved.

This problematic was related to the creation of a penal code included in the reglamento. The democratic spirit that characterized the election of the officers also translated into infractions and crimes since it established the same penalties for everyone equally: commanding officers, officers, and militiamen.

The various penalties included jail or prison. All the same, most arrests were served in militia company quarters, and more than anything else, as penalties paid off by fines. Table 8.1 is a list of offenses and their corresponding penalties.

Table 8.1. Civic Militia's Offenses and Penalties

Offense	*Penalty*
Simple disobedience	One day's detention
Insulting an officer	Three days' detention or one day in jail
Lack of service	Fine of from 10 to 100 pesos
Abandonment of watch post	Eight days in prison
Falling asleep on guard duty	Six days in prison
Taking up arms to harm another	Eight days in prison
Inciting insubordination	Eight days in prison
Recidivism of a crime	Double the imposed penalty

The civic militia's obligations included comprising the "principal" guard in the ayuntamiento and in those city emplacements assigned to it by local authorities. The militia also had to patrol the city and act as a riot squad in ludic celebrations when army forces or the permanent militia did not have sufficient men for those duties. In addition, the militia was used to pursue "criminals and deserters" within the limits of each town and to escort prisoners and national funds to their destinations. The official list of militia responsibilities concluded with a patriotic statement that encouraged militiamen to "defend the homes of the people under their jurisdiction against any internal or external enemy." This clause manifested the particularity of the civic militia at the time. It was organized and directed as much to defend a possible invasion by the Spanish monarchy as to act as an armed force under the orders of civil, local, and provincial authorities against any absolutist or conservative attempts from the executive branch to assume local control.

Unlike the case of the Spanish national militia, tasks were entrusted to the civic militia that fell outside the urban limits of the population in which it was constituted. In general, the Spanish national militia, except in exceptional cases that required the permission or the order of military command, was conceived as an eminently urban and defensive force. In addition, a mobile force of the Spanish militia was created only when faced with the gravity of the war against the Carlistas in 1837; it was a force composed mostly of volunteer militiamen who joined the army on specific occasions against the parties of Carlista guerillas.

These continuing responsibilities of the civic militiamen reflected the scarcity of soldiers in the Mexican army. In its first reglamento, the civic militia was established as an armed force to complement the army's role in defending the nation against possible foreign invaders, such as the Spanish, as well as assisting the army with quotidian assignments that the latter could not perform. In addition, the civic militia proved to be indispensable as a police force, which, while planned, was still not a reality. Among the reasons for the militia's responsibilities for external defense was the lack of funds in the treasury.

These realities explain some contradictions. The civic militia was created as a civil force, composed of citizens and, later, of "mexicanos," with authority for internal order, but—and here lies a substantial difference with the Spanish militia—with authority and powers complementary to the army and dedicated both to defending the borders from outside attack and to the complete defeat of the Spanish troops that still occupied San Juan de Ulúa. These necessities caused an increase in the number of militiamen in the decade of the 1820s, a time of contradictions: social (class), political (liberal versus democratic), national (conflicts between the regions and the "Mexican" center), and state (center-periphery, provincial-executive, state-executive).

THE ECONOMIC PROBLEM

The civic militia's financing was a significant problem. The ayuntamiento responsible for the militia had the necessary authority to use public funds to buy armament, uniforms, and the necessary equipment. Until 1824, this required the permission (supervision) of the diputación provincial. If there were not sufficient funds, the diputación assumed the responsibility of levying new taxes to supplement the budget. The jefes políticos could even demand the donation of armaments from the military commanders in their provinces, provoking numerous conflicts between them.

The funds for the militia were deposited in the ayuntamiento in a chest with three keys held by the magistrate, the treasurer, and a high-ranking militia officer. With this tripartite division, the financial co-responsibility among the local authority, its administration, and the militia command was guaranteed.

Nevertheless, the reglamento also provided for another resource, more practical and common, for acquiring armaments: the militiamen themselves furnished their own weapons. The documentation concerning this provision demonstrates one of the characteristics of Mexican society, the proliferation of arms—generally blades but also some firearms—it contained. An eminently armed society was now militarized . . . civilly.

In the case of the cavalry squadrons, the militiamen had to furnish the horses and riding equipment. Thus the cavalry became an elite and smaller body comprising, generally, renters, landowners, and liberal professionals. This social composition gave the squadrons a politically conservative orientation. Finally, in a nationalist fervor and "as a patriotic act," the militiamen were urged to wear uniforms and armaments from the "national factories."[26] This idea was not unfounded. Three forms of nationalism combined: armed, economic, and ideological. One had to "create the Patria," buying national products and developing a market that aspired to become national; and the militia constituted an incentive for increased production.

But the civil militia had yet another mission. The nation needed not only militiamen—that is, armed vecinos—but also cívicos. For the state this meant that they were civilians, in contradistinction with the military caste, and also that they were aware of their rights and, above all, obligations as citizens, an older concept that gained new meaning after the liberal revolution.

At its birth, the Mexican nation not only needed an armed force, but also one that would organize itself according to the new liberal principles that involved assuming and propagating national values. This included also developing and extending a hegemonic nationalism. Since an armed force with these characteristics did not exist after independence, it had to be created ex novo, the same as the nation. But, as in the case of other institutions, concepts, and aspects, the liberal revolution changed the meaning of many signifiers.

The militiamen had to act according to their oath of enlistment. It was not just any act; the liberal paraphernalia had begun. The militiaman had to be of an elevated civic category. The state ideologues had studied the symbolic value and the transcendence of the militiaman. Thus, after an ayuntamiento agreed that it was appropriate to organize militia companies in its territory, the following Sunday all militiamen gathered to take an oath to support liberal political and military institutions. A mass was then celebrated for which the parish priest had used the militia reglamento to prepare the content of his sermon, which dealt with the militiamen's obligations to the Patria and his commitment to defend its independence, civil liberty, and the nation's constitution in effect since 1824.

The oath reads as follows:

> Do you swear to God our Lord to employ the arms that the nation places in your hands in defense of the Catholic, Apostolic, and Roman Religion, to maintain the internal order of the State, to obey and to enforce the obedience of that which is sanctioned by the National Congress, maintaining strict fidelity to Congress as the repository of [national] sovereignty, to obey strictly local civil authorities, and to show due consideration to other citizens?
>
> Yes, I swear.

And the civilian commitment, although it may have been confessional, transformed the citizen into a military man, a militiaman. Each battalion possessed its own flag. The instructions for the flag were precise and uniform. It was to be made from taffeta with three vertical stripes in green, white, and red. On the white stripe there should be an eagle about to take flight surrounded by the mottos "Religion, Independence, and Union," and underneath, "Mexican Constitution," with the name of the province on top. In short, they were symbols that French historiography likes to call, although without sufficient explanation, "collective imaginary."

The flags held both symbolic and ideological value in their watchwords: religious, liberal, constitutional, and, especially, national. One of the symbolic values of Mexican nationalism was forged in the flag. But in the militia's case this was realized from the symbolic perspective of armed Mexican-citizens.

Uniformity, homogeneity, especially in national symbols, was a requirement in the process of forming the nation. And despite the emphasis on uniformity, the flag offered a concession to particularity: the name of the province of each battalion. Latent federalism thus began to appear, and the civic militia became a fundamental part of its gestation and support.

One of the required ceremonies involved the blessing of the militia flags, an act that had characteristics similar to those of the Spanish national militia. A solemn and well-attended event, it brought together all civil, ecclesiastical, and military authorities. Significantly, in addition to the obligatory nature of the event, the regulation contained a passage that the civil authorities were to read to all militiamen. It was designed to harangue troops who happened to be civic militiamen:

> Militiamen: all of us who have the honor of being enlisted under this national flag that God our Lord has deigned to bless so that it will serve us as a symbol of unity against the enemies of our independence and civil liberty, are obligated to defend it with our lives if necessary. The glory of nations demands it. The reputation of our unit and our personal honor depend upon the fulfillment of the solemn promise we have made to employ the arms that our nation has placed in our hands in defense of its political Constitution: and as a testament and as a sign that thus we promise . . . ready . . . aim . . . fire . . .

The organization of the militia represented the armed aspect of the national question since the achievement of independence. The civic militia was conceived in Mexico, as in Spain, as not only an armed force, but also as an ideological and political one capable of transferring Mexican national and liberal values to the population. The role of the militia changed with the reform of the reglamento in 1827, which granted the states all responsibility concerning the civic militia. This reform is one of the keys to understanding the nature of federalism in Mexico. That is, apart from political, economic, historical, and cultural considerations, federalism granted each state of the Mexican union its own civic militia. As a result, an indispensable element of state autonomy was won: the possession of armed coercive agents. Moreover, the size of the militia in certain states made the federal army incapable of engaging it with any surety of success. The history of nineteenth-century Mexico can only be understood if one realizes that power resided in the states and not in the nation's capital. The militias of the states of Mexico contributed significantly to that relation of power.

NOTES

1. Manuel Chust, *La cuestión nacional Americana en las Cortes de Cádiz* (Valencia & Mexico: UNED-Fundación Instituto de Historia Social & Universidad Nacional Autónoma de México, 1999).

2. See Ivana Frasquet, "America 1812: ¿Una Constitución Hispána?" *Mexican Studies/Estudios Mexicanos* 20: 1 (winter 2004), 24–46.

3. Mexico, *Actas del Congreso Constituyente*, vol I (Mexico: Universidad Nacional Autónoma de México, 1980), (hereafter cited as ACC), (March 1, 1822), 30.

4. See Christon Archer, *El ejército en el México borbónico, 1760–1810* (Mexico: Fondo de Cultura Económica, 1983); Juan Ortiz, *Guerra y gobierno. Los pueblos y la independencia de México* (Sevilla: Instituto Mora-Universidad de Sevilla, 1997); Josefina Vázquez, "Iglesia, ejército y centralismo," *Historia Mexicana* 39: 1 (July–September, 1989); and "Los pronunciamientos de 1832: Aspirantismo político e ideología," in Jaime E. Rodríguez O., ed., *Patterns of Contention in Mexican History* (Wilmington, Delaware: Scholarly Resources, Inc., 1992), 163–187.

5. ACC, (March 1, 1822), 30.

6. ACC, (May 13, 1822), 226.

7. Ibid., 219.

8. Ibid., 224.

9. Ibid., 214–215.

10. ACC, (May 15, 1822), 264.

11. Jaime E. Rodríguez O., "Las Cortes Mexicanas y el Congreso Constituyente" in Virginia Guedea, coord., *La independencia de México y el proceso autonomista novohispano, 1808–1824* (Mexico: Universidad Nacional Autónoma de México, 2001), 285–320; and Jaime E. Rodríguez O., "The Struggle for Dominance: The Legislature versus the Executive in Early Mexico," in Christon I. Archer, ed., *The Birth of Modern Mexico* (Wilmington: SR Books, 2003), 205–228.

12. For a superb study from this historical and interpretive understanding, see José Antonio Serrano "Liberalismo gaditano y milicias cívicas en Guanajuato, 1820–1836," in Carlos Illades and Ariel Rodríguez Kuri, eds., *Construcción de la legitimidad en México* (Mexico: El Colegio de Michoacán-Universidad Autónoma de México, 1998); and "Villas fuertes, ciudades débiles: milicias y jerarquía territorial en Guanajuato, 1790–1847," in Salvador Broseta, Carmen Corona, Manuel Chust et al., eds., *Las ciudades y la guerra* (Castellón: Universitat Jaume I, 2002), 381–421; and Juan Ortiz, "Las fuerzas militares y el proyecto de estado en México, 1767–1835," in Alicia Hernández Chávez, ed., *Cincuenta años de historia en México*, vol. II (Mexico: El Colegio de México, 1991), 261–282.

13. Archivo Histórico del Estado de Zacatecas, Fondo Ayuntamiento de Zacatecas. Sección Milicias, caja 2.

14. Archivo Histórico Municipal de México, Milicias cívicas, caja 3274.

15. I am currently engaged in a far-ranging study of the civic militia in Mexico.

16. Jaime E. Rodríguez O., *The Emergence of Spanish America: Vicente Rocafuerte and Spanish Americanism, 1808–1832* (Berkeley: University of California Press, 1975).

17. José Antonio Serrano, *El contingente de la sangre. Los métodos de reclutamiento del ejército mexicano, 1824–1844* (Mexico: Instituto Nacional de Antropología e Historia, 1993).

18. Archivo Histórico Municipal de México, Milicias cívicas, caja 3274.

19. Archivo Histórico del Estado de Zacatecas, Jefatura política de Zacatecas. XVIII. Milicias.

20. Manuel Chust, *Ciudadanos en armas* (Valencia: IVEI, 1987); Juan Sisinio Pérez Garzón, *Milicia nacional y revolución burguesa* (Madrid: CSIC, 1978); and Roberto Blanco Valdés, *Rey, Cortes y fuerzas armadas en los orígenes de la España liberal, 1808–1823* (Madrid: Siglo XXI, 1988).

21. ACC, (April 18, 1822), 54.

22. Archivo Histórico del Estado de Zacatecas, Poder Legislativo, caja VIII.

23. Article 37 of the *Reglamento*.

24. Observe here also the requirement "americano."

25. Archivo Histórico del Estado de Zacatecas, Poder Legislativo, caja VIII, milicias.

26. Article 67 of the *Reglamento*.

IV

THE ECONOMY

9

Cádiz Liberalism and Public Finances: Direct Contributions in Mexico, 1810–1835

José Antonio Serrano Ortega

On September 13, 1813, the Cortes of Cádiz announced a decree that established a new constitutional principle on taxation in the Spanish Monarchy: "All citizens, without exception or privilege, are obliged to contribute to the burdens of the state according to their wealth." Liberal deputies were overjoyed with the promulgation of the decree and, from the podium of the parliament, observed that the month of September inaugurated a new stage in the financial system of the Spanish Nation, as the Monarchy was now called.

Why did this decree create such euphoria? Liberals hoped that direct contributions would replace the tax system of the *antiguo régimen*. Their hopes rested on the expectation that the new tax law would promote the establishment of three liberal principles diametrically opposed to the previous operation of the royal treasury.[1]

The first principle was *equal* tax burden. All citizens, "without exception or privilege," were directed to contribute. The key word is "everybody." The antiguo régimen had been founded on tax exemptions for the "privileged," but the September resolution would force all inhabitants of the Monarchy to contribute to the burden of the state.

The second principle was fiscal *uniformity*. The Cortes of Cádiz had the right to determine the amount of tax that each citizen was obliged to pay, and officials from the Ministry of Finance had the power to collect the tax throughout the Monarchy. As a result, a direct relationship was created between the contributors and public finances, a very different bond than the one that had been at work in the royal treasury of the antiguo régimen. Previously, the Spanish Crown, at least in the Iberian Peninsula, had negotiated with the authorities from each kingdom—be they called cortes, diputación of the cortes, or royal councils—the total tax sum that was to be paid by the subjects of these territories.[2] Direct taxes would annul "territorial *fueros* [privileges]" by instituting fiscal uniformity throughout the Spanish Monarchy.

The third principle was *tax proportionality*. The amount of the contribution was fixed by the Cortes according to the total wealth of each contributor, which implied that the state was to be sustained primarily by the "privileged"—the wealthiest citizens—those who benefited the most from the activities of the government.[3] Through direct contribution, deputies sought to create an institutional, political, and social place for the three doctrinaire principles of *gaditano* (Cádiz) fiscal liberalism: *equality, uniformity,* and *proportionality.*

The new tax decree soon reached New Spain. From 1813 to 1821, the liberal tax became a source of income for the treasury of the viceroyalty of New Spain. Furthermore, the direct contribution became a fundamental principle of public finance of the First Mexican Empire, from 1822 to 1823, and also of the national and state governments during the Federal Republic between 1824 and 1835. How well were the expectations of the liberal deputies of the Cortes of Cádiz fulfilled in Mexico? To what extent did the direct contribution transform the nature of the financial system of New Spain? How did this tax policy influence the development of the Mexican financial system? How did the tax promote public acceptance and institutionalization of the principles of *equality, uniformity,* and *proportionality?* This essay proposes answers to these broad questions.

The impact of gaditano liberalism in Mexico during the first half of the nineteenth century has been examined from a number of perspectives. Books and articles describe how that liberalism spread and was put into practice by political elites, they examine its influence on peasant communities and Indian towns, and they demonstrate its incorporation into the judicial system. However, there are only a few articles on gaditano liberalism written from the perspective of public finances. Fiscal history is an optimal way to identify the new aspects of liberalism in nineteenth-century Mexico, as well as to reconsider previously studied issues.

"THE CUSTOM OF PAYING PROGRESSIVE TAXES": THE WAR OF INDEPENDENCE, 1810–1821

Under the concept of "direct contribution," the deputies of the Cortes of Cádiz imposed two forms of direct taxes—the product tax and the income tax—that adhered to the three liberal principles mentioned above. The first taxed separately the sources of income that made up the taxpayer's personal fortune. In this sense, contributions were "direct product taxes—also called objective taxes—because they burdened the source that generated taxable earnings."[4] With direct product taxes the contributor was defined according to the sources of his wealth: a merchant's capital or an "industrialist's" wealth was taxed, as well as property rents, luxury items, and a farmer's crop. Direct product contributions "pursued" the sources of wealth rather than specific persons; the tax was calculated on the products of those sources of riches rather than on the total wealth of the taxpayer. In contrast, the direct income tax was applied to the total riches of each individual taxpayer, "regardless of the source." In this way, gaditano deputies promoted an income tax.

Only a few months after they went into effect, the Cádiz decrees on direct contributions were hastily enforced in an unstable and nearly bankrupt New Spain. By the end of 1811, the war between the royalists and the insurgents had left New Spain's public treasury in a deep state of crisis: ordinary income, such as that generated by tobacco, had disappeared; sales taxes were rarely collected; and taxes on minting coins and on tithes were inadequate. The weakened administrative links between the regional and central treasuries had increased the poverty of the Royal Treasury, since most of the funds collected never left the outlying regions and only a small percentage reached Mexico City. Due to the lack of resources, the authorities frequently resorted to extraordinary fund-raising measures such as donations and loans. These were insufficient to resolve the financial crisis in New Spain.[5]

Under these conditions of fiscal poverty, the authorities of the viceroyalty of New Spain welcomed the direct contributions decree as a new opportunity to restore the treasury. In February 1812, Viceroy Francisco Javier Venegas ordered all homeowners to contribute 5 percent of rental income to the royal chest. In addition, tenants were expected to contribute 5 percent of their total yearly rent payments. Finally, "those who lived in their own houses will contribute 10 percent [of the rental value of the property] as both owners and tenants."[6] Intendants, who were in charge of collecting this property tax, appointed the appraisers who determined the taxation value of each house.

In order to obtain more resources for the "*buena causa*" (the "good cause" or the war against the insurgents), Viceroy Félix María Calleja applied the direct tax to individual wealth. Closely following gaditano regulations "so as to verify extraordinary war contributions (September 1812),"[7] Calleja issued, on November 15, 1813, the "Extraordinary War Contributions Regulations,"[8] which established that a proportional tax would be collected on every citizen's income and fortune. All the inhabitants of New Spain, except day laborers and those who earned less than 300 pesos annually, were to present a sworn account of their capital, earnings, and liquid assets, so that "the *ayuntamientos* (town councils) could assign the tax that, according to the tax table, corresponded to each contributor." If a taxpayer refused to present the sworn list or falsified information, the municipal body had the right to determine the tax "according to the information or opinion held of his fortune or assets." The municipal authorities were instructed to update their lists of contributors every six months to reflect increases or decreases in the liquid assets of local inhabitants. In "towns" that did not have ayuntamientos, subdelegates and *tenientes de justicia* (assistant magistrates) would "elect two honest citizens from each parish and together with them assign the tax quotas."

Despite the viceroy's preparations, the institutions that represented New Spain's taxpayers, especially the ayuntamientos and the recently established *diputaciones provinciales* (provincial deputations), rejected direct contributions based both on income and amassed wealth. The ayuntamientos of the cities of León and Mérida and the Diputación Provincial of New Galicia used the same argument to justify their opposition: the Constitution of 1812 authorized only the Cortes to establish taxes within the Monarchy. Viceroys Venegas and Calleja, therefore, did not have the authority to impose taxes. Furthermore, both viceroys had infringed on the Constitution with their edicts of February 1812 and November 1813. The *regidores* (aldermen) and syndics of the Ayuntamiento of Mérida, as representatives of all the citizens of the municipality, declared that article 172 of "the Holy Constitution, the source and origin of happiness for all Spaniards," expressly prohibited the authorities from either "imposing direct or indirect contributions or making any [financial] demand under any name or for any reason whatsoever; such decrees must always be made by the Cortes."[9] Therefore, Viceroy Venegas, as the king's alter ego, could not impose contributions without the permission of the deputies of the Cortes of the Monarchy.

The deputies of the Provincial Deputation of New Galicia, for their part, refused to accept the direct contribution edict of November 1813. They also based their argument on article 172 of the Constitution. However, they emphasized the fact that the "Sacred Code" had separated the "Kingdom of New Galicia" from its earlier political dependence on the "Viceroyalty of Mexico."[10] According to article 324 of the Constitution and the Instructions of 1813, New Galicia had been established as a constitutional province "entirely" independent of New Spain's *jefe político* (political chief, the official in charge of a province under the Constitution)—that is to say, the former viceroy. Thus, the provincial deputation recognized the jefe político of New Galicia as its only immediate superior authority and the only official with authority to receive and fulfill orders from the Cortes. In this sense, General José de la Cruz, the jefe político of New Galicia, was not a subaltern of the authorities in Mexico City and thus "could not receive orders from the viceroyalty related to the government of the kingdom [of Nueva Galicia] or be forced to fulfill them."

Viceroy Calleja, in March and again in October of 1813, rejected the arguments set forth by the municipal officials of Mérida in opposition to property taxes. First, he argued, the tax was just since it was based on "a mathematical proportion of each individual's possessions." Implicitly, Calleja was asserting that the tax that burdened tenants and homeowners followed the principle of proportionality established by the Cortes. Also, he indicated that the February 1812 edict had preceded the promulgation of the Charter of Cádiz and that no order had been issued to suspend or abolish it. Finally, Calleja accused Mérida's syndics and regidores of lacking patriotism for refusing to support the causa buena, especially at a moment when insurgents threatened New Spain. Suspending the collection of property tax was not justified, considering "the extraordinary occurrences in the kingdom caused by the insurrection." It was also elemental, he added, "that the obligation to help out our brothers [is stipulated by] not only natural law, but by civil, human, and political law."[11] Consequently, Calleja ordered that the February 1812 edict be put into effect as soon as possible.

In spite of the viceroy's forceful order, the Diputación Provincial of New Galicia and the ayuntamientos of Mérida, Léon, and other cities in New Spain refused to name *comisionados* (assessors) to survey houses and collect the extraordinary war tax. The resistance was generally successful, since the February 1812 edict was fulfilled in only a few areas of the viceroyalty.

Paradoxically, the abolition of the Constitution of Cádiz in 1814 favored the operation and collection of direct contributions in New Spain. A few months after Fernando VII ordered "a return to the status quo ante of 1808," Viceroy Calleja again assumed political and administrative control of the entire territory of New Spain. He abolished all new gaditano institutions, such as the diputaciones provinciales, and annulled almost every decision taken by the Cortes. As an exception, in October 1814 he declared valid the direct contribution sanctioned in September of 1813 "by the outlawed Cortes," after consulting with the *junta de arbitros* (committee of arbitration) in Mexico City and considering, on the one hand, the "evident paucity of the Royal Treasury," and on the other, "the pressing need for a just government to levy contributions in such a way that no one is burdened more than any other." The viceroy ordered that throughout the Viceroyalty of New Spain, the "progressive direct contribution" was to be collected according to the rules of the 1813 edict, such as the 1812 ruling on property taxes.[12] The order specified again that each provincial capital was to form a council made up of the commissioners of the ayuntamiento and representatives of the Church, the merchant class, as well as another group versed in "all class of matters." In towns without an ayuntamiento, the subdelegates and the tenientes de justicia "will elect two honest citizens from each parish, who will together establish the quotas." As before, day laborers and those who made less than 300 pesos annually were exempt from payment, and a table was created that specified the percentages each "individual" was to pay according to his assets.

Although a closer and more detailed study is needed of the development of direct contributions during the decade of the War for Independence, documentary evidence exists that product and individual wealth taxes were collected in most areas of New Spain, especially from 1815 onwards. One piece of documentary evidence is an 1823 Finance Ministry report on the revenues from the different branches of public finances that had not been collected since 1810.[13] The report lists all properties on which sales tax had not been collected, as well as uncollected taxes on alcoholic beverages, mescal, tobacco, salt mines, and, of course, "war contribution rights,"—in other words, direct contributions, both on individual fortunes and on different products of wealth. The report shows that from 1812 to 1814 such taxes were collected only in certain areas, but from 1815 to 1816, they were collected regularly in most of New Spain, except in the Intendancy of Michoacán and in certain regions of the intendancies of Guanajuato and of México. These areas were characterized by continued violent conflicts between insurgents and royalists. Nevertheless, after 1817, direct taxes were collected even in these areas.

The War for Independence and the constant penury of the royal treasury forced the authorities of New Spain to continue to collect the direct taxes established by the Cortes of Cádiz. Thus, it could be concluded that the war "naturalized" liberal taxes in New Spain. In the words of a deputy of the *Junta Nacional Instituyente* (the body established by Emperor Agustín de Iturbide to replace the Mexican Cortes that he had dissolved) in 1822, "[S]ince 1810 the inhabitants of Mexico have become accustomed, in spite of their complaints, to paying direct contributions." During the war, the population of New Spain became used to such taxes, as well as to fiscal institutions—be they the royal bureaucracy, ayuntamientos, or juntas de arbitros. In effect, New Spain had accepted the direct taxes first imposed by the Cortes of Cádiz.

TAXATION PROPORTIONALITY:
ALL MUST CONTRIBUTE, ACCORDING TO THEIR MEANS?

Following independence, between March and June of 1821, Agustín de Iturbide—then president of the Council of Regency—abolished most "extraordinary *pensiones* [taxes] imposed by the Mexican Government from the year 1810 to the present," such as direct contributions and a number of mining and agricultural taxes.[14] Nonetheless, at the end of December 1821, the government coffers held only 6,647 pesos.[15] Iturbide and the members of the *Soberana Junta Provisional Gubernativa* (Sovereign Provisional Governing Junta) were forced to propose "direct contributions," to address the "chronic penury of the national treasury."[16] In February 1822 the Finance Ministry presented to the recently elected Mexican Cortes a proposal on "direct contributions," the contents of which are not known.[17] The debate that followed forced the different economic and social interests represented in the imperial legislature to state their positions vis à vis the principle that justified direct contributions: "Every citizen is obligated to contribute to the burdens of the state according to their wealth." In April 1822, the finance commission, made up mainly of deputies representing mining and commercial interests, proposed that Mexico establish a tax system that would force each hacienda, farm, and small landholding to pay a tax of 5 percent of its gross production, including everything harvested and all animals sold. This so-called "direct rural pensión [was to function as] a mortgage to moneylenders that assisted the national treasury in its emergency or to create an amortization fund for the public debt."[18] In exchange for this rural tax, farmers would be exempt from the *alcabala* (sales tax) on the sale of cereals and flocks. The provincial deputations and the ayuntamientos would be authorized, first, to conduct property surveys, and second, to collect the contributions. Finally, they would have the authority to deliver the collected taxes to the public treasury.

According to the legislators from the finance committee, three considerations justified the land tax. The first was habit: the people of Mexico were accustomed to paying tithes, a direct colonial tax. While one of the impediments to collecting direct contributions was the social opposition to a new tax, the rural pensión was really an addendum to the tithes. Second, it was impossible in so short a time to conduct a survey of the nation's public wealth that would provide an accurate account of the capital in circulation, as well as agricultural and industrial products and earned salaries. Also, it was impossible to "appraise the value of the income, capital, or industry of each citizen," since establishing a "sole direct contribution" implied creating an extensive bureaucratic apparatus in each province that would "assign and appraise the riches of each citizen." Due to the lack of a register of wealth, the finance committee deputies argued, it was impossible to establish a direct tax that would apply to all citizens and would eliminate those "taxes that affected consumption and that, as most celebrated economists believe, burden society unequally."[19]

But according to Benifacio Fernández, representative from the Province of Chiapas, the project of the finance committee was an assault against "healthy liberalism" because it only affected one economic sector, i.e., farmers. "I oppose land taxes since they go against liberal principles," he said in justification. According to this deputy, the unimpeachable principle that should structure Mexican public finances was that "All citizens are obliged to contribute to the burdens of the state according to their wealth."[20] For the same reason, Fernández criticized the proposal of the finance minister and other "*publicistas*" (commentators) who maintained that only the "wealthy" should contribute to the government. Moreover, he argued that the poor should not be excluded because all Mexican citizens received benefits from the state.

Deputy Fernández also rejected a number of other projects proposed by the finance minister and publicistas for this same reason. Finance Minister Rafael Pérez Maldonado had proposed, among other measures, a direct contribution based on the principle of a progressive distribution of the tax burden. Without further details, the minister stated that citizens must be divided according to class—depending on their wealth—and those with highest incomes and capital should shoulder the burden of the public treasury. Under this structure, day laborers and the "poor" would be excluded from tax distribution. A number of publicistas announced their support for such a tax system. José Ignacio Negreiros Sordo,[21] author of a public finance project, agreed with Pérez Maldonado that taxpayers should be divided into four groups according to their "wealth." The members of the poorest group, that is, day laborers, servants, and poor artisans, would be taxed only one peso annually. Negreiros Sordo calculated that out of the Empire's six million inhabitants, only 500,000 actually supported the tax burden. The rest provided only a minimal sum that was not needed by the Ministry of Finance.[22]

In December 1822, the finance commission of the Junta Nacional Instituyente presented a project that tried to establish a balance among the different interpretations of the liberal principle "all citizens . . . according to their wealth." The commission, chaired by Lorenzo de Zavala, proposed collecting a capitación [head tax] that would help to mitigate the Empire's fiscal crisis.[23] As its name indicates, the proposal required every man and woman over the age of fourteen to pay a tax of four *reales* per year. Each inhabitant of the Mexican Empire, no matter his or her fortune, would pay the treasury "the same quantity." Zavala gave three arguments in support of the tax. First, it followed the principle that all Mexicans were obliged to contribute to the public coffers. Second, it would not be burdensome to any citizen, no matter how poor. "There is no person, no matter how miserable, that does not have an income of at least thirty-five pesos—the salary of the lowest day laborer—and the least that could be expected is a contribution of one and a half percent." Finally, it would be fairly easy to collect: the municipal commission in charge of collecting taxes would simply include all men and women over the age of fourteen. He expected to collect close to two million pesos through the capacitación.

Simultaneously, the finance commission of the Junta Nacional Instituyente proposed seeking plentiful, but "just and equitable," taxes. In fact, throughout the debate, commission legislators frequently stated that the only way the inhabitants of the empire would pay their taxes was if a tax system were established that took into account "differences in fortune." The principle they defended was that "everyone should contribute according to their possibilities." Taxes should, therefore, be distributed in a differentiated manner: "the wealthiest" should contribute more than those who "only have their person." In this brief sentence, "everyone should contribute according to their possibilities," the finance commission reopened a debate that dated to the initial discussions by the Cortes of Cádiz in 1813, when some of its members argued that the state should be sustained by the wealthiest individuals who most benefited from governmental activities, such as economic development, the building of infrastructure needed for commercial enterprises, and actions taken to ensure public order.[24]

Consistent with the principle of equal distribution, the deputies of the finance commission established a "direct contribution" that would proportionately tax all homeowners both in the city and the countryside. Based on the April 1811 decree of the Cortes of Cádiz, the Mexican deputies ordered a widespread tax based on the value of real property that would give the treasury "four times the annual rent of the house each family occupied; . . . they [the family] would be taxed on the total and this would result in a one time ten percent tax."[25] Inhabitants with more than one property would be taxed "for the property with the highest value." Individuals with houses located in haciendas, farms, and rural smallholdings would pay 2 percent of the total value of the annual rent of the house they inhabited. All the Church's rural and urban properties would pay 2 percent of the amount calculated to be in their confraternities, schools, hospitals, and other charities. The value of the houses was to be assessed by a commission, created in each town, composed of the parish priest, a finance ministry employee, and a town council representative. The commission was to survey the properties within its jurisdiction and name appraisers, who, in the presence of tenants, "would assess that part of the building that serves as home to the interested party."

The capitación and the real property tax created, within and without the legislature, a heated debate that once again made evident the different interpretations of the liberal principle, "All citizens must contribute to the burdens of the state according to their wealth." Deputies Francisco Argandar and José María Covarrubias and attorney Wenceslao de la Barquera considered that the capitación was by definition an antiliberal tax that should not feed the public coffers of Mexico: "we are dealing with a head tax, which according to [Charles de Secondat, baron de] Montesquieu is closer to servitude and therefore, a commentator declared, closer to a feudal system, and according to [Adam] Smith, a sign of slavery."[26] Aside from being antiliberal, the capitación condemned the poor to lack the resources to even feed themselves, much less save or invest in their workshops, stores, or land. As deputy for Jalisco, Covarrubias declared, "[N]evertheless, not all the wealth of each member of the state is equal. If the Indian—wracked with cold and burned by the sun, in back of the plow—contributes, then, he whom the heavens have blessed, giving him much more than the Indian, in order to access public goods should contribute according to the blessings that have been handed to him."[27] For all these reasons, they argued, it was best to reject the head tax and, instead, resort to a direct contribution that would burden the inhabitants of the empire proportionally. It was the only tax that complied with the liberal precept that "all should contribute according to their wealth."

Deputy Lorenzo Zavala defended the capitación by declaring that although he agreed with the critics, it was the only means by which the public treasury could collect two million pesos. It would be easy to collect and only provisional, subject to revision when the Ministry of Finance had sufficient resources to initiate reforms. Zavalas's arguments settled the controversy, and the Junta Nacional Instituyente approved the head tax and the land tax.

Nevertheless, the tax law was short-lived. A few months later discontented groups pronounced the *Plan de Casa Mata,* leading to the dissolution of the Junta Nacional Instuyente, the reconvening of the dissolved 1822 Mexican Cortes, and Agustín de Iturbide's abdication. The reconvened Cortes again took up discussion of the bases of public finances. In June 1823, the new finance committee also tried to reconcile the positions about direct contributions and about the liberal principle, "all citizens . . . according to their wealth." In this sense, it proposed a "direct contribution, the oldest [tax]"; in other words, a "personal, direct, and proportional tax," requiring all individuals "of any class, sex, or age that enjoy income, salary, or personal industry, to contribute to the state the profit or income corresponding to three days of the year."[28] Two distinct positions were drawn between those who considered personal tax to be just another form of head tax (and therefore unjust for not taking into account the proportionality of assets) and those who defended the personal tax because of the empire's financial crisis. Deputy Miguel Muñoz argued: "I cannot agree to make these demands of day laborers who do not earn 100 pesos, since this would mean that the extreme poor would be forced to contribute while many rich landowners or merchants might be exempt." Deputy Covarrubias described the personal tax as a form of capitación that went against the fundamental principle that "proportionality must be considered when contributions are established."[29]

Deputies Manuel Sánchez de Tagle and Lorenzo Zavala, members of the finance committee, insisted that the personal tax was easy to collect and would supply the government with immediate funds. They also rejected the argument that the new proposal was simply a restatement of the 1822 head tax proposal, because the new proposal took into account the fundamental liberal principle of proportionality. "The committee, when proposing this article, intended to help the government with its current needs, and tried to establish contributions according to the income or earnings of citizens; the capitación would not have been as fair."[30]

Finally, in June 1823, the legislature approved the personal tax because the Ministry of Finance urgently needed funds. But the deputies of the nation also approved a change important to the development of direct contribution in Mexico: every provincial government, and not the national government, would collect and use personal tax, as well as other indirect taxes. National legislators surely took this step to ensure the support of regional political and economic elites, at a time when the Plan de Casa Mata had raised regionalist and autonomist passions. The provinces were, therefore, included in fiscal administration, allowing local authorities to establish both the taxable base and the means of collecting taxes.

After 1821, the debates on direct contribution posed two contradictory positions: on the one hand, the distribution of the tax burden among the different economic groups and sectors through a land tax, or contribution that would affect both individual income and the products of wealth, and on the other hand, a different interpretation of the liberal principle of "all citizens . . . according to their wealth." In other words, either everyone must be considered a subject of direct contribution or only the wealthy, excluding day laborers and those living in extreme poverty. These two positions marked the operation of liberal taxes in Mexico during most of the nineteenth century.

FISCAL EQUALITY: DIRECT TAXES ARE DISTRIBUTED REGIONALLY

The elites of various regions reacted in diverse ways to the national congress's authorization of provincial/state governments to administer and use the different direct taxes. In certain regions, such as Jalisco and Tamaulipas, it was expected that the direct tax would become the main source of taxation for their treasuries. In these states, fiscal reform was based on citizens' wealth. In clear contrast, the economic elites of Zacatecas, Yucatán, Oaxaca, and Guanajuato agreed (each for different reasons) on a systematic rejection of any form of direct contribution and fought for a continuation of the colonial fiscal structure. Also, a group of states composed of Puebla, Querétaro, Nuevo León, Tabasco, and México promoted a direct product tax as an important supplement: direct taxes were only one among many means of fiscal reform in these states.

This shows a very diverse map of tax contribution in Mexico. For example, in an exceptional case, the Jalisco legislature ordered in 1824 that public income should derive mostly from a direct tax on the wealth of each citizen. This decision was elevated to the constitutional level in Article 251: "One single direct contribution will be established as soon as possible in the state to cover all expenditures."[31] Soon after, the direct tax regulations were printed, and in March 1825 the state legislature established a tax "on the capital used by every citizen of the state; this will include amounts from 200 to 200,000 pesos."[32] The tax was applied to all individuals who had a capital of more than 200 pesos invested in "rural or urban land destined for private use, in rural activities . . . , [in] commercial ventures of any kind, and [in] all other ventures that require investment of capital."[33] "Individuals" were divided into twelve categories according to their capital in "operation," and each category was assigned a fixed quota, established yearly by the state legislature. In March 1825, state deputies decided that those with capital of more than 200,000 pesos would pay 1,000 pesos in direct tax yearly; capital between 150,000 and 200,000 pesos would be taxed 500 pesos; and capital greater than 20,000 but lower than 40,000 pesos would be taxed 300 pesos. The contributions established by the state of Jalisco were an attempt to individualize each fiscal subject by taxing all capital held by each and every one of the "individuals that contribute to the treasury."

Jefes de cantón (district chiefs) or of *policía* (public tranquility, public works, provisions, et cetera) and officials named by the governor were responsible for the proper administration of the tax on individual wealth. They had the authority to supervise, evaluate, and approve the survey of capital holders created by the juntas de cantón established by the commissioners of the ayuntamiento and the *directores de rentas* (directors of revenue). "If the chief of policía or the junta de cantón finds a notable decrease in capital, to vary the tax rate in detriment of the public treasury or of the capitalist, they will rectify the rate and fine the administrator, director, or commissioner up to 500 pesos."[34] Also, the jefes de cantón were allowed to resolve "without appeal" the complaints presented by capital holders who considered the tax sum assigned to them to be unfair. Administrators, *receptores* (collectors), and *subreceptores de rentas* (sub-collectors of revenue)—all employed by the jefe de cantón—"would verify the collection of direct taxes."

Jalisco authorities used various arguments to promote the direct tax based on individual capital. Deputy Antonio Pacheco Leal stated one advantage: "The constituent legislature, always seeking the greater happiness of the people of the state of Jalisco, approved the direct contribution, since it is without doubt the fairest option. Truthfully, in comparison with the head tax that was once almost imposed on us, what great inequality exists in this system? It would be intolerable for the day laborer to contribute equally with the great landowner because citizens should contribute according to the benefits they receive from society."[35] In his statement, Pacheco Leal was attacking the "menacing uniformity" of taxes and placing emphasis on the second part of the liberal principle, "all citizens are obliged to contribute to the burdens of the state according to their wealth." The 1825 Jalisco law excluded all individuals with a capital of less than 200 pesos or a yearly income of less than that amount, demonstrating that large sectors of the political and economic elite of Jalisco believed that those who received the greatest benefits from society should also contribute the most to the public treasury.

Deputy Pacheco Leal also offered another reason for supporting direct taxes: the same April 1825 decree had established that by the end of the year alcabalas on national and foreign effects would be abolished. Sales taxes were considered by the economic elites of Jalisco, especially merchants, as an obstacle to internal trade. Deputies hoped that the direct contribution would simplify tax collection, reduce tax evasion, and free regional trade and production.[36] Antonio Ibarra also rightly observed that Jalisco legislators hoped that the direct contribution would allow for "a programmatic stability of the budget, in this way ending extraordinary contributions or forced or voluntary loans. For this reason, fiscal reform also implied a substantial change in the conception of the budget: the latter would define the level and expansion of income from a stable fiscal base."[37]

What allowed the state of Jalisco to approve a form of direct contribution that individualized the taxpayer? There are at least three explanations. The first is that the direct contribution had the support of local merchants who considered it a means to end sales taxes. With a tax proportional to an individual's capital, merchants hoped to reverse the local fiscal system's increasing dependency on taxing merchandise. By the end of the eighteenth century there had been an exponential increase in sales tax collection—from 50,000 pesos in 1780 to more than 250,000 in 1800[38]—accompanied by a notable decrease in other forms of royal treasury income, such as mining. In 1823, Intendant Antonio Gutiérrez y Ulloa estimated that sales taxes represented 63 percent of all fiscal income, while tithes and other ecclesiastic branches were responsible for 13 percent of total income.[39] With direct contribution, Jalisco merchants hoped to end the fiscal burden that affected their capital and only caused "inconveniences, worries and bother of carrying documents, enduring *garitas* [sentry posts guarding the city], transit detentions, and horrible searches."[40] Merchants also considered this liberal tax as a means to reduce their own tax burden by incorporating other economic sectors such as, specifically, day laborers. According to the governor's financial plan, rural and agricultural sectors would contribute 60 percent of total direct tax collection, urban properties 27 percent, and trade only 10.8 percent. Thus, the financial plan relied on taxing rural property.[41]

The second reason Jalisco was able to implement an individualized tax was that, during 1824–1825, Governor Prisciliano Sánchez and the state legislative deputies believed that a state bureaucracy was capable of efficiently collecting taxes on individual wealth. Although in February of 1825 the governor proposed the creation of *jefaturas de partido* (offices of chiefs of districts) so as to "improve tax collection,"[42] he also stated that collectors and sub-collectors of revenues were capable of gathering direct taxes without help from the ayuntamientos.[43] Hence, in Jalisco, unlike other states, the ayuntamientos were not given an important role in the creation and operation of direct contributions. An 1825 law specified that the syndics and regidores of ayuntamientos would work with receptores de rentas to carry out a census of capital holders. They were also in charge of receiving complaints from contributors when a quota was wrongfully assigned. But it was public state officials who would be directly responsible for conducting the census and dealing with the complaints of taxpayers, and not the ayuntamientos, as was the case in other areas of the republic.

The governor of Jalisco and the deputies of the state legislature were not mistaken in believing that in 1825 they had available a fiscal bureaucracy that covered the taxation area of the state and answered directly to the state treasury. In the Intendancy of Guadalajara, unlike other areas of New Spain, such as Guanajuato and Oaxaca,[44] the war between royalists and insurgents did not disorganize the bureaucracy of the royal treasury. Between 1810 and 1821, General José de la Cruz, commander of New Galicia, ordered officials under the direct jurisdiction of the military command to collect, within their political and administrative jurisdictions, sales, tobacco, and extraordinary war taxes.[45] One important factor that allowed José de la Cruz to maintain control over fiscal bureaucracy in Guadalajara was that the provincial deputation and the *audiencia* (high court) did not limit de la Cruz's fiscal authority, as occurred in other regions of the Viceroyalty of New Spain, where both institutions demanded that royal authorities, such as the intendants or even the viceroy, not intervene in "matters of royal finances." In New Galicia, on the other hand, the provincial deputation ordered the ayuntamientos to leave the collection of war taxes to subdelegates.[46] On their part, the attorneys of the Audiencia of New Galicia recommended that Commander de la Cruz continue intervening in contentious issues, so as to "not affect their development."[47]

There is a final reason for the fiscal relevance that direct taxation assumed in Jalisco. Starting in 1820, local economic and political elites supported and tried to implement a number of principles of liberal doctrine, such as freedom of the press, an emphasis on political and economic individualism, the secularization of society, and the distribution of the property of indigenous communities. As Brian Connaughton has pointed out, the 1820s produced a clash between the Church and civil authorities over the supremacy of the state, the administration and use of tithes, and the corporate nature of society, among other issues. Even members of the political elite, such as the *Polares* (polaresques, referring to the poles of the earth), adopted a number of liberalist principles.[48] Starting in 1824, wide distribution of the property of the indigenous communities began in Jalisco, with the aim of promoting economic individualism. The ideological context helped other liberal principles (i.e., direct contributions) to be accepted in Jalisco.

Jalisco, as previously stated, was an exceptional case in the landscape of direct contributions in Mexico. It was the only state that began broad fiscal reform with the objective of using progressive taxes on individual capital as the basis of the public treasury. The course of direct contribution policy was very different in Zacatecas and Yucatán. In both states there was a systematic, unanimous rejection of direct taxes on income or on personal wealth, but each state had different reasons for this position.

The important link between the establishment of direct contributions and fiscal crisis applies to the case of Zacatecas, but in reverse. Since there was no deficit, direct taxes were not palatable. During most of the early period of the first federal republic, the state of Zacatecas held "an excess of resources," as Governor Francisco García Salinas correctly stated.[49] In 1826, the state's public treasury reported a surplus of over 74,000 pesos, after paying the *contingente* (the contributions from the states to the federal government established by the Constitution of 1824) and for the tobacco leaf received from the growers in the State of Veracruz; in 1828, the state treasury reported 133,000 pesos in surplus; and 170,000 in 1833. In 1831, the public coffers received income of just under two million pesos, a figure that was not matched by any other state. Taxes generated by mining, particularly, the 3-percent tariff on minting silver, only partly explain the abundance in Zacatecas. Unlike Guanajuato and Pachuca, mines in Zacatecas were not affected by the War for Independence. Starting in 1821, a mint was established, and British investment helped to increase production and, therefore, tax collection.

Zacatecas's prosperity explains why the state's political elites did not consider it necessary to reform the fiscal system created during colonial times. In 1823 a public finance commission from the Provincial Deputation of Zacatecas clearly stated that "new theories or imposing new contributions are not necessary or convenient; . . . present ones are enough and people are used to them; . . . no new rules are needed, nor is wasting energy in inventing a new tax system; . . . current rules are good enough to collect sufficient public funds."[50] The tax system needed only a few minor administrative changes in the areas of mining, tobacco, and tithes. New forms of taxes were rejected, since they implied an important change in the organization and conception of the state's fiscal system. Therefore, it is not surprising that toward the end of 1823 local deputies rejected the national congress's decree that personal tax was to be collected in "their province."[51] The projects presented to the state legislature in 1826 by deputies Juan José de Mata Jiménez, José Esparza Narváez, and Cayetano Martínez for the implementation of direct taxes on mescal, production from rural and urban real estate, and merchant capital all suffered the same fate.[52]

The state of Yucatán, on the other hand, tried to implement direct contribution in a way similar in certain aspects to the state of Jalisco. Under extraordinary circumstances, at a moment when a "foreign invasion" was feared—that is, by the government in Mexico City—the constituent legislature of Yucatán decreed, in December 1823, that a "war contribution" would be collected from "every landowner, merchant or person of income" according to his wealth. This decree categorized contributors according to their capital or monetary income, ranging from 200 to 25,000 pesos.[53] The one-time tax on the lowest category, 200 pesos, was four reales, and on the highest, 25,000 pesos, two pesos per thousand. The committees in charge of classifying contributors consisted in Mérida and Campeche of the intendant or the subdelegate, the *sindico procurador* (the ayuntamiento's attorney), and four individuals well-versed in commercial issues; and in rural haciendas and *partidos* (districts) of the subdelegate, the parish priest, the *alcalde primero* (the senior magistrate of the ayuntamiento), and four individuals.

Nevertheless, efforts to tax personal wealth soon failed, and a few months later, in April 1824, the legislature of Yucatán passed a personal pension or, to give it a just name, a capitación or head tax that was not even progressive. "All men in the state from the age of 16 to 60 will contribute 12 reales."[54] The subdelegados, with the help of a committee that consisted of the alcalde primero, the parish priest, the sindico procurador, and two local citizens, were in charge of collection. To ease tax gathering, a few months later, in July 1824, the *repúblicas de indios* (Indian government under the Spanish Monarchy), which had been abolished by the Constitution of 1812, were reestablished. "So as to remove the obstacles to tax collection, contain the dispersion of the indigenous population and obtain for them an honest occupation, . . . the former repúblicas de indios will be temporarily reestablished . . . in the form held at the moment they were abolished in 1820."[55]

In this way, in 1824, a head tax almost identical to the tribute was established: the officials of the repúblicas created taxpayer lists and collected the tax, and for this they received 6 percent of what was collected. The subdelegados would be responsible for making sure indigenous authorities fulfilled their obligation and delivered the money collected to the treasury. The difference between capitación and tribute was that the first was not paid by only the indigenous sector but also by the white population. All men in Yucatán paid a head tax. In this sense liberalism struck a very minor victory within the elite sector of Yucatán.

Although the Provincial Deputation of Yucatán proposed tax reforms based on direct taxes, all reformist tendencies soon were abandoned due to the economic elites' refusal to accept the burden of the local tax system. In fact, they preferred to continue with the colonial tax system, based on the extraction of resources from indigenous communities.[56] The head tax was a means to distribute the tax burden without its weight resting on the capital and the properties of local economic elites. Although these forms of wealth had to pay 12 reales annually, most of the revenue came from the indigenous communities. It was easier to continue taxing the Indians than local merchants or hacendados.

As a final example, in the state of México a direct land tax was implemented as part of a series of reforms to overcome fiscal deficits. This solution was accepted only as a last resort. The first option considered was sources of taxation that would not incur high administrative and collection costs, such as the tithe.[57] The tobacco state monopoly appeared to be a sure source of funds, but initial expectations were not met. Between 1826 and 1827, the tobacco monopoly generated more than half a million pesos, the second-largest source of income in the state of México, but the net profit—after covering all costs—was only 12,683 pesos.[58] The government of the state of Mexico had been one of the first to establish its own tobacco factory so as to merchandise cigarettes and cigars. Nevertheless, contraband, the high costs of administration and production, as well as the high costs of purchasing tobacco leaf yielded to the public treasury only a pitiful amount. As a result of the gap between expectation and reality, the public treasury was struck with a large deficit between 1825 and 1827.

To address the situation, in 1828 the governor of the state of México, Lorenzo de Zavala, proposed a direct product tax on *aguardiente* (liquor) and pulque. The May 9, 1828, law established a tax of two pesos on each *quintal* (100 kilograms) barrel of *aguardiente de caña* (rum) and one real for every six grams of maguey. In compensation, cotton, cane syrup, *panocha* (ear of corn), and brown sugar were to be exempt from all taxes.[59]

Protests were heard immediately. In the *"Representación que hacen al Congreso del Estado los propietarios de haciendas de caña"* (Representation that the Owners of Sugar Haciendas Make to the State Congress), the principal landowners of the state complained of the "abusive" May 1828 decree.[60] Antonio Velasco de la Torre, José del Monte, Andrés Quintana Roo, and Antonio Icaza declared that taxation should be ruled by the principles of necessity and equality. The governor argued that a new tax was needed to address the 200,000-peso public deficit. Sugar-mill owners answered that it would be wiser for the government to reduce costs in areas such as the civic militias and the salaries of public officials. The new tax was not equitable and, therefore, unjust, since it affected only one agricultural sector, sugar mill owners, maguey producers, and liquor factories, while all others were exempt. The targeted sectors argued that the public burden should be distributed more equitably through indirect taxes on other products.

The hacendados complained that Zavala was using direct taxes to increase public treasury funds. They argued that this form of taxation had been abandoned by "liberal governments" such as Great Britain's, since they were in the end counterproductive. Experience showed that increasing taxes on personal wealth diminished the amount of capital invested in the industrial, agricultural, and commercial sectors, affecting both economic growth as well as government revenues. With direct contributions everyone lost, even the public treasury. Implicitly, the hacendados also warned that direct tax collection would affect public order and pointed to the fact that the direct taxes implemented by the Cortes of Cádiz had provoked peasant uprisings.[61]

Due to the opposition of the hacendados, Zavala recommended to the state legislature that the May 1828 law be repealed. In his 1829 *Memoria de*

Gobierno, the governor recognized that the law could not have been implemented, not only because of opposition from the hacendados, but also because of opposition from the indigenous communities who owned the maguey plants. He cautioned the legislature, "The indigenous community threatened to revolt and had begun to examine the justice and the convenience of orders from higher authorities."[62] To avoid the risk that the Indians would refuse to obey the government, Zavala proposed that the land tax be abolished and that government land be distributed. Such actions would promote trade as well as the circulation of capital and would prevent the emergence of a "revolutionary" who might be able to lead to insurgency "day laborers and small land owners."[63]

Several factors explain the different reception and application of direct taxes, i.e., fiscal liberalism, in Mexico. Support or opposition to direct contributions was directly related to the implementation, suspension, or rejection of fiscal reforms. The magnitude of the post-independence economic crisis, as well as large fiscal deficits, also played a significant role. Furthermore, it is important to note the reactions of regional elites to the concept of direct contribution. In Jalisco the elites, particularly the merchants, readily accepted a liberal tax on individual wealth so as to expand the burden of taxation; economic groups in Yucatán—and possibly those in Chiapas and Oaxaca as well—preferred to continue with the tribute, which had been a central element of the colonial tax system, disguised as head tax. The southeastern region rejected fiscal liberalism and opted to continue to extract resources from indigenous communities. Further study of the reactions of regional elites would provide a more complete account of the impact of liberalism in the many Mexicos of the time.

TAX UNIFORMITY: DIRECT
CONTRIBUTION AND FEDERALISM

In 1829, liberal taxation acquired a new dynamic in the fiscal and political tensions between the national government and the regional elites. Direct contributions and centralism became, for many, interchangeable terms. This is not surprising considering that, for the liberal deputies of the Cortes of Cádiz in 1812, direct contributions constituted the preferred measure for reducing the fiscal privileges of the regions of the Spanish Monarchy. In Mexico, the Ministry of Finance promoted liberal taxes to reduce the fiscal sovereignty of the states.

On April 1, 1829, Vicente Guerrero succeeded Guadalupe Victoria as president; a few days later he named Lorenzo de Zavala minister of finance. In his *"Exposición al Congreso de la Unión"* on April 17, 1829, the new minister presented a bleak picture of the public treasury.[64] The large debt the country had incurred had become unmanageable, since internal capitalists and those from "overseas nations" had abandoned Guerrero's government. In addition, state governments were not paying the contingente, the annual fiscal quota to the federal government established by the Constitution of 1824. Of the three million pesos that the Ministry of Finance should have received annually from the states, only 150,000 pesos had entered the public treasury. Tobacco and customs revenues were not providing adequate resources. Minister Zavala declared, "A commercial house has more order and method than we do in our administration of public wealth."

To improve this situation, Zavala proposed that the federal congress establish a direct and proportional tax on the wealth of the richest property owners in the country. Following a close vote on May 22, a law was passed that taxed annual income greater than 1,000 pesos.[65] Zavala again tried to impose taxes according to individual wealth, but with proposals different from those he had advanced as a member of the Junta Nacional Instituyente in 1822 and as governor of the state of México in 1828. The new tax was, for lack of a better term, much more radical. The 1822 proposal taxed real estate, and the 1828 tax, hacendados, owners of sugar mills, and pulque. The 1829 measure, on the other hand, directly affected taxpayers' wealth, independently of the sources that created it: "Throughout the Republic, a contribution of five percent annually on income of *any nature* higher than 1,000 pesos will be applied; income of more than 10,000 pesos will incur a 10 percent contribution."[66] Thus, in 1829, Zavala tried to tax the total amount of a contributor's income, independently of whether it came from agricultural, industrial, or urban property; from salaries, pensions or retirement funds.

In 1829, Zavala promoted the largest national fiscal reform in Mexico since 1821; it could be said that he set in motion one of the most radical transformations to the tax structure inherited from colonial times. To quote the French ambassador to Mexico in 1829, the minister sought "a fiscal system that would be in tune with the most modern practices in Europe."[67] Most of the sources of revenues for the royal treasury and the post-independence tax system were indirect (based on use); a few were direct, such as the tithe, which affected, in a different way, the various income sources of an individual. On the other hand, "Zavala's contribución" merged into one single tax— "income from any source"—the different parts of individual wealth. Taxpayers became individuals and defined as real people. A modern income tax was established at the national level.

The May 1829 law brought about another important change: taxation was imposed only on the country's richest citizens. Here, Zavala was rescuing the principle he had defended in 1822: equitable taxation. The tax burden should fall on those who benefited the most from society and the state's activities. In that year, direct contribution had established amounts that affected all real estate owners. In 1829, taxation was limited to the people with the highest incomes. Fiscal responsibilities were concentrated on the most powerful landowners of Mexican society.

The new law also established the federal government's authority to collect taxes directly, without intermediaries. The tax law charged state legislatures with the responsibility of preparing a taxpayer list, which would be delivered to "agents" of the national government. It also stated that "if for any reason the arrangements for tax collections were not complete in a state by the end of the first quarter, the national government would complete them. If payments were not made within the first 15 days of the stated deadlines . . . agents of the national government will collect them, according to the laws of the federation."[68] This measure annulled one of the fiscal principles that had been established by the federal Constitution of 1824: the freedom states had had to establish rules for their internal administration, including fiscal matters. While state governments had been responsible for assessing and collecting taxes within their "sovereign" territories, in 1829 federal officials were authorized to directly collect taxes in each state, without the approval of state authorities.

Regional economic elites strongly rejected direct progressive contributions on individual wealth. State congresses demanded that Vicente Guerrero's government and the national congress abolish the "Zavala Law." The major objection was that the May law allowed the national government to meddle with "the homes of citizens." Deputies from a number of state legislatures argued that one of the main attributes of sovereignty was local ability to design fiscal systems according to the character of each region. The May 1829 law violated the federal agreement because it ignored the specifics of each state, which should distribute taxes according to the characteristics of local taxpayers. Newspapers, such as *El Sol,* maintained that the law promoted the "evil" central system by ignoring the fiscal autonomy of every state.[69] Opposition was so widespread in the states that U.S. Minister to Mexico Joel Poinsett was afraid the country would break up and that the states would unite in opposition to the "centralized policies" of the national government.[70]

Along with this argument in favor of federalism, newspapers insisted that the law denied the basic principle of liberal doctrine: the inviolability of the homes of citizens. As Carlos María de Bustamante argued in the *Voz de la Patria,* "Who would like their possessions and wealth to be public knowledge? Not out of curiosity, but to establish the sum of contribution and then tomorrow or the day after, this information entered into the record of landowners so as to be later taken when the patriotism that rules us so demands it."[71] Establishing a census of landowners would be dangerous, because once an individual's wealth was known, the government could tax it repeatedly.

Minister Zavala contested these accusations in *El Correo de la Federación.* Taxes, he wrote, were not in themselves good or bad, centralist or federalist, but "liberal or despotic according to their use and the manner of their collection."[72] He argued that state legislatures who criticized the direct contribution had misunderstood the concept and meaning of the national pact. Federations were agreements between parties that granted the national government the responsibility and authority to promulgate laws that would benefit the entire republic. "The general assembly must have the faculty to determine the sum of subsidies needed to carry out a specific goal and to establish the responsibility each party must fulfill."[73] With this Zavala was implicitly questioning the efficiency of the August 1824 law, which had imprudently divided funds between the states and the federal government.

In the *Correo*, Zavala argued that the new taxes did not favor centralism, but rather were aimed at creating solid foundations for the national public treasury and, with this, for the federation. "The federation can only be threatened by a lack of funds. Is there a more obvious way [to threaten the union] than to deny these funds? Without money, there will be no army."[74] Controversies had to be avoided, and support was needed for a law that would strengthen the national government: "We must avoid the fate of the Greeks in the Middle Ages. While they debated the origins of the Holy Spirit, the Muslims were dividing up the Empire of the Caesars."[75] Extended discussion of the law would allow the Spaniards, who were armed and ready in Havana, to enter through Veracruz and reconquer Mexico.

With the polemics surrounding the May law, Zavala divided the discussion into two concepts that had marked the republic's political life: federalism or confederalism.[76] Minister Zavala was on the side of federalism. As was evident in the law he proposed, the Minister of Finance intended to increase the national government's fiscal authority through measures that led to a strong national government. With this, Zavala became, according to the confederalists, a traitor, and without the support of regional elites he was forced to resign. This ended the federal government's attempt at collecting direct contributions.

From the perspective of regional elites, most national governments—be they centralist or federalist, liberal or monarchic—saw direct taxation as a way to weaken the autonomy of the states and to increase the range of resources controlled by the national Ministry of Finance. By 1829, the practice of direct contributions was charged with a political meaning that would continue during a large part of the nineteenth century. Direct contributions and centralism became, in the eyes of regional leaders, interchangeable. They were right. The various national governments, in spite of different ideological characteristics, used income tax to limit the fiscal sovereignty of the states, since it was a useful tool for controlling "peripheral powers." In this sense, regional elites opposed granting the national Ministry of Finance the power to administer direct taxes. Paradoxically, regional administrations had no choice but to implement direct taxes to cover the growing debts of their public finances.

FORCED CONSENSUS: REGIONAL ELITES AND
DIRECT CONTRIBUTIONS, 1830–1835

While regional elites opposed national taxes, after 1830 state governments were forced to use the same strategies to fill their bankrupt coffers. Even the state of Zacatecas, where mining contributed significantly, was in the red, and most states were in even worse fiscal condition. There are a number of explanations for this general crisis in local finances. First, with the law of August 24, 1824, deputies representing regional elites had established that income from tobacco sales would be divided between the national government and the fiscal administrations of each state, and this resulted in significant loss of local revenue.[77] In states such as Tabasco, Sonora, Sinaloa, Durango, and Coahuila and Texas, tobacco was the most important source of income; cigarette and cigar sales generated the second most important form of income in the states of Guanajuato, Michoacán, San Luis Potosí, México, Querétaro, Zacatecas, and Jalisco. The national government established a number of measures that affected the sum collected by public treasuries of the states. In 1829, the Guerrero administration granted the Wilson and Garay Company the right to sell tobacco grown in Veracruz throughout the country, as well as to merchandize the cigarettes and cigars made in the Mexico City factory. Although, the states succeeded in revoking the measures, during the following administration of Vice President Anastasio Bustamante, many suffered great losses due to increased competition when the tobacco monopoly was abolished in 1833. After June of that year, a decree established the freedom to plant tobacco, as well as the manufacturing and sale of cigarettes and cigars.

In addition, a change in the fiscal nature of *contingente* significantly diminished state revenues. In 1824 the Constituent Congress had determined that each state must contribute, according to its population and wealth, a specific annual sum to the federal coffers. However, in 1830 the national government, with the backing of Congress, determined that each state must surrender a *contingente* equal to 40 percent of its total annual tax collection. This measure completely changed the way taxes were determined: no longer on the basis of population and wealth—which in 1824 would have been difficult to establish, and had not been updated since then—but by annual income, a number very easy to calculate from the annual reports presented by state governors to their legislatures. Although the state legislatures of México, Querétaro, Michoacán, and Guanajuato protested this measure, in the end it was enforced.[78]

Finally, the abolition of tithe payments increased the state's fiscal crisis. In June of 1833, the national administration of the so-called men of progress freed agriculture from tithe payments, part of which had ended up in public coffers.

Even states that had systematically opposed direct contributions, such as Veracruz, Guanajuato, and Michoacán, were forced to use this liberal tax to overcome their own fiscal crises. The Veracruz state legislature, for example, refused to tax its population with the progressive personal tax established in 1823, even though from 1824 its governors had repeatedly cautioned that the state was in deficit. In 1828, Governor Antonio López de Santa Anna maintained that it was a mistake to "adopt the Spanish tax system, which is a body of dislocated heterogeneous elements and a monstrous combination that is not in tune with economic rules. Far from spreading the burden of public consumption on citizen wealth . . . it limits economic growth, complicates labor, paralyzes industry, attacks capital, and causes uncomfortable inquiries."[79] In the 1831 *Memoria*, Governor Sebastián Camacho proposed a number of measures needed to control the fiscal crisis, including reducing the contingente paid to the federation, increasing taxes on foreign textiles, controlling tobacco contraband and the illegal sale of cigarettes and cigars, and the timely payment of sales tax.[80] It was not until May 13, 1833, that the Veracruz legislature ordered the collection of a direct tax on the products of all rural and urban properties in the state. Owners of houses were forced to pay 20 percent of their rent collections, and rural property owners had to pay a similar percentage on their crops.[81]

The Guanajuato state legislature also was forced to impose a direct contribution—first, to address the bankruptcy of state coffers, and, second, to obtain funds to arm the local civil militia.[82] In February 1832, the state legislature published law 149, which created a war tax that was proportional to individual wealth. Article 4 established that "artisans, merchants, day laborers, owners of buildings or rural land, those with properties of any kind, or those with capital in circulation of less than 1,000 pesos will contribute two reales per month;"[83] those with capital of more than 1,000 and less than 2,000 pesos, 4 reales; between 2,000 and 4,000 pesos, 1 peso; between 4,000 and 10,000 pesos, 2 pesos; and more than 10,000 pesos, 3 pesos. The principle of proportionality was established as "an effort to maintain civic militias." The ayuntamientos were to be in charge of creating tax rolls, grouping taxpayers according to wealth, receiving complaints related to distribution, and penalizing evasion. The law exempted from taxation those residents who received a salary of less than two reales per day. This measure, the state governor acknowledged, excluded most of the population—the so-called day laborers—from the burden of "financing the war." In this way the state government and legislature included proportionality in the war effort, a mechanism that had proven useful during the counterinsurgent war.

Economic elites, oligarchic groups from the ayuntamientos of Guanajuato, León, Celaya, and San Miguel did not approve all sections of the decree, especially those dealing with proportionality for extraordinary taxes. They considered that the so-called "civic pension" taxed the state population unequally by placing the burden of war costs on one sector.[84] Instead, they proposed distributing taxation among the social groups of Guanajuato, employing three measures. First, all taxpayers should be forced to contribute the amount assigned as the civic quota; second, the ayuntamientos of the towns that ignored tax evasion should be penalized; and third, indirect taxes should be established. Although direct taxes had been abolished in 1833, during 1834 and 1835 progressive direct taxes once again were used to overcome the economic crisis and help arm the civic militia for its participation in the 1834 civil war.

In this way, the fiscal crisis and civil wars of 1832 and 1834 caused substantial transformation in the taxation structure of Guanajuato. The collection of direct contributions marked an important change in the state's fiscal organization, which had remained unchanged since 1823. The state government was forced to impose extraordinary taxes on mining and agricultural properties, as well as establishing the principle of progressive taxation. The strategy of local oligarchic groups to avoid progressive and direct contributions at all costs finally collapsed. That strategy had become an "institution" in reaction to the fiscal structure imposed by the viceregal government in the 1810s as a form of financing the counterinsurgency. But by 1832, the state government was forced to employ the fiscal methods that had once financed military actions against the insurgents, as well as to implement proportional contributions to the war effort.

After 1812, the liberal direct contributions forged in the Cortes of Cádiz began to spread among the institutional and social groups of New Spain. Between 1830 and 1835, fiscal liberalism—especially direct contributions—became the predominant doctrine among Mexico's regional and national political elites. By 1835 an agreement, sometimes forced, had been reached among the different components of the fiscal system that liberal taxes were to be the foundation of the fiscal system. Fiscal liberalism was established—to stay—in Mexico.

NOTES

1. For an overview of the liberal principle of direct contributions, see Fernando López Castellanos, *Liberalismo económico y reforma fiscal. La contribución directa de 1813* (Granada: Universidad de Granada-Fundación Caja de Granda, 1995). For a general study of the royal finances of the antiguo régimen, see Miguel Artola, *La hacienda del antiguo régimen* (Madrid: Alianza Editorial-Banco de España, 1982); and Richard Bonney, ed., *Economic Systems and State Finance* (Oxford: Clarendon Press, 1995).

2. María Cruz Mina Apat, *Fueros y revolución liberal en Navarra* (Madrid: Alianza Editorial, 1981).

3. Jean Pierre Gross, "Progressive Taxation and Social Justice in Eighteenth Century France," *Past and Present* 140 (August 1993): 79–126; and López Castellanos, *Liberalismo económico.*

4. Enrique Fuentes Quintana, "El estilo tributario latino: características principales y problemas de su reforma," in Francisco Comín Comín, ed., *Las reformas tributarias de España* (Barcelona: Crítica, 1990); and Francisco Comín, *Historia de la hacienda pública. Europa* (Barcelona: Grijalbo Mondadori, 1996), 207.

5. Luis Jáuregui, *La real hacienda de la Nueva España. Su administración en la época de los intendentes, 1786–1821* (Mexico: Universidad Nacional Autónoma de México, 1990), 6.

6. Centro de Estudios de Historia de México de la Fundación Cultural de Condumex (hereafter Condumex), Bando del 24 de febrero de 1812; and Jáuregui, *La real hacienda de Nueva España*, 259–260.

7. "Reglamento para verificar la contribución extraordinaria de guerra" (September 1812); Roberto Fontana and Roberto Garrabou, *Guerra y hacienda. La hacienda del gobierno central en los años de la guerra de independencia (1808–1814)* (Alicante: Instituto de Estudios Juan Gil-Albert, 1986), 225.

8. "Bando de Calleja, 15 de diciembre de 1813," Condumex, XLI-1, folder 143.

9. "Ayuntamiento de Mérida, 22 de octubre de 1812," Archivo General de la Nación (hereafter AGN): Propios y arbitros, 143, file 1, ff. 16–17v.

10. "Diputaciones provinciales al jefe político José de la Cruz, 14 de mayo de 1814," Archivo Histórico de Jalisco (hereafter AHCJ): 114, box 4, file 5.

11. "Calleja, marzo de 1813 y 2 de octubre de 1813," AGN: Propios y arbitros, 143, ff. 12–13 and 22–24.

12. "Bando de 14 de octubre de 1814," Condumex.

13. "Razón de las cuentas de oficina y ramos que no se han presentado por sus respectivos responsables en los años que se esperan," 1823, AGN: Archivo Histórico de Hacienda, 2329, file 31.

14. For an overview of public finances during the First Empire, see Barbara Tenenbaum, *México en la época de los agiotistas, 1821–1857* (Mexico: Fondo de Cultura Económica, 1985); Barbara Tenenbaum, "Sistema tributario y tiranía: la finanzas públicas durante el régimen de Iturbide, 1821–1823," in Luis Jáuregui and José Antonio Serrano, coords., *Las finanzas públicas en los siglos XVII–XIX* (Mexico: El Colegio de México, El Colegio de Michoacán, Instituto Mora, and Universidad Nacional Autónoma de México, 1998), 209–226; Timothy Anna, *El imperio de Iturbide* (Mexico: Conaculta-Grijalbo, 1992); Leonor Ludlow, "Elites y finanzas públicas durante la gestación del Estado independiente, 1821–1824," in José Serrano Ortega and Luis Jáuregui, eds., *Hacienda y política. Las finanzas públicas y los grupos de poder en la primera república federal mexicana* (Mexico: El Colegio de Michoacán-Instituto Mora, 1998), 79–114. Carlos Rodríguez, "Un acercamiento a las propuestas de organización del sistema impositivo en México, 1821–1823," in Serrano Ortega and Jáuregui, eds., *Hacienda y política*, 291–316.

15. Tenenbaum, "Sistema tributario y tiranía," 215.

16. Anna, *El imperio de Iturbide*, 48; and Ludlow, "Elites y finanzas públicas."

17. "Sesión de la Junta Provisional Gubernativa, 10 de febrero de 1822," *Diario de las sesiones de la soberana junta provisional gubernativa del Imperio mexicano* (Mexico: Imprenta de Valdés, 1821), facsimile edition in José Barragán Barragán, ed., *Actas constitucionales mexicanas (1821–1824)*, 10 vols. (Mexico: Universidad Nacional Autónoma de México, 1980), 1: 22

18. *Actas del Congreso contituyente de México* (Mexico: Imprenta de Valdés, 1822), facsimile edition in Barragán Barragán, *Actas constitucionales mexicanas*, vol. 2 (hereafter, *Congreso, 1822*)

19. *Congreso, 1822*, 2: 2.

20. *Congreso, 1822*, 2:70–73.

21. Rodríguez, "Un acercamiento a las propuestas."

22. Ibid., 306.

23. Lorenzo de Zavala, "Dictamen de la comisión de Hacienda sobre el presupuesto de gastos para el año económico de 1823, 6 de diciembre de 1822," in Lorenzo Zavala, ed., *Obras. El historiador y el representante popular* (Mexico: Editorial Porrúa, 1969), 720.

24. Enrique Fuentes Quintana, "El estilo tributario latino: características principales y problemas de su reforma," in Francisco Comín, *Las reformas tributarias de España* (Barcelona: Crítica, 1990); Francisco Comín, *Las cuentas de la hacienda preliberal en España, 1801–1855* (Madrid: Banco de España, 1990); López Castellanos, *Liberalismo económico*; and Comín, *Historia de la hacienda pública*.

25. Zavala, "Dictamen de la comisión de Hacienda."

26. "Sesión del 16 de septiembre de 1822," *Diario de la Junta Nacional Instituyente, 1822* (Mexico: Imprenda de Valdés), facsimile edition in Barragán Barragán, *Actas constitucionales mexicanas*, 1: 121; and Juan Wencenlaos Barquera, "Plan de contribución directa para sustituir a la de cas y abolir las alcabalas," January 1823, AGN: Interior Ministry, file 15, f. 67.

27. "Sesión del 17 de diciembre de 1822," *Diario de la Junta Nacional Instituyente*, 1: 136.

28. "Sesión del 23 de junio de 1823," in Luis Muro, ed., *Historia parlamentario. Crónicas del soberano congreso constituyente mexicano* (Mexico: Cámara de Diputados-Instituto de Investigaciónes Legislativas, 1983), 1: 151–154.

29. Ibid., 1: 153.

30. Ibid.

31. *Constitución de Jalisco*, November 1824

32. "Ley orgánica de Hacienda, 10 de marzo de 1825, artículo 7," Jalisco, *Colección de decretos, circulares y órdenes de los Poderes Legislativo y Ejecutivo del Estado de Jalisco* (Guadalajara: Jalisco, Tipología de Pérez Lete, 1876), 2: 26.

33. "Ley orgánica de Hacienda, 10 de marzo de 1825, artículo 9," 2: 26–47.

34. "Ley orgánica de Hacienda, 10 de marzo de 1825, capítulo III," 2: 26–47.

35. Antonio Ibarra, "Reformas y fiscalidad republicana en Jalisco: ingresos estatales, contribución directa y pacto federal, 1824–1835," in Serrano Ortega and Jáuregui, eds., *Hacienda y política*, 142, note 18.

36. Ibid., 136.

37. Ibid.

38. Antonio Ibarra, *La organización regional del mercado interno novohispano. La economía colonial de Guadalajara, 1770–1804* (Mexico: Universidad Nacional Autónoma de México-Universidad Autónoma de Puebla, 2000), graph 5.

39. Ibarra, "Reformas y fiscalidad republicana en Jalisco," 138, note 9.

40. "Gobernador al congreso, febrero de 1826," AHCJ, 1826, box 21, 40–43.

41. Ibarra, *La organización regional del mercado interno novohispano*, 46, note 33.

42. "Gobernador al congreso, febrero de 1826," AHCJ, 1825, 16, file 1.

43. "Contestación, 1825," AHCJ, 1825, 16, file 1.

44. For more on this issue in the state of Guanajuato see José Antonio Serrano, *Jerarquía territorial y transición política: Guanajuato, 1790–1836* (Mexico: El Colegio de Michoacán and Instituto Mora, 2001); and for the case of Oaxaca see AGN: Propios y arbitros 26, file 31, f. 433–440, and AGN: Propios y arbitros, 43, file 16, f. 248–257.

45. On the new politics in Jalisco see: Jaime E. Rodríguez O, *"Rey, religión, independencia y Unión": el proceso político de la Independencia de Guadalajara* (México: Instituto Mora, 2003).

46. "Diputación provincial, dictamen del 3 de noviembre de 1813," AHCJ, box 2, file 13.

47. "Audiencia, julio de 1814," Archivo de la Audiencia de Nueva Galicia, box 260, file 3.

48. Brian Connaughton, *Ideología y sociedad en Guadalajara, 1788–1853* (Mexico: Conaculta, 1992).

49. Zacatecas, *Memoria* (Guadalajara: Imprenta del Urbano San Roman, 1825); *Memoria* (Zacatecas: Imprenta Pedro Pineda, 1826); *Memoria* (Zacatecas: Imprenta de Pedro Pineda, 1828); *Memoria* (Zacatecas, 1831); and *Memoria* (Zacatecas: Imprenta del Supremo Gobierno, 1833).

50. Quoted by Mercedes de la Vega, "Los dilemas de la organización autónoma. Zacatecas, 1808–1835" (Doctoral dissertation: El Colegio de México, 1997), 308.

51. "Sesión extraordinaria del 21 de agosto de 1823," in Beatriz Rojas, ed., *Actas de la diputación provincial de Zacatecas* (Mexico: Instituto de Investigaciones José María Luis Mora, 2003), 176–177.

52. "Proyecto de ley que ha dirigido el ciudadano José Esparza Navaez, 6 de marzo de 1826" and "Proyecto de Jiménez, Naváez y Calvillo, 12 de agosto de 1826," Archivo Histórico del Estado de Zacatecas: Poder Ejecutivo, box 2.

53. "Decretos del 12 de diciembre de 1823," Yucatán, *Colección de leyes, decretos y órdenes del augusto congreso del estado de Yucatán*, 2 vol. (Mérida: Imprenta de Lorenzo Seguí, 1832).

54. "Decreto del 30 de abril de 1824," in ibid.

55. "Decreto del 26 de julio de 1824, artículo I," in ibid.

56. Marco Bellingeri, "El tributo los indios y el estado de los criollos. Las obvenciones eclesiáticas en Yucatán en el siglo XIX," in Othon Báños Ramírez, ed., *Sociedad, estrucura agraria y estado en Yucatán* (Merida: Universidad Autónoma de Yucatán, 1993); Marco Bellingeri, "De una constitución a otra: conflictos de jurisdicción y dispersión de poderes en Yucatán, 1789–1831," in Raymond Buve and Antonio Annino, coords., *Liberalismo en México. Cuadernos de Historia Latinoamericana* (Hamburg: AHILA, 1993), 49–78; Marco Bellingeri, "Soberanía o representación: la legitimidad de los cabildos y la conformación de las instituciones liberales en Yucatán," in María Justina Sarabia Viejo, ed., *Europa e Iberoamérica: cinco siglos de intercambio.* (Sevilla: AHILA, 1992), 2: 365–381; and Terry Rugeley, *Yucatan's Maya Peasantry and the Origins of the Caste War.* (Austin: University of Texas Press, 1996).

57. Carlos Marichal, "La hacienda pública del Estado de México desde la Independencia hasta la república restaurada, 1824–1870," in Carlos Marichal, Manuel Miño, and Paolo Riguzzi, eds., *El primer siglo de la Hacienda Pública del Estado de México, 1824–1923*, 4 vols. (Toluca: Gobierno del Estado de México-El Colegio Mexiquense, 1994), 1: 122.

58. Charles Macune, *El Estado de México y la federación mexicana* (Mexico: Fondo de Cultura Económica, 1978), 86.

59. "Decreto del 9 de mayo de 1828," in Estado de Mexico, *Colección de decretos del congreso Constituyente del Estado libre y soberano de México* (Toluca: Imprenta de Quijano, 1850).

60. *Representación que hacen al congreso del estado de México los propietarios de Haciendas de caña del mismo* (Mexico: Imprenta de Márquez, 1828); and José Delmos, *Representación de los cosecheros de pulque al Honorable Congreso del Estado de México* (México: Imprenta del Aguila, 1828).

61. *Representación que hacen . . . los propietarios de Haciendas de caña*, 10.

62. Lorenzo de Zavala, *Memoria del Estado de México presentada el 20 de marzo de 1829* (Mexico: Imprenta del Gobierno, 1829), 46.

63. Ibid., 21.

64. Lorenzo de Zavala, *Ensayo Histórico de las Revoluciones de México desde 1808 hasta 1830*. Edición facsimilar, 2 vols. (Mexico: FCE-Instituto Cultural Helénico, 1985), 2: 118.

65. "Ley. Contribución de un 5 por ciento sobre rentas que pasen de 1000," in Manuel Dublán and José María Lozano, *Legislación mexicana, o colección completa de las disposiciones legislativas expedidas desde la independencia de la República*, 34 vols. (Mexico: Dublán y Lozano Hijos, 1876–1911), I2: 110.

66. Ibid., Art. 1 (italics added).

67. Cited in Torcuato Di Tella, *Política nacional y popular en México, 1820–1847* (Mexico: Fondo de Cultura Económica, 1994).

68. "Ley. Contribución de un 5 por ciento sobre rentas que pasen de 1000," in Dublán and Lozano, *Legislación mexicana*, 2: 110, Art. 5.

69. Michael Costeloe, *La primera república federal de México, 1824–1835. Un estudio de los partidos políticos en el México independiente* (Mexico: Fondo de Cultura Económica, 1975), 233.

70. Stanley Green, *The Mexican Republic: The First Decade, 1823–1832* (Pittsburgh: University of Pittsburgh Press, 1987), 167.

71. *Voz de la Patria* (June 3, 1829).

72. "Editorial," *El Correo* (June 6, 1829).

73. "Editorial," *El Correo de la Federación* (June 17, 1829).

74. *El Correo de la Federación* (June 27, 1829).

75. "Sesión del 23 de abril de 1829," in Juan Antonio Mateos, *Historia Parlamentaria* (Mexico: PRI, 1976), 1: 471.

76. Josefina Zoraida Vásquez, "El federalismo mexicano, 1823–1847," in Marcello Carmagnani, ed., *Federalismos latinoamericanos: México, Brasil y Argentina* (Mexico: Fondo de Cultura Económica, 1993).

77. José Antonio Serrano, "El humo de la discordia: los gobiernos estatales, el gobierno nacional y el estanco del tabaco, 1824–1836," in José Antonio Serrano and Luis Jáuregui, eds., *Hacienda y política. Las finanzas públicas y los grupos de poder en la primera república federal mexicana* (Mexico: El Colegio de Michoacán, 1998).

78. Ibid.

79. Veracruz, *Memoria relativa a la situación del erario público del Estado de Veracruz* (Veracruz: Imprenta de Alburto, 1828), 18.

80. Veracruz, *Esposición formada por la administración general de rentas del Estado de Veracruz* (Veracruz: Imprenta de Alburto, 1831).

81. Veracruz, *Memoria de Hacienda desde el 1 de junio de 1832 hasta 21 de mayo de 1834* (Veracruz: Imprenta de Alburto, 1834).

82. Serrano, *Jerarquía territorial y transición política.*

83. "Decreto 149, 21 de febrero de 1832," in Guanajuato, *Decretos del Congreso Cuarto y Quinto Constitucional del Estado de Guanajuato* (Mexico: Imprenta de Ximeno, 1845).

84. "Ayuntamiento de Guanajuato, 5 de abril de 1832," Archivo Histórico de Guanajuato, Municipios, 115, exp. 8.

10

Vectors of Liberal Economic Culture in Mexico

Marcello Carmagnani

This chapter advances the proposition that an analysis of the role of economic liberalism is central to an understanding of the evolution of Mexican politics. The analytical framework is based on the author's previous studies of the performance of Mexico's public economy and its economic and political context and grounded in the author's explorations of various other aspects of nineteenth-century Mexico, which demonstrate the imbalance that exists between the expectations for and the performance of modern economies.[1] In this essay, the author illustrates the processes that contributed to the spread of liberal economic culture. Special emphasis is placed on the anti-corporate tendencies present in Mexican society during the nineteenth century; on the creation of a public opinion receptive to liberal ideology; and on the role played by institutions that advocated economic freedom.

Postmodern syncretisms have generated widespread confusion about what constitutes political culture. The author defines political culture as a group of individual and collective behavioral codes constructed by a limited number of individuals with distinct and shared intellectual, social, economic, and political referents. These codes are formalized within a political party, association, or group of individuals, and are later disseminated among one or more social groups without necessarily being of interest to a country's entire population. In other words, political culture, of which the economy is only one of many aspects, can be understood as an ensemble of representations that transmit norms, practices, and values that constitute the temporal identity of different political or interest groups, which in turn interact in a specific historical, national, regional, local, or international space.[2]

Political cultures do not constitute a single worldview that is imposed on a society as a whole; rather, they coexist with other similar or alternative cultures, which explains why liberal culture, the subject of this essay, formed in opposition to other preexisting cultures, such as the monarchic and the mercantile. At the same time, liberal culture in Mexico had to coexist with other cultures, especially the republican and the Catholic, resulting in a process of exchange, contamination, and accommodation with the other political cultures. In other words, "national" cultures do not exist because none is able to cover an entire society; no culture can be considered hegemonic because the characteristic of political cultures is that they develop in a specific temporal space and among specific social groups.[3]

The uniqueness of liberal culture is that it established, for the first time in modern history, an interdependent relationship between the political and economic dimension that is visible in the interaction between political freedom (opinion and association) and economic freedom (exchange and property security). Liberal culture also establishes a new equilibrium between liberty and the power of the state and of governments to control both personal dictatorships and the despotism of the majority, through a balance among the branches of government, and by defining and implementing property rights—all with the objective of controlling the excesses of the groups who wield power.[4]

Although it can be said that liberal principles had circulated in Mexican society since the promulgation of the Constitution of Cádiz, the introduction of free international trade, and the establishment of the federal republic in 1824, the foundational moment of liberal culture occurred between 1840 and 1860, when favorable national and international conditions allowed for the creation of a doctrinary corpus of liberalism.[5] The development of liberal culture, of which the economy is an important part, occurred with close contact—permeated and permeating—among contemporary political cultures in the Mexican space, especially the republican culture with its strong popular roots and its egalitarian tendencies; the modernist and social Catholic culture, which underscores family and community values; and, later on, the influence of socialist, libertarian, and egalitarian culture. Thus, liberal political culture was only one of the many cultures present in the Mexican space, and could not boast of being the "national culture." Such a claim can be made only by the corporate and state-centered national-populist culture of the twentieth century, owing to its instrumental use of the ideological entelechy of identity.

It is difficult to present the different aspects of liberal political culture, as the field of study still lacks elements that would permit one to establish strong links between the intellectual, political, social, and economic trajectories and the ideological, cultural, and historical representations that existed throughout the liberal period. For these reasons, this essay is limited to exploring some of the factors that favored the widespread influence of the idea of economic freedom in Mexican society during the second half of the nineteenth century.

TOWARD THE DISSOLUTION OF CORPORATE FORMS

It has been rightly noted that all political culture is characterized by significant inconsistencies, and that some—those without a monolithic ideology, such as the ones supporting right- or left-wing totalitarian regimes—are created taking into account tensions between the historical actors and the political regime. In Mexican liberalism, the tension exists between the freedom of the historical actors and the power held by the state apparatus. The tension between liberty and power is the result of the pessimism contained in the belief that the nature of the social and political body is uncontrollable—as illustrated by the historical experiences of the independence and the rebellions that occurred during the 1840s and the 1850s—and the realization that state power tends toward despotism and individual dictatorships, as demonstrated by the dictatorship of Antonio López de Santa Anna in the 1850s. To avoid a dictatorship of the majority or individual despotism, liberalism offers the possibility of creating barriers against cyclical outbursts of despotism or of demagogy through the new institutions included in the constitution.[6]

Unlike the other cultures, the liberal culture was handicapped because it includes human actions institutionally but is not able to mobilize them. This lack of interest in mobilization is probably the result of the importance liberal doctrine places on rationality as a way of resisting and restricting the excesses of heads of state, congresses, and judiciaries. Due to these motivations, one of the fundamental features of liberal culture is the tension created between natural-rights doctrines—its ideological and philosophical underpinning—and the institutional rationale that translates these doctrines into a political order. A natural-rights doctrine favors the development of a liberal society through the establishment of the rights to security, property, freedom of speech, and equality before the law. Rationality strengthens liberal society thanks to the balance and concurrence of the branches of government and the importance given to the rights of congress and institutions of control. The tension between natural-rights doctrine and institutionalization explains the preference of liberal culture for the definition of a non-natural, empirical, political, and economic legal system capable of organizing and, at times, limiting those same natural-rights principles. As a result of these tensions, liberalism places a growing importance on the sphere of government and on the exercise of public authority, which in turn favors restrictions on suffrage and on freedom of speech and can create obstacles both to freedom of trade and production as well as on the expansion of the rights of men and citizens.

If liberal culture is, as stated here, a culture that frames and limits within its own sphere both the freedom of actors and the power of government apparatus, then it could be said that if more were known about the way concepts of economic freedom (visible in the relatively early acceptance of free trade) were originally transmitted, it would be possible to trace the changes that, at times formally and at others informally, preceded at the level of economic restructuring the formation of a liberal economic culture. The fact that at the beginning of the nineteenth century the legal order was still essentially a colonial legacy explains why ecclesiastic and military *fueros* (privileges) persisted side by side with *ancien regime*–type mercantile corporations,[7] in spite of the formal abolition of the tribunals of the *Consulado* (merchants' guild) and the tribunal of *Minería* (miners' guild) and their governing bodies, the *diputaciones*. In fact, although the Cortes of Cádiz abolished corporations in 1813, the law provided exemptions for ecclesiastical, military, mineral, and mercantile corporations.

Starting in 1822, government policy shifted constantly with regard to commercial institutions. Despite a tendency to dismantle existing consulados, the chambers of commerce and commercial courts, authorized in 1841, were created in all state capitals, ports, and commercial centers with more than 15,000 inhabitants. Although the details of their operation remain unknown, the new chambers of commerce, like the colonial consulados, adopted the pre-existing norms and practices to the new context, thereby limiting the transformation of pre-liberal economic values.[8]

The Mercantile Code of 1854 institutionalized the commercial courts and determined that for legal purposes a merchant was someone who registered with a commercial court establishing that his regular occupation consisted of commercial traffic or exchange limited to the purchase or sale of products, goods, merchandise, and other materials and that he possessed the required amount of capital, the minimum sum of which was determined by the local mercantile tribunal. The code established that instruments of payment and mercantile services were auxiliary to the commercial activity and could not be used independent of the physical goods that were being traded. A limitation to economic freedom can be found in the 1854 code, which contains a regulation establishing that mercantile contracts are not valid if they contradict canon law and good manners. In addition, the code provides that mercantile cases must be tried before a tribunal made up of a lawyer and two judges from the mercantile community with experience in the ways and customs of trade.[9]

A similar case can be found in the mining sector. Even after the Tribunal de Minería and its provincial representatives were eliminated and replaced in 1826 by the Establecimiento de Minería, in practice the new institution continued to function within the colonial tradition of corporate representation and law enforcement. In fact, the continuity of corporate practice was so strong that foreigners were not allowed to own either real estate or mines until 1842. The new Junta de Fomento y Administrativa de Minería, created in 1842, had the same authority as the old tribunal since mining justice fell under the jurisdiction of mining diputaciones, leading to the creation of courts of appeals in each department seat. In 1854, as occurred in the mercantile sector, the Tribunal de Minería was converted into an administrative body of the state. It assumed the role of representing miners and encouraging production. These corporate tribunals were still functioning through the end of the 1860s.[10]

In this brief overview of the persistence of corporate economic institutions, it is worth considering the corporate tendencies present in the Church and military. These corporations defended their fueros, that is, their privileges, with equal, if not greater, force than they had in the colonial era. The Church relied on the financial needs of the state and the military on its role as regulator of the country's governability and apparent defender of national sovereignty to protect their interests.[11] Furthermore, as late as the 1840s some attempted to structure political representation in accordance with the estates into which society was divided: landowners, miners, merchants, and manufacturers. In an effort to organize manufacturers, the Dirección General de la Industria Nacional was established in 1831 to create a new corporation that would be able—as envisioned by José Luis Mora—to reduce competition among producers and help generate an esprit de corps to counter the freedom of association supported by liberals.[12] Under the name of the Secretaría de Fomento, the Dirección General de la Industria Nacional existed until the Restored Republic (1867–1874), owing to the fact that manufacturers were able to defend their sectoral interests by invoking the protection offered to manufacturing by the state.

The reaction to these persistent corporate forms and to the old and new barriers to the entrance of new actors into production and trade was the rapid spread of illegal activities such as contraband and tax evasion; opposition to economic actors protected by the renewed corporate structures; and the strengthening of free-trade clubs in the country's main trade and production centers. As Matías Romero stated, only a small percentage of the total silver production was minted by the Casas de Moneda (mints) because of government prohibitions. In addition, these restrictions favored old regime-style manufacturers' corporations because of the persistence of colonial *alcabalas* (sales taxes) on interstate trade.[13]

The persistence of a culture created during the antiguo régimen delayed the birth of new institutions based on objective economic law—in other words, a law that took into account only the objects produced by mining, manufacturing, or agriculture as well as the goods exchanged in commercial contracts and that differentiated the goods produced and traded from the social and economic conditions of the individuals involved in the transactions.

Anti-corporate outcry began in the period from 1830 to 1850, was openly manifested in the Constituent Congress of 1857, and gained momentum from 1860 to 1880. The triggering event was probably the expansion of illegal trade and especially the great expansion of professional, patriotic, mutual help, instructional, and economic development associations both in the nation's capital and the states of Puebla, Veracruz, Michoacán, Jalisco, Yucatán, San Luis Potosí, and Durango. These associations encouraged individuals and families to favor the secularization of society and the liberalization of antiguo régimen-style corporate links.[14]

It is safe to say that the key element in the dissolution of corporativism was initially the battle for, and later, the enactment of laws to reform civil institutions and the disamortization of ecclesiastic property. After freedom of the press was established in 1855, the number of liberal newspapers grew rapidly and most portrayed the Church as the principal obstacle to political and economic freedom: on the one hand, as an informal political institution capable of influencing the behavior of the conservatives, and on the other, as an informal economic institution that defended the interests of the proprietary class.[15]

It is important to keep in mind that opposition to the Church had strong support from towns, small communities, and villages. That is why the regulations disamortizing commonly held town lands, which were distributed among heads of families by the municipalities, were not implemented until 1870. Popular opposition to the fees and obventions demanded by the Church, as well as the charges for religious services demanded by the parish priest, favored the rapid implementation in many municipalities of laws for the establishment of the office of civil registry and the creation of lay cemeteries. Even in Indian communities in the state of Oaxaca, for example, the new laws were rapidly internalized because they liberated indigenous families from the iniquitous ecclesiastic rights against which the Indians had battled since the end of the eighteenth century.[16]

INSTITUTIONAL VECTORS

This essay stresses the anti-corporate tendencies that emerged from Mexican society to point to a problem that has not been given sufficient attention. Liberalism came into existence, as has been noted, by giving voice to and using the anti-corporate tendencies of different social components and trying to institutionalize them. Liberals feared that these social manifestations would lead to demagogy and a dictatorship of the majority, something they considered even more damaging than Santa Anna's dictatorship. It is evident that, unlike other political cultures, especially totalitarian ones, liberal culture does not present a project or a pre-constituted design of a new society.

Moreover, it exhibits a strong distrust of the capacity of political parties, clubs, and lay associations to prevent the unleashing of political passions among citizens.

If we take into account the contemporary interpretations of the Constitution of 1857 offered by Francisco Zarco, Guillermo Prieto, Ignacio Altamirano, or Ignacio Ramírez, we can see that they identify work and the daily toil of men as the disciplinary mechanism of life in a society. These authors refer to a concrete, not an abstract, form of political or economic freedom when they insist—with regard to economic life—on freedom of work and the enjoyment of its fruits, as long as this freedom does not create conflicts of interest that would block the entrance of new actors into economic activity. The interaction between economic and political freedom can be found even in a guidebook to political economy published in the mid-nineteenth century. The author asks how "the security of the citizen's civil and political rights influences the implementation of political economy" and responds that the economy offers citizens "the means to produce, by their own accord or through their representatives, the social compact of which they are a part and have, in some cases, helped to create. In this way, as owners of a portion of the public wealth and benefiting from the advantages produced by the whole, citizens are obliged to take part in the measures that affect this wealth because they have a direct interest in its increase. The security of civil rights places citizens under the protection of the law, which also protects property and work and, therefore, promotes that which constitutes national wealth."[17]

In Mexico, as in other Western settings, freedom of trade was the first vector for the spread of a liberal economic culture. It is mercantile freedom that diffuses the notion of exchange as a voluntary written or verbal contract that brings to life a chain of agreements that lead to multilateral exchange.[18] This idea is clearly stated in the mercantile code proposed in 1869 that defines acts of trade as "all operations that are made with the intent of trafficking for profit."[19] With this idea as a starting point, a jurist of the time held that mercantile acts generate new operations, agents, and judicial relationships with the result that "these agreements acquire a serious and transcendental nature that require removing them from customary to a defined and positive law."[20]

It is not a coincidence that to secure this constitutional guarantee, the customs system had to be reformed. The reform started in 1872 and slowly began a process of foreign trade liberalization that gained momentum between 1888 and 1900.[21] Free foreign trade was strengthened between 1870 and 1880 as a result of new commercial treaties signed with the United States and various European countries. Unlike the accords signed in the 1820s and 1830s, the new treaties fully recognized Mexican sovereignty and eliminated the partial extraterritoriality that had benefited foreign actors, creating trade relations with greater symmetry.

The institutionalization of free trade within the Mexican space proved to be more difficult; it was only achieved—and not fully—twenty years later. The setbacks in the unification of a commercial space, a requirement for the creation of a sole or national market, were in part due to the resistance of the states to the expansion of federal power and also by regional protectionist interests. These interests opposed the spread of the liberal principle of fiscal equality, according to which every citizen must pay consumption taxes in order to sustain the constitutionally assigned tasks of the government.[22] It is worth noting that resistance to liberalism's fiscal equality was related to concerns about possible demands that the payment of a universal tax on consumption also grant all tax-paying citizens the right to vote and be elected.

After the institutionalization of free trade, which promoted voluntary mercantile contracts, a series of new mechanisms developed that allowed the progressive separation of the public and private economic spheres and recognized the autonomy of market forces within a constitutional regulatory framework. It is important to establish the milestones of a process that began with the Restored Republic, continued during the *Porfiriato* (the regime of Porfirio Díaz, 1876–1911), and culminated during the first decades of the twentieth century. It is also important to stress the continuity of this institutional effort and to challenge the widely held belief that liberal institutionalization only took place during the Restored Republic. That version of events presents liberal institutionalization as an incomplete process unable to recover from setbacks in the performance of the economy, in government stability, or in the progress of economic culture during that period.

To understand the continuity that characterized the institutionalization period, we must consider the relationship between the 1870 civil code reform and the 1872 customs reform of the civil procedures code. Although they initially applied only to the Federal District and the national territories, they were later adapted, reformulated, and modified by the states. The link between civil regulations and preexistent mercantile norms and practices is reflected in the individualization of the social actor. This individualization, which characterized both civil and commercial society, is present in the reformed Civil Code of 1884 for the Federal District and national territories and later in the civil codes of the different states.[23]

The swiftness with which commercial freedom disseminated the idea that there should be only one national economic space is illustrated by the constitutional reform of 1883 that transferred to the federal government the authority to regulate mining, trade, and banks. Because of the constitutional reform, Congress issued trade codes in 1884 and 1889.[24] The 1884 Code recognized that the value of merchandise results from the voluntary transaction between seller and buyer and that the price is the one established through negotiation between the parties. In other words, the 1884 Code grants legal value to market prices, overcoming the idea of a just price, which is found in the first Civil Code of 1870. The latter code recognized the possibility of canceling contracts in cases where the value of the traded goods exceeds half the just price. The full recognition of economic freedom was in this way established both in the mercantile Code of 1884 as well as the reformed 1889 Code. Both recognized that "it has at its base civil [law] whose precepts modify only the part strictly necessary to establish the nature of mercantile businesses and to determine the rights and obligations derived from them."[25] The importance of the new codes lies in the fact that they helped to establish the distinction between the public and the private sphere, a distinction demonstrated by the public sphere's exclusive authority to issue currency, control purely public services—such as the mail, telegraph, and telephone systems and all services related to internal security and national sovereignty—, and to recognize intellectual property, industrial trademarks, and literary property.

The 1884 code was grounded on the principle that all individuals could participate in commerce without the need to register. The code also defined trade as "the collection of acts related to production, transport, and other forms authorized by legislation or habit" and "whose sole purpose is profit."[26] The code of 1889 expanded free trade to cover individuals who engage in commerce and the financial instruments that sustain the physical exchange of goods and services. The new code, therefore, included and expanded the 1888 limited liability company law by establishing regulations for its organizations; limits on shareholder responsibility to creditors; and establishing the amount of shareholder capital in the company. Furthermore, it required that the company's capital be underwritten 10 percent in cash or 100 percent in the case the contributions consisted of titles, securities, goods, movable property, or real estate. The 1889 code thus introduced the first distinction between variable capital and fixed capital companies.[27] The 1889 code was important for laying the foundation for the creation of a financial economy by defining as mercantile activities all credit titles and their emission, distribution, endorsement, approval, or acceptance, as well as all activities that today would be considered financial mediation.[28]

In effect, the commercial code of 1884 legalized the emission of bank bills and established that all bank operations had to be authorized by the Ministry of Finance.[29] The 1889 code stated that credit institutions would be "regulated by a special law" and that, until the law was enacted, banks would have to obtain authorization from the Ministry of Finance to operate and each contract to form a credit institution would be approved "on a case per case basis by the Congress of the Union."[30] The interregnum that preceded the 1897 law of credit institutions was characterized by numerous concessions to banks of issue, which were able to present a minimum capital of 500,000 pesos, half in liquid capital and the rest in public debt bonds. Under this law, banks also agreed to keep cash in their vaults equal to at least half the amount of the bills in circulation, and to accept a federal auditor, appointed by the Finance Ministry, to supervise the operations and balances of the banks of issue.[31]

The law of 1897 established the regulatory framework for banks, stock exchanges, and credit institutions based on the principle of banking freedom. Moreover, the law did not create a central bank, thus continuing to permit private institutions to issue currency. The Ministry of Finance became the top monetary and credit authority, which French author Jean Favre described as having "limitless [power] over banks." It exercised an excessive authority over the entire banking system and public trust.

It was precisely because the credit system was founded on almost limitless freedom that the system was divided into two levels: the state and the federal. This way, the regional banks benefited from local capital linked to local interests, and the national banks (with regional presence thanks to local branches) interacted with state institutions, which created a national credit system that was able to self-regulate interest rates. This in turn made the creation of a federal monetary authority unnecessary. Therefore, in 1897 a law divided banking institutions into specialized categories: banks of issue, circulation, and discount—an activity reserved exclusively for national banks authorized to issue currency and discount letters of payment and loans; mortgage banks, in charge of offering short- and medium-term loans, underwritten by real estate, and authorized to issue mortgage bonds, accept short-term deposits, and loan to the federal government, the states, and municipalities; and commercial banks for mining and agricultural enterprises, with the authority to emit credit titles redeemable within a period of three months to two years. The law also regulated general warehouses, pawnshops, and the stock exchanges. The latter institutions could negotiate public credit titles, company stocks, bills of exchange, loans, bearer bonds, precious metals, merchandise deposit certificates, shipments, insurance policies, and cargo and transports.[32]

The subordination of bank freedom to the political power of the Ministry of Finance did not allow the development of policies—similar to that of the United States—whereby part of the currency in circulation was guaranteed by government bonds, thus favoring the circulation of public titles and their acquisition by investors. Banking freedom, however, prevented the creation of a multiple banking system capable of generating better synergy among the different credit modalities. This obstacle was partially obviated by widespread use in the Mexican financial system of "current account credit that offered clients the advantage of paying interest only on the sum used; repayment of that credit did not have to be made on a fixed date during the duration of the account; the entire line of credit could be disposed at once; and, finally, interest was due every six months."[33] Although these banking practices helped overcome the limits imposed by commercial credit, they also created a series of obstacles to the development of banking institutions and the creation of medium-term forms of credit.

Just as trade freedom rapidly eroded the barter exchange present in Mexico's regions and favored the emergence of a modern credit for production, free economy also was compromised by the slow implementation of the constitutional articles relating to property rights and the security of possessions, as well as compensation for expropriations carried out for public utility. It is important to emphasize the absolute novelty in Mexico of constitutional principles related to property rights. As Andrés Molina Enríquez correctly observed, Mexico was characterized by exhibiting "every form of society that humanity offered except for the one evident in the final period [of evolution] towards territorial rights" or "property rights not linked to the territorial portion itself." That is why an existing property title *"did not allow title holders any other rights than those related to the limited value they represent."* Beyond his critique of the large landed estates, Molina Enríquez gave great importance (as was the case with the liberal generation that paved the way for the Revolution) to the coexistence of a plurality of rights derived from the simple possession of resources to the de facto use of those resources and, finally, to the existence of de facto property, lacking legal title, the result of the traditional property rights due to long-term occupation of the land.[34]

In spite of his positivist obsession with classification, Molina Enríquez understood perfectly that the central problems of property rights were the result of the "lack of accuracy in the assignment of private property titles," "the lack of security of property," and the fact that the so-called private property "has reached us without being defined in a precise, irreversible, and definitive way." The result is that "due to the rigor of juridical principles, public authorities could revoke the occupation or possession of private property held by any individual. In doing so, the public authorities were not at any moment forced to act outside the law."[35]

The concept of property rights as a mixed bag of different rights that did not provide security or certainty to their holders can be seen in the first liberal law on *terrenos baldíos* (uncultivated lands). This law was based on the constitutional principle of property entitlement as it evolved from legal decisions on land.[36] Such entitlement is not an act that annuls preexistent rights because it was obtained without prejudice to historical or customary rights held by *hacendados*, small landowners, communities, and towns. Starting with the first law of 1863, all the regulations supporting the Constitution of 1857 recognize that the nation acquires "all the Republic's land that has not been either destined for public use by the appropriate authorities nor transferred by the same authorities through an onerous or lucrative title to individuals or corporations authorized to purchase them."[37]

As a result of the implementation of this constitutional norm, property rights and the security they implied were divided into new or titled rights and preexistent or historic rights, known as primordial titles—in other words, rights founded on customary law, on the uses and practices of the land. Unlike "primordial rights," the new titles were of an objective nature, since the boundaries of land solicited by individuals were demarcated by the interested party and purchased from the government. To stress the link between primordial and new rights, the law gave priority to usufructuaries who had occupied national lands productively for a period of no less than ten years. National lands were then sold to them for a sum below market price.

The institutional path taken to reform property rights was firmly established with the colonization law of 1883 and with the uncultivated-land law of 1894. The first perfected the transition from primordial rights to the new property rights that would become important in regulating the activities of the companies authorized to survey public lands. The law was designed, as Joaquín Casasús wrote in 1888, to force "land owners to regularize their property, and cease being usurpers."[38] The 1894 uncultivated land law transferred land from the public domain to private use. The transfer included land "discovered and surveyed by official commissions or authorized companies," surplus land or "land possessed by individuals with primordial titles that included an area larger than established by it [the primordial title]," *excedencias*, that is, "land possessed by private individuals for twenty years or more not included in the boundaries established by the primordial title, but adjacent to the land covered by that title."[39]

Both laws were aimed at implementing constitutional property rights. In this way, a complete recognition of property rights was established as the economic right of private individuals and companies, as stated in the mercantile code. It is important to note that in Mexico private property rights did not annul other preexisting property rights. The earlier property rights became secondary, but offered the possibility of being converted to private property. The new foundation of property law was its objectivity, which was based on "the identification of property on the law that favored private interests."[40]

A process similar to the reinforcement of agrarian property rights took place in the mining sector with the approval, in 1884, of a mining code that, as in the case of commerce and the uncultivated land laws, established mining under federal jurisdiction. However, it was the mining law of 1892 that established "the three conditions absolutely necessary for the development and prosperity of mining: the facility to acquire, freedom to exploit, and security to retain." The new 1892 mining law, reformed in 1909, recognized freedom for mining exploration and made mining property "irrevocable and perpetual" with titles granted by the Minister of Development. The law marked the end of the informal colonial institution of *avío*, which gave preference to merchants and impoverished the producers by providing for the creation of mining societies and the mortgaging of mining properties.[41]

As in the case of land, mining sector property rights were framed with the same economic logic: the reduction of transaction costs for mining production to facilitate its entrance into the market and to provide certainty not only to existing proprietors, but to all newcomers to that activity, regardless of nationality. These new property rights contributed to the reduction of transaction costs because producers were now able to acquire bank credits and were free from usurious practices imposed by merchants through avío or *habilitación*, a practice of colonial origin that allowed producers to obtain production materials and money in exchange for future production sold well below market prices.

DISSEMINATION AND REPRESENTATION OF ECONOMIC CULTURE

The foregoing discussion of freedom of trade and contractual and property rights demonstrates that new liberal economic culture favored a new relationship between the producers and receivers of that culture. On the side of the producers were those who worked with state and federal governments, such as federal and state administrative officials. Among the receivers of the new liberal culture were those who benefited from the institutional transformations as well as those who sustained ideologically, electorally, and even through clientelism the construction of a new Mexican reality based on the new political order.

With the studies currently available, it is very hard to understand the timing and degree to which the evolution of cultural and political imaginaries converged. It is also difficult to understand the temporal relationship in Mexico, as well as other Western lands, between political freedom and economic freedom—in other words, between liberalism and free trade. At the same time, precisely because liberal political culture was not the only one present in the Mexican space, its circulation was favored by the egalitarianism that emerged from republicanism, which some erroneously characterize as "popular liberalism," as well as restrained by a communitarianism promoted by a renovated Catholic political culture. Nevertheless, many liberal elements influenced other political cultures present in the Mexican space. This did not result, as is widely believed, in a dichotomy between elite or high political culture and popular or low political culture. On the contrary, the notable inequality between the cultures slowly closed and became westernized due to the spread of the written word, public readings, and schools.

Literacy and education were, in fact, the main promoters of liberalism. The preference for written over oral culture is explained by its relative advantages in meeting the need to generate greater interaction between the government and its people and, at the same time, among interest groups. This interaction was aimed at distributing material progress throughout the different regions of the country. Even though it could be said that the new property rights mainly benefited the large holders of preexistent primordial rights, they also helped smaller primordial rights holders, such as Indians, mestizos, and mulattos. Among those affected by the disamortization of ecclesiastic properties were the lower clergy because parishes were forced to turn over their land to the municipalities so they could be sold to the new social actors promoted by the liberal revolution. According to the partial data currently available, the new individual private property rights that granted titles to land—much of which had belonged to the old *ejidos* or communal town lands—benefited 19,983 heads of families and affected more than one million hectares of land between 1877 and 1906. As a result of the new title granting facilities established in 1906, another 14,415 heads of families received land titles between 1906 and 1911.[42]

Little, if anything, is known about the circulation of liberal culture among different social strata and its capacity to encourage the creation of new forms of social association. It was these movements that contributed to the assimilation of a secularized economic culture with strong anti-corporate, anti-protectionist, and anti-prohibitionist tendencies. Other political cultures contemporary to liberalism probably were influenced by the liberal proposal of creating institutions capable of guaranteeing and strengthening the freedom of social actors in ways that would allow them to improve their individual and their families' economic condition.

Presidential discourse of the time sought to disseminate a view of the economic world based on the characterization of the government's economic priorities. These priorities could be found in a limited number of actions that provided the economic actors, who were the receptors of that image, a sense of support so they might act autonomously because they knew their actions were guaranteed by the new institutions. Thus, contrary to common assertions, liberal economic culture never considered the market as a force independent of institutional actions, which had no interest in dominating market forces, as that would constitute an attack against the freedom of economic actors.

The priorities assigned by the presidency of the republic to different economic issues help to explain how an institution fosters liberal economic culture throughout society. For more than a century, the executive branch and public opinion considered that the state's economic role was essentially the regulation and implementation of economic freedom through budget policies, regulation of currency and of private and public credit, and the economic promotion of individuals and companies. The latter task was to be accomplished through trade and the supply of public goods, including those developed and administered directly by the state as well as those sustained through its subsidies to private companies for the improvement of infrastructure throughout the country and particularly in its urban centers.

These general parameters may be found in the presidential addresses on the state of the national economy, even though the addresses are only a rough indicator of the view of the economic forces that the executive branch offered to the public. The only issue common to all presidential addresses was the budget, since, as Ignacio Manuel Altamirano declared, "without the Ministry of Finance there is no government; without taxes, no Ministry of Finance; without the law there is no obligation to pay taxes; [and] without the budget law there is no possible way of organizing of a country." The executive branch fostered, especially between 1867 and 1880, an optimistic vision of trade, particularly foreign trade, and "material improvements" (in other words, railroads, telegraph, infrastructure, and ports), as demonstrated in Mexico's participation in international exhibitions.[43] In this period, increased interest in the new image of economic growth is evident; less importance is given to institutions for the consolidation of economic freedom. The change was probably an attempt to minimize the conflicts set in motion with the financial reforms in the period between 1868 and 1874.

The birth of the liberal order offers a view of the economy according to which the government guarantees the nation's material progress as long as the different regional, social, and economic interests agree to reduce the level of conflict. The new image is one of increased wealth and well-being due to the modernization of administration and infrastructure, which in turn improves the material condition of the population and expands the resources available to the government for the development of public services and education.

In the years following the 1880s and 1890s there was a greater insistence on the new economic realities promoted by the new monetary and public credit order. By emphasizing the new economic forms, the government sought to demonstrate to the economic actors the possibilities offered by the financial economy, provided that they accepted and utilized the opportunities created by freedom of trade and public subsidies to corporations. At the start of the twentieth century, the financial dimensions of the economy and the increase of public works were the vectors used by the government to generate a consensus that allowed for strengthening the state's role in the economic sphere.

The actions taken by the legislative branch, which had greater importance than typically acknowledged, constituted another vector of great importance for new economic culture. While the executive branch promoted its message hierarchically, the Congress of the Union acted in a seemingly quotidian manner through the press, which frequently reported that body's debates. Indeed, it published summaries, and even extracts of proposed laws being discussed by legislative commissions. Thus, the link between Congress and public opinion—as well as the relationship between elected representatives and citizens—was strengthened. Especially after 1874, with the re-establishment of the senate, the congress managed to increase its capacity for the transmission of political culture. Both senators and deputies issued a plural message, relying on the different political factions and groups of the press and by participating in public demonstrations that reflected the different interpretations of the country's political and economic reality. The spread of the economic views formed in the Congress of the Union may be followed through the debates about legislative initiatives, the discussions of congressional commissions, and the votes of the two chambers of Congress.[44]

One may evaluate the transformations that occurred in the new interpretation of economic life by considering the growing role of the federal government. These changes coincided with the new economic culture that asserted that "the states did not have either sovereignty or independence, but instead possessed freedom because they were free to act within the limits established by the federal pact and [were free] to do anything that is not prohibited by law." It was the federal government's responsibility to preserve a framework of freedom and "foster the development of reciprocal interests" between the federal government and the states, as well as to encourage cooperation between the federal government and economic actors. Such mutual cooperation ensured the emergence of "a peace that some have called mechanical" which, with the passing of time, "became a social institution, in principle, fundamental [to the general social well-being]."[45]

The three studies conducted by Pablo Macedo for the centenary of independence provide a valuable indicator of assimilation of the new economic culture as observed by one of its proponents at that time. In order of appearance, these works are: *La evolución mercantil* (The Evolution of Trade), *Las comunicaciones y obras públicas* (Communications and Public Works), and *La Hacienda Publica* (Public Finances).[46] The sequence itself is interesting, since it shows the mental order on which the image of the liberal economic process was founded. According to Macedo, economic freedom, visible in the commercial sphere, was the guiding force behind the transformations that took place in the country. It led to the development of communications and public works, and these, in turn, resulted in the unification of a national economic space. The transformation occurred as a result of the increasing collaboration between the government and the classes that sustained it with their taxes and their keen desire for progress. That collaboration allowed the interaction between the state and the market, facilitated by the constant allotment of public funds for material progress.

The unfolding nineteenth-century liberal culture favored the creation of an economic space, for both social actors and the government, which protected the general interest; that is, the interest of consumers, above the specific interests of a producer or a group of producers. It sought a unified image of society in contrast to the previously divided notions of liberal culture of an included majority and an excluded minority. By the end of the century, the proponents of liberal culture understood that those excluded must be offered the possibility of inclusion. They concluded that exclusion was a deplorable state of affairs that threatened both individual dignity and the universality of consumption and thus created conflicts that could disrupt the rational order that liberalism sought to build.

NOTES

1. See Marcello Carmagnani, *Estado y mercado. La economía pública del liberalismo mexicano 1857–1911* (Mexico: Fondo de Cultura Económica-Fideocomiso Historia de las Américas-El Colegio de México, 1994); "Instituciones financieras internacionales del orden liberal mexicano," in Marcello Carmagnani, ed., *Constitucionalismo y orden liberal en América Latina, 1850–1920* (Turin: Otto Editore, 2000), 315–339; and "Towards a New Financial Order, 1857–1912," in Michael Bordo and Roberto Cortés-Conde, eds., *Transferring Wealth and Power from the Old to the New World. Monetary and Fiscal Institutions in the 17th through the 19th Century* (Cambridge: Cambridge University Press, 2001), 303–326.

2. On the different forms of political culture, cf. S. Bernstein, comp., *Les cultures politiques en France* (Paris: Seuil, 1999); and in the same volume, on liberal culture see N. Roussellier, "La culture politique libérale," 69–112.

3. For a full understanding of how a "national" culture is constructed, cf. Ernest Gellner, *Nations and Nationalism* (Ithaca: Cornell University Press, 1983), 39–62, 88–109.

4. See Norberto Bobbio, "Libertà e democrazia," in Gian Mario Bravo and S. Rota Ghibaudi, comps., *Il pensiero politico contemporaneo*, vol. 1 (Milán: F. Angeli, 1985), 21–88.

5. Alicia Hernández Chávez, *México. Breve historia contemporanea* (Mexico: Fondo de Cultura Económica, 2000), 215–240.

6. Certain elements are found in Marcello Carmagnani, "La libertad, el poder y el estado en la segunda mitad del siglo XIX," *Historias* 15 (1986): 55–63; and also in M. Luna Argudín, "El Congreso de la Unión y las transformaciones del liberalismo y federalismo mexicanos 1857–1910" (Ph.D. diss., El Colegio de México, 2001).

7. The term "corporation" in this case does not refer to modern business and industrial corporations, which were invented as legal entities in the middle of the nineteenth century, but to the corporate institutions of the *ancien regime*, such as the Church, the military, Indian communities, and many other guild-like bodies.

8. *Tribunal Mercantil* (1842), Lafragua Colection, vol. 346, part 5. Certain references are found in G. M. Armstrong, *Law and Market Society in Mexico* (New York: Praeger, 1989), 27–28.

9. José Tornel y Mendevil, *Manual de derecho mercantil mexicano* (Mexico: Imprenta de Vicente Segura, 1854). Cf also María del Refugio González, "Comercio y comerciantes en México en el siglo XIX," in Instituto de Investigaciones Jurídicas, *Centenario del Código de Comercio* (Mexico: Universidad Nacional Autónoma de

México, 1991), 225–233; Alejandra Araya, "Prácticas financieras en los actos mercantiles: comerciantes, comisionistas y corredores en el México decimonónico" (Centro de Estudios Históricos-El Colegio de México, 2000 [unpublished]); J. A.Cosamalón Aguilar, "Hacia una nueva ética: un manual de comerciante y los códigos de comercio de 1884–1889" (Centro de Estudios Históricos-El Colegio de México, 2001 [unpublished]); and M. J. Rhi Sausi, "El derecho mercantil frente a las leyes civiles" (Centro de Estudios Históricos-El Colegio de México, 2001 [unpublished]).

10. J. Olmedo y Lama, *Ordenanzas de Minería y colección de leyes* (Mexico: Imprenta de Vicente García Torres, 1873), 68–74; María del Refugio González, "La Legislación minera durante el siglo XIX," in *Minería Mexicana* (Mexico: Comisión de Fomento Minero, 1984), 250–255; Cuauhtémoc Velasco Avila et al., *Estado y minería en México (1867–1910)* (Mexico: Fondo de Cultura Económica, 1988), 121–129. On the persistence of *diputaciones* in the state of Mexico until 1875, cf. Mario Téllez González, *La Legislación minera en el Estado de México, 1824–1883* (Toluca: El Colegio Mexiquense, 1996), 167–197.

11. On the persistence of the Church and the military's colonial corporations, cf. Michael P. Costeloe, *Church and State in Independent Mexico. A Study of the Patronage Debate* (London: Royal Historical Society, 1978); and Günter Kahle, *El ejército y la formación del Estado en los comienzos de la Independencia de México* (Mexico: FCE, 1997). An excellent study on the existence of corporativism is Michael P. Costeloe, *The Central Republic in Mexico, 1835–1846. Hombres de bien in the Age of Santa Anna* (Cambridge: Cambridge University Press, 1993).

12. S. Niccolai, "Industria manuale e industria meccanica in Messico, 1780–1850" (Ph.D. diss., Universidad de Turín, 1998); Armstrong, *Law and Society,* 31–34.

13. M. Romero, *Geographical and Statistical Notes on Mexico* (New York: Knickerbocher Press, 1898), 186–192.

14. An excellent study on associationism, although marred by a lack of understanding of the nature of the Spanish Monarchy, is Carlos A. Forment, *Democracy in Latin America, 1760–1900* (Chicago: University of Chicago Press, 2003). See also Hernández Chávez, *México,* 215–239; J. F. Leal, *Del mutualismo al sindicalismo en México, 1843–1910* (Mexico: Universidad Nacional Autónoma de México, 1991); R. Rojas Coria, *Tratado de cooperativismo mexicano* (Mexico: Universidad Nacional Autónoma de México, 1952); and Carlos Illades, *Hacia la república del trabajo* (Mexico: Universidad Autónoma Metropolitana-El Colegio de México, 1996), 67–113.

15. Cf. Gerald L. McGowan, *Prensa y poder, 1854–1857* (Mexico: El Colegio de México, 1978), 157–181, 226–234; Jacqueline Covo, *Las ideas de la reforma en México (1855–1861)* (Mexico: Universidad Nacional Autónoma de México, 1983), 479–498, 511–536. On the impact of desamortization on moderate public opinion, cf. Silvestre Villegas Revueltas, *El liberalismo moderado en México 1852–1864* (Mexico: Universidad Nacional Autónoma de México, 1997), 129–149.

16. For a study of the elements of hostility against the Church and the reception of the reform laws, see Robert J. Knowlton, "La individualización de la propriedad corporativa civil en el siglo XIX. Notas sobre Jalisco," *Historia Mexicana* 109 (1978): 24–61; and, by the same author, "La división de la tierras de los pueblos durante el siglo XIX: el caso de Michoacán," *Historia Mexicana* 157 (1990): 3–25; D. J. Fraser, "La política de desamortización en las comunidades indígenas," *Historia Mexicana* 84 (1972): 615–652; F. Schenk, "La desamortización de las tierras comunales en el Es-

tado de México (1856–1911)," *Historia Mexicana* 177 (1995): 3–38; D. Traffano, "Y el Registro Civil no es más que un engaño del Gobierno, Sociedad civil e Iglesia frente a un nuevo registro de los datos vitales: Oaxaca en la segunda mitad del siglo XIX," in Marcello Carmagnani, ed., *Constitucionalismo y orden liberal*, 201–225.

17. L. Pinal, *Catecismo de economía política*, Part II (Mexico: Imprenta de Ignacio Cumplido, 1856), 79–80.

18. On the relationship between trade and contractual obligations, cf. A. Greif, "The Fundamental Problem of Exchange. A Research Agenda in Historical Institutional Analysis," *European Review of Economic History* 4 (2000): 251–284.

19. *Proyecto de Código Mercantil* (Mexico: Imprenta de Gobierno, 1869), 3.

20. J. Pallares, *Derecho mercantil mexicano*, vol. I (Mexico: J. Guerra, 1891), 747–748.

21. Cf. Sandra Kuntz Ficker, "The Import Trade Policy of the Liberal Regime in Mexico, 1870–1900," in this volume.

22. Marcello Carmagnani, "El liberalismo, los impuestos internos y el estado federal mexicano 1857–1911," *Historia Mexicana* 3 (1989): 471–496.

23. A. Salinas Martínez, "Las sociedades mercantiles en el código de comercio de 1889," in Instituto de Investigaciones Jurídicas, *Centenario del Código de comercio* (Mexico: UNAM, 1991), 566–570.

24. J. Barrera Graf, "Codificación en México. Antecedentes, código de comercio de 1889, perspectivas," in Instituto de Investigaciones Jurídicas, *Centenario del Código de comercio*, 75–79; and María del Refugio González, "Comercio y comerciantes en México en el siglo XIX," ibid., 239–240.

25. *Código de Comercio de los Estados Unidos Mexicanos 1883* (Mexico: Tipografía Gonzalo Esteva, 1884), art. 4.

26. Ibid., art. 1.

27. W. Frisch Philipp, "Los viejos códigos y las leyes modernas," in Instituto de Investigaciones Jurídicas, *Centenario del Código de comercio*, 214–218; and Salinas Martínez, "Las sociedades mercantiles," in ibid., 576–580.

28. Barrera Graf, "Codificación en México," in Instituto de Investigaciones Jurídicas, *Centenario del Código de comercio*, 77–79. See also A. J. Lozano, *Código de comercio de los Estados Unidos Mexicanos* (Mexico: Imprenta de Lozano, 1890).

29. *Código de comercio de los Estados Unidos Mexicanos*, 1883, arts. 954–994.

30. *Código de comercio de los Estados Unidos Mexicanos*, 1889, art. 640.

31. P. Macedo, *La evolución mercantil* (1903) (Mexico: UNAM, 1970), 156–159; and J. Favre, *Les banques au Méxique* (Paris: Marcel Rivière, 1907), 30–34.

32. On the banking law, cf. Macedo, *La evolución mercantile*, 157–159; Favre, *Les banques*; J. D. Casasús, *Las instituciones de crédito* (Mexico: Secretaria de Fomento, 1890), 393–412; and, by the same author, *Las reformas a la ley de instituciones de crédito* (Mexico: Palacio Nacional, 1908).

33. Casasús, *Las reformas*, 206. A good introduction to the formation of a financial economy is P. Riguzzi, "Los pobres por pobres, los ricos por ignorancia. El mercado financiero en México, 1880–1925," in Marcello Carmagnani, Alicia Hernández Chávez, R. Romano, coords., *Para una historia de América. Los Nudos*, vol. I (Mexico: Fideicomiso Historia de las Américas-El Colegio de México-FCE, 1999), 352–365.

34. Andrés Molina Enríquez, *Los grandes problemas nacionales* (1909) (Mexico: Era, 1978), 151–152. Italics are mine.

35. Ibid., 200–204.

36. Robert J. Knowlton, "Tribunales federales y terrenos rurales en el México del siglo XIX: el Semanario Judicial de la Federación," *Historia Mexicana* 181 (1996): 71–98.

37. Law on uncultivated lands 23.07.1863, in Manuel Dublán and José María Lozano, *Legislación Mexicana*, (Mexico, 1902) tome IX, 637. For an understanding of the reorganization process of agrarian property rights, especially customary law, cf. W. L. Orozco, *Legislación y jurisprudencia sobre terrenos baldíos* (Mexico: Imprenta El Tiempo, 1895). On the relationship between land and water rights, cf. C. B. Kroeber, *El hombre, la tierra y el agua. Las políticas en torno a la irrigación en la agricultura de México* (Mexico: CIESAS, 1994), 191–223.

38. Quoted by R. H. Holden, *Mexico and the Survey of Public Lands. The Management of Modernization 1876–1911* (De Kalb: Northern Illinois University Press, 1994), 12. On the recognition and transference of traditional, customary rights, cf. *Disposiciones sobre designación y fraccionamiento de los ejidos de los pueblos mandados compilar y publicar por el Sr. Ministro de Fomento Gral Carlos Pacheco* (Mexico: Secretaría de Fomento, 1889).

39. Carmagnani, *Estado y mercado*, 40–41. George McCutchen McBride, *Los sistemas de propiedad rural en México* (1925) (Mexico: Conaculta, 1993) is the first study to state the due importance of the reorganization of agrarian property rights.

40. C. A. de Medina y Ormachea, *Garantía de la propiedad raíz en Mexico* (México: Secretaría de Fomento, 1901), 5–6.

41. Carmagnani, *Estado y mercado*, 41–42. One of the best analyses of mining rights published during the liberal period is R. Reyes and F. F. Barker, *The Mining Laws of Mexico* (Mexico: The American Book, 1910), 3–35.

42. Romero, *Geographical*, 226–227; and Robert J. Knowlton, "El ejido mexicano en el siglo XIX," *Historia Mexicana* 189 (1998): 91–92.

43. The analysis of government actions that facilitated the spread of liberal economic culture was carried out with the references contained in the presidential addresses published in *La hacienda pública de México a través de los informes presidenciales* (Mexico: Secretaría de Hacienda y Crédito Público, 1963), 136–177. A future task should be the detailed analysis of the actions of the Interior Ministry and the Finance and Development Ministries. On the new image of Mexico, cf. Mauricio Tenorio Trillo, *Artilugios de la nación. México en las exposiciones universales, 1880–1930* (Mexico: Fondo de Cultura Económica, 1998), 51–65.

44. I have discussed the importance of political coalitions in the creation of budget policies in *Estado y mercado*, 101–165. Also of great importance is Luna, *El Congreso de la Unión*, which is an excellent analysis of the active role played by Congress in the institutional changes within the economic sphere.

45. R. de Zayas Enríquez, *Los Estados Unidos Mexicanos. Sus progresos en veinte años de paz* (New York: H. A. Host, 1897), 41–42.

46. The three monographs provide a sense of aspects of Mexico's economic evolution: La *evolución mercantil; Las comunicaciones y obras públicas;* and *La Hacienda Publica* (Mexico: J. Ballescá, 1905).

11

The Import Trade Policy of the Liberal Regime in Mexico, 1870–1900

Sandra Kuntz Ficker

There has existed in Mexico a striking contrast between our eagerness to adopt political and social reforms, even when they were accompanied by the greatest of difficulties, and our resistant opposition to economic and fiscal reform, even when they would have been of the greatest benefit to the people.

—Matías Romero, 1869.[1]

We meet the challenges of politics with the energy of a Cyclops, yet we face economic problems with the timidity of a virgin [. . .]. The proof is that even after 80 years of independence [. . .], our domestic industry, that most powerful metaphysical vestige of our antiquated beliefs, remains omnipotent in our lives, and inviolable in our consciences. I have struggled against it, and I will continue to do so, as long as it is based not in freedom, but in exploitation.

—Francisco Bulnes, 1886.[2]

In 1867 the Liberal party returned to power, consolidating its rule after having defeated the Conservatives and the Empire of Maximilian. At the start of this period, Mexico's was one of the most closed economies in Latin America. Its connections with the international economy were meager; foreign capital investment, foreign loans, immigration, and international trade all were at low levels.[3] The Mexican government had traditionally pursued an extremely restrictive trade policy, which included high duties and import prohibitions on a broad range of products. In the thirty years that followed, this landscape changed dramatically, thanks in part to an effort to develop the country's resources by opening their exploitation to foreign interests, while at the same time providing selective protection to some industrial activities. This essay analyzes the pace and scope of the change in trade policy during the first three decades of Liberal rule. It examines when and to what extent trade policy began to be liberalized following the long tradition of protectionism, moving toward what usually has been understood as a liberal trade policy.[4] The chapter also identifies some of the obstacles that slowed down and limited this process.

The hypothesis is threefold. First, contrary to what might be expected, the turn toward a more liberal trade policy did not take place as soon as the Liberals came to power. As Matías Romero stated, political and social change seemed to be easier to implement than economic reform in Mexico, despite the importance ascribed to the latter. Second, changes in this field were not linear, i.e., they did not evolve as a progressive, incremental process, but rather as one composed of advances and retreats. Third, the dominating factor that determined the pace and direction of change in trade policy was probably the degree to which the government depended on customs revenue for its functioning and survival.

Three stages in the evolution of the trade policy of the Liberal regime during the last three decades of the nineteenth century can be identified, each of them corresponding approximately to one of the decades of the period. In the first sub-period, starting in 1872, the government expressed the opinion that the excessively restrictive policies and practices followed since independence should be liberalized. This intention, however, came into conflict with the same government's heavy dependence on customs duties as the main source of public revenue. The result was that protectionism prevailed. In the second stage, starting in 1880, new and growing financial commitments acquired by the government prevented any attempt at liberalizing trade policy, reinforcing instead a protectionist stance that was strongly informed by fiscal motives. Only when the financial situation of the government was somewhat improved due to more promising economic performance and to the development of internal sources of revenue, could trade policy begin a genuine, albeit moderate, trend toward liberalization. This trend characterized the third stage, which evolved during the 1890s. It included a lower overall tariff barrier, cascading rates that granted selective protection while at the same time reducing duties across the board, and a set of regulatory reforms that facilitated foreign trade operations considerably.

This essay is part of a broader study of the evolution of Mexico's trade policy in the late nineteenth and early twentieth centuries, but its purposes are more limited. The present aim is to analyze the evolution of import trade policy as reflected in the various tariff laws enacted during the first three decades of the Liberal regime. The variety of positions that evolved in the congressional debates around the tariff are described, and the motives underlying the policy adopted by the government in each stage are analyzed.

Not addressed are other aspects of trade policy, such as export duties or trade agreements, as well as the influences originating from various economic and interest groups that may have driven the government to the adoption of particular measures.

THE BACKGROUND: MEXICO'S FOREIGN TRADE AND COMMERCIAL POLICY CA. 1870

In 1870 Mexico imported about 19 million dollars worth of merchandise, roughly the same as in 1825. As in those early years of Mexico's independent life, three-fourths of the import basket consisted of textiles, haberdashery, and wines.[5] The import mix was thus characteristic of a traditional economy, oriented to supplying the small, relatively inelastic demand for luxury goods generated by the upper classes. The character of the market had little to do with the role played by imports in modern or modernizing societies; namely, to contribute to the expansion of the productive capacity of the country and to supplement the domestic supply of goods for general consumption.

This import mix filled another purpose at the time; it provided government with the largest component of its revenues. The small but inelastic demand for luxury goods allowed the government to levy high duties on imports without serious risk of decreasing them or depriving the domestic economy of essential commodities. In 1868, total customs duties of about 9 million pesos represented 64 percent of the total revenue collected by the government.[6]

According to the 1856 tariff law still in force at the time, imports bore two types of duties, import duties in the strict sense, and the so-called additional duties, which, calculated as a percentage of regular import duties and paid in addition to them, were allocated to meet particular purposes: amortization of the public debt (25 percent), material improvements (20 percent), *internación*—the actual introduction of goods—(19 percent), and *contra-registro*—paid upon arrival to destination—(20 percent). Although the particular duties paid in addition to regular import duties varied with time, by 1871 they still represented more than 70 percent in excess of regular import duties. See table 11.1 for instance, the total duties charged to a standard shipment that arrived to Tepic in September 1871.[7]

There were, of course, great variations as to duties paid by each particular type of merchandise. In this case, regular import duties amounted to 17 percent of the shipment's value, and total duties represented 32 percent of it, a moderate amount for the standards of the time. To this one should add the duty levied upon the exportation of coin (used to pay for the merchandise imported) and consumption duties of variable amount that were charged upon imports in most of the republic's states and territories.[8] According to

Table 11.1.   Total Duties Charged on a Standard Shipment to Tepic, September 1871

Concept		Amount (in pesos)
Value of merchandise		2,004.64
1. Import duties		349.30
2. Additional duties		
Material improvements (20%)	69.86	
Railroads (15%)	52.39	
Internación (10%)	34.93	
Contrarregistro (25%)	87.32	
Roads	35.38	
Municipal tax	11.96	
add up to		291.84
Total duties paid (1 + 2)		641.14

some estimates, the total of both import and additional duties amounted to an average tariff burden of 50 percent on total import value.[9]

Import duties were specific, that is, calculated on the quantity rather than the value of a wide range of specifically listed items. For those products not included in the list, import duty was calculated as a percent of the local market value. The 1856 tariff law did not employ a uniform system of weights and measures, and duties established in pesos coexisted with some taxes fixed in *reales*. Thirty-four items were duty free, including machinery, coal, plows, salt, railroad wagons and rails, marble, books and maps, and printing ink. The law also continued the traditional prohibition on the import of eighteen specific items, including sugar, rice, coffee, shoes, brakes, wheat and wheat flour, wax, *sarapes* and *rebozos* (traditional Mexican cloaks and shawls) made of cotton and wool, lard, tobacco, seeds, and grains, although many exceptions applied to particular customshouses, to the government, and to specially licensed importers.

FIRST STAGE: THE FIRST (NOT SO LIBERAL) TARIFF LAW OF THE LIBERAL PERIOD

In some respects, the tariff law designed by Matías Romero during his term as Minister of the Treasury and enacted in 1872 to replace the 1856 *Ordenanza* was Mexico's most liberal since shortly after Independence.[10] It extended the list of duty-free goods from thirty-four to seventy-three items and eliminated prohibitions;[11] it simplified the payment of duties to some extent; and it attempted to provide nationwide uniformity in tariffs and regulations. However, it could hardly be argued that this tariff law represented true liberalization of the traditionally protective and restrictive trade policy.[12] Furthermore, some of the liberal provisions it contained were short-lived; Congress abolished them only five months after its enactment. As Romero's successor at the Treasury, Francisco Mejía, would put it, it was necessary to "sacrifice [. . .] liberal theory to the special circumstances of the country."[13]

The 1872 tariff law incorporated two crucial improvements. The first attempted to put an end to variations between customshouses across the country by introducing uniform rates, regulations, and procedures. The centrifugal forces that had long dominated Mexico's political landscape and the weakness of the national government had brought about a state of affairs in which the tariff law was not always locally enforced, or in which a regional boss was able to impose his own tariff law.[14] For example, during the late 1850s the so-called "tarifa Cevallos" was in force in Veracruz and (in a slightly different version) in the Pacific customshouses, while in the Northeast the "Vidaurri tariff" applied. In general, "there were two tariff laws; the official one and a private one, the latter depending on the negotiations among private parties."[15] Moreover, the sole fact that in many cases import duties were charged as a percentage of the price of imports in the local market (*aforo*) implied considerable diversity in the duties charged by different customshouses.[16] The new tariff law was an improvement in that it established specific duties for a much wider range of products, eliminated exceptions, and set a uniform ad valorem duty of 55 percent of market value for goods not included in the tariff list.[17] At the same time, however, these changes, which were intended to achieve nationwide consistency, often caused a significant increase in duties compared to amounts previously paid.[18] On the other hand, some other innovations of the 1872 *Arancel* (tariff law) represented a net improvement of the existing situation, such as adoption of the metric system and the establishment of uniform import procedures.

The creation of a standardized institutional framework to regulate foreign trade can certainly be understood as a part of the liberal view that tried to eliminate privileges and avoid differential treatment for particular groups, and that considered all individuals to be equal before the law.[19] However, the law established restrictive and burdensome directives and inflicted severe punishments not only for major illegal practices such as smuggling, but also for less serious faults committed in the course of normal customs operations. It was as though the government was trying to use stringent legislation to compensate for its inability to check smuggling and watch over the country's territory. For these reasons, the enactment of the 1872 tariff law brought no degree of liberalization to traditionally restrictive practices beyond a basic principle of nominal equality.

In fact, the impetus toward nationwide consistency in international trade faced clear limits, which the government of the time was not able to overcome. A good example was the regime's inability to enforce the regulation contained in the 1872 tariff law that no duties could be levied on imported merchandise by state and municipal authorities. This was no more than the corollary to the constitutional principle that only the national government could levy taxes on foreign trade. However, such a simple notion faced the strong opposition of state governments, which had long profited from transit and consumption duties on imports. It was not long (May 1872) until this prescription was eliminated from the legislation and a 6 percent consumption duty on foreign goods was introduced in Mexico City and the territory of Baja California, implicitly suggesting that state governments were authorized to proceed in the same way. It was only in 1886 that Congress limited the consumption duties that could be levied by state governments, setting them at a maximum of 5 percent of import duties.[20]

The second significant improvement of the 1872 tariff law was that it simplified the payment of customs duties by combining what had been divided into import duties and additional duties. In the introductory section of the arancel, Treasury Minister Matías Romero explained that the executive branch did not find it appropriate to introduce any radical change in rates with respect to the 1856 tariff.[21] Later on his successor, Francisco Mejía, admitted that such an attempt had been made but had encountered strong opposition in Congress.[22] Apparently, the only liberalizing measure in regard to tariffs therefore consisted of procedural simplification; instead of several taxes, some of them at different places, a single import duty was to be paid. This was a rather limited achievement for a liberal regime, particularly in view of the liberal convictions of the author of the tariff law.

The extent to which prevailing import duties were modified by this simplification was a subject for discussion at the time. According to Romero's own estimates in the introduction to the law, by combining customs duties, the total of fees and duties was reduced by 12 percent. However, the perception of merchants was that the operation actually produced a slight increase in total import duties. Apparently their complaints were well founded, since only five months later the government decreed an overall 10 percent reduction to the tariff.[23] It is hard to estimate to what extent duties were in fact changed by the 1872 tariff law, in particular because quantitative information for the years before 1870 is scarce and fragmentary. According to some estimates, in the five decades after Independence the average tariff rate was about 50 percent of the value of imports.[24] If this is accurate, the reduction was, in fact, small or even nil. Calculated on Mexican official import trade figures, the average tariff was 52 percent between 1872 and 1874, in spite of the 10 percent overall reduction implemented by Congress in 1872.[25] Using alternative estimates of import figures, the overall level of protection amounted to 49 percent of the total value of imports in 1870 and to 47 percent in the following three years.[26] It was not a substantial change for a liberal regime.

In any event, no one at the time seemed to believe that the 1872 *Ordenanza* was as liberal as had been hoped. Treasury Minister Francisco Mejía promised on more than one occasion that it was soon to be reformed "in an entirely liberal direction, as is appropriate for our institutions."[27] Far from doing that, in 1875 the government decreed the full application of the 1872 tariff (thus canceling the 10 percent discount granted in 1872), in order to deal with the "disturbances to the peace" in some states.[28] Although the government justified the increase in import duties as an emergency measure, it remained in force until a new tariff law was issued in 1880. Reality was harsh, indeed.

In 1878 the government completed a study of the 1872 *Arancel* in preparation for its reform. In the resulting document, the Treasury Ministry explained some of the most serious shortcomings of the *ordenanza*, and the reasons why they were so difficult to remedy.[29] The main flaw of the 1872 tariff law was that it basically adopted in their entirety import duties originally established in 1856, without regard to changes in prices that had taken place since then. As prices for manufactured products were generally declining in the international market, the actual ad valorem charged on most products could only have risen considerably since that year. The document provided a list of products for which ad valorem rates were calculated using the specific duties in force and 1878 production prices. Although for some items the ad valorem equivalent was very low, particularly among groceries and wines, for a majority of the most heavily traded items it was well above what could be considered a reasonable level of protection. As an example, the rate was 145 percent for two of the most important types of cotton manufactures imported into the country, and as high as 250 percent of the production cost for some specific items.[30]

The document accepted that since high import duties were the main incentive for smuggling, it could be argued that a significant reduction in duties would actually be beneficial to the Treasury because of the considerable increase in legal imports that would follow. Besides, in the opinion of merchants, the protection granted by those duties was so high as to make cotton manufacturing in Mexico an extremely lucrative business. The government was aware that a reduction in duties would not ruin the industry, "but only reduce its profits."[31] Why, then, was it so difficult to institute reform in a more liberal direction? The document took a detour before answering this question. First, it argued, experience had shown that a reduction in import duties did not necessarily lead to an increase in revenues. Such a course of action had been followed for a brief period in 1842, and abandoned quickly in 1843.[32] In any event, the government had limited room for experimentation, as the document made clear:

If the Mexican Treasury were not burdened by troubles, if it could cope without a part of its income for a time and not thereby incur peril; if it could experiment without the risk of serious upset, then a reduction in certain imported articles would already have been decreed. But the situation is so hazardous that the failure of such an experiment would seriously compromise the peace and the future of our Republic. In the face of such grave danger, it would be foolhardy to put to the test any levies in whose success we could not fully confide.[33]

Here the document came finally to the point; the real (and only) reason the government could not implement a liberal reform to the tariff was that it could not do without the income from import duties. The modest domestic textile industry may well have needed protection to survive, but cotton textile imports were more important, because they alone provided the government with 60 percent of the annual total import revenue collected between 1872 and 1875. In fact, the government was more willing to reduce subsidies to the textile industry by imposing a small tax on textile factories, as it actually did, than by reducing duties on textile imports.[34]

The financial needs of the Mexican government were not new, nor was the excessive reliance upon import duties to meet these needs. In 1869, Matías Romero questioned the wisdom of depending so heavily on customs revenue and stressed the need to seek alternative sources of income:

> Customs duties are the basis of our national income; its proceeds are equivalent to two thirds of our total income. This is the system which has been in place almost without exception since Independence, and in the judgment of the Executive, one which it would be in the national interest to change, albeit gradually, and to the extent possible.[35]

However, Romero observed that he himself did not dare propose that import duties should be "attacked," because without them "functioning of the administration would not be possible."[36]

The argument still held ten years later. On several occasions, the fiscal priorities of the government, hidden beneath supposedly protectionist motives, were exposed. A few examples may serve to illustrate the point. In the late 1870s, Congress raised the duties on imports of raw cotton. After a bitter debate about the conflicting interests of cotton growers and textile manufacturers, the decisive argument was that "the distressed situation of the Treasury being evident, [the proposed increase] can do no less than alleviate it . . ."[37] In the same years, a proposal for duty-free importation of paper for printing was discussed in the chamber of deputies. During the debate it was admitted that this was hardly a case for industrial protection, since the only "industry" that could be damaged by the measure was very small and unable to supply the domestic demand. Furthermore, there was an apparent consensus that the proposed measure would yield important benefits to the newspaper and publishing industry. Finally, although an ad valorem duty of almost 60 percent was paid on imported printing paper, it provided the government with less than ten thousand pesos of yearly revenue. After a long debate about such a trivial issue, the same time-honored reasoning prevailed. As Congressman Joaquín Alcalde put it, all the arguments were nothing but speculation about the possible effects of adopting the measure; the only certain outcome was the reduction in income that it would cause an unbalanced Treasury. Congress rejected the project, tacitly affirming that the government could not afford to do without ten thousand pesos per year.[38]

In summary, the first tariff law of the liberal regime was far from what could be considered a "liberal" trade policy. It might be defined as protectionist, inasmuch as it was quite restrictive, included high duties under the pretext of protectionist motives, and did in fact create a substantial shelter for a small sector of the economy. One would wonder, however, to what extent it was protectionist in the original meaning of the term—namely, a tariff that is primarily designed to promote the development of a viable domestic industry through the aid of a reasonable temporary barrier to competing imports.[39] Apart from the strong fiscal motivation of the tariff (and probably because of it), the 1872 *Arancel* had some features that were not consistent with a coherent policy of industrial protection.[40] First, it levied high duties on a broad range of imports that did not compete with domestic production, or that competed with incipient activities that could hardly be defined as more than handicrafts.[41] Second, in the case of competing imports, the tariff did not calculate what amount of protection would be needed to stimulate domestic production without compromising efficient long-term development. Third, it imposed duties on raw materials as well as on finished products, reducing the effective protection granted to domestic industries.[42] Fourth, it did not provide for the gradual decline in tariffs that would have been necessary to create both protection for current production and an incentive to improve technology. Nonetheless, if one considers that the 1872 tariff law tried to modernize the old ordenanzas by eliminating prohibitions, standardizing fees, adopting a uniform system of measures, and establishing nationwide regulations and procedures, it should be acknowledged that there was some liberalizing intention in it, perhaps waiting for a more propitious moment to be fully expressed. In the meantime, it could be suggested that the 1872 tariff law represented little more than the old protectionism, perhaps wearing slightly more liberal clothes.

A STEP BACKWARDS: THE REINFORCEMENT OF PROTECTIONISM IN THE 1880S

During the 1880s, the Mexican government faced two important new challenges. Trying to recover the international credit of the country, the Porfirio Díaz administration undertook a reorganization of the external debt and began its repayment again after fifty years of virtual default. Second, the government granted the first and most important concessions for railroad construction, which placed the laying of Mexico's main railroad lines in the hands of foreign (mostly U.S.) companies. The railroad contracts affected public finances in two ways: first, because they included a monetary subsidy per kilometer built, and second, because they granted duty-free importation to all inputs and capital goods related to railroad construction. The financial needs of the government would therefore rise considerably, while foreign investment in the railroads would yield little immediate benefit to the Treasury in the form of import duties.[43]

How was the Mexican government, traditionally short of money to cover existing administrative spending, supposed to meet these new commitments? It was true that since the mid 1870s, the government had begun to develop new sources of internal revenue that provided it with an increasing income. In 1875 the "stamp tax," as it was called, had been created to replace the old *papel sellado* (stamped paper), and by 1879 it was providing 18 percent of government revenue at 3.8 million pesos per year.[44] During the 1880s the stamp tax became in fact the most important instrument in the government's strategy to create a more flexible taxation system, and its scope was progressively broadened through the inclusion of articles formerly exempted.[45] As a result, revenue from this source grew rapidly throughout the decade, amounting to 9.5 million pesos by 1889.[46] However, this gradual turn to domestic revenue sources would only yield its fruits in the mid-term, and could only partially contribute to meeting the immediate needs of the government. For the time being, import duties were still by far the main source of public revenue, providing about 50 percent of total income between 1880 and 1883. For this reason, it is no wonder that they became the main tool in the government's efforts to increase the resources available to it.

Hence, both the stamp tax and the tariff played crucial roles in the government's fiscal strategy during the 1880s. In the shaping of this strategy, decision-making was divided between the legislative and the executive branches. The chamber of deputies was in charge of discussing and approving the yearly budget, and some changes in taxes and duties were often introduced by this means.[47] However, the design of the tariff law as such was progressively left in the hands of the executive branch, thanks to the authorizations contained in the annual income laws enacted by Congress. During the 1870s, these authorizations were provisional and ad hoc, as the income laws empowered the executive to modify the existing tariff law, and then to combine the reforms in a single piece of legislation. This gave way to the 1880 tariff law, issued by the executive. Following this, during the early 1880s, Congress authorized the executive to modify particular aspects of the tariff law, as those related to the introduction of goods by railroad.[48] As soon as Porfirio Díaz returned to power in 1884, Congress gave him a "vote of confidence" to modify the tax system, in view of the urgent need to reorganize the public treasury.[49] Using these powers, the government issued a new tariff law in 1885. Then, starting in 1886, the Treasury Committee of the chamber of deputies claimed not to have enough time to analyze such complex matters as "the most important tax laws." Thus, it considered that, having granted the executive ample powers to deal with those issues, "there was nothing more natural" than to leave the study of the matter in its hands.[50] Because the income law included broad authorization for the executive to reform the tariff annually, its design became to a large extent the province of the executive branch.[51] In fact, all the ordenanzas and any reforms to them enacted during these decades were decreed by the executive, not by Congress.[52] Nevertheless, although Congress surrendered the discussion of trade policy in practice, it exercised the power to affect import duties through the income law.

During the 1880s, the Mexican government issued three tariff laws. The first, in 1880, was enacted only for the purpose of consolidating reforms made since 1872. A new arancel was issued in 1885, to be replaced by another in 1887. The ephemeral nature of these laws may be explained as the result of the need to adapt to the rapid, major changes that Mexico's international trade was undergoing at the time. Europe's traditional importance to Mexico was being seriously challenged by the United States, and the emergence of a new main partner brought about changes in routes and ports of entry for Mexico's import trade. Moreover, as these events were taking place, the main railroad lines were being built in Mexico, which in itself meant significant changes in foreign trade operations. The existence of railroads dramatically increased the volume of goods that could be introduced into the country, creating new challenges and placing higher demands on the customs administration. Finally, the whole process was accompanied by significant change in the composition of Mexico's imports. The traditional basket made up largely of textiles and luxuries began to include an increasing proportion of railroad equipment, coal, mining machinery, and other capital goods. Moreover, a considerable share of these new articles was imported free of duty, due to the exemptions granted by the government for railroad construction. Some indicators of these changes based on the available Mexican figures have been summarized in table 11.2.

As far as can be deduced from legislation enacted during the 1880s, the government attempted to obtain more resources from imports by three principal means: tariff adjustments, stricter regulation, and stronger control over the national territory. Tariffs during the early 1880s were subjected to overall increases decreed by Congress through the annual income law, and the 1885 *Ordenanza* further increased import duties for a wide range of products.[53] This tariff generated a strong reaction among merchants and a sector of the press, a response that led to the enactment of a new arancel in 1887.

Table 11.2. Changes in Mexico's Import Trade: Some Indicators, 1874–1889

	(percentages)		
	1874	*1885*	*1889*
Origin of imports			
United States	27	42	56
Europe	73	58	44
Port of entrance			
Northern border	14	26	44
All other	86	74	56
Import basket:*			
1. textiles and groceries	70	57	33
2. inputs, fuels, and capital goods	21	33	55
3. all other	9	10	12
Fiscal classification			
Duty-free imports	15	24	41
Dutiable imports	85	76	59

*This is a rough distribution of imports based upon the official division into fiscal categories. It assumes that all duty free importations belong to the second group (inputs, fuels, and capital goods).

Sources: Own elaboration based upon the information contained in: *Noticia,* 1880; *Noticias de las mercancías importadas en los dos primeros semestres de los años fiscales de 1884 a 1885 y 1885 a 1886. Formadas bajo la dirección de J. Stávoli,* Mexico, 1888; *Importaciones 1889 a 1890. Primer semestre-año fiscal. Noticias formadas bajo la dirección de Javier Stávoli,* México, 1892.

Although some duties were reduced by this law, ad valorem protection for certain goods continued to be extremely high, to the point that some scholars have considered the Mexican tariffs of the 1880s "among the highest in the world."[54] In addition to a heavier tariff burden, the government implemented other measures in an attempt to check smuggling. First, it enacted stricter legislation, in which a rigid regulatory framework was accompanied by severe punishments for illegal practices. Then, in 1885, it created a fiscal police, the *Gendarmería Fiscal,* in order to increase surveillance. This armed corps had a widespread presence in northern Mexico, and enjoyed ample powers to chase and apprehend smugglers. By these means, the government achieved to some extent its purpose of controlling smuggling and increasing resources deriving from imports, but it came at the cost of making import operations more burdensome and costly. These changes were significant.

In 1880 the budget committee of the chamber of deputies proposed a 10 percent overall reduction in tariffs for the 1880–1881 fiscal year. It was not a radical proposal, as a 10 percent discount had already applied for some years in the 1870s, and its lifting in 1875 had been justified as a temporary measure. However, the proposal was rejected on the grounds that the government had just been authorized to subsidize railroad construction, and thus could not be deprived of part of its already scarce financial resources.[55] Later that year the executive issued a new arancel with the main purpose of combining the various partial reforms enacted within the previous decade into a single piece of legislation, which included slight increases in duties charged on some cotton articles and other particular items.[56] One year later a more significant increase in duties was implemented with the approval of a "*derecho de bulto*" or bulk duty by Congress. The chamber of deputies budget committee proposed this new duty together with other tax increases as part of the income law for 1881–1882. This particular duty consisted of an extra payment of 50 to 100 cents per hundred kilos of merchandise imported, and was defended as a minor and harmless tax that would hardly be resented by importers. The novel aspect was that, with the exception of railroad companies, which enjoyed duty-free importation, this tax was to be charged even on duty-free imports such as machinery and coal. Again, the argument for approving such an increase was, as Congressman Manuel Payno put it, the need to face "inescapable [. . .] commitments," as those arising from the railroad contracts.[57]

This was a wholly fiscal duty aimed explicitly at reducing the deficit incurred by the government. It affected bulk commodities far more than costly goods, and thus left practically intact the burden on luxury merchandise while reducing the effective protection granted to manufacturing. Apparently its proponents were well aware of the changes in trade composition that were taking place, and wished to charge a somewhat concealed import duty on cheap products and on goods on the duty-free list. It is difficult to estimate the impact of this duty on actual import values, because the official records of imports for these years are scarce and fragmentary, and those that exist do not contain complete information on the weight of articles imported. However, contrary to what might be expected, the impact was not insignificant for certain goods with a high weight-to-value ratio, as may be deduced from estimates made for purely illustrative purposes in table 11.3.

The estimates shown in table 11.3 of the impact of the bulk duty are purely hypothetical, because they are based on import data from a year in which that duty no longer existed. However, it gives an idea of the practical implication of this apparently innocuous tax. The table provides a lower-bound estimate, assuming a uniform duty of 50 cents per 100 kg. Imports that were officially duty-free were burdened by this tax with an ad valorem of between 14 and 70 percent of their invoice value, while some bulky dutiable imports bore an additional load of about 20 percent, which added to the regular import duties established by the tariff. Had this duty still been in force in 1889, it would have yielded revenues of at least 3.5 million pesos to the government, or 14 percent more than the actual import revenues that year.

Apparently the bulk duty was created as a temporary device to produce an immediate increase in import revenues while the new tariff law was being prepared. It remained in force during the next fiscal year, although some goods were then excluded: plows, mercury, bricks, cotton seed, tobacco, and coffee.[58] As the studies for reforming the arancel took longer than expected,

Table 11.3. Hypothetical Impact of the "Derecho de Bulto" of Bulk Duty*
(Calculated upon 1889–1890 import values. Selected products)

	a Weight	b Invoice Value	c Import Duties	d Bulk Duty	e % c:b	f % d:b
Duty-free imports						
barbed wire	15,395,038	176,206	0	76,975	0	44
iron or plumb pipes	12,027,785	333,311	0	60,139	0	18
coal	207,517,765	1,486,313	0	1,037,589	0	70
construction wood	96,239,695	2,375,683	0	481,198	0	20
machinery	81,767,114	3,019,776	0	408,836	0	14
Dutiable imports						
wheat flour	3,394,622	230,987	373,408	16,973	162	7
common bricks	4,126,933	57,025	7,428	20,635	13	36
cast iron	4,676,589	224,492	233,829	23,383	104	10

*Lower-bound estimate, assuming a uniform duty of 50 cents per 100kg weight
Source: Estimated from real imports according to *Importaciones*, 1892, pp. 64–126.

this type of compensatory mechanism appeared again in the following two years. In 1882 Congress decreed the duty-free exportation of gold and silver, but established a compensatory surcharge of 2 percent on import duties.[59] The latter were further increased by a 5 percent overall raise decreed in 1883.[60]

The growth in both imports and duties affected the government's resources positively; import revenues grew by one third (from 12 to 18 million pesos) between 1879–1880 and 1882–1883. However, public spending was growing even faster; railroad subsidies alone consumed 12 million pesos in 1882–1883.[61] In 1884, the Treasury Ministry announced that railroad subsidies and the duty-free importation granted to railroad companies had become "the most serious obstacle to functioning of the public credit." According to the Treasury report, about 80 percent of the total revenue collected at customshouses was used for payment of railroad subsidies, the National Bank subsidy, and the public debt.[62] Thus, in spite of expanding revenues, the budget could not be balanced. This situation helped exacerbate the protectionist trend already observed at the beginning of the decade, leading to the enactment of the 1885 tariff law.[63] The new ordenanza reduced the number of duty-free items from sixty-six to twenty-one, and instituted a considerable increase in the specific duties for a broad range of products. The Mexico City *Cámara de Comercio* (Chamber of Commerce) considered the duties imposed on some articles "extremely high," and many newspapers claimed that they were so damaging to commercial activity that they would in practice cancel out the beneficial impact of railroads.[64] In the chamber of deputies some congressmen responded vigorously to the law; Francisco Bulnes offered bitter criticisms against what he considered disproportionate rates for some articles, while Manuel Sánchez Facio proposed an entirely new and far more liberal tariff law. In his proposal, most duties were 40 to 50 percent lower than those in force, and regulations and procedures were considerably less demanding than those prescribed by the 1885 *Arancel*. Although there is no evidence that this proposal had even been considered for discussion, it made clear the strongly restrictive nature of the 1885 *Ordenanza*.[65] Apparently as a reaction to this widespread criticism, the government issued a new tariff law in 1887, which broadened the duty-free list to sixty-eight items and reduced to some extent duties charged on the more sensitive items.[66] The following table provides an overall picture of the changes in ad valorem duties for some important categories during the 1870s and 1880s.

Table 11.4 illustrates the high levels of protection that affected some of the most traded groups of products while the 1885 tariff law was in force. It also makes clear that despite the reduction in duties brought about by the 1887 tariff, in most cases duties were considerably higher in the late 1880s than they had been during the 1870s. The strengthening of protectionism during the 1880s has often been ignored in the literature because it has been

Table 11.4. Implicit ad valorem duty according to the fiscal classification of imports 1874, 1885, 1889.

(Selected fiscal groups)	1874	1885	1889
textiles (overall)	76	126	106
groceries	69	85	78
crystal and glass	77	106	111
drugs and chemicals	82	67	60

Note: In the Mexican official records for 1885 and 1889 there is no explicit mention of the currency in which import values are recorded. Following qualitative sources, ad valorem equivalents are here calculated assuming that import values were recorded in pesos.

Sources: *Noticia*, 1880, passim; *Memoria [1891–92]*, 1892, p. 53; *Importaciones*, 1892, pp. 247–249.

concealed by a particular feature of Mexico's foreign trade during these years, namely, the exceptionally large share of imports that were introduced free of duty. The estimates presented in figure 11.1, based on official data, illustrate the situation.

As the figure shows, during the 1870s most of Mexico's imports were subject to duty. For this reason, the ratio of import duties to total imports was similar to that of import duties to dutiable imports (there was only a 10 percent difference between them). It means that the tariff burden was fairly evenly distributed across total import trade. In contrast, in the late 1880s about 40 percent of imports were introduced free of duty, and thus import duties were paid on only 60 percent of import trade. For this reason, the decline in overall tariff burden is rather misleading, as duties paid on dutiable imports were on the average 13 percent higher than in the 1870s.

Together with a more protective tariff policy, during the 1880s the government produced a more restrictive set of regulations for foreign trade operations.[67] The regulatory part of the tariff law was already burdensome in the 1872 *Ordenanza*, as it contained more detailed rules for international trade than previous *aranceles*. It included very specific instructions for the procedures to be followed by exporters, consuls, ship captains, and importers. Each procedure required writing out up to five documents in identical originals, containing precise, detailed information about the merchandise. The information requested consisted essentially of the characteristics of the cargo; the number and weight of packages; and for each article contained in the packages, its trademark, material, class, number, weight, length, cost, and fiscal classification. In addition, each procedure involved the payment of some kind of duty, and most of them also required the cargo to be inspected by the corresponding official. All tariff laws enacted during this period prescribed monetary penalties for smuggling, substitution in quality or quantity, fraud, and for minor faults, such as inaccurate description of the imported goods.

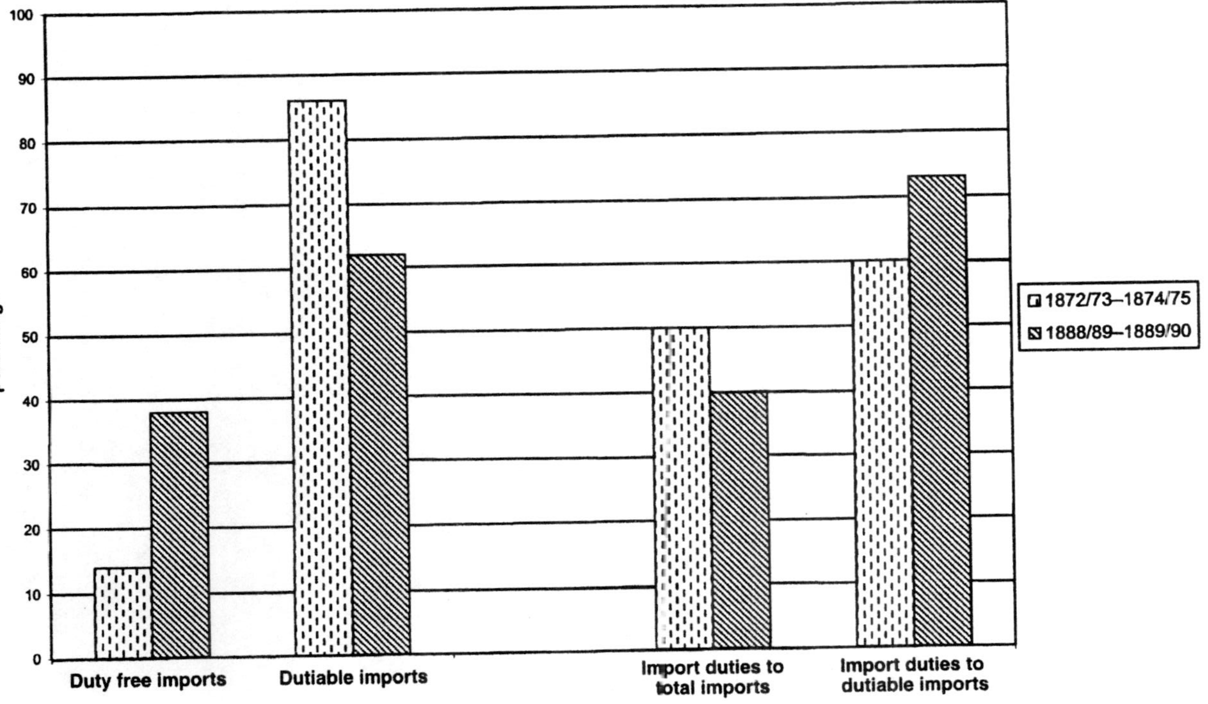

Figure 11.1. Duty-free/Dutiable Imports and the Average Height of the Tariff Barrier (average for the fiscal years 1872–1874 and 1888–1889)

Sources: *Noticia*, 1880; *Importaciones*, 1892; Ministerio de Fomento, *Boletín semestral de la estadística de la República Mexicana, a cargo del Dr. Antonio Peñafiel*, Núm. 4, México, 1889.

Penalties ranged from confiscation (in the case of contraband), double or triple duties for substitution, to lesser fines for minor faults. Finally, in order to avoid corruption within the customs administration, the 1872 tariff law contained a provision by which, after paying duties owed to the Treasury, the proceeds obtained from fines and confiscation would be distributed among customs employees.

This already troublesome regulation was tightened during the 1880s by several measures. Stricter procedural guidelines were implemented for customs declarations and clearance,[68] and also for particular aspects of import operations such as storage, rail transport, and arrival of ships at more than one port. Regarding the latter, the law prescribed that ship captains had to present a document in duplicate bearing details of the entire cargo (even the part not destined for Mexico) to Mexican customs, including weight, trademarks, and characteristics of each package.[69] In addition, the actual introduction of goods into Mexico after customs revision had been successfully passed was subject to a rigid set of controls; the cargo had to be sealed and accompanied by an official document throughout its journey, and this document had to be returned to the customshouse within a certain period of time after being checked at the final destination; moreover, the cargo could be inspected any number of times by tax authorities during its journey. The number of handwritten documents that had to be provided both by merchants and customs officials was increased, and strict rules were established as to how they should be written. The customs manager at Paso del Norte noted how absurd this prescription was in a letter to the treasury minister in 1886:

> Article 132 stipulates that the consignee provide a list in duplicate of the brands, countermarks, and number of bundles contained in his shipping application. If he is to be guided literally by this instruction, each import application forwarded by the consignee, even if it derives from a single invoice, and corresponds to a single record, will generate two lists. For example, if one invoice gives rise to twenty-five applications, the governor's office will require fifty lists and twenty-five cards, a task which will occupy not inconsiderable time, . . . with unwieldy results.[70]

The legislation also became more punitive, both by increasing the number of practices subject to penalization and by raising penalties for nearly all infractions. The most important change was that along with the economic sanctions already in force, smuggling in every form was now punished by imprisonment for periods ranging from two months to five years, depending on the gravity of the crime.[71] This included all the individuals involved in an act of smuggling, from the actual perpetrators to accomplices and customs officials.[72] As for monetary penalties, double and triple duties applied to undeclared goods, and double duties for inaccurate declarations in which the discrepancy exceeded 3 percent of the true amount imported. This 3 percent tolerance was eliminated in the 1885 tariff law, which instead charged double duties for what merchants considered "insignificant differences" that might be found in the inspection of goods.[73] Moreover, fines were instituted for a large variety of minor or inadvertent faults. Double duties applied if the consular invoice did not give enough detail about the merchandise to be imported; almost any amendment to customs declarations was subject to fines that ranged from 10 percent to double the regular amount of import duties. Simple "ambiguities" in the exporters' invoices, as well as erasures or rubbing out in documents provided by them or by consuls, ship captains, or importers, were subject to some sort of fine.

There is little doubt that this set of regulations was in itself onerous and that the penalties it inflicted were far too strict. However, the practice of distributing the yields of this punitive system among customs officials made it even more perverse. The commercial press published numerous complaints about the dubious role played by customs officials, who were at the same time both judges and participants, and about a system that involved severe penalties for honest merchants but no penalization whatsoever of customs employees who abused their powers. According to these opinions, proceeds from fines and confiscations at times represented double or even triple the regular salary of a customs official. Although such claims are hard to corroborate, there is evidence that in the late 1880s and early 1890s fines did in fact represent a regular and non-negligible source of personal income, particularly for mid- and top-ranked customs officials. Moreover, the evidence indicates that many of these fines arose from what could be considered minor faults, or from subjective judgments about the specific quality of the merchandise imported.[74]

It is not difficult to understand how this regulatory system might have affected the import business, delaying the dispatch of goods at customs, increasing costs and making them less predictable, and forcing merchants to hire brokers who were experts in the intricacies of the law. In fact, despite the rising tax burden, most of the grievances expressed by merchants during the 1880s were directed against the burdensome and even absurd practices prescribed by the law. Merchants from various parts of the country joined together in the Mexico City *Cámara de Comercio* to address a letter to President Díaz requesting a reform of the 1885 tariff law. They summed up their claims against it in the following words:

> The practical difficulties, at times insurmountable, arise daily at border and seaport customs posts. A number of foreign manufacturers and producers already demur at shipping directly to Mexico. Endless fines are levied on hones importers. There are ceaseless obstacles, nuisances, delays of every kind, explanatory directives from the Treasury Department . . .

For these reasons, the letter continued, the business community unanimously agreed on "the indispensable need to [undertake] a vigorous, radical reform of the ordenanza" in order to achieve the following aims: "moderate rates, fair and simple regulations, and a salary increase for customs employees, who must cease to profit by the fines that are imposed upon trade."[75] Even the *Semana Mercantil*, a newspaper that usually favored protectionism and opposed constant changes in the tariff, found the 1885 tariff law extremely restrictive. As stated in the preface of the law, "an exaggerated fear of smuggling has prevailed, and from it have arisen the excessive precautions and useless hindrances that are so abundant in the regulation, which it is prudent to eliminate, leaving only those prescripts that are a true safeguard of fiscal interests."[76] However, institutional reform was a much more complex task than tariff reform. Thus, whereas the government was able to change some rates in a more liberal direction in the following several years, it took longer to begin to liberalize the regulatory aspects of Mexico's international trade.

Finally, as a part of its strategy against smuggling, the federal government carried out one further step. The *Gendarmería Fiscal*, organized in 1885, consolidated a corps of rural forces, military colonial squadrons, and the tax police. The Gendarmería Fiscal was an armed corps with a widespread presence in northern Mexico and a broad mandate to watch over its territory, inspect cargo transported by any means, and to pursue and apprehend smugglers. It appears to have been fairly successful in controlling smuggling, as reported by the authorities and acknowledged by the public.[77] According to the government, the combined effect of stricter regulation and tighter policing nearly eliminated smuggling by the early 1890s.

During the 1880s several factors contributed to intensify restrictive policies and delay the implementation of a more liberal view in international trade. The expanding financial needs of the government, compounded by a still incipient internal revenue system, forced it to rely largely on import duties to keep its revenues growing. On the other hand, seized by the idea that smuggling was diverting much-needed resources, the administration created a strict body of regulations and punishments to deter illegal practices of every sort. In the government's view, the efficiency of this regulatory framework was guaranteed by the distribution of its yields among customs employees and by the creation of an armed corps that considerably enhanced the surveillance capabilities of the state. Presumably, this protective system had a negative impact on the development of foreign trade and on the economy as a whole. Such an impact, however, is hard to measure and even to perceive, however, since both Mexico's economy and its international trade continued to grow during the 1880s under the powerful stimulus created by the beginning of railroad expansion and foreign investment. On the other hand, in the short term the government saw increased revenues,[78] and industrial entrepreneurs benefited from the rents generated under the shelter of protection.

TARIFF AND REGULATORY LIBERALIZATION IN THE 1890S

A significant increase in import trade due to foreign investment and domestic economic development, successful diversification of revenue sources, and the consolidation of the Porfirian administration allowed the government to begin a progressive liberalization of trade policy during the last decade of the century. With regard to import duties, the decision to reduce legislated tariffs also may have been fostered by the continuing depreciation of the Mexican peso, which rendered imports more costly as they were priced in gold.[79] As for relaxation of regulations and procedures, the main factor was probably the success in checking smuggling and increased confidence of the administration in its own strength and its material ability to enforce the law.

The new tariff law enacted in 1891 was clearly more liberal than its predecessors.[80] It expanded the duty-free list to 115 items, including parts and machinery, wire and a number of iron and steel goods, agricultural and mining implements, bulky construction materials, fuels, certain chemicals, and other inputs to industrial activities. Furthermore, although changes in fiscal classification prevent a systematic comparison with previous tariffs, it is apparent that most of the items included in the dutiable list were affected by reductions in duties. However, at the same time that liberalization was being introduced in Mexico, a protectionist tariff was enacted in the United States. The McKinley tariff imposed high duties on, among other products, ores with lead content, one of Mexico's most rapidly growing exports to that country.[81] In retaliation against the policy, several reforms were made to Mexican tariffs during the next several years, reducing considerably the duty-free list and imposing small, purely fiscal duties on machinery, wire and iron goods, agricultural implements, and chemical products.[82] With rather more protectionist motives, duties were raised on tobacco goods, jute rope and sacking, and dynamite. In contrast, further reductions in duties were introduced for some animal products, raw wool, and some cotton goods.[83] In the balance, and despite a partial reconsideration of the liberalizing turn, the results were consistent and unambiguous; the average level of the tariff barrier was significantly reduced in the 1890s in comparison to levels in the previous decade, and the tax burden was more evenly distributed across the entire import trade. Figure 11.2 illustrates these changes, showing the evolution of the tariff barrier between 1870 and 1900.

The figure shows two different measures of the average tariff level; the ratio of duties to the total value of imports and that of duties to the value of dutiable imports. Since there is no complete official record of the yearly value of imports before 1892, the first ratio was calculated on estimated trade values.[84] Although some of the annual figures may not be exact, together they give an accurate picture of changes in trade throughout the period, and thus

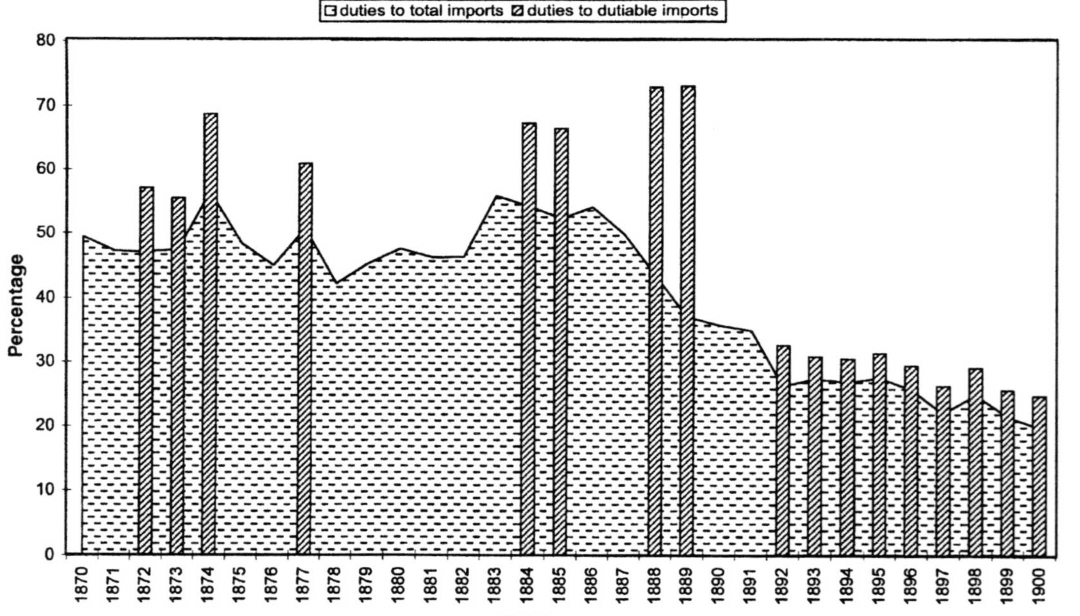

Figure 11.2.   The Average Height of the Tariff: 1870–1900

Note: The ratio of duties to total imports was calculated upon the new yearly series of import values estimated in Kuntz Ficker, "Nuevas series," cuadro 2. The percentage of duties to dutiable imports was calculated upon official values. Since the official figures of duties collected vary from one source to another, both series should be considered as approximate.

Sources: *Noticia*, 1880; *Noticias*, 1888; *Importaciones*, 1892; *Boletín de Estadística Fiscal* [1893–1900], México, 1895–1901; *Comercio exterior y navegación* [1898–99], México, 1901.

of the trend followed by the tariff barrier as well. The second ratio can only be calculated for those years in which official figures of dutiable imports are available. Despite these limitations, some significant features of Mexico's protection levels emerge clearly from the figure. First, a declining trend in the ratio of duties to total import values appeared in the late 1880s, reached its lowest point in the early 1890s, and consolidated during that decade. Second, and more important, the percentage of duties levied on dutiable imports fell considerably in 1892 compared to any of the previous years. This happened even though the percentage of imports introduced free of duty was very similar to that in the 1870s (about 15 percent), and thus it must have been the result of an across-the-board reduction in rates within the dutiable list. By any of these two standards, it seems clear that during the 1890s the average level of the tariff barrier was considerably lower than it had been since the 1870s, perhaps even the lowest reached by Mexico in its history as an independent nation.

The importance of this liberalizing turn should not be underestimated, particularly in view of the strengthening of protectionism that had characterized the previous decade. However, neither should the significance of this new stance in Mexico's trade policy veil the fact that, even then, liberalization was partial and moderate. In the early 1890s Matías Romero expressed this opinion during his last term as secretary of the treasury, stating that under the special circumstances of Mexico, the adoption of an "enlightened protectionism" was understandable and justifiable.[85] Later on, he declared more frankly that he was not convinced of the practical virtues of protectionism, but understood why such a system had come to predominate in Mexico and why it was so hard to eliminate. In fact, even in the late 1890s, when the tariff had been significantly reduced by Mexican standards, Romero highlighted its protective nature:

> Our tariff is a highly protective one [. . .] The causes which have induced such a high tariff are twofold; first, that, in great measure, protectionist ideas have prevailed; secondly, and especially, the need for revenue, and the idea that the higher the rate of duties, the larger the revenue collected [. . .] The protectionist policy in Mexico has been so deeply rooted that although I incline to freer trade, and I have been three times at the head of the Treasury Department [. . .], I was never able to modify that policy substantially, because the condition of the Treasury was so precarious, that [. . .] a great reduction of an insufficient revenue [. . .] would have brought about disastrous results.[86]

In summary, it is apparent that some liberalization was taking place in tariff policy, and that this meant an important departure from the traditionally restrictive stance of the Mexican government. The result was not, however, the embracing of a liberal trade policy, if this is understood as the implementation of low tariffs across the board with purely fiscal purposes and minimal public interference in trade. The process would be better described by saying that during the 1890s the government exercised increased room to maneuver, broadening the definition of trade policy. Under the new conditions, the administration was able to implement a policy that was less constrained by its own fiscal needs and more informed by development issues.[87] Indiscriminate high duties, largely aimed at supplying the needs of the government, gradually gave way to a more liberal tariff with a more efficient design. The new structure of the tariff consisted of two clearly identifiable types of duties; small duties were charged on a wide range of capital goods and materials in order to provide for the fiscal needs of the administration, while a cascading system was designed to provide varying degrees of protection to selected sectors of industry.[88] It was still a protectionist policy, but for the first time in the nineteenth century, selective protection was balanced by overall reduction in the tariff burden, providing more favorable conditions for the development of foreign trade.

This moderate liberalization in the tariff policy was accompanied by a slow but significant reduction in trade barriers imposed by the regulations.[89] As smuggling was checked and the administrative capabilities of the state enhanced, the government implemented a series of measures to facilitate import operations, to simplify the clearing of goods through customs, and to reduce the controls imposed on the introduction and transport of merchandise within the country. The customs administration was reorganized more efficiently beginning in 1893 with a law that established customshouse hierarchies, jurisdictions, and staff, in a process that culminated in 1900 with the creation of the *Dirección General de Aduanas*. During the same period, import operations were simplified through reduction of some of the strictest regulations and fines. For example, deadlines and fines formerly imposed for the amendment of consular invoices were eliminated, and the obligations of ship captains and carriers were reduced. Introduction and transit of goods was facilitated in several ways. First, the rigid prescription of times and routes for transporting imported merchandise within Mexico was somewhat loosened. Second, the powers of the fiscal police were curtailed, for instance, by permitting only one inspection of cargo per journey. Moreover, the jurisdiction of this corps was progressively reduced and eventually confined to the northern border.[90] It was likely not by chance that these provisions took effect in the same years that the *alcabalas*, the old taxes levied on transit of goods from one state to another, were abolished. In any event, taken together, these measures had an important meaning; for the first time, free and uninterrupted transit of merchandise was allowed throughout Mexico and guaranteed by law. Finally, it must be pointed out that, notwithstanding these important improvements, liberalization of the tariff regulations during the 1890s was uneven and incomplete. For example, the government continued to require strict conditions and bonds for the transport of merchandise by railroads, increased the fines for substitution (in order to compensate for the reduction in fines for minor faults), and was unable to eliminate the objectionable practice of distributing proceeds collected from fines among customs employees.[91]

CONCLUDING REMARKS

In the Mexican experience, political liberalism and economic liberalization did not go hand in hand, at least as far as foreign trade is concerned. The adoption of a more liberal trade policy was delayed, as the Liberals argued, by the "special circumstances of the country." Although protectionist motives were always claimed, it seems clear that the real reason why the tariff could not be liberalized during the first decade of liberal rule was that import duties were by far the most important source of revenue for the federal government, and that a more efficient fiscal system could not be created overnight. By claiming protectionist motives, the government could justify its policies to interest groups and before public opinion; the truth was, however, that only by imposing extremely high duties upon a relatively price-inelastic basket of imports could the administration survive. The best evidence of this is perhaps the reinforcement of protectionism in the 1880s. Were there any new economic activities that deserved protection? Were there special circumstances that justified increased protection for traditional activities? Not necessarily. What is certain is that there were new and growing financial obligations that had to be met, and that despite reforms to the taxation system already underway, customs revenue was still the most important—and apparently the most flexible—source of public revenue.

On the other hand, it is obvious that even if it is not their primary purpose, high import duties do provide an umbrella under which protected activities can flourish. But it does make a difference whether the protective tariff is designed to promote economic activity. The protection granted by a policy motivated mainly by fiscal considerations seeks to set the highest duties possible to generate income, not duties optimized to protect industry without making it vulnerable in the long run. Besides, such a trade policy lacks the coherence and structure that is needed to foster industrial growth without at the same time hampering foreign trade. In fact, a policy informed by developmental motives is probably in a much better position to pursue both aims simultaneously with some degree of consistency.

Interestingly enough, the first time that Mexico adopted a sound, coherent protectionist trade policy was when foreign trade policy began to be liberalized. This could not take place until the government diversified its sources of revenue, thereby becoming less dependent on customs income to survive. Only then was it able to design a tariff policy shaped more by development goals than by stringent fiscal demands. The trade policy adopted during the

1890s was part of a broader strategy to progressively open up the Mexican economy. Consistent with this purpose, the government gradually began to ease the conditions under which foreign trade had evolved, conditions that were characteristic of a closed, traditional economy. Within the framework of this broader project, there was explicit recognition of the twofold purpose of the tariff; on the one hand, a broad list of products that paid small duties to produce revenue, while on the other, a selective group of economic activities that the government had decided (for whatever reasons) to protect. Furthermore, soon after the tariff barrier began to fall, the government began a progressive liberalization of the laws regulating foreign trade operations. This development was fully consistent with the liberal purpose of creating more scope for individual action and initiative, while restricting latitude for government intervention. Liberalization of the rules of the game was a more complex task than tariff liberalization, as it entailed numerous changes in formal and informal standards in a number of arenas. It was also difficult to implement, since it implied putting an end to old practices and vested interests *within* the customs administration, and fully reorganizing an antiquated system that had not been designed for the promotion of international trade.

The process was, of course, more complex and onerous than I have been able to portray in this first approach. Thus, in the trade policy of the 1890s not only was liberalization limited, but there were also inconsistencies and dark spots that undermined the declared intentions of the government. These were demonstrated, for instance, by the persistence of high duties for some materials, which reduced effective protection, or in the lack of a strategic view that anticipated the need to gradually reduce levels of protection in order to foster development of industrial competitivity. After all, a tariff is always an unfinished product, designed amid conflicting interests, opposing needs, and changing circumstances, rather than out of pure ideological or academic principles. It is this set of constraining forces that provides the true dimension and significance of the liberalization in trade policy that took place in the last decade of the nineteenth century.

NOTES

1. [Secretaría de Hacienda y Crédito Público], *Memoria que el Secretario de Hacienda y Crédito Público presenta al Quinto Congreso de la Unión el 16 de Setiembre de 1869, y que comprende el año fiscal de 1°. De julio de 1868 al 30 de junio de 1869* (Mexico: 1869), 21. (Hereafter a short form of reference to these reports will be used as follows: SHCP, *Memoria* [corresponding year], year of publication.)

2. *Diario de los Debates de la Cámara de Diputados. Año de 1886* (Mexico: 1888), 664. (Hereafter cited as *Diario de Debates* [corresponding year and volume], year of publication.)

3. Paolo Riguzzi, "Libre cambio y libertad económica en la experiencia liberal mexicana, 1850–1896," in Marcello Carmagnani, ed., *Constitucionalismo y orden liberal en América Latina, 1850–1920* (Torino: Otto Editore, 2000), 287–314. For comparisons with other Latin American countries see Victor Bulmer-Thomas, *The Economic History of Latin America since Independence* (Cambridge: Cambridge University Press, 1994), chapters 1, 2.

4. Although a definition of the concept is rarely to be found in the international economics literature, the criterion that underlies its use is, in my opinion, captured in the following paragraph: a liberal trade policy is "a trade policy aimed at allowing a country's residents to take part in international trade with the minimum of interference. This involves the reduction of tariffs, the relaxation or removal of quantitative trade controls, and replacement of discretionary controls by rules. [. . .] Trade policy is capable of many degrees of *dirigisme*, and liberalization of trade policy does not necessarily involve a shift to complete laissez-faire." John Black, *A Dictionary of Economics* (Oxford/New York: Oxford University Press, 1997), 269. The idea of minimal government interference as essential to a free-trade policy is generally present throughout the literature, although its contents may vary. See, for instance, Miltiades Chacholiades, *Economía internacional*, 2d ed. (Mexico: McGraw-Hill, 1992), 163, 194; Paul R. Krugman and Maurice Obstfeld, *Economía internacional. Teoría y práctica* 4th ed. (Mexico: McGraw-Hill, 1999), 178. In any case, this essay does not attempt to measure Mexican trade policy against a static concept of free trade; instead, it focuses on the dynamic process of liberalization, which understands change as variation from a previous state of affairs.

5. Matías Romero, *Geographical and Statistical Notes on Mexico* (New York and London: G. P. Putnam's Sons, 1898), 155; Inés Herrera Canales, *El comercio exterior de México. 1821–1875* (Mexico: El Colegio de Mexico, 1977), 26.

6. SHCP, *Memoria [1868–69]* (1869), 8.

7. [Ministerio de Hacienda y Crédito Público], *Documentos de la Secretaría de Hacienda relativos a un contrabando traído por la goleta americana "Minna Bell" procedente de San Francisco (Alta California) y aprehendido por el resguardo de la Aduana Marítima de San Blas en la ensenada del "Custodio" el día 10 de Agosto de 1871 y reclamación entablada con ese motivo* (México: 1879), 13.

8. *Arancel de aduanas marítimas y fronterizas [de 1º de enero de 1872]*, in Manuel Dublán and José María Lozano, *Legislación mexicana o Colección completa de las disposiciones legislativas expedidas desde la independencia de la República* (Mexico: Imprenta y Litografía de Eduardo Dublán y Comp., 1877–1912), 12: 4–5. (Hereafter cited as: Dublán y Lozano, *Legislación*, year of publication, vol.).

9. *Ordenanza General de Aduanas Marítimas y Fronterizas de la República Mexicana*, enero 31 de 1856, in Dublán and Lozano, *Legislación mexicana*, 8: 42–94. For the estimate of the average tariff burden see Richard Salvucci and Linda Salvucci, "The Politics of Protection: Interpreting Trade Policy in Late Bourbon and Early National Mexico," in Kenneth J. Andrien and Lyman L. Johnson eds., *The Political Economy of Spanish America in the Age of Revolution. 1750–1850* (Albuquerque: University of New Mexico Press, 1994), 103.

10. In what follows, the Spanish terms *arancel* and *ordenanza* are used interchangeably to refer to the tariff laws. There was supposedly a free-trade tariff between 1821 and 1824, which nonetheless contained some protectionist and even

prohibitionist features. Another "liberal" tariff law was in force between April 1842 and September 1843. It set overall import duties at 25 percent upon the value of imports, but failed to produce the expected effects (a substantial increase in imports) and was therefore shortly replaced by another protectionist tariff law. Except for these two brief periods, Mexican *aranceles* were strongly protectionist and contained numerous prohibitions. Araceli Ibarra Bellón, *El comercio y el poder en México, 1821–1864. La lucha por las fuentes financieras entre el Estado central y las regiones* (Mexico: Fondo de Cultura Económica, 1998), 65–70; Daniel Cosío Villegas, *La cuestión arancelaria en México* (Mexico: Universidad Nacional Autónoma de México, 1989), 21–33. See also SHCP, *Memoria [1878]*, 1879, 56.

11. Which, by the way, had been eliminated in the reformed 1856 tariff that was in force during the Maximilian Empire, with banned books being the only exception. Eugenio Maillefert, *Directorio del Comercio del Imperio Mexicano* [1867] (facsimile edition) (Mexico: Instituto Mora, 1992), 101.

12. Riguzzi, "Libre cambio," 293.

13. Secretaría de Hacienda y Crédito Público, *Informe presentado al Congreso de la Unión el 16 de setiembre de 1873, en cumplimiento del precepto constitucional por el C. Francisco Mejía, Secretario de Estado y del Despacho de Hacienda y Crédito Público de los Estados Unidos Mexicanos* (Mexico, 1872–1873), 17. (Hereafter cited as SHCP, *Informe* [corresponding year], year of publication).

14. Cosío Villegas, *La cuestión*, 31.

15. Ibarra Bellón, *El comercio*, 72.

16. *Arancel de aduanas marítimas y fronterizas [de 1º de enero de 1872]*, in Dublán y Lozano, *Legislación*, 1882, 12: 4.

17. Art. 21 of the 1872 *Arancel*, in Dublán y Lozano, *Legislación*, 1882, 12: 39.

18. Riguzzi, "Libre cambio," 294.

19. Marcello Carmagnani, "Introducción," in Carmagnani, ed., *Constitucionalismo*, 3.

20. SHCP, *Memoria [1886–87]*, 1888, xxviii.

21. The treasury minister was well aware that "a wise reduction in import tariffs" could only take place "once internal revenue had been systematized." Quoted in Banco Nacional de Comercio Exterior, *Colección de documentos para la historia del comercio exterior de México. VII: Del centralismo proteccionista al régimen liberal, 1837–1872*, Segunda Serie (Mexico, 1876), 320.

22. SHCP, *Memoria [1878]* (1879), 49.

23. SHCP, *Informe [1873]* (1872–1873), 9.

24. Salvucci and Salvucci, "The Politics," 103.

25. Official import data as well as liquid import duties collected were taken from *Noticia de la importación y exportación de mercancías, en los años fiscales de 1872 a 1873, 1873 a 1874 y 1874 a 1875 formada bajo la dirección de José Ma. Garmendia* (Mexico: Tipografía de Gonzalo A Esteva, 1880), passim. Since figures for duties collected differ among the various official sources, these estimates, as those made in the text following, should be regarded with caution.

26. For the reconstruction of the yearly import values see Sandra Kuntz Ficker, "Nuevas series del comercio exterior de México, 1870–1929," *Revista de Historia Económica* 20: 2 (2002), passim. Regarding the evolution of the average tariff level between 1870 and 1911 see Sandra Kuntz Ficker, "Institutional Change and Foreign Trade in Mexico, 1870–1911," in Stephen Haber and Jeffrey Bortz, eds. *The Mexican*

Economy, 1870–1930: Essays on the Economic History of Institutions, Revolution, and Growth (Stanford: Stanford University Press, 2003). Since that article was submitted, some adjustments have been made to my estimated import values, which produce slight differences in the average tariff level for some years.

27. SHCP, *Informe [1874]*, (1873–1874), xiv.

28. The government obtained approval for this increase in exchange for a reduction in the *"derecho de consumo"* (consumption duty), from 6 percent to 2 percent. The *"derecho de consumo"* had been established in 1872 to compensate for the 10 percent discount granted to import duties, and was payable in Mexico City and Baja California. SHCP, *Informe [1875]*, (1874–1875), 48–49. See also SHCP, *Documentos anexos al informe presentado al congreso de los Estados Unidos Mexicanos el 16 de setiembre de 1875 por el C. Francisco Mejía*, n.d., cxxiii–cxxci.

29. SHCP, *Memoria [1878]* (1879), 49–75 y anexos. See also SHCP, *Noticia pormenorizada del costo que tienen las mercancías extranjeras que se importan por el puerto de Veracruz mandada formar por el secretario de Hacienda a Luis N. Márquez* (Mexico, 1879).

30. The two articles mentioned are bleached and colored cotton clothing, which in 1874 represented 66 percent of total cotton imports. Among the articles with ad valorem duties above 200 percent were some types of cotton and silk handkerchiefs, some types of glass, and some types of socks and stockings. SHCP, *Memoria [1878]* (1879), 50–52.

31. SHCP, *Memoria [1878]* (1879), 59.

32. Apparently, in that case import revenues did not grow because merchants and smugglers had sufficient supply of merchandise to satisfy the current demand. One wonders if there was also another factor at play; since the Mexican import basket was made up of luxury products, and the market for such imports was small and inelastic, a temporary reduction in import duties was unlikely to produce a visible effect in such a short span of time.

33. *"Si el Erario mexicano no tuviera las dificultades que lo agobian; si pudiera prescindir por algún tiempo y sin peligro de una parte de sus ingresos; si pudiera hacer ensayos sin exponerse a graves trastornos, podría haberse decretado ya una rebaja en algunos de los artículos de importación, y conocerse sus resultados prácticamente; pero la situación es tan difícil, que el mal éxito de un ensayo podría comprometer seriamente la paz y el porvenir de la República, y ante este grave y trascendental peligro, parece hasta temerario ensayar arbitrios, en cuyo buen éxito no puede confiarse con plena seguridad."* SHCP, *Memoria [1878]* (1879), 55.

34. The tax on textile factories was contained in the 1879 income law and modified one year later.

35. *"Los derechos aduanales forman la base de nuestras rentas nacionales, y sus productos equivalen a dos terceras partes del importe de todas las rentas. Este es el sistema que se ha seguido casi sin excepción desde la independencia, y que a juicio del Ejecutivo sería conveniente a los intereses nacionales cambiar paulatinamente y en cuanto fuere posible."* SHCP, *Memoria [1868–1869]* (1869), 13.

36. SHCP, *Memoria [1868–1869]* (1869), 13.

37. The law was passed 77 to 43. *Diario de Debates [1880, Tomo III]* (1880), 359–385.

38. *Diario de Debates [1878]* (1878), 269–271, 351–362, 519–534, and passim.

39. About the conditions under which some economic activities deserved protection according to the classic protectionist argument, see Federico List, *Sistema*

nacional de economía política (Mexico: Fondo de Cultura Económica, 1979), 150–173.

40. Regarding the role of tariffs as a source of revenue, as opposed to those intended to reduce imports, see for instance Chacholiades, *Economía*, 206.

41. This was the case of wool and silk manufactured goods, carts and coaches, and some types of paper and cardboard. In regards to the ad valorem equivalent paid by these and other articles in 1878 see SHCP, *Noticia* (1879), 2–15.

42. This was clearly the case with the cotton textile sector; duties were imposed on raw cotton, cotton thread, and manufactured cotton goods, so that effective protection was much smaller than the nominal protection granted to manufacturers. SHCP, *Noticia* (1879), 2–15.

43. In the years 1881 to 1883 alone, about 3,600 kilometers of subsidized railroad lines were built. Calculating an average subsidy of 8,000 pesos per kilometer, this would mean a total payment of about 30 million pesos for the Treasury. Considering that total public revenue averaged 25 million pesos yearly between 1872 and 1880, and that this amount was hardly enough to meet regular expenses, the extra burden posed by this subsidy was considerable. For data on annual railroad construction and public revenue see Romero, *Geographical*, 119, 140.

44. Marcello Carmagnani, *Estado y mercado. La economía pública del liberalismo mexicano, 1850–1911* (Mexico: Fondo de Cultura Económica and Fideicomiso Historia de las Américas-El Colegio de México, 1994), appendices.

45. This happened in 1881 and again in 1884. The stamp tax was subsequently broadened into an overall consumption tax, and eventually became the most important source of public revenue. Carmagnani, *Estado*, 264–269.

46. Carmagnani, *Estado*, 259 and appendix 3.

47. A thorough analysis of this process is provided in Carmagnani, *Estado*, passim.

48. *Diario de Debates [1882, Vol. IV]* (1882), 1043–1044; *Diario de Debates [1884, Vol. IV]* (1905), 484, 843.

49. *Diario de Debates [1884, Vol. I]* (1884), 393, 416.

50. *Diario de Debates [1886]* (1887), 21. As the committee put it in 1887: "There is another reason to be considered [...] in abstaining from proposing reforms to the tax laws; the Executive having ample powers to verify these laws in regard to the stamp tax, import duties and other abundant levies which contribute to the Treasury, there would be nothing more natural than to leave the way clear for it to have the liberty to institute these reforms, having made a careful study of them and subsequently subjecting them to the approval of the Legislative power." *Diario de Debates [1887]* (1889), 28.

51. This peculiar feature of decision-making in late nineteenth-century Mexico was first noted in Riguzzi, "Libre cambio," 296.

52. All decrees reforming the tariff law were preceded by the following statement: "*Que usando la autorización que concede al Ejecutivo de la Unión la fracción I del art. 10. de la ley de ingresos vigente..., he tenido a bien decretar lo siguiente.*" ("Exercising the authority granted to the Executive Power of the Union in Paragraph 1 of Article 19 of the Income Law [...], I decree the following.") See, for instance, Dublán y Lozano, *Legislación*, 1898, 24: 64.

53. Taken together, the reforms made to the tariff in the 1880s have been considered as an expression of intensified trade policy protectionism. See Riguzzi, "Libre cambio," 294–295 and note 29.

54. Richard Salvucci, "The Origins and Progress of U.S. Mexican Trade, 1825–1884: 'Hoc opus, hic labor est,'" *Hispanic American Historical Review* 71: 4 (1991), 722, 726.

55. *Diario de Debates [1880, Vol. IV]* (1880), 680, 682.

56. The 1880 *Arancel* was published in *Memoria [1880–81]* (1881), 9–69.

57. *Diario de Debates [1881, Vol. II]* (1881), 28–29, 527–528. About the debate on this duty see: 693–696.

58. *Diario de Debates [1882, Vol. IV]* (1882), 498.

59. *Diario de Debates [1882, Vol. IV]* (1882), 1043–1044.

60. SHCP, *Memoria [1883–1884]* (1884), xix.

61. Carmagnani, *Estado*, appendices.

62. SHCP, *Memoria [1883–84]* (1884), lxxi. See also Jan S. Bazant, *Historia de la deuda exterior de México, 1823–1946* (Mexico: El Colegio de México, 1968), 114–115.

63. The 1885 *Ordenanza* is found in *Memoria [1884–85]* (1884), 411–441.

64. Consider, for instance, the following remarks published in *El Nacional*: "General Díaz has decided to keep the arancel in force, to our insult and disgrace both within and without the country. [. . .] It is necessary to admit, no matter how much it may pain those who govern us, that such measures are impediments which work against the movement of goods. Following such a system would make the railroads useless, as is happening with the line from Nogales to Guaymas [. . . Such a perverse act causes] the immense harm which business throughout Mexico is suffering." *El Nacional* (December 17, 1885), 144. See also *Semana Mercantil* (August 3, 1885), 295.

65. For Bulnes's speeches, see *Diario de Debates [1886]* (1888), 662–666; for Sánchez Facio's law project see *Diario de Debates [1885]* (1886), 668–738.

66. The 1887 *Ordenanza* is included in Dublán y Lozano, *Legislación*, 1887, 18: 35–174.

67. For an analysis of the regulatory aspects of trade policy, see Kuntz Ficker, "Institutional Change."

68. For example, Wells Fargo complained in 1885 that the Mazatlán customshouse obliged it to list every single item separately in the consular invoices, even if they consisted of a quarter pound package. Archivo General de la Nación, Fondo *Aduanas Marítimas y Fronterizas*, (hereafter cited as AGN, *AMF*), 1885, Sección de Aranceles, caja s.n., exp. 32, (March 16, 1885).

69. Just before the enactment of the 1885 tariff law, John Frisbie wrote the treasury minister on behalf of the Compañía de Vapores de la Mala del Pacífico to explain the inconvenience of this order. The company's ships were headed for various ports in the United States and the Orient, and only secondarily for Mexico, where a rather small part of their shipment was to be landed. His understanding was that this order was aimed at checking the small smuggling operations made by boat along Mexican shores, so it was pointless to impose it on a company like that which he represented. Moreover, such a condition was almost impossible for the company to meet, to the point where its enforcement "would hinder enormously its operations." The Treasury answered with a rather cold apology for the inconvenience. AGN, *AMF*, Sección de Aranceles, 1885, caja s.n., exp. 35, (May 26, 1885).

70. AGN, *AMF*, Sección 1ª, 1886, Paso del Norte, Caja 6, exp. 3189, (Feb. 22, 1886).

71. Imprisonment was prescribed for smugglers by a decree in June 1879. Carlos J. Sierra and Rogelio Martínez Vera, *Historia y legislación aduanera de México* (Mexico: Secretaría de Hacienda y Crédito Público, 1973), 180–181. According to the 1880

tariff law, this punishment applied when the amount of duty owed to the Treasury exceeded 200 pesos.

72. According to the 1880 tariff law, the punishment for customs officials was to be at least double the time imposed on the actual perpetrator. This provision disappeared in later reforms to the law, but others remained, such as publication of the name and crimes committed by the customs employee, exclusion for life from public administration, etc.

73. *Semana Mercantil* (August 31, 1885), 358. Taken from the *Diario Comercial.*

74. A detailed, although fragmentary account of fines collected at different customshouses can be found in AGN, *AMF.* See for example Confiscaciones y Multas, 1892, Ciudad Juárez, caja 32; ibid., 1886, Paso del Norte, caja 6; ibid., 1884, Nogales, caja 16; ibid, 1884, Mazatlán (actas de multas), caja s.n.

75. AGN, *AMF,* Sección 1ª, Indiferente, 1885, Todas las Aduanas del Norte, caja 23, exp. 410, s.f., (Sept. 2 de 1885).

76. *Semana Mercantil* (September 7, 1885), 372.

77. See for example *Informe que el general Hipólito Charles, comandante en jefe del cuerpo "Gendarmería fiscal", presenta al Secretario de Hacienda y Crédito Público. 1885–1886* (Mexico: 1886), passim; SHCP, *Memoria [1886–87]* (1888), xxxi.

78. Income from import tariffs increased from 14 million pesos in 1880 to about 20 million in 1890, still providing a considerable share (47 percent) of public revenue in the latter year. Carmagnani, *Estado,* appendix 3.

79. The problem was explicitly acknowledged by the Treasury Ministry in its annual report for the fiscal year 1891–1892. See SHCP, *Memoria [1891–92]* (1892), 17. For an estimate of the effect of silver depreciation on ad valorem tariff rates see Graciela Márquez, "Tariff Protection in Mexico, 1892–1909: Ad Valorem Tariff Rates and Sources of Variation," in John Coatsworth and Alan M. Taylor, eds., *Latin America and the World Economy Since 1800* (Cambridge: The Rockefeller Center Series on Latin American Studies, Harvard University, 1998), passim.

80. The 1891 tariff law is included in Dublán y Lozano, *Legislación,* 1898, 21: 179–483. For reforms to the law enacted during the 1890s, see Dublán y Lozano, *Legislación,* 1898, 22: 311–312 (October 1892); 1898, 23: 69–72 (February 1893); 1898, 24: 64–65 (April, 1894); 1898, 25: 33–34 (February, 1895); 1898, 27: 92–93 (February 1897), and 27: 288–289 (June 1897); and 1899, 29: 454–456 (December 1898).

81. For more about the McKinley tariff and the reaction of the Mexican government toward it, see Paolo Riguzzi, "La diplomacia de la reciprocidad: comercio y política entre México y Estados Unidos, 1875–1897," *Secuencia,* nueva época, 48 (Sept–Dec 2000), 161–163.

82. Paolo Riguzzi states that, despite its liberalizing contents, the 1891 *Ordenanza* already included some retaliatory rates for a few sensitive items that were important in the import basket originating in the United States. This is indeed likely, considering that the McKinley tariff was enacted in 1890 and the new Mexican arancel in June 1891. Although it was probably too late for a radical turn, there was enough time for the Mexican government to introduce slight changes in the arancel that was being prepared. See Paolo Riguzzi, *La política del comercio. Negociaciones comerciales entre México y Estados Unidos, 1857–1918,* chapter 4, forthcoming.

83. For reforms to the tariff in 1892 and 1893 see Dublán y Lozano, *Legislación,* 1898, 22: 311–312 (October 18, 1892), and 1898, 23: 69–72 (February 22, 1893).

84. See Kuntz Ficker, "Nuevas series," table 2.

85. SHCP, *Memoria [1891–92]* (1892), 17. Limantour also admitted that import duties, which were directed mainly at providing the government with revenue, had at times reached such high proportions that they hardly fulfilled their intended purpose.

86. Romero, *Geographical,* 143.

87. About the role of tariff protection and other policies aimed at promoting industrial development during the Porfiriato see Edward Beatty, *Institutions and Investment. The Political Basis of Industrialization in Mexico before 1911* (Stanford: Stanford University Press, 2001).

88. For an in-depth analysis of the cascade structure of the tariff in the 1890s and early 1900s see Edward Beatty, "Trade policy in Porfirian Mexico: The Structure of Protection," in Stephen Haber and Jeffery L. Bortz, *The Mexican Economy, 1870–1930* (Stanford: Stanford University Press, 2002).

89. This task was largely undertaken by José Yves Limantour starting from the moment he took over the Treasury Ministry in 1893. Limantour, who might be defined as an academic liberal with practical common sense, explained in his memoirs that among the most urgent steps to be taken in the early 1890s was the reform of the arancel in three principal aspects: "suppress some of the most objectionable customs formalities, furnish the Government with weapons against smuggling, and modify a good number of Import Tariffs in a liberal direction." José Yves Limantour, *Apuntes sobre mi vida pública* (Mexico: Editorial Porrúa, 1965), 32. The importance he gave to the regulatory aspects of trade policy is also apparent on p. 55.

90. The surveillance zone was reduced first to 100 km and then to 40 km along the border in 1896. Only in 1901 did the executive consider that it was "a good idea to pull the *Gendarmería Fiscal* back towards the north," in order to facilitate trade. Dublán y Lozano, *Legislación,* 1898, 26, and 1907, 33, passim.

91. This account of the changes in the regulatory part of the tariff is based on numerous memos and reforms issued by the government during the decade and published in Dublán y Lozano, *Legislación,* 1897–1904, 20 to 32, passim.

Conclusion

Legitimacy, Sequencing, and Credibility: Challenges of Mexico's Liberal Reforms in the Nineteenth Century

Aldo Flores-Quiroga

Reforming political and economic systems is difficult; attempting both at the same time is thoroughly challenging. Achievement of either goal is quite remarkable, and a special environment is required for their implementation and survival. The evidence presented in this volume confirms that few of the conditions necessary for successful economic and political reform were in place in nineteenth-century Mexico. Accomplishing the reform of political and economic systems was for decades beyond the institutional, political, and managerial capacity of the Mexican government. This commentary explores some reasons for this outcome.

In addition to Mexico's well-known domestic political constraints, the argument presented here highlights limitations in the country's design and implementation of policies during the nineteenth century. Three related concepts borrowed from recent analyses of structural reforms implemented in Latin America during the 1980s were needed to provide the building blocks for success: legitimacy, sequencing, and credibility. Absent a broad agreement on the legitimacy of successive presidential administrations, the Mexican government's mandate for advancing liberal reforms was severely constrained. Coupled with the poor design of the sequence of policy and institutional adjustments, reform had little chance of success. Finally, the lack of confidence in the government's commitment and ability to enact change only compounded the difficulties.

This essay explains the relevance of each of these three factors (legitimacy, sequencing, and credibility) and provides examples to illustrate their impact in the episodes analyzed in this volume, especially those addressing problems of economic reform. Some comparisons with the late twentieth century are offered, along with conclusions and a few policy lessons.

ECONOMIC AND POLITICAL CHALLENGES
OF STRUCTURAL REFORM

For several reasons, legitimate governments are better able to advance a reform agenda. The mandate for change is questioned less, and tough proposals are met with patience and good will. Discussion of the merits of various policy proposals does not escalate into demands for regime change. The ordinary business of politics is conducted within existing institutional structures because a broad consensus prevails in favor of the dominant decision-making rules.

The sustainability and efficiency of a reform program relies on its sequence. Opening the political regime before attempting economic reforms can break down the consensus for change. Economic reforms are sure to generate winners and losers, possibly weakening the foundations of the ruling coalition and threatening the execution of new policies. Certain economic measures cannot be taken simultaneously without jeopardizing the reform agenda itself. Growing fiscal deficits and high inflation rates, for instance, make trade liberalization harder to sustain. If the government is unable to control economic factors before lowering trade barriers, it will put the reform at high risk.

Credibility interacts with both legitimacy and sequencing to determine the sustainability of the reform. If the public believes that the government's commitment to change is weak, it will not adjust its behavior in the manner intended by the reforms. For example, if the public harbors doubts about the government's ability to maintain low trade barriers, it will increase imports today in the expectation that tomorrow tariffs will be higher. Today's import increase will worsen the trade deficit, and will therefore be seen as justification for increasing tariffs. As a consequence, the reform program will fail and the efficiency gains of reform will be lost.

Questions of credibility extend to the speed of implementation. Is a shock reform more likely to survive than a gradual one? Is one more efficient than the other? Examples of success with either strategy can be provided, but it is evident that political will and strength are required to fulfill the agenda each strategy dictates.

That the conditions of legitimacy, sequence, and credibility almost never coincide in the episodes analyzed in this book helps to explain why it was so hard for Mexico to achieve the liberal goal in the nineteenth century. More frequently than not, the legitimacy of governments was open to question and political instability ensued. When governments were legitimate, they frequently lacked the credibility necessary to implement fully their reform agendas because of insufficient institutional capacity (human resources, laws, enforcement procedures); failure to select the best sequence for policy change; and/or because they were fighting foreign invasions.

LEGITIMACY

The incidence of the legitimacy problem is most apparent in the debates and power struggles that surrounded the choice of political regime and the method for levying taxes—in other words, in the absence of consensus around the rules for political participation and the distribution of economic gains and losses. The quarrels explored in this book between liberals and conservatives, the supporters of the old and new regimes, local and central governments, the Church and the state reveal elites too polarized to configure a formula for governance that included most of their concerns. Important policy decisions, such as tax reform or protection of the borders, were therefore delayed for too long. This created a difficult dilemma: Mexican governments had to clear doubts about their legitimacy in order to enact tax reform, but without tax revenues, the foundation of their own legitimacy was in doubt. The reorganization of public institutions to improve governance structures suffered delay as a consequence.

Alicia Hernández Chávez provides evidence to this effect. She notes that the choice of a liberal republic was neither immediately appealing to Mexican elites nor pre-ordained after independence. The formula proposed at the outset for a legitimate government involved a constitutional monarchy that failed to provoke the imagination of either the Spanish Crown or Mexican liberals; therefore, Mexican conservatives were deprived of the resources to enforce the adoption of such a form of government. Without a legitimate claim to establish an empire, conservative elites could not raise tax revenues, and without tax revenues, they could not even begin to work to legitimize their mandate. Agustín de Iturbide's fall can be seen in this light; his regime proved unable to muster the economic and military support of those who could have benefited from it. The liberal establishment ended up toppling his regime, opening a new wave of debates about the proper form of government. Nearly the same observation can be made of Maximilian, although his claim to legitimacy was weaker, since it rested on the support of a foreign army.

The shortcomings of the proposal for a constitutional monarchy combined with the repeated setbacks in the design of a federal structure to further delay reforms. Jaime E. Rodríguez O. gives us through his analysis of the Oaxacan experience a glimpse of the arduous process for establishing the dividing lines between local sovereignty and national authority. The evidence shows that pressures from the center and other federal units helped keep Oaxaca in the union (as it probably did in other states), but it also emphasizes the gap that separated local elites favoring closer links with the center from those who wanted a more autonomous arrangement. Until that gap was closed, it was nearly impossible to deal with the problem of fiscal federalism.

To complicate the equation, a role had to be found for a subset of the elite that had already developed an economic way of life outside the state's supervision: the army. Christon Archer and Manuel Chust portray some local army chiefs as little more than local mafia, offering to protect the shipments of merchants in exchange for a fee. These practices suggest that the army in some cases deprived the state of valuable fiscal revenues and retarded the creation of a truly federal market. It is plausible that they played a useful role in protecting the property of those willing and able to pay for their services, but one can hardly argue that competition between them was a mechanism to increase the new nation's welfare, or to strengthen the government's ability to coordinate the federal units. Inevitably, the quest for legitimacy had to include some form of compensation to the local warlords in order to have them renounce the rents they were already enjoying from their extortion business.

Last, but not least, the problem of the Church's claims to political participation compounded the government's conundrum. As Brian Connaughton confirms, the Church opposed any reform that reduced its influence, and in so doing it contributed to the delay in making important decisions.

Without an institutional solution that addressed these governance issues it was nearly impossible to begin reforming the tax system, especially one that paid attention to three challenges identified by various authors in this book: the choice of a decision-making procedure that respected diverse, and often opposing, demands for representation; the distribution of the tax burden between the central and local government; and the imposition of losses on diverse social groups.

Rodríguez notes that the dissolution of the Spanish Crown posed a puzzle to New Spain's elites: in the absence of a king, who should rule? The answer to the question had ramifications far beyond the identity of the ruler, be it "the people," an individual, or a small group. It entailed ascertaining who should have the power to assess and collect tax. Lacking a clear guideline—much less a consensus—elites constantly fought over each of these questions.

Take the cases examined by José Antonio Serrano Ortega of the debates around the liberal's preferred principle of taxation—"Each citizen . . . according to his means." What does this principle mean in terms of actual policy? For Mexican elites it provided little help in determining who was to be included as a citizen, what tax levels were most appropriate, whether direct taxation was superior to indirect taxation on grounds of efficiency and fairness, and whether direct taxation should be collected on the basis of individual income or output. In addition, the debate occurred in the context of whether the Cortes or the local governments had precedence in this matter, given that the issue of sovereignty had not yet been solved.

The technical and political challenges of implementing progressive taxation and fiscal federalism take a central role as well. Iturbide, in a move apparently intended to satisfy Creole elites, had eliminated indirect (sales) taxes on what today we would call luxury goods and any direct contributions forced upon the population by the no-longer legitimate Spanish Cortes, but financial demands compelled his government to reinstitute both types of taxes. Direct taxes provided a way out, since they would compensate for the lost revenues from sales taxes resulting from reduced domestic commerce.

The ensuing problem involved the administration and the liberal credentials of such a tax; the issue was whether to assess it on the basis of an individual's wealth or income. In the absence of precise accounting of land and property values, a 5 percent production tax was proposed. Some elites deemed taxes on land ownership to be unfair because they put most of the burden on the wealthy. The Finance Ministry compounded the problem with a proposal to tax individuals progressively, exempting the poor from payment. This principle was strongly supported by Lorenzo de Zavala, chair of the Finance Committee, who believed that the wealthy had an obligation to support the state. Others felt a flat tax per head went against liberal economic principles.

In the end, the principle that people should pay according to their wealth triumphed, due to its easy administration. But the principle addressed only the question of the type of tax to be levied, not of its federal distribution or administration. States were inclined against direct taxes because they associated them with centralization and redistribution of wealth in favor of the national government—too similar to a distribution in favor of the crown.

It is hardly surprising that when local governments were entrusted with the task of assessing and collecting these new taxes, they did not unanimously receive it with outright enthusiasm. Jalisco adopted the tax because local merchants saw it as a substitute for sales taxes. It was both credibly managed by government authorities and compatible with liberal economic ideas. Yucatán toyed with the concept because it saw direct taxes as a way to finance local troops against an invasion from Mexico City. The State of Mexico did not approve the scheme, despite Governor Zavala's proposal, because elites found its application to be unfair (it taxed some agricultural sectors, especially those linked to liquor production, to the exclusion of others) and too onerous. And Zacatecas, which escaped a fiscal crisis after independence, did not need to resort to taxation.

SEQUENCING

Eventually, the state's inability to enforce payment of taxes played a major role in delaying, even reversing, liberal trade reforms. The problem involved aspects of sequencing and credibility. Sandra Kuntz observes that tariff reductions at the end of the nineteenth century had to be designed and implemented under harsh budgetary constraints; tariffs were the government's main source of revenues. Any sustainable trade reform had to wait until alternative sources of fiscal revenues were developed to support it. Officials in the Porfirio Díaz regime were well aware of this challenge as they attempted to liberalize trade in a series of steps, starting with customs reform and moving on to reduced tariffs. But institutional shortcomings, insufficient resources for customs administration, and a thin tax base forced them to follow a less direct path toward trade reform.

Kuntz explains this aspect of the reform process in a review of the three main stages of the *Porfiriato's* trade liberalization program. In Stage I (1872–1880s) illegal activities and an inefficient customs administration occupied most of the government's efforts, since they threatened to increase imports when tariffs fell. The government enacted a new law establishing specific duties for a wider range of products, eliminated exceptions and privileges, set a uniform *ad valorem* duty of 55 percent of market value of goods not included in the tariff list, regularized duties on different customs offices, increased the number of exempted products from thirty-four to seventy-three, and simplified procedures for payment of duties. In Stage II (1880s) tariff reductions were reversed because of low governmental revenues and increased foreign competition. Protective tariffs and anti-smuggling regulations were enacted to increase government revenues, shield producers affected by the rise of competition associated with the advent of the railroad, and punish traffickers. It was not until Stage III (1890s)—as greater foreign investment, diversified sources of capital inflows, and a revamped customs administration increased revenues—that the opportunity opened for the progressive trade liberalization implemented by the Díaz regime.

This experience lends support to a now-common proposition for structural reform programs: stabilize the macroeconomic aggregates before opening the economy; otherwise the risks of failure increase significantly. For Mexico this implied stabilizing capital inflows and keeping a strong fiscal stance, so that the expected increase in imports would not undermine the balance-of-payments position. The Díaz regime took some time to learn or apply this lesson, but fortunately for its survival and its economic reforms it had sufficient political control to restart and sustain the reform soon after the reversal.

Sequencing challenges applied as well to political reforms. When was it best to begin opening a political regime? The experiences analyzed in this book confirm there is no straightforward answer, because increasing spaces for political participation entailed giving up some of the power necessary to make the political reforms themselves possible. To include local governments in the design of a federal structure coordinated by a national authority was to block its very creation, because local governments had for a long time yearned for greater autonomy from the center. To include conservatives in the creation of a liberal regime was a contradiction in terms, as it was to include liberals in the creation of an empire.

The Mexican regimes that neglected these contradictions paid dearly for their mistakes. Iturbide had to give up his imperial aspirations. Maximilian lost his life, despite his progressive economic reform agenda. The governments between them had a short shelf life. The Díaz regime ended in a revolution. As Robert Duncan vividly illustrates with his study of Maximilian's experience, the most progressive and forward-looking reform agenda can dissolve in the face of major political incompatibilities. The policy challenge is to internalize these lessons when designing new institutions.

CREDIBILITY

The difficulties successive nineteenth-century Mexican governments faced in advancing liberalism also derive from at least two questions: whether to reform politics or economics first, and whether appropriate domestic enforcement mechanisms existed to make enacted reforms effective.

Mexican elites understood that the choice of a political regime was inseparable from the choice of economic policies, yet they held conflicting preferences toward each. Some supported an empire, but not the taxes required to sustain it. Others sought a more democratic model, but were not ready to endure the economic hardships required to achieve it. This made for a very tricky choice of a sequence of reform. As soon as a regime attempted either, it lost support from important political groups. Iturbide and Maximilian, who attempted to reform the political and economic systems at the same time, failed. Both sought to create an empire in an environment where demands for less government intervention were high. Their proposals for economic reform therefore lost political momentum. The many administrations between them failed for similar reasons, while trying to implement the dual program of political and economic liberalization. The apparent success story, that of Díaz, with its motto of "much administration and little politics," secured political power before implementing economic reform.

This history suggests that fast and all-encompassing reforms were doomed to failure because the state lacked either the political strength to carry it forward, or the economic base to finance it, or both. In the absence of a preponderant political force to enforce them, shock reforms never stood a chance. The most that weak governments could do was to attempt to change one policy area at a time.

This interpretation can be supported with some observations contained in Marcelo Carmagnani's chapter that imply Mexican governments were, more than failing, learning. What we actually see, following his argument, is a gradual reform process increasing the freedom to trade and contract (guild privileges disappear, for example; new trade laws are enacted) and improving protection of property rights. That is, as the state became strong enough to protect property rights, it also gained the strength required to credibly open the economy. Liberal reforms survived when Mexicans understood that in order to have free markets they needed a strong state.

Enhanced protection for property rights relied in turn on an improved law-enforcement apparatus. Since the democratic-federal formula proved wanting in this regard, it is not surprising the authoritarian track attracted many and proved workable at the century's end. Authoritarianism supported by foreign military intervention was repeatedly seen as a way out of the enforcement problem, and implicitly as a way of improving the credibility of the investment regime. Conservative Mexicans who believed that neither democracy nor domestic institutions could create the type of regime that would protect their interests inaugurated the era of Maximilian. In northern Mexico the demand for new distribution of land ownership, a sort of land reform in reverse, clashed with the position of the central government. Northerners addressed the clash by coalescing with Texan inhabitants, undermining the national government's efforts to control the borders.

These are instances of searches for what it is now called a policy or an institutional "anchor"—a mechanism that ties the government's hands, blocking it from reversing a course of action. Policy anchors, such as a fixed exchange rate to control inflation or a free-trade agreement to block tariff increases, are frequently the focus of most attention, but they require the support of institutional procedures that make it difficult to lift them. The institutional procedures can be managed domestically, as in the fixed exchange-rate case, or jointly with other countries, as with free-trade agreements, or through rules, as with currency boards. In the Mexican case it is apparent that anchors lacking domestic support structures were not likely to succeed. Maximilian's liberal reforms, for instance, did not prosper while they were enforced with the aid of a foreign army, but they survived when the Juárez administration imposed them. A combination of this administration's preponderance of power and legitimacy helped to keep such anchors in place.

PARALLELS AND CONTRASTS WITH
THE TWENTIETH CENTURY

Mexico's economic and political reforms of the late twentieth century offer parallels with the stories told above. To appreciate them, a brief review is in order.

The debt crisis of 1982 triggered an economic and political crisis that thrust the three consecutive presidencies of Miguel de la Madrid Hurtado, Carlos Salinas de Gortari, and Ernesto Zedillo Ponce into the most wide-ranging reform agenda Mexico had seen in decades. The agenda was liberal in the eighteenth-nineteenth century sense. It sought to implant free markets and legislative oversight of the executive. To succeed, it also had to dodge opposition from entrenched interests, a disadvantage that slowed its progress. To survive, it had to find solutions to similar legitimacy, sequencing, and credibility problems.

The legitimacy issue bedeviled these presidencies because of two main factors. First, the PRI had been in power for too long, while Mexican society had become more pluralistic. Demands for greater access to the channels of political participation and decision-making had long accumulated without the government opening significant concessions.

Second, when the debt crisis exploded, the government of José López Portillo attempted to improve its fiscal stance by expropriating wealth from Mexican elites. It nationalized the banking industry, raised taxes and tariffs, froze dollar-denominated bank accounts and converted to pesos at an uncompetitive market rate, and imposed exchange controls. This massive redistribution of wealth from the private to the public sector motivated a strong and wide political mobilization to transform the country's institutional framework. Its aim was to create a new political reality, where power was less concentrated in one individual and less centralized in the federal government. Such a system would no longer permit the president to spend excessively and expropriate wealth easily. The new political reality required guaranteeing free and fair elections, removing from the presidency the control of the legislative and judicial powers, and giving more power to local governments with respect to the national government.

To accomplish such an ambitious political change in the face of major economic challenges was, however, extremely difficult. A more convenient sequence of reform would concentrate first on economic change and wait until it was accomplished to begin opening the political system. That way the risk of a political stalemate would decrease, allowing the implementation of emergency economic measures and structural adjustment without delay. Presidents de la Madrid and Salinas de Gortari thus privileged economic over political reform. Between 1985 and 1993 they focused on lowering trade barriers, privatizing state-owned enterprises and deregulating markets, while trying to control inflation and restore fiscal health.

Once most of these reforms were anchored with measures that changed the institutional makeup of the economic regime, such as the North American Free Trade Agreement, which made it difficult to reverse trade liberalization, or the independence of the Central Bank, which blocked the government from financing its deficits by printing money automatically, the Salinas administration accelerated the pace of political reform. It introduced a new electoral code that, in providing for the most credible voter registration system ever, paved the way for the most transparent presidential elections in Mexico's recent history, from which Ernesto Zedillo emerged the winner.

By the time Zedillo took office the fundamental aspects of the economic and electoral reforms had been addressed. His administration had no choice but to negotiate constantly with opposition parties to enact new policies. Significantly, since 1997 no budget in Mexico's congress has been approved without the concurrence of at least two political parties. The legitimation of the budget is no longer an issue. But the problem of fiscal federalism is yet unsolved: Mexican states demand more resources and more independence in collecting and spending them.

The parallels of this experience with the liberal agenda of the nineteenth century are many, despite the differences in the length of the periods involved. In both cases economic reform preceded political reform, and it was triggered by a fiscal crisis derived from a legitimacy crisis. The legitimacy crisis was closely linked with the problem of concentration of power, serious policy blunders, and ineffective government. The reforms that survived relied on institutional anchors that protected them from groups opposing them. When measures to enhance the credibility of a new regime were insufficient, the reforms were reversed or delayed. Economic reform was rarely sustainable in isolation; political change usually followed.

Consider the following examples. Iturbide's and López Portillo's attempts at solving a fiscal crisis by forced expropriation of private-sector wealth (through debatable taxes or decrees) backfired and triggered a political crisis that started a movement toward liberal reforms. The trade reforms of the Díaz regime and the de la Madrid and Salinas administrations were not credible and sustainable until tight control of the fiscal deficit, higher foreign investment, and new institutional anchors were adopted. In modern parlance, setbacks in the process of liberalization were produced by inconsistent macroeconomic policies and weak institutional commitment. Market-oriented reforms, like those of Maximilian, Díaz, or Salinas, stimulated regime change: the opening of spaces for economic exchange and their associated distributive effects evolved into demands for political participation by more diverse groups. In the long run, market-oriented reforms were not compatible with institutions that concentrated power in one individual.

Certainly, differences between both periods are prominent. At the end of the twentieth century the Church did not pose a real obstacle to the liberal agenda; it in fact benefited from it when President Salinas reestablished relations with the Vatican. Free trade between Mexico's regions was a nonissue, despite the drawbacks of the prevailing structure's dominance over federal and local government relations. No foreign army invaded the country as the march toward democracy advanced.

CONCLUSION

Political and technical obstacles difficult to overcome for a government in search of legitimacy slowed the march toward liberalism in nineteenth-century Mexico. As elites espousing liberalism gained political clout, learned to address the demands of local units, and designed better sequences of economic and political reform, their ideals began to take shape as concrete, sustainable policies.

Their experiences, as analyzed in this book, suggest some policy-making lessons applicable to the nineteenth and twentieth centuries alike:

1. Trade reform is impossible if it compromises fiscal health.
2. Economic liberalization is in the long run incompatible with centralization and concentration of power.
3. Policy and institutional anchors require a domestic support base to survive; foreign enforcement is not sufficient.
4. The lack of competent bureaucracies and the inefficient coordination between federal and local governments slow the pace and endanger the success of reform.
5. Weak or uncertain protection of property rights hinders investment and economic growth.

Mexican policymakers continue today to struggle with the challenges of political and economic change, working in some ways to fulfill the ideals of their nineteenth-century predecessors. Perhaps it would be to their advantage to take some of these lessons to heart, for history displays the habit of repeating itself.

Bibliography

ARCHIVES AND SPECIAL COLLECTIONS

Archivo de la Audiencia de Nueva Galicia, Guadalajara
Archivo del Ayuntamiento de Jalapa
Archivo del Ayuntamiento de Oaxaca
Archivo del Congreso de Diputados de las Cortes, Madrid
    Documentación Electoral
Archivo General de Indias, Sevilla
Archivo General de la Nación, Mexico
    Aduanas Marítimas y Fronterizas
    Archivo Histórico de Hacienda
    Ayuntamientos
    Colección José López Portillo
    Gobernación
    Gobernación: Sin Sección
    Historia
    Ministerio del Interior
    Propios y arbitros
Archivo Histórico de Guanajuato, Guanajuato
    Municipios
Archivo Histórico del Ayuntamiento de la Ciudad de Oaxaca
Archivo Histórico del Centro de Estudios de Historia de México Condumex
Archivo Histórico del Estado de Zacatecas, Zacatecas
    Fondo Ayuntamiento de Zacatecas
    Jefatura política de Zacatecas

Poder Ejecutivo
Poder Legislativo
Archivo Histórico de Jalisco, Guadalajara
Archivo Histórico Municipal de México
    Milicias cívicas
Archivo de la Secretaría de Defensa, Mexico
Bancroft Library, University of California, Berkeley
    Bolton Papers
Beinecke Library, Yale University
Benson Latin American Collection, University of Texas at Austin
    Nettie Lee Benson Papers
    García Collection
Béxar Archives, Austin
Biblioteca del Estado de Oaxaca, Oaxaca
    Colección de Mariano Martínez Grácida
Biblioteca Nacional de México
    Lafragua Colection
Daughters of the Republic of Texas at the Alamo
    Casiano-Pérez Collection
General Land Office of Texas, Austin
Library of Congress, Washington, D.C.
    Agustín de Iturbide Papers.
Museo Nacional de Títeres, Humantla, Tlaxcala.
    El Archivo de la familia Rosette Aranda, Libros del Cuentos,
Nacogdoches Archives
Texas State Archives, Austin
    Comptroller of Public Accounts Collection
    Unpaid Claims Collection

PERIODICALS

Aguila Mexicana, 1823
Diario de México, 1806, 1809, 1810.
El Correo, 1829
El Correo de la Federación, 1829
El Nacional, 1885
Gazeta del Gobierno de México, 1820
Gazeta de Madrid, 1776
Gaceta Imperial de México, 1822
La Sociedad, 1866
Mercurio histórico y político, 1776
Semana Mercantil, 1885
Voz de la Patria, 1829

PRINTED SOURCES

A.T. *Hablen los predicadores y confundan la impiedad.* Guadalajara: Imprenta de Dionisio Rodríguez, 1833.

Adams, John. "A Defense of the Constitution of the Government of the United States," in John Adams, *The Works of John Adams.* Boston: Little, Brown, and Company, 1850., 4: 271–588, 5: 3–490.

———. *The Works of John Adams.* 10 vols. Boston: Little, Brown, and Company, 1850.

Addy, George M. *The Enlightenment in the University of Salamanca.* Durham: Duke University Press, 1966.

Advenimiento de SS.MM.II Maximiliano y Carlota al trono de México. Edición de "La Sociedad." Mexico: Andrade y Escalante, 1864.

Agostoni, Claudia. *Monuments of Progress: Modernization and Public Health, 1876–1910.* Calgary: University of Calgary Press, 2003.

Alamán, Lucas. *Historia de Méjico desde los primeros movimientos que prepararon su Independencia en el año de 1808 hasta la época presente.* 5 vols. Mexico: Fondo de Cultura Económica, 1985.

———. *Historia de Méjico desde los primeros movimientos que prepararon su independencia en el año de 1808 hasta la época presente.* Mexico: J. Mario Lara, 1852.

Alba, Rafael, ed. *La Constitución de 1812 en la Nueva España.* 2 vols. Mexico: Archivo General de la Nación, 1912–1913.

Alessio Robles, Vito. *Coahuila y Texas desde la consumación de la independencia hasta el tratado de paz de Guadalupe Hidalgo.* 2 vols. Mexico City: Jus, 1945.

Alonso, Manuel Moreno. *La forja del liberalismo en España. Los amigos españoles de Lord Holland, 1793–1840.* Madrid: Publicaciones del Congreso de Diputados, 1997.

Alzate, José Antonio. *Obras,* vol 1. *Periódicos.* Edited by Roberto Moreno. Mexico: Universidad Nacional Autónoma de México, 1980.

Anna, Timothy E. *Forging Mexico, 1821–1835.* Lincoln: University of Nebraska Press, 1998.

———. *El imperio de Iturbide.* Mexico: Conaculta-Grijalbo, 1992.

———. *The Mexican Empire of Iturbide.* Lincoln: University of Nebraska Press, 1990.

Annino, Antonio. "Cádiz y la revolución territorial de los pueblos mexicanos, 1812–1821." In *Historia de las elecciones en Iberoamérica, siglo XIX.* Edited by Antonio Annino. Buenos Aires: Fondo de Cultura Económica, 1995.

Appleby, Joyce. *Economic Thought and Ideology in 17th Century England.* Princeton: Princeton University Press, 1978.

Archer, Christon I. *El ejército en el México borbónico, 1760–1810.* Mexico: Fondo de Cultura Económica, 1983.

———. "Fighting for Small Worlds: Wars of the People during the Independence Era in New Spain, 1810–1821." *Cuadernos de Historia de América* 6 (1998): 87–92.

———. "The Militarization of Mexican Politics: The Role of the Army, 1815–1821." In *Five Centuries of Mexican History/Cinco siglos de historia de México*. 2 vols. Edited by Virginia Guedea and Jaime E. Rodríguez O. Mexico: Instituto Mora, 1992, 1: 285–302.

———. "Politicization of the Army of New Spain during the War of Independence, 1810–1821." In *The Evolution of the Mexican Political System*, edited by Jaime E. Rodríguez O. Wilmington, Delaware: Scholarly Resources Inc., 1993, 17–43.

———. "The Royalist Army of New Spain, 1810–1821: Militarism, Praetorianism, or Protection of Interests?" *Armed Forces & Society* 17: 1 (fall 1990): 99–116.

———. "Where Did All the Royalists Go? New Light on the Military Collapse of New Spain, 1810–1821." In *The Mexican and Mexican American Experience in the 19th Century*, edited by Jaime E. Rodríguez O. Tempe: Bilingual Press, 1989.

Armstrong, George M. *Law and Market Society in Mexico*. New York: Praeger, 1989.

Arrangoiz y Berzábel, Francisco de Paula de. *Apuntes para la historia del segundo imperio mexicano*. Madrid: Imprenta de M. Rivadeneyra, 1869.

———. *Méjico desde 1808 hasta 1867*. Madrid: Imprenta de Estrada, 1872.

Artola, Miguel. *La hacienda del antiguo régimen*. Madrid: Alianza Editorial-Banco de España, 1982.

Austin, Moses. *The Austin Papers*. 3 vols. Edited by Eugene C. Barker. Vols. 1 and 2. Washington, D.C.: American Historical Association, 1924, 1928. Vol. 3. Austin: University of Texas Press, 1927.

Avila Rueda, Alfredo. "Para la libertad. Los republicanos en tiempos del imperio, 1821–23." Ph.D. diss.: Universidad Nacional Autónoma de México, 2001.

Bacarisse, Charles A. "The Union of Coahuila and Texas." *Southwestern Historical Quarterly* 51: 3 (Jan. 1958): 340–349.

Banco Nacional de Comercio Exterior. *Colección de documentos para la historia del comercio exterior de México. VII: Del centralismo proteccionista al régimen liberal, 1837–1872*. Segunda Serie. Mexico, 1876.

Barker, Eugene C. *The Life of Stephen F. Austin, Founder of Texas, 1793–1836*. New York: Da Capo Press, 1968.

Barker, Nancy Nichols. "Monarchy in Mexico: Harebrained Scheme or Well-considered Prospect." *Journal of Modern History* 48 (March 1976): 51–68.

Barragán Barragán, José, ed. *Actas constitucionales mexicanas (1821–1824)*. 10 vols. Mexico: Universidad Nacional Autónoma de México, 1980.

———. *Introdución al federalismo (la formación de los poderes 1824)*. México: Universidad Nacional Autónoma de México, 1978.

Barrera Graf, J. "Codificación en México. Antecedentes, código de comercio de 1889, perspectivas." In *Centenario del Código de comercio*, Instituto de Investigaciones Jurídicas. Mexico: Universidad Nacional Autónoma de México, 1991.

Barroso Díaz, Angel. "Maximiliano: Legislador Liberal." In *Memoria del II Congreso de historia del derecho Mexicano (1980)*, edited by José Luis Soberanes Fernández. Mexico: Universidad Nacional Autónoma de Mexico, 1981.

Bartolache, Ignacio. *Mercurio volante*. Edited by Roberto Moreno. Mexico: Universidad Nacional Autónoma de México, 1979.

Bases Provisionales con que se Emancipó la Provincia de Oajaca. Oaxaca, n.p., 1823.

Baskes, Jeremy. "Coerced or Voluntary? The *Repartimiento* and Market Participation of Peasants in Late Colonial Oaxaca." *Journal of Latin American Studies* 28: 1 (Feb. 1996): 1–28.

————. *Indians, Merchants, and Markets: A reinterpretation of the Repartimiento and Spanish-Indian Economic Relations in Colonial Oaxaca, 1750–1821.* Stanford: Stanford University Press, 2000.

Bastian, Jean-Pierre. "Una ausencia notoria: la francmasonería en la historiografía mexicana." *Historia Mexicana* 175 (Jan.–Mar. 1995): 439–460.

Bazant, Jan S.. *Antonio Haro y Tamariz y sus aventuras políticas, 1811–1869.* Mexico: El Colegio de México, 1985.

————. *Historia de la deuda exterior de México, 1823–1946.* Mexico: El Colegio de México, 1968.

————. *Los bienes de la Iglesia en México (1856–1875). Aspectos económicos y sociales de la Revolución liberal.* Mexico: El Colegio de México, 1971.

Beezley, William H. "Amending Memories: The Formation of National Identity in Nineteenth-century Mexico." (Work in Progress).

————. *Judas at the Jockey Club and Other Episodes of Porfirian Mexico.* Lincoln: University of Nebraska Press, 1987.

Bellingeri, Marco. "De una constitución a otra: conflictos de jurisdicción y dispersión de poderes en Yucatán, 1789–1831." In *Liberalismo en México. Cuadernos de Historia Latinoamericana,* coordinated by Antonio Annino and Raymond Buve. Hamburg: AHILA, 1993, 49–77.

————. "Soberanía o representación: la legitimidad de los cabildos y la conformación de las instituciones liberales en Yucatán." In *Europa e Iberoamérica: cinco siglos de intercambio,* edited by Ma. Justina Sarabia Viejo. Sevilla: AHILA, 1992.

————. "El tributo de los indios y el estado de los criollos. Las obvenciones eclesiáticas en Yucatán en el siglo XIX." In *Sociedad, estrucura agraria y estado en Yucatán,* edited by Othon Báños Ramírez. Merida: Universidad Autónoma de Yucatán, 1993.

Benson, Nettie Lee. "The Contested Mexican Election of 1812." *Hispanic American Historical Review* 26 (August 1946): 336–350.

————. *La diputación Provincial y el federalismo mexicano.* Mexico: El Colegio de México, 1955.

————. *La Diputación Provincial y el Federalism Mexicano.* 2d ed. Mexico City: El Colegio de México, 1994.

————. "Iturbide y los planes de Independencia." *Historia Mexicana* 2: 3 (January–March 1953): 442.

————. ed. *Mexico and the Spanish Cortes, 1810–1822.* Austin: University of Texas Press, 1966.

————. "The Plan of Casa Mata." *Hispanic American Historical Review* 25 (February 1945): 45–56.

————. *The Provincial Deputation in Mexico: Harbinger of Provincial Autonomy, Independence, and Federalism.* Austin: University of Texas Press, 1992.

————. "Territorial Integrity in Mexican Politics, 1821–1833." In *The Independence of Mexico and the Creation of the New Nation,* edited by Jaime E. Rodríguez O. Los Angeles: UCLA Latin American Center Publications, 1989, 275–307.

————. "Texas as Viewed from Mexico, 1820–1834." *Southwestern Historical Quarterly* (January 1987): 219–291.

Berninger, Dieter George. *La inmigración en México, 1821–1857*. Mexico City: Sep-Setentas, 1974.

Bernstein, Harry. *Dom Pedro II*. New York: Twayne Publishers, Inc., 1973.

Bernstein, Michael A. "Numerable Knowledge and its Discontents." *Reviews in American History* 18 (1990), 151–164.

Bernstein, Serge, comp. *Les cultures politiques en France*. Paris: Seuil, 1999.

Bitar Letayf, Marcelo. *Los economistas españoles del siglo XVII y sus ideas sobre el comercio con las Indias*. Mexico: Instituto Mexicano de Comercio Exterior, 1975.

Black, John. *A Dictionary of Economics*. Oxford/New York: Oxford University Press, 1997.

Black, Shirley. *Napoleon III and Mexican Silver*. Silverton, Colorado: Ferrell Publications, 2000.

Blanco Valdés, Roberto. *Rey, Cortes y fuerzas armadas en los orígenes de la España liberal, 1808–1823*. Madrid: Siglo XXI, 1988.

Blumberg, Arnold. "The Diplomacy of the Mexican Empire, 1863–1867." *Transactions of the American Philosophical Society*. New Series, 61: 8. Philadelphia: The American Philosophical Society, 1971.

Bobbio, Norberto. "Libertà e democrazia." In *Il pensiero politico contemporaneo*, vol. 1, compiled by Gian Mario Bravo and S. Rota Ghibaudi. Milán: F. Angeli, 1985.

———, Nicola Matteucci, and Gianfranco Pasquino, eds. *Diccionario de Política*. 2 vols. Mexico: Siglo XXI, 1995.

Bocanegra, José María. *Memorias para la historia de México independiente, 1822–1846*. 3 vols. Mexico: Fondo de Cultura Económica, 1987.

Bonney, Richard, ed. *Economic Systems and State Finance*. Oxford: Clarendon Press, 1995.

Brading, David A. *The First America: The Spanish Monarchy, Creole Patriots, and the Liberal State, 1492–1867*. Cambridge: University of Cambridge Press, 1991.

———. *The Origins of Mexican Nationalism*. Cambridge: Centre of Latin American Studies, 1985.

Brett, Annabel S. *Nature, Right, and Liberty: Individual Rights in Later Scholastic Thought*. Cambridge: Cambridge University Press, 1997.

Bulmer-Thomas, Victor. *The Economic History of Latin America since Independence*. Cambridge: Cambridge University Press, 1994.

Burns, E. Bradford, and Thomas E. Skidmore. *Elites, Masses, and Modernization in Latin America, 1850–1930*. Austin: University of Texas Press, 1979.

Bustamante, Carlos María de. *Cuadro histórico de la revolución mexicana*. 4 vols. Mexico: Cámara de Diputados, 1961.

———. *Diario histórico de México*. 3 vols. Mexico: Instituto Nacional de Antropología e Historia, 1980.

———. *Examen crítico sobre la federación de las provincias del territorio mexicano. Carta primera a un oaxaqueño*. Mexico: Imprenta del Ciudadano Alejandro Valdés, 1823.

Calvillo, Manuel. *La consumación de la Independencia y la Instauración de la República Federal Mexicana. Gestación y Nacimiento*. Mexico: Distrito Federal, 1974.

Canales, Inés Herrera. *El comercio exterior de México, 1821–1875*. Mexico: El Colegio de Mexico, 1977.

Cañizares–Esguerra, Jorge. *How to Write the History of the New World: Historiographies, Epistomologies, and Identities in the Eighteenth-Century Atlantic World.* Stanford: Stanford University Press, 2001.

Cantrell, Gregg. *Stephen F. Austin: Empresario of Texas.* New Haven: Yale University Press, 1999.

Cardozo Galue, Germán. *Michoacán en El Siglo de las Luces.* Mexico: El Colegio de México, 1973.

Carmagnani, Marcello. *Estado y mercado. La economía pública del liberalismo mexicano, 1857–1911.* Mexico: Fondo de Cultura Económica-Fideocomiso Historia de las Américas-El Colegio de México, 1994.

———. "Instituciones financieras internacionales del orden liberal mexicano." In *Constitucionalismo y orden liberal en América Latina, 1850–1920*, edited by Marcello Carmagnani. Turin: Otto Editore, 2000.

———. "Introducción." In *Constitucionalismo y orden liberal en América Latina, 1850–1920,* edited by Marcello Carmagnani. Torino: Otto Editore, 2000, 1–7.

———. "El liberalismo, los impuestos internos y el estado federal mexicano 1857–1911." *Historia Mexicana* 3 (1989): 471–496.

———. "La libertad, el poder y el estado en la segunda mitad del siglo XIX." *Historias* 15 (1986): 55–63.

———. *El regreso de los dioses. El proceso de reconstitución de la entidad étnica en Oaxaca. Siglos XVII y XVIII.* Mexico: Fondo de Cultura Económica, 1988.

———. "Del territorio a la region." In *Cincuenta años de historia en México en el cincuentenario del Centro de Estudios Históricos.* 2 vols. Coordinated by Alicia Hernández Chávez and Manuel Miño Grijalva. Mexico: El Colegio de México, 1991, 2: 221–241.

———. "Towards a New Financial Order, 1857–1912." In *Transferring Wealth and Power from the Old to the New World. Monetary and Fiscal Institutions in the 17th through the 19th Century,* edited by Michael Bordo and Roberto Cortés-Conde. Cambridge: Cambridge University Press, 2001.

Carreño, Alberto M. *Jefes del Ejército Mexicano en 1847: Biografías de Generales de División y de Brigada y de Coroneles del Ejército Mexicano por fines del año de 1847.* Mexico: Imprenta y Fototipia de la Secretaría de Fomento, 1914.

Carroll, Patrick J. *Blacks in Colonial Veracruz.* Austin: University of Texas Press, 1991.

Carta pastoral del . . . Deán y Cabildo Gobernador de la Santa Iglesia Metropolitana de México. Mexico: Imprenta de Galván a cargo de Mariano Arévalo, 1833.

Carter, James David. *Masonry in Texas: Background, History, and Influence to 1846.* Waco: Committee on Masonic Education and Service for the Grand Lodge of Texas, 1955.

Casasús, Joaquín D. *Las instituciones de crédito.* Mexico: Secretaria de Fomento, 1890.

———. *Las reformas a la ley de instituciones de crédito.* Mexico: Palacio Nacional, 1908.

Casillas R., Rodolfo. "Del Patronato al nombramiento de obispos: El inicio de un nuevo entendimiento." *Religiones y Sociedad* 6 (May–Aug. 1999): 83–110.

Castán, José. *La influencia de la literatura jurídica española en las codificaciones americanas.* Madrid: Instituto de Estudios Jurídicos, 1984.

Castañeda, Carmen. *La educación en Guadalajara durante la colonia, 1552–1821.* Mexico: El Colegio de México, 1984.

Castellanos Hernández, Eduardo. "Formas de gobierno y sistemas electorales durante el periodo 1857–1867." In *La definición del estado mexicano 1857–1867,* edited by Patricia Galeana de Valadés. Mexico: Archivo General de la Nación, 1999.

Castillo Crimm, Ana Carolina. "Success in Adversity: The Mexican Americans of Victoria County, Texas, 1800–1880." Ph.D. diss.: University of Texas, Austin, 1994.

Catálogo del Museo Nacional de Títeres. Huamantla, Tlaxcala: n.p., n.d.

Cayetano Orozco, J. M. *Discurso sobre la necesidad que hay en el día, de dedicar a la juventud al estudio de las humanidades. Y principalmente sobre la elocuencia sagrada: escrito por Dr. D. . . . Catedrático de Elocuencia y de Historia en el Seminario de esta ciudad.* Guadalajara: Imprenta de Manuel Brambila, 1848.

Ceballos Ramírez, Manuel. *El catolicismo social: Un tercero en discordia. Rerum Novarum, la 'cuestión social' y la movilización de los católicos mexicanos (1891–1911).* Mexico: El Colegio de México, 1991.

———. "Las fuentes del catolicismo social." In *Catolicismo social en México, Teoría, Fuentes e Historiografía,* coordinated by Manuel Ceballos Ramírez and Alejandro Garza Rangel. Monterrey: Academia de Investigación Humanística, A.C., 2000.

Cervantes Bello, Francisco J. "La piedad en la catedral angelopolitana: capellanías, aniversarios y misas, 1830–1840." In *Memoria del I Coloquio Historia de la Iglesia en el Siglo XIX,* compiled by Manuel Ramos Medina. Mexico: Condumex, 1998.

Chabot, Frederick C. *With The Makers of San Antonio.* San Antonio: Artes Gráficas, 1937.

Chacholiades, Miltiades. *Economía internacional.* 2d ed. Mexico: McGraw-Hill, 1992.

Chance, John K. *Race and Class in Colonial Oaxaca.* Stanford: Stanford University Press, 1978.

Chiaramonte, José Carlos. "Fundamentos iusnaturalistas de los movimientos de independencia." In *Las guerras de independencia en la América española,* edited by Marta Terán and José Antonio Serrano Ortega. Zamora: El Colegio de Michoacán, 2002, 99–122.

Chust, Manuel. *Ciudadanos en armas.* Valencia: IVEI, 1987.

———. *La cuestión nacional Americana en las Cortes de Cádiz.* Valencia and Mexico: UNED-Fundación Instituto de Historia Social & Universidad Nacional Autónoma de México, 1999.

———. "De esclavos, encomenderos y mitayos. El anticolonialismo en las Cortes de Cádiz." *Mexican Studies/Estudios Mexicanos* 11: 2 (summer 1995): 179–202.

———. "Legislar y revolucionar. La trascendencia de los diptados novohispanos en las Cortes hispanas, 1810–1814." In *La independencia de México y el proceso autonomista novohispano, 1808–1824,* coordinated by Virginia Guedea. México: Universidad Nacional Autónoma de México and Instituto Mora, 2001, 23–82.

Coffey, David. "Brothers of the Sword: The Bond of Nationalist Struggle in Porfirian Mexico." Unpublished seminar paper, Texas Christian University, 1996.

Comín, Francisco. *Las cuentas de la hacienda preliberal en España, 1801–1855.* Madrid: Banco de España, 1990.

———. *Historia de la hacienda pública. Europa.* Barcelona: Grijalbo Mondadori, 1996.

Connaughton, Brian F. "Ágape en disputa: fiesta cívica, cultura política y la frágil urdimbre nacional antes del Plan de Ayutla." *Historia Mexicana* 45: 2 (Oct.–Dec. 1995): 281–316.

———. "Agio, clero y bancarrota fiscal, 1846–1847." *Mexican Studies/Estudios Mexicanos* 14: 2 (summer 1998): 263–285.

———. "Conjuring the body politic from the 'corpus mysticum': the post-independent pursuit of public opinion in Mexico, 1821–1854." *The Americas* 55: 3 (1998): 459–479.

———, ed. *Construcción de la legitimidad política en México*. Mexico: Universidad Autónoma Metropolitana, 1999.

———. "Cultura, política y discurso religioso en Puebla: los caminos entrecruzados de la primera ciudadanía, 1821–1854." *Iztapalapa* 39: 69–92.

———. *Dimesiones de la identidad patriótica*. Mexico: Miguel Angel Porrúa, 2001.

———. "El federalismo: las élites secular y clerical en los 1820." *Estudios Jaliscienses* 22 (1995): 23–38.

———. "Hegemonía desafiada: libertad, nación e impugnación clerical de la jerarquía eclesiástica. Guadalajara 1821–1860." In *La Iglesia Católica en México*, edited by Nelly Sigaut. Mexico: El Colegio de Michoacán and Secretaría de Gobernación, 1997.

———. *Ideología y sociedad en Guadalajara, 1788–1853*. Mexico: Consejo Nacional para la Cultura y las Artes and Universidad Nacional Autónoma de México, 1992.

———. "La Iglesia y el Estado en México mexicana, 1821–1856." *Gran Historia de México Ilustrada* 36. Mexico: Editorial Planeta, 2001.

———. "El ocaso del proyecto de 'Nación Católica.' Patronato virtual, préstamos, y presiones regionales, 1821–1856." In *Construcción de la legitimidad política en México en el siglo XIX*, edited by Brian Connaughton, Carlos Illades, and Sonia Pérez Toledo. Mexico: El Colegio de Michoacán, Universidad Autónoma Metropolitana, UNAM/Instituto de Investigaciones Históricas, El Colegio de México, 1999, 227–262.

———, ed. *Poder y legitimidad en México, siglo xix: Instituciones y cultura política*. Mexico: Miguel Angel Porrúa, 2003.

———. "Providencia y progreso, Cultura política en Guadalajara, 1821–1853." In *Dimensiones de la identidad patriótica. Religión política y regiones en México, Siglo XIX*. Mexico: Universidad Autónoma Metropolitana–Iztapalapa and Miguel Ángel Porrúa, 2001, 123–135.

———, ed.. "¿Ruptura o continuidad? Federalismo, centralismo y cultura político-religiosa, 1821–1854." *Eslabones* 13 (Jan.–June 1997): 6–19.

———. "La sacralización de lo cívico: la imagen religiosa en el discurso cívico-patriótico del México independiente. Puebla (1827–1853)." In *Estado, Iglesia y Sociedad en México, Siglo XIX*, coordinated by Álvaro Matute, Evelia Trejo, and Brian Connaughton. Mexico: Universidad Nacional Autónoma de México and Miguel Ángel Porrúa, 1995, 223–250.

———. "La Secretaría de Justicia y Negocios Eclesiásticos y la evolución de las sensibilidades nacionales: una óptica a partir de los papeles ministeriales, 1821–1854." In *Memoria del I Coloquio Historia de la Iglesia en el Siglo XIX*, compiled by Manuel Ramos Medina. Mexico: Condumex, 1998, 127–147.

———. "Troublemakers, Priests and Public Opinion in Mexico, 1821–1860." *Mexican Studies/Estudios Mexicanos* 17: 1 (winter 2001): 41–69.

Contreras, Carlos Alberto, and Peter L. Reich. "Numbers and the State: An overview of Government Statistical Compilation in Mexico Since the Colonial Period." In *Statistical Abstract of Latin America* 31, part 2, James W. Wilkie, Carlos Alberto Contreras, and Catherine Komisaruk, eds., Los Angeles: UCLA Latin American Center Publications, 1995, 1254–1264.

Corti, Egon Caesar Count. *Maximilian and Charlotte of Mexico*, translated by Catherine Alison Phillips. New York: Archon Books, 1968.

Cortina, José Gómez de la. *Cartilla Social o Breve Instrucción sobre los Derechos y Obligaciones del Hombre en la Sociedad Civil.* 1st ed. Mexico: Imprenta Galván, 1833.

———. *Cartilla Social o Breve Instrucción sobre los Derechos y Obligaciones del Hombre en la Sociedad Civil.* 2d ed. Mexico: Ignacio Cumplido, 1836.

Cosío Villegas, Daniel. *La cuestión arancelaria en México.* Mexico: Universidad Nacional Autónoma de México, 1989.

Costeloe, Michael P. *The Central Republic in Mexico, 1835–1846. Hombres de bien in the Age of Santa Anna.* Cambridge: Cambridge University Press, 1993.

———. *Church and State in Independent Mexico. A Study of the Patronage Debate.* London: Royal Historical Society, 1978.

———. "The Junta Patriótica and the Celebration of Independence Day in Mexico City, 1825–1855." *Mexican Studies/Estudios Mexicanos* 13: 1 (Winter 1997): 21–53.

———. "Mariano Arista y la élite de la Ciudad de México, 1851–1852." In *El conservadurismo mexicano en el siglo XIX (1810–1910)*, coordinated by Humberto Morales and William Fowler. Puebla: Benemérita Universidad Autónoma de Puebla, Saint-Andrews University, Secretaría de Cultura del Gobierno del Estado de Puebla, 1999, 169–186.

———. *La primera república federal de México, 1824–1835. Un estudio de los partidos políticos en el México independiente.* Mexico: Fondo de Cultura Económica, 1975.

———. *La república central en México, 1835–1846. "Hombres de bien" en la época de Santa Anna.* Mexico: Fondo de Cultura Económica, 2000.

Covarruvias, José de. *Memorias históricas de la última guerra con la Gran Bretaña, desde el año de 1774: Estados Unidos de América.* Madrid: Imprenta de Antonio Ramírez, 1783.

Covo, Jacqueline. *Las ideas de la reforma en México (1855–1861).* Mexico: Universidad Nacional Autónoma de México, 1983.

Crimm, Ana Carolina Castillo. "Finding Their Ways." In *Tejano Journey, 1770–1860*, edited by Gerald E. Poyo. Austin: University of Texas Press, 1996.

Cruz Mina Apat, María. *Fueros y revolución liberal en Navarra.* Madrid: Alianza Editorial, 1981.

Cumberland, Charles C. *The Mexican Revolution; Genesis under Madero.* Austin: University of Texas Press, 1952.

D. J. C. *Catecismo político arreglado a la constitución de la Monarquía Española.* Palma: en octavo por Miguel Domingo, 1812

———. *Catecismo político arreglado a la Constitución de la Monarquía Española; para la ilustración del Pueblo, instrucción de la juventud, y uso de las escuelas de primeras letras.* 2d ed. Puebla: Imprenta San Felipe Neri, 1820.

Davenport, Harbert. "General José María Jesús Carabajal." *Southwestern Historical Quarterly* 40 (April 1952).

Dawson, Daniel. *The Mexican Adventure*. London: G. Bell and Sons, Ltd. 1935.

Defensa de algunos puntos de la Doctrina Católica, o sea contestación a las "Nuevas observaciones sobre el opúsculo 'Lo del Señor Espinosa contra el Retrato a la Virgen.'" Guadalajara: Tipografía de Dionisio Rodríguez, 1851.

Delmos, José. *Representación de los cosecheros de pulque al Honorable Congreso del Estado de México*. Mexico: Imprenta del Aguila, 1828.

Dublán, Manuel, and José María Lozano. *Legislación mexicana o colección de las disposiciones legislativas expedidas desde la independencia de la República*. 34 vols. Mexico: Imprenta Dublan y Lozano, 1876–1904.

———. *Legislación mexicana, o colección completa de las disposiciones legislativas expedidas desde la independencia de la República*. 34 vols. Mexico: Dublán y Lozano Hijos, 1876–1911.

———. *Legislación mexicana o Colección completa de las disposiciones legislativas expedidas desde la independencia de la República*. 51 vols. Mexico: Imprenta y Litografía de Eduardo Dublán y Comp, 1877–1912.

Ducey, Michael T. "Village, Nation, and Constitution: Insurgent Politics in Papantla, Veracruz, 1810–1821." *Hispanic American Historical Review* 79: 3 (Aug. 1999): 463–493.

Duncan, Robert H., "For the Good of the Country: State and Nation Building during Maximilian's Mexican Empire, 1864–67." Ph.D. diss.: University of California, Irvine, 2001.

Edicto del . . . Dr. D. Toribio González, prebendado de la santa iglesia catedral y vicario capitular del obispado de Guadalajara, en sedevacante. Guadalajara: Imprenta de la viuda de Romero, December 12, 1824.

Esparza, Manuel. "Arzobispo Eulogio G. Gillow, ¿un liberal?" In *A Dios lo que es de Dios*, edited by Carlos Martínez Assad. Mexico: Aguilar, 1994.

Espinosa, Pedro. *Patronato en la nación. Núm. 2º, Contestación al dictamen de la comisión eclesiástica del Senado sobre que el patronato de la Iglesia mexicana reside radicalmente en la nación*. Guadalajara: Imprenta de Dionisio Rodríguez, 1833.

———. *Rentas eclesiásticas o sea impugnación de la disertación que sobre la materia se ha publicado de orden del Honorable Congreso de Zacatecas*. Guadalajara: Imprenta a cargo de Teodosio Cruz-Aedo, 1834.

Esposito, Matthew D. "Memorializing Modern Mexico: The State Funerals of the Porfirian Era, 1876–1911." Ph.D. dissertation, Texas Christian University, 1997.

Estrada Martínez, Rosa Isabel. "Legislación y política agraria de la Reforma y del Segundo Imperio." In *Memoria del II Congreso del Historia del Derecho Mexicano*. Mexico: Universidad Nacional Autónoma de México, 1981.

Examen crítico de la administracion del Principe Maximiliano de Austria en México. Mexico: Vicente G. Torres, 1867.

Exposición hecha por el M. I. Ayuntameinto de esta ciudad al Señor Prefecto del Primer Distrito, de los motivos que determinaron al primero á no contratar funciones de opera en cuaresma. Guadalajara: Imprenta de Dionisio Rodríguez, 1844.

Favre, J. *Les banques au Méxique*. Paris: Marcel Rivière, 1907.

Fernández, Isabel, y Carmen Nava Nava, "He de comer de esa tuna: Ensayo histórico iconográfico sobre el esudo nacional." Unpublished presentation at the American Historical Association, 1996.

Filisola, Vicente. *Memorias para la historia de la Guerra de Tejas*. 2 vols. Mexico: Imprenta de I. Cumplido, 1849.

Fisher, Lillian Estelle. "Early Masonry in Mexico (1806–1828)." *Southwestern Historical Quarterly* 40: 3 (Jan. 1939): 198–214.

Florescano, Enrique. "La construcción de identidades colectivas en México: Etnia, estado y nación." Unpublished essay, presented at the coloquio "México en Francia: Tradición, Modernidad, Actualidad de la Investigación Mexicana en Ciencias Sociales." Paris, May 1995.

———. "La creación de la bandera nacional: un encuentro de tres tradiciones." Unpublished essay presented at the coloquio "México en Francia: tradición. modernidad: Actualidad de la investigación mexicana en ciencias socials." Paris, May 1995.

———. *Memoria Mexicana*. México: Fondo de Cultura Económica, 1994.

Fontana, Roberto, and Roberto Garrabou. *Guerra y hacienda. La hacienda del gobierno central en los años de la guerra de independencia (1808–1814)*. Alicante: Instituto de Estudios Juan Gil-Albert, 1986.

Forment, Carlos A. *Democracy in Latin America, 1760–1900*. Chicago: University of Chicago Press, 2003.

Fowler, William. "Carlos María Bustamante: un tradicionalista liberal." In *El conservadurismo mexicano en el siglo XIX (1810–1910)*, coordinated by Humberto Morales and William Fowler. Puebla: Benemérita Universidad Autónoma de Puebla, Saint-Andrews University, Secretaría de Cultura del Gobierno del Estado de Puebla, 1999.

———. *Tornel and Santa Anna: The Writer and the Caudillo, Mexico 1795–1853*. Westport, Connecticut: Greenwood Press, 2000.

Frank, Ross. *From Settler to Citizen: New Mexican Economic Development and the Creation of Vecino Society, 1750–1820*. Berkeley: University of California Press, 2000.

Fraser, D. J. "La política de desamortización en las comunidades indígenas." *Historia Mexicana* 84 (1972): 615–652.

Frisch Philipp, W. "Los viejos códigos y las leyes modernas." In *Centenario del Código de comercio*, Instituto de Investigaciones Jurídicas. Mexico: Universidad Nacional Autónoma de México, 1991.

Fritz, Naomi. "José Antonio Navarro." MA thesis: Saint Mary's University of Saint Antonio, 1941.

Fuentes Quintana, Enrique. "El estilo tributario latino: características principales y problemas de su reforma." In *Las reformas tributarias de España*, edited by Francisco Comín Comín. Barcelona: Crítica, 1990.

Galeana de Valadés, Patricia. "El concepto de soberanía en la definición del Estado mexicano." In *La definición del estado mexicano 1857–1867*, edited by Patricia Galeana de Valadés. Mexico: Archivo General de la Nación, 1999.

———, ed. *La definición del estado mexicano 1857–1867*. Mexico: Archivo General de la Nación, 1999.

———. *Las relaciones iglesia-estado durante el segundo imperio*. Mexico: Universidad Nacional Autónoma de México, 1991.

García, Genaro. *Documentos históricos mexicanos*. 7 vols. Mexico: Museo Nacional de Arqueología Historia y Etnología, 1910.

García Cantú, Gastón. *El pensamiento de la reacción mexicana*. 3 vols. Mexico: Universidad Nacional Autónoma de México, 1994–1997.

García Melero, Luis Angel. *La independencia de los Estados Unidos de Norteamérica a través de la prensa española.* Madrid: Ministerio de Asuntos Exteriores, 1977.

Garritz, Amaya, Virginia Guedea, and Teresa Lozano, eds. *Impresos novohispanos, 1808–1821.* 2 vols. Mexico: Universidad Nacional Autónoma de Mexico, 1990.

Gellner, Ernest. *Nations and Nationalism.* Ithaca: Cornell University Press, 1983.

Giron, Nicole. "El proyecto de Folletería Mexicana del Siglo XIX: alcances y límites." *Secuencia* 39, nueva época (Sept.–Dec. 1997): 7–24.

Goddard, Jorge Adame. *El pensamiento político y social de los católicos mexicanos 1867–1914.* Mexico: Universidad Nacional Autónoma de México, 1981.

Gómez, Felipe Victoria. *Guadalupe Victoria: Primer Presidente de México.* Mexico: Ediciones Botas, 1962.

González, Julio V. *Filiación histórica del gobierno representativo argentino.* 2 vols. Buenos Aires: Editorial "La Vanguardia," 1937–1938.

González, María del Refugio. "Comercio y comerciantes en México en el siglo XIX." In *Centenario del Código de Comercio,* Instituto de Investigaciones Jurídicas. Mexico: Universidad Nacional Autónoma de México, 1991.

———. "La Legislación minera durante el siglo XIX." *Minería Mexicana.* Mexico: Comisión de Fomento Minero, 1984, 249–263.

Gortari Rabiela, Hira de. "Julio-agosto de 1808: 'La lealtad mexicana.'" *Historia Mexicana* 39: 1 (July–Sept. 1989): 201.

Grandner, Margarete. "Conservative Social Politics in Austria, 1880–1890." *Austrian History Yearbook* 27 (1996): 77–107.

Green, Stanley C. *The Mexican Republic: The First Decade 1823–1832.* Pittsburgh: University of Pittsburgh Press, 1987.

Greif, A. "The Fundamental Problem of Exchange. A Research Agenda in Historical Institutional Analysis." *European Review of Economic History* 4 (2000): 251–284.

Gross, Jean Pierre. "Progressive Taxation and Social Justice in Eighteenth Century France." *Past and Present* 140 (Aug. 1993): 79–126.

Guanajuato. *Decretos del Congreso Cuarto y Quinto Constitucional del Estado de Guanajuato.* Mexico: Imprenta de Ximeno, 1845.

Guardino, Peter F. *Peasants, Politics, and the Formation of Mexico's National State: Guerrero, 1800–1857.* Stanford: Stanford University Press, 1996.

———. "'Toda libertad para emitir sus votos': Plebeyos, campesinos, y elecciones en Oaxaca, 1808–1850." *Cuadernos del Sur* 6: 15 (June 2000): 87–114.

Guedea, Virginia. *En busca de un gobierno alterno: Los Guadalupes de México.* Mexico: Universidad Nacional Autónoma de México, 1992.

———. "The First Popular Elections in Mexico City, 1812–1823." In *The Evolution of the Mexican Political System,* edited by Jaime E. Rodríguez O. Wilmington: SR Books, 1993, 45–69.

———. *Las gacetas de México y la medicina: Un índice.* Mexico: Universidad Nacional Autónoma de México, 1991.

———, ed. *La independencia de México y el proceso autonomista novohispano.* Mexico: Universidad Nacional Autónoma de México, 2001.

———. *José María Morelos y Pavón.* Mexico: Universidad Nacional Autónoma de México, 1981.

———. "México en 1812: Control político y bebidas prohibidas." *Estudios de Historia Moderna y Contemporánea de México* 8 (1980): 23–65.

———. "Las primeras elecciones populares en la ciudad de México, 1812–1813." *Mexican Studies/Estudios Mexicanos* 7: 1 (winter 1991): 1–28.

———. "Los procesos electorales insurgentes." *Estudios de Historia Novohispana* 11 (1991): 222–248.

———. "El pueblo de México y la política capitalina, 1808–1812." *Mexican Studies/Estudios mexicanos* 10: 1 (winter 1994): 27–61.

———. "Las sociedades secretas durante el movimiento de independencia." In *The Independence of Mexico and the Creation of the New Nation*, edited by Jaime E. Rodríguez O. Los Angeles: UCLA Latin American Center, 1989, 45–62.

Guerra, François-Xavier. *México: Del Antiguo Régimen a la Revolución.* 2 vols. Mexico: Fondo de Cultura Económica, 1988.

———. *Le Mexique de l'ancien regime a la revolution.* 2 vols. Paris: Editions L'Harmattan, 1985.

———. *Modernidad e independencias. Ensayos sobre las revoluciones hispánicas.* Madrid: Editorial MAPFRE, 1992, and Fondo de Cultura Económica, 1993.

———. "El soberano y su reino: Reflexiones sobre la génesis del ciudadano en América Latina." In *Ciudadanía política y formación de la naciones: Perspectivas históricas de América Latina,* coordinated by Hilda Sabato. Mexico: Fondo de Cultura Económica, 1999, 33–61.

Gulick, Charles A., ed. *Papers of Mirabeau Buonaparte Lamar.* 6 vols. Austin: A. C. Balwin Printers, [1921].

Gutiérrez de Estrada, José María. *Carta dirigida al excelentísimo señor presidente de la República sobre la necesidad de buscar en una convención el posible remedio de los males que aquejan a la República, México.* Mexico: Ignacio Cumplido, 1840.

———. *Discurso pronunciado por D. J. M. Gutiérrez de Estrada presidente de la diputación, el 3 de octobre de 1863, al ofrecer en el palacio de Miramar, a nombre de la asamblea de los Notables de Mexico, la corona imperial AS.A.I. Y R. el archiduque Fernando Maximiliano.* Querétaro: Imprenta del Gobierno, 1863.

Habermas, Jürgen. *The Structural Transformation of the Public Sphere: An Inquiry into a Bourgeois Category.* Cambridge: MIT Press, 1989.

Hacking, Ian. *The Taming of Chance.* Cambridge: Cambridge University Press, 1990.

Hale, Charles A. *El liberalismo mexicano en la época de Mora, 1821–1853.* Mexico: Siglo XXI, 1968.

———. *El liberalismo mexicano en la época de Mora, 1821–1853.* Mexico: Siglo Veintiuno Editores, 1972.

———. *Mexican Liberalism in the Age of Mora, 1821–1853.* New Haven: Yale University Press, 1968.

———. *The Transformation of Liberalism in Late Nineteenth-Century Mexico.* Princeton: Princeton University Press, 1989.

Hamill, Hugh M. *The Hidalgo Revolt: Prelude to Mexican Independence.* Gainesville: University of Florida Press, 1966.

Hamnett, Brian R. *Juárez.* New York: Longman, 1994.

———. *Politics and Trade in Southern Mexico, 1750–1821.* Cambridge: Cambridge University Press, 1971.

———. "Royalist Counterinsurgency and the Continuity of Rebellion: Guanajuato and Michoacán, 1813–20." *Hispanic American Historical Review* 62: 1 (Feb. 1982): 19–48.

John H. Hann. "The Role of the Mexican Deputies in the Proposal and Enactment of Measures of Economic Reform Applicable to Mexico." In *Mexico and the Spanish Cortes, 1810–1822*, edited by Nettie Lee Benson. Austin: University of Texas Press, 1966, 167–168.

Hanson, Randall S. "The Day of Ideals: Catholic Social Action in the Age of the Mexican Revolution, 1867–1929." Ph.D. diss.: Indiana University, 1994.

Hardin, Stephen L. "Efficient in the Cause." In *Tejano Journey, 1770–1860*, edited by Gerald E. Poyo. Austin: University of Texas Press, 1996.

Haslip, Joan. *The Crown of Mexico*. New York: Holt, Rinehart, and Winston, 1971.

Henderson, Mary Virginia. "Minor Empresario Contracts for the Colonization of Texas, 1825–1834." *Southwestern Historical Quarterly* 31: 4 (1928): 295–324.

Hensel, Silke. *Die Entstenhung des Foderalismus in Mexiko. Die politische Elite Oaxacas zwischen Stadt, Region un Staat, 1786–1835*. Stuttgart: Franz Steiner Verlag, 1997.

———. "Los orígenes del federalismo en México. Una perspectiva desde la provincia de Oaxaca de finales del siglo XVIII a la Primera República." *Ibero-Amerikanisches Archiv* (1999): 235.

Hernández Chávez, Alicia. *Anenecuilco. Memoria y vida de un pueblo*. Mexico: Fideicomiso Historia de las Américas/El Colegio de México/Fondo de Cultura Económica, 1993

———. *México. Breve historia contemporánea*. Colección Popular. Mexico: Fondo de Cultura Económica, 2000.

———. *La tradición republicana del buen gobierno*. Mexico: Fideicomiso Historia de las Américas/El Colegio de México/Fondo de Cultura Económica, 1993.

Hernández y Dávalos, J. E. *Colección de documentos para la historia de la guerra de independencia de México de 1808–1821*. 6 vols. Mexico: José María Sandoval, 1882.

Herr, Richard. *The Eighteenth-Century Revolution in Spain*. Princeton: Princeton University Press, 1958.

Herrejón Peredo, Carlos, ed. *Actas de la Diputación Provincial de Nueva España, 1820–1821*. Mexico: Camara de Diputados, 1985.

———. "México: Luces de Hidalgo y de Abad y Queipo." *CARAVELLE: Cahiers du Monde Hispanique el Luso-Brasilien* 54 (1990): 107–135.

Holden, R. H. *Mexico and the Survey of Public Lands. The Management of Modernization 1876–1911*. De Kalb: Northern Illinois University Press, 1994.

Hutchinson, C. Alan. "General José Antonio Mexía and His Texas Interests." *Southwestern Historical Quarterly* 85 (Oct. 1978): 117–142.

———. "Mexican Federalists in New Orleans and the Texas Revolution." *Louisiana Historical Quarterly* 30 (Jan. 1956): 1–47.

Ibarra, Antonio. *La organización regional del mercado interno novohispano. La economía colonial de Guadalajara, 1770–1804*. Mexico: Universidad Nacional Autónoma de México-Universidad Autónoma de Puebla, 2000.

———. "Reformas y fiscalidad republicana en Jalisco: ingresos estatales, contribución directa y pacto federal, 1824–1835." In *Hacienda y política. Las finanzas públicas y los grupos de poder en la primera república federal mexicana*, edited by José Serrano Ortega and Luis Jáuregui. Mexico: El Colegio de Michoacán-Instituto Mora, 1998, 133–174.

Ibarra Bellón, Araceli. *El comercio y el poder en México, 1821–1864. La lucha por las fuentes financieras entre el Estado central y las regiones.* Mexico: Fondo de Cultura Económica, 1998.

Iglesias Cabrera, Sonia, and Guillermo Murray Prisant. *Piel de Papel, Manos de Palo; Historia de los Títeres en México.* México: Espase-Calpe Mexicana, 1995.

Iguíniz, Juan B. *Catálogo Biobibliográfico de los Doctores, Licenciados y Maestros de la Antigua Universidad de Guadalajara.* Mexico: Universidad Nacional Autónoma de México, 1963.

Illades, Carlos. *Hacia la república del trabajo.* Mexico: Universidad Autónoma Metropolitana-El Colegio de México, 1996.

Iturbide, Agustín de. *Memorias escritas desde Liorna.* México: Editorial Jus, 1973.

J. H. *El liberalismo y sus efectos en la República Mexicana.* Mexico: Imprenta de A. Boix, 1858.

Jalisco. *Colección de decretos, circulares y órdenes de los Poderes Legislativo y Ejecutivo del Estado de Jalisco.* Guadalajara: Jalisco, Tipoligía de Pérez Lete, 1876.

———. *Constitución de Jalisco.* November 1824.

Jáuregui, Luis. *La real hacienda de la Nueva España. Su administración en la época de los intendentes, 1786–1821.* Mexico: Universidad Nacional Autónoma de México, 1990.

Jenkins, John H., ed., *Papers of the Texas Revolution, 1835–1836.* 10 vols. Austin: Presidial Press, 1973.

Kahle, Günter. *El ejército y la formación del Estado en los comienzos de la Independencia de México.* Mexico: Fondo de Cultura Económica, 1997.

Kamen, Henry. *Empire: How Spain Became a World Power, 1492–1763.* New York: Harper Collins Publishers, 2003.

Knowlton, Robert J. *Los bienes del clero y la Reforma mexicana, 1856–1910.* Mexico: Fondo de Cultura Económica, 1985.

———. "La división de la tierras de los pueblos durante el siglo XIX: el caso de Michoacán." *Historia Mexicana* 157 (1990): 3–25

———. "El ejido mexicano en el siglo XIX." *Historia Mexicana* 189 (1998): 91–92.

———. "La individualización de la propriedad corporativa civil en el siglo XIX. Notas sobre Jalisco." *Historia Mexicana* 109 (1978): 24–61.

———. "Tribunales federales y terrenos rurales en el México del siglo XIX: el Semanario Judicial de la Federación." *Historia Mexicana* 181 (1996): 71–98.

Krause, Enrique. *Mexico: Biography of Power: A History of Modern Mexico, 1810–1996,* translated by Hank Heifetz. New York: Harper Collins, 1997.

Kroeber, C. B. *El hombre, la tierra y el agua. Las políticas en torno a la irrigación en la agricultura de México.* Mexico: CIESAS, 1994.

Krugman, Paul R., and Maurice Obstfeld. *Economía internacional. Teoría y práctica.* 4th ed. Mexico: McGraw-Hill, 1999.

Kuntz Ficker, Sandra. "Nuevas series del comercio exterior de México, 1870–1929," *Revista de Historia Económica* 20: 2 (2002), 213–270.

———. "Institutional Change and Foreign Trade in Mexico, 1870–1911." In *The Mexican Economy, 1870–1930: Essays on the Economic History of Institutions, Revolution, and Growth,* edited by Stephen Haber and Jeffrey Bortz. Stanford: Stanford University Press, 2003, 161–204.

Lack, Paul. *The Texas Revolutionary Experience, A Political and Social History, 1835–1836*. College Station: Texas A&M University Press, 1992.

Las chinches de la Europa, ó comparación de los franceses con este odioso animal. Por el autor del juego de las provincias. Mexico: Imprenta de la calle del Espiritu Santo, c. 1809.

Lato Monte, Lodovico. *Catecismo de la Independencia en Siete Declaraciones, por. . . . Quien lo dedica al Excmo. Señor don Agustín de Iturbide y Aramburu, Generalísimo de las armas de mar y tierra, y Presidente de la Regencia Gobernadora del Imperio Mexicano*. Mexico: Imprenta de Mariano Ontiverso, 1821.

Leal, Juan Felipe. *Del mutualismo al sindicalismo en México, 1843–1910*. Mexico: Universidad Nacional Autónoma de México, 1991.

Lee, James H. "Church and State in Mexican Higher Education, 1821–1861." *Journal of Church and State* 20: 1 (winter 1978).

Lempériere, Annick. "Reflexiones sobre la terminología política del liberalismo." In *Construcción de la legitimidad política en México,* edited by Brian Connaughton, Carlos Illades, and Sonia Pérez Toledo. Zamora and Mexico: El Colegio de Michoacán, Universidad Autónoma Metropolitana, Universidad Nacional Autónoma de México, and El Colegio de México, 1999, 35–56.

Lerdo de Tejada, Miguel. *Apuntes históricos de la heróica ciudad de Veracruz*. 2 vols. Mexico: Secretaría de Educación Pública, 1940.

Limantour, José Yves. *Apuntes sobre mi vida pública*. Mexico: Editorial Porrúa, 1965.

List, Federico. *Sistema nacional de economía política*. Mexico: Fondo de Cultura Económica, 1979.

López Castellanos, Fernando. *Liberalismo económico y reforma fiscal. La contribución directa de 1813*. Granada: Universidad de Granada-Fundación Caja de Granda, 1995.

Lozano, A. J. *Código de comercio de los Estados Unidos Mexicanos*. Mexico: Imprenta de Lozano, 1890.

Lubienski, Johann. "Una monarquía liberal en 1863." In *La definición del estado mexicano 1857–1867,* edited by Patricia Galeana de Valadés. Mexico: Archivo General de la Nación, 1999.

Ludlow, Leonor. "Elites y finanzas públicas durante la gestación del Estado independiente, 1821–1824." In *Hacienda y política. Las finanzas públicas y los grupos de poder en la primera república federal mexicana,* edited by José Serrano Ortega and Luis Jáuregui. Mexico: El Colegio de Michoacán-Instituto Mora, 1998, 79–114.

Macedo, P. *La evolución mercantil* (1903). Mexico: Universidad Nacional Autónoma de México, 1970.

Macedo, Pablo. *La evolución mercantil; Las Comunicaciones y obras públicas; La Hacienda Pública. Tres monografías . . .* Mexico: J. Ballescá, 1905.

Macías, Ana. *Génesis del gobierno constitucional en México, 1808–1820*. Mexico: Secretaría de Educación Pública, 1973.

Macune, Charles. *El Estado de México y la federación mexicana*. Mexico: Fondo de Cultura Económica, 1978.

Maillefert, Eugenio. *Directorio del Comercio del Imperio Mexicano para el año de 1867*. Facsimile edition. Mexico: Instituto de Investigaciones Dr. José María Luis Mora, 1992.

Mallon, Florencia. *Peasant and Nation: The Making of Postcolonial Mexico and Peru*. Berkeley: University of California Press, 1995.

Manifiesto que sobre la instalación de la Junta provisional gubernativa de Oajaca, se hace a los habitantes de la provincia. Puebla: Pedro de la Rosa, 1823.

Maravall, José Antonio. *La philosophie politique espagnole au XVIIe siècle dans ses rapports avec l'esprit de la contre-réforme.* Paris: J. Vrin, 1955.

Marichal, Carlos. "La hacienda pública del Estado de México desde la Independencia hasta la república restaurada, 1824–1870." In *El primer siglo de la Hacienda Pública del Estado de México, 1824–1923.* 4 vols. Edited by Carlos Marichal, Manuel Miño, and Paolo Riguzzi. Toluca: Gobierno del Estado de México-El Colegio Mexiquense, 1994.

Marichal, Juan. "From Pistoia to Cádiz: A Generation's Itinerary, 1786–1812." In *The Ibero-American Enlightenment,* edited by A. Owen Aldridge. Urbana: University of Illinois Press, 1971.

Márquez, Graciela. "Tariff Protection in Mexico, 1892–1909: Ad Valorem Tariff Rates and Sources of Variation." In *Latin America and the World Economy Since 1800,* edited by John Coatsworth and Alan M. Taylor. Cambridge: The Rockefeller Center Series on Latin American Studies, Harvard University, 1998, 407–442.

Martin, L. Aymé. *Censura y prohibición del libro titulado "Educación de las madres de familia, o de la civilización del género humano por medio de las mujeres."* Guadalajara: Tipografía de Dionisio Rodríguez, 1850.

Martínez Marina, Francisco. "Introduction" to the *Siete Partidas.* Vol. 194 of Biblioteca de Autores Españoles. Madrid: Ediciones Atlas, 1966.

———. *Teoría de las Cortes.* 2 vols. Biblioteca de Autores Españoles. Madrid: Ediciones Atlas, 1968–1969.

Mateos, Juan Antonio. *Historia Parlamentaria.* Mexico: PRI, 1976.

Mateos, Juan A. *Historia Parlamentaria.* Mexico: Congress of the Union. Instituto de Estudios Parlamentarios, 1997.

Maximilian. *Recollections of My Life by Maximilian I. Emperor of Mexico.* London: Richard Bentley, 1868.

Mayer Celis, Leticia. *Entre el infierno de una realidad y el cielo de un imaginario: Estadística y comunidad científica en el México de la primera mitad del siglo xix.* México: El Colegio de México, 1999.

———. "La *Ley de los Grandes Números* y La Cultura Liberal en México, 1856– 1885." In *Imaginar la nación,* edited by François-Xavier Guerra and Mónica Quijada. Münster, Germany: Cuadernos de historia latinoamericana, 1994, 51–82.

McBride, George McCutchen. *Los sistemas de propiedad rural en México (1925).* Mexico: Conaculta, 1993.

McPharlin, Paul. *The Puppet Theatre in America: A History.* New York: Harper & Brothers, 1949.

McGowan, Gerald L. *Prensa y poder, 1854–1857.* Mexico: El Colegio de México, 1978.

McLean, Malcolm D. *Papers Concerning Robertson's Colony in Texas.* 16 vols. Fort Worth and Arlington: University of Texas at Arlington Press, 1974–1990.

Medina y Ormachea, C. A. de. *Garantía de la propiedad raíz en Mexico.* Mexico: Secretaría de Fomento, 1901.

Merriman, Roger B. *The Rise of the Spanish Empire in the Old World and the New.* 4 vols. New York: The Macmillan Co., 1918–1934.

Mexico. Archivo General de la Nación. "La consumación de independencia 175 años." Documentary exposition held in 1996.

———. Cámara de Diputados. *Diario de los Debates de la Cámara de Diputados.* 1878, 1880, 1881, 1882, 1884, 1886, 1887, 1888, 1889, 1905.

———. *Código de Comercio de los Estados Unidos Mexicanos 1883.* Mexico: Tipografía Gonzalo Esteva, 1884.

———. *Colección de leyes, decretos y reglamentos que interinamente forman el sistema político, administrativo y judicial del Imperio.* 8 vols. Mexico: A Boix, 1865.

———. Congress. *Actas del Congreso contituyente de México.* Mexico: Imprenta de Valdés, 1822.

———. Congress. *Actas del Congreso Constituyente.* Mexico: Universidad Nacional Autónoma de México, 1980.

———. Congress. *Decreto del Soberano Congreso Mexicano para las elecciones que deberán hacer las Provincias, de los Diputados que han de componer el que constituya la Nación.* Mexico: Imprenta del Supremo Gobierno en Palacio, 1823.

———. Congress. *Representación de los comisionados de las provincias al Soberano Congreso.* Mexico: Imprenta del Ciudadano Alejandro Valdés, 1823.

———. *Diario de la Junta Nacional Instituyente, 1822.* Mexico: Imprenda de Valdés.

———. *Diario de las sesiones de la soberana junta provisional gubernativa del Imperio mexicano.* Mexico: Imprenta de Valdés, 1821.

———. Secretaría de Fomento. *Disposiciones sobre designación y fraccionamiento de los ejidos de los pueblos mandados compilar y publicar por el Sr. Ministro de Fomento Gral Carlos Pacheco.* Mexico: Secretaría de Fomento, 1889.

———. Secretaría de Hacienda y Crédito Público. *Informe presentado al Congreso de la Unión . . . en cumplimiento del precepto constitucional por el C. Francisco Mejía, Secretario de Estado y del Despacho de Hacinda y Crédito Público de los Estado Unidos Mexicanos.* Mexico: 1872–1873; 1873–1874; 1874–1875.

———. Secretaría de Hacienda y Crédito Público. *La hacienda pública de México a través de los informes presidenciales.* Mexico: Secretaría de Hacienda y Crédito Público, 1963–1977.

———. Secretaría de Hacienda y Crédito Público. *Memoria que el Secretario de Hacienda y Crédito Público presenta al Quinto Congreso de la Unión . . .* Mexico: 1869, 1879, 1884, 1888, and 1892.

———. Secretaría de Hacienda y Crédito Público. *Noticia pormenorizada del costo que tienen las mercancias extranjeras que se importan por el puerto de Veracruz mandada formar por el secretario de Hacienda a Luis N. Márquez.* Mexico, 1879.

Mexico, Ayuntamiento. In *Leyes Fundamentales de México, 1808–1983*, edited by Felipe Tena Ramírez. Mexico: Porrúa, 1983.

Mexico, Estado de. *Colección de decretos del congreso Constituyente del Estado libre y soberano de México.* Toluca: Imprenta de Quijano, 1850.

———. *Representación que hacen al congreso del estado de México los propietarios de Haciendas de caña del mismo.* Mexico: Imprenta de Márquez, 1828.

Meyer, Jean. "La Junta Protectora de las clases menesterosas. Indigenismo y agrarismo en el segundo imperio." In *Indio, nación y comunidad en el México del siglo XIX*, coordinated by Antonio Escobar. Mexico: Centro de Estudios Mexicanos y Centroamericanos, 1993.

Meza Olivier, Rocío, and Luis Olivera López, eds. *Catálogo de la colección LaFragua de la Biblioteca Nacional de México, 1800–1810.* Mexico: Universidad Nacional Autónoma de México, 1993.

———, eds. *Catálogo de la colección LaFragua de la Biblioteca Nacional de México, 1811–1821.* Mexico: Universidad Nacional Autónoma de México, 1996.

Mier, Servando Teresa de. *La formación de un republicano.* Compilation and introduction by Jaime E. Rodríguez O. Mexico: Universidad Nacional Autónoma de México, 1988.

———. "Idea de la Constitución dada a las Américas por los reyes de España antes de la invasión del antiguo despotismo." In *Obras completas de Servando Teresa de Mier. Vol. 4, La formación de un republicano,* edited by Jaime E. Rodríguez O. México: UNAM, 1988.

Miranda, José. *Humboldt y México.* Mexico: Universidad Nacional Autónoma de México, 1962.

———. *Las ideas y las instituciones políticas mexicanas, primera parte, 1521–1820.* 2d ed. Mexico: Universidad Nacional Autónoma de México, 1978.

Molina Enríquez, Andrés. *Los grandes problemas nacionales* (1909). Mexico: Era, 1978.

Montiel, Rosalba, ed. *Documentos de la guerra de independencia en Oaxaca.* Oaxaca: Archivo General del Estado de Oaxaca, 1986.

Mora, José María Luis. *Obras Completas. Política.* 3 vols. Mexico: Instituto Mora–Secrataría Educación Pública, 1986.

———. *Obras sueltas de . . . , Ciudadano mejicano.* 2 vols. París: Librería de Rosa, 1837.

Morán y Crivelli, Tomás. *Observaciones al proyecto de reglamento presentado por la Junta protectora de las clases menesterosas sobre el trabajo de los peones y sirvientes de fincas rústicas.* Mexico: Imprenta Literaria, 1865.

Munguía, Clemente. *Los principios de la Iglesia Católica comparados con los de las escuelas racionalistas, en sus aplicaciones a la enseñanza y educacion pública, y en sus relaciones con los progresos de las ciencias, de las letras y de las artes, la mejora de las costumbres y la perfeccion de la sociedad. Por el Lic. . . . , Rector del Seminario, Canónigo de esta Santa Iglesia Catedral, Provisor y Vicario general de este Obispado.* Morelia: Imprenta de Y. Arango, 1849.

Muñoz, Manuel Ferrer. *La formación de un estado nacional en México. El Imperio y la República Federal: 1821–1835.* Mexico: Universidad Nacional Autónoma de México, 1995.

Muro, Luis, ed. *Historia parlamentaria. Crónicas del soberano congreso constituyente mexicano.* Mexico: Cámara de Diputados-Instituto de Investigaciónes Legislativas, 1983.

Muzzarelli, Conde. *Cartas del Conde Muzzarelli, sobre el juramento de la Constitución Cispadana,* translated by Fr. José María Guzmán. Guadalajara: Imprenta del Gobiero, 1843.

Navarro, Bernabé. *La introducción de la filosofía moderna en México.* Mexico: El Colegio de México, 1948.

Neufeld, Stephan. "The Preformative Porfirian Army." M.A. thesis: University of British Columbia, 2003.

Noriega Elío, Cecilia. *El Constituyente de 1842.* Mexico: Universidad Nacional Autónoma de México, 1986.

Noticia de la importación y exportación de mercancías, en los años fiscales de 1872 a 1873, 1873 a 1874 y 1874 a 1875 formada bajo la dirección de José Ma. Garmendia. Mexico: Tipografía de Gonzalo A Esteva, 1880.

O se descoyota a la nación o cesa su libertad. Puebla: Imprenta Liberal de Moreno Hermanos, 1824.

Oaxaca *Bases para el Gobierno Provincial de este Estado interin se da la Constitución General de la Nación.* Oaxaca: n.p., 1823.

————. *Voto particular del Señor Ordoño, Diputado del Congreso Provincial de Oajaca sobre el pase a Convocatoria de México. Con notas de un Ciudadano del Estado libre de Xalisco.* Guadalajara: Imprenta del Ciudadano Urbano Sanroman, 1823.

Oaxaqueños. Oaxaca: Impreso en la Oficina del R. P. Preposito D. José María Idiaquez, 1820.

Observaciones contra la impugnación del libro titulado El retrato de la Virgen, y su contestación por el Dr. D. Pedro Espinosa, Canónigo de Guadalajara. México: Tipografía de R. Rafael, Calle de la Cadena número 13, 1850.

Observaciones que hace el Venerable Cabildo de Guadalajara al Soberano Congreso Constituyente, sobre el proyecto de Constitución. Guadalajara: Imprenta del Gobierno, 1842.

Observaciones sobre el dictamen del Señor Licenciado don Manuel de la Peña y Peña relativo al decreto de 31 de agosto de 1843. Guadalajara: Imprenta del Gobierno, 1847.

O'Callaghan, Joseph F. *The Cortes of Castile-León, 1188–1350.* Philadelphia: University of Pennsylvannia Press, 1989.

Ocampo López, Javier. *Los Catecismos Políticos de la Independencia de Hispanoamérica. De la Monarquía a la República.* Tunja: Publicación del Magister en Historia, Universidad Pedagógica y Tecnológica de Colombia, 1988.

O'Dogherty, Laura. "El ascenso de una jerarquía eclesial intransigente, 1890–1914." In *Memoria del I Coloquio Historia de la Iglesia en el Siglo XIX,* compiled by Manuel Ramos Medina. Mexico: Condumex, 1998.

O'Gorman, Edmundo. *Historia de las Divisiones Territoriales de México.* Mexico: Editorial Porrúa, 1985.Olavarría y Ferrari, Enrique. *Episodios históricos mexicanos.* 4 vols. Mexico City: ICH-FCE, 1987.

Olimón Nolasco, Manuel. "Una revista católica europea y la Reforma mexicana." In *Las fuentes eclesiásticas para la historia social de México,* coordinated by Brian F. Connaughton and Andrés Lira González. Mexico: Universidad Autónoma Metropolitana-Iztapalapa and Instituto Mora, 1996.

Olmedo y Lama, J. *Ordenanzas de Minería y colección de leyes.* Mexico: Imprenta de Vicente García Torres, 1873.

Olmos Sánchez, Isabel. *La sociedad mexicana en vísperas de la independencia (1787–1821).* Murcia: Universidad de Murcia, 1989.

Orozco, W. L. *Legislación y jurisprudencia sobre terrenos baldíos.* Mexico: Imprenta El Tiempo, 1895.

Ortiz, Juan. "Las fuerzas militares y el proyecto de estado en México, 1767–1835." In *Cincuenta años de historia en México.* Vol. 2. Edited by Alicia Hernández Chávez. Mexico: El Colegio de México, 1991.

————. *Guerra y gobierno. Los pueblos y la independencia de México.* Sevilla: Instituto Mora-Universidad de Sevilla, 1997.

Ortiz, Tadeo. *México considerado como Nación Independiente y Libre según algunas indicaciones sobre los Deberes más Esenciales de los Mexicanos.* Mexico: Cien de México, 1996.

Pagden, Anthony. *Lords of all the Word: Ideologies of Empire in Spain, Britain, and France c. 1500–c.1800*. New Haven: Yale University Press, 1995.

Pallares, J. *Derecho mercantil mexicano*, vol. 1. Mexico: J. Guerra, 1891.

Pani, Erika. *Para mexicanizar el Segundo Imperio: el imaginario político de los imperialistas*. Mexico: El Colegio de México and Instituto José María Luis Mora, 2001.

———. "La tentación de la dictadura 1857–1861." In *La definición del estado mexicano 1857–1867*, edited by Patricia Galeana de Valadés. Mexico: Archivo General de la Nación, 1999.

Paret, Peter. *Clausewitz and the State. The Man, His Theories and His Times*. Princeton: Princeton University Press, 1985.

Peloso, Vicent C., and Barbara A. Tenenbaum, eds. *Liberals, Politics, and Power: State Formation in Nineteenth-Century Latin America*. Athens: University of Georgia Press, 1999.

Pérez Garzón, Juan Sisinio. *Milicia nacional y revolución burguesa*. Madrid: CSIC, 1978.

Pérez-Rioja, José Antonio. *Proyección y actualidad de Feijoo (ensayo de interpretación)*. Madrid: Instituto de Estudios Políticos, 1965.

Pérez Sánchez, Alfonso E., and Eleanor A. Sayre. *Goya and the Spirit of the Enlightenment*. Boston: Little, Brown, 1989.

Perry, Laurens Ballard. *Juárez and Díaz: Machine Politics in Mexico*. DeKalb: Northern Illinois University Press, 1978.

Phelan, John L. *The People and the King: The Comunero Revolution in Colombia, 1781*. Madison: University of Wisconsin Press, 1978.

Pimentel, Francisco. *La economía política aplicada a la propiedad territorial en México*. Mexico: Andrade y Escalante, 1866.

Pinal, L. *Catecismo de economía política*, Part II. Mexico: Imprenta de Ignacio Cumplido, 1856.

Piskorski, Wladimiro. *Las Cortes de castilla en el periodo de tránsito de la Edad Media a la Moderna 1188–1520*. Barcelona: Ediciones El Albir, S. A., 1977.

Pocock, John G. A. *The Machiavellian Moment: Florentine Political Thought and the Atlantic Republican Tradition*. Princeton: Princeton University Press, 1975.

Poinsett, Joel R. *Notes on Mexico made in the Autum of 1822*. Philadelphia: H. C. Carey and Lea, 1824.

Polt, John H. R. *Jovellanos and His English Sources, Economic, Philosophical, and Political Writings*. Philadelphia: Transactions of the American Philosophical Society, 1964.

Poyo, Gerald E., ed. *Tejano Journey, 1770–1850*. Austin: University of Texas Press, 1996.

———, and Gilberto M. Hinojosa. "Spanish Texas and Borderlands Historiography in Transition: Implications for United States History." *Journal of American History*, 75: 2 (September 1988): 395–416.

———, and Gilberto M. Hinojosa, eds. *Tejano Origins in Eighteenth-Century San Antonio*. Austin: University of Texas Press, 1991.

Primera Parte de las Coplas de Don Simón. Puebla: Imprenta de Jesús Franco é hijo, 1907.

Prohibición del libro titulado. "El retrato de la Virgen María en los cielos." Guadalajara: Tipografía de Rodríguez, 1850.

Proyecto de Código Mercantil. Mexico: Imprenta de Gobierno, 1869.

Puebla. *Breve Noticia del recibimiento y permanencia de SS. MM. II. en la ciudad de Puebla*. Puebla: T.F. Neve, 1864.

———, Ayuntamiento de. *Representación que hace a S. M. Las Cortes el . . . , para que en esta ciudad, cabeza de provincia, se establezca Diputación provincial, como dispone la Constitución*. Puebla: Imprenta del Gobierno, 1820.

———, Junta de. *Acta de la Junta de Puebla sobre la reinstalación del Congreso Mexicano*. Puebla: Pedro de la Rosa, 1823.

———, Junta Electoral. *Representación, que hace al soberano congreso de Cortes la . . . de la provincia de Puebla conforme al artículo 325 de la Constitución*. Puebla: Imprenta de Pedro de la Rosa, 1820.

Quiñónez, Isabel. *Mexicanos en su tinta: Calendarios*. Mexico: Instituto Nacional de Antropología e Historia, 1994.

Quiroz-Martínez, Olga Victoria. *La introducción de la filosofía moderna en España*. Mexico: El Colegio de México, 1949.

Radding, Cynthia. *Wandering Peoples: Colonialism, Ethnic Spaces, and Ecological Frontiers in Northwestern Mexico, 1700–1850*. Durham: Duke University Press, 1997.

Ramón, Regino F. *Historia general del estado de Coahuila*. 2 vols. Saltillo: Universidad Autónoma de Coahuila, 1990, c. 1917.

Ramos Gómez-Pérez, Luis. "Escuela católica y sociedad a principios del Siglo XX." In *La Iglesia Católica en México*, edited by Nelly Sigaut. Mexico: El Colegio de Michoacán and Secretaría de Gobernación, 1997.

———. "El Emperador, el Nuncio y el Vaticano." In *Estado, Iglesia y Sociedad en México, Siglo XIX*, coordinated by Álvaro Matute, Evelia Trejo, and Brian Connaughton. Mexico: Universidad Nacional Autónoma de México and Miguel Ángel Porrúa, 1995, 251–265.

Rangel Rojas, Guillermo. *General Antonio de León. Consumador de la Independencia de Oaxaca y Benemérito del Estado de Oaxaca*. Oaxaca: Ayuntamiento de Oaxaca de Juárez, 1997.

Reichstein, Andreas V. *Rise of the Lone Star*. Translated by Jeanne R. Willson. College Station: Texas A&M University Press, 1989.

Reyes, R., and F. F. Barker. *The Mining Laws of Mexico*. Mexico: The American Book, 1910.

Ridley, Jasper. *Maximilian and Juárez*. New York: Ticknor and Fields, 1992.

Riguzzi, Paolo. "La diplomacia de la reciprocidad: comercio y política entre México y Estados Unidos, 1875–1897." *Secuencia*, nueva época, 48 (Sep.–Dec. 2000): 151–170.

———. "Libre cambio y libertad económica en la experiencia liberal mexicana, 1850–1896." In *Constitucionalismo y orden liberal en América Latina, 1850–1920*, edited by Marcello Carmagnani. Torino: Otto Editore, 2000, 287–314.

———. "Los pobres por pobres, los ricos por ignorancia. El mercado financiero en México, 1880–1925." In *Para una historia de América. Los Nudos*, vol. I, coordinated by Marcello Carmagnani, Alicia Hernández Chávez, and R. Romano. Mexico: Fideicomiso Historia de las Américas-El Colegio de México-FCE, 1999.

Robertson, William Spence. *Iturbide of Mexico*. Durham: Duke University Press, 1952.

Rocafuerte, Vicente. *Bosquejo ligerísimo de la Revolución de Mégico [sic] desde el grito de Iguala hasta la proclamación imperial de Iturbide*. Philadelphia: Imprenta de Teracruef y Naroajeb, 1822.

Rodríguez, Carlos. "Un acercamiento a las propuestas de organización del sistemas impositivo en México, 1821–1823." In *Hacienda y política. Las finanzas públicas y los grupos de poder en la primera república federal mexicana*, edited by José Serrano Ortega and Luis Jáuregui. Mexico: El Colegio de Michoacán-Instituto Mora, 1998, 291–316.

Rodríguez, Mario. *La revolución Americana de 1776 y el mundo hispánico: ensayos y documentos*. Madrid: Editorial Tecnos, 1976.

Rodríguez O., Jaime E. "La Constitución de 1824 y la formación del Estado mexicano." *Historia Mexicana* 40: 3 (Jan.–Mar. 1991): 507–535.

———. "The Constitution of 1824 and the Formation of the Mexican State." *The Evolution of the Mexican Political System*, edited by Jaime E. Rodríguez O. Wilmington, Delaware: SR Books, 1993, 71–90.

———. "Las Cortes Mexicanas y el Congreso Constituyente." In *La independencia de México y el proceso autonomista novohispano, 1808–1824*, coordinated by Virginia Guedea. Mexico: Universidad Nacional Autónoma de México and Instituto Mora, 2001, 285–320.

———. "Down from Colonialism: Mexico's Nineteenth-Century Crisis." In *The Mexican and Mexican American Experience in the 19th Century*, edited by Jaime E. Rodríguez O. Tempe: Bilingual Press, 1989, 7–23.

———. "Las elecciones a las Cortes Constituyentes Mexicanas." In *Ensayos en homenaje a José María Muriá*, coordinated by Louis Cardaillac and Angélica Peregrina. Zapopan: El Colegio de Jalisco, 2002, 79–110.

———. *The Emergence of Spanish America: Vicente Rocafuerte and Spanish Americanism, 1808–1832*. Berkeley: University of California Press, 1975.

———. "The Formation of the Federal Republic." In *Five Centuries of Mexican History/Cinco siglos de historia de México*. 2 vols. Edited by Virginia Guedea and Jaime E. Rodríguez O. Mexico: Instituto Mora, 1992, 1: 316–328.

———. "From Royal Subject to Republican Citizen: The Role of the Autonomists in the Independence of Mexico." In *The Independence of Mexico and the Creation of the New Nation*, edited by Jaime E. Rodríguez O. Los Angeles: UCLA Latin American Center, 1989, 19–43.

———. *La independencia de la América Española*. Mexico: Fideicomiso Historia de las Américas/El Colegio de México/Fondo de Cultura Económica, 1996.

———. *The Independence of Spanish America*. Cambridge: Cambridge University Press, 1998.

———. "La revolución hispánica en el Reino de Quito: las elecciones de 1809–1814 y 1821–1822." In *Las guerras de Independencia en la América española*, edited by Marta Terán and José Antonio Serrano Ortega. Zamora, México, and Morelia: El Colegio de Michoacán, INAH y Universidad Michoacana de San Nicolás de Hidalgo, 2002, 485–508.

———. *"Rey, religion, Yndependencia, y Unión": el proceso político de la Independencia de Guadalajara*. Mexico: Instituto de Investigaciones José Luis Mora, 2003.

———. "The Struggle for Dominance: The Legislature versus the Executive in Early Mexico." In *The Birth of Modern Mexico, 1780–1824*, edited by Christon I. Archer. Wilmington: SR Books, 2003, 205–298.

———. "The Struggle for the Nation: The First Centralist-Federalist Conflict in Mexico." *The Americas* 49: 1 (July 1992): 1–22.

———. "La transición de colonia a nación: Nueva España, 1820–1821." *Historia Mexicana* 43: 170 (Sep.–Dec. 1993): 265–232.

———. "The Transition from Colony to Nation: New Spain, 1820–1821." In *Mexico in the Age of Democratic Revolutions, 1750–1850*, edited by Jaime E. Rodríguez O. Boulder: Lynne Rienner, 1994, 97–132.

Rojas, Beatriz, ed. *Actas de la diputación provincial de Zacatecas*. Mexico: Instituto de Investigaciones José María Luis Mora, 2003.

Rojas Coria, Rosendo. *Tratado de cooperativismo mexicano*. Mexico: Universidad Nacional Autónoma de México, 1952.

Romero, Matías. *Geographical and Statistical Notes on Mexico*. New York: Knickerbocker Press, 1898.

———. *Geographical and Statistical Notes on Mexico*. New York and London: G. P. Putnam's Sons, 1898.

Rosete Aranda, Francisco. *La compañía de títeres de los Rosete Aranda*. Tlaxcala: Instituto Tlaxcalteca de la Cultura, 1983.

Roussellier, N. "La culture politique libérale." In *Les cultures politiques en France*, compiled by Serge Bernstein. Paris: Seuil, 1999.

Rueda Smithers, Salvador. *El diablo de Semana Santa: El discurso político y el orden social en la ciudad de México en 1950*. México: Instituto Nacional de Antropología e Historia.

Rugeley, Terry. *Yucatan´s Maya Peasantry and the Origins of the Caste War*. Austin: University of Texas Press, 1996.

Safford, Frank. "Politics, ideology, and society in post-Independence Spanish America." In *The Cambridge History of Latin America*. 8 vols. Edited by Leslie Bethell. Cambridge: Cambridge University Press, 1984–1992, 3: 347–421.

Salinas Martínez, A. "Las sociedades mercantiles en el código de comercio de 1889." In *Centenario del Código de comercio*, Instituto de Investigaciones Jurídicas. Mexico: Universidad Nacional Autónoma de México, 1991.

Salvucci, Richard. "The Origins and Progress of U.S. Mexican Trade, 1825–1884: 'Hoc opus, hic labor est.'" *Hispanic American Historical Review* 71: 4 (1991): 697–735.

———, and Linda Salvucci. "The Politics of Protection: Interpreting Trade Policy in Late Bourbon and Early National Mexico." In *The Political Economy of Spanish America in the Age of Revolution, 1750–1850*, edited by Kenneth J. Andrien and Lyman L. Johnson. Albuquerque: University of New Mexico Press, 1994, 115–136.

San Miguel, Juan Rodríguez de. *Discurso pronunciado en [sic] 14 de noviembre de 1842 por el Sr. Diputado . . . contra el proyecto de Constitución en su discusión general. Tomado del Siglo Diez y Nueve Num. 410*. Guadalajara: Imprenta del Gobierno, 1842.

Santibañez, Manuel. *Reseña histórica del cuerpo de ejercito de oriente*. México: Oficina impresora del timbre, 1893.

Santillán, Gustavo. "La tolerancia religiosa y el Congreso Constituyente, 1823–1824." *Religiones y Sociedad* 6 (May–Aug. 1999): 67–80.

Schenk, F. "La desamortización de las tierras comunales en el Estado de México (1856–1911)." *Historia Mexicana* 177 (1995): 3–38.

Seguín, Juan N. *A Revolution Remembered: The Memoirs and Selected Correspondence of Juan N. Seguín*, edited by Jesús F. de la Teja. Austin: State House Press, 1991.

Segur, Monseñor. *Ofrenda a los jovenes católicos liberales por . . . Vertida al castellano de la cuarta edición francesa por el C. De A.* Guadalajara: Tipografía de Rodríguez, 1875.

Serrano, José Antonio. *El contingente de la sangre. Los métodos de reclutamiento del ejército mexicano, 1824–1844.* Mexico: Instituto Nacional de Antropología e Historia, 1993.

———. "El humo de la discordia: los gobiernos estatales, el gobierno nacional y el estanco del tabaco, 1824–1836." In *Hacienda y política. Las finanzas públicas y los grupos de poder en la primera república federal mexicana,* edited by José Serrano Ortega and Luis Jáuregui. Mexico: El Colegio de Michoacán-Instituto Mora, 1998, 203–226.

———. *Jerarquía territorial y transición política: Guanajuato, 1790–1836.* Zamora and Mexico: El Colegio de Michoacán and Instituto Mora, 2001.

———. "Liberalismo gaditano y milicias cívicas en Guanajuato, 1820–1836." In *Construcción de la legitimidad en México,* edited by Carlos Illades and Ariel Rodríguez Kuri. Mexico: El Colegio de Michoacán-Universidad Autónoma de México, 1998, 169–192.

———. "Villas fuertes, ciudades débiles: milicias y jerarquía territorial en Guanajuato, 1790–1847." In *Las ciudades y la guerra,* edited by Salvador Broseta, Carmen Corona, Manuel Chust et al. Castellón: Universitat Jaume I, 2002, 381–419.

Shafer, Robert J. *The Economic Societies in the Spanish World, 1763–1821.* Syracuse: Syracuse University Press, 1958.

Shershow, Scott Cutler. *Puppets and "Popular" Culture.* Ithaca: Cornell University Press, 1995.

Siebzehner, Batia B. *La universidad americana y la ilustración: Autoridad y conocimiento en Nueva España y el Río de la Plata.* Madrid: Editorial MAPFRE, 1992.

Sierra, Carlos J., and Rogelio Martínez Vera. *Historia y legislación aduanera de México.* Mexico: Secretaría de Hacienda y Crédito Público, 1973.

Sierra, Justo. *The Political Evolution of the Mexican People.* Translated by Charles Ramsdell. Austin: University of Texas Press, 1969.

Simms, Harold Dana. *The Expulsion of Mexico's Spaniards, 1821–1836.* Pittsburgh: University of Pittsburgh Press, 1990.

Skinner, Quentin. *The Foundations of Modern Political Thought.* 2 vols. Cambridge: Cambridge University Press, 1978.

Smith, Robert Sidney. "The *Wealth of Nations* in Spain and Hispanic America, 1780–1830." *The Journal of Political Economy* 65: 2 (April 1957): 104–125.

Sordo Cedeño, Reynaldo. *El congreso en la primera república centralista.* Mexico: El Colegio de México and Instituto Tecnológico Autónomo de México, 1993.

———. "El General Tornel y la Guerra de Texas." *Historia Mexicana* 42: 4 (1993): 934–935.

Soto, Miguel. *La conspiración monárquica.* Mexico: EOSA, 1988.

Spain. "Constitución política de la Monarquía Española." *In Leyes fundamentales de México, 1808–1991.* 16th ed. Edited by Felipe Tena Ramirez. Mexico: Editorial Porrúa, 1991.

Spain. Cortes. *Colección de decretos y órdenes de las Cortes de Cádiz.* 2 vols. Madrid: Publicaciones de las Cortes Generales, 1987.

Staples, Anne. *La Iglesia en la primera república federal mexicana (1824–1835)*. México: Secretaría de Educación Pública, Colección SepSetentas, 1976.

———. "Un balance histórico: el papel de los conventos mexicanos de monjas, siglo XIX." In *Memoria del I Coloquio Historia de la Iglesia en el Siglo XIX*, compiled by Manuel Ramos Medina. Mexico: Condumex, 1998.

Stevens, Donald Fithian. "Autonomists, Nativists, Republicans, and Monarchists: Conspiracy and Political History in Nineteenth-Century Mexico." *Mexican Studies/Estudios Mexicanos* 10 (winter 1994): 251.

Stoetzer, O. Carlos. *The Scholastic Roots of the Spanish American Revolution*. New York: Fordham University Press, 1979.

Suárez, Francisco. *Tratado de las leyes y de Dios legislador*. Translated by Jaime Torrubiano Ripoll. Madrid: Reus, 1918.

T.B.M. *Disertación contra la tolerancia religiosa*. Mexico: Imprenta de Galván a cargo de Mariano Arévalo, 1833.

Tafolla Pérez, Rafael. *La Junta de Notables de 1863*. México: Editorial Jus, 1977.

Tanck de Estrada, Dorothy. *La educación ilustrada (1786–1836)*. Mexico: El Colegio de México, 1977.

———. *Pueblos de indios y educación en el México colonial, 1750–1821*. Mexico: El Colegio de México, 1999.

Teja, Jesús F. de la "The Colonization and Independence of Texas: A Tejano Perspective." In *Myths, Misdeeds, and Misunderstandings: The Roots of Conflict in U.S.-Mexican Relations*, edited by Jaime E. Rodríguez O. and Kathryn Vincent. Wilmington, Delaware: SR Books, 1997, 79–95.

———. *San Antonio de Bexar: A Community on New Spain's Northern Frontier*. Albuquerque: University of New Mexico Press, 1996.

Tella, Torcuato Di. *Política nacional y popular en México, 1820–1847*. Mexico: Fondo de Cultura Económica, 1994.

Téllez González, Mario. *La Legislación minera en el Estado de México, 1824–1883*. Toluca: El Colegio Mexiquense, 1996.

Tena Ramírez, Felipe. *Leyes fundamentales de México, 1808–1991*. 16th ed. México: Editorial Porrúa, 1991.

Tenenbaum, Barbara. "Development and Sovereignty: Intellectuals and the Second Empire." In *Intellectuals and Power in Mexico*, edited by Roderic A. Camp, Charles A. Hale, and Josefina Zoraida Vázquez. Los Angeles: UCLA Latin American Center Publications, 1981, 77–88.

———. *México en la época de los agiotistas, 1821–1857*. Mexico: Fondo Nacional de Cultura Económica, 1985.

———. "Sistema tributario y tiranía: la finanzas públicas durante el régimen de Iturbide, 1821–1823." In *La finanzas públicas en los siglos XVII–XIX*, coordinated by Luis Jáuregui and José Antonio Serrano. Mexico: El Colegio de México, El Colegio de Michoacán, Instituto Mora, and Universidad Nacional Autónoma de México, 1998.

Tenorio Trillo, Mauricio. *Artilugios de la nación. México en las exposiciones universales, 1880–1930*. Mexico: Fondo de Cultura Económica, 1998.

Thomson, Guy P. C. "Bulwarks of Patriotic Liberalism: The National Guard, Philharmonic Corps and Patriotic Juntas in Mexico, 1847–88." *Journal of Latin American Studies* 22: 1 (Feb. 1990): 31–68.

———. "The Ceremonial and Political Roles of Village Bands, 1846–1974." In *Rituals of Rule, Rituals of Resistance: Public Celebrations and Popular Culture in Mexico*, edited by William H. Beezley, Cheryl English Martin, and William E. French (Wilmington, DE: SR Books, 1994), 307–342.

———. "La contrarreforma en Puebla, 1854–1886." In *El conservadurismo mexicano en el siglo XIX (1810–1910)*, coordinated by Humberto Morales and William Fowler. Puebla: Benemérita Universidad Autónoma de Puebla, Saint-Andrews University, Secretaría de Cultura del Gobierno del Estado de Puebla, 1999, 239–263.

———. "Popular Aspects of Liberalism in Mexico, 1848–1888." *Bulletin of Latin American Research* 10: 3 (1991), 265–292.

———. *Puebla de los Ángeles, Industry and Society in a Mexican City, 1700–1850*. Boulder: Westview Press, Dellplain Latin American Studies, 1989.

Tijerina, Andrés. *Tejanos & Texas under the Mexican Flag, 1821–1836*. College Station: Texas A & M University Press, 1994.

Tornel, José María. *Tejas y los Estados Unidos de América. Mexico City, 1837*. In *The Mexican Side of the Texan Revolution*, translated by Carlos E. Castañeda. Dallas: P. L. Turner Co., 1928.

Tornel y Mendevil, José. *Manual de derecho mercantil mexicano*. Mexico: Imprenta de Vicente Segura, 1854.

Traffano, D. "Y el Registro Civil no es más que un engaño del Gobierno, Sociedad civil e Iglesia frente a un nuevo registro de los datos vitales: Oaxaca en la segunda mitad del siglo XIX." In *Constitucionalismo y orden liberal en América Latina, 1850–1920*, edited by Marcello Carmagnani. Turin: Otto Editore, 2000.

Un jalisciense. *Tendencias de la demagogia mexicana, manifestadas por sus propios hechos*. Guadalajara: Tipografía de Rodríguez, 1857.

Un quidam. *Contestación a los enemigos de los predicadores*. Guadalajara: Imprenta de Dionisio Rodríguez a cargo de Trinidad Buitrón, 1833.

Valadés, José C. *Maximiliano y Carlota en México: Historia del Segundo Imperio*. México: Editorial Diana, 1976.

Van Young, Eric. *The Other Rebellion: Popular Violence, Ideology, and the Mexican Struggle for Independence, 1810–1821*. Stanford: Stanford University Press, 2001.

Varey, J. E. *Historia de los títeres en España (desde sus origines hasta mediados del siglo XVIII)*. Madrid: Revista de Occidente, 1957.

Vázquez, Josefina Zoraida. "Centralistas, conservadores y monarquistas 1830–1853." In *El conservadurismo mexicano en el siglo XIX (1810–1910)*, coordinated by Humberto Morales and William Fowler. Puebla, Mexico: Benemérita Universidad Autónoma de Puebla, Saint-Andrews University, Secretaría de Cultura del Gobierno del Estado de Puebla, 1999, 115–133.

———. "The Colonization and Loss of Texas: A Mexican Perspective." In *Myths, Misdeeds, and Misunderstandings: The Roots of Conflict in U.S.-Mexican Relations*, edited by Jaime E. Rodriguez O. and Kathryn Vincent. Wilmington: SR Books, 1997, 47–77.

———. "El federalismo mexicano, 1823–1847." In *Federalismos latinoamericanos: México, Brasil y Argentina*, edited by Marcello Carmagnani. Mexico: Fondo de Cultura Económica, 1993, 15–50.

———. "Federalismo, reconocimiento e Iglesia." In *Memoria del I Coloquio Historia de la Iglesia en el Siglo XIX*, compiled by Manuel Ramos Medina. Mexico: Condumex, 1998, 93–112.

———. "Iglesia, ejército y centralismo." *Historia Mexicana* 39: 1 (July–September, 1989), 205–234.

———. "Los pronunciamientos de 1832: Aspirantismo político e ideología." In *Patterns of Contention in Mexican History*, edited by Jaime E. Rodríguez O. Wilmington, Delaware: Scholarly Resources, Inc., 1992, 163–186.

Vázquez Mantecón, Carmen. *Santa Anna y la encrucijada del Estado. La dictadura (1853–1854)*. Mexico: Fondo de Cultura Económica, 1986.

Velasco Avila, Cuauhtémoc, et al. *Estado y minería en México (1867–1910)*. Mexico: Fondo de Cultura Económica, 1988.

Véliz, Claudio. *The Centralist Tradition in Latin America*. Princeton: Princeton University Press, 1980.

Ventura Beleño, Eusebio. *Recopilación sumaria de los autos acordados de la Real Audiencia y Sala del Crimen de esta Nueva España*. 2 vols. Edited by María del Refugio González. México: Universidad Nacional Autónoma de México, 1981.

Veracruz. *Esposición formada por la administración general de rentas del Estado de Veracruz*. Veracruz: Imprenta de Alburto, 1831.

———. *Memoria de Hacienda desde el 1 de junio de 1832 hasta 21 de mayo de 1834*. Veracruz: Imprenta de Alburto, 1834.

———. *Memoria relativa a la situación del erario público del Estado de Veracruz*. Veracruz: Imprenta de Alburto, 1828.

Villegas Revueltas, Silvestre. *El liberalismo moderado en México 1852–1864*. Mexico: Universidad Nacional Autónoma de México, 1997.

Viroli, Maurizio. *For Love of Country: An Essay on Patriotism and Nationalism*. New York: Oxford University Press, 1995.

Warren, Richard A. *Vagrants and Citizens: Politics and the Masses in Mexico City from Colony to Republic*. Wilmington: SR Books, 2001.

Weber, David J. *Myth and the History of the Hispanic Southwest*. Albuquerque: University of New Mexico Press, 1988.

White, Gifford, ed. *The 1840 Census of the Republic of Texas*. Austin, Texas: Pemberton Press, 1966.

Wold, Ruth. *Diario de México: Primer cotidiano de Nueva España*. Madrid: Editorial Gredos, 1970.

Y. M. O. *Invitación que hace un oaxaqueño a su suelo Patrio*. Oaxaca: n.p., 1823.

Yucatán. *Colección de leyes, decretos y órdenes del augusto congreso del estado de Yucatán*. 2 vols. Mérida: Imprenta de Lorenzo Seguí, 1832.

Zacatecas. *Memoria*. Guadalajara: Imprenta del Urbano San Roman, 1825.

———. *Memoria*. Zacatecas: Imprenta Pedro Pineda, 1826.

———. *Memoria*. Zacatecas: Imprenta de Pedro Pineda, 1828.

———. *Memoria*. Zacatecas: n.p., 1831.

———. *Memorias*. Zacatecas: Imprenta del Supremo Gobierno, 1833.

Zamacois, Niceto de. *Historia de Méjico desde sus tiempos mas remotos hasta nuestros días*. Mexico: J. F. Parras y Compañía, 1881.

Zavala, Lorenzo de. "Dictamen de la comisión de Hacienda sobre el presupuesto de gastos para el año económico de 1823, 6 de diciembre de 1822." In *Obras. El historiador y el representante popular*, edited by Lorenzo Zavala. Mexico: Editorial Porrúa, 1969.

———. *Ensayo crítico de las revoluciones de México desde 1808 hasta 1830*. Mexico City: Editorial Porrúa, 1969.

———. *Ensayo Histórico de las Revoluciones de México desde 1808 hasta 1830*. Edición facsimilar. 2 vols. Mexico: FCE-Instituto Cultural Helénico, 1985.

———. *Memoria del Estado de México presentada el 20 de marzo de 1829*. Mexico: Imprenta del Gobierno, 1829.

Zavala, Silvio. "Tres acercamientos de la Ilustración Francesa a Nuestra Historia." In *La Revolución Francesa en México*, coordinated by Solange Alberro, Alicia Hernández Chávez, and Elías Trabulse. Mexico: El Colegio de México, CIESAS, 1991, 9–46.

Zayas Enríquez, R. de. *Los Estados Unidos Mexicanos. Sus progresos en veinte años de paz*. New York: H. A. Host, 1897.

Index

Jiménez, Juan José de Mata, 269
Johnson, Francis W., 122
Jovellanos, Gaspar Melchor, 5–6
Juárez, Benito, 25, 137, 141, 142, 151,
    159, 168, 171, 173, 175, 176, 346
Juarismo, 133
juaristas, 152, 158
judiciary power, 187
junta de arbitros, 259
Junta de Fomento y Administrativa de
    Minería, 289
Junta de Guerra, Oaxaca, 89
Junta Electoral de Provincia, 77
Junta Nacional Instituyente, 81, 260,
    262, 264
Junta Preparatoria de México, 76
Junta Provisional Administrativa,
    Yucatán, 85
Junta Provisional Gubernativa of
    Oaxaca, 84, 85, 89, 92
Junta Suprema Central Gubernativa del
    Reino (Spanish Monarchy), 11, 39,
    69; instructions of American
    representatives to, 12

king, authority of, 135
Kuntz, Sandra, 343, 344

Labarrieta, Antonio, 227, 228
Labastida, Antonio Pelagio (bishop of
    Puebla), 145, 153
Labayru, Pedro, 81
labor, 158; child, 156; laws, European,
    156; reform under Maximilian,
    156–58
laissez-faire economics, 5
laity, 191–92, 193
land: commissioners, 117; communal,
    154; grants, 113–15, 117–18, 120,
    122; law of 1894, 296; local control
    of 171; national, 296; ownership,
    346; vacant, 110, 112, 295
Lanuza, Pedro José, 237–38
Lares, Teodosio, 154, 158
Las comunicaciones y obras públicas
    (Macedo), 300
Laws of the Indies (*derecho indiano*), 6

Leftwich, Robert, 113
legislative branch, 299; dominance, vs.
    executive power, 20, 21, 347
legislature: power of, 24, 135, 141, 187;
    role in tariff policy, 314, 315
legitimacy, government, 339–42, 347
Lent, 188
Leo XII, 192
Leo XIII, 196
León, Antonio de, 79, 80, 83, 87–88,
    95–96
León, *ayuntamiento* of, 258, 259
León, Fernando de, 121
León, Martín de, 116, 121
Leopold I, 134, 138, 140, 141, 152
Lerdo de Tejada, Miguel, 171, 206
Ley agraria del imperio, 155
ley de trabajo, 156, 157
Ley lerdo, 152, 153
*Ley para dirimir las diferencias sobre
    tierras y aguas entre los pueblos*, 154
liberal: Catholic alliance, 194; culture,
    286, 288, 290–91, 298, 300–301;
    economic culture, 291, 297; ideology,
    xv; institutionalization, 292; order,
    299; origination of term, 136; Party,
    return to power, 305; pluralism, 194;
    political culture, 297; project, 158;
    reforms, challenges of, 339–49;
    regalism, 189; republicanism, 183.
    See also liberals; liberalism
liberalism, 23, 109, 118–19, 125, 134,
    290; and Catholic Church, 183–97;
    Catholic, 167; centralist, 190;
    defined by Juárez, 169; 1867
    triumph of, 24; fiscal, 278; folk,
    170–71; and free trade, 297;
    gaditano fiscal, 256; in Hispanic
    political culture, xiii; in Hispanic
    world, 1; individualistic, 195; of
    Maximilian 134; military issue of,
    172; moderate, 195; in New Spain,
    xv; in Oaxaca, 68; patriotic, 167,
    170; popular, 167, 297; radical, 133;
    Republican, 196; scientific, 167;
    social, 154; ultra-, 184. *See also*
    liberal, liberals

About the Contributors

Christon I. Archer is professor of history at the University of Calgary. He has written extensively on the army of New Spain and on the era of independence as well as on the Northwest Coast in the eighteenth century. His works include *The Army in Bourbon Mexico* (Albuquerque, 1977), which won the Bolton Prize. He coauthored with John R. Ferris, Holger H. Herwig, and Timothy H. E. Travers *World History of Warfare* (Lincoln, 2002). He has edited *The Wars of Independence in Spanish America* (Wilmington, 2000); and *The Birth of Modern Mexico, 1780-1824* (Wilmington, 2003). He is currently working on the insurgency and counterinsurgency during the wars of independence in New Spain and on Spanish oceanic exploration of the Northwest Coast in the eighteenth century.

William H. Beezley is professor of history at the University of Arizona. He has written extensively on Mexico. His works include *Insurgent Governor: Abraham González and the Mexican Revolution* (Lincoln, 1973); *Judas at the Jockey Club and Other Episodes of Porfirian Mexico* (Lincoln, 1987); *El Gran Pueblo: A History of Greater Mexico* (with Colin M. MacLachlan) (Upper Saddle River, 1999); *Rituals of Rule, Rituals of Resistance: Public Celebrations and Popular Culture in Mexico* (with Cheryl English Martin and William E. French) (Wilmington, 1994). He is currently working on a book tentatively entitled: "Amending Memories: The Formation of National Identity in Nineteenth-century Mexico."

Marcello Carmagnani is professor in the Dipartimento di Studi Politici at the Universsitá di Torino as well as professor in the Centro de Estudios Históricos at El Colegio de México. He is the author of numerous socioeconomic studies of Mexico and Latin America. His works include *El regreso de los dioses: El proceso de reconstitución de la identidad étnica en Oaxaca, siglos XVII y XVIII* (Mexico, 1990); *Estado y Mercado. La economía pública del liberalismo mexicano* (Mexico, 1994); and *L'altro Occidente: L'America Latina dallinvasione europea al nouvo millenio* (Torino, 2003). He is currently working on Latin America's role in world affairs.

Brian Connaughton is professor and researcher at the Universidad Autónoma Metropolitana, Iztapalapa. He has published widely on late-eighteenth- and early-nineteenth-century political cultural and Catholicism in Mexico. His works include *España y Nueva España ante la crisis de la modernidad* (Mexico, 1983); *Ideología y sociedad en Guadalajara (1788-1853)* (Mexico, 1992), which won the Marcus Mauss prize and has appeared in English as *Clerical Ideology in a Revolutionary Age: The Guadalajara Church and the Idea of the Mexican Nation (1788-1853)* (Calgary, 2003); *and Dimensiones de la identidad patriótica: Religión, política y regiones en México. Siglo XIX* (Mexico, 2001). He is currently working on questions of political culture and national identity in nineteenth-century Mexico.

Manuel Chust is profesor in the Departamento de Historia, Geografía y Arte and Vice Rector of the Universitat Jaume I. He has published widely on the political transformation of the Hispanic world at the beginning of the nineteenth century. His works include *La cuestión americana en las Cortes de Cádiz* (Valencia y México, 1999); *Revoluciones y revolucionarios en el mundo hispano* (Castellón, 2000); and *Las ciudades y la guerra, 1750-1898* (Castellón, 2002). He is currently working on the formation of the Mexican state in the early nineteenth century.

Robert H. Duncan received a Ph.D. from the University of California, Irvine. His research focuses on the role of the Mexican state during the second half of the nineteenth century. His publications include "The Chinese and the Economic Development of Southern Baja California," *Hispanic American Historical Review* 74: 4 (November 1994); "Political Legitimation and Maximilian's Second Empire, 1864-1867," *Mexican Studies/Estudios Mexicanos* 12: 1 (winter 1996); and "Embracing a Suitable Past: Independence Celebrations under Mexico's Second Empire, 1864-6," *Journal of Latin American Studies* 30 (May 1998): 249-277. He is currently completing a book on state and nation building during Maximilian's Mexican Empire, 1864-1867.

Aldo Flores-Quiroga is assistant professor at the School of Politics and Economics of the Claremont Graduate University. He has published widely on the economic and political determinants of Mexico's structural reforms. His publications include *Proteccionismo versus librecambio: La economía* *política de la protección comercial en México, 1970-1994* (Mexico, 1998). He is currently working on contemporary issues of international trade between Mexico and the rest of the world.

Alicia Hernández Chávez is professor and researcher at the Centro de Estudios Históricos of El Colegio de México. She has published widely on politics during the nineteenth and twentieth century. She is also the founder and president of the Fedeicomiso Historia de las Américas. Her works include *La mecánica cárdenista* (Mexico, 1979); *Anenecuilco, memoria y vida de un pueblo* (Mexico, 1993); *La tradición republicana del buen gobierno* (Mexico, 1993); and *México. Breve historia contemporánea* (Mexico, 2000), which is being published in English by the University of California Press. She is currently working on the ideology of nineteenth-century Mexico.

Sandra Kuntz Ficker is professor and researcher at the Centro de Estudios Históricos of El Colegio de México. In 1999, she was a Tinker Visiting Professor at Stanford University. She has published widely on economic history. Her works include *Empresa extrangera y Mercado interno. El Ferrocarril Central Mexicano* (Mexico, 1995); and *Ferrocarriles y vida económica en México, 1850-1950: Del surgimiento tardío al decaimiento precoz* (Mexico, 1996). She is currently working on the evolution of foreign trade and commercial policy in the late nineteenth- and early twentieth-century Mexico.

Andrés Reséndez is assistant professor of history at the University of California, Davis. He has just completed *Changing National Identities at the Frontier: Texas and New Mexico, 1800–1850*, which will appear in 2005 and will be published by Cambridge University Press.

Jaime E. Rodríguez O. is professor of history and director of Latin American Studies at the University of California, Irvine. He is also editor of the journal *Mexican Studies/Estudios Mexicanos*. He has published widely on Mexico and on early nineteenth-century Spanish America. His works include *The Emergence of Spanish America: Vicente Rocafuerte and Spanish Americanism, 1808-1832* (Berkeley, 1975); with Colin M. MacLachlan, *The Forging of the Cosmic Race: A Reinterpretation of Colonial Mexico* (Berkeley, 1980 & 1990); *El proceso de la independencia de México* (Mexico, 1992); *The Independence of Spanish America* (Cambridge, 1998); and *"Rey, religion, Yndependencia y unión": El proceso político de la independencia de Guadalajara* (Mexico, 2003). He has also edited a dozen volumes on Mexican politics. He is currently completing a book on the Formation of the Federal Republic of Mexico.

José Antonio Serrano Ortega is professor and researcher at the Centro de Estudios Históricos at El Colegio de Michoacán. He has published widely on politics, the military, and government finances in early-nineteenth-century Mexico. His works include *El contingente de sangre: Los gobiernos estatales y departamentales y los métodos de reclutamiento del ejército permanente mexicano, 1824-1844* (Mexico, 1993); *Jerarquía territorial y transición política: Guanajuato, 1790-1836* (Zamora & Mexico, 2001); *Hacienda y política: Las finanzas públicas y grupos de poder en la primera República Federal Mexicana,* (ed. with Luis Jéregui) (Zamora & Mexico, 1998); and *Las guerras de independencia en la América española* (ed. with Marta Terán) (Zamora & Mexico, 2002). He is currently working on public finances in Mexico during the first half of the nineteenth century.

Series Editors: William H. Beezley and Judith Ewell

Recent Titles in the Series

For a complete listing of series titles, visit www.rowmanlittlefield.com.